Approaching Monumentality
in Archaeology

APPROACHING MONUMENTALITY IN ARCHAEOLOGY

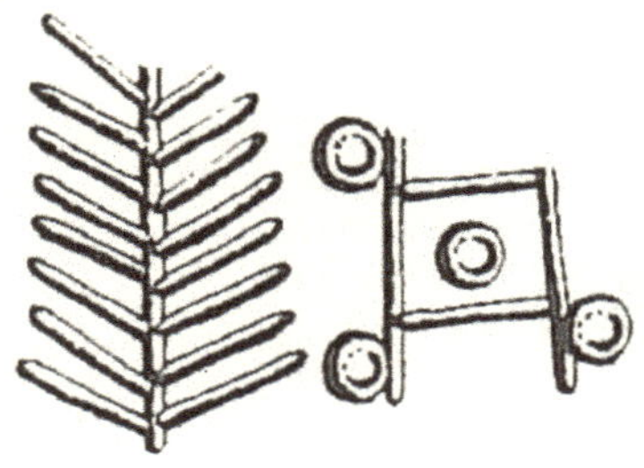

IEMA Proceedings,
Volume 3

EDITED BY

James F. Osborne

STATE UNIVERSITY OF
NEW YORK PRESS

Logo and cover/interior art: A vessel with wagon motifs from Bronocice, Poland, 3400 B.C. Courtesy of Sarunas Milisauskas and Janusz Kruk, 1982, Die Wagendarstellung auf einem Trichterbecher au Bronocice, Polen, *Archäologisches Korrespondenzblatt* 12: 141–144

Published by
State University of New York Press, Albany

For information, contact
State University of New York Press, Albany, NY
www.sunypress.edu

Production, Eileen Nizer
Marketing, Michael Campochiaro

Library of Congress Cataloging-in-Publication Data

Approaching monumentality in archaeology / edited by James F. Osborne.
        pages cm. — (The Institute for European and Mediterranean
Archaeology distinguished monograph series)
    Includes bibliographical references and index.
    ISBN 978-1-4384-5325-5 (hc : alk paper) 978-1-4384-5326-2 (pb : alk paper)
    ISBN 978-1-4384-5327-9 (ebook)
    1. Monuments—History.   2. Archaeology—History.   3. Symbolism
in architecture.   4. Architecture and society.   5. Urban anthropology.
I. Osborne, James F., editor of compilation.

NA9335.A67 2014
722—dc23   2013046282

10 9 8 7 6 5 4 3 2 1

Contents

Illustrations

Tables

CHAPTER ONE

Monuments and Monumentality

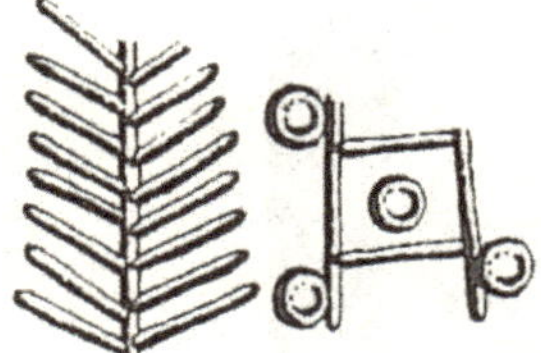

James F. Osborne

On December 5, 2007, the august Sotheby's auction house sold the Guennol Lioness, an ancient statue from Mesopotamia, for the then-unprecedented sum of $57.2 million. Many aspects of this remarkable sale warrant contemplation. The first and most obvious of these is the statue's astronomical price tag, at the time rendering it the most expensive sculpture ever sold; still today the lioness holds the record for the most expensive object from antiquity.[1] Another is the Guennol Lioness's murky provenance—the history of the object's ownership, knowledge of which confirms the legality of its sale—and the complete lack of provenience information—its original context and "find spot," the *sine qua non* of archaeological interpretation without which we can neither authenticate the antiquity of the piece, nor understand its original function (Witmore and Harmanşah 2007). With this crucial information lacking, we can only guess at the Guennol Lioness's place and time of origin, currently assumed, on the basis of stylistic parallels with other, more securely dated objects, to derive from the Proto-Elamite culture of southwestern Iran sometime around 3,000 B.C.E. (Porada 1950:223).

Though certainly intriguing and worthwhile, these economic and ethical issues distract us from the Guennol Lioness itself and its material qualities as a work of art. Given the statue's sale price one might be surprised by its physical properties: the Guennol Lioness is a mere 8.4 cm, or 3.25 inches, in length, fitting easily into the palm of one's hand (Figure 1.1).

Such a diminutive stature has not prevented scholars and laypeople alike from describing the lioness in the grandest of terms, however. Porada's (1950) original publication of the object, still the only dedicated analysis of it in art historical literature, wastes no time in praising the lioness, opening her article with the following statement: "Perhaps the most striking feature of this sculpture is the impression of monumental

FIGURE 1.1 The Guennol Lioness, (likely) a proto-Elamite statue from 3,000 B.C.E.
Height: 3.25 inches (source: Wikimedia).

power which it conveys. When seen in the original, the figure seems to fill the entire
field of mental vision" (1950:223).[2] Likewise, Hugh Hildesley, executive vice president of
Sotheby's, described the Guennol Lioness in a pre-auction publicity pitch using similar
terms: "It is one of those objects which catches your imagination immediately because
although it is tiny, it is monumental."[3]

The counterintuitive application of this adjective—*monumental*—to so diminutive
an object raises several intriguing questions: Can something that is tiny really be considered monumental? More to the point, just what do we mean by the terms *monument,*

monumental, and *monumentality?* The use of these words is commonly found across several academic disciplines, archaeology, architecture, and art history in particular; is there common ground in the ways these fields deploy this terminology, or have diverging disciplinary traditions created a scenario in which the same terms are used with different meaning and intent? To what extent can it be argued that monumentality is a cross-cultural characteristic of the human species? Perhaps most important, what is the social and political significance of monumentality as it is manifested in particular ways around the world?

I posed these questions to the participants in the conference *Approaching Monumentality in the Archaeological Record,* which was hosted by the Institute for European and Mediterranean Archaeology at SUNY Buffalo in May 2012. The answers they provided through a series of case studies are contained in this volume. But before readers turn to the regions or time periods in the following chapters that concern them directly, it is worthwhile to consider the topic of monumentality more generally, and how it is has been treated over the past century or so by the humanities and social sciences. Though the literature is vast and often disparate, there do exist themes that recur in often surprising places.

In what follows, I would like to propose that approaching monumentality requires a two-step process. First, one must distinguish between monument and monumentality as two closely related, but nevertheless distinct, phenomena. A helpful way to conceptualize this problem is by likening their relationship to the art historian's familiar distinction of form and meaning. Second, and with this analogy in mind, it is most productive to see in monumentality an ongoing, constantly renegotiated *relationship* between thing and person, between the monument(s) and the person(s) experiencing the monument. Such a relational approach to monumentality offers the possibility of forging a unifying discourse to the topic, and one that might act as a guide for future research.

≈

The precise meaning of the word *monument* is frustratingly difficult to isolate, and seems only to recede further from grasp as one approaches it. The *Oxford English Dictionary,* in theory the arbiter of terminological disputes (in reality, of course, a participant in them) provides two major subdivisions of "monument," the first being what is today recognized as the standard usage: an object that is generally large in size, that commemorates or memorializes, that is historically significant, and that has longevity. It is important to note monument's etymological origin, however: the word derives from the Latin verb *monēre,* "to remind." Monument's Latin source contains a crucial element of meaning that tends to be overlooked in everyday speech: that monuments are not simply things, they are things-that-do, motionless objects that nevertheless possess an active force, accomplishing real work among those surrounding them. This same active force is the sense of monument's second major definitional subdivision in the *OED,* now wholly obsolete: a transitive verb meaning to cause to be memorialized, to commemorate with a monument.[4]

Art historian Wu Hung argues that what might be considered the normative definition of monument—large, permanent, public objects; in short, the main definition provided by the *OED*—is, though universal in ambition, little more than a construct of our own time, place, and cultural history (Wu 1995:1). Since any meaning associated with a monument can and will change over time as the culture that surrounds an object evolves, it is futile to ascribe an absolute meaning to any given monument. Hence, Wu's (1995:4) analogy to art history's form and meaning: though a monument may physically stay the same over long durations of time, monumentality, or the meanings we associate with a monument, continuously change (cf. Meyers 2012:13, Thomas 2007:4). Riegl (1903) even noted the tendency for sculptures and buildings to become monumental unintentionally, insofar as they are ascribed monumental associations long after—potentially many generations after—their creation.

A monument, then, should be considered an object, or suite of objects, that possesses an agreed-upon special meaning to a community of people.[5] But since this meaning can never be immutable, we can only consider an object's monumentality in the context of its relationship to the community of which it forms a part. Appreciating relationality is thus essential to understanding the monumentality of any object, for just as we assign to material things their meaning, so they exert their own agency on us, influencing our thoughts, beliefs, even physical actions (Hoskins 2006). Perhaps it is time to resuscitate the *OED*'s transitive sense of the word: the active meaning of monument that has become obsolete should once again gain currency.

This is not to downplay or disregard the genuine contributions that formal analyses of monuments can provide. This is particularly apparent in pre- or nonhistoric contexts, where identifying and understanding meaning with any degree of confidence is notoriously difficult. In extreme situations, formal analysis may be the only option available. But more to the point, an archaeological interpretation operating under a relational framework has to consider equally the formal properties of the monument(s) under investigation as well as the monumentality that exists in the relationship between objects and subjects. The two are inextricably intertwined, and considering one without the other does justice to neither.

The following pages present a handful of examples of the ways in which various scholars from several disciplines, archaeology especially, have considered either side of this form/meaning dialectic.

FORM AND MONUMENT

In 1950, eminent archaeologist V. Gordon Childe published what would become his most famous work, "The Urban Revolution" (1950). According to one informal study, Childe's piece on the origins of urbanism has since become the single most-cited archaeological article on ancient complex society (Smith 2009:3). Using Lewis Henry Morgan's (1877) social evolutionary rubric of savagery-barbarism-civilization as a baseline for human culture over time, Childe equated these stages to the hunting-gathering, agricultural, and urban stages of demography, respectively.

Childe's arguments for the social changes that occurred with the advent of urbanism—essentially, a shift from mechanical to organic social solidarity, in Durkheim's (1893) terms—and his lifelong predilection for Marxian social theory (Trigger 1989:259–263) are well-trodden ground. Less commonly noted is his assertion that one of the primary distinguishing characteristics of cities, and thus of urban civilization (as distinct from villages and agricultural civilization), is the presence of monumental architecture. In his words, "Truly monumental public buildings not only distinguish each known city from any village but also symbolize the concentration of the social surplus" (1950:12). In ancient Sumer, for example, whose cities were in part characterized by enormous temples with attached magazines and granaries, Childe proposes that "the social surplus was first effectively concentrated in the hands of a god and stored in his granary. . . . But of course the imaginary deities were served by quite real priests who . . . administered their divine masters' earthly estates" (1950:12).

Seeing architectural scale as directly correlated with power and with the social and political control of commoners by elites is among the most common interpretations of monumental buildings offered by archaeologists (see Potts this volume). Occasionally, the influence of Marxian thought is explicitly noted, as in the case of Mesopotamian archaeologist Susan Pollock, who uses an appeal to Gramsci's notion of cultural hegemony to argue that monumental buildings are physical embodiments of relations of domination/subordination, and are thus inherently ideological statements (1999:175). In other studies, the same or similar principles are present, though with reference to more contemporary anthropologists such as Godelier (1986) instead of Marx (e.g., Kolb 1994).

The primary difference between Childe's programmatic article and the more recent case studies is the latter's implementation of a thermodynamic approach to monumental architecture, according to which monumentality can be measured quantitatively in terms of energy expenditure. The foundational text in this branch of the archaeology of architecture is Trigger's study, which defines monumental architecture as buildings whose "scale and elaboration exceed the requirements of any practical functions that a building is intended to perform" (1990:119). Though thermodynamics reduces monumentality to scale and little else, archaeologists are at least offered the ability to proceed measuring monumentality in a formal fashion. This is done by assessing the amount of energy that is involved in building a structure: since, according to principles of least effort, humans seek to conserve energy wherever possible, it follows that situations in which much energy has been expended in construction activities must speak to the ability of a ruler to marshal resources and human loyalties (1990:122–124). Although some scholars argue that this principle results in simplistic conclusions that can be summarized as "the bigger the building, the more powerful the builder" (see Marcus 2003), and understanding the duration of monumental building events is rarely taken into consideration (cf. Bayliss et al. 2007), the idea remains prominent in archaeology (e.g., Rosenswig and Burger 2012:4–5). Adherents to this approach typically quantify energy investiture in a building by estimating the number of labor-hours or days that was necessary to build it (Abrams 1989; Abrams and Bolland 1999). The procedure first estimates the original volume of a building,[6] then multiplies that volume by construction rates determined either from ethnographic or ethnoarchaeological examples (Pollock 1999:179), experimental archaeology (Kolb 1994:525), or, ideally, from ancient texts (Ristvet 2007:199).[7]

Though less transparently reductive, other approaches are only slightly less instrumentalist in their assumption that the scale of large public structures functions to perpetuate and consolidate political power on the part of elites, and that monuments and monumental architecture are thus useful indices for social complexity. Moore, for example, notes that architecture is more than merely a passive byproduct of labor investment; rather, the form of buildings actually helps shape social interaction (1996:3). At the same time, however, his assessment of the visibility of large structures in the Andes comes to similar conclusions, such as that high visual angles of incidence and large viewsheds from buildings suggest those structures' use in communicating control (1996:116–118). Likewise, Inomata (2006:811–813) and Gilibert (2011:101–106) calculate the size of open spaces (plazas, courtyards, and so on) that stood before public buildings in order to estimate the number of individuals that could fit in the space. That number is then taken as a proxy for the degree to which rulers were able to use these open spaces as venues for political performances, performances that are argued to have been crucial to the efficacy and legitimacy of the state.

Archaeologists will occasionally go so far as to argue that monumental works can be directly correlated with particular complex social formations, as Renfrew (1973; 1976) did when he used Service's (1962) and Sahlins's (1968) neo-evolutionary framework to propose that the presence and distribution of long barrows in Neolithic Wessex corresponded to the territorial divisions of local chiefdoms. The association of monumentality with particular neo-evolutionary stages of complexity has recently been challenged (Howey 2012; cf. Notroff et al. this volume), and more sophisticated modeling of the relationship of landscape monuments and territory is now prevalent, such as Glatz and Plourde's (2011) use of costly signaling theory to understand Late Bronze Age monuments in Anatolia (cf. Neiman 1997; see also Glatz this volume). Very common is the general interpretive stance that sees social complexity and monuments as inextricably related (e.g., Dillehay 1990; Kolb this volume; Sherratt 1990). DeMarrais et al.'s well-known study proposed that monumental buildings "associate a group with a place and represent the power and authority of its leaders . . . often expressing relatively unambiguous messages of power" (1996:18); thus, the presence of a southern Moche monumental ceremonial complex in a non-Moche area is taken as an indicator of the expansionist nature of the Moche state (1996:26). Such works are characterized by a similar underlying assumption—that size can be equated with political power and social complexity, and thus that the construction of monumental works is undertaken in order to facilitate political subjectivity (cf. Caraher this volume; Notroff et al. this volume).

Another aspect of the archaeological record that archaeologists have examined with an eye toward the formal properties of monuments is in the layout of ancient cities. The presence of coordinated monuments across urban centers has often been taken to suggest the presence of urban planning. For example, following Trigger's definition of monumental architecture discussed above, Smith argues that a series of spatially coordinated buildings and sculptures can be taken to suggest that urban construction took place in a top-down fashion in which political rulers decreed the layout of a city and deliberately and conspicuously staged the city to emphasize their own ability and strength (Smith

2007:8–12). The temple compound of Angkor Wat in Cambodia is a good example of such a planned monumental urban center.

Whereas archaeologists will typically look at an ancient city plan and assess its monumental layout to determine cases of top-down city planning, studies of contemporary monumentality in urban planning conventionally take the equation of political power and monumental architecture as a given and proceed from there (Therborn this volume). Ford, for example, notes the paradox that although grand monumental places and structures are among our most treasured urban attractions (think Olmstead's Central Park in Manhattan, or the Palais Garnier in Paris), it takes governmental regimes that are nearly totalitarian in strength to see them actually built (2008:237–238).[8] Nowhere is this more clearly attested than in China, where strong governmental authority has permitted the construction of 2,800 high-rise buildings in the city of Shanghai (and an additional 2,000 planned) as well as iconic "megaprojects" being undertaken in every city across the country (C. J. Smith 2008:266–267).

However, the wealth of information for modern cities renders them all the more visible and interpretable, and thus studies of places more modern than the ancient past can offer insights and caveats regarding political authority that might not otherwise occur to the archaeologist. Political geographer John Agnew looks to twentieth-century Rome, and especially its infamous Beaux-Arts memorial to Victor Emmanuel II, which has been relentlessly mocked since even before the completion of its construction (Atkinson and Cosgrove 1998:28–29), to point out that "[s]*imply because they were built* does not mean that they [monumental structures] inevitably served to solidify the regimes among the national populace and necessarily sacralize their claims" (Agnew 1998:236, original emphasis). The difference between conceived intent and perceived outcome is something archaeologists would do well to keep in mind, since the discrepancy challenges the correlation of scale and power that so many assume is inherent to ancient building projects.

Finally, this brief turn to contemporary urban planning reminds us of the discipline of architecture and the contributions it has made to the study of the formal properties of monuments. Architecture has long had a difficult relationship with monumental buildings; during the early days of the Modern Movement especially, architects were reluctant to discuss monumentality openly or to pursue monumental goals given their own complicity in furthering the causes of the totalitarian regimes of the 1920s and 1930s by designing and constructing their monumental state apparatuses (Collins and Collins 1984:17). Furthermore, those same regimes were stylistically obsessed with excessive Beaux-Arts constructions (see, e.g., Speer 1970), the very architectural fashion that the modernists were so desperate to avoid. Lewis Mumford went so far as to write, "If it is a monument, it is not modern, and if it is modern, it cannot be a monument" (1938:438).

Nevertheless, prominent architects from the Modern Movement eventually became closely associated with monumentality, including Louis Kahn, Sigfried Giedion, and Josep Lluís Sert, particularly when the need for monumental memorials became apparent in the aftermath of World War II (Goldhagen 2001:25). A programmatic statement penned during the height of the conflict scorned monumental efforts of the preceding century and offered many pieces of advice, including the use of new materials and techniques. It also demanded the close collaboration of architects, landscapists, painters, sculptors, and urban planners in creating works that symbolize a culture's ideals and that offer people more than mere functional fulfillment (Sert et al. 1984), recalling Trigger's definition of monumental architecture discussed above. At the same time, however, the lofty cultural ambition of the modernists reminds us as archaeologists that monumental buildings and sculptures can be much more than works possessing certain criteria of form. They also influence us in multifarious ways, participating in our ongoing and unceasing social negotiations long after their creators have departed (Sert et al. 1984).

MEANING AND MONUMENTALITY

If the studies cited above are lacking in any respect, it is in their general tendency to overemphasize form at the expense of meaning, to concentrate too closely on the nature of the monument itself and not enough on the monumentality created in its interaction with people and things around it (Thomas 2007:10–12; this volume). In the past two decades or so there have been several attempts in archaeology and other disciplines to move the discussion of ancient monuments along new avenues of research, often exploring new theoretical areas as they arise in neighboring disciplines. Only occasionally is a study dedicated to monuments or monumentality specifically; more frequently, we will see their relevance to the present work applied indirectly.

One of the most commonly discussed topics in theoretical archaeological literature in recent years has been the theme of agency—that of common individuals as active participants in the creation of social structure as opposed to the "great men" purview of traditional history, typically using the work of Bourdieu (1977) and Giddens (1984) as a foundation, as well as the agency of material objects themselves influencing the negotiation of social engagements (Olsen 2003; 2010). This burgeoning literature has inevitably spilled over into monumentality, perhaps most famously in Pauketat's (2000) analysis of the gradual construction of the enormous Monks Mound at the Mississippian site of Cahokia (cf. Blitz and Livingood 2004). Drawing upon his excavations at the site, which show clear evidence for annual construction cycles, Pauketat uses Giddens's concept of unintended consequences to construct a narrative that sees the commoners who were, of course, the actual builders of the mound, as the unwitting agents of their own subjection, assembling the apparatus of their own domination over too long a time span to anticipate the consequences of their actions (2000). A highly similar approach has been adopted in Formative Period Mesoamerica by Joyce (2004), who proposes that the iconic pyramids of the later classic Maya and Aztecs were simply the end point of a long trajectory of monument building that began with relatively modest structures newly built out of clay. These clay buildings lasted much longer than previous materials, and thus changed the spatial arena in which political interaction occurred, eventually—and unintentionally—becoming the sites of new political practices that over time became standardized and thus necessitated ever larger physical settings. Likewise, Johansen (2004) documents how Neolithic ashmounds in southern India, though originally created by a process of repetitive and mundane activities such as cattle penning and dung storage, later became sites of megalith construction and the expression of political power (see also Fisher this volume).

The contrast with the approach advocated by Trigger, and adopted indirectly by scholars such as Kolb and Pollock, is clear. Agency-based reconstructions of the origins of monuments turn the traditional explanation on its head by removing powerful political actors altogether and replacing them with common people as the monumental agents. Far from being indexes for how much labor a political ruler was able to mobilize, Joyce and Pauketat reverse Trigger's understanding of cause and consequence in monumental constructions by rendering political power an outcome of monumental architecture instead of its creator.

Not unrelated to concepts of agency in the creation of monuments is the notion of how individuals experience monuments once construction is completed (Pauketat this volume). The so-called phenomenological approach to the built environment has encouraged much speculation—some productive, some less so—on how ancient buildings and sculptures were actually understood and perceived by individuals. In the case of architecture, one might point not to a particular architect, but to the writing of prominent social theorist Henri Lefebvre, godfather of the "spatial turn" in the humanities and social sciences, who argues that the power of a cathedral, for example, lies in how its visitors become aware of their own footsteps, listen to the singing, smell the incense—in short, they "experience a total being in a total space" (1990:221).[9]

In archaeology, the phenomenological approach to monuments is most closely tied to landscape archaeology (Johnson 2012) where scholars, especially those working in Great Britain and continental Europe, have attempted to interpret the meaning of megaliths, cairns, henges, and other built landscape features without the aid of native historical documents as a guide (e.g., Cummings et al. 2002; Müller this volume). One researcher frequently concerned with monuments in the landscape is Bradley (1993, 1998, 2000), who turns to built features of ancient circular henges such as distinctions in sight lines between interior and exterior to postulate about ancient principles of inclusivity and exclusivity, among other things. Equally important is the work of Tilley (1994, 1996) who, following a lengthy theoretical explication and justification of the phenomenological approach, speculates about whether cairns in the coastal area of Wales were placed deliberately to draw one's attention to distant landscape features like mountains, or to nearby natural features such as rivers within earshot of a given monument (1994:93–109). One does not have to be a dyed-in-the-wool positivist to challenge the credibility of such reconstructions, and several strong negative reactions have been penned (e.g., Fleming 2005). Regardless of how one feels about the phenomenological approach to landscape, however, it is critical to keep in mind the landscape setting of ancient monuments, and to consider the possibility—or even likelihood—that a given ancient culture may not have had the same conceptual dichotomy between culture and physical landscape that we do today (Scarre 2002a, 2002b:6–8, 2007). Related theoretical positions and interpretations are often held by archaeologists interested in monumentality and the sacred

(Barrett 1990; Howey 2012; Johansen 2004; Scarre 2011; Thomas 1990; Thompson and Pluckhahn 2012) and in urban symbolism and settlement planning according to principles of cosmology, where lie longstanding debates concerning the verifiability of results (Ashmore 1991; Ashmore and Sabloff 2002, 2003; Carl et al. 2000; Smith 2003, 2007; Wheatley 1971).

Even if some phenomenological interpretations of ancient monumentality flounder on account of our inability to confirm or reject them, rendering reconstructions of ancient perception a challenge in the best of times, it is nevertheless worth recalling phenomenology's basic tenet that humans in all times and in all places are trapped within their own particular worldview and can only ever view the world through the perspective of their own cultural environment. This is important to any study of ancient monumentality (and, indeed, to any study of the past), for how are we to evaluate rival interpretive claims of a given body of evidence, particularly in the case of nonliterate societies? Consider the experiment posed by the Environmental Protection Agency, who requested that a deterring symbol be placed permanently above New Mexico's underground Waste Isolation Pilot Plant (WIPP). The symbol chosen has to last in the desert at least 10,000 years, and thus in addition to being durable must also be an effective communicator well beyond the demise of our civilization that produces it (Bryan-Wilson 2003). The sheer futility of the proposals made by a committee of anthropologists, archaeologists, linguists, and engineers—ranging from huge skulls and crossbones to a vast desert landscape of black thorn-shaped monoliths—would be comical were it not for the disquieting fact that the failed suggestions effectively shatter any confidence we might otherwise have possessed regarding our ability to understand accurately the intent behind ancient monuments.

Part of the problem in the WIPP case is humans' inability to perpetuate genuinely long-term social memory beyond the cyclical rise and fall of civilizations; phenomenology teaches us that attempts to do so are doomed to fail. Nevertheless, the maintenance of social memory at a smaller time scale is one of monuments' most visible, and most frequently discussed, functions. One case of monuments being used as tools to activate social memory is the so-called unintentional monument, which refers to buildings and sculptures that, though not intended to have a special relationship with people at the time of their construction, later are mobilized to serve the social needs of the present (think Baltimore's Poe House, or the Paul Revere House in Boston) (Riegl 1903). Perhaps more obvious manifestations of the materialization of memory are those monuments, especially memorial sculptures, that are created with the explicit goal of reminding people about significant places, events, or people. This phenomenon began in earnest following the Renaissance (Choay 2001), and accelerated exponentially in the second half of the twentieth century (Huyssen 2000).

It is important to recall, however, that deliberately created memorials are by no means exclusively positive in their associations (Savage 1997). Perhaps the most famous memorial to have been built in North America in the past decade is Michael Arad's 9/11 Memorial, commemorating the September 11 attacks of 2001 (Arad 2009). Far less famous, though equally revealing of the delicate nature of monumentality as a social memory device, is The Eye that Cries (*El Ojo que Llora*), a rock art installation placed in a public park in Lima comprising several thousand pebbles, each inscribed with the name of a victim from Peru's violent civil conflict during the 1980s and 1990s. When it was discovered that several dozen names of Shining Path terrorists who had been killed in a prison uprising were inadvertently included in the monument, The Eye that Cries was vandalized, revealing that a sculpture explicitly intended to symbolize a nation in healing can in fact do quite the opposite, reopening painful wounds by activating disturbing memories (Drinot 2009).[10] Similarly, artists have been struggling to find effective ways to commemorate traumatic or shameful national events without glorifying them inadvertently by constructing large, permanent sculptures; what is the appropriate way to commemorate the Holocaust in Germany, for example? One innovative solution has been the rise of the "counter-monument," monuments that self-consciously challenge expected norms of scale and endurance, such as the Harburg Monument against Fascism, a twelve-meter high square pillar that invited pedestrians to scrawl personal messages on its soft aluminum siding before being slowly sunk into the ground to rest (cf. Huyssen 1996; Moshenska 2010; Young 1992, 1999).

Time will tell how monuments such as the 9/11 Memorial or The Eye that Cries are received in future centuries—if, indeed, they are even still standing. As we have seen, monuments, even deliberately constructed memorials, have an uncomfortable habit of changing meanings with the passage of the years (Harmanşah 2011). For archaeologists, one of the greatest challenges is articulating how these meanings changed in the past, for of course ancient societies had social memories too—and how are we to tell to what stage in the evolution of memory an excavated feature belongs? Can a building we bring to light have its memory-history accurately reconstructed, from its creation to its use, reuse, and eventual abandonment? Building on the work of scholars such as Halbwachs (1950) and Connerton (1989), Alcock (2002) asks similar questions in her study of memory in the landscape and monuments of ancient Greece. She argues convincingly that, far from representing merely a shift in political status from independent democracy to subjugated province, the architectural infilling of the Athenian Agora during the occupation of the Roman Empire was a deliberate attempt to highlight Greece's former Hellenistic glories, showcasing earlier Hellenistic art and architecture as both a reassurance to themselves and a reminder of their accomplished legacy to their conquerors (Alcock 2002:51–67). The relative wealth of information pertaining to the Classical world makes it an ideal venue for studies of monumentality and memory (Alexandridis this volume; Boschung this volume).

The Athenians' attempt to use architecture as a means of conveying messages to their Roman occupiers raises another way individuals have approached monuments and monumental buildings, and that is as a text whose social meanings can, with judicious and careful treatment of physical and historical evidence, be "read" by scholars seeking insight into social relations. Victor Hugo is perhaps the writer who most explicitly makes the analogy. At one point (Book V, chapter 2), Hugo leaves the narrative of *The Hunchback of Notre-Dame* for a lengthy discourse likening architecture to books that compile and represent cultures' memories, traditions, and values, writing that for 6,000 years—in biblical terms the entire span of earth's history—"architecture was the great handwriting of the human race. And this is so true, that not only every religious symbol, but every human thought, has its page and its monument in that immense book." Hugo opines a strong pessimism for the survival of architecture as the poetry of humankind in the face of competition from the printing press; the antagonist Claude Frollo ominously declares, "This will kill that," when looking up from a printed volume to the towering cathedral.

Hugo need not have worried, since reading monumental architecture as social text has continued well into the present day. Ethnohistorian Gary Urton, for example, wrote a social history of the Andean village of Pacariqtambo based on the construction sequence of the courtyard wall, what in antiquity would be referred to as a temenos wall, that surrounds the village's public church (1988). Since the village's ten clans, or *ayllu*s, were each responsible for a section of the wall, the patchy evolution of the wall's morphology over time reflects the oscillating hierarchies that exist between the *ayllu*s, and serves as a testament of the public interaction and dialogue between them. Monumental sculpture can be similarly "read" (Ibarra this volume; Langin-Hooper this volume), as in the case of the Patna Massacre Memorial, a statue erected to commemorate the deaths of several dozen British soldiers during the eighteenth-century occupation of India. Over time, subtle changes were made to the monument's form as well as to its accompanying inscription, which Brown (2006) argues were both a result of, and a contributing factor to, the changing dynamics between the English and their colonial subjects.

There is one final theme pertaining to meaning and monumentality that has appeared in scholarly literature, though much more subtly, and that is several scholars' challenge to the typically assumed association of monuments and permanence. Monuments do not necessarily remain in place where they were erected, but can be uprooted and transplanted with accompanying changes of meaning (Parker 2003; this volume). Because it is the case that many, if not most, monuments are built to last, it is worth ruminating on those monuments that seem to be characterized, at least in part, by their proclivity for change (Savage 2009:21). For example, in the previous section I described how open courtyards and plazas in ancient cities have been interpreted as proxies for state control via political performances. Though certainly true in many instances, Smith looks to modern examples of open spaces and notes that unlike buildings, whose form and meaning are comparatively rigid, open spaces contain the capacity for almost instantaneous changes in meaning (2008:220). Tiananmen Square is one example, a carefully constructed venue of state authority that became, almost overnight, the locus of revolution in 1989.[11]

For a very brief period—just five days, from May 30 to June 4—Tiananmen contained what must surely be one of the shortest-lived monuments in history: the Goddess of Democracy, a statue erected by the demonstrating students as a deliberate provocation to the regime, who was then obliged either to allow the statue to remain standing, or to destroy it in an embarrassing public spectacle (Wu 2005). The regime chose the latter, and replicas of the Goddess of Democracy have gone on to become symbols of political freedom around the world, a powerful example of how a monument's efficacy can lie in its temporariness, not its permanence, as standard definitions would have us believe. More contrived, perhaps, but no less fascinating is the case of Gerz and Shalev-Gerz's Holocaust Memorial in Hamburg, consisting of an 8-m-tall column that was slowly lowered into the ground beneath as people inscribed their thoughts and feelings onto its surface. Here we again see the monument's meaning and its relationship with its viewers being negotiated in its disappearance, not its immutability.

CONCLUSION

The numerous studies described above, in addition to providing a general overview of the themes that are found across the vast and disparate literature that exists on monuments and monumentality, illustrate the point with which I opened this chapter: that no definition of "monument" can ever aspire to be absolute unless it locates a monument's monumentality in the relationship that exists between it and the people experiencing it. Such an approach is both flexible and encompassing, incorporating many disciplines and methodologies without expecting researchers to adhere to strict definitional properties. A relational viewpoint is absent from formal treatments of monuments, and generally only hinted at in the more interpretive works just described. Both aspects of the topic are necessary to any study, though not sufficient individually; form and meaning must be considered together. Monumentality is something more than the shape, or size, or visibility, or permanence of the monument—though these variables absolutely carry their own significance. Monumentality lies in the meaning created by the relationship that is negotiated between object and person, and between object and the surrounding constellation of values and symbols in a culture. This introductory chapter—and the case studies that are presented in the chapters that follow—has demonstrated this in numerous studies of monuments of all kinds, and from all times and places.

To return, then, to the question with which I opened this chapter—can the tiny Guennol Lioness truly be considered monumental?—we are faced with the stark reality that without provenience information the miniature statue's relationship with the people that used it and its relational status within its larger cultural system are all but irretrievable. And yet, there is a tantalizing clue in the ancient art historical record. The one other place in which the image of the muscular lioness appears is in seal impressions from the site of Susa. Here one sees the same lioness standing beside stylized mountains, and in two cases even holding the mountains above her head (Porada 1950:fig. 6). Porada writes,

> [T]he enormous size of the leonine figures in comparison with the small mountains could . . . be interpreted as indicating that the lion-demons had great power over the mountainous country through which they stride (fig. 6: a) or which they support on their raised paws (fig. 6: f, g). (1950:225)

Whether or not the lioness had "great power" over the mountains, it seems undeniable that the animal was somehow related to this massive feature of the natural landscape—perhaps the only culturally held relationship of any kind to which we can point. Though the evidence is exiguous at best, it does appear that the instinctive inclination to refer to the lioness statue as "monumental" despite its tiny stature might have some ancient relational justification after all. Furthermore, we cannot disregard the relationship that our own culture has chosen to associate with it. For better or for worse, and for reasons many of us may not agree with, in our multimillion dollar purchase of the object we have chosen to ascribe to the Guennol Lioness a meaning that is only marginally related to its size. As one archaeologist has written, "Monuments, it turns out, are in the eye of the beholder" (Hole 2012:457).

Though we can interpret such ascriptions of meaning in the present with relative ease, the challenge for the archaeologist is to make such determinations using only inconsistent and fragmentary evidence from the past. The chapters contained in this volume, which is divided into five major parts—(I) Monumental Architecture and Social Transformation (Potts, Caraher, Thomas, and Notroff et al.); (II) Monumentality and Landscape (Glatz, Ibarra, Kolb, and Müller); (III) Monuments and Memory Work (Bogucki, Alexandridis, Boschung, and Parker); (IV) Monuments, Settlements, and Cities (Bachhuber, Novák, and Therborn); and (V) The Experience of Monuments (Fisher, Langin-Hooper, Wendrich, and Pauketat)—take up this challenge with rigor and resolve, and it is my pleasure to present their findings here.

Notes

1. The previous record holders for most expensive sculpture, modern or ancient, were the ancient Roman piece *Artemis and the Stag*, which sold for $28.6 million in June 2007, and then Picasso's *Tête de Femme (Dora Maar)*, which fetched $29.1 million in November of that year. This record lasted less than a month, when the Guennol Lioness was sold for nearly double that price. Though the lioness still stands at the top of the pile for most highly priced antiquity, the record for the most expensive sculpture was surpassed yet again in early 2010, when Alberto Giacometti's *L'Homme qui marche I* sold for $104.3 million, a record that remains intact today.

2. A contemporary art historian whom I invited to participate in the monumentality conference whose proceedings are contained in the present volume (and who politely declined the invitation) mentioned in passing, "You should get someone to present on the Guennol Lioness. Talk about *monumental!*"

3. See http://www.youtube.com/watch?v=T-K7PNw1_dw for Hildesley's presentation of the statue, as interesting for its artful persuasion of the viewer as it is for the lioness itself.

4. "monument, v.." *OED* Online. September 2012. Oxford University Press, accessed 14 November 2012, http://www.oed.com/view/Entry/121853?rskey=Oz7z5V&result=2.

5. In the same analogical spirit as Wu, Lefebvre declares that "[b]uildings are to monuments as everyday life is to festival" (1990:223).

6. The degree to which this part of the process is speculative is directly correlated with the amount of the building that is preserved in the archaeological record. Though a crucial stage of the quantification process, the degree of confidence in archaeologists' volumetric reconstructions is rarely specified and never statistically evaluated.

7. Of course, the same procedure can be used to argue *against* a particular building's monumentality, with the reasoning that buildings with low energy investiture must be fairly conventional, nonmonumental structures. Such is the case with Banning's (2011) recent reassessment of the massive 11,000-year-old buildings excavated at Göbekli Tepe, whose size and uniqueness leads most scholars (including their excavator, Klaus Schmidt†) to assume that the buildings must be monumental.

8. The interminable struggles surrounding the construction of One World Trade Center (formerly known as the Freedom Tower) in downtown Manhattan are emblematic of the difficulties nontotalitarian regimes face when trying to launch major monumental building projects.

9. A lengthier passage perhaps better summarizes Lefbvre's intent: "Inasmuch as the poet through a poem gives voices to a way of living (living, feeling, thinking, taking pleasure, or suffering), the experience of monumental space may be said to have some similarity to entering and sojourning in the poetic world" (1990:224).

10. As an interesting aside, it is worth noting that the sculptor, Lika Mutal, was not aware of the presence of Shining Path activists in the list of victims' names she was handed, and claims she would not have included them if given the choice (Drinot 2009:23). Here again we see the agency of the object itself exerting itself, this time not only without the sculptor's intent, but in direct contradiction to it.

11. The iconic photograph of the still-anonymous "Tank Man" who defied a line of tanks by standing before them with nothing more than a grocery bag is emblematic of monumental open spaces' remarkable ability to undergo 180° turns of meaning at dizzying speeds.

References Cited

Abrams, E. M. 1989 Architecture and Energy: An Evolutionary Perspective. *Archaeological Method and Theory* 1:47–88.

Abrams, E. M., and T. W. Bolland 1999 Architectural Energetics, Ancient Monuments and Operations Management. *Journal of Archaeological Method and Theory* 6:263–291.

Agnew, J. 1998 The Impossible Capital: Monumental Rome under Liberal and Fascist Regimes, 1870–1943. *Geografiska Annaler. Series B, Human Geography* 80(4):229–240.

Alcock, S. E. 2002 *Archaeologies of the Greek Past: Landscape, Monuments, and Memories*. Cambridge University Press, Cambridge.

Arad, M. 2009 Reflecting Absence. *Places* 21(1):42–51.

Ashmore, W. 1991 Site-Planning Principles and Concepts of Directionality among the Ancient Maya. *Latin American Antiquity* 2(3):199–226.

Ashmore, W., and J. A. Sabloff 2002 Spatial Orders in Maya Civic Plans. *Latin American Antiquity* 13(2):201–215.

Ashmore, W., and J. A. Sabloff 2003 Interpreting Ancient Maya Civic Plans: Reply to Smith. *Latin American Antiquity* 24(2):229–236.

Atkinson, D., and D. Cosgrove 1998 Urban Rhetoric and Embodied Identities: City, Nation, and Empire at the Vittorio Emanuele II Monument in Rome, 1870–1945. *Annals of the Association of American Geographers* 88(1):28–49.

Banning, E. B. 2011 So Fair a House: Göbekli Tepe and the Identification of Temples in the Pre-Pottery Neolithic. *Current Anthropology* 52(5):619–660.

Barrett, J. C. 1990 The Monumentality of Death: The Character of Early Bronze Age Mortuary Mounds in Southern Britain. *World Archaeology* 22(2):179–189.

Bayliss, A., F. McAvoy, and A. Whittle 2007 The World Recreated: Redating Silbury Hill in its Monumental Landscape. *Antiquity* 81:26–53.

Blitz, J. H., and P. Livingood 2004 Sociopolitical Implications of Mississippian Mound Volume. *American Antiquity* 69:291–301.

Bourdieu, P. 1977 *Outline of a Theory of Practice*. Cambridge University Press, Cambridge.

Bradley, R. 1993 *Altering the Earth: The Origins of Monuments in Britain and Continental Europe*. Society of Antiquaries of Scotland, Edinburgh.

Bradley, R. 1998 *The Significance of Monuments: On the Shaping of Human Experience in Neolithic and Bronze Age Europe.* Routledge, London.

Bradley, R. 2000 *An Archaeology of Natural Places.* Routledge, London and New York.

Brown, R. M. 2006 Inscribing Colonial Monumentality: A Case Study of the 1763 Patna Massacre Memorial. *The Journal of Asian Studies* 65(1):91–113.

Bryan-Wilson, J. 2003 Building a Marker of Nuclear Warning. In *Monuments and Memory, Made and Unmade,* edited by R. S. Nelson and M. Olin, pp. 183–204. The University of Chicago Press, Chicago and London.

Çambel, H. 1999 *Corpus of Hieroglyphic Luwian Inscriptions vol. II: Karatepe-Arslantaş.* Walter de Gruyter, Berlin and New York.

Carl, P., B. Kemp, R. Laurence, R. Coningham, C. Hingham, and G. Cowgill 2000 Were Cities Built As Images? *Cambridge Archaeological Journal* 10(2):327–365.

Childe, V. G. 1950 The Urban Revolution. *The Town Planning Review* 2(1):3–17.

Choay, F. 2001 *The Invention of the Historic Monument.* Translated by L. M. O'Connell. Cambridge University Press, Cambridge.

Collins, C. C., and G. R. Collins 1984 Monumentality: A Critical Matter in Modern Architecture. *Harvard Architecture Review* 4:15–35.

Connerton, P. 1989 *How Societies Remember.* Cambridge University Press, Cambridge and New York.

Cummings, V., J. Jones, and A. Watson 2002 Divided Places: Phenomenology and Asymmetry in the Monuments of the Black Mountains, Southeast Wales. *Cambridge Archaeological Journal* 12(1):57–70.

DeMarrais, E., L. J. Castillo, and T. Earle 1996 Ideology, Materialization, and Power Strategies. *Current Anthropology* 37(1):15–31.

Dillehay, T. D. 1990 Mapuche Ceremonial Landscape, Social Recruitment and Resources Rights. *World Archaeology* 22(2):223–241.

Drinot, P. 2009 For Whom the Eye Cries: Memory, Monumentality, and the Ontologies of Violence in Peru. *Journal of Latin American Cultural Studies* 18(1):15–32.

Durkheim, É. 1893 *De la division du travail social.* F. Alcan, Paris.

Fleming, A. 2005 Megaliths and Post-Modernism: the Case of Wales. *Antiquity* 79:921–932.

Ford, L. R. 2008 World Cities and Global Change: Observations on Monumentality in Urban Design. *Eurasian Geography and Economics* 49(3):237–262.

Giddens, A. 1984 *The Constitution of Society: Outline of the Theory of Structuration.* University of California Press, Berkeley.

Gilibert, A. 2011 *Syro-Hittite Monumental Art and the Archaeology of Performance: The Stone Reliefs at Carchemish and Zincirli in the Earlier First Millennium BCE.* Topoi: Berlin Studies of the Ancient World. De Gruyter, Berlin.

Glatz, C., and A. Plourde 2011 Landscape Monuments and Political Competition in Late Bronze Age Anatolia: An Investigation of Costly Signaling Theory. *Bulletin of the American Schools of Oriental Research* 361:33–66.

Godelier, M. 1986 *The Mental and the Material: Thought, Economy and Society.* Verso, London.

Goldhagen, S. W. 2001 *Louis Kahn's Situated Modernism.* Yale University Press, New Haven and London.

Halbwachs, M. 1950 *La Mémoire Collective.* Paris, Presses Universitaires de France.

Harmanşah, Ö. 2011 Monuments and Memory: Architecture and Visual Culture in Ancient Anatolian History. In *The Oxford Handbook of Ancient Anatolia, 10,000–323 B.C.E.,* edited by S. R. Steadman and G. McMahon, pp. 623–656. Oxford University Press, New York.

Hole, F. 2012 A West Asian Perspective on Early Monuments. In *Early New World Monumentality*, edited by R. L. Burger and R. M. Rosenswig, pp. 457–465. University Press of Florida, Gainesville.

Hoskins, J. 2006 Agency, Biography, and Objects. In *Handbook of Material Culture,* edited by C. Tilley, W. Keane, S. Küchler, M. Rowlands, and P. Spyer, pp. 74–84. Sage, London.

Howey, M. C. L. 2012 *Mound Builders and Monument Makers of the Northern Great Lakes, 1200–1600.* University of Oklahoma Press, Norman.

Huyssen, A. 1996 Monumental Seduction. *New German Critique* 69:181–200.

Huyssen, A. 2000 Present Pasts: Media, Politics, Amnesia. *Public Culture* 12(1):21–38.

Inomata, T. 2006 Plazas, Performers, and Spectators: Political Theaters of the Classic Maya. *Current Anthropology* 47(5):805–842.

Johansen, P. G. 2004 Landscape, Monumental Architecture, and Ritual: A Reconsideration of the South Indian Ashmounds. *Journal of Anthropological Archaeology* 23:309–330.

Johnson, M. H. 2012 Phenomenological Approaches in Landscape Archaeology. *Annual Review of Anthropology* 41:269–284.

Joyce, R. A. 2004 Unintended Consequences? Monumentality as a Novel Experience in Formative Mesoamerica. *Journal of Archaeological Method and Theory* 11(1):5–29.

Kolb, M. J. 1994 Monumentality and the Rise of Religious Authority in Precontact Hawai'i. *Current Anthropology* 35(5):521–547.

Marcus, J. 2003 Monumentality in Archaic States: Lessons Learned from Large-Scale Excavations of the Past. In *Theory and Practice in Mediterranean Archaeology: Old World and New World Perspectives,* edited by J. K. Papadopoulos and R. M. Leventhal, pp. 115–134. Cotsen Institute, UCLA, Los Angeles.

Meyers, G. E. 2012 Introduction: The Experience of Monumentality in Etruscan and Early Roman Architecture. In *Monumentality in Etruscan and Early Roman Architecture: Ideology and Innovation,* edited by M. L. Thomas and G. E. Meyers, pp. 1–20. University of Texas Press, Austin.

Moore, J. D. 1996 *Architecture and Power in the Ancient Andes: The Archaeology of Public Buildings.* Cambridge University Press, Cambridge.

Morgan, L. H. 1877 *Ancient Society.* H. Holt, New York.

Moshenska, G. 2010 Charred Churches or Iron Harvests? Counter-Monumentality and the Commemoration of the London Blitz. *Journal of Social Archaeology* 10(1):5–27.

Mumford, L. 1938 *The Culture of Cities.* Harcourt, Brace, New York.

Neiman, F. D. 1997 Conspicuous Consumption as Wasteful Advertising: A Darwinian Perspective on Spatial Patterns in Classic Maya Terminal Monument Dates. *Archeological Papers of the American Anthropological Association* 7:267–290.

Olsen, B. 2003 Material Culture after Text: Re-Membering Things. *Norwegian Archaological Review* 36(2):87–104.

Olsen, B. 2010 *In Defense of Things: Archaeology and the Ontology of Objects.* Altamira Press, Lanham.

Parker, G. 2003 Narrating Monumentality: The Piazza Navona Obelisk. *Journal of Mediterranean Archaeology* 16(2):193–215.

Pauketat, T. R. 2000 The Tragedy of the Commoners. In *Agency in Archaeology,* edited by M.-A. Dobres and J. Robb, pp. 113–129. Routledge, London and New York.

Pollock, S. 1999 *Ancient Mesopotamia: The Eden that Never Was.* Cambridge University Press, Cambridge.

Porada, E. 1950 A Leonine Figure of the Protoliterate Period of Mesopotamia. *Journal of the American Oriental Society* 70(4):223–226.

Renfrew, C. 1973 Monuments, Mobilization, and Social Organization in Neolithic Wessex. In *The Explanation of Culture Change: Models in Prehistory*, edited by C. Renfrew, pp. 539–558. Duckworth, London.

Renfrew, C. 1976 Megaliths, Territories, and Populations. In *Acculturation and Continuity in Atlantic Europe*, edited by S. J. d. Laet, pp. 198–220. De Tempel, Brugge.

Riegl, A. 1903 *Der Moderne Denkmalkultus: Sein Wesen und seine Entstehung*. W. Braumhuller, Vienna = The Modern Cult of Monuments: Its Character and its Origin, *Oppositions* 25 (1982):21–51.

Ristvet, L. 2007 The Third Millennium City Wall at Tell Leilan, Syria: Identity, Authority, and Urbanism. In *Power and Architecture: Monumental Public Architecture in the Bronze Age Near East and Aegean*, edited by J. Bretschneider; J. Driessen and K. V. Lerberghe, pp. 183–211. Peeters, Leuven.

Rosenswig, R. M., and R. L. Burger 2012 Considering Early New World Monumentality. In *Early New World Monumentality*, edited by R. L. Burger and R. M. Rosenswig, pp. 4–22. University Press of Florida, Gainesville.

Sahlins, M. D. 1968 *Tribesmen*. Prentice-Hall, Englewood Cliffs.

Savage, K. 1997 *Standing Soldiers, Kneeling Slaves: Race, War, and Monument in Nineteenth-Century America*. Princeton University Press, Princeton.

Savage, K. 2009 *Monument Wars: Washington, D.C., the National Mall, and the Transformation of the Memorial Landscape*. University of California Press, Berkeley, Los Angeles, London.

Scarre, C. 2002a *Monuments and Landscape in Atlantic Europe: Perception and Society During the Neolithic and Early Bronze Age*. Routledge, London and New York.

Scarre, C. 2002b Introduction: Situating Monuments. The Dialogue between Built Form and Landform in Atlantic Europe. In *Monuments and Landscape in Atlantic Europe: Perception and Society During the Neolithic and Early Bronze Age*, edited by C. Scarre, pp. 1–14. Routledge, London and New York.

Scarre, C. 2007 *The Megalithic Monuments of Britain and Ireland*. Thames and Hudson, London, New York.

Scarre, C. 2011 Monumentality. In *The Oxford Handbook of the Archaeology of Ritual*, edited by T. Insoll, pp. 9–23. Oxford University Press, Oxford.

Sert, J. L., F. Leger, and S. Giedion 1984 Nine Points on Monumentality. *Harvard Architecture Review* 4:62–63.

Service, E. R. 1962 *Primitive Social Organization*. Random House, New York.

Sherratt, A. 1990 The Genesis of Megaliths: Monumentality, Ethnicity, and Social Complexity in Neolithic North-West Europe. *World Archaeology* 22(2):147–167.

Smith, A. T. 2003 *The Political Landscape: Constellations of Authority in Early Complex Polities*. University of California Press, Berkeley.

Smith, C. J. 2008 Monumentality in Urban Design: The Case of China. *Eurasian Geography and Economics* 49(3):263–279.

Smith, M. E. 2003 Can We Read Cosmology from Maya City Plans? Comment on Ashmore and Sabloff. *Latin American Antiquity* 14:221–228.

Smith, M. E. 2007 Form and Meaning in the Earliest Cities: A New Approach to Ancient Urban Planning. *Journal of Planning History* 6(1):3–47.

Smith, M. E. 2009 V. Gordon Childe and the Urban Revolution: A Historical Perspective on a Revolution in Urban Studies. *Town Planning Review* 80(1):3–29.

Smith, M. L. 2008 Urban Empty Spaces. Contentious Places for Consensus-Building. *Archaeological Dialogues* 15(2):216–231.

Speer, A. 1970. *Inside the Third Reich: Memoirs*. Macmillan, New York.

Steadman, S. R., and J. C. Ross, eds. 2010 *Agency and Identity in the Ancient Near East: New Paths Forward*. Equinox, London and Oakville, CT.

Thomas, E. 2007 *Monumentality and the Roman Empire: Architecture in the Antonine Age*. Oxford University Press, Oxford.

Thomas, J. 1990 Monuments from the Inside: The Case of the Irish Megalithic Tombs. *World Archaeology* 22(2):168–178.

Thompson, V. D., and T. J. Pluckhahn 2012 Monumentalization and Ritual Landscapes at Fort Center in the Lake Okeechobee Basin of South Florida. *Journal of Anthropological Archaeology* 31(1):49–65.

Thompson, V. D., and T. J. Pluckhahn 1994 *A Phenomenology of Landscape: Places, Paths and Monuments*. Berg, Oxford.

Tilley, C. 1996 The Powers of Rocks: Topography and Monument Construction on Bodmin Moor. *World Archaeology* 28(2):161–176.

Trigger, B. G. 1989 *A History of Archaeological Thought*. Cambridge University Press, Cambridge and New York.

Trigger, B. G. 1990 Monumental Architecture: A Thermodynamic Explanation of Symbolic Behaviour. *World Archaeology* 22(2):119–132.

Urton, G. 1988 La Arquitectura Publica como Texto Social: La Historia de un Muro de Adobe en Pacariqtambo, Peru (1915–1985). *Revista Andina* 6(1):225–261.

Wheatley, P. 1971 *The Pivot of the Four Quarters: A Preliminary Enquiry Into the Origins and Character of the Ancient Chinese City*. Aldine, Chicago.

Winter, I. J. 1992 "Idols of the King": Royal Images as Recipients of Ritual Action in Ancient Mesopotamia. *Journal of Ritual Studies* 6(1):13–42.

Witmore, C., and Ö. Harmanşah 2007 The Endangered Future of the Past. *New York Times*, http://www.nytimes.com/2007/12/21/opinion/21iht-edwhitmore.html?pagewanted=all.

Wu, H. 1995 *Monumentality in Early Chinese Art and Architecture*. Stanford University Press, Stanford.

Wu, H. 2005 *Remaking Beijing: Tiananmen Square and the Creation of a Political Space*. University of Chicago Press, Chicago.

Young, J. E. 1992 The Counter-Monument: Memory against Itself in Germany Today. *Critical Inquiry*, 18(2):267–96.

Young, J. E. 1999 Memory and Counter-Memory: The End of the Monument in Germany. *Harvard Design Magazine* 9:1–10.

PART I

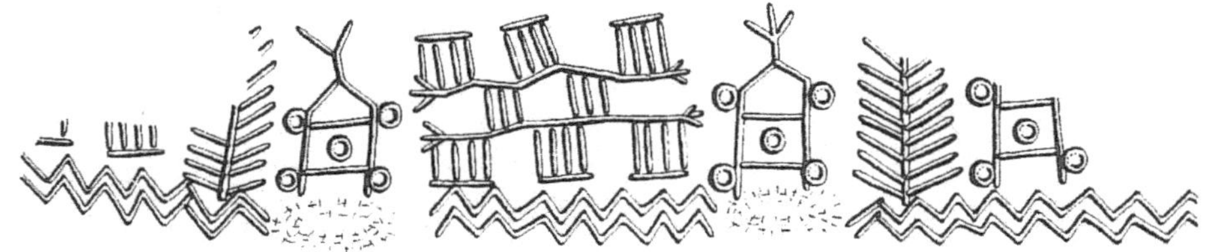

Monumental Architecture and Social Transformation

CHAPTER TWO

Elamite Monumentality and Architectural Scale

Lessons from Susa and Choga Zanbil

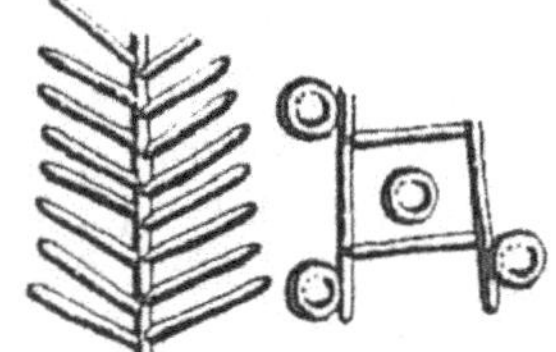

Daniel T. Potts

Abstract *Architectural monumentality in Elam (southwestern Iran) may be defined by a number of variables including material consumption, scale, elevation, and labor input. While little evidence of Elamite palatial architecture survives outside of the cuneiform sources, several examples of monumental religious structures are attested. This chapter looks at the high terrace on the Acropole mound at Susa, dated to c. 4000 B.C., and the Late Bronze Age ziqqurrat built by Untaš-Napiriša at Choga Zanbil (ancient Al Untaš-Napiriša). Each was impressive as a feat of engineering, requiring the mobilization of significant human resources and the production of millions of bricks. In order to appreciate the scale of these structures and the resources required to build them, comparisons are drawn with the much better documented Etemenanki at Babylon.*

Elam was the dominant political force in southwestern Iran (modern Khuzestan and Fars provinces) from about 2000 B.C. until the appearance of the Achaemenid Persian empire in the sixth century B.C. Despite the imposing scale of the major architectural monuments at Susa and Choga Zanbil (Figure 2.1)—two of the most intensively and extensively excavated sites in Elam—the monumentality of Elamite architecture has been overshadowed by that of its better known Mesopotamian neighbors to the west. This study aims to provide a corrective to this perspective by discussing two major monuments from southwestern Iran that are relevant to any discussion of monumentality in the ancient Near East: the late prehistoric, high terrace (*haute terrasse*) at Susa, erected c. 4000 B.C.; and the stepped temple platform (*ziqqurrat*) and associated precinct at Choga Zanbil, built in the late fourteenth century B.C. by the Middle Elamite king Untaš-Napiriša.

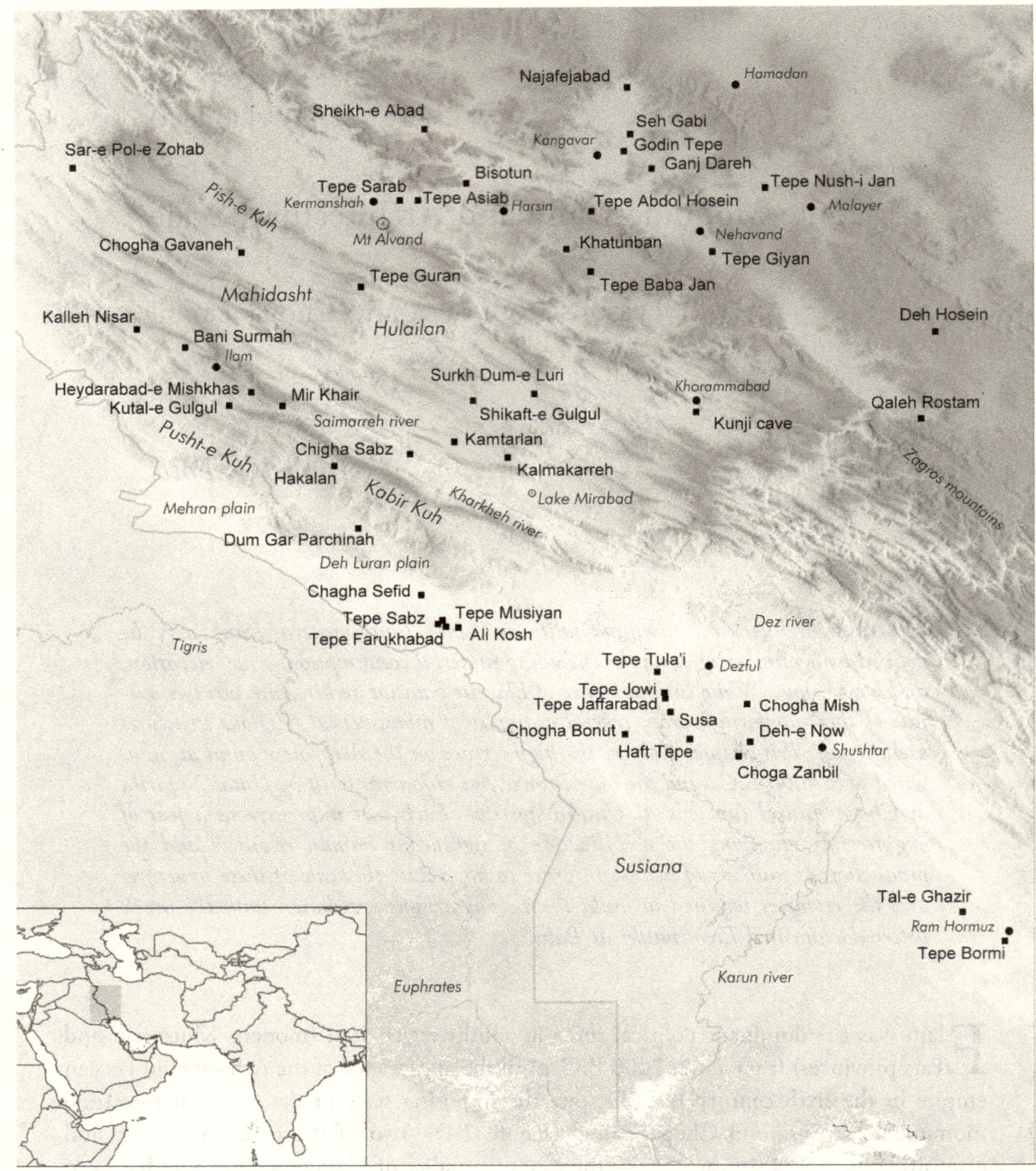

FIGURE 2.1 Map of southwestern Iran showing the location of Susa and Choga Zanbil.

Monuments are and probably always were multifunctional in the sense that the pragmatic rationale that lay behind their construction was but one of many uses to which they were put. In the case of the *haute terrasse* at Susa and the *ziqqurrat* at Choga Zanbil both served as platforms for the elevation of a temple, bringing it closer to the heavens. But each undoubtedly functioned as a symbol of much more. Like a lighthouse that evokes sensations of home, safety, warmth, or even salvation in the minds of terrorized sailors caught in a storm who may be contemplating their own imminent demise, the monuments of Susa and Choga Zanbil towered above the surrounding public and domestic buildings and were visible from a great distance (particularly in the case of Choga Zanbil, the temple of which was faced with multicolored, glazed bricks). Monuments such as these may well have evoked an Elamite equivalent of the Roman notion of *civitas* or *res publica,* a feeling of social solidarity and identification with the city, the city-state, and, eventually, the empire. As Anthony Tuck has noted in discussing pre-Roman Italy, "Monumentalized contexts . . . seize upon preexisting quotidian behaviors and seek to impress an audience through a radical rescaling of otherwise normative actions" (Tuck 2012:42). It is certainly true that religious expressions are quotidian in the sense that rituals may be performed by small numbers of worshippers in modest surroundings. In this sense, the monumental expressions of religious piety chosen for discussion here do represent a monumentalization and rescaling of something that was originally nested in a much humbler setting. On the other hand, what becomes clear in examining the architectural requirements of the monumental structures discussed below, as well as the more famous Etemenanki of Babylon, introduced here for comparison, is the utter impossibility of achieving anything remotely like the size and scale of these structures without access to the resources of a state over an extended period of years. Herein lies the real essence of monumentality in Elam.

Late Prehistoric Susa

Located along the Karkheh River on the Susiana plain in Khuzestan, Susa was founded *ab novo* around 4000 B.C., just on the cusp of the late or post-Ubaid/Early Uruk centuries of the early fourth millennium B.C. The portion of the site christened the "Acropole" (acropolis) by the early French excavators who worked there in the 1880s was established on a natural hill of yellow loess that rose about 9 m above the plain (Canal 1978a) and thus enjoyed an elevated position. This was a topographic situation in marked contrast to settlements on the flat alluvial plain of southern Mesopotamia (cf. Pollock 1989:283–285).

Many scholars have pointed to the Ubaid period examples of raised terraces that elevated temples in Mesopotamia as comparanda for the remains at prehistoric Susa (for a discussion of the ideological bases of this phenomenon see, e.g., Allinger-Csollich 1996, 2005; Lenzen 1966). Notable examples include the terrace at Eridu and the late Ubaid archaic terrace beneath the Anu *ziqqurrat* of first-millennium B.C. date at Uruk (for bibliography see Schmid 1995:96–103). Few scholars not specialized in Iran, however, are aware that the so-called *haute terrasse* of Susa I absolutely dwarfs the Mesopotamian examples. This monumental structure covered 6,400 sq. m (80 m on a side). Moreover, it was stepped like the Ur III and later temple platforms known as *ziqqurrats* (Sumerian u_6-*nir*, Akkadian *ziqqurratu*), discussed below. The lowest level stood 2 m high, and thus would have consisted originally of 12,800 cu. m of bricks (80 x 80 x 2 m); while the second step measured 74.5 x 78 m for a total surface area of 5811 sq. m (Canal 1978b:34). Compare this with the 375 sq. m terrace that supported Temple VIII at Eridu or the much larger terrace on which the Painted Temple at Tell 'Uqair stood, which covered an area of 2,700 sq. m (Schmid 1995:100–103).

While we do not know how high the second level stood, let alone how high the presumed temple on top of this stepped terrace rose, it is clear, when one adds the 9 m of elevation afforded by the natural loess hill on which Susa was founded, that from a distance, the *haute terrasse* would have been an imposing site, rising more than 11 m above the surface of the plain. Little wonder, then, that much later the native Elamite designation for the Acropole, where the main shrine of Susa's city-god, Inšušinak, stood, was *alumelu*, a term that was probably derived from Akkadian *ālu elû*, meaning "high/ high-rising city." Thus, it is perfectly understandable that Inšušinak bore the epithet *temti alieliri* or *temti alimelu*, "lord of the Acropole/high-rising city" (Poebel 1933:133; Potts 2010:54).

As for origins and antecedents, the older, nearby site of Chogha Mish, destroyed by fire shortly before Susa was founded, is sometimes cited as the source both of Susa's founding population (see Potts 1999:46 with earlier bibliography) and its high terrace (Hole 2010:231). The alleged remains of a platform and terrace at Chogha Mish (Alizadeh 2008:41; Delougaz and Kantor 1996:28–35), however, were so poorly preserved that it is difficult to seriously consider them related to later developments at Susa. One might look to the earliest terrace at Eridu, supporting Temple XI, which dates to the Ubaid 3 period and is thus older than the Susa I example by several centuries, but it seems clear that both in concept and in scale, the two were very different. There is nothing to suggest that the Eridu terrace was stepped and, as noted above, it was certainly much smaller (375 sq. m). Nor is there any reason to think that Susa's first settlers came from the Eridu region or for that matter any other part of southern Iraq. In any case, the point here is not to argue for the precedence of Susa in a debate over the origins of the temple terrace, but rather to highlight a precocious example of monumentality in Iran that historians of Mesopotamian architecture, such as Lenzen (1966) and Schmid (1995), completely overlooked in their discussions of the late prehistoric architectural antecedents of the *ziqqurrat*.

Whether the *haute terrasse* of Susa supported a temple of the city-god Inšušinak we cannot say, anymore than we can assume that the Late Uruk representation of a two-stage building with horn-like projections on a cylinder seal impression from Susa (Amiet 1987:Fig. 1) is an image of the *haute terrasse* founded in Susa I times. Nor can we say whether the temple that one assumes stood on the *haute terrasse*, or the building shown on the Susa seal impression, was the *kizzum labiram*, "the old sanctuary" of Susa referred to in later texts from the site (Malbran-Labat 1995:31–32; Potts 2010:54). Nevertheless, it is interesting to note that it was apparently in this area of the Acropole that a number of typically Early Dynastic limestone wall-plaques—common adornments in temples during the mid-third millennium B.C.—were found during the early excavations at Susa (Boese 1971; Pelzel 1977).

Moreover, there is certainly no question that the evocative image on the Late Uruk Susa sealing calls to mind the much later testimony of Assurbanipal who, in 647 B.C., sacked Susa and broke the bronze horns off its *ziqqurrat* (Streck 1916:53)—a building clearly shown as a four-tiered structure in a relief adorning one of the walls of Room I in Assurbanipal's palace at Nineveh (Dombart 1928:Abb. 1; Potts 1990)—before destroying the structure. This stepped platform may well have been the *zagratume*, an Elamite loanword derived from Akkadian *ziqquratu*, built by the Middle Elamite king Untaš-Napiriša at Susa in the fourteenth century B.C., according to a text inscribed on more than 120 bricks found at the site (Potts 2010:56–57). We may even have a stylized depiction of the Susa *ziqqurrat* on the famous bronze *sit šamsi* or "sunrise," commissioned by the twelfth-century Elamite king Shilhak-Inšušinak, where two crouching nude males appear before two stepped features that have often been likened to stepped terraces or, in the case of the larger example, a *ziqqurrat* (Potts 1999:Pl. 7.8). As for Assurbanipal's reference to bronze horns on the *ziqqurrat* of Susa (Potts 2010:57), the likelihood that horns crowned the *ziqqurrat* of Susa is supported not only by the Nineveh relief, but by an inscription on a badly damaged stele of Shilhak-Inšušinak's which refers to the casting of horns for a place of sacrifice (König 1965:106 §15). A Middle Elamite text from Tal-e Malyan (ancient Anšan) also records a transfer of 25 minas 5 shekels of gold for "horn(s)" (Potts 1999:284; Stolper 1984:68–69).

Choga Zanbil

Although Untaš-Napiriša built a *ziqqurrat* at Susa in the late fourteenth century B.C., he is better known for the one that he erected in the center of Choga Zanbil (Figure 2.2), a sprawling, 100 ha site located 40 km southeast of Susa (Potts 1999:222–230; 2010:60–62 and Table 1). With an outer perimeter wall more than 4 km long and an inner precinct, the perimeter wall of which was 1.625 km long, Choga Zanbil seems to have been intended by Untaš-Napiriša to serve as a religious center, and perhaps also a destination for pilgrimage, at which the deities of the Elamite highlands and lowlands were to be worshipped on an equal footing. According to texts inscribed on more than 5,000 bricks, at least 18 different deities were worshipped in more than 50 shrines at the site. The Choga Zanbil *ziqqurrat* was built principally of sundried mud-bricks covered with a 2 m thick shell of baked brick. Every tenth course of bricks was inscribed with a text proclaiming that Untaš-Napiriša raised a *ziqqurrat* to the sky in honor of Inšušinak of the sacred precinct and built a *kukunnum* of baked brick in order to ensure his own life, health, and prosperity (Potts 2010:490, no. 47). The Elamite term *kukkunum*, a loanword from Sumerian *gi-gú-na/gi-gun$_4$-na*, Akkadian *gigunû*, designated the temple that stood atop a terrace or *ziqqurrat*. In Elamite texts it is clearly distinguished from the *ziqqurrat* itself, for which another Elamite loanword, *zagratume*, was used (Potts 2010:57).

FIGURE 2.2 Untaš-Napiriša's *ziqqurrat* at Choga Zanbil, late fourteenth century B.C.

The four-stage structure at Choga Zanbil stood on a socle 105.2 m on a side, the successive levels of which measured 99.4, 67 (on a socle 71.2 m. long on each side), 51 (on an eroded socle the dimensions of which could not be reconstructed), and 35.2 m (the socle of which was no longer extant) on a side. The *kukunnum* on top, dedicated to both Inšušinak, lord of Susa, and Napirisha, the great god of Anšan (i.e., highland Elam, the capital of which was Tal-e Malyan near the later Achaemenid capital Persepolis), was faced with glazed bricks, gleaming in blue, green, gold, and silver. In contrast to the external staircases of Mesopotamian *ziqqurrats,* that of Choga Zanbil was largely internal (Potts 1999:225). Ghirshman estimated that the *ziqqurrat* stood to a height of about 12 m., broadly comparable with the minimum elevation of the temple that stood on the high terrace at Susa (including the natural loess hill on which it was built). When one considers the size of the overall architectural program at Choga Zanbil, which integrated 52 shrines attested in hundreds of brick inscriptions into a massive religious complex dominated by the *ziqqurrat,* then it is no exaggeration to suggest that Choga Zanbil is possibly the most striking example of a deliberately constructed suite of integrated monuments and architectural structures ever built in the ancient Near East.

As noted above, the *ziqqurrat* was an innovation of Ur-Nammu's. Regardless of the structural innovations introduced by Untaš-Napiriša, like the largely internal staircase ascending to the *kukunnum,* it is obvious that precedence in the development of the *ziqqurrat* must be accorded to Mesopotamia, rather than Elam. Given the proximity of Elam to the cities of southern Mesopotamia, and the fact that Susa and its hinterland were incorporated into the Ur III empire founded by Ur-Nammu (Potts 1999:130ff), it is not difficult to imagine how a knowledge of this distinctive form of monumental architecture came to be known there. Yet the appearance of *ziqqurrats* at Choga Zanbil and Susa may have been due to more than a simple case of stimulus diffusion from Elam's nearest western neighbor.

It is surely no coincidence that the Elamite examples of this quintessentially monumental architectural form date to the Middle Elamite period when, as we know from an extraordinary text in Berlin (Goldberg 2004; Van Dijk 1986), at least five generations of Elamite kings were married to Kassite princesses. In fact, Untaš-Napiriša was himself half-Kassite, for he was the son of an Elamite king, Humban-Numena, and a Kassite princess whose father was the great Kassite monarch, Kurigalzu I. Thus, Kurigalzu I was Untaš-Napiriša's maternal grandfather. Moreover, Untaš-Napiriša's wife, Napir-Asu, immortalized in one of the most extraordinary examples of Late Bronze lost-wax cast metalwork ever found in the Near East (Potts 1999:Pl. 7.3), was a daughter of the Kassite king Burnaburiaš II, in whose honor Untaš-Napiriša dedicated a statue of the god Immiriya at Choga Zanbil (Vallat 1999). Given the frequency of interdynastic marriage between the royal houses of Elam and the Kassite dynasty, it is inconceivable that the great *ziqqurrat* built by Untaš-Napiriša's grandfather, Kurigalzu I, at his capital, Dur-Kurigalzu (Baqir 1944, 1945; Gerster 2005:322), was unknown to Untaš-Napiriša. This monument, therefore, could well have served as the inspiration for the *ziqqurrats* built at Susa and Choga Zanbil by Untaš-Napiriša. That Elamite equivalents of Babylonian and Assyrian building rituals involving the construction of new buildings may have been followed by Untaš-Napiriša is also indicated by the discovery at Susa of an Elamite version of the calendrical omen series *Iqqur ipuš* ("he demolishes and reconstructs"), a handbook for determining propitious times to undertake building work (Ambos 2010:233–234; Scheil 1925).

THE ETEMENANKI OF BABYLON

Based solely on their dimensions and the labor that must have been involved in constructing them, the *haute terrasse* at Susa and the *ziqqurrat* at Choga Zanbil fully deserve their place in any discussion of monumentality in the ancient Near East. Yet to put these structures in perspective it may be helpful to review some of the Babylonian evidence, as this provides a convenient metric against which the architectural achievements of the Elamites may be judged. Since few monuments in Mesopotamia are as bound up with the notion of monumentality as the Etemenanki of Babylon—literally the "house foundation platform of heaven and underworld" (George 2011:154), but better known as the "tower of Babel" (Genesis 11.5, 9)—this may serve as a helpful yardstick against which to assess the monumentality of the high terrace at Susa and the *ziqqurrat* at Choga Zanbil.

Perpetuating an interest in the "tower of Babel" that stretches back to mediaeval and Early Modern times (Ooghe 2007), modern scholars have generated an enormous number of studies on Mesopotamian *ziqqurrats* (Schmid 1995:xv–xix). Herodotus's famous description of the *ziqqurrat* of Babylon has been the subject of extensive commentary (e.g., Boiy 2004; George 2005/6; Heller 2010; Henkelman et al. 2011; Nesselrath 1999; Ravn 1942; van der Spek 2006), as have several relevant cuneiform tablets. One of these, the so-called E-sangil Tablet (AO 6555; Louvre Museum), dating to 229 B.C., gives a description of a seven-stage *ziqqurrat* (Schmid 1995:20, 128ff with earlier lit. and Taf. 38a-b), consisting of six "steps" plus the temple on top (Table 2.1). The other relevant text (BM 38217; British Museum) has a schematic drawing of the seven stages labeled with their dimensions (Bagg 2011: 576, no. 30 and Abb. 30a; Schmid 1995: Taf. 39b-c). Finally, a recently published stele (Figure 2.3) of Nebuchadnezzar II's in the Schøyen Collection (MS 2063) shows a remarkable image of a seven-stage *ziqqurrat,* complete with

Table 2.1
Metric data in the E-sangil Tablet (AO 6555; Louvre Museum),
detailing a seven-stage *ziqqurrat* at Babylon consisting
of six "steps" plus the temple on top

Stage	in cubits Length	Width	Height	in meters Length	Width	Height	in square meters
1	180	180	66	90	90	33	8100
2	156	156	36	78	78	18	6084
3	120	120	12	60	60	6	3600
4	102	102	12	51	51	6	2601
5	84	84	12	42	42	6	1764
6	—	—	—	—	—	—	—
7	48	48	30	25	22.50	15	562.50

an epigraph which reads, "Etemenanki, the *ziqqurrat* of Babylon" (George 2011:154). As George has emphasized, the E-Sangil Tablet "is not an eyewitness's description of a standing building, nor is it an architect's blueprint for an eventual construction. It is a compilation of mathematical exercises and very probably draws its figures from an ideal, not from reality" (George 2011:156). Nevertheless, while it differs in the relative heights of the steps depicted, the image of the *ziqqurrat* on the stele in the Schøyen Collection also shows seven stages, including the temple on top, as does the text in the British Museum. Whether or not these, too, represent an idealized *ziqqurrat*, it is surely significant and hardly a coincidence that all three sources—the two cuneiform tablets and the Schøyen stele—depict a seven-stage structure, though whether this reflects an architectonic reality or not is difficult to say. It may simply reflect the importance of the number seven in ancient Mesopotamia (Heeßel 2011:173 and n. 8 with earlier lit.). What none of these texts provide, of course, is any information on access to the temple on the uppermost stage. For this, one must consult the archaeological evidence of *ziqqurats* at sites such as Ur. As we know from the Neo-Assyrian and Neo-Babylonian "*ziqqurrat* lists" (George 1993:45–49), many other Mesopotamian cities, including Borsippa, Nippur, Dur-Kurigalzu, Sippar, Akkade, Kish, Kutha, Dilbat, Marad, Larsa, Uruk, Eridu, Karkara, and of course Babylon had *ziqqurats*, but Ur's is by far the best preserved.

In the case of the Etemenanki, we are fortunate in having several copies of the foundation cylinders buried beneath it by Nabopolassar (r. 626–605 B.C.) and his son Nebuchadnezzar II (r. 605–562 B.C.) that provide extraordinary detail on its construction. When his son Aššur-nadin-šumi was carried off and murdered by the invading Elamites in 694 B.C. and Babylonia entered into open rebellion against its Assyrian overlords (Frame 1992:52), Sennacherib (r. 705–681 B.C.) launched a brutal attack on his erstwhile southern vassal. After a protracted and bloody siege, the capital Babylon fell to Assyrian forces in 689 B.C. The city was burned and many of its buildings razed.

FIGURE 2.3 Stele of Nebuchadnezzar II (The Schøyen Collection MS 2063; courtesy of The Schøyen Collection, Oslo and London).

Thereafter it was flooded; its city elders killed; and the cult statue of Marduk, the city god, seized and taken to Assyria, as we know from a text conventionally referred to as the *Marduk ordeal*. Sennacherib's son Esarhaddon (r. 681–669 B.C.) and grandson Assurbanipal (r. 668–627 B.C.) both set to work repairing the damage wrought by the Assyrian forces and, as their building inscriptions attest, restoring the Etemenanki (Porter 1993:51ff.). But the most detailed account of this restoration is provided by Nabopolassar, the founder of the Neo-Babylonian dynasty who, after subduing Assyria between 614 and 610 B.C., received Marduk's command to restore the Etemenanki (Schaudig 2010:151).

Befitting the sacred nature of the enterprise upon which he was embarking, amply illustrated in the corpus of building ritual texts recently studied by Claus Ambos (2010), Nabopolassar says he had hoes, spades, and brick-molds made of sissoo wood, ebony, and ivory. His numerous troops performed the work. He had bricks "without number" fired in kilns, as uncountable, he says, as drops of rain. Like a flood, asphalt to be used as mortar was transported along the Araḫtu canal to the building site. The surveyor measured the distances with his measuring rod; the master builder pulled the measuring tapes and laid out the work. Nabopolassar consulted the omens of Šamaš, Adad, and Marduk, and when the foundations had been dug he "spread gold and silver, stones of the mountains and the sea over its foundations." He continues: "Below its bricks, I heaped up bright powders, fine oil, perfumes and golden paste. I made an image of my royal person carrying a basket and I placed it in the foundation." He then goes on to say that he bowed his neck, gathered up his royal dress, and carried bricks and mortar on his own head. "I had baskets clad in gold and silver and I had Nebuchadnezzar, my first born, the beloved of my heart, mix with my workmen clay that had wine, oil, and cuttings [of fragrant wood]." His younger brother wielded "a hoe and a spade" and was presented by Nabopolassar to Marduk as a votive gift (Schaudig 2010:152–153).

The Etemenanki measures 91.53 m ± 1 cm (180 cubits) on each side (Schmid 1995:90), just slightly more than the figure given in the E-sangil tablet (Table 2.1). According to a foundation cylinder of Nebuchadnezzar II, his father Nabopolassar brought the Etemenanki to a height of 30 cubits (15.25 m), only about one-sixth of its intended height (for Babylonian units of lineal measurement see Powell 1990). In fact, Nabopolassar had only built the "lower part of the first platform" (Pedersén 2011:14). Hansjörg Schmid estimated that Nabopolassar, whose reconstruction project lasted about 20 years, used about 10,000,000 baked bricks (Schmid 1995:91). By the time of Nebuchadnezzar's death in 562 B.C., the reconstruction of the Etemenanki was complete. Schmid has estimated that the work carried out under Nebuchadnezzar probably lasted 25 years and required an additional 32,000,000 bricks. Hence, the reconstruction effort lasted c. 45 years under two successive Babylonian kings. Interestingly, this compare well with the figure of 43 years given to complete the entire project in the *Book of Jubilees* (10.21), a Midrashic commentary on Genesis and Exodus dating to the second century B.C. (Charles 1902:lviii ff.).

But we have far more evidence to draw on than just the Assyrian and Babylonian royal inscriptions in trying to gauge the scale of a construction project such as this for, in addition to actual bricks from Babylon, we have dozens of cuneiform texts that inform us about the digging of clay to make bricks, work-rates for their manufacture, their dimensions, their weights, their carriage, their stacking, etc., which have been discussed in detail by numerous scholars, including Jöran Friberg (1996), Marvin Powell (1990), Andrew George (1995), Eleanor Robson (1999), and Paul-Alain Beaulieu (2005). These texts reveal the organizational and economic dimensions of industrial-scale brick production as well as the logistics involved in construction projects involving thousands of laborers and many millions of bricks. While some of these texts take the form of mathematical exercises, others are without question grounded in reality. To cite just one example, a text of unknown provenance, but probably from Uruk, in the Yale Babylonian Collection (NBC 4786), books the receipt and inspection of 459,600 "kiln-fired bricks" that were paid for "with the silver of the king" (Beaulieu 2005:67). The text dates to the year Nebuchadnezzar 26, that is, March 579 to March 578 B.C. (for the conversion of the date see Parker and Dubberstein 1956:28). These bricks were produced by workers attached to the Eanna temple at Uruk in fulfillment of the temple's obligation to supply bricks for the construction of Nebuchadnezzar's North Palace at Babylon. When a single delivery from a single institution could consist of nearly a half-million baked bricks, then it is obvious that the construction of a structure as monumental as the Etemenanki, regardless of the fact that it entailed tens of millions of bricks, was well within the capabilities of the Neo-Babylonian state.

Another, equally interesting perspective on the Etemenanki is afforded by sources relating to its demise. In his description of Xerxes's destruction of the so-called "tomb of Belus" at Babylon, Strabo describes it as "a quadrangular pyramid of baked brick, not only being a stadium in height but also having sides a stadium in length" (*Geog.* 16.1.6). It has long been recognized that Strabo was undoubtedly referring not to the tomb of Belus, or, Marduk, chief god of the pantheon of Babylon, but to the Etemenanki. Strabo continues: "Alexander intended to repair this pyramid; but it would have been a large task and would have required a long time (for merely the clearing away of the mound was a task for 10,000 men for two months)" (*Geog.* 16.1.6).

We have no way of knowing whether Strabo's intelligence on the labor involved in clearing away the debris after the later destruction caused by Xerxes is correct, but it is certainly not fanciful. It is not just the fact, noted above, that something on the order of 42,000,000 baked bricks may have gone into the reconstruction of the Etemenanki. Rather, it is the nature of the number given by Strabo—10,000 man days for two months, that is, 60 days, for a total of 600,000 man days. This has an unquestionably Babylonian, sexagesimal ring to it and it is doubtful that Strabo came up with the figure himself. As the Swedish historian of mathematics Jöran Friberg has noted, "The predominantly Semitic population in Mesopotamia in the 2nd and 1st millennia BC normally counted with decimal numbers, using their own Semitic decimal number words. Only educated scribes had learned how to count with the originally Sumerian sexagesimal numbers" (Friberg 2007:5). This suggests that the information transmitted by Strabo was drawn from an official source, probably a Babylonian priest or scribe, and although we have no confirmation in cuneiform sources that Alexander set 10,000 soldiers to work on the project, four texts dating to 327 and 325 B.C.—thus postdating Alexander's first entry into Babylon and predating his return from the east—document sums of money expended for the cleanup of the entire Esagila precinct at Babylon (Boiy 2010:213–214).

These were apparently desultory efforts. The three texts with legible numbers record the expenditure of only 391.5 shekels of silver. As another text from 321 B.C. shows, the wages of the workers employed on this project amounted to 4 shekels per month. Thus, 391.5 shekels would have supported only about 98 men for a month of cleanup duty (van der Spek 2006:16). This is a far cry from the 10,000 men that Strabo says were deployed by Alexander, who, Strabo emphasizes, was "not able to execute what he had attempted" due to his untimely death on June 11, 323 B.C. (for the date see Depuydt 1997). However, although Strabo specifically says that "none of the persons who succeeded him [i.e., Alexander] attended to this undertaking," this is patently untrue. Cuneiform texts confirm that the operation continued after Alexander's death. An astronomical diary from 322 B.C., for example, notes "the debris of Esagil was removed to the opposite west bank" of the Euphrates and the work continued, with some interruptions, under the Diadochi—Philip and Alexander IV—and, according to the later Babylonian chronicles, under two of the early Seleucids—Seleucus I and Antiochus I (van der Spek 2006:17)—all of which goes to show what a massive undertaking this was, lasting for at least 47 years possibly as long as 66 years. However, there was probably more than civic pride and cleanliness at work here for the debris from the Etemenanki, including a fragmentary foundation cylinder of Nebuchadnezzar's, was reused. The Greek theater at Babylon was built of recycled bricks taken from the Etemenanki, a fact which explained to Robert Koldewey, the original excavator of the site, the absence of brick debris around the Etemenanki that he had observed at the time of its excavation (Koldewey 1913:300; Potts 2011:240).

CONCLUSION

As noted at the beginning of this study, the greatest expressions of monumentality in the Elamite world are to be found in the realm of religious architecture. The late prehistoric *haute terrasse* at Susa surpasses the largest Mesopotamian temple platforms of the pre-*ziqqurrat* era, while the basal dimensions of the *ziqqurrat* of Choga Zanbil exceed those of even the Etemenanki at Babylon, in ground plan, if not in height. While it will always be contentious to nominate a threshold of height, length, or square meters below which something was not monumental and above which it was, the cuneiform sources demonstrate that size does matter for when the *chaîne opératoire* behind size is examined it reveals a level of complexity that far surpassed the capacity of an individual, household, village, or town and was plainly beyond the means of all but kings and major institutions, such as temples, often entailing multiyear building projects that mobilized immense natural resources as well as a large, systematically organized labor force of both skilled and unskilled, free and unfree workers. A comparison with the Etemenanki, which took more than four decades to restore, at a staggering cost of both manpower and materiel, involving tens of millions of bricks, not to mention untold quantities of bitumen, fuel for brickmaking, foodstuffs for the labor force, and ideological capital (in terms of the strictly regulated royal/religious rituals, priestly interventions, and so on), suggests that the temple platforms and *ziqqurrats* of Elam must have been equally costly in both material and social capital.

Projects such as these, lasting decades and employing thousands of laborers, were monumental in every sense of the word. Monumental architecture in Babylonia and Elam was marked as much by grandiosity of design, strict adherence to religious protocols, highly complex work-flow, deployment of massive numbers of laborers, and temporal duration, as it was by actual bricks and mortar. Only the state could mobilize, feed, house, and equip such large numbers of participants. Only the state had the ideological capital necessary to stage the theater of divine sanction prescribed by the highly specific requirements of temple building. Therein lies the main difference between monumentality in the sense used here, and other forms of major construction. Secular buildings, irrigation canals, land reclamation, long-distance trade, and many other activities often required resources surpassing those at the disposal of individuals or even institutions. Few, if any, undertakings can compare, however, with the multi-decadal construction of major religious monuments in Mesopotamia and Elam.

References Cited

Alizadeh, Abbas 2008 *Chogha Mish II: The Development of a Prehistoric Regional Center in Lowland Susiana, Southwestern Iran. Final Report on the Last Six Seasons of Excavations, 1972–1978.* Oriental Institute Publications, vol. 130. The Oriental Institute, Chicago.

Allinger-Csollich, Wilfrid 1998 Birs-Nimrud II: "Tieftempel"—"Hochtempel." Vergleichende Studien Borsippa—Babylon. *Baghdader Mitteilungen* 29:95–330.

Allinger-Csollich, Wilfrid 2005 Die Größe und Lage der Heiligtümer im Esaĝil von Babylon. In *Von Sumer bis Homer: Festschrift für Manfred Schretter zum 60. Geburtstag am 25. Februar 2004,* edited by Robert Rollinger, pp. 7–19. Alter Orient und Altes Testament, vol. 325. Ugarit-Verlag, Münster.

Ambos, Claus 2010 Building Rituals from the First Millennium BC. In *From the Foundations to the Crenellations: Essays on Temple Building in the Ancient Near East and Hebrew Bible,* edited by Mark J. Boda and Jamie Novotny, pp. 221–237. Alter Orient und Altes Testament, vol. 366. Ugarit-Verlag, Münster.

Amiet, Pierre 1987 Temple sur terrasse ou forteresse? *Revue d'Assyriologie* 81:99–104.

Bagg, Ariel 2011 Mesopotamische Bauzeichnungen. In *The Empirical Dimension in Ancient Near Eastern Studies/Die empirische Dimension altorientalischer Forschungen,* edited by Gebhard J. Selz with the collaboration of Klaus Wagensonner, pp. 543–586. Wiener Offene Orientalistik, vol. 6. Lit Verlag, Vienna.

Baqir, Taha 1944 Iraq Government Excavations at 'Aqar Quf: First Interim Report, 1942–43. *Iraq Supplement:*3–16.

Baqir, Taha 1945 Iraq Government Excavations at 'Aqar Quf: Second Interim Report, 1943–44. *Iraq Supplement:*1–15.

Beaulieu, Paul-Alain 2005 Eanna's Contribution to the Construction of the North Palace at Babylon. In *Approaching the Babylonian Economy: Proceedings of the START Project Symposium Held in Vienna, 1–3 July 2004,* edited by Heather D. Baker and Michael Jursa, pp. 45–73. Alter Orient und Altes Testament, vol. 330. Ugarit-Verlag, Münster.

Boese, Johannes 1971 *Altmesopotamische Weihplatten: Eine sumerische Denkmalsgattung des 3. Jahrtausends v. Chr.* Walter De Gruyter, Berlin and New York.

Boiy, Tom 2004 *Late Achaemenid and Hellenistic Babylon.* Orientalia Lovaniensia Analecta, vol. 136. Peeters, Leuven.

Boiy, Tom 2010 Temple Building in Hellenistic Babylonia. In *From the Foundations to the Crenellations: Essays on Temple Building in the Ancient Near East and Hebrew Bible,* edited by Mark J. Boda and Jamie Novotny, pp. 211–219. Alter Orient und Altes Testament, vol. 366. Ugarit-Verlag, Münster.

Canal, Denis 1978a La haute terrasse de l'Acropole de Suse. *Paléorient* 4/4:169–176.

Canal, Denis 1978b Travaux à la terrasse haute de l'Acropole de Suse I. Historique, stratigraphie et structures. *Cahiers de la Délégation archéologique française en Iran* 9:11–55.

Charles, Robert H. 1902 *The Book of Jubilees or the Little Genesis, translated from the editor's Ethiopic text.* Adam and Charles Black, London.

Delougaz, Pinhas, and Helene J. Kantor 1996 *Chogha Mish Volume I. The First Five Seasons of Excavations, 1961–1971.* Oriental Institute Publications, vol. 101. The Oriental Institute, Chicago.

Depuydt, Leo 1997 The Time of Death of Alexander the Great: 11 June 323 BC, ca. 4:00–5:00 PM. *Die Welt des Orients* 28:117–135.

Dombart, Theodor 1928 Das Zikkurratrelief aus Kujundschik. *Zeitschrift für Assyriologie und vorderasiatische Archäologie* 38:39–64.

Frame, Grant 1992 *Babylonia 689–627 B.C.: A Political History.* Uitgaven van het Nederlands Historisch-Archaeologisch Instituut te Istanbul, vol. 69. Nederlands Instituut voor het Nabije Oosten, Leiden.

Friberg, Jöran 1996 *Bricks and Mud in Metro-Mathematical Cuneiform Texts.* Max-Planck-Institut für Wissenschaftsgeschichte Preprint 32. Max-Planck-Institut für Wissenschaftsgeschichte, Berlin.

Friberg, Jöran 2007 *A Remarkable Collection of Babylonian Mathematical texts: Manuscripts in the Schøyen Collection, Cuneiform Texts I.* Springer, New York.

Frymer-Kensky, Tikva 1983 The Tribulations of Marduk: The So-called "Marduk Ordeal Text." *Journal of the American Oriental Society* 103:131–141.

George, Andrew R. 1993 *House most high: The temples of Ancient Mesopotamia.* Eisenbrauns, Winona Lake.

George, Andrew R. 1995 The Bricks of E-Sagil. *Iraq* 57:173–197.

George, Andrew R. 2005/6 The Tower of Babel: Archaeology, History, and Cuneiform Texts. *Archiv für Orientforschung* 51:75–95.

George, Andrew R. 2011 A Stele of Nebuchadnezzar II. In *Cuneiform Royal Inscriptions and Related Texts in the Schøyen Collection,* edited by A. R. George, pp. 153–169. Cornell University Studies in Assyriology and Sumerology, vol. 17. CDL Press, Bethesda.

Gerster, Georg 2005 *The past from above.* Frances Lincoln, London.

Goldberg, Jacob 2004 The Berlin Letter, Middle Elamite Chronology, and Šutruk-Nahhunte I's genealogy. *Iranica Antiqua* 39:33–42.

Heeßel, Nils P. 2011 "Sieben Tafeln aus sieben Städten"—Überlegungen zum Prozess der Serialisierung von Texten in Babylonien in der zweiten Hälfte des zweiten Jahrtausends v. Chr. In *Babylon: Wissenskultur in Orient und Okzident,* edited by Eva Cancik-Kirschbaum, Margarete van Ess, and Joachim Marzahn, pp. 171–195. Topoi: Berlin Studies of the Ancient World, vol. 1. De Gruyter, Berlin.

Heller, André 2010 *Das Babylonien der Spätzeit (7.–4. Jh.) in den klassischen und keilschriftlichen Quellen.* Oikumene, vol. 7. Verlag Antike, Berlin.

Henkelman, Wouter, Amélie Kuhrt, Robert Rollinger, and Josef Wiesehöfer 2011 Herodotus and Babylon Reconsidered. In *Herodot und das Persische Weltreich/ Herodotus and the Persian Empire,* edited by Robert Rollinger, Brigitte Truschnegg, and Reinhold Bichler, pp. 449–470. Classica et Orientalia, vol. 3. Harrassowitz, Wiesbaden.

Herles, Michael 2012 Ziggurat. *Encyclopaedia Iranica* online edition.

Hole, Frank 2010 A Monumental Failure: The Collapse of Susa. In *Beyond the Ubaid: Transformation and Integration in the Late Prehistoric Societies of the Middle East,* edited by Robert A. Carter and Graham Philip, pp. 227–243. Studies in Ancient Oriental Civilization, no. 63. The Oriental Institute, Chicago.

Koldewey, Robert 1913 *Das wieder erstehende Babylon: Die bisherigen Ergebnisse der deutschen Ausgrabungen.* J. C. Hinrichs'sche Buchhandlung, Leipzig.

König, Friedrich Wilhelm 1965 *Die elamischen Königsinschriften.* Archiv für Orientforschung Beiheft, vol. 16. Ernst Weidner, Graz.

Lenzen, Heinz J. 1966 Gedanken über die Entstehung der Zikurrat. *Iranica Antiqua* 6:25–33.

Malbran-Labat, Florence 1995 *Les inscriptions royales de Suse: Briques de l'époque paléo-élamite à l'Empire néo-élamite.* Réunion des Musées Nationaux, Paris.

Nesselrath, Heinz-Günther 1999 Herodot und Babylon: Der Hauptort Mesopotamiens in den Augen eines Griechen des 5. Jh.s v. Chr. In *Babylon: Focus mesopotamischer Geschichte, Wiege früher Gelehrsamkeit, Mythos in der Moderne,* edited by Johannes Renger. Colloquien der Deutschen Orient-Gesellschaft, vol. 2. Saarbrücker Druckerei und Verlag, Saarbrücken.

Ooghe, Bart 2007 The Rediscovery of Babylonia: European Travellers and the Development of Knowledge on Lower Mesopotamia, Sixteenth to Early Nineteenth Century. *Journal of the Royal Asiatic Society,* Ser. 3, 17/3:231–252.

Parker, Richard A., and Waldo H. Dubberstein 1956 *Babylonian Chronology 626 B.C.–A.D. 75.* Brown University Press, Providence.

Pedersén, Olaf 2011 Work on a Digital Model of Babylon Using Archaeological and Textual Evidence. *Mesopotamia* 46:9–22.

Pelzel, Suzanne M. 1977 Dating the Early Dynastic Votive Plaques from Susa. *Journal of Near Eastern Studies* 36:1–15.

Poebel, Arno 1933 The Acropolis of Susa in the Elamite Inscriptions. *American Journal of Semitic Languages* 49:125–140.

Pollock, Susan 1989 Power Politics in the Susa A Period. In *Upon This Foundation—The 'Ubaid Reconsidered: Proceedings from the 'Ubaid Symposium, Elsinore, May 30th–June 1st 1988,* edited by Elizabeth F. Henrickson and Ingolf Thuesen, pp. 281–292. Carsten Niebuhr Institute Publications, vol. 10. Museum Tusculanum, Copenhagen.

Porter, Barbara N. 1993 *Images, Power, and Politics: Figurative Aspects of Esarhaddon's Babylonian Policy.* American Philosophical Society, Philadelphia.

Potts, D. T. 1990 Notes on Some Horned Buildings in Iran, Mesopotamia, and Arabia. *Revue d'Assyriologie* 84:33–40.

Potts, D. T. 1999 *The Archaeology of Elam: Formation and Transformation of an Ancient Iranian State.* Cambridge University Press, Cambridge.

Potts, D. T. 2010 Elamite Temple-Building. In *From the Foundations to the Crenellations: Essays on Temple Building in the Ancient Near East and Hebrew Bible,* edited by Mark J. Boda and Jamie Novotny, pp. 49–70 and 479–509. Alter Orient und Altes Testament, vol. 366. Ugarit-Verlag, Münster.

Potts, D. T. 2011 The *politai* and the *bīt tāmartu*: The Seleucid and Parthian Theatres of the Greek Citizens of Babylon. In *Babylon: Wissenskultur in Orient und Okzident,* edited by

Eva Cancik-Kirschbaum, Margarete van Ess, and Joachim Marzahn, pp. 239–251. Topoi: Berlin Studies of the Ancient World, vol. 1. De Gruyter, Berlin.

Powell, Marvin 1990 Maße und Gewichte. *Reallexikon der Assyriologie* 7:457–517.

Ravn, Otto E. 1942 *Herodotus' Description of Babylon*. Nyt Nordisk Forlag, Copenhagen.

Robson, Eleanor 1999 *Mesopotamian Mathematics, 2100–1600 BC: Technical Constants in Bureaucracy and Education*. Oxford Editions of Cuneiform Texts, vol. 14. Clarendon Press, Oxford.

Schaudig, Hanspeter 2010 The Restoration of Temples in the Neo- and Late Babylonian Periods: A Royal Prerogative as the Setting for Political Argument. In *From the Foundations to the Crenellations: Essays on Temple Building in the Ancient Near East and Hebrew Bible*, edited by Mark J. Boda and Jamie Novotny, pp. 141–164. Alter Orient und Altes Testament, vol. 366. Ugarit-Verlag, Münster.

Scheil, Vincent 1925 Hémérologie élamite. *Revue d'Assyriologie* 22:157–158.

Schmid, Hansjörg 1995 *Der Tempelturm Etemenanki in Babylon*. Baghdader Forschungen 17. Philipp von Zabern, Mainz.

Stolper, Matthew W. 1984 *Texts from Tall-i Malyan I. Elamite Administrative Texts (1972–1974)*. Occasional Publications of the Babylonian Fund, vol. 6. University Museum, Philadelphia.

Streck, Maximilian 1916 *Assurbanipal und die letzten assyrischen Könige bis zum Untergange Niniveh's*. Vorderasiatische Bibliothek, vol. 7. Hinrichs, Leipzig.

Tuck, Anthony 2012 The Performance of Death: Monumentality, Burial Practice, and Community Identity in Central Italy's Urbanizing Period. In *Monumentality in Etruscan and Early Roman Architecture: Ideology and Innovation*, edited by Michael L. Thomas and Gretchen E. Meyers, pp. 41–60. The University of Texas Press, Austin.

Vallat, François 1999 L'hommage de l'élamite Untash-Napirisha au Cassite Burnaburiash. *Akkadica* 114–115:109–117.

van der Spek, Robartus J. 2006 The Size and Significance of the Babylonian Temples under the Successors. In *La transition entre l'empire achéménide et les royaumes hellénistiques (vers 350–300 av. J.-C.)*, edited by Pierre Briant and Francis Joannès, pp. 261–307. Persika 9. Collège de France, Paris.

Van Dijk, Johannes J. 1986 Die dynastischen Heiraten zwischen Kassiten und Elamern: eine verhängnisvolle Politik. *Orientalia* 55:159–170.

Chapter Three

Patronage and Reception in the Monumental Architecture of Early Christian Greece

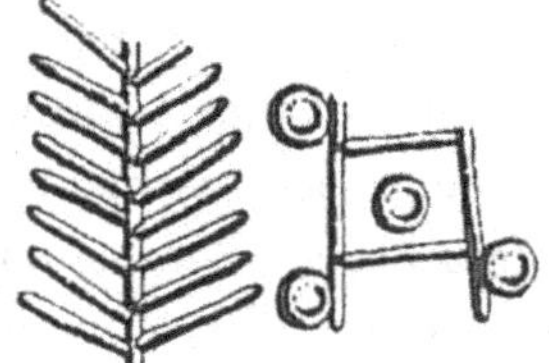

William R. Caraher

Abstract *The emergence of Christianity in the Mediterranean was marked by a rise in a distinct form of monumental architecture. This contribution uses the more than 200 basilica-style churches from the Peloponnesus and Central Greece as case studies for the rise in a new standard and form of monumentality. It explores how the ritual context of these buildings communicated changing social expectations, the role of patronage practices in using monumental architecture to promote authority, the interaction of these buildings and labor practices, and the faint evidence for how visitors understood these buildings. By locating Christian architecture at the intersection of architectural, economic, social, and religious change, we begin to understand how monumentality produced meaning in the Early Christian world.*

Introduction

Issues of monumentality play a particularly significant role in the ongoing conversations about Late Antique or Early Christian architecture. Like many other places and periods represented in this volume, the production of monumental Early Christian architecture in Greece stands at the intersection of changing forms of economic organization and shifts in the perception of monumental religious space. The scale and extent of Early Christian monumental architecture both around the Mediterranean generally, but also within particular regions, emphasized the deliberate character of the architectural change. From the early fourth to the seventh century, the Mediterranean basin saw the emergence of a new form of monumental architecture—the Christian basilica-style church—and the abandonment of many older forms associated with paganism and the structure of Roman urban life.

As James Osborne sagely noted in his introduction to this volume, a definition of the monumental remains unstable and dependent upon economic and social relations, political concerns, formal criteria, and other discursive features that shift both historically and across a single community. It is no surprise, then, that during Late Antiquity, a time of particularly dynamic social, political, religious, and economic change, a consistent definition of monumentality can be elusive. Late Antiquity did, however, witness an expansion of public buildings, fortification walls, religious architecture, and sprawling urban and rural houses of the emerging Late Roman elite (e.g., Dey 2010; L'Orange 1965; Wharton 1995). The structures were large, often attracted private patronage, and served various public and private functions. Moreover, these buildings were related to one another architecturally, aesthetically, spatially, and through the status of their patrons. As much as these buildings absorbed resources, occupied well-defined places within the landscape, and engaged other similar buildings, they contributed to a larger monumental discourse of Late Antiquity. As Osborne noted (this volume), the discourse of monumentality is relational both in terms of the relationship between the viewer and the object or building, but also in the relationships between buildings and objects.

Early Christian churches carry the additional significance of being religious buildings that represent a particularly distinct space within the discourse of monumentality. If, as Osborne notes, monuments served both to persist and commemorate, then Christian churches certainly fulfilled the formal definition of the monumental to contemporary viewers. The commemorative function of the Christian liturgy—the main ritual housed in Late Antique churches—worked to remind the congregation of the redemptive events of the Passion and present in earthly form the continuous liturgical celebrations of the celestial hierarchy (Taft 1992). Some churches served more specifically to commemorate the deaths and sanctification of martyrs and to mark the burials of members of the community, weaving together the central and universal narratives of the Christian faith with events of local concern (Grabar 1946; Yasin 2009). Churches, then, played a key role in producing a Christian community in the ancient world by commemorating a sacred past in the context of the present. The position of churches at the intersection of a newly articulated Christian community and a changing architectural and aesthetic discourse captures many of the key themes central to current discussions of the monumental and monumentality.

The changing standards of monumentality in Late Antiquity marked this period as significant and distinct from those before. In fact, for many scholars the abandonment of ancient pagan temples and the decline of traditional forms of urban monumentality represent archaeological and architectural evidence for the end of the ancient world and the emergence of its Byzantine and Medieval successors (for a short survey see Caraher 2010). As early as the first year of the twentieth century, traditional views of monumentality, which privileged Classical forms, understood the spread of Christianity as concomitant with the transformation of the ancient world. For some scholars, such "late" architecture forms were decadent and represented the beginning of a period of economic, political, and cultural regression (for an important summary of this transformation see Elsner 2002, a critique of Reigl 1901 and Strzygowski 1901; Marchand 1994; Wharton 1995). While recent scholarship has done much to revise these views, they remain common enough in the literature to serve as critical foils within studies of Late Antiquity and to direct attention to issues of continuity and change in the function and meaning of monumental architecture (Liebeshuetz 2001; Ward Perkins 2005). Thus, changing ideas of monumentality not only informed ancient practices, but also played a key role in modern debates. However the denizens of the sixth and seventh-century Mediterranean understood the character of their own architectural environment, modern scholars have singled out religious buildings as central to the fabric and structure of Late Antiquity as a historically constructed period.

My contribution to the discourse of monumentality examines the rise of basilica-style church architecture in Greece where such churches are effectively synonymous with the rise of Christianity. My chapter in this volume concentrates, in particular, on the Early Christian architecture of southern and central Greece where more than 200 monumental Christian churches stand as the first widespread indication of the presence of significant and evidently prosperous Christian communities (Avramea 1997; Caraher 2003; Orlandos 1957; Sweetman 2010). These churches are generally similar in form. Three parallel aisles divide the buildings longitudinally, and the central aisle, or nave, ends with an eastern apse. They vary widely in size with maximum dimensions ranging from just over 10 m to well over 100 m. As a group, these churches are rather poorly published, found mostly in Greek journals, and none have received a full monograph-length final publication with stratigraphy, finds, and detailed architectural study. Several recent catalogues do, however, make the case for considering this group of churches as a coherent, more or less contemporary, corpus of buildings (Figure 3.1) (Caraher 2003; Sweetman 2010).

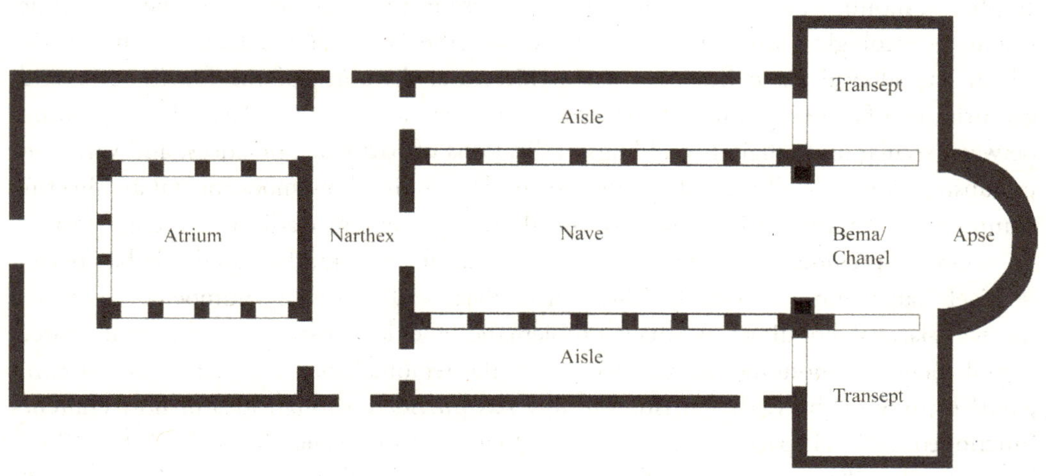

FIGURE 3.1 Typical Greek Basilica-Style Church (W. Caraher).

These Early Christian basilicas provide the first significant evidence for the widespread presence of Christian communities in Greece. Textual and epigraphic sources for the region provide only scant indications that Christian communities of any marked size existed in Greece prior to the middle decades of the fifth century (Rothaus 2000; Trombley 2001). This rather well-defined monumental moment in early Christianity has often led scholars to understand the "boom" in large-scale Christian architecture as an indication for the rapid demographic expansion of Christianity presumably fed by large-scale conversions (Sanders 2005; Sweetman 2010). The demographic growth of Christianity almost certainly influenced the construction of basilica-style churches. Recent readings of the so-called Late Antique building boom, however, have moved away from such functional interpretations of Early Christian church architecture and toward readings of monumentality that see churches as manifestations of the growing power of the ecclesiastical elite, local responses to tensions in imperial and church politics, shifts in economic priorities and practices of euergetism, and theological and philosophical changes in how Christians understood the nature of sacred space (Bowes 2008; Yasin 2009). As many of the chapters in this volume reflect, monumental architecture cross-culturally played a key role in regimes of visual, social, and economic power, and as a result provided an avenue for various forms of authority and resistance. The best understanding of how monumental architecture functioned in any particular historical context, of course, takes into account all of these influences and how they refracted on both a local and regional level.

This chapter considers how the reception and response to monumental Christian architecture defined monumentality in a Christian context and shaped the character of patronage, function, and even construction practices in the Mediterranean landscape (Elsner 2007; Nasrallah 2010). The archaeological approaches presented in this volume have particular significance for understanding monumental Christian architecture, as circumstances surrounding its construction and reception remain difficult to track in our sources, which tend to be biased toward the elite, have significant regional gaps, and emphasize monumental urban buildings over those in the countryside. At the same time, recent archaeological work has revealed more of the fabric of the Late Antique world, which has allowed us to flesh out the architectural discourse of the fourth to seventh centuries in a far more robust way than previous generations of scholars. The relationship between secular and religious buildings, indications of patronage practices, and variations in construction style all present avenues for understanding how monumental architecture communicated meaning in situations outside the purview of traditional literary texts.

Greece provides a particularly suitable venue for this kind of study. It has both a relatively large number of Early Christian basilicas and a growing number of excavated nonecclesiastical buildings. A small, problematic, and lacunose body of textual sources complement the monumental architecture in the region. Moreover, a tradition of comparative study of the Early Christian liturgy has provided a rough idea of how churches functioned as ritual space (Mathews 1971; Orlandos 1957; Pallas 1979, 1979/80, 1984). While no specific liturgy exists for Greece, comparanda from elsewhere in the Mediterranean basin have allowed scholars to reconstruct a plausible liturgical form for the

Greek church and shed important light on the ritual organization of monumental Early Christian architecture.

This chapter interrogates Early Christian architecture in Greece along four interrelated lines. First, I will consider the relationship between ritual and access in Early Christian churches. The clergy had privileged access to certain areas within the church and rituals reinforced the architectural limits experienced by both the clergy and the congregation. These limits provide an important method for understanding how monumental architecture and ritual attempted to create a distinctly Christian discourse for the relationship between the ecclesiastical power of the clergy and social organization (Bowes 2008). Next, I will consider the role of patronage in the construction and spread of monumental architecture, suggesting that lay patronage practices, in particular, challenged the social structuring presented by architectural limits and rituals as it allowed a whole range of individuals to shape ritual space. Third, the physical labor and architectural and decorative models involved in building the churches provide another set of keys to understanding the role of monumental architecture in the changing landscape of Late Antique Greece. Thus far, scholars have paid little attention to processes involved in the construction and design of Late Antique churches (for the Byzantine period see Ousterhout 1999; for secular architecture see Kardulias 1995; for a larger context see Given 2004; Knapp 2009; Trigger 1990). The construction of the church relied upon traditional building practices, architectural forms, decorative motifs, and both local and nonlocal workers to produce monumental ritual space. The process of construction contributed additional complexity to the relationship between monumentality, the laity, and ecclesiastical authority. Finally, as means of a conclusion, this chapter will look at how architecture, ritual, patronage, and construction processes provide ways to understand the reception of Early Christian monumental architecture in Greece. Recent scholarship on monumental architecture in Mediterranean antiquity has increasingly explored the reception of these buildings as a way to see how monumentality, authority, and various forms of social perception intersect to produce meaning in the landscape.

ACCESS

Scholars have long noted the relative consistency in the spatial organization of Early Christian churches in Greece (Krautheimer 1986; Orlandos 1957). The primary function of these buildings was to accommodate movements associated with the liturgy and to house the mystical, sacred space associated with the eastern end of the church building. As a result—and regardless of the other functions of basilica-style churches—this architecture provides an important context for considering the point of contact between celestial cosmology and terrestrial social order (Mathews 1971). From the perspective of the clergy, the combination of ritual and architecture produced a heterotopic space for the earthly performance of the celestial liturgy (Foucault 1986; Taft 1992; Wharton 1995:127–139; Yasin 2009). Foucault defined the term *heterotopia* as the manifestation of the idealized space of a utopia in the real world. This manifestation of the celestial order in the world of the living distinguished Christian sacred space from the profane world, faintly echoing Eliade's (1959) ideas for how the mundane can understand the sacred. Thus, for the church at least, the Early Christian basilica represented both sacred and social space. The intense attention given to the *taxis* (order) of liturgy and architecture within existing liturgical manuals provides ample evidence for the intentionality of the clergy (Taft 1992).

The basilican form adopted by most Early Christian basilicas in Greece had precedents in Roman architecture (Krautheimer 1986:39–43; Ward Perkins 1954). Basilica-shaped buildings often served as audience halls and courts for imperial officials. Their pronounced longitudinal axis and apsidal end provided an ideal venue for processions toward the source of power and established the distance between a presiding magistrate or aristocrat and a visitor to the audience chamber. In some instances, to reinforce the power of the presiding official, a statue of the emperor would stand in the apsidal space and confer tacit authority to the individual who sat in its shadow (Elsner 1998:131–132). By Late Antiquity, basilica-style spaces that were common in public buildings during the Roman period began to appear in elaborate urban and rural villas throughout the Mediterranean and in Greece (Bowden 2003; Frantz 1988:34–47). Most scholars see the appearance of apsidal audience halls in private villas as representing the shifting locus of authority from traditional urban elites to a new class of elites based in the countryside and possessing as much personal as institutional power and authority (Bowden 2003).

The typical Early Christian church was oriented west to east with the entrance through an enclosed courtyard typically located at the western end of the building. In most cases, the entrance to the atrium was not particularly monumental and was seemingly oriented to face local roads or to avoid other buildings rather than according to the orientation of the church. Once inside the atrium, however, the colonnaded courtyard typically provided a monumental, but inward facing, area that prepared one to enter the narthex, which is the outer most part of the church's ritual space. In Greece, access to the narthex most frequently occurred through two doors set to either side of the main axis of the main building of the church. In other words, the atrium does not provide visual or physical access to the main axis of the church; this is gained only through the narthex. The narthex consists of a narrow hallway running the entire width of the church. Traditionally, the narthex represents an area where the clergy would prepare for the main procession into the church and it served as a buffer between the world outside the church and the more sacred space inside (Spieser 1995).

The main body of the church consisted of a central hall, or nave, flanked by two aisles. In Greece, the aisles were separated from the nave by a high stylobate and a series of parapet screens that limited passage from the lateral aisles to the central nave. Most scholars have assumed that women stood in one aisle and men in the other based on evidence for similar divisions elsewhere in the Mediterranean (Krautheimer 1986:159; Orlandos 1957:265; Pallas 1984). Catechumens, pre-baptismal individuals awaiting full admission into the Christian community, would have stood in galleries above the aisle, if present, or above the narthex (Sanders 2005; Taft 1998). These galleries would have allowed catechumens to depart the building before the most sacred parts of the service without disrupting the ritual taking place in the main area of the church.

Thus separated from the aisles, the central nave became the space for liturgical processions (Mathews 1971:148–151). The clergy, assembled in the narthex after the congregation had entered the aisles of the church, would process toward the eastern end (Mathews 1971:145; Taft 1992:33–34). If this procession followed traditional rules for processions in the Late Antique world, then it was organized according to rank with the more senior clergy either at the end or at the beginning of procession in a recognizable and consistent order (Baldovin 1987; MacCormack 1981; Sanders 2005). From their place in the aisles, the congregation would effectively watch this procession framed by the nave colonnade which would limit their view of the western and eastern termini of the clerical procession. Windows in the high clerestory that covered the main nave and lamps at night would have illuminated the procession; the aisles, in contrast, may have been less well lit at least in the daytime, once more emphasizing the importance of the processional space.

The eastern part of the church typically featured another set of barriers including a chancel screen and a step separating the eastern part of the nave from the main aisle (Orlandos 1957:206–224; Xydis 1947). The eastern end of the main nave terminated in an apse covered by a half-dome. Scholars have long pondered the symbolism of the eastern half-dome and found parallels with the vault of heaven (Lehmann 1945 is the *locus classicus* for this symbolism). While scholars have challenged many of these universal, symbolic connections (e.g., Mathews 1982, 2003), most scholars continue to recognize the half-dome as an ideal place for large-scale figural programs designed to draw the eye eastward and emphasize the sacred space of the church (Mathews 2003:167–176). The eastern part of the church was the main focus of the Christian ritual and the interment of a sacred relic often reinforced the sanctity of the rituals taking place there.

Thus arranged, church architecture reinforced ritual practices that served to express the relationship between the ecclesiastical hierarchy and the congregation. The rigid divisions between various groups in the church, the barriers between the exterior of the building and the interior of the building, and the effort to block visual or physical access to the processional axis of the church reflect an interest in creating a heterotopic space distinct from the outside world and structured around the clergy (for church as heterotopia see Foucault 1986; Wharton 1995:127–139). Within the church, access to spaces defined architecturally were reinforced by ritual practices associating privileges of access with one's rank in the Christian ecclesiastical hierarchy. The architecture both accentuated the movements of the clergy and the experience of the space and continued to evoke and commemorate the ritual of the liturgy even when it was not taking place.

Efforts to limit access to ritual space in Early Christian architecture find parallels in the growing political effort on the part of the clergy to limit access to their ritual authority (Bowes 2008; Yasin 2009). The famous story of St. Ambrose of Milan ousting the Emperor Theodosios from the chancel area of his cathedral communicates in spatial terms the increasingly tense political conflict between political and religious authority (and their overlapping interests) in the late ancient world (Theodoret, *EH* 5.17). In Greece the institutional church looked to the pope in Rome, and traditional political authorities, with no little interest in the role of Christianity in promoting it own goals, looked to the Emperor at Constantinople. As a result, church architecture likely played a key role in these disputed lines of authority (Pietri 1984; Sotinel 1992, 2005).

PATRONAGE

Many of the chapters in this volume have emphasized the idea that monumental architecture served to produce and reinforce social distinctions and worked to establish an obvious locus of authority. Basilica-style churches in Greece, however, are particularly good examples for how the production of seemingly rigid hierarchical space could support both the rapid spread of Christianity as the dominant form of public, religious expression in Greece, and the expansion of the clergy as a source of social, political, and economic power. It remains tempting to imagine that the expansion of "public," monumental Christianity and the expansion of the ecclesiastical hierarchy were interdependent and, as a result, to assume that the institutional church was largely responsible for the spread and organization of Early Christian ritual space.

While it remains undeniable that the institutional church and monumental architecture are interrelated, evidence for the patronage and construction of monumental buildings—particularly from inscriptions located in and on the buildings themselves—demonstrates that the tie between the expansion of the church as an institution and the spread of monumental architecture is rather complex. Patronage practices suggest a wide range of strategies used to finance church construction, which involved individuals, communities, and institutions (Bowden 2003; Caillet 1993; Jones 1960, 1964:899–903). Thus, the institutional church was only one of a number of players involved in the spread of monumental Christian architecture and in the communication of privileged access afforded the clergy.

In Greece, there are at least four kinds of patronage practices visible in Early Christian basilicas. A relatively small group of churches appear to have been constructed by members of the ecclesiastical hierarchy themselves and perhaps represent the economic strength of the institutional church or members of the ecclesiastical hierarchy in particularly important towns such as the episcopal see of Nikopolis in Epirus Vetus (Bowden 2003:130–131). Other churches, including the impressive Lechaion basilica in the Corinthia, appear to have been the product of imperial patronage. While there is no epigraphic evidence to support this attribution, its massive size, unconventional architecture and furnishing, and extensive use of imperially controlled Proconnesian marble point to imperial involvement in its construction (Pallas 1979:95–96; Sanders 2005:439). Some buildings appear to be the products of individual, nonecclesiastical patronage with attributions to individual members of the local elite. The basilica at Demetrias, for example, preserves a dedicatory inscription by a woman of senatorial rank (Habicht 1987:292–295). Finally, there are a number of buildings that appear to have been built and decorated by numerous members of the community, each of whom contributed a small amount to construction of the church. The practice of families or individuals donating sections of mosaic floor is visible at the church at Kallion, and would seem to reflect a tradition common in the northern Adriatic and elsewhere in Italy during Late Antiquity (Yasin 2009:132).

Imperial, ecclesiastical, and aristocratic patronage fit well within traditions of elite patronage that functioned from Classical times to the end of antiquity (Veyne 1990). In fact, scholars have tended to see the investment by members of the elite or powerful, nonlocal institutions—such as the Christian church—as a way to explain the concurrent decline in monumental secular or pagan architecture and boom in Early Christian building (Bowden 2003). As a result, scholars have conflated the working of these two processes without taking into account the peculiarities of secular, pagan, and Christian architecture. Elite munificence of pagan and secular architecture often served to reinforce the standing of the local aristocracy themselves and supported institutions and leadership positions to which they had privileged access. In contrast, elite, "secular"—or at least nonclerical—patronage of Early Christian architecture tended to support the clergy's growing and rival claim to economic, social, and political power (Bowes 2008:219; Rapp 2005).

Despite this apparent contradiction, the patronage of Early Christian architecture by either private individuals or members of the community presented a way for individuals outside the ecclesiastical elite to be present, albeit by proxy, in the ritual space of the church and challenge the hierarchical arrangement of the architecture. In this way, The laity could make donations that allowed their names to be present in areas that they could not physically enter with their bodies. This continued a tradition of building private churches on their estates or even in urban centers of the empire (Bowes 2008). For Greece, the archaeological evidence for private churches' building remains elusive, but it seems probable that some private churches served the needs of the growing Christian communities in the century prior to the fifth-century Late Roman building boom. The fifth-century building boom in Greece would coincide with efforts by the institutional church to curb elite involvement in church construction and lay influence over the liturgy in an effort to leverage the ritual space of the church and to promote more ambitious understandings of ecclesiastical authority. There is no indication that the church's efforts were successful. Private churches continued to appear throughout Late Antiquity despite efforts to legislate against their construction (Bowes 2008:179–187, 217–226; Ruggieri 1991:9–14, 40–46).

Not all examples of elite patronage of church architecture involved the construction of an entire building. Communities sometimes relied on smaller gifts to build, furnish, and decorate their buildings. The best preserved evidence for smaller gifts are floor mosaics, which offered relatively affordable ways for members of the community to contribute to the decoration of the church (Caillet 1993; Janes 1998:136–140). For example, the church at Kalion featured a series of donor inscriptions commemorating modest gifts of a single solidus and a half solidus (Caraher 2003:332, Yasin 2009:132). Inscriptions celebrating the generosity of the donor appear, for example, in the processional space of the main nave and the most sacred eastern parts of the church. At the church at Klapsi in Eurytania there are numerous donor inscriptions throughout the church (Figure 3.2). While these largely name members of the clergy, the position of the texts would

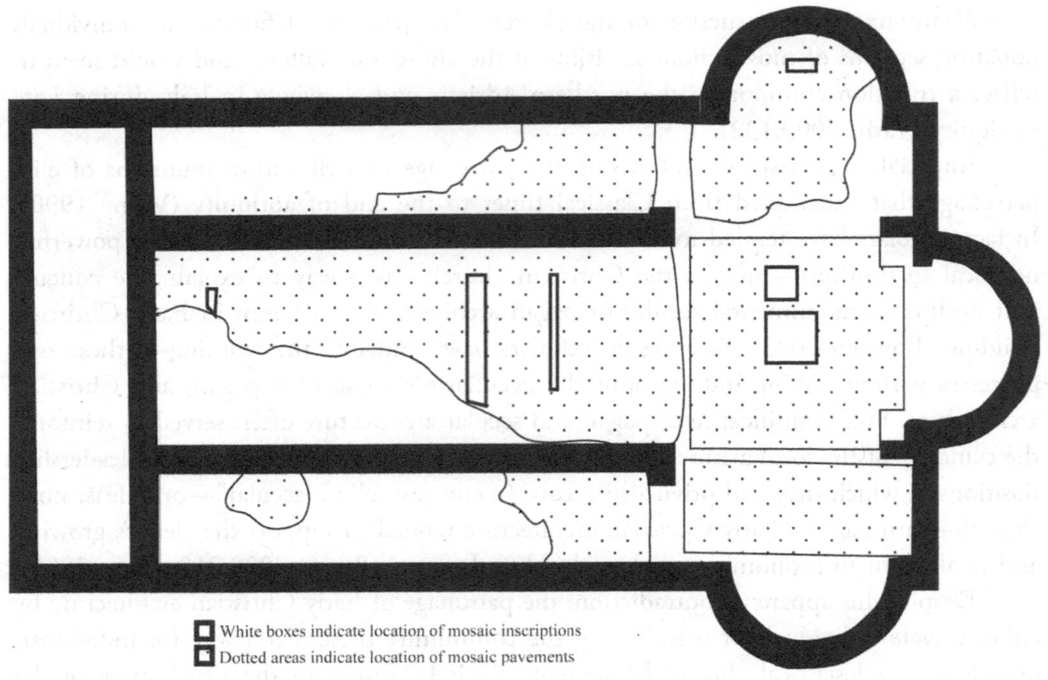

FIGURE 3.2 Plan of the basilica at Klapsi (modified by the author from Assimako-poulou-Atzaka 1987, fig. 271).

have provided access to the most sacred areas of the church for members of the clergy who likely had little involvement with the key components of the Christian ritual. Two members of the lower clergy, a deaconess and a reader, donated the mosaic nearest to the altar table, thus gaining a kind of permanent, if virtual, access to the most important ritual space of the building (Caraher 2003:327 with references).

Small donations and strategies that allowed these modest donors access to ritual space of the church show how monumental architecture stood at the intersection of both lay and clerical strategies for accessing and producing social and religious power. This was made all the more visible in light of the tendency for these donor inscriptions to feature language associated with small-scale, personal ritual acts typically associated with votive offerings or prayers for salvation (for a recent study of this phenomenon in a Christian context see Moralee 2004). Locating these prayers within the church further obscures the rigid boundaries between the space of the clergy and the space of the congregation. Thus, floor mosaics enable individuals to locate their names and to conduct personal prayers and rituals in places where their bodies could not enter. From an architectural perspective, Early Christian architecture features numerous strategies to limit access to the most sacred areas of the building and to reinforce the privileged position of the clergy. A brief study of patronage, however, suggests that patronage practices provided means to infiltrate, if not subvert, the ritual authority of the clergy by co-opting the space of the church and crossing the carefully articulated boundaries that framed the Christian liturgy.

Construction

If patronage practices determined the various groups who paid for the church, the construction and design of the church also provided a series of processes through which the community came to understand the sacred space. The methods used to construct the churches, the material used in the church buildings, the decorative motifs and architectural styles available to the builders all located churches within a complex cultural, social, political, and economic matrix. The process of constructing a church as well as the physical fabric of the buildings worked to communicate the process of Christianization across a substantial cross-section of the population in distinctive ways.

Contextualizing the Early Christian basilicas of Greece in local building, architectural, and decorative traditions represents a challenge for our current body of archaeological evidence. The evidence for construction practices remains scant in the archaeological record and the uneven and growing body of excavated and published Late Antique buildings provides only an incomplete guide to local traditions, schools of artisans, and lines of influence. There has been some work on mosaic pavements (Assimakopoulou-Atzaka 1987; Spiro 1978), various architectural elements (Vemi 1989), imported marble and church furnishings (Jakobs 1987), and spolia (Frey 2006) but almost no work on the organization of production and practices outside of a few regional studies (Bowden 2003:130–151; Sodini 1977, 1978; Sweetman 2001). As a result, our understanding of building practices, the organization of labor, and the range of influences on architecture and decoration is more suggestive than definitive.

From the start of the fifth century to the middle of the sixth century, both urban areas and the countryside saw the construction of numerous basilica-style churches, many of which had truly monumental character. The labor necessary to construct these buildings alone and the substantial changes that they brought to the Greek countryside suggest that the arrival of monumental Christianity was more than the redeployment of existing labor and construction practices in the service of the new faith, but rather a significant shift in productive practices in the service of a new architectural vocabulary (Bowden 2003:151–154; Kardulias 2005:101–106).

Unfortunately, we know relatively little about the organization of construction labor in Greece during Late Antiquity, although there is some evidence that the local extraction of resources and building trades were organized into guilds. The occasional appearance of fish incised in the mortar of various buildings around Corinth, for example, might represent the mark of a particular group of masons (Athanasoulis 1998; Sanders 2005:428). Skilled regional laborers certainly played a role in the production of Early Christian architecture in Greece. The mosaic floors, for example, appear to represent both local schools as well as those connected to trans-Mediterranean networks of production. Scholars have argued that mobile workmen travelled with Proconnesian marble column capitals and other pieces of decorative sculpture to put the finishing touches on the objects before they were put into place within the building (Frey 2006:82 with references). In short, the emergence of monumental Early Christian architecture in Greece involved a reorientation of a range of building practices toward church construction, and in this way connected labor and Christian ritual space.

The designs of the buildings were clearly negotiated between patrons, requirements of the church ritual, the ecclesiastical elite, the communities, and existing building practices, resources, and expertise. The resulting buildings transformed local traditions and forms in the service of Christian space. The most prominent example of this is the use of spolia, architectural fragments quarried from earlier buildings, which played a prominent role in Late Antique building practices in Greece (Bowden 2003:147–151; Frey 2006). While the use of spolia in Late Antique churches in Greece remains relatively unstudied owing largely to the incomplete publication of many of the major monuments, there is evidence that it occurred on a fairly widespread scale. Large marble columns used in the architecturally prominent colonnades often derived from older buildings. Recycled marble appeared frequently in various furnishings—parapet screens, altar tables, and thresholds—cut from discarded monumental sculpture. There is likewise evidence that collapsed buildings were quarried for marble and sold perhaps on-site (Frey 2006:84–85; Rothaus 2000:41). The traditional view of spolia is that it reflected more difficult economic times in Late Antiquity, but more recently scholars have seen the use of spolia as part of a series of aesthetic and ideological decisions (Frey 2006; Hansen 1993; Kinney 1995, 1997). The reuse of marble columns in Greece (Orlandos 1957:263–264), for example, invoked older structures and located the power of the church within the history of local architectural practices. The incorporation of older architectural members particularly in highly visible areas such as the nave colonnade tied the church quite literally to earlier traditions of monumental architecture.

For the modern viewer, the relationship between the spolia and the earlier building from which it derived usually appears obscure, but for an ancient viewer the references might have been more obvious. Thus, in some ways, the use of spolia has parallels with the less common practice of converting pagan structures to Christian use. The destruction of the Asklepeion in Athens and the modification and reuse of its members in a Christian church is among the better-known examples of this practice in Greece (Frantz 1965:195; Gregory 1986:237–241). Elsewhere in Greece, the reuse of the so-called "workshop of Phidias" as a Christian basilica at Olympia decorated with marbles quarried from the ancient sanctuary shows how these two practices can share common ground (Speiser 1976). The outright conversion of pagan temples or secular buildings to Christian churches remains relatively rare in Greece. The Parthenon in Athens is perhaps the most famous exception (Kaldellis 2009 is only the most recent treatment of this important and long-lived building). This famous monument continued to serve the city of Athens as the Christian cathedral of Athens (and later a mosque) for centuries after the end of paganism. The conversion of these temples may have been part of the same phenomena that saw the reuse of architectural members in the construction of Christian buildings.

To take the allusive potential of Christian architecture a step farther, it is worth noting that the architectural form of Early Christian basilicas relied upon a relatively well-established architectural vocabulary. As we have already noted, Early Christian basilica-style churches echoed the design of civic basilicas and monumental reception halls frequently associated with elite villas. The basilican form of the reception hall at the fourth-century imperial residence at Trier is merely the best-known example (Elsner 1998:130–132); smaller-scale examples of apsidal spaces exist throughout the Mediterranean. If the use of the apse represented a recognizable way to draw attention to the locus of power within Late Antique architecture, the colonnade of the main nave evoked, in processions, the quintessential public ritual space of the Late Empire (Mathews 2003:167). Colonnaded avenues of the empire framed regular processions by visiting dignitaries, provided a backdrop for public liturgical rituals, and typified Late Antique forms of urban monumentality (MacCormack 1981; Mathews 1993:142–173; Wharton 1995:64–65). Thus, the use of the central nave as a space for procession evoked the architecture of public space in the Late Antique city, which served to frame processional movements and the hierarchical arrangement of dignitaries.

The use of brilliant and sometimes elaborate mosaic floors executed by skilled workmen or workshops represents perhaps the best point of contact between the architecture of the church building and other forms of monumental Late Antique architecture. Themes in church mosaics regularly appear in a domestic context and, in Greece at least, mosaics in a Christian context rarely evoke unambiguously Christian themes. The calendar mosaic on the floor of the Thysos basilica has clear parallels with the calendar mosaic preserved at the villa of the falconer in Argos (Äkerström-Hougen 1974; Maguire 1987). The scenes of hunting putti from Nikopolis and the violent scene at the center of the basilica at Delphi (Figure 3.3) both find parallels in domestic and ecclesiastical contexts

FIGURE 3.3 Delphi Central Nave Emblema (photo: W. Caraher).

(Kitzinger 1951; Maguire 1987:21–28). The quotations from Homer at Nikopolis and the use of epic meter at the Thysos basilica at Tegea tie ecclesiastical space explicitly to long-standing elite intellectual practices (Kitzinger 1951; Pallas 1973/1974).

The Early Christian churches of Greece evoked through their design and decorations new modes of monumental expression, but they did this through combining traditional architectural forms and decorative themes. This use of the older forms to produce new meanings contributed to a continuity of authority in this period, while at the same time creating a series of new social and economic relationships. Thus, monumentality both manifested and produced social transformation.

RECEPTION

Ritual, patronage, architecture, and construction practice provide useful structural perspectives on the archaeology of monumental Christian space, but they also begin to offer some indication of how this new Christian space produced meaning in Late Antique Greek society. Recently, attention to reception in the context of monumental architecture has led scholars to regard monumentality less as a manifestation of elite authority and more as the locus for the performance of social strategies and attitudes toward power (some of the best recent work has come from scholars working in the Mediterranean Bronze Age and Iron Age, e.g., Kearns 2011; Knapp 2009; Wright 2006).

Scholars have long appreciated that ecclesiastical control over the ritual context of church architecture allowed the clergy to leverage traditional forms of elite ritual, architecture, and decoration—from apsidal halls to the themes of elaborate mosaic floors— to articulate their new positions within Late Antique society. At the same time, lay patronage opened the doors for individuals outside of the ecclesiastical hierarchy to use church architecture to express their positions of authority, privilege, wealthy, or piety in Christian terms. Between these two poles there likely existed a whole range of attitudes that engaged the complex processes that produced meaning both in elite and Christian space and ritual in a variety of ways. The experience of constructing the church or even watching churches bloom across the Late Roman Mediterranean created an experience of monumental architecture in the bodies and senses of the residents of Greece. In other words, monumental architecture produced Christian culture not through the projection of a set of values onto Late Roman Greek society, but, in part, through society's reception of new forms of monumental architecture that rely upon and embody a plurality of perspectives, competing social and ideological statements, and ritual contexts. Monumental buildings provided a framework in which an audience performed new cultural meanings. The combination of recognizable features associated with the long-standing architectural and decorative "language" of elite authority and the arrangement of space to position bodies in relation to Christian sacred space presented a place well suited for a range of interpretations grounded across Christian and non-Christian discourses of authority.

The roots of Christian space in architectural and decorative allusions to public space and elite residences created an uncanny environment that reinforced the hybrid nature of Christian authority for a Greek audience. This hybridity not only destabilized longstanding elite modes of self-representation, but participated in the process of embedding them within the emerging and explicitly totalizing Christian discourse (Cameron 1994; for hybridity see Bhabha 1994; Young 1995). While many scholars have looked toward the social confluence of traditional Mediterranean elites and positions of leadership within the institutional church (e.g., Rapp 2005), this chapter has suggested that monumental Early Christian architecture provided a place for the blending of elite and Christian themes (or its rejection) before a diverse audience. Thus, the architecture itself embodied tensions between different articulations of authority in Late Antique society rather than resolving them. The ambivalence of Christian space played a key role in the transformation of Late Antique society.

Monumentality in Early Christian architecture created a context for the performance of new forms of authority. The new Christian monumental architecture was a space that neither promoted a linear transition from pre-Christian to Christian times nor grounded Christian authority in the traditions of aristocratic representation in antiquity. Instead, monumental architecture in a Christian context provided a space where the audience negotiated new social, political, economic, and religious relationships.

REFERENCES CITED

Äkerström-Hougen 1974 *The Calendar and Hunting Mosaics of the Villa of the Falconer in Argos: A Study in Early Byzantine Iconography.* Svenska Institutet i Athen, Stockholm.

Asimakopoulou-Atzaka, P. 1987 Σύνταγμα τών παλαιο χριστιανικών ψηφιδωτών δαπέδων της Έλλάόος, II. Πελοπόν- νησος-Στερεά Έλλάόα. Kentro Byzantinon Erevnon, Thessaloniki.

Athanasoulis, D. 1998 Λουτρική εγκατάσταση στην Κοκκινόκρραχι Σπάρτης. Πρακτικά τοῦ Ε' Διεθνούς Συνεδρίου Πελοποννησαικών Σπουδών 2:209–244.

Avramea, A. 1997. *Le Péloponnèse du IVe au VIIIe siècle: changements et persistances.* Publications de la Sorbonne, Paris.

Baldovin, J. F. 1987 *The Urban Character of Christian Worship: The Origins, Development, and Meaning of Stational Liturgy. Orientalia Christiana Analecta* 228. Pont. Institutum Studiorum Orientalium, Rome.

Bhabha, H. 1994 Signs Taken for Wonders: Questions of Ambivalence and Authority under a Tree outside Delhi, May 1817. In *Location of Culture,* pp. 145–174. Routledge, London.

Bowden, W. 2003 *Epirus Vetus: The Archaeology of a Late Antique Province.* Duckworth, London.

Bowes, K. 2008 *Private Worship, Public Values, and Religious Change in Late Antiquity.* Cambridge University Press, Cambridge.

Caillet, J.-P. 1993 *L'evergetisme Monumental Chretien en Italie et a ses Marges: D'apres l'epigraphy des pavements de mosaique (IVè–VIIè s.).* Collection de l'École Française de Rome, Rome.

Cameron, A. 1994 *Christianity and the Rhetoric of Empire: The Development of Christian Discourse.* University of California Press, Berkeley.

Caraher, W. 2010 Abandonment, Authority, and Religious Continuity in Post-Classical Greece. *International Journal of Historical Archaeology* 14:241–254.

Caraher, W. 2003 *Church, Society, and the Sacred in Earth Christian Greece.* PhD dissertation. Ohio State University, Columbus.

Dey, H. 2010. Art, Ceremony, and City Walls: The Aesthetics of Imperial Resurgence in the Late Roman West. *Journal of Late Antiquity* 3:3–37.

Eliade, M. 1956 *The Sacred and the Profane: The Nature of Religion*. Translated by William Trask. Harcourt, Brace, New York.

Elsner, J. 1998 *Imperial Rome and Christian Triumph*. Oxford University Press, Oxford.

Elsner, J. 2002 The Birth of Late Antiquity: Riegl and Strzygowski in 1901. *Art History* 25:358–379.

Elsner, J. 2007 *Roman Eyes: Visuality and Subjectivity in Art and Text*. Princeton University Press, Princeton.

Foucault, M. 1986 Of Other Spaces. *Diacritics* 16:22–27.

Frantz, A. 1965 From Paganism to Christianity in the Temples of Athens. *Dumbarton Oaks Papers* 19:185–205.

Frantz, A.1988 *The Athenian Agora XXIV: Late Antiquity: A.D. 267–700*. American School of Classical Studies, Princeton.

Frey, J. 2006 *Speaking through Spolia: The Language of Architectural Reuse in Late Roman Greece*. PhD dissertation. University of California, Berkeley.

Given, M. 2004 *Archaeology of the Colonized*. Routledge, London.

Grabar, A. 1946. *Martyrium. Recherches sur le culte des reliques et l'art chrétien antique*. Collège de France, Paris.

Gregory, T. E. 1986 The Survival of Paganism in Christian Greece: A Critical Essay. *American Journal of Philology* 107:229–242.

Habicht, C. 1987 *"Neue Inschriften aus Demetrias"* in 1987. In *Demetrias 5*, edited by Simon Cornelis Bakhuizen, Fritz Gschnitzer, and Christian Habicht, pp. 269–306. R. Habelt, Bonn.

Hansen, F. B. 1993 *The Eloquence of Appropriation: Prolegomena to an Understanding of Spolia in Early Christian Rome*. L'Erma di Bretschneider, Rome.

Jakobs, P. H. F. 1987 *Die Frühchristlichen Ambone Griechenlands*. Reihe Klassische Archäologie, Bonn.

Janes, D. 1988 *God and Gold in Late Antiquity*. Cambridge University Press, New York.

Jones, A. H. M. 1960 Church Finance in the Fifth and Sixth Centuries. *Journal of Theological Studies* 11:84–94.

Jones, A. H. M. 1964 *The Later Roman Empire 284–602: A Social, Economic and Administrative Survey*. University of Oklahoma Press, Norman.

Kaldellis, A. 2009 *The Christian Parthenon: Classicism and Pilgrimage in Byzantine Athens*. Cambridge University Press, New York.

Kardulias, P. N. 1995 Architecture, Energy, and Social Evolution at Isthmia, Greece: Some Thoughts about Late Antiquity in the Korinthia. *Journal of Mediterranean Archaeology* 8:33–59.

Kearns, C. 2011 Building Social Boundaries at the Hybridizing First-Millennium BC Complex of Vouni (Cyprus). *Journal of Mediterranean Archaeology* 24:147–170.

Kinney, D. 1995 Rape or Restitution of the Past? Interpreting Spolia. In *The Art of Interpreting*, edited by S. C. Scott, pp. 52–67. Pennsylvania State University Press, University Park.

Kinney, D. 1997 Spolia. Damnatio and renovatio memoriae. *Memoirs of the American Academy in Rome* 42:117–148.

Kitzinger, E. 1951 Studies on Late Antique and Early Byzantine Floor Mosaics I: Mosaics at Nikopolis. *Dumbarton Oaks Papers* 6:83–122.

Knapp, A. B. 2009 Monumental Architecture, Identity and Memory. In *Proceedings of the Symposium: Bronze Age Architectural Traditions in the East Mediterranean: Diffusion and Diversity* (Gasteig, Munich, 7–8 May, 2008), pp. 47–59. Verein zur Förderung der Aufarbeitung der Hellenischen Geschichte e.V., Weilheim.

Krautheimer, R., with Slobodan Ćurčić 1986 *Early Christian and Byzantine Architecture*. Yale University Press, New Haven.

Lehmann, K. 1945 The Dome of Heaven. *Art Bulletin* 27:1–28.

Liebeschuetz, J. H. W. G. 2001 *The Decline and Fall of the Roman City.* Oxford University Press, New York.

L'Orange, H.-P. 1965 *Art Form and Civic Life in the Later Roman Empire.* Princeton University Press, Princeton.

MacCormack, S. 1981 *Art and Ceremony in Late Antiquity.* University of California Press, Berkeley.

Maguire, H. 1987 *Earth and Ocean: The Terrestrial World in Early Byzantine Art.* Pennsylvania State University Press, University Park.

Marchand, S. L. 1994 The Rhetoric of Artifacts and the Decline of Classical Humanism: The Case of Josef Strzygowski. *History and Theory* 33:106–130.

Mathews, T. 1971 *The Early Churches of Constantinople: Architecture and Liturgy.* Pennsylvania State University Press, University Park.

Mathews, T. 1982 Cracks in Lehmann's "Dome of Heaven." *Source: Notes in the History of Art* 3:12–16.

Mathews, T. 2003 *The Clash of the Gods: A Reinterpretation of Early Christian Art.* Rev. ed. Princeton University Press, Princeton.

Moralee, J. 2004 *"For Salvation's Sake": Provincial Loyalty, Personal Religion, and Epigraphic Production in the Roman and Late Antique Near East.* Routledge, New York.

Nasrallah, L. S. 2010 *Christian Responses to Roman Art and Architecture: The Second-Century Church amid the Spaces of Empire.* Cambridge University Press, New York.

Orlandos, A. 1957 *Η Ξυλόστεγος Παλαιοχριστιανική Βασιλική Της Μεσογειακής Λεκάνης: Μελέτη Περί Της Γενέσεως, Της Καταγωγής, Της Αρχιτεκτονικής Μορφής Και Της Διακοσμήσεως Των Χριστιανικών Οίκων Λατρείας Από Των Αποστολικών Χρόνων Μέχρις Ιουστινιανού.* Bibliothiki tis en Athinais Archaiologikis Etaireias, Athens.

Ousterhout, R. 1999 *Master Builders of Byzantium.* Princeton University Press, Princeton.

Pallas, D. 1973/1974. *Παλαιαχριστιανικές ρυθμικές ἐπιγραφές.* Rivista di Studi Bizantini e Neoellenici 10/11:17–56.

Pallas, D. 1979 Corinth et Nicopolis pendant le haut moyen-âge. *Felix Ravenna* 18:93–142.

Pallas, D. 1979/80 Monuments et texts: rémarques sur la liturgie dans quelques basiliques paléochrétiens. *EEBS* 44:37–116.

Pallas, D. 1984 L'édifice culturel chrétien et la liturgie dans l'Illuricum oriental. *Studi Antichita Cristiana* 1:544–557.

Pietri, C. 1984 La géographie de l'Illyricum ecclésiastique et ses relations avec l'Églize de Rome (Ve–VIe siècles). In *Villes et peuplement dan l'Illyricum protobyzanin,* pp. 21–59. Ecole Française de Rome, Rome.

Rapp, C. 2005 *Holy bishops in Late Antiquity: The Nature of Christian Leadership in an Age of Transition.* University of California Press, Berkeley.

Reigl, A. 1901 *Die Spätrömische Kunst-Industrie, nach den Funden in Österreich-Ungarn.* K. K. Hof- und Staatsdruckerei, Vienna.

Rothaus, R. M. 2000 *Corinth, the First city of Greece: an Urban History of Late Antique Cult and Religion.* Brill, Leiden.

Ruggieri, V. 1991 *Byzantine Religious Architecture (582–867): Its History and Structural Elements.* Pontificium Institutum Studiorum Orientalium, Rome.

Sanders, G. D. R. 2005 Archaeological Evidence for Early Christianity and the End of Hellenic Religion in Corinth. In *Urban Religion in Roman Corinth: Interdisciplinary Approaches,* edited by D. N. Schowalter and S. J. Friesen, pp. 419–442. Harvard University Press, Cambridge.

Sodini, J.-P. 1977 Remarques sur la sculpture architecturale d'Attique, de Béotie, ed du Péloponnése à l'Époque Paléochrétienne. *BCH* 101:423–450.

Sodini, J.-P. 1978 Mosaiques Paléochrétiennes de Grece: L'atelier de Klapsi et de Loutra Hypatis. *BCH* 102:557–561.

Sotinel, C. 1992 Autorité pontificale et pouvoir impérial sous le règne de Justinien: Le Pape Vigile. *Mélange d'archéologie et d'histoire de l'École français de Rome* 104:439–463.

Sotinel, C. 2005 Emperors and Popes in the Sixth Century: The Western View. In *The Cambridge Companion to the Age of Justinian,* edited by M. Maas, pp. 267–290. Cambridge University Press, Cambridge.

Spieser, J.-M. 1976 La christianisation des sanctuaires païens en Grèce. In *Neue Forschungen in griechischen Heiligtümern,* edited by Ulf Jantzen, pp. 309–320. Wasmuth, Tübingen.

Spieser, J.-M. 1995 Portes, limites et organisation de l'espace dans les églises paléochrétiennes. *Klio* 77:433–445.

Spiro, M. 1978 *Critical Corpus of the Mosaic Pavements on the Greek Mainland Fourth/Sixth Centuries with Architectural Surveys.* Garland, New York.

Strzygowski, J. 1901 *Orient oder Rom: Beiträge zur Geschichte der Spätantiken und Frühchristlichen Kunst.* J. C. Hinrichs'sche Buchhandlung, Leipzig.

Sweetman, R. 2001 The Evidence of Itinerant Craftpeople from the Mosaics of Roman Crete. In *La Mosaïque gréco-romaine VIII: actes du VIIIème Colloque international pour l'étude de la mosaïque antique et médiévale: Lausanne (Suisse): 6–11 Octobre 1997,* edited by D. Paunier and C. Schmidt, pp. 249–260. Cahiers d'arch'elogie romande, Lausanne.

Sweetman, R. 2010 The Christianization of the Peloponnese: The Topography and Function of Late Antique Churches. *Journal of Late Antiquity* 3:203–261.

Taft. R. 1992 *The Byzantine Rite: A Short History.* Liturgical Press, Collegeville, Minnesota.

Taft. R. 1998 Women at Church in Byzantium: Where, When—and Why?" *Dumbarton Oaks Papers* 52:27–87.

Trigger, B. 1990 Monumental Architecture: A Thermodynamic Explanation of Symbolic Behavior. *World Archaeology* 22:119–132.

Trombley, F. R. 2001 *Hellenic Religion and Christianization c. 370–529.* 2nd ed. Brill, Leiden.

Vemi, V. 1989 *Les Chapiteaux Ioniques à Imposte de Grèce à L'Époque Paléochrétienne.* BCH Supp. 17. Ecole française d'Athènes, Athens.

Veyne. P. 1990 *Bread and Circuses: Historical Sociology and Political Pluralism.* Penguin, London.

Ward Perkins, B. 2005 *The Fall of Rome and the End of Civilization.* Oxford University Press, New York.

Ward Perkins, J. B. 1954 Constantine and the Origins of the Christian Basilica. *Papers of the British School at Rome* 22:69–90.

Wharton, A. 1995 *Refiguring the Post Classical City: Dura Europos, Jerash, Jerusalem, and Ravenna.* Cambridge University Press, New York.

Wright, J. 2006 The Social Production of Space and the Architectural Reproduction of Society in the Bronze Age Aegean during the 2nd Millennium B.C.E. In *Constructing Power: Architecture, Ideology, and Social Practice/Konstrukton Der Macht: Architektur, Ideologie und soziales Handeln,* edited by J. Maran, C. Juwig, H. Schwengel, and U. Thaler, pp. 49–69. Lit Verlag, Hamburg.

Xydis, S. G. The Chancel Barrier, Solea, and Ambo of Hagia Sophia. *Art Bulletin* 29:1–24.

Yasin, Ann Marie. 2009 *Saints and Church Spaces in the Late Antique Mediterranean: Architecture, Cult, and Community.* Cambridge University Press, New York.

Young, R. 1995 *Colonial Desire: Hybridity in Theory, Culture, and Race.* Routledge, New York.

CHAPTER FOUR

The Monumentality of Text

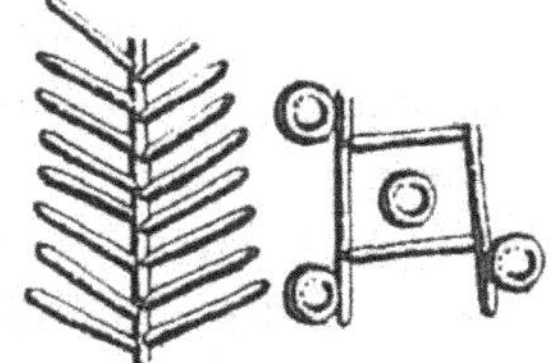

Edmund Thomas

Abstract *Monumentality is usually understood as a characteristic of physical structures in their own right, without taking into account the role of visible writing upon them. This chapter, however, considers the impact of inscribed writing on Greek and Roman architecture and highlights the contribution of the physical lettering to the status of a monument. It questions what writing adds to a building and why some buildings are inscribed and others not. It asks if a building is more or less monumental because of the presence or absence of inscribed lettering, and how far different forms, sizes, and scripts affect the impact of a building as a monument. Writing may define monumentality or merely consolidate it. The analogy of the tomb suggests that monuments were defined by the text or texts around them, so it might be inferred that a building's monumentality was a function of the writing inscribed upon it. Yet in public and sacred architecture what is today frequently described as "monumental writing" had, by contrast, a humanizing role. After considering both formal inscriptions and graffiti from a range of sites and periods, the paper concludes that writing can play a central role, not only in conferring monumentality on a building, but also in denying it.*

WRITING MONUMENTS

"Now is not the time to be thinking of monumentality": so the architectural historian James Ackerman (1981) admonished a gathering of American architects discussing the theme of "Monumentality and the City" some thirty years ago. In similar vein, a generation earlier, on the five hundredth anniversary of Alberti's *De Re Aedificatoria,*

Henry Hope Reed (1952:42) had lamented the loss of the monumental: "Even if we should wish to build monumentally, we would fail miserably. The tools to create the monument have been lost." Yet others insisted that *not* to think about monumentality is dangerous because "it seeks to extinguish a facet of cultural life." The problem was that architects could hardly agree on what monumentality was. To C. H. Reilly forty years earlier it had been obvious: "If we consider what we mean by the word monumental as applied to a building," he wrote, "we see at once that we mean some quality in it which isolates it from its practical and immediate use and gives it a peculiar appeal to our imagination" (Reilly 1912). That represents an idealized version of Bruce Trigger's functionalist definition, that monumental architecture had "a scale and elaboration that exceeds the requirements of any practical functions that a building is intended to perform" (Trigger 1990:119). For Reilly, monumentality could be broken down further into four distinct qualities: first, overall mass and unity of conception; second, the skillful direction of labor and craft; third, large scale; and, finally, refinement and delicacy of detail. But, as I have discussed elsewhere, ancient writers also saw monumentality as a visionary and in some sense superhuman quality, taking the building beyond the bounds of the living and beyond the present to something that represents the past to a future world (Thomas 2007). Like the literary Sublime, the Monumental can be regarded as "a figure of history that never had a discrete present and is as much a continuous past as a continuous present" (Budick 2000:69).

To many architects in search of the monumental, texts offered reassurance that their buildings might continue to reach to an audience. Yet, even in the most famous case, of Sir Christopher Wren (Elmes 1852:411), his text in St Paul's Cathedral had an inhibiting effect. On the west jamb of the window recess in the crypt below the choir containing his tomb the following words are inscribed in the sunken panel of a marble slab framed by egg-and-dart mouldings:

SUBTUS CONDITUR
HUIUS ECCLESIAE ET URBIS CONDITOR
CHRISTOPHORUS WREN
QUI VIXIT ANNOS ULTRA NONAGENTA
NON SIBI SED BONO PUBLICO.
LECTOR, SI MONUMENTUM REQUIRIS
CIRCUMSPICE.
OBIIT XXV FEB. ANNO MDCCXXIII

(Buried below is the founder of this church and city, Christopher Wren, who lived for over ninety years, not for himself, but for the public good. Reader, if you want a monument, look around you! He died on the 25th February in the Year 1723.)

The punning lines evoke the contrast between the importance of the deceased and his self-effacing humility, now buried in the crypt. Given that the overall and monumental aspect of the work could only be appreciated from a distance, this inscription, concealed below the main cathedral interior, only served to show either that text was no substitute for the building or that the reader was no match for the monument (Bold and Hinchcliffe 2009:172). But Wren's biographer, James Elmes, suspected a more sinister motive. He argued that the text, which in its present location "appealed in vain to the few readers who had scanned its contents," had been originally intended for the body of the cathedral, accessible to the worshipping congregation and visiting public, but had been relegated to "the dim religious light of the crypt" by the malicious intrigues of the Commissioners after Wren's death (Elmes 1852:412). On such an interpretation the initial pun of the *conditor conditur* appears vengeful, the proclaimed modesty of Wren takes on a far from delicious irony, and the command to the reader to inspect his architectural work not only becomes a frustrating challenge to the viewer, but puts the proud architect firmly in his place.

This chapter explores further the kinds of monumentality that visible, inscribed text could offer to buildings in classical antiquity. According to the prevailing view among archaeologists that monumental buildings are correlated with power and with the social and political control of elites, one might expect that an inscription imposed on a monument at the time of its dedication was an instrument of power and that its primary role was to publicize the message of the agent behind the program. Countless examples seem to endorse this view, from the works of Eastern monarchs to those of Roman emperors (Figure 4.1). The monument requires a written marker, but also one fitted to

FIGURE 4.1 "Porta Maggiore," Rome, carrying the Aqua Claudia and Anio Novus. Detail of inscriptions of Claudius (top), Vespasian (middle), and Titus (below). Photo: author.

the grandeur of the building in materials and proportion. Tombs need labels; temples invite dedicatory scripts. But this is just one aspect of ancient inscriptions on buildings, and to see them only in this way is not only overly reductive of their complexity of meaning, but also to misunderstand their very nature.

An inscription on a building can be said to consist of three elements, from which its monumentality is derived: the *text,* which can be subdivided into *content* (the primary message, or historical record) and *form* (the linguistic style, which gives evidence of its culture from literary to very modest); the *writing* (graphic design of lettering and frame, which can reach the level of art); and, thirdly, the *monument* (the physical integration of a text into a structure, not just like a document or inscribed artifact, but inserted in an artistic context or sometimes into a preexisting artistic monument) (Campana 1984:363). To understand how this works, one may consider the text on the plinth of Trajan's Column in Rome (Figure 4.2):

FIGURE 4.2 Pedestal of Trajan's Column. Photo: DAI Rome.

SENATVS POPVLVSQVE ROMANVS

IMP(eratori) CAESARI DIVI NERVAE F(ilio) NERVAE

TRAIANO AVG(usto) GER(manico) DACICO PONTIF(ici)

MAXIMO TRIB(uniciae) POT(estatis) XVII IMP(eratori) VI CO(n)S(uli) VI P(atri) P(atriae)

AD DECLARANDVM QVANTAE ALTITVDINIS

MONS ET LOCVS TANT[is ope]RIBVS SIT EGESTVS

(The Senate and People of Rome

To the Emperor Caesar, son of the divine Nerva,

Trajan Augustus Germanicus Dacicus Pontifex Maximus, 17 times awarded Tribunician Power, 6 times called Emperor, 6 times Consul, Father of the Country,

In order to make clear of what great height was the hill, and the site

For such great works, that was cleared away) (*CIL* 6.960 = *ILS* 294; translation after Lepper and Frere [1988:203–207])

As *text,* its *content* communicates the primary message of the "program," the honorific dedication of the column to Trajan by Senate and People, and records that honor for posterity. But it also signals the monumentality of the Forum as a whole, at the edge of which it stands and which it surveys from the upper gallery of the column. It not only serves as historical record, a fossilization of the column's dedication by Trajan in person, which seems to have taken place on May 12, A.D. 113 (Vidman 1982:48), but even hints that the column marks the height of the Quirinal hill from which the Forum was excavated, whether in a rhetorical and impressionistic way (as translated here) or more precisely like a measuring rod—the grammar is ambiguous. The *form* of the text is both official and solemn (in the dedicatory first part) and embellished and rhetorical (in the second), highlighting both a formal and a high level of literary culture. As *monument,* like any inscription on an artifact, it not only comments on the function of the column as honor and yardstick, but highlights the commemorative aspect of those functions for posterity; yet within a few years, after Trajan's death, it could also be interpreted as hinting in retrospect at the personal memory of the emperor and his ashes, stored in a gold urn "at the foot of" the column (*sub columna* [Eutropius 8.5.2]), perhaps in a roofed shrine directly behind the plinth that faced his temple with its own proper funerary inscription (Claridge 2007:88). As *writing,* the text is not only framed as an artifact with the same emphasis on proportion as the plinth—the epigraphic field occupies a double square, the plinth a 21-foot square—but presented in highly regular, proportionate, and artistic lettering, in the arrangement of both the lines and the individual letters (Grasby 1996:99–103 Figures 2–5). On either side, winged victories frame and support the text, just as in large-scale architecture similar figures are used to frame architectural points of focus or to give the impression of holding up a building.

Formally, the inscription conveys all of the four distinct qualities ascribed by Reilly to monumentality in architecture: mass and unity of conception (Ohlsen 1981); the skillful direction of labor and craft, both in its own combination of the stonecutting,

sculpture, and architecture and through its textual reference to the excavation of the hill;
large scale, reinforced by the consistent height of the square lettering, 11.4 mm in lines
1–4, drawing the reader's eye vertically to the "hundred-foot column" and horizontally
to the broad expanse of imperial space beyond; and, finally, refinement and delicacy of
detail in the precision and proportion of the serif lettering (Catich 1968). Moreover, as
an artistic monument, the text's isolation from any immediate practical function gives
it a peculiar appeal to the viewer's imagination (Land 1994:42; Nasrallah 2010:156).
It is therefore hardly surprising that attention has been drawn to the Roman monumental inscription as an art form. "The attic inscription of the Arch of Titus," writes
Ross Holloway, "was meant to be seen, appreciated and understood. If one considers
the relative scale of the sculpture visible on the exterior of the Arch of Titus and the
monumental inscription of the attic (Figure 4.3), there is every reason to feel that the
arch was intended as a pedestal for a written message. The sculpture is an addition."
(Holloway 1987:187) This kind of monumentality of text is well known: the grand scale,
making visual impact and a physical impression; the high art with both visual impact and
artistic value; the public message, promoting a program. But this view risks reading the
monument through modern spectacles, tinted by visions of banner-like Baroque *trionfi
d'acqua* such as the Acqua Felice or Acqua Paola (Figure 4.4) which reused the Roman
triumphal arch as Counter-Reformation celebration (Petrucci 1993:37, 41), or turning
it into a postmodernist idealization of the self-reflective monument like Robert Venturi's
(1977:100 Figure). Similarly, one should beware of reading Roman band inscriptions
(Figure 4.5) through the lens of Renaissance imitators such as Lorenzo Manili (Figure
4.6). The deep-cut incision of writing (Figure 4.7) carved into the wall's "skin" (Fabre et
al. 1992:71) is of a different order to the mannered self-presentation of the Renaissance
antiquarian (Tucci 2001).

It is therefore important to assess the text and the medium together. What is the
effect of the text? Does it monumentalize? Is a work of architecture more of a monument with or without it? The Manilian inscription, for example, is not just related
to the building on which it stands, the house of Manili, but proudly announces the
rebirth of Rome (*Have Roma*), gestures toward the ancient Roman *gens Manlia* and the
ancient "Forum of the Jewish people" (*Forum Iudeorum*), which had stood on the site,
and is dated with mock-archaizing solemnity from the Foundation of the City. Without
the inscription, heightened by its imitation of classical lettering and boldly protruding
cornices framing the text field, this typical row of orange plastered houses in the ancient
ghetto could hardly be considered "monumental." The inscription at Spoleto, by contrast,
is cut deeply into a leveled course of the city wall, apparently in the second half of the
first century B.C., to judge from its letter forms and distinctive triangular interpuncts
(*CIL* 11.4809; Di Marco 1975: Plate XIX). Most of the wall circuit, however, used the
remnants of the original polygonal wall built when the town was established as a Latin
colony in 241 B.C. (Becker 2008:150–152; Fontaine 1990:150–151). The inscription is
therefore thought to commemorate a restoration after an earthquake in 63 B.C. (Becker
2008:63). But this explanation seems unlikely, since the earthquake recorded by ancient
sources must have occurred by 65 B.C. and its epicenter lay much farther east, in the

FIGURE 4.3 Arch of Titus, Rome. East face. Photo: DAI Rome.

area of northern Syria and the Crimea, rather than central Italy (Traina 1995). Thus, the primary effect of the inscription was not to memorialize a completely new structure, or even to commemorate restoration after its supposed devastation by an earthquake, but to appropriate a structure that was already physically monumental and visually impressive. Like later Augustan texts on the Republican city gates of Rome (Thomas 2007:108, 298 n. 28), the text simply appropriated the monumentality of the city walls, with the names of the principal magistrates of the city—which since 82 B.C. had had the higher status of a *municipium*—literally carved into the local stone and into the fabric of the urban boundary. Taking the unusual form of a single line (Bispham 2007:493), it presented a marker of authority. Raised several meters above the ground, the foot-high lettering carved into a course of finished ashlar blocks, whose smooth surface presents a visible contrast with the other courses of the wall, accentuates the physical grandeur of the

FIGURE 4.4 Fontanone dell'Acqua Paola, Gianicolo, Rome. Detail. Photo: author.

FIGURE 4.5 Wall inscription from the Roman city walls of Spoletium (Spoleto). Photo: author.

FIGURE 4.6 Casa di Lorenzo Manili, Rome. Photo: Wikicommons.

FIGURE 4.7 Detail of lettering on the wall inscription from the Roman city walls of Spoletium (Spoleto). Photo: author.

fortifications. But here it was not the text that made the monument, but the monument which made the text.

The famous inscription of the Pantheon, formed of gilded bronze letters three-quarters of a meter high, is even more incidental to the building on which it stands. The original letters of gilded bronze provided a similar physical adornment to the frieze equivalent to figured ornament. Yet, stripped of that relief-like lettering in the early Middle Ages, the building lost none of its imposing grandeur (Scherer 1955:Plate 192); indeed, the letters of metal alloy jammed into the surviving matrices in 1887 at the instruction of the education minister Guido Baccelli (Alföldy 1990:73) seemed, rather than restoring a lost ornament or a forgotten meaning, almost to jar with its very monumentality. So what does writing add to a building? Does the text make the monument, or, as may be asked in the Pantheon's case, does the monument make the text? If inscribed writing was always a monumentalizing device, why are some buildings inscribed, while others are left free of writing? A classic example is the Parthenon. It hardly needed the Emperor Nero's interspacing of bronze shields and bronze letters alternately below the metopes and triglyphs of the Doric frieze (Carroll 1982), whether as objects of dedication or elements of beautification, to confirm its status as a monument. Yet for Nero the Parthenon's historic immensity and counterintuitive blankness invited his self-gratifying insertion of monumental writing, as if to confirm the ancient belief that an uninscribed building was only half complete (Koenen 1985; *P. Leiden* I. 396.59–62).

I have argued previously that inscriptions played an important role in celebrating the monumentality of a building, not least through the use of formal devices such as the *tabula ansata* and other decorative frames; this was particularly the case in funerary monuments where both the commemoration of the dead and the monumentality of the tomb were enhanced by the aggregation there of votive and memorial texts (Thomas 2007:191–193). A striking example of such monumentalization is at the Roman theater of Patara, where a record of the decoration of the *proscaenium* by Quintus Vilius Proculus and the addition of awnings by his daughter Claudia Vilia Proc(u)la in 147 was displayed at the southern parodos entrance in self-consciously publicist form, its recessed profile blended inevitably into the architecture (Thomas 2007:82 Figure 83). But it is worth considering the nature of writing. While some argued that it was secondary to speech, others maintained that written discourse was an enduring memorial (*monumentum*) of the spoken version (Quintilian, *Inst. Or.* 12.10.5). Thus, the words written on a building, and above all those incised into its fabric to become part of it, could be considered as a *voix scriptible,* or "writable voice" (Desbordes 1990:101). Just as the human voice was thought to consist of letters (*charaktēres,* literally "things engraved," or *tupoi,* literally physical "impressions"), so, conversely, inscriptions had a phonetic and phonographic quality. For legal texts such as the Great Law Code at Gortyn, which has been seen "first and foremost as a monument, and not a text . . . there to represent the majesty of the law to a population that was largely illiterate . . . [and] to present the particular regulations and practices of a small city-state as eternal and immutable" (Whitley 1998:322–323), the phonetic aspect of the words also gave the inscription a performative dimension, displayed as if to reverberate acoustically in the vaulted passageway curving around the building of the city's legislative assembly. In monumental dedicatory inscriptions the "golden letters" (in fact, of resonant, gilded bronze) inserted into a temple frieze had a special power to highlight the dedicator's voice; the single golden letter E at Delphi dedicated by Livia was perhaps intended to upstage the earlier wooden and bronze *anathēmata,* although it was the oldest one of wood that was attributed to "the Wise Men" (Plutarch, *De E apud Delphos* 385 f 6-386 a 3). It was such a voice, repeatedly set out in three rows beneath each triglyph of the Parthenon façade like a musical incantation, at which the performer Nero surely aimed.

An unusually stark manifestation of the inscription as voice appears in the Temple of Artemis at Sardis, in one of the columns of the east (front) colonnade, just beside the central intercolumniation at the entrance to the temple. Engraved in a single line on the vertical fillet below the apophyge a little more than a meter above the stylobate (Figure 4.8) are these words: "The torus and the base [literally, 'root'] are each a single stone, and of all (the columns) I am the first to rise again from entire stones, not furnished by the people (*dēmoteuktos*), but given by friends (*oikeios*)" (Buckler and Robinson 1932:143–144 no. 181; Yegül 2014). Here the dedication of the columns acquires special authority by

FIGURE 4.8 Temple of Artemis, Sardis. Detail of inscription on the base of a column. Photo: author.

being presented not as the contribution of an external agent, but, through explicit plant metaphors—the base is called *rhizaios*, the "root (stone)"—as a literally organic process. The epigraphic voice of this self-confessedly animate structure should be distinguished from dedicatory texts that were simply attached to the building. In some cases, the latter were viewed as potentially destructive to the structure: hence, the construction at the sanctuary of Apollo Delphinios in Miletus of a "new stoa," horseshoe-shaped, for the posting of citizen and proxeny lists and, when this quickly became filled with votive wooden tablets (*pinakes*), the formal prohibition of their spreading, almost like a contagion, to other parts of the sanctuary (Kawerau and Rehm 1914:172 n. 32, 284).

Some 2,200 years earlier than Wren, a Greek architect or state official (*epistates*) in Syracuse left a record at the Temple of Apollo similar in effect to Wren's memorial in St Paul's (Engelmann 1981; Guarducci 1967–1978:1:343, 1987; Umholtz 2002:263–265). It was not his tomb memorial, but a statement of an individual official's provision of columns of the temple, carefully punctuated to separate its different elements (name; purpose; patronymic; object of construction). Like the Wren tablet, the dedication occupies a low-key position in comparison with later monumental texts, inscribed on the vertical face of the stylobate in letters minuscule in proportion to the temple. Yet to the reader ascending the stylobate of the temple or, perhaps more likely, looking up at it from below, the letters were high enough (15–18 cm) to be clearly visible and monumental. In addition to the clear message of self-promotion (Holloway 1999) and the squared lettering of the text—remarkable at this date, even if it should be attributed to a fifth-century restoration, rather than to the period of the columns' erection in the sixth century B.C.—the inscription's position at the foot of the columns, like a text at the base of a statue, makes clear its effect in indicating the artistic status of the object, toward which, like Wren's tombstone, but in this case without visual interruption, it directs the reader to gaze upward. It could thus be said to make the temple a monument. But by highlighting the act of construction by a mortal identified through name and patronymic the text also humanizes the colossal temple columns of the house of the god.

An extreme version of this urge to inscribe stone surfaces with clearly visible writing are the monstrous inscriptions of the village of Gerga in the hills of Caria, with lettering larger even than that of the Pantheon and achieving a monumentality of their own in terms of scale alone, cut deep into gigantic boulders and across the pediment of a simple shrine (Bean 1969; Held 2008). Such writing is unparalleled in the Roman world and presents a simple name, rather than an articulated message. In some cases it stands by itself, carved on a rock and not so much speaking as shouting to viewers all around that wild mountainous region above the valley of the river Marsyas; and in another case the script is placed more conventionally within the tympanum of a little prostyle temple, but at an excessive and disproportionate scale. The lettering on the citadel at the Hernician settlement of Ferentinum in central Italy presents a scale of its own, marking the monumentality of this gigantic structure (D'Alessio 2007). But to highlight the monumentalizing aspect of this architectural text is only half the story. Writing on buildings did not only emphasize their superhuman dimensions, real or imagined; it also had the opposite, humanizing effect. As the smaller stylobate text of the Syracusan architect brought that monumental temple into the human plane, so the local censors' text high up on the acropolis wall, militarily secured by a row of defensive emplacements for catapults above (Figure 4.9), signaled the place of what had previously looked like nameless, "Cyclopaean" foundations within its local context of civic administration and defense (Solin 1980–82). In so bringing a building down to size, and into the human domain, the text did not so much magnify as *de*-monumentalize the work.

Defacing/Rewriting Monuments

In 283/282 B.C., the architect Sostratus of Cnidus carved his name into the exterior fabric of a great lighthouse on the island of Pharos off the coast of Alexandria that would later become known as one of the Seven Wonders of the World and an icon of monumentality. He was conscious that the stonework was soon to be covered with plaster, on which the dedication of his royal patron, Ptolemy Philadelphus, would be inscribed. As he foresaw, in time the plaster surface flaked away, taking the royal inscription with it and leaving the architect's own dedication exposed underneath: "Sostratus, son of Dexiphanes,

FIGURE 4.9 Citadel wall with band inscription, Ferentinum (Ferentino). Photo: author.

of Cnidus, to the saviour gods for those who sail on the sea" (Lucian, *Hist. conscr.* 62: *Sōstratos Dexiphanous Knidios Theois sōtērsin huper tōn plōizomenōn*). Thus, unlike Wren, the ancient architect had the last laugh on those who tried to suppress his voice and to camouflage his attempt to make his building his monument. We are not told if Sostratus himself ever saw the outcome of his clever game with the materiality of architecture and the inevitability of time and decay. But for the satirist Lucian, who recounted this story in the second century A.D. as a message to those contemporaries who chose to write obsequious histories of imperial campaigns, it was a solid testimony to how a structure presented as the work of a royal "founder" might ultimately become a monument to its architect, and was thus an illustration of the need of the architect/writer to have an eye on the future, rather than the present (Eck et al. 2007:215–217).

His narrative was a travesty of the actual dedication. In fact, it seems that King Ptolemy had permitted the architect to leave an inscription (Pliny, *HN* 36.83). Its text is elsewhere quoted: "*Sōstratos Dexiphanous Knidios Theois philos tōn basileōn tēs tōn plōi- zomenōn sōtērias charin anethēke* [Sostratus of Cnidus, son of Dexiphanes, to the Gods, friend of kings dedicated (this) for the safety of sailors]" (Strabo 17.1.6, C791). This confirms the aspect of the building's dedication on behalf of sea travelers, which also provides an important intimation of the intended audience of the inscribed text. Howev- er, Lucian conveniently ignored the detail that Sostratus called himself "friend of kings" and that, as other surviving inscriptions confirm, this designer of hanging gardens in his home city of Cnidus was not just an architect, but also a high-ranking diplomat in the Ptolemaic court (Perdrizet 1899). The architect's dedication thus perpetuated both the king's and his own memory.

In his reconstruction a century ago, Herman Thiersch (1909; Eck et al. 2007:217 Figure 3) imagined the text as standing high up like the inscription at Ferentinum and legible from afar to travelers by sea. This restoration now finds some corroboration in the rediscovery ten years ago of the Emperor Nero's dedication of the lighthouse at Patara on the Lycian coast. Looking across the Mediterranean at the Alexandrian wonder off its southern shore, this Roman structure carried an inscription consisting of letters of gilded bronze attached by dowels to at least six courses of the building's stonework, so that it extended in all nearly four meters high. The exact height from the ground can- not yet be established (Işkan-Işik et al. 2008:93–94); but the wording of the inscription makes it likely that Nero's dedication at Patara was a deliberate echo of the Alexandrian text (Işkan-Işik et al. 2008:110). By comparison, the dedications of architects at such structures were much more unobtrusive. A military architect's dedication to Mars at the "Tower of Hercules" at La Coruña was carved in a smaller rectangular frame in the natural rock (Hutter 1973:12). The account transmitted by Lucian might therefore have originated from a wish to explain how such a royal monument carried a dedication by its architect at all, let alone in such a prominent position, and lacked the kind of direct statement of monarchical achievement that was *de rigueur* under the Roman emperors. His suggestion about the furtiveness of Sostratus's intentions recalls the ancient tradition, possibly apocryphal, that some architects' signatures were not even explicit, but concealed in visual form, such as the rebuses of the architects Batrachus ('Frog') and Saurus ('Lizard') carved on the columns of the Republican temples in the Portico of Octavia (Vell. Pat. 1.11.3; Pliny, *HN* 36.42), and the modern theory that the two tiny rings, or "eyeglasses," between the dentils on Flavian entablatures in Rome were a "signature" of Domitian's architect Rabirius (MacDonald 1982:128; Toynbee 1975:12 n. 4) or, less romantically, the "house style" of a workshop (Wilson Jones 2000:29). Although it is now largely discredited, the latter theory appealed to the Italian archaeologist Giuseppe Lugli and others as a means through which the architect could escape the emperor's prohibition to leave his own name on the buildings (Crema 1959:315; Lugli 1918 and 1965), and this suggestion continues to be reiterated by some well-respected archaeologists today (Salza Prina Ricotti 2006). There is, in fact, no evidence for such a veto by Domitian on architects' self-commemoration, but it may be more than coincidence that the original suggestion was made in Heinrich Brunn's monumental work on Greek artists alongside his reference to Lucian's narrative (Brunn 1889,II: 254–256). At any rate, in highlighting the ephemerality of the official text and the permanence of the Cnidian's illicit addition, the story also provides an interesting commentary on potential archaeological evidence where the imperial letters were later removed while the architect's inscription survived.

Indeed, Lucian's story helps us think more closely about the monumentality of the act of writing on buildings in general and about the shifting notions of fragility and durability that were inevitably involved in the act of placing a meaningful string of letters into or upon a work of architecture. For those seeking an understanding of such texts in the classical world, it is strangely discomforting. The destruction of the official statement and endurance of the illicit signature is the very opposite of what we find in the remains of built Roman architecture. In ancient cities, as in modern urban space, it is the transitory graffiti texts scratched into plaster that too often elude our grasp as the surface disappears or the letters are eroded, while the official inscriptions cut into a building's fabric endure to catch the eye of posterity and frequently become recycled. Lucian was well aware of this paradox in his account of the wily Cnidian, who turned his royal patron's official dedication into a transitory graffito and defacement of his structure and his own subversive intervention into a more fundamental and lasting monument. We in turn are challenged to take graffiti more seriously as monumental writing.

The many graffiti that have thwarted the forces of time and decay and left their trace on the remains of Roman buildings in Italy and farther afield were written in pen or scratched with a sharp implement on the stucco or plaster walls of buildings. But they should not therefore be regarded as "random" or "intrusive" interventions into the architectural fabric or classed as "informal writing," but recognized "as a form of writing practice" (Baird and Taylor 2011:7). Indeed, they are often deployed in an intentional engagement with notions of celebrity and monumentality and in a conscious dialogue with more "monumental" forms of architectural writing. When a suburban villa at Gigthis in southern Tunisia was partially excavated in two campaigns of 1902–1903 and 1911, abundant and mostly indecipherable graffiti were observed to cover the interior walls (Constans 1916:100–104). One example merits particular attention. Painted in red letters 2 cm high, it belongs to the category termed *dipinti,* marks painted more or less skillfully on walls (Kruschwitz 2010:157). Its bright color stood out on a band of white stucco, which was later transported to the Musée Alaoui (now Bardo) at Tunis. The text consists of two disconnected fragments put together as follows (*CIL* 8.22754a; Merlin, in Gauckler et al. 1910: 101 no. 1065):

NVNC TIBI IN OPERE S— — NIDIFICAS.

Now you build a nest for yourself in construction—

As the excavators recognized, this text can be explained with the help of a well-known story preserved in Donatus's *Life of Virgil* (Donatus Auctus, *Vita Vergilii* 69–70, in Diehl 1911: 35). The celebrated poet is supposed to have written a couplet in praise of Augustus and "fixed" it (*infixisset*) anonymously on a door. The verb here might be thought to imply nailing a wooden tablet to the door (cf. Cicero, *Philippics* 2.36) rather than a painted graffito, but, since there is no mention of such a medium but the lines are the direct object of the verb *infigere,* it may be better to interpret the action as the driving of a sharp object such as a nail into the door to scratch the words and leave their imprint in the wooden panel. In any case, its anonymity makes it analogous. The location of the door is not specified further. As this portentous anecdote would become a "hackneyed quotation" (Toynbee 1957:11), the words were assumed to have been written in a public place (Russell 1897:379) or even on the walls of Maecenas's villa (Miller 1919:174); but the context of the story suggests that the door more likely belonged to the emperor's Palatine house. The sycophantic couplet ran as follows:

NOCTE PLVIT TOTA REDEVNT SPECTACVLA MANE
COMMVNE IMPERIVM CVM IOVE CAESAR HABET.

It rains all night, but the shows return in the morning:
Caesar shares power with Jupiter.

The lines are rationalized to explain that it rained all night before the "feast-day [i.e., birth-day?] of Augustus" and the sun shone on the day itself (Russell 1897:379). But the point of the anecdote is to show the status of the text as an anonymous, graffito-like intervention. After Augustus had enquired for a long time as to the author of these lines, no one said anything, until eventually a mediocre poet called Bathyllus—perhaps the Alexandrian pan-tomime dancer freed by Maecenas (Suetonius, 17 *Maecenas* 1; Cassius Dio 54.17)—falsely claimed responsibility and, in accordance with the authority accruing from his acknowl-edged authorship (Lowrie 2009), was duly honored by the emperor. In response to this Virgil put a second text on the same door consisting of a single half-line repeated four times:

SIC VOS NON VOBIS
SIC VOS NON VOBIS
SIC VOS NON VOBIS
SIC VOS NON VOBIS

(So not for yourselves you . . .
So not for yourselves you . . .
So not for yourselves you . . .
So not for yourselves you . . .)

When Augustus asked for these seemingly nonsensical half-lines to be completed, no one was able to complete them until Virgil added a hexameter before the lines and completed the quatrain as follows:

HOS EGO VERSICVLOS FECI TVLIT ALTER HONOREM
SIC VOS NON VOBIS NIDIFICATIS AVES
SIC VOS NON VOBIS VELLERA FERTIS OVES
SIC VOS NON VOBIS MELLIFICATIS APES
SIC VOS NON VOBIS FERTIS ARATRA BOVES

(I made these little verses myself: another took the credit:
So not for yourselves you build nests, O birds,
So not for yourselves you wear fleeces, O sheep,
So not for yourselves you make honey, O bees,
So not for yourselves you carry the plough, O cattle.)

Students of Pompeii are familiar with the licentious mauling of quotable lines from the poets (Beard 2008:52); Virgil was a particular favorite (Petrucci 1981). In this context of recycled poetry the line in the Gigthis dipinto has another, ironically self-referential meaning. The phenomenon owed much for its effect to the words' monumental setting, like modern *bons mots* scrawled along the walls of public buildings today. Lines that played on physical features such as the perceived impenetrability of a door or the hardness of stone walls were particularly popular (*CIL* 4.1893–1895; cf. Ovid, *Amores* 1.8.77–78, *Ars Am.* 1.475–476; Propertius 4.5.47–48).

However, the Gigthis dipinto is no precise quotation, but an *amendment* of the Virgilian lines with a positive meaning and a further architectural dimension. By answering the negative sense of the Virgilian text with a positive version applied not to animals but to a person, the "speaker" of the graffito alludes to a concept of *nidificatio* ("nest-building"), a playfully diminutive and self-disparaging antithesis of normal, "monumental" building (*aedificatio*) referring to smaller-scale domestic architecture (Thomas 2007:255). On this interpretation it is natural to assume that the owner of the house was the addressee of the lines, and that he was an architect, accustomed to building houses for others, who had now made one for himself (Constans 1916:103). The text might be assumed to be the work of a guest, with or without the owner's consent, or indeed to have been written by the owner to himself. Yet the context of the Virgilian story, which concerns unattributed, graffito-like texts, implies that the author's identity can remain only a guess. Like monumental inscriptions, unsigned graffiti are essentially anonymous. At the same time, the text has a quasi-monumental aspect because it masquerades as a kind of building inscription, albeit presented as an address, rather than in the third person. It offers a statement about the construction of the whole building around it, although the exact character of that construction (*OPERE*) is now unclear because of the gap between the two preserved fragments. Yet its nature as part of a dialogue suggests greater spontaneity, and the present tense, in place of the past used in monumental texts, points to a graffito-like, continuing engagement. The form of the inscription confirms this ambiguity in the status of the text and its dialogue between the monumental/public and domestic/private. Painted in red *minium* on a small band of white stucco along the upper part of a vermilion wall, which invites a monumental text like the fresh, smoothed stone work of a public façade, it is presented to the viewer as if to evoke a monumental inscription along a frieze. The red paint of the dipinto echoes the scarlet *minium* applied to both books and inscriptions (Pliny, *HN* 33.122; Warga 2001) and so plays out the constant dialogue between literary texts, painted stucco, and cut stone. Yet with the small size and irregular form of the lettering the text resembles a graffito. For educated élite visitors to the house, it could have suggested a caricature of grand building projects.

Graffiti and dipinti gain monumentality and celebrity from being presented in the manner of more durable texts. The visibility, permanence, and orderliness of architectural writing are what the graffito artist cherishes, but, while he lacks the expertise, he enjoys the privilege, unknown for monumental texts, of putting in place a text that he has composed himself (Solin 1970:12); the dipinto, executed by a professional scribe, is magnified by its more orderly writing and frame, however banal or indecent its content, and shouts more loudly at a busy location, pressing passers-by to show continence while they pass that spot (*CIL* 4.6641, translated in Beard 2008:56). Conversely, the imperial inscriptions of Claudius, Vespasian, and Titus incised on the "Porta Maggiore" in Rome (Coates-Stephens 2004), an archway carrying the Aqua Claudia and Anio Novus across the ancient Via Praenestina, are like successive graffiti in dialogue with each other (Figure 4.1). Both the lack of correspondence between lines of text and courses of masonry and the defacing of existing architectural ornament are graffito-like in their abandon. It is no surprise that Claudius employs a typical strategy of graffiti, using a physical text as a vehicle of denunciation, in his inscription over the arches of the Aqua Virgo at Via del Nazareno, which he claims had previously been "disturbed by Gaius Caesar [Caligula]" (Ramage 1983). This denunciative aspect reveals how the monumental text engages with an implicit audience. Even more disruptive are the imperial inscriptions added to the archway that carried the Augustan Aqua Julia and the rebuilt Aquae Marcia and Tepula and proclaimed Augustus's restoration of the water supply to the whole city (Figure 4.10). The original pedimented architecture of this structure, which, situated just inside the Porta Tiburtina of the later Aurelianic Walls, appeared as a city-gate within the arcaded barrier of the aqueduct between the Augustan city and its suburb, was mutilated to make room for a later, Caracallan text vying for the attention of traffic coming toward the city from the fork of the Via Tiburtina and Via Collatina (Malmberg and Bjur 2011:374). The inscription quite literally defaced the Augustan gateway more than any graffito artist could have dreamed.

By contrast, multiple graffiti could exploit or endorse the monumentality of a public building. The best single example is the basilica at Pompeii, which has the highest density of graffiti per square meter of any public building in the city (Keegan 2011:172). The vast majority of its 193 recorded instances were painted or scratched into the stucco

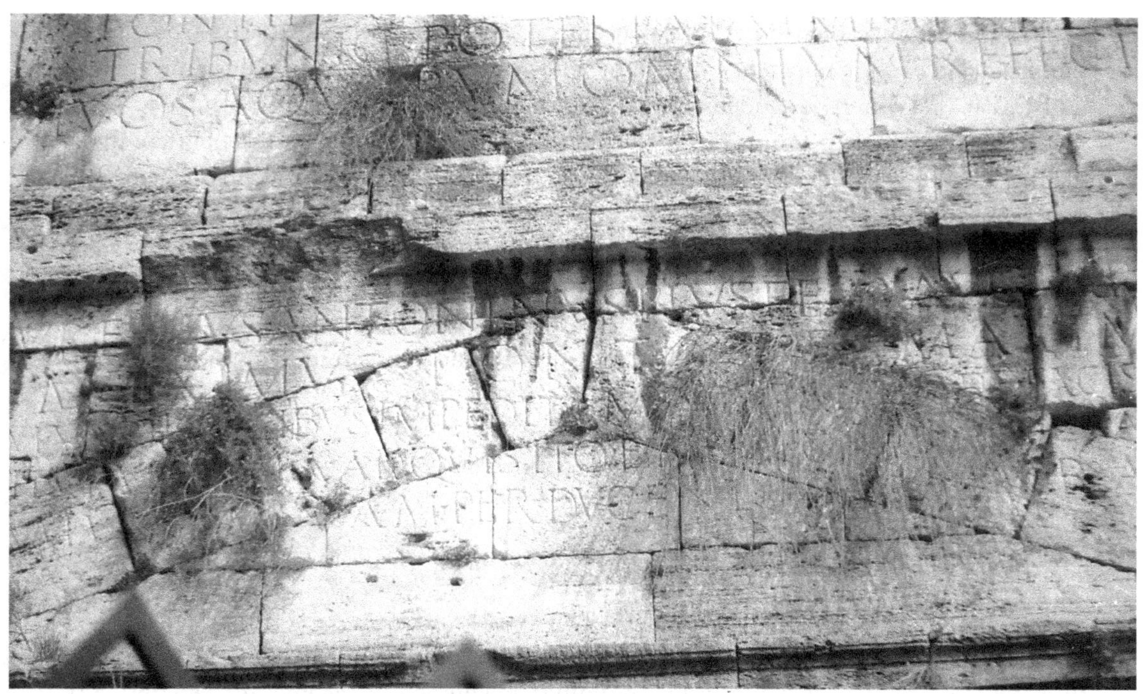

FIGURE 4.10 "Porta Tiburtina," Rome: detail of the attic. Photo: author.

of the building's north interior wall, where in the nineteenth century William Gell (1832) and Christopher Wordsworth (1837) observed a remarkable density of graffito text (*CIL* 4.1780–1952). Some remains, cut with a nail into the yellowish stucco surface, were captured and preserved in the Museo Nazionale at Naples and recorded as *CIL* 4.1880–1904. This wall of inscriptions is an unlicensed version of the official whitewashed boards (*tabulae dealbatae*) in Roman public spaces (Bollini 1984) or of stone walls given over to fixed public notices, as at Assisi (Gros-Theodorescu 1985). But it is not just the overall look of the wall that mimics official architectural writing. The pseudo-monumental character of many of the individual texts preserved is remarkable, claiming authority by their pretentious dating formula *ab urbe condita* ("from the Foundation of the City"), some of them as early as 78 B.C., barely a generation after the completion of the building (*CIL* 4.1842). Also striking is the way in which the name of the building itself is scrawled repeatedly over the exterior wall. Each time the word is spelled with a double S (*CIL* 4.1458, 1459a). Wordsworth's classical education taught him to be aghast at such continued bad orthography (Wordsworth 1837:14), whereas an English middle-class audience might now chuckle with amusement in recalling the corrections made across architectural space on a much larger scale in Monty Python's *Life of Brian* by its clueless hero (Zadorojnyi 2011:111). But who are we to fault or mock the spelling of a Hellenistic Roman import into a Samnite town? What seems to us incorrect may then have been common usage (Kruschwitz 2010:163–164). More significant here is the apparent impulse to scratch the name of the building into its very walls, as if the writers, excluded from the socially higher activities of the interior (Vitr. *De Arch.* 5.1.5), sought to mimic the deictic function of monumental texts by repeatedly identifying the building on its exterior. It was as if the definition and nomenclature of this novel form of public space erected before the imposition of the Sullan colony, and among the earliest of the type attested outside Rome (Gros 1996–2001:1:240–243), now needed constant reiteration by the new Roman colonists or acculturated local families.

A strikingly self-reflective graffito from the interior "wall of inscriptions" consists of the following two damaged lines, scratched into the stucco in two different places, which present an elegiac couplet (*CIL* 4.1904, 1906; Zangemeister 1867:51):

ADMIROR O PARIENS TE NON CECIDISSE [ruin?]IS QVI TOT
SCRIPTORVM TAEDIA SVSTINEAS

(I marvel, O wall, that you have not collapsed [in ruin]s, when you hold up so many writers' scribbles.)

The same couplet reflecting humorously on the physical impact of text on architecture recurs on two other major public buildings at Pompeii (Zangemeister 1867:50–52). The distribution of these instances can be said to form a "discursive network" across the city and, because of the different ways of reading this text, from noticing the metrical solecism to seeing the self-irony of its participation in the very process it disparages, to capture "the various levels by which a pedestrian might participate in the Rabelaisian cultural streetscape of Pompeii" (Keegan 2011:174). But one of the most immediate meanings of the text is its foregrounding of the issue of monumentality in the everyday pedestrian experience and the way in which it puts writing at the center of the question of the durability of the city's most monumental buildings. In the vaulted passage of the amphitheater, to the left of the main entrance from the north, another version of the same couplet was incised into blackened stucco, preserved perhaps because of the darkness of the spot and the accumulation of hardened ash (*CIL* 4.2487):

ADMIROR TII PARIES NON CECIDISSE___
QVI TOT SCRIPTORVM TAEDIA SVSTINEAS

(I marvel at you, wall, that you have not fallen down. . . .
When you support so many writers' scribbles.)

On the outside of the east wall of the stage building of the large theater, the initial hexameter of the same couplet could be read in very fine characters (*CIL* 4.2461):

AD MIROR PARIIIS
TII NON CIICIDISII RVNA . . .

(I marvel at you, wall, that you have not fallen down . . .)

The last four letters can be restored as *ru[i]na* to complete the hexameter. Raised a little above the second line, they depict the very process that they describe, with the words appearing to "fall" on the wall's surface. But in this case there is a difference from the previous instances of this aphorism. The closing pentameter is omitted, as the hexameter is sufficient to bring the popular couplet to the reader's mind. The half-completion of a well-known literary quotation is a familiar tactic of both modern and ancient graffiti explicable by more than a simple lapse of memory (Carande Herrero and Fernández Martínez 2005:278–279). Yet in avoiding its completion the graffiti writer achieves a further verbal coup. He appears to save the stage building from collapse by *not* adding the weight of *taedia* in the pentameter, which might otherwise have brought it to the ground.

The idea of an identical monumental text repeated across different buildings in the city was only too familiar to readers in the imperial Roman city. The notion of the physical weight of that added text, as a material burden imposed on the building, plays on a long-standing idea that inscribed text is a sensible addition. In the last case in particular, the conceit is aided by the common perception of theater stage buildings as top-heavy accumulations of material (Pliny, *HN* 36.113–120). But architecture in general is victim to the same problematic. Tombs, trophies, and victory monuments were all piles of masonry liable to the risk of falling from their own weight (Thomas 2007:171–172). The inscription, for all its real lack of mass, was an intervention that was regarded as adding further to the fabric. But its effect of threatening the building's stability was anti-monumental. Too much writing could erode the structure, like the monumental inscriptions for which the Emperor Trajan earned the nickname "wall weed" (Amm. Marc. 27.3.7; Aur. Vict *Epit. de Caes.* 41).

Conclusion

We have come full circle. The Pharos of Alexandria at risk from its own attrition reduced the royal dedication to perishable graffiti and left the text of Sostratus, incised into its fabric, as its monument: the structure's own decay took the official inscription with it. In Pompeii, however, it is the public buildings that seem to be pulled down by the weight of their graffiti. Writing is not, as with the Pharos, revealed as a result of the building's gradual decay, but is itself responsible for its very dilapidation. But all inscriptions, whether formally laid out (*ordinatus*) and cut with a chisel (*sculptus*) (Susini 1973:9–13) or illicitly scratched with a nail, are incised intrusions into the architectural surface. What separates them is only the manner of their writing and its durability, both of which are open to question.

The relational approach to monumentality outlined in the introduction to this volume offers a key to interpreting the monumentality of ancient inscriptions (Osborne, this volume). The inscribed text is the medium between a potentially monumental building and its audience. The words imposed on buildings or inscribed into their fabric are an attempt to construct a narrative of monumentality for contemporary and future readers. Some texts proclaim in a loud and highly visible manner the origin or dedicatory purpose of a building, emphasizing the relationship between the architecture and its sponsors. Other texts bring to the fore the work of the building's architect in a more or less obscure manner; and the additional advantage of the architect in being able to communicate through form as well as by text leaves later readers, both in antiquity and today, the dilemma of interpreting nonverbal features as possible "messages," as we have seen in the case of Rabirius. Further texts are interventions by later viewers taking on the role of both composer and carver in order to establish a dialogue with the passing audience through the fabric and surface of a building in the manner of more monumental examples. Finally, in some cases the physical interaction between the statements of sponsors, architects, and viewers provides evidence of real or potential conflicts between them. But this is to say nothing of the vast bulk of text on architecture in antiquity that made no mention of the building at all. For this, the architecture was simply a blank surface ready to be used for writing. The numerous civic, political, religious, or even philosophical texts added to the analemma wall of a theatre, the anta walls of a temple, or the back wall of a stoa undoubtedly had the effect of making the content of these texts appear more monumental. But the same cannot be so confidently maintained for their impact on the buildings. Such writings had, rather, an anti-monumental impact, bringing the architecture into the human domain.

It is hard to claim that without text buildings lack monumentality. What one *can* claim is that without text they have less humanity. A bronze clamp from the site of Verulamium (St Alban's) shaped on its short end to look like a human thumb with the impression of a fingernail is thought to have been used to hold in place the marble dedicatory inscription of the basilica (http://www.stalbansmuseums.org.uk/content/view/full/13490). If this interpretation is correct, it reinforces how the adding of text to a building was regarded in antiquity as a human intervention. Writing and architecture were mutually reinforcing activities in the ancient world. The collapse of one endangered the whole.

REFERENCES CITED

Ackerman, James 1984 Monumentality and the City. *The Harvard Architecture Review* 4 (Spring).

Alföldy, Géza 1990 *Der Obelisk auf dem Petersplatz in Rome: ein historisches Monument der Antike.* Sitzungsberichte der Heidelberger Akademie der Wissenschaften, Philosophisch-historische Klasse, 1990/2. Carl Winter, Heidelberg.

Baird, Jennifer A., and Claire Taylor 2011 Ancient Graffiti in Context: Introduction. In *Ancient Graffiti in Context,* edited by Jennifer A. Baird and Claire Taylor, pp. 1–19. Routledge, New York and Abingdon.

Bean, George E. 1969 Gerga in Caria. *Anatolian Studies* 19:179–182.

Bispham, Edward 2007 *From Asculum to Actium: The Municipalization of Italy from the Social War to Augustus.* Oxford University Press, Oxford.

Bold, John, and Tanis Hinchcliffe 2009 *Discovering London's Buildings: With Twelve Walks.* Frances Lincoln, London.

Brunn, Heinrich 1889 *Geschichte der Griechischen Künstler.* 2 vols. 2nd ed. Ebner & Seubert (Paul Neff), Stuttgart.

Buckler, William H., and David M. Robinson 1932 *Greek and Latin Inscriptions, Part I.* Publications of the American Society for the Excavation of Sardis, 7. Brill, Leiden.

Campana, Augusto 1984 La testimonianza delle iscrizioni. In *Lanfranco e Wiligelmo. Il duomo di Modena,* edited by Marina Armandi Barbolini, pp. 363–373. Edizioni Panini, Modena.

Carande Herrero, Rocío, and Concepción Fernández Martínez 2005 Virgil on a Brick from Itálica. *Mnemosyne* 58:277–282.

Carettoni, G. 1961 Il fregio figurato della Basilica Aemilia. *Rivista dell'Istituto Nazionale d'archeologia e storia dell'arte* 10:5–78.

Carroll, Kevin K. 1982 *The Parthenon Inscription.* Greek, Roman and Byzantine monographs, no. 9. Duke University, Durham.

Catich, Edward M. 1968 *The Origin of the Serif: Brush Writing & Roman Letters.* Catfish Press, Davenport, Iowa.

Claridge, Amanda 2007 Hadrian's lost Temple of Trajan. *Journal of Roman Archaeology* 20:54–94.

Coates-Stephens, Robert 2004 *Porta Maggiore, Monument and Landscape. Archaeology and Topography of the Southern Esquiline from the Late Republican Period to the Present.* «L'Erma» di Bretschneider, Rome.

Constans, Léopold Albert 1916 *Rapport sur une mission archéologique à Bou-Ghara (Gigthis) (1914 et 1915).* Nouvelles Archives des Missions Scientifiques et Littéraires, new series 14. Imprimerie Nationale, Paris.

Crema, Luigi 1959 *L'architettura romana.* Società editrice internazionale, Turin.

D'Alessio, Alessandro 2007 L'avancorpo dell'acropoli di Ferentino. Vecchi e nuovi dati per la lettura storica del monumento. *Archeologia Classica* 58:397–433.

Diehl, Ernst 1911 *Die Vitae Vergilianae und ihre antiken Quellen.* A. Marcus and E. Weber, Bonn.

Di Marco, Liana 1975 *Spoletium: topografia e urbanistica.* Edizioni dell'Accademia spoletina, Spoleto.

Di Stefano Manzella, Ivan 1987 *Mestiere di epigrafista. Guida alla schedatura del materiale epigrafico lapideo.* Quasar, Rome.

Eck, Werner, Henner von Hesberg, and Monika Gronke 2007 Die Stimme der Bauten—Schrift am Bau. In *Kosmos der Zeichen. Schriftbild und Bildformel in Antike und Mittelalter,* edited by Dietrich Boschung and Hansgerd Hellenkemper, pp. 211–234. Reichert Verlag, Wiesbaden.

Elmes, James 1852 *Sir Christopher Wren and His Times.* Chapman & Hall, London.

Engelmann, Helmut 1981 Die Bauinschrift am Apollonion von Syrakus. *Zeitschrift für Papyrologie und Epigraphik* 44:91–94.

Fabre, Guilhem 1992 *The Pont du Gard: Water and the Roman Town.* Translated by Janice Abbott. Caisse nationale des monuments historiques et des sites, Paris.

Gauckler, Paul, et al. 1910 *Catalogue du Musée Alaoui (Supplément).* Ernest Leroux, Paris.

Grasby, Richard 1996 A Comparative Study of Five Latin Inscriptions: Measurement and Making. *Papers of the British School at Rome* 64:95–138.

Gros, Pierre 1996–2001 *L'architecture romaine du début du IIIe siécle av. J.-C. à la fin du Haut-Empire.* 2 vols. Éditions A. and J. Picard, Paris.

Gros, Pierre, and Dinu Theodorescu 1985 Le mur nord du "forum" d'Assise: ornementation pariétale et spécialisation des espaces. *MEFRA* 97:879–898.

Guarducci, Margherita 1967–1978 *Epigrafia greca.* 4 vols. Istituto Poligrafico dello Stato, Libreria dello Stato, Rome.

Guarducci, Margherita 1987 Il tempio arcaico di Apollo a Siracusa: riflessi nuove. In *Saggi in onore di Guglielmo de Angelis d'Ossat,* edited by Sandro Benedetti and Gaetano Miarelli Mariani, with Laura Marcucci, pp. 43–45. Multigrafica, Rome.

Held, Winfried 2008 *Gergakome. Ein "altehrwürdiges" Heiligtum im kaiserzeitlichen Karien.* Istanbuler Forschungen, Vol. 49. Wasmuth, Tübingen.

Holloway, R. Ross 1987 Some Remarks on the Arch of Titus. *L'Antiquité Classique* 56:183–191.

Holloway, R. Ross 1999 *The Hand of Daedalus*. Published for electronic distribution, online at http://brown.edu/Departments/Joukowsky_Institute/publications/papers/daedalus/index.html.

Hutter, Siegfried 1973 *Der römische Leuchtturm von La Coruña*. Philipp von Zabern, Mainz.

Işkan-Işik, Havva, Werner Eck, and Helmut Engelmann 2008 Der Leuchtturm von Patara und Sex. Marcius Priscus als Statthalter der Provinz Lycia von Nero bis Vespasian. *Zeitschrift für Papyrologie und Epigraphik* 164:91–121.

Kawerau, Georg, and Albert Rehm 1914 *Das Delphinion in Milet*. Milet, Vol. 3. Reimer, Berlin.

Keegan, Peter 2011 Blogging Rome: Graffiti as Speech Act and Cultural Discourse. In *Ancient Graffiti in Context*, edited by Jennifer A. Baird and Claire Taylor, pp. 165–190. Routledge, New York and Abingdon.

Koenen, Ludwig 1985 The Dream of Nektanebos. *Bulletin of the American Society of Papyrologists* 22:171–194.

Kruschwitz, P. 2010 Romanes eunt domus! Linguistic Aspects of the Subliterary Latin in Roman Wall Inscriptions. In *The Language of the Papyri*, edited by T. V. Evans and Dirk D. Obbink, pp. 156–170. Oxford University Press, Oxford.

Land, Norman E. 1994 *The Viewer as Poet: The Renaissance Response to Art*. Pennsylvania State University Press, University Park.

Le Roux, P. 1992 Le Phare, l'architecte et le soldat: l'inscription rupestre de la Corogne (*CIL* II, 2559). In *Miscellanea greca e romana* 15:133–145.

Lepper, Frank, and Sheppard Frere 1988 *Trajan's Column. A New Edition of the Cichorius Plates*. Alan Sutton, Gloucester and Wolfboro, New Hampshire.

Lowrie, Michelle 2009 *Writing, Performance, and Authority in Augustan Rome*. Oxford University Press, Oxford.

Lugli, Giuseppe 1918 La villa di Domiziano sui Colli Albani. *Bullettino della Committenza Archeologica Comunale* 46:3–68.

Lugli, Giuseppe 1965 Rabirius. In *Enciclopedia dell'Arte antica, classica, e orientale. Vol. 6*. Istituto della Enciclopedia Italiana, Rome.

MacDonald, William L. 1982 *The Architecture of the Roman Empire. Vol. 1 An Introductory Study*. 2nd ed. Yale University Press, New Haven and London.

Malmberg, Simon, and Hans Bjur 2011 Movement and Urban Development at Two City Gates in Rome. The Porta Esquilina and Porta Tiburtina. In *Rome, Ostia, Pompeii. Movement and Space*, edited by Ray Laurence and David J. Newsome, pp. 361–385. Oxford University Press, Oxford.

Miller, Frank J. 1919 On a Translation of Vergil's Quatrain, *Sic vos non vobis*. *The Classical Journal* 15(3):174–175.

Nasrallah, Laura Salah 2010 *Christian Responses to Roman Art and Architecture: The Second-Century Church amid the Spaces of Empire*. Cambridge University Press, Cambridge.

Ohlsen, Walter 1981 *Monumentalschrift, Monument, Mass: Proportionierung des Inschriftalphabule in Rom*. Wittig, Hamburg.

Perdrizet, Paul 1899 Sostrate de Cnide, architecte du Phare. *Revue des Études Anciennes* 1:261–272.

Petrucci, Armando 1981 Virgilio nella cultura scritta romana. In *Virgilio e noi, Atti delle None Giornate Filologiche Genovesi, 23–24 febbraio 1981*, Istituto di filologia classica Pubblicazioni, 71, pp. 51–72. Istituto di Filologia Classica e Medievale, Genoa.

Petrucci, Armando 1993 *Public Lettering: Script, Power, and Culture*. Translated by Linda Lappin. University of Chicago Press, Chicago and London.

Picard, Charles 1965 Sur les dédicaces monumentales apposées en Grèce aux entablements de façades d'édifices sacrés ou civils. In Χαριστήριον, εις Αναστάσιον Κ. Ορλάνδον, vol. I, pp. 91–107. Athens.

Reed, Henry Hope 1952 Monumental Architecture or the Art of Pleasing in Civic Design. *Perspecta* i (Summer):42.

Reilly, C. H. 1912 The Monumental Qualities in Architecture. *Town Planning Review* 3(1) (April):11–18.

Rimell, Victoria 2008 *Martial's Rome: Empire and the Ideology of Epigram.* Cambridge University Press, Cambridge.

R[ussell], M[atthew] 1897 Sic vos non Vobis. *The Irish Monthly* 25(289):379–382.

Salza Prina Ricotti, Eugenia 2006 Gli architetti romani. Online at http://www.espr-archeologia. it/articoli/146/Gli-architetti-romani.

Solin, Heikki 1970 *L'interpretazione delle iscrizioni parietali.* F.lli Lega, Faenza.

Solin, Heikki 1980–1982 Le iscrizioni antiche di Ferentino. Introduzione alla problematica dell'epigrafia classica ferentinate. *Atti della Pontificia Accademia. Rendiconti* 53–54:91–143.

Susini, Giancarlo 1973 *The Roman Stonecutter.* Translated by A. M. Dabrowski. Blackwell, Oxford.

Thiersch, Herman 1909 *Pharos, Antike, Islam und Occident: ein Beitrag zur Architekturgeschichte.* B. G. Teubner, Leipzig.

Thomas, Edmund 2007 *Monumentality and the Roman Empire: Architecture in the Antonine Age.* Oxford University Press, Oxford.

Thomas, Edmund, and Christian Witschel 1992 Constructing Reconstruction: Claim and Reality of Latin Rebuilding Inscriptions from the Latin West. *PBSR* 60:135–177.

Toynbee, Arnold J. 1957 *A Study of History.* Abridgement of Vols. 7–10 by David C. Somervell. Oxford University Press, London.

Toynbee, Jocelyn M. C. 1975 *Some Notes on Artists in the Roman World.* Collection Latomus, 6. Latomus, Brussels.

Traina, Giusto 1995 From Crimea to Syria. Re-defining the Alleged Historical Earthquake of 63 B.C. *Annali di Geofisica* 38(5–6):479–489.

Tucci, Pier Luigi 2001 *Laurentius Manlius: la riscoperta dell'antica Roma, la nuova Roma di Sisto IV.* Quaderni di Eutopia, Vol. 3. Quasar, Rome.

Umholtz, Gretchen 2002 Architraval Arrogance? Dedicatory Inscriptions in Greek Architecture of the Classical Period. *Hesperia* 71(3):261–293.

Venturi, Robert 1977 *Learning from Las Vegas: The Forgotten Symbolism of Architectural Form.* Rev. ed. MIT Press, Cambridge.

Vidman, Ladislav 1982 *Fasti Ostienses.* 2nd ed. Academia, Prague.

Visconti, Pietro Ercole 1867 *La stazione della Coorte VII dei Vigili e i ricordi istorici segnati a graffito nelle pareti di essa,* 3rd ed. Tipografia delle Scienze Matematiche, Rome.

Warga, Richard G. Jr. 2001 The Paintbrush and the Chisel. *Illinois Classical Studies* 26:137–144.

Whitley, James 1998 Literacy and Lawmaking: The Case of Archaic Crete. In *Archaic Greece: New Approaches and New Evidence,* edited by Nick Fisher and Hans Van Wees, pp. 311–331. Duckworth, London, with the Classical Press of Wales, Swansea.

Wilson Jones, Mark 2000 *Principles of Roman Architecture.* Yale University Press, New Haven and London.

Yegül, Fikret K. 2014 A Victor's Message: The Talking Column of the Temple of Artemis at Sardis. *Journal of the Society of Architectural Historians* 73:204–225.

Zadorojnyi, Alexei V. 2011 Transcripts of Dissent? Political Graffiti and Elite Ideology under the Principate. In *Ancient Graffiti in Context,* edited by Jennifer A. Baird and Claire Taylor, pp. 110–133. Routledge, New York and Abingdon.

Zangemeister, Karl 1867 Graffiti e dipinti pompeiani. *Bullettino dell'Instituto di Corrispondenza Archeologica* (1867):50–57.

CHAPTER FIVE

Building Monuments, Creating Communities

Early Monumental Architecture at Pre-Pottery Neolithic Göbekli Tepe

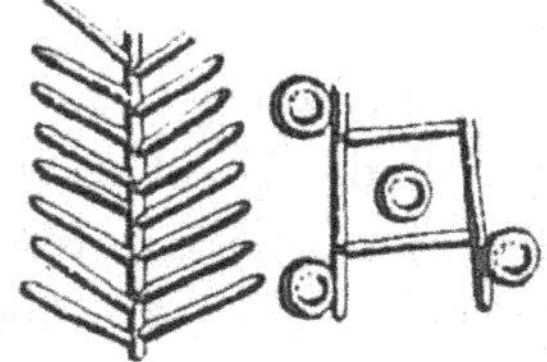

*Jens Notroff, Oliver Dietrich,
Klaus Schmidt†*

Abstract *The meaning of monumental buildings as an indicator of social complexity and the visible expression of power and authority has been a lasting topos in the field of archaeology. Now new evidence is coming from southeastern Turkey, showing that the origins of monumental architecture have to be sought as early as with the hunter-gatherer groups at the end of the last Ice Age in the Near East twelve thousand years ago. At Göbekli Tepe, monumental, monolithic T-shaped pillars were erected by mobile groups of the Early Neolithic constituting large circular enclosures and indicating a degree of coordination and cooperation among these people hitherto not suspected.*

INTRODUCTION: THE CASE OF EARLY MONUMENTALITY

The appearance and construction of monumental architecture has often been discussed as a major element in the process of evolution toward complex societies. Increasing social complexity and the emergence of elites centralizing power was thought to find its architectural expression in the form of monuments displaying prestige as well as visualizing the boundaries of territorial control. Next to their historico-cultural denotation in means as focal point of commemoration and communication, monumental structures also became of central significance in the discussion of prehistoric perception, relation, and use of landscape (e.g. Bradley 1993; Richards 1996), as well as in the development of mathematical models toward understanding patterns of human movement and the development of corporate territories (e.g., Renfrew and Level 1979). Still, an essential factor at the basis of considerations like these is the ability of prehistoric societies to generate and motivate the labor force necessary for monumental constructions culminating in a scale and complexity sufficient to reach into the symbolic sphere. Monumental architecture has a strong symbolic connotation, serving in a communication process of collective interaction as well as in the creation of a group's identity and cohesion. A cultural landscape defined by monumental architectonic expressions therefore offers valuable clues to the social structure and degree of complexity of the societies building them. Following in the footprints of Childe's "Urban Revolution" (Childe 1950), monumental buildings have been interpreted as the result of rising elites and the concentration of social and political power, and thus were seen as expression of a complex social hierarchy within a framework of advancing social-territorial structures (see also Osborne, this volume).

With the excavation of the Pre-Pottery Neolithic site of Göbekli Tepe in southeastern Turkey, evidence for monumental architecture in a hunter-gatherer milieu was brought to light for the first time in this number and scale, suggesting a social complexity and a degree of organization hitherto unsuspected for such an early period. Rather small groups of hunter-gatherers with a high degree of mobility apparently were investing a surprising amount of time, material, and effort in the construction of large enclosures of standing monoliths, walls, and benches. The buildings they created were of a specific kind lacking any attributes of domestic architecture, but aiming instead at special activities of a communal, most likely ritual, character (Dietrich and Notroff in press; Schmidt† 2001, 2010, 2012). The finds of such monumental architecture at Göbekli Tepe, requiring a large amount of organization and coordination not expected in emerging Early Neolithic cultures so far raise a number of questions and challenge the traditional picture of monumentality as representation of political authority.

Göbekli Tepe: An Early Neolithic Sanctuary in Southeastern Turkey

Located 15 km northeast of the modern town of Şanlıurfa in southeastern Turkey, the site of Göbekli Tepe (Figure 5.1) is situated at the foothills of the Taurus Mountains, between the upper reaches of the Euphrates and Tigris Rivers. The site measures about 9 ha in area and 300 m in diameter, and stands 15 m in height. It is completely man-made, formed through a series of deliberate backfilling events that covered the monumental enclosures erected there.

At least three stratigraphic layers can be distinguished at Göbekli Tepe at the current state of research. The oldest layer, Layer III (Figure 5.2) belongs to the material culture of the Pre-Pottery Neolithic A (PPN A), that is, the tenth millennium B.C. by archaeological dating (e.g., typical projectile points), which is also confirmed by a number of radiocarbon dates (Dietrich 2011; Dietrich and Schmidt† 2010; Dietrich et al. 2013). The characteristic architecture associated with this layer can be described as monumental 10–30 m wide circular or semicircular structures formed by huge monolithic limestone pillars of a distinct T-shape. These pillars, reaching up to 4 m in height, are always orientated toward a central pair of even larger pillars of the same shape. These central pairs of pillars stand in surprisingly shallow pedestals cut out of the bedrock, which are known from at least

FIGURE 5.1 The tell of Göbekli Tepe, view from south (photo: K. Schmidt†, DAI).

three of the enclosures discovered so far. In some areas a later layer, Layer II[1] (see Figure 5.2), dating to the early and middle PPN B, that is to say, the ninth millennium B.C., is superimposed on top of the monumental architecture from Layer III. The buildings of Layer II can be summarized as rectangular rooms measuring about 3 x 4 m, whose floors usually consist of a terrazzo-like pavement. These smaller structures may be understood as a reduction of the larger older enclosures. The quantity and height of the T-shaped pillars are reduced: often only two small central pillars are present, the largest among them not exceeding a height of 2 m. Sometimes these rooms possess only one or even no pillars at all. Finally, Layer I describes the surface soil resulting from erosion processes as well as a plough zone that bears witness to the use of the fertile soil for agricultural activities in more recent centuries. The soil matrix of this layer comprises an amalgam of material from the older layers and therefore also generates relevant finds.

After the end of their use, the circular buildings of Layer III were not left open, but rather were backfilled intentionally, thereby creating the mound visible today. The fill material consists of limestone rubble, bones, fragments of flint artefacts (tools are more rare), and fragmented ground stone objects; its rather homogenous character makes the whole process of backfilling similar to a burial, which seems to have been a part of the use-concept of these enclosures from the very beginning.

FIGURE 5.2 Schematic plan of the excavation at Göbekli Tepe (main excavation area plus southwestern hilltop) and its stratigraphical units. Also depicted is the stratum producing small, near-surface structures of yet uncertain relative-chronological position (plan: K. Schmidt† and J. Notroff, DAI).

Due to the results of geophysical surveys, including ground penetrating radar, it can be safely stated that these monumental enclosures are not restricted to the particular part of the mound where they have been found in excavation, but instead exist all over the site. More than ten such enclosures were located through geophysical mapping, confirming predictions based on the archaeological surface investigation and adding to those enclosures already unearthed and numbered A to H in the order of their discovery. Five of these structures—Enclosures A, B, C, D, and G—were discovered in the main excavation area at Göbekli Tepe's southern depression (Figure 5.3). Enclosure F was excavated at the southwestern hilltop (Figure 5.4), Enclosure E situated at the western plateau, and Enclosure H, recently discovered at the northwestern hilltop (Dietrich et al. 2014). While Enclosures A, B, F, and G are still under excavation, E was recognized as a completely cleared enclosure of which only the floor and two pedestals cut out of the bedrock are still visible (Figure 5.5). Enclosures C and D were excavated to their ground levels in recent campaigns. Enclosure D, which is the largest and best preserved structure so far, may serve as an example of the general layout and character of the older circular PPN A enclosures in the following.

FIGURE 5.3 Main excavation area at Göbekli Tepe with Enclosures A, B, C, D, and G (photo: E. Küçük).

At the current state of excavation, 11 T-shaped pillars with a height of up to 4 m were gathered around a pair of even larger central pillars of the same shape (Figure 5.6).[2] The surrounding pillars are decorated with depictions of a variety of animals, with foxes, birds, and snakes being the most common species in Enclosure D, but the iconography of the whole site offers a wide range of other motifs, including boars, aurochs, gazelles, wild donkeys, and more (Figure 5.7). In the case of Enclosure D, the two pillars in the center, measuring about 5.5 m in height and weighing some 10 metric tons, stand in pedestals with a height of not more than 20 cm, which are—like the rest of the floor level—carved out of the carefully smoothed bedrock. Outstanding also in their decora-

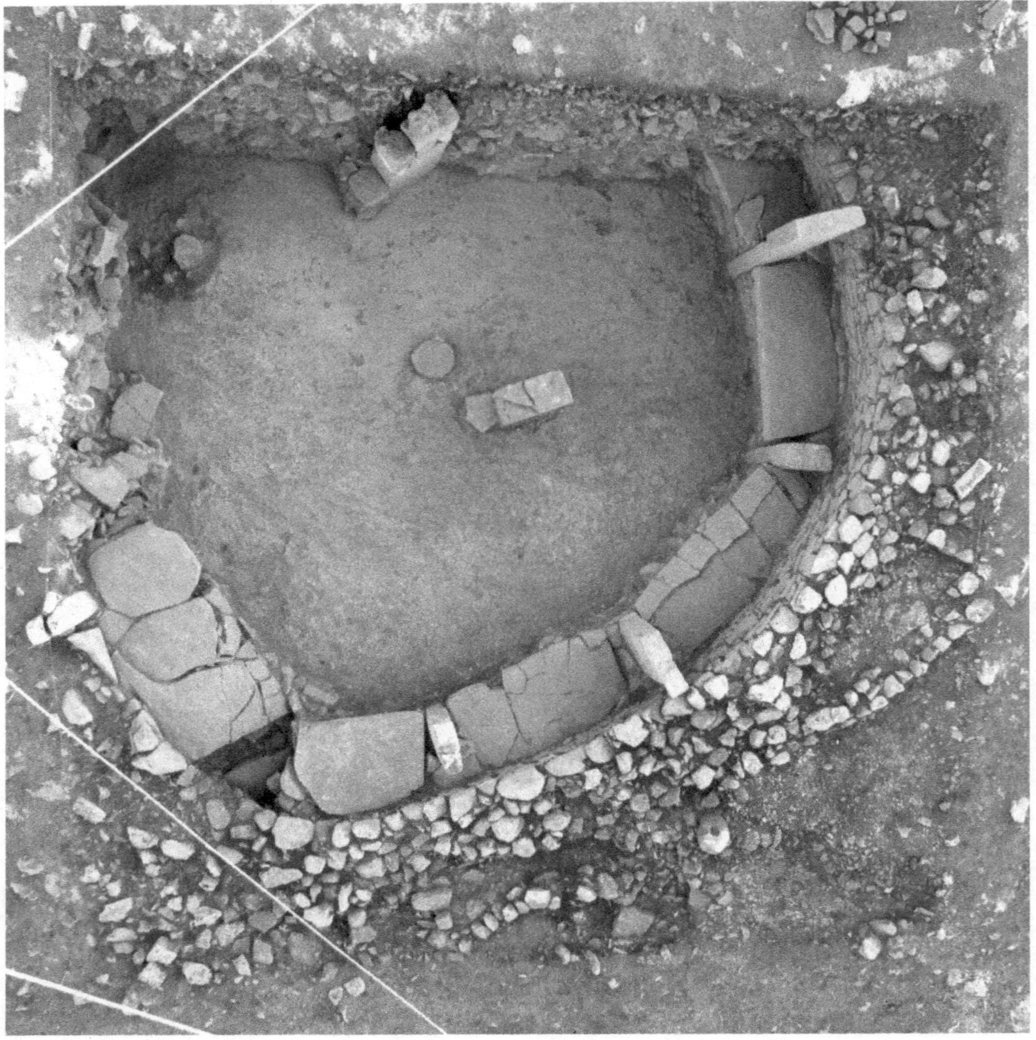

FIGURE 5.4 Enclosure F at the southwestern hilltop (photo: K. Schmidt†, DAI).

tion, these central pillars clearly demonstrate that the T-shaped pillars possess an anthropomorphic identity and therefore should more accurately be referred to as pillar-statues. The oblong T-heads represent the human head in an abstract manner, with the smaller side representing the face. On the pillars' shafts, arms are clearly recognizable, ending in hands brought together above the abdomen. Furthermore, belts and loincloths in the shape of animal skins are depicted in relief, underlining the human-like appearance of the T-shaped pillars (Figure 5.8). By covering the genital area of the pillar-statues, these loincloth-reliefs are hiding the sex of the two individuals depicted here. However, some insight may be drawn from the clay figurines—a find group totally absent from Göbekli

FIGURE 5.5 Enclosure E at the western rock plateau (photo: M. Morsch, DAI).

FIGURE 5.6 Enclosure D serves as example of the general layout of the monumental circular enclosures: a number of T-shaped pillars are gathered around a central pair of larger pillars of the same shape (photo: N. Becker, DAI).

Tepe so far—that were discovered at the PPN B site of Nevalı Çori (Morsch 2002:148, 151). Situated about 60 km north of Göbekli Tepe, Nevalı Çori—known for having produced T-shaped pillars of the smaller type paralleling those of Layer II—also produced a variety of figurines depicting male and female individuals of which only the male ones are wearing belts. Thus, it seems probable to regard the two central pillars in Enclosure D as male individuals as well. This also confirms the observation that the iconography and symbolism visible at Göbekli Tepe seem to be dominated by masculinity in general. Whenever the sex of one of the animals depicted is indicated, it is a male specimen. Among the depictions of human beings, ithyphallic individuals are prevalent. The only clear depiction of a female is a graffito that was apparently added later on a stone slab in one of the buildings of Layer II (Schmidt† 2012:221–226). Taken together with the fact that the remains of animals and plants identified at Göbekli Tepe so far are clearly wild forms while domesticated species are completely absent, the animal iconography corroborates the interpretation of the site as a place of male hunters.

This highly symbolic iconography and the remarkable amount of monumentality marks the outstanding character of the site of Göbekli Tepe. Although the site's cultic

FIGURE 5.7 A number of pillars illustrating the rich iconographic repertoire of the reliefs depicted on the T-shaped pillars at Göbekli Tepe: Pillar 1 in Enclosure A (upper left) shows a "net" of snakes above what might be a ram; Pillar 9 in Enclosure B (upper right) depicts a fox; Pillar 12 in Enclosure C (lower left) shows five water birds above a boar and a fox, and Pillar 43 in Enclosure D (lower right) is richly decorated with a number of birds (among them a large vulture), a scorpion and an acephalic ithyphallic man (photo: Ch. Gerber, D. Johannes, and K. Schmidt†, DAI).

FIGURE 5.8 Pillar 31, one of the two central pillars of Enclosure D, illustrates their anthropomorphic appearance due to the depiction of arms, hands, and elements of clothing (photo: N. Becker, DAI).

nature has recently been called into question (Banning 2011), the symbolism and scale of the buildings, together with the lack of other domestic features such as fire pits and hearths as well as the absence of find categories typical from settlement contexts (cf. Schmidt† 2005), for instance, clay figurines, awls, and points of bone, clearly contradict a domestic character of the enclosures in our opinion.[3] According to Banning, Göbekli Tepe has to be seen as a settlement with buildings yielding a rich symbolism but still of domestic nature. However, contemporaneous domestic architecture is well known in this region due to the stratigraphy at Çayönü Tepesi (Özdoğan 1999; Schirmer 1983, 1988, 1990) as well as the excavations at Nevalı Çori (Hauptmann 1988), for example. Both sites, which can be addressed as settlements due to a variety of domestic structures and a respective material culture, are situated in favorable environmental positions for subsistence strategies with easy access to water supply and fertile land (which has to be emphasized in contrast to the erratic topographical situation of Göbekli Tepe). The buildings of Çayönü's "grill-plan phase" (PPN A), as well as those with "channeled" ground plans and the "cobble paved buildings" (early respectively middle PPN B; cf. Özdoğan 1999:41; Schirmer 1988, 1990:365–377), can be considered contemporaneous with Göbekli Tepe; "channeled-plan" buildings are also known from Nevalı Çori, too. But none of these building types have been detected at Göbekli Tepe as of yet (and the results of geophysical surveys are not indicating that such structures may be expected in future excavations). Furthermore, in the context of these settlement sites a number of single constructions stand out, noticeably differing in layout and other characteristics from the rest of architecture. They are termed "special purpose" or "cult" buildings, interpreted as communal structures within a settlement (cf. Kornienko 2009; Kurapkat 2010) and share distinct commonalities with the enclosures at Göbekli Tepe. The examples from Çayönü and Nevalı Çori show benches hinting at gatherings, an elaborate interior as well as special installations and finds including depositions of human skulls in Çayönü (Schirmer 1990:378–382) and a variety of T-shaped pillars, as well as a rich inventory of stone sculptures in Nevalı Çori (Hauptmann 1993:50, 52–53 Figures 19–26). The list could be expanded with further examples of comparable "special" or communal buildings in settlements, as nearly every PPN site excavated on an appropriate scale seems to feature such architecture (cf. Dietrich et al. 2012:691–692; with further literature), but we may content ourselves with these examples, outlining that at Göbekli Tepe apparently no hints of the well-documented PPN domestic architecture exist, while instead strong similarities to exceptional, outstanding structures within these settlements are evident.[4]

COOPERATIVE GROUPS CREATING MONUMENTS

A prominent and peculiar attribute of the architecture at Göbekli Tepe, as discussed above, underlining its special communal character, is their denotative layout and setup. Benches along the walls suggest places of gathering and congregation; the anthropomorphic pillars themselves seem to represent an assembly of some kind, with about a dozen stone figures grouped around a pair at the center. This gathering aspect also gains relevance with regard to the mode of the enclosures' construction. The labor force necessary to carve such large pillars from the rock, for transporting and finally erecting them, probably outnumbers the members of a single band of hunter-gatherers. Any attempt to exactly calculate the size of these groups and the corresponding number of individuals is confronted with a lack of data, naturally caused by the mode of living of these mobile groups, which left few traces (e.g., representative burials) evaluable in terms of demography. This means that we have to rely on estimations based on historic, respectively ethnographic, analogies mostly. Several examples and calculations collected in a number of studies (Helbling 1987; Hultkrantz and Vorren 1982; Kelly 1995; Lee and DeVore 1968) suggest rather small groups of 25 to maximum 50 individuals; larger numbers (as in the case of the sedentary foraging indigenous peoples of the Pacific Northwest Coast) being the exception (cf. Kelly 1995:209–213; Petrasch 2010). Ethnologic observations furthermore imply a common identity (based on material culture, language, etc.) among 10 to 20 of such independent groups or bands, adding up to a number of 250 to 1,000 individuals interacting in a collective sphere of communication (Petrasch 2010). No less vague, but showing a much larger variety, are estimations of labor costs and man-hours necessary for the construction of monumental structures. Figures for the erection of the giant *moai* statues of Rapa Nui (Easter Island) with (despite a few larger exceptions) a typical height of 4 m and a weight of 12 t (Kolb 2011:140; Lipo et al. 2013:2865)— somewhat smaller than the larger of the pillars of Göbekli Tepe—have been reckoned to include anything from a period of only days or a few weeks (Routledge 1920) to a year (Pavel 1990) and more (Heyerdahl 1958:138). While according to Pavel (1990) a total of 20 individuals was sufficient to carve such a statue in their spare time within one year, at least 50 to 75 people were assumed to be required to move it a distance of 15 km over the course of a week (Van Tilburg and Ralston 2005). In contrast to this and other calculations (e.g., Heyerdahl et al. 1989), recent experiments have demonstrated that efficient transport could be engineered by a comparably smaller number of about 18 individuals using a special technique by forward leaning and side rocking the statues with the help of ropes (Lipo et al. 2013).

Yet ethnographic records from the early twentieth century report that on the Indonesian Island of Nias even up to 525 men were involved in hauling a megalith of 4 m³ over a distance of 3 km to its final location in three days using a wooden sledge (Schröder 1917). Another example from Indonesia points out that such a large number of participants was not necessarily required exclusively for the labor involved, but that other factors have to be considered as well. In Kodi, West Sumba, the transport of the stones themselves used for the construction of megalithic tombs was ritualized and required a large number of people to be involved as witnesses (Hoskins 1986). Thus, other social aspects such as the acquisition and maintenance of prestige among the individuals participating need to be incorporated into the models of the erection of monumental structures.

However, at Göbekli Tepe the enclosures of Layer III consist of several megalithic elements cut into the surrounding limestone plateaus, as for example an unfinished T-pillar with a size of nearly 7 m and volume of 20 m³ illustrates.[5] Recent practical experiments of preparing and cutting limestone comparable to but considerably harder than the material used at Göbekli Tepe, conducted by Claudia Beuger from the Martin Luther University of Halle-Wittenberg, have shown that about 22 to 44 individuals[6] could have quarried a single pillar of the dimensions mentioned above within four to five months (Beuger forthcoming).[7] Furthermore, up to 60 persons were calculated in the preparation of an additional experiment (not conducted yet) as needed to lift and move such a work piece. Thus, the numbers given here may be in need of some extrapolation when projecting them onto about a dozen of these pillars forming one enclosure (cf. Schmidt† 2012:102–104). This gains importance with consideration of the amount of time that these mobile groups may have been able to invest, time they then could not invest in nourishment, for example which meant that yet other group members had to compensate for this gap. This suggests a certain degree of cooperation and organization among several of such groups, since—apparently—a significant number of people from the wider area had to be drawn together. A common mode for executing large communal tasks like this has been described under the term *collective work events,* usually achieved through the prospect of a lavish feast (Dietler and Herbich 1995) emphasizing the voluntaristic character of this labor force. Already acknowledged as an integral part of Epipaleolithic (Munro and Grosman 2010) and early Neolithic societies (Benz 2006), such extensive feasting also fuels the discussion of cooperative action. This could shed some light on the character of gatherings held at Göbekli Tepe as noted above and finds confirmation in closer inspection of the fill material of the enclosures. In addition to the limestone rubble, flakes of flint, and fragments of ground stone tools already mentioned, numerous animal bones are present in the filling. These bones represent hunting game exclusively—primarily gazelle, but in terms of weight of meat, wild cattle seems to be the most important species. The sheer amount of bones speaks in favor of large feasts including the consumption of enormous amounts of meat and possibly alcoholic beverages (Dietrich et al. 2012).

Gathering at particular places on certain occasions must have had a long tradition for hunter-gatherer groups, serving social purposes such as the exchange of goods and marriage partners. Marking these meeting places by creating monumental architecture meant going a step further, especially if these monuments served strictly ritual purposes, as seems to be the case at Göbekli Tepe. While the question regarding the use and purpose of the enclosures still cannot be answered conclusively, it seems rather clear that Göbekli Tepe occupied a unique role among the PPN sites of the Near East as a place of cult and ritual, lacking domestic features compared to other known contemporary settlement sites. Instead, the structures unearthed at Göbekli Tepe rather seem to reflect a type of specialized building within these settlements that served communal purposes. In addition to their function as gathering places (Dietrich et al. 2012), as well as a symbolic storage system and a nodal point in a communication network that preserved and passed on cultural knowledge among these groups (Morenz & Schmidt† 2009; Watkins 2004, 2010), the enclosures at Göbekli Tepe may also have played an important role in death cult and burial rituals (Notroff et al. in press), bringing together a number of mobile groups.

From a social and economic point of view, investing in collective work made sense for single groups and individuals due to the benefits they gained from this collective action, which thus may be regarded as the motivating force in the genesis of larger communities. The megalithic enclosures of Göbekli Tepe challenge such models, which suggests that monumental architecture marked the culmination of a development toward complex social entities with institutionalized power, that is to say, potent rulers, who were able to gather and control the necessary resources, material and human.

Monuments Generating Communities

T-shaped pillars resembling the smaller examples from Göbekli Tepe's Layer II were first recorded at the settlement site of Nevalı Çori (Hauptmann 1993). Three more sites in the near vicinity—Sefer Tepe, Karahan, and Hamzan Tepe (cf. Çelik 2011a; Moetz and Çelik 2012)—are known to have similar pillars, but no excavation work has been carried out so far. With the Neolithic site of Urfa-Yeni Yol, which seems to have revealed a small T-shaped pillar in the course of construction work in that area (cf. Çelik 2011b: 142. Figure 19), with Gusir Höyük (Karul 2011, 2013), and with Taşlı Tepe (Çelik et al. 2011), three more related sites were added to this list recently. While these places form an inner circle of sites that clearly belong to a community sharing a common background of material and spiritual culture, its sphere of influence exceeded this region. This is proven by a common set of symbols used over a wide area within Upper Mesopotamia, defining a larger cultic community (Costello 2011; Schmidt† 2012:193–200). Shaft-straighteners and plaquettes from Jerf el Ahmar (Stordeur and Abbès 2002: Figure 16/1–3) and Tell Qaramel (Mazurowski 2003:Figure 12, 2004:Figure 10; Mazurowski and Jamous 2000:341 Figures 7–8; Mazurowski and Yartah 2001:304 Figures 10–11), as well as Tell 'Abr 3 (Yartah 2004:155 Figure 18/3) and Körtik Tepe (Özkaya and San 2007: Figure 19) feature decorations in the form of snakes and scorpions, quadruped animals, and birds strongly reminiscent of the iconography of Göbekli Tepe, and are known from this site as well. The same motifs occur on thin-walled stone cups and bowls of the Hallan Çemi type (Rosenberg and Redding 2000:50 Figure 5). Fragments of this vessel type are known from Göbekli Tepe, Çayönü (Özdoğan 1999:59), Nevalı Çori, Jerf el Ahmar (Stordeur and Abbès 2002:583 Figure 12/1–4), Tell 'Abr 3 (Yartah 2004:155 Figure 18/2, 4–5), and Tell Qaramel (Mazurowski 2003:369 Figure 11/1–2), while complete vessels have been discovered at Körtik Tepe recently in large numbers (Özkaya and San 2007:Figure 6 15–18) as part of rich grave inventories. Another connection is suggested by the zoomorphic scepters of the Nemrik type, which are present at Hallan Çemi, Nevalı Çori, Çayönü, Göbekli Tepe, Abu Hureyra, Mureybet, Jerf el Ahmar, and Dja'de (Kozłowski 2002:77–80).

Without many forerunners in Paleolithic art, the sudden variety of imagery represents a new symbolic world shared among the residents of PPN sites in Upper Mesopotamia. These commonalities in symbolism and iconography suggest a high degree of communication and a shared ideology even beyond the circle of sites producing T-shaped pillars and monuments and thus illustrate a spiritual concept that must have linked these sites to each other, testifying to the existence of extensive networks of supra-regional contacts sustained on a regular basis (Watkins 2008, 2010). It seems that a cultic community developed in the PPN around Göbekli Tepe.

In this light, the emphasis on communal cooperative processes in creating the monumental architecture at Göbekli Tepe seems to gain some weight. Based on the effort necessary to cut, transport, and erect even a single one of the T-shaped pillars, the labor force estimated above, which exceeded the options of any individual hunter-gatherer groups, clearly required a notable degree of cooperation. While also certain (inter- or even intragroup) competitive aspects in the erection of the individual pillars may have to be taken into account, the final common layout of the enclosures—circular, with benches at the inner walls—accentuates the communal character of these buildings (cf. Figure 5.4). The encircling walls may also express a certain degree of exclusion. Since the chronological relation of the individual enclosures to each other is still not fully clarified, and represents a topic of ongoing research, the possibility of competitive behavior among different groups creating several enclosures remains (cf. van Wees 2011:14–23). According to this line of thought, the monuments at Göbekli Tepe are the culminating expression of a community's (or its leaders') success in competition with other groups for superiority. The enclosures' construction in the frame of ritual feasts is thus seen as displaying economic success to neighboring groups or—in the case of a whole community—to outsiders (van Wees 2001:18–19, 21).

The enclosures of Göbekli Tepe show a variation in the animal species depicted prominently in the iconography of each circle. While in Enclosure A the snake prevails, in Enclosure B (which has produced only a few reliefs so far), foxes are dominant, for example. In Enclosure C, boars seem to take over this role, and in Enclosure D, foxes, birds, and snakes play an important role (Figure 5.9). Interpreting these differences as figurative expression of community patterns might hint at the different groups building the particular enclosures. Distinct enclosures may have served different social entities (cf. Becker et al. 2012:33–37). Regarding these buildings as visible material expressions of group affiliations highlights the cooperative effort of their creation as a basis of community formation. With their expression of a common ideology, iconography, and a congregational layout, the monumental circular enclosures of Göbekli Tepe's Layer III emphasize a collective unity accentuating cooperative action and ritual. Renfrew and Level highlighted the meaning of a monumental site's size and location for its sphere of influence in a process of emerging elites controlling ritual practice and finally centralizing territorial control and power (Renfrew 1981; Renfrew and Level 1979). At the moment, we do not know enough about the social structure of those PPN groups constructing and using the monumental architecture at Göbekli Tepe to elaborate such thoughts in an appropriate context of secured data. Approaches to determine territorial influence operating with a center-periphery model hardly work in the case of Göbekli Tepe due to the assumed segmentary character of the hunter-gatherer groups in question and the uniqueness of the site for the nonce.[8] However, the exposed and widely visible position at the highest point of the surrounding landscape and its communal character as discussed above give reason to suggest that Göbekli Tepe must have taken on a prominent role of

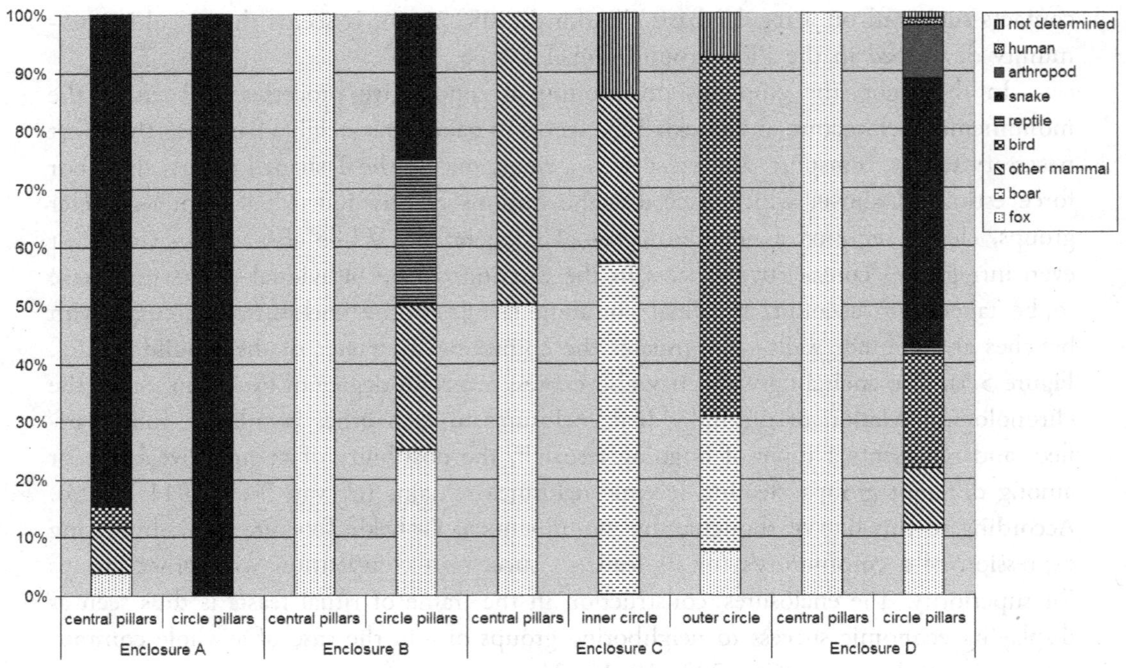

FIGURE 5.9 Distribution of the appearance of figurative representations in the enclosures of Göbekli Tepe. Note: The differing state of excavation as well as a possible chronological depth in the construction period of the particular enclosures have to be considered. Furthermore, later added graffiti as well as symbolically reduced icons were not included (graphic: J. Notroff and N. Becker, DAI).

actually central importance to a number of these hunter-gatherer groups. This large-scale influence is supported by evidence of a cultic community developing in its surroundings and furthermore indicated by the large variety of obsidian from the site. Although somewhat underrepresented compared to the numbers known from settlement sites and the large amount of flint, seven different kinds of obsidian raw material coming from four different volcanic regions within a distance of up to 500 km have been detected at Göbekli Tepe (pers. comm. T. Carter, Toronto).

Considering the structure and size of these groups of people and with a view to agency-based reconstructions of the origins of monuments (as pointed out by Osborne, this volume; cf. also Joyce 2004; Pauketat 2000), the amount of monumentality visible at Göbekli Tepe may demonstrate that responsibility for the construction of monumental structures does not necessarily have to be attributed to single powerful political actors, but could as well lie within a community as a whole. Instead of being the result and expression of institutionalized political power and control, the creation of monumental megalithic architecture may as well have acted as its impetus by setting up an arena for gatherings of large groups in an intragroup communication network (cf. Schmidt† 2000).

Conclusion

The monumentality of the architecture unearthed with the PPN A enclosures at Göbekli Tepe necessitates a shift in our paradigms regarding hunter-gatherer groups following the end of the Ice Age in the Near East as well as the meaning of monumentality as the outcome of complex, hierarchic societies. Regarded as the result of corporate, cooperative strategies, the monumental structures give witness to a social complexity among these groups hitherto unknown.

To attract the large number of individuals needed for the erection of the huge T-shaped pillars and their composition into circular enclosures, supposedly huge feasts were held—again strongly emphasizing the cooperative aspect of these building projects. These projects themselves have been shown to be of integral importance for the genesis of networked communities forming among the residents of PPN sites in Upper Mesopotamia. Furthermore, it seems likely that the whole process of monument construction at Göbekli Tepe, their repeated alteration and modification, was an intended reason for the particular participants within the communication network to continually come together.

While the role of feasting as the basis for this construction work was highlighted, it also has to be considered an important activity to strengthen a group's coherence (Rosenberg & Redding 2000:44). However, acquiring the supply of food needed for such a large number of people as gathered at Göbekli Tepe to build the monumental constructions described above must have been a difficult task when it depended on hunted game only. To use the example of the erection of the *moai* at Rapa Nui again, it was noted that food requirement increased by about 25 percent over the course of 300 years of construction activity (Van Tilburg and Ralston 2005). It seems reasonable to suggest that in response to a similar growing demand at Göbekli Tepe, new food sources and processing techniques were sought. According to this scenario, religious ritual and the construction of monumental architecture may be seen as one factor in the adoption of intensive cultivation and the transition to food production (Dietrich et al. 2012).

Against this background, the reduction of the monumental circular enclosures with numerous T-pillars in Layer III to smaller rectangular buildings containing only smaller or even no pillars at all in Layer II (Figure 5.10) could somehow be interpreted as a diminution of effort and labor force to some degree.[9] This may express a transformation of the community's structure in the course of the adaption to this new mode of living. Perhaps with the accessibility of new resources, a rising number of individuals within these groups was advancing, finally leading to a dissolution of larger social units into smaller clusters, which was reflected in the architectural features. Whether this new social structure also involved the emergence and rise of elites and the centralization of power cannot be answered satisfactorily at the current state of research. But the scenario described above, in preliminary thoughts based on the state of excavation and research at Göbekli Tepe, clearly accentuates the importance of an emerging monumentality for the genesis of complex social structures as early as the PPN of the Near East.

FIGURE 5.10 The so-called Lions' Pillar Building (named after the depiction of lions at its pillars) shows the change in layout toward smaller, rectangular buildings with a reduced number of T-pillars in Layer II (PPN B) (photo: D. Johannes, DAI).

NOTES

1.   In the framework of first stratigraphic considerations in the field, Layer II had been subdivided preliminarily in IIa and IIb as in some surface-near areas also circular, but considerably smaller structures have been unearthed, whose layout clearly differs from the usual rectangular buildings. The character of these constructions is not yet understood completely, so the former denotations as IIa and IIb have been waived, since they implied a close relation between these different structures. Layer II refers exclusively to the rectangular building phase.

2. Since the northern wall of this enclosure is not yet completely excavated, the number of pillars may have to be calculated higher; at least one more pillar must be expected to be still hidden in the northern baulk.

3. While it has been, certainly correctly, argued that a strict differentiation between "sacred" and "profane" in everyday life of primordial societies should hardly be expected (cf. Eliade 1959; also Banning 2011:624–627), spatial focal points of the holy and cult may be well attested also detached from domestic architecture (Dietrich and Notroff in press).

4. For a more detailed comment on and discussion of Banning's suggestions, cf. Dietrich and Notroff in press.

5. This could also hint at multiple stages in the process of cutting and working the stones at different localities, i.e., larger rough pieces were brought from the quarries to the construction site, where the final sculpting then took place; the pillars eventually erected have a height of up to 5.50 m and a weight of approximately 10 t.

6. This rather large range is explained by the level of training and experience of the individuals in question. The experiment was conducted with male and female students lacking the physique and know-how we might have to assume for the hunter-gatherer groups of the PPN. According to experience, a modern mason, trained and skilled, works twice as quickly as the students in this experiment, so maybe a Neolithic craftsman may be assumed to fit somewhere in the middle between these two extremes.

7. Beuger (forthcoming) also emphasizes that these preliminary results are calculated on the basis of a model including the use of fire in the quarrying processes, which helped to reduce labor time.

8. Although this probably might be considered a research void; it seems not unlikely that indeed other important ritual places of a similar or—even more likely—completely different character, such as Göbekli Tepe, have existed, albeit they are unknown to us at present. Regarding the scarcity of respective settlement sites, it might be assumed that up to 90 percent of relevant sites have not yet been discovered.

9. In developing his model of rivalry in history, van Wees suggests interpreting this change as reflecting a resumed rivalry at a more modest level after the old form of competition went too far and turned out not to be viable anymore (van Wees 2011:22).

REFERENCES CITED

Banning, E. B. 2011 So Fair a House: Göbekli Tepe and the Identification of Temples in the Pre-Pottery Neolithic. *Current Anthropology* 52(5):619–660.

Becker, N., O. Dietrich, Th. Götzelt, Th., Ç. Köksal-Schmidt, J. Notroff, and K. Schmidt† 2012 Materialien zur Deutung der zentralen Pfeilerpaare des Göbekli Tepe und weiterer Orte des obermesopotamischen Frühneolithikums. *Zeitschrift für Orient-Archäologie* 5:14–43.

Benz, M. 2006 Zur Bedeutung von Festen während der Neolithisierung im Vorderen Orient. *Ethnographisch-Archäologische Zeitschrift* 47(4):439–462.

Beuger, C. Forthcoming. *The Tools of the Stone Age Masons of Göbekli Tepe—An Experimental Approach.*

Bradley, R. 1993 *Altering the Earth: The Origins of Monuments in Britain and Continental Europe.* Society of Antiquaries of Scotland, Edinburgh.

Çelik, B. 2011a Karahan Tepe: A New Cultural Centre in the Urfa Area in Turkey. *Documenta Praehistorica* 38:241–253.

Çelik, B. 2011b Şanlıurfa—Yeni Mahalle. In *The Neolithic in Turkey 2. The Euphrates Basin,* edited by M. Özdoğan, N. Başgelen, and P. Kuniholm, pp. 139–164. Archaeology & Art Publications, Istanbul.

Çelik, B., M. Güler, and G. Güler 2011 Türkiye'nin güneydoğusunda yeni bir çanak çömleksiz neolitik yerleşim: Taşlı Tepe. *Anadolu/Anatolia* 37:225–236.

Childe, V. G. 1950 The Urban Revolution. *The Town Planning Review* 2(1):3–17.

Costello, S. K. 2011 Image, Memory, and Ritual: Re-viewing the Antecedents of Writing. *Cambridge Archaeological Journal* 21(2):247–262.

Dietler, M., and I. Herbich 1995 Feasts and Labor Mobilization. Dissecting a Fundamental Economic Practice. In *Feasts. Archaeological and Ethnographic Perspectives on Food, Politics, and Power,* edited by M. Dietler and B. Hayden, pp. 260–264. Smithsonian Institution Press, Washington, D.C. and London.

Dietrich, O. 2011 Radiocarbon Dating the First Temples of Mankind. Comments on 14C-Dates from Göbekli Tepe. *Zeitschrift für Orient-Archäologie* 4:12–25.

Dietrich, O., M. Heun, J. Notroff, K. Schmidt†, and M. Zarnkow 2012 The Role of Cult and Feasting in the Emergence of Neolithic Communities. New Evidence from Göbekli Tepe, South-Eastern Turkey. *Antiquity* 86:674–695.

Dietrich, O., and J. Notroff In Press. A Sanctuary or So Fair a House? In Defense of an Archaeology of Ritual and Cult at Pre-Pottery Neolithic Göbekli Tepe. In *Defining the Sacred: Approaches to the Archaeology of Religion in the Near East,* edited by N. Laneri. Oxbow, Oxford.

Dietrich, O., and K. Schmidt† 2010 A Radiocarbon Date from the Wall Plaster of Enclosure D of Göbekli Tepe. *Neo-Lithics* 2:82–83.

Dietrich, O., Ç. Köksal-Schmidt, J. Notroff, and K. Schmidt† 2013 Establishing a Radiocarbon Sequence for Göbekli Tepe. State of Research and New Data. *Neo-Lithics* 1/13:36–41.

Dietrich, O., Ç. Köksal-Schmidt, C. Kürkçüoğlu, J. Notroff, and K. Schmidt† 2014 Göbekli Tepe. Preliminary Report on the 2012 and 2013 Excavation Seasons. *Neo-Lithics* 1/14:11–17.

Eliade, M. 1959 *The Sacred and the Profane.* Harcourt Brace and World, New York.

Hauptmann, H. 1993 Ein Kultgebäude in Nevali Çori. In *Between the Rivers and over the Mountains. Archaeologica Anatolica et Mesopotamica Alba Palmieri dedicate,* edited by M. Frangipane, H. Hauptmann, M. Liverani, P. Matthias, and M. Mellink. Dipartimento di Scienze Storiche Archaeologiche e Anthropologiche dell'Antichità, Università di Roma "La Sapienza," Roma.

Hauptmann, H. 1988 Nevalı Çori: Architektur. *Anatolica* XV: 99–110.

Hauptmann, H. 1999 The Urfa Region. In *Neolithic in Turkey: The Cradle of Civilization* (Ancient Anatolian Civilizations Series 3), edited by M. Özdoğan and N. Başgelen, pp. 65–86. Arkeoloji ve Sanat Yaınları, Istanbul.

Helbling, J. 1987 *Theorie der Wildbeutergesellschaft: Eine ethnosoziologische Studie.* Campus, Frankfurt/Main, New York.

Heyerdahl, T. 1958 *Aku-Aku: The Secrets of Easter Island.* George Allen and Unwin, London.

Heyerdahl, T., A. Skjølsvold, and P. Pavel 1989 The "Walking" Moai of Easter Island. *Occasional Papers of the Kon-Tiki Museum* 1:55.

Hoskins, J. A. 1986 So My Name Shall Live: Stone-Dragging and Grave-Building in Kodi, West Sumba. *Bijdragen tot de Taal-, Land- en Volkenkunde* 142(1) (Anthropologica XXVIII):31–51.

Hultkrantz, Å., and Ø. Vorren, eds. 1982 *The Hunters: Their Culture and Way of Life.* Tromsø Museums Skrifter 18. Universitetsforlage, Tromsø.

Joyce, R. A. 2004 Unintended Consequences? Monumentality as a Novel Experience in Formative Mesoamerica. *Journal of Archaeological Method and Theory* 11(1):5–29.

Karul, N. 2011 Gusir Höyük. In *The Neolithic in Turkey 1. The Tigris Basin,* edited by M. Özdoğan; N. Başgelen, and P. Kuniholm, pp. 1–17. Archaeology & Art Publications, Istanbul.

Karul, N. 2013 Gusir Höyük/Siirt. Yerleşik Avcılar. *Arkeo Atlas* 8:22–29.

Kelly, R. L. 1995 *The Foraging Spectrum. Diversity in Hunter-Gatherer Lifeways.* Smithsonian Institution Press, Washington, D. C.

Kolb, M. J. 2011 The Genesis of Monuments in Island Societies. In *The Comparative Archaeology of Complex Societies,* edited by M. E. Smith, pp. 138–164. Cambridge University Press, Cambridge.

Kornienko, T. V. 2009 Notes on the Cult Buildings of Northern Mesopotamia in the Aceramic Neolithic Period. *Journal of Near Eastern Studies* 68(2):81–101.

Kozłowski, S. K. 2002 *Nemrik: An Aceramic Village in Northern Iraq.* Institute of Archaeology, Warsaw University, Warsaw.

Kurapkat, D. 2010 Frühneolithische Sondergebäude auf dem Göbekli Tepe in Obermesopotamien und vergleichbare Bauten in Vorderasien. Unpublished dissertation. Berlin.

Lee, R. B., and I. DeVore, eds. 1968 *Man the Hunter. The First Intensive Survey of a Single, Crucial Stage of Human Development—Man's once Universal Hunting Way of Life.* Aldine, Chicago.

Lipo, C. P., T. L. Hunt, and S. R. Haoa 2013 The "Walking" Megalithic Statues (Moai) of Easter Island. *Journal of Archaeological Science* 40(6):2859–2866.

Mazurowski, R. F. 2003 Tell Qaramel. Excavations 2003. *Polish Archaeology in the Mediterranean* 15:355–70.

Mazurowski, R. F., and B. Jamous 2000 Tell Qaramel. Excavations 2000. *Polish Archaeology in the Mediterranean* 12:327–41.

Mazurowski, R. F., and T. Yartah 2001 Tell Qaramel. Excavations 2001. *Polish Archaeology in the Mediterranean* 13:295–307.

Moetz, F. K., and B. Çelik 2012 T-shaped Pillar Sites in the Landscape around Urfa. In *Proceedings of the 7th International Congress on the Archaeology of the Ancient Near East. 12 April–16 April 2010, the British Museum and UCL, London. Volume 1: Mega-cities & Mega-sites. The Archaeology of Consumption & Disposal. Landscape, Transport & Communication,* edited by R. Matthews and J. Curtis, pp. 695–703. Harrassowitz Verlag, Wiesbaden.

Morenz, L. D., and K. Schmidt† 2009 Große Reliefpfeiler und kleine Zeichentäfelchen. Ein frühneolithisches Zeichensystem in Obermesopotamien. In *Non-Textual Marking Systems. Writing and Pseudo Script from Prehistory to Modern Times,* edited by P. Andrássy, J. Budka, and F. Kammerzell, pp. 13–31. Seminar für Ägyptologie und Koptologie, Göttingen.

Morsch, M. 2002 Magic Figurines? Some Remarks about the Clay Objects of Nevali Cori. In *Magic Practices and Ritual in the Near Eastern Neolithic.* Proceedings of a Workshop held at the 2nd International Congress on the Archaeology of the Ancient Near East (ICAANE) in Copenhagen 2000 (Studies in Early Near Eastern Production Subsistence and Environment 8), edited by H. G. Gebel, B. Dahl Hermansen, and C. Hoffmann Jensen, pp. 145–162. ex oriente, Berlin.

Munro, N. D., and L. Grosman 2010 Early Evidence (ca. 12,000 BP) for Feasting at a Burial Cave in Israel. *Proceedings of the National Academy of Sciences* 107:15362–15366.

Notroff, J., O. Dietrich, and K. Schmidt† In Press. Gathering of the Dead? The Early Neolithic Sanctuaries of Göbekli Tepe, Southeastern Turkey. In *Death Shall Have No Dominion: The Archaeology of Mortality and Immortality—A Worldwide Perspective,* edited by C. Renfrew, M. J. Boyd, and Iain Morley. Cambridge.

Özdoğan, A. 1999 Çayönü. In *Neolithic in Turkey: The Cradle of Civilization* (Ancient Anatolian civilizations series 3), edited by M. Özdoğan and N. Başgelen, pp. 35–63. Arkeoloji ve Sanat Yaınları, Istanbul.

Özkaya, V., and O. San 2007 Körtik Tepe. Bulgular ışığında kültürel doku üzerine ilk gözlemler. In *Türkiye'de neolitik dönem*, edited by M. Özdoğan and N. Başgelen, pp. 21–36. Arkeoloji ve Sanat Yaınları, Istanbul.

Pauketat, T. R. 2000 The Tragedy of the Commoners. In *Agency in Archaeology*, edited by M.-A. Dobres and J. Robb, pp. 113–129. Routledge, London, New York.

Pavel, P. 1990 Reconstruction of the Transport of Moai. In *State and Perspectives of Scientific Research in Easter Island Culture*, ed. H.-M. Esen-Bauer, pp. 141–144. Courier Forschungsinstitut Senckenberg, Frankfurt am Main.

Petrasch, J. 2010 Demografischer Wandel während der Neolithisierung in Mitteleuropa. In *Die Neolithisierung Mitteleuropas/The Spread of the Neolithic to Central Europe*. Internationale Tagung, Mainz 24. bis 26. Juni 2005/International Symposium, Mainz 24 June–26 June 2005, edited by D. Gronenborn and J. Petrasch, pp. 351–363. Römisch-Germanisches Zentralmuseum, Mainz.

Renfrew, C. 1981 Space, Time, and Man. *Transactions of the Institute of the British Geographers*, New Series 6(3):257–278.

Renfrew, C., and E. V. Level 1979 Exploring Dominance: Predicting Polities from Centers. In *Transformations: Mathematical Approaches to Culture Change*, edited by C. Renfrew and L. L. Cooke, pp. 145–167. Academic Press, New York.

Richards, C. 1996 Monuments as Landscape: Creating the Centre of the World in Late Neolithic Orkney. *World Archaeology* 28(2):190–208.

Rosenberg, M., and R. W. Redding 2000 Hallan Çemi and Early Village Organization in Eastern Anatolia. In *Life in Neolithic Farming Communities. Social Organization, Identity, and Differenziation*, edited by I. Kuijt, pp. 39–61. Kluwer Academic/Plenum Publishers, New York.

Routledge, S. 1920 *The Mystery of Easter Island: The Story of an Expedition*. Hazell, Watson and Viney, London.

Schirmer, W. 1983 Drei Bauten des Çayönü Tepesi. In *Beiträge zur Altertumskunde Kleinasiens*. Festschrift Kurt Bittel, edited by H. Hauptmann and R. M. Boehmer, pp. 463–476. Philipp von Zabern, Mainz.

Schirmer, W. 1988 Zu den Bauten des Çayönü Tepesi. *Anatolica* XV:139–159.

Schirmer, W. 1990 Some Aspects of Building at the "Aceramic-Neolithic" Settlement of Çayönü Tepesi. *World Archaeology* 21(3):363–387.

Schmidt†, K. 2000 "Zuerst kam der Tempel, dann die Stadt." Vorläufiger Bericht zu den Grabungen am Göbekli Tepe und am Gürcütepe 1995–1999. *Istanbuler Mitteilungen* 50:5–41.

Schmidt†, K. 2001 Göbekli Tepe, Southeastern Turkey. A Preliminary Report on the 1995–1999 Excavations. *Paléorient* 26(1):45–54.

Schmidt†, K. 2005 Die "Stadt" der Steinzeit. In *Wege zur Stadt—Entwicklung und Formen urbanen Lebens in der alten Welt*, edited by H. Falk, pp. 25–38. Hempen, Bremen.

Schmidt†, K. 2010 Göbekli Tepe—The Stone Age Sanctuaries. New Results of Ongoing Excavations with a Special Focus on Sculptures and High Reliefs. *Documenta Praehistorica* 37:239–256.

Schmidt†, K. 2012 *Göbekli Tepe. A Stone Age Sanctuary in South-Eastern Anatolia* (English translation of Schmidt†, K. 2007 *Sie bauten die ersten Tempel. Das rätselhafte Heiligtum der Steinzeitjäger*. C. H. Beck, München). ex oriente, Berlin.

Schröder, E. E. W. 1917 *Nias, ethnographische, geographische en historische aanteekeningen en studien.* Brill, Leiden.

Stordeur, D., and F. Abbès 2002 Du PPNA au PPNB: mise en lumière d'une phase de transition à Jerf al Ahmar (Syrie). *Bulletin de la Société Préhistorique Française* 99(3):563–595.

Van Tilburg, J. A., and T. Ralston 2005 Megaliths and Mariners: Experimental Archaeology on Easter Island. In *Onward and Upward: Papers in Honor of Clement W. Meighan,* edited by K. L. Johnson, pp. 279–306. Stansbury Publishing, Chico, California.

van Wees, H. 2011 Rivalry in History: An Introduction. In *Competition in the Ancient World,* edited by N. Fisher and H. van Wees, pp. 1–36. The Classical Press of Wales, Swansea.

Watkins, T. 2004 Building Houses, Framing Concepts, Constructing Worlds. *Paléorient* 30(1):5–23.

Watkins, T. 2008 Supra-Regional Networks in the Neolithic of Southwest Asia. *Journal of World Prehistory* 21:139–171. 2010 New Light on Neolithic Revolution in South-West Asia. *Antiquity* 84:621–634.

Yartah, T. 2004 Tell 'Abr 3, un village du néolithique précéramique (PPNA) sur le moyen Euphrate. Première approche. *Paléorient* 30(2):141–158.

PART II

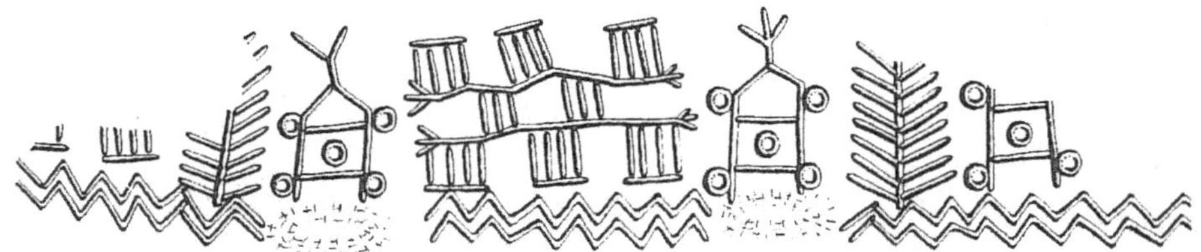

Monumentality and Landscape

CHAPTER SIX

Monuments and Landscape

Exploring Issues of Place, Distance, and Scale in Early Political Contest

Claudia Glatz

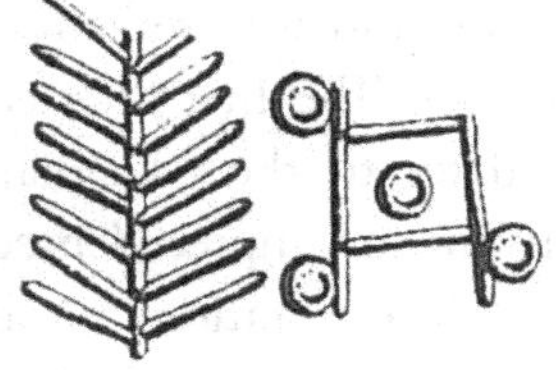

Abstract *The marking of special places in the landscape and the creation of collective memories through the modification of living rocks and the construction of stone monuments is by no means the prerogative of early complex and expansive societies. However, the sociopolitically motivated monumental displays of individual rulers' authority in landscape settings, as well as the representation and reimagination of distant landscapes in urban monuments, track the emergence of the first expansive polities in the ancient Near East. The practice of monument construction forms an integral part of the (re)production and negotiation of social space. In this chapter, I explore the relationship between depictive monumental display, landscape, and sociopolitical scale. The main focus of this chapter will be the monuments of the late third and early second millennium B.C. societies of Mesopotamia and the Zagros piedmont.*

The making and marking of socially significant places in the landscape through monuments and—in the process of their construction and celebration—the production of collective memory and cultural meaning constitute an important strategy in the production and negotiation of social authority (Harmanşah 2007; Lefebvre 1991:220–228; Smith 2003). Landscape monuments can take a wide variety of forms, including reliefs carved into the living rock, monumentalized natural features such as springs, or large-scale landscape transformations in the form of dams and canals and associated commemorative monuments. Although not exclusive to expansive polities, the most extensive corpora of landscape monuments in the ancient Near East are closely related to large-scale political networks such as those of Hittite Anatolia and the Neo-Assyrian empire. Increasing territorial scales of interaction, it would therefore seem, required new, geographically expansive, strategies of political production and competition (Glatz and Plourde 2011:35, 58) and new ways of imagining and symbolically incorporating expanded social spaces (Harmanşah 2012:55). Representation—in word, image, or a combination thereof—is one means by which landscapes and people are reimagined and conquered (Said 1978:32). Neo-Assyrian palace reliefs, for instance, carefully differentiate people and landscapes from the distant corners of their realm (e.g., Albenda 1983; Thomason 2001). Plants and animals from across Assyria's and other Near Eastern polities' areas of influence and beyond were displayed as three-dimensional representations of distant landscapes in gardens and zoos (Pollinger Forster 1998; Stronach 1990; Wiseman 1983).

The exertion of symbolic control over distant regions by way of representation, as well as the modification of social and political landscapes through the production of monuments, may have reached a temporary apex in the late second and first millennia B.C., but both practices first developed almost a millennium earlier. The first attested monumental representation of a distant landscape and people dates to the Akkadian period (ca. 2350–2150 B.C.), when south Mesopotamia underwent an unprecedented process of political centralization and expansion that resulted in the incorporation—or at least its attempt—of regions that are geographically distant and topographically distinct from those of the Mesopotamian plains (Kuhrt 1995). At the same time, or shortly thereafter, landscape monuments in the form of rock reliefs made their first appearance in the Taurus and Zagros foothills in a political climate of Mesopotamian expansionism and intraregional competition. In this chapter, I want to explore this apparent connection between monumental production, landscape, and an expansive scale of sociopolitical competition.

LANDSCAPES AND MONUMENTS

Landscapes are social spaces that are constituted by overlapping physical characteristics, cultural practices, and meaning. Such spaces are produced, reproduced, and transformed through social practices at a range of social and spatial scales (Lefebvre 1991; Mitchell 2002:14). Landscapes are, thus, continuously evolving both in terms of their physical characteristics, which are shaped by natural and anthropogenic forces, and the ways in which they are conceptualized and imbued with meaning by those living in them and by observers farther afield. Political landscapes, in particular those of early complex societies, are often short-term and highly contested configurations. Toponyms drop in and out of textual sources or disappear entirely while boundaries undergo often violent, short-term oscillations that no political map can ever hope to capture (Harmanşah 2012:54 for a similar point). This is because social power as a negotiated relationship with multiple sources of dissent and resistance is in need of continued performance (Foucault 1978:92–102). Power is, therefore, never absolute nor is it evenly distributed across space. The spatial gaps in authority that are created by practices of governance of varying intensity and sustainability are the loci in which resistance is mounted and alternative power bases emerge (Smith 2003:76–77, 110). As a consequence, landscapes, and especially political landscapes, are always in the making. Practices that aim for the (re)production or transformation of spatial authority such as monument construction are, thus, signs of the ongoing negotiation of power relationships rather than commemorative symbols of hegemony.

The monuments of interest here either deliberately modify, and in the process symbolically appropriate, the very landscapes over which hegemony is sought, or do so through the monumentalized representation of such landscapes in distant political centers. Urban monuments and those constructed in landscape settings are two distinct yet related strategies of political production that operate on a range of different planes of cultural communication and geographical scales.

The overall physical characteristics of a particular monument, its pictorial theme, iconographic style, form and content of accompanying inscriptions, and the activities surrounding its construction, maintenance, or commemoration, are products of culturally specific systems of representation and symbolic communication. In other words, the primary target audience for such monuments forms part of the same cultural and social sphere as the monument patron. Shafer (2007), for instance, proposed that Neo-Assyrian rock carvings and stele in provincial settings and on political boundaries represent Assyrian rulers' kingship in a standardized and symbolically coded format, which is directed toward an internal elite audience and discourse.

However, cross-culturally understood representations of royal, male authority, and the mere ability to carve or construct monuments, do convey a more general message of political strength to both subordinates and potential competitors. As costly signals of political strength, monuments acquire an active role in the negotiation of both internal and external power relationships. They convey honest information about the social standing and economic prowess of the monument patron to competitors and provide the basis on which future decisions about the most advantageous modes of interaction can reliably be based (e.g., Bliege Bird and Smith 2005). Monument production requires economic and intellectual resources, and only those in command of such resources have the ability to produce monuments and, by extension, the political landscape (Smith 2003:70–71). The cost of monument construction—the wealth and social influence necessary to rally sufficient labor power and specialist knowledge—therefore acts as the guarantor for the honesty of the signal, even if monuments may be placed beyond one's sphere of effective control as a means of staking territorial claims over contested regions (Morrison and Lycett 1994), and even if accompanying boastful inscriptions are not "true" in a literal sense. With monument construction, the medium is the message (McLuhan 1964).

Ancient Near Eastern textual sources are not only well aware of the economics and logistics of monument construction such as city walls or ziggurats, but see them fundamentally connected to the projection and reproduction of social power (Potts, this volume; Ristvet 2007:198–204). Size in this context clearly matters: it sends a strong signal of economic wealth and political importance (Trigger 1990:118). Not everything we would define as monumental is necessarily exceedingly large in size, however (Osborne, this volume). The monuments that are the focus of this chapter range in size from life-size depictions of human actors to about half that. The knowledge and specialist workmanship involved in their construction, however, attests to the substantial economic and social expenditures required for their production. In the case of monuments in the landscape it is often their strategic and dramatic settings that make them awe inspiring. In terms of their culturally specific significance, depictive monuments of royalty, Akkadian *ṣalmu*, derive their power not from their size but from the fact that the representation is ontologically equivalent to the person depicted and therefore present at the location of the monument or personified by it (Bahrani 2003:127). For these reasons, the objects under investigation here are considered monuments.

The location of a monument, whether in an urban center or in a distant landscape setting, also provides insights into the geographical scale of communication and competition. A costly signaling system of political strength is only successful if the signal can reach the target audience, and so monument construction within the confines of urban centers would suggest a geographically limited interaction sphere that is characterized by small competing polities (Neiman 1997). Monuments placed outside of urban centers, by contrast, may be argued to form part of a political and symbolic dialogue that reaches beyond competition among city states and points to a more expansive spatial scale of interaction (Glatz and Plourde 2011).

Depictive monuments, whether they are displayed in urban settings or carved on the living rock, are capable of expressing a further spatial dimension, that of cultural and geographical distance and difference. With military and political expansion comes knowledge of distant people and cultures as well as geographical knowledge. Knowledge, to return to Foucault (1980), is fundamental to the production and exercise of power, and knowledge of the "other" is fundamental to a colonial discourse that represents and distorts colonial societies in text and image through the prism of this knowledge (Said 1978:32). The victory stele of Naram Sîn, to which we will return in the following section, is the first time such knowledge is monumentalized and manipulated in the ancient Near East. Likewise, later Neo-Assyrian and Persian architectural reliefs are concerned with the representation of defeated enemies and deferent subjects, whose dress, hairstyle, material culture, and physique distinguish them from their conquerors and overlords, as well as the detailed depiction of the landscapes they inhabit.

MONUMENTAL BEGINNINGS

Large-scale stone sculpture first develops in the ancient Near East during the mid-third millennium B.C. in southern Mesopotamia (Pollock 1999:181). The first monumental sculptures are associated with Early Dynastic (ca. 2900–2300 B.C.) and Akkadian-period urban centers and almost exclusively focus on the depiction of victorious royal males (Börker-Klähn 1982:14; Cooper 1990:40).

During the Early Dynastic period, the Mesopotamian alluvium underwent a dramatic demographic increase and the concentration of the vast majority of its population in large cities (e.g., Adams and Nissen 1972:12, 87). These cities formed the centers of a mosaic of competing polities embedded within a larger regional cultural sphere. Intercity conflict and territorial competition is well attested for this period, and it is this unsettled, competitive political climate that appears to have facilitated the emergence of the palace as the most powerful city institution during this period (Stone 1995:236). The most famous of intercity conflicts is the struggle over land between Lagash and Umma around 2500 B.C., which lasted more than 150 years and was decided by a military victory of Eannatum of Lagash. The war was commemorated in the so-called Stele of the Vultures, the first public narrative monument in the ancient Near East (Winter 1985:13). The stele, with a reconstructed height of about 1.8 m, would likely have been displayed in the temple of Ningirsu in Girsu (Hansen 2003:190–191 Figures 52, 53). Eannatum's successful military assault on Umma is depicted on the stele in several registers, including detailed portrayals of the Lagash phalanx and Ningirsu's divine support. Fallen enemies are shown, but the geographical setting of the encounter receives no attention in the preserved fragments. An inscription details the same historical event.

Several larger polities and alliances incorporating formerly independent cities emerged toward the end of the Early Dynastic period. Around 2400 B.C., Uruk was able to exert control over the territories of both Ur and Umma, and subsequently claimed control of the entire region. The first attempts were made by Lugalzagesi of Uruk, who distributed land grants to local rulers to consolidate his expanded realm (Kuhrt 1995:42–44).

The following Akkadian period continues both the tradition of territorial contest and expansion as well as the production of victory stele (*narû*). Unlike in the previous phase, however, Sargon (r. 2334–2279 B.C.) and his successors were the first to successfully centralize control over southern Mesopotamia and surrounding regions in the hands of a single dynasty through military success, political appointments, administrative restructuring, and strategic land redistribution. The Akkadian polity reached its maximum spatial extent under the rulership of Sargon's grandson, Naram Sîn (r. 2254–2218 B.C.). The textual sources attest to garrisons delimiting the boundaries of Akkad's influence from north Syria to western Iran. Under subsequent rulers, the realm of Akkad gradually shrank back to the city of Akkad and its hinterland and the traditional patchwork of powerful cities vying for supremacy (Kuhrt 1995:44–55).

In addition to fragments of stele and other monuments coming from Mesopotamian cities such as Telloh (Foster 1985), a series of fragmentary Akkadian period monuments were excavated at Susa, where they had been taken from Mesopotamian cities by Shutruk-Nahhunte in the late second millennium B.C. They include diorite stele fragments commemorating Sargon's victories and the lower part of a statue of Manishtushu and his fragmented inscribed obelisk, which, like their Early Dynastic predecessors, would have been displayed within the confines of southern Mesopotamian cities (Hansen 2003). Also among the Susa collection of Akkadian monuments is the two-meter-tall, freestanding sandstone Victory Stele of Naram Sîn, which marks a radical new approach to royal power and its spatial dimensions.

LANDSCAPE ON A MONUMENT

The Victory Stele of the Akkadian king, Naram Sîn, depicts the defeat of the Lullubi, a people of the western Zagros region, by Naram Sîn and his soldiers (Figure 6.1) (Hansen

FIGURE 6.1 Stela of Naram Sîn (Musée du Louvre; photograph by 'Rama' via wiki-media commons).

2003:191–198). An accompanying inscription recounts the battle against the Lullubi and their ruler Sidur. A second inscription was added later when the stele was removed from Sippar to Susa more ·than a millennium later. The stele can be dated to ca. 2254–2218 B.C. on the basis of the first inscription.

Naram Sîn is the central, dominant figure on the monument. He is clad in a short tunic and horned helmet—a mark of his status as divine ruler—and equipped with bow, spear, and battleaxe. He stands underneath starburst emblems and above registers of Akkadian soldiers orderly marching up the mountain on the lefthand side and Lullubi enemies falling off it in turmoil or pleading for their life on the right.

Unlike the many generic representations of victory and conquest in ancient Near Eastern art, the stele depicts a specific historical event and it does so in the context of a specific, foreign landscape. Naram Sîn's victory takes place on the side of a rugged, tree-clad mountain. Although the landscape is formalized in order to correspond to the hierarchical composition of the scene, there are several topographic and faunal elements that point toward an explicit concern with a specific geographical region, one that is foreign to lowland Mesopotamia and which Naram Sîn claims to have conquered. The two trees on the stele seemingly represent a variety of oak native to the western Zagros, and even the sandstone from which the stele is carved may have been quarried in the region (Winter 1999:69–70, 71 suggests the Jebel Hamrin range between the Diyala and the Little Zab as a possible source).

This is the first monumental depiction of landscape in the ancient Near East, but it is not landscape for its own sake. The trees on the Naram Sîn stele "do not signal an identification with place, but rather an identification of a place" (Winter 1999:72). The detailed foreign representation of the fallen Lullubi wearing animal skins and long, pleated hair in the very landscape of their defeat marks the beginning of a colonial discourse of "otherness" in ancient Near Eastern public monuments. Fundamental to this discourse is the knowledge of distant peoples and landscapes, acquired on military expeditions such as the one depicted on the stele, and reproduced to enhance Naram Sîn's personal achievement and symbolic hold over both the Lullubi and their land.

Bahrani (2008:102–104) recently suggested that through its depiction of Naram Sîn as a divine ruler, the stele both marks and helps produce the transformation of Mesopotamian kingship from the limited powers of the ruler of a city-state to sovereign power. The demonstration of an expanded geographical sphere of control over remote landscapes and people forms integral part of the ideology of a newly centralized and expansive state and its ruler.

Until the Akkadian period, other depictive genres, such as cylinder seals, depict landscapes only in a highly stylized manner that serves as decoration rather than holds a specific narrative quality. Depicted are the domesticated canal and garden landscapes typical of lowland Mesopotamia. During the Akkadian period, however, mountain landscapes begin to appear on cylinder seals both as divine attributes as well as settings for hunting activities (Figure 6.2) (Kantor 1966:146–147). Although royal victory themes such as those on the Naram Sîn stele are absent from Akkadian glyptic (Kantor 1966:146), victory scenes over gods from the mountains are attested. The legend of one such seal, for

FIGURE 6.2 Akkadian cylinder seals depicting scenes in mountainous landscapes (a) Metropolitan Museum of Art No. 41.160.192 (after Kantor 1966:Figure 8) (b) Boston Museum of Fine Arts No. 34.194 (after Kantor 1966:Figure 9).

instance, reads "As long as Ištar-anunitum holds sway over the mountain gods, ^{d}x and Ea provide abundant yields at home" (Westenholz 1999:49, note 161 cf. Ahmed 2012:87).

No landscape monuments such as rock reliefs can be ascribed with any degree of confidence to Akkadian rulers. From later copies of inscriptions, however, it would appear that many more victory stele stood in city-shrines across the region controlled by Akkad (Kuhrt 1995:47–49; 54). A diorite stele fragment depicting Naram Sîn from the area of Pir Hüseyin in Dyarbakır province, eastern Turkey, and the lower half of a hollow-cast copper-alloy sculpture of a sitting nude male from Bassetki near Dohuk (Hansen 2003:195, Figure 58) may represent the use of monumental display as a means

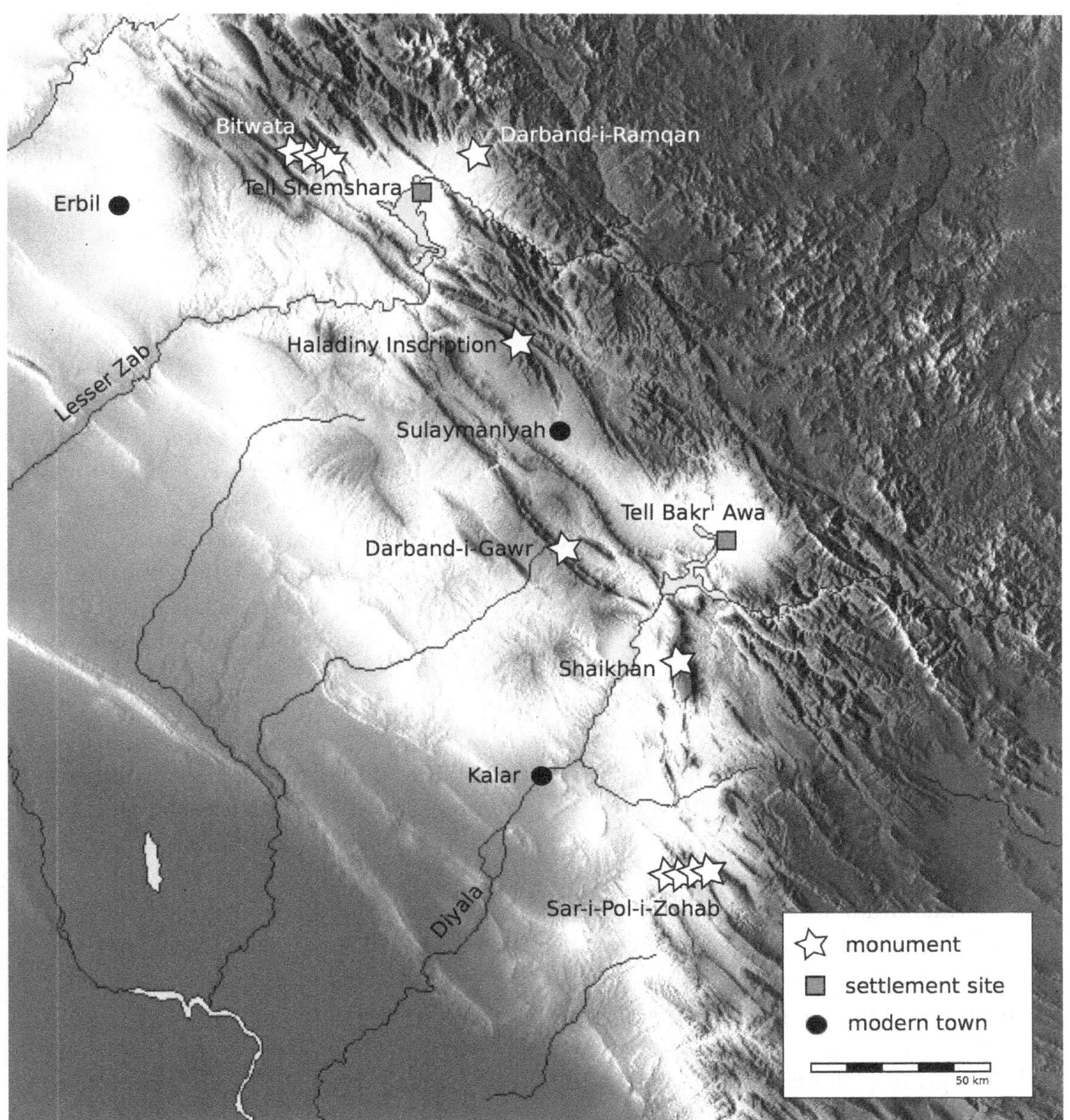

FIGURE 6.3 Map showing the location of third and early second millennium B.C. landscape monuments around the Sharezor plain and the upper Diyala/Sirwan river.

of projecting political power in regions over which limited effective control was exerted. It is, however, also possible that both monuments were displaced from more southerly urban centers in the same manner in which Akkadian sculptures arrived at Susa many centuries later.

MONUMENTS IN THE LANDSCAPE

Landscape monuments make their first appearance in northeast Iraq and western Iran during the late third millennium B.C. (Figure 6.3). A relief probably dating to the mid-third millennium is known from Gündük, near Akre northwest of Erbil, and a total of 13 reliefs and inscriptions spanning the late third and early second millennium B.C. skirt the mountainous fringes of the Sharezor plain and the upper reaches of the Diyala River. (Two additional roughly contemporary landscape monuments are known from Kurangun in Fars [Potts 1999:182; Seidl 1986], but are not considered here in any more detail.) The reliefs in the western Zagros are located in dramatic as well as strategic parts of the landscape, usually controlling communication routes of either local or more wide-ranging significance at important highland-lowland intersections. With the exception of the Gündük relief and three purely inscriptive fragments from Bitwata, the rock reliefs all depict variations on the theme of the triumphant warrior and thus share a thematic tradition with the urban Victory Stele of Naram Sîn. On the basis of overall iconographic theme and details in composition, posture, and clothing, the Zagros rock reliefs are traditionally assigned dates in the Ur III (ca. 2100–2000 B.C.) or the first Babylonian dynasty (ca. 1830–1531 B.C.) (Börker-Klähn 1982:44–46), but a more precise dating of many of the rock reliefs and a relative chronological sequence of monument construction remain difficult to establish.

With the exception of the Gündük reliefs (Ahmed 2012:93–94, Figures 18, 19; Böker-Klähn 1982:No. 274–276, 234), which were carved at some distance from the other reliefs and which also differ from them thematically, the geographical distribution of the majority of rock reliefs as well as the cuneiform inscriptions which accompany some of them, connect these landscape monuments with the highland polities of Simurrum and Lullubum.

Simurrum and Lullubum are relatively well attested in the late third and early second millennium B.C. in south Mesopotamian as well as local textual sources. First attested in the Akkadian period, the relationship between lowland Mesopotamia and this highland region was one of repeated military conflict and lowland attempts to exert control over the region. Limited archaeological research in the region means that reconstructs of the region's political geography are broadly agreed upon but with much variation in detail. Most recently, the polity of Simurrum has been located in the Sharezor plain and Lullubum in the high plateau between the Qara Dagh and the Binzird and Beranan ranges to the southwest of the Sharezor, extending from the Lesser Zab to the Diyala River (Altaweel et al. 2012:21–22; Frayne 2011:511; but see, for instance, Sallaberger 1999:158 for a location of Lullubum to the north of Simurrum; or Frayne 1997:104 for a localization of the center of Simurrum along the upper Diyala).

Three Akkadian year names commemorate the victories of Sargon and Naram Sîn over Simurrum, which is characterized as a polity centered on a city of the same name (ENSI2, Altaweel et al. 2012:22). The Lullubi and their conflict with Akkad, as we have seen already, are immortalized in the Victory Stele of Naram Sîn. More peaceful exchange relations involving the export of barley, horses, and slaves to Gasur and later Nuzi in exchange for livestock and metals (Fincke 1993:192 cf. Ahmed 2012:78; Meek

1935:HSS X 99 and 176) are also attested in the textual sources. A similar picture emerges for subsequent periods, where the region appears to fluctuate in and out of south Mesopotamian control (see Altaweel et al. 2012 for a summary).

In the following section, I will provide an overview of the landscape monuments in the vicinity of the Sharezor plain and the Diyala river that are both the product and media of these local and more wide-ranging political struggles.

Darband-i Gawra

The rock relief of Darband-i Gawra (Figure 6.4) is generally thought to be the oldest of the reliefs in the western Zagros region due to its close resemblance to the Victory

FIGURE 6.4 Sketch of the rock relief at Darband-i Gawra (after Postgate and Roaf 1995:Figure 5).

Stele of Naram Sîn (Börker-Klähn 1987:44–45, no. 29; Strommenger 1962, 1963). The relief is hewn into a rock face above the only passage through the 3,500 m high Qara Dagh mountain range, which delimits the Sharezor plain in the west and southwest. In preparation for the carving of the relief, the rock surface was smoothed and a niche created with an overhanging roof. A near life-size triumphant male warrior is depicted equipped with bow, axe, and dagger, and wearing a short skirt, a roll-brimmed hat, and a long curly beard. Two fallen enemies with long braided hair lie naked and with twisted limbs under the warrior's feet. Unlike some of the other Zagros reliefs, no inscription accompanies Darband-i Gawra.

The execution of the relief, which is carved with much care and attention to detail, points to an expert stonemason. The sculptor appears to have been familiar with the Naram Sîn stela or another similar but now lost monument. Alternatively, Darband-i Gawra may have provided the inspiration for the Akkadian stele. Some scholars ascribe the relief to Naram Sîn (Huot 2004:142; Strommenger 1962:26), but other than an a priori allocation of creative agency to lowland elites and their crafts specialists, there is no reason why it should not be the work of a local ruler and stonemason. The most broadly accepted dating of the relief places it in the post-Akkadian period on the basis of the headdress of the central male figure, the so-called roll-brimmed hat (Boese 1973:15–25). The roll-brimmed hat is first attested on the statue of Gudea of Lagash (r. 2150–2125 B.C.), who ruled in southern Mesopotamia after the fall of Akkad. The Gudea statue shares connections with Early Dynastic and Akkadian iconographic traditions, but the roll-brimmed hat is not attested on earlier depictions and presents a new item of dress in lowland Mesopotamia. The sudden appearance of the roll-brimmed hat in this period and the lack of lowland predecessors, however, raise the possibility that it is a cultural adoption from outside the Mesopotamian sphere, and presumably one with a long-standing tradition as royal headgear. Thus, it is plausible, albeit impossible to prove conclusively, that the roll-brimmed hat originates in the Zagros region and that it was subsequently adopted by Gudea as an alternative, non-Akkadian, royal headgear.[1] As a consequence, it remains possible that the Darband-i Gawra relief could have provided the inspiration for Naram Sîn's victory stele.

BITWATA RELIEFS

To the north of the Sharezor, in a side valley of the Rania plain at Bitwata, four fragmentary inscriptions and a relief carving from a now destroyed locality can be attributed to Iddi(n)-Sîn, king of Simurrum and/or his son Anzabazuna (Figure 6.5). The relatively small figural relief (93 x 92 cm) is carved into a smoothed and framed limestone surface in bas relief and surrounded by a vertical cuneiform inscription in eight rectilinear columns (Shaffer et al. 2003:3). The relief depicts, in much detail, a variation on the triumphant warrior theme. Striding to the right and facing a goddess, the male warrior steps onto an enemy, who has fallen on his back but is still alive. He carries a bow in his left hand and sword in his right. He wears a knee-length skirt, a bracelet on his right wrist, a necklace, and a brimmed hat with four crescent-shaped ornaments. His

FIGURE 6.5 Rock relief and inscription of Iddi(n)-Sîn of Simurrum from Bitawta (after Shaffer et al. 2003:Figure 1).

hair appears to be short and he is clean-shaven. The fallen enemy also wears a short skirt and, in contrast to his victorious opponent, has a pointed beard. The goddess wears a hat adorned with four pairs of horns, a long dress over a short-sleeved shirt and a necklace. In her left hand she holds a bi-voluted item.

The Akkadian cuneiform inscription tell us how Iddi(n)-Sîn, king of Simurrum held sway over nine *kulišu*, a regional political unit equivalent to a district or province.

One of these, the formerly independent *kulišum* of Nimun, had been turned into a tribute-bearing subordinate of Simurrum and was forced to hand over the district/province of Kulun(n)num to Simurrum. Kulun(n)num subsequently rebelled and a monument was erected in its territory to commemorate the crushing of the uprising. Following a curse to befall anyone attempting to destroy it, Kulun(n)num's tribute requirements in the form of livestock are stated (Shaffer et al. 2003:11).

Three additional stone blocks with fragmentary inscriptions from Bitwata also mention the rebellion of Kulun(n)num and its crushing (Frayne 1990:709, E4.19.1.1–3.), but seem to be written from a different perspective. Although Iddi(n)-Sîn is mentioned in the first line of each inscription, all subsequent activity appears associated with Anzabazuna, Iddi(n)-Sîn's son. Each inscription commemorates the erection of dedications to these gods, with whose divine support the rebellion was defeated by Anzabazuna. By contrast, Anzabazuna is not mentioned at all in the inscription that accompanies the relief (Shaffer et al. 2003:29) and it would appear, therefore, that father and son disagreed as to who was instrumental in securing Simurrum's grasp over this northern district/province (see Al-Fouadi 1978:128; Gelb and Kienast 1990:379–381; Shaffer et al. 2003:30–31 for various scenarios). Whatever the precise historical context of the production of the four Bitwata monuments, it is clear that they form part of an ongoing reproduction and subtle transformation of a politically significant and contested landscape.

Both Iddi(n)-Sîn and Anzabazuna are attested in southern Mesopotamian textual sources dating to the end of the Ur III period, a date that is confirmed by the paleography of the inscriptions and art-historical considerations. Historically, this would place the inscriptions at a time when south Mesopotamia lost direct control over the Zagros piedmont and local principalities began to regain independence and expanded in their own right (Shaffer et al. 2003:39).

DARBAND-I RAMQAN

The remains of two probably more or less contemporary but badly damaged reliefs are carved on the sides of a rugged rock face above the Lesser Zab between the Rania plain and Dizah and along a key juncture in communication routes from the lowland plains to the south and east into the highland regions of Iran (Börker-Klähn 1982:no. 34, 140–141). One relief shows a sun and crescent symbol above a human figure (Westernolz 2000:108 interprets it as a triumphant warrior). Only the sun and crescent are visible on the second relief.

HALADINY INSCRIPTION

An inscribed limestone slab (76 x 37 x 27 cm), which was found in a field near the village of Qarachatan at the foot of the Pir-a Magrun range can also be attributed to Iddi(n)-Sîn of Simurrum (Ahmed 2012:255–273). A lengthy inscription details the victories of Iddi(n)-Sîn over a large number of local polities located in a wide region stretching from the Rania and farther to the north and west to where the Khorasan highway cuts through the Zagros in the southeast. This inscription, together with the Bitwata evidence, points to the reigns of Iddi(n)-Sîn and his son as a phase of military expansionism that brought Simurrum into conflict with a wide array of neighboring polities. Also mentioned in a fragmented passage is Anubanini, king of Lullubum, who is depicted on the Sar-e Pol-e Zohab II relief (see below) and who, from this new evidence, appears to have been a contemporary and rival of Iddi(n)-Sîn for control over the westernmost stretch of the Khorasan highway (Ahmed 2012:258, 286–293).

Sar-e Pol-e Zohab

Four reliefs dating to the early second millennium B.C. frame the rocky flanks of the river Alwand at Sar-e Pol-e Zohab in western Iran, where the river breaks through the Zagros. The Khorasan highway, which connects the Mesopotamian plains with the Iranian highlands and central Asia, runs only a few kilometers to the south. The four reliefs range in size between ca. 150 cm and life-size and two have accompanying Akkadian cuneiform inscriptions.

The relief of Sar-e Pol-e Zohab I (Börker-Klähn 1982:No. 30, 138) (144 x 150 cm) is carved atop an artificial ledge. Depicted is a triumphant male warrior equipped with bow and two further weapons and wearing a short skirt, roll-brimmed hat, and pointy shoes, which tread on a fallen enemy (Figure 6.6). Sun and crescent symbols hover over the king's head. A damaged inscription can be read only partially. Frayne (1990:4.18.1) reads the personal name Zaba[zuna], son of x. The text further seems to mention a victory and the erection of a Salam on mount Batir, followed by a lengthy curse formula. Different readings of the inscription have resulted in wildly varying dating of the monument, from the Akkadian period (Börker-Klähn 1982:138) to the late Ur III or early Old Babylonian period on the basis of similarities with the Iddi(n)-Sîn inscription at Bitwata (Frayne 1990:712; Shaffer et al. 2003:21–22 Table 1; Walker 1985:188–190).

Sar-e Pol-e Zohab II (Börker-Klähn 1982:No. 31, 138–139) is located about 200 m from Sar-e Pol-e Zohab I on the other side of the river (Figure 6.7). The life-size relief is carved ca. 30 m above the modern Baghdad-Hamadan road and close to a major bitumen source. Against a flattened surface, another triumphant—but this time bearded—male is depicted wearing a short skirt, sandals, and a roll-brimmed hat and holding a bow and battleaxe. He is stepping on a fallen, pleading bearded enemy. Opposite the male warrior stands a female goddess in a long skirt and horned headdress, holding two kneeling captives on a leash. A star symbol hovers between the two main figures. A second register shows a row of six further naked, bound enemies, whose leader appears to wear a feathered crown. An accompanying inscription reads, "Anubanini, the mighty king, king of Lullubum, erected a Salam of himself and a Salam of Ištar in the Mountains of Batir," followed by a lengthy curse formula (Frayne 1990:E4.18.1). The dating of the relief, again, ranges from the Akkadian to the Old Babylonian period (Shaffer et al. 2003:51; Börker-Klähn 1982:46), but the newly translated Haladiny inscription suggests a chronological overlap between Iddi(n)-Sîn and Anubanini and a date in the early second millennium B.C. (Ahmed 2012:258).

FIGURE 6.6 Sketch of the rock relief at Sar-e Pol-e Zohab I (after Postgate and Roaf 1995:Figure 6).

Two further reliefs, Sar-e Pol-e Zohab III and IV (Börker-Klähn 1982:No. 34, 140), which are both badly weathered and damaged, depict scenes that closely resemble Sar-e Pol-e Zohab II, except for the headdress of the goddess, the astral symbol, and the clean-shaven hero. There are no accompanying inscriptions and their dating is not agreed upon. Most recently a date in the late Ur III to early Old Babylonian period and a close link with the Iddi(n)-Sîn relief at Bitwata has been proposed on the basis of similarities in the composition and iconographic detail (Shaffer et al. 2003:49–50).

SHAIKHAN/DARBAND-I BALULA

Possibly of a somewhat later second millennium B.C. date is the relief of Shaikhan (Figure 6.8), which was carved high up on a vertical cliff near the entrance of the Darband-i Balula ravine at the southern tip of a mountain range running parallel to the upper Diyala (Börker-Klähn 1982:No. 33; 139–140; Postgate and Roaf 1997). Nearby runs

FIGURE 6.7 Sketch of the rock relief at Sar-e Pol-e Zohab II (after Postgate and Roaf 1995:Figure 7).

the Abassan River, a tributary of the Diyala. From there, the Sar-Kal'ah pass provides access to the Zohab valley of western Iran, where the rock reliefs of Sar-e Pol-e Zohab are located and the Khorasan highway leads on to the Iranian plateau and beyond. With less than one square meter in size (89 x 83 cm) and hewn into the rock high above the bottom of the Darband-i Balula ravine, the visibility of this rock carving is, at least at present, very low (see especially photographs by Postgate and Roaf 1997:Pl. 1a, b and d).

Depicted in low relief and in about half life-size is a male figure in triumphal pose, treading on one pleading adversary and facing another kneeling figure. The figure holds a bow in his left hand, a dagger in his right, and an axe is stuck in his belt. A quiver is standing behind the figure. He wears a short skirt, a cape with marked fillet, and a necklace with a large round pendant as well as an earring in his right ear. He is clean-shaven. The figure stands facing northwest toward the entrance of the ravine (Postgate and Roaf 1997:146).

FIGURE 6.8 Sketch of the rock relief at Shaikhan (after Postgate and Roaf 1995: Figure 4).

The three figures are cut into a hard limestone surface, with minimal surface preparation, and in low relief (Börker-Klähn 1982:141). To the left of the figures is a cuneiform inscription arranged in vertical panels, which is generally thought to be contemporary with the depiction (Postgate and Roaf 1997:149; contra Herzfeld 1968:156). Fragments of the names of a ruler and his father can be reconstructed, and that the relief was carved in commemoration of a military victory. Dates proposed for the monument range from the Akkadian to the Middle Babylonian periods, but most seem to favor a later date on the basis of iconography and style as well as the palaeography of the inscription (Börker-Klähn 1982:139–140; Faber 1975; Postgate and Roaf 1997:149). Although similar in theme to many of the other reliefs, the proportions of the depicted ruler are different and mistakes or idiosyncrasies in the inscription seem to point toward less-skilled scribal expertise or a stone mason unfamiliar with the genre and its local conventions.

Summary and Discussion

Landscape as a social space is produced and altered, among many other practices, through the construction of monuments, which either deliberately transform the very landscapes in which they are built or attempt to do so through representation and reimagination. All social landscapes are subject to continuous change, but political ones in particular can be transformed at a very fast pace, as practices of political authority—particularly in early complex societies—provide ample opportunity for power to be contested. Monument production is one means by which such authority is produced as well as challenged.

Monuments as costly signals are honest in that the political strength projected by a monument is directly related to its patron's social standing and economic wealth and the ability to assemble the necessary labor force, crafts expertise, and specialist knowledge to mount or carve a monument. As a primary means of communication rather than commemoration, monument construction implies an ongoing political contest, not its conclusion, as is often proposed. Evidence from later periods in the ancient Near Eastern, as well as cross-cultural evidence, suggests that the location of monument display is closely related to the spatial scale of the political contest (see Glatz and Plourde 2011 for a more detailed outline of this model). The aim of this chapter was to investigate this proposition on the basis of the earliest public monumental representations of landscapes and landscape monuments in the ancient Near East.

The first attestations of large-scale politically motivated depictive monuments are associated with the rulers of south Mesopotamian city-states during a time when intercity conflict and competition reached a temporary apex beginning in the mid-third millennium B.C. At this time, military victories over neighboring city-states were narrated and depicted on free-standing stele. The political centralization of south Mesopotamia under Akkadian rule, and the expansion of Akkad's influence beyond the familiar alluvial landscapes, sees the beginning of a new awareness of distant people and landscapes and the harnessing of this knowledge in an incipient colonial discourse of distance and difference. The degree of integration of the Akkadian polity is disputed, as is the spatial extent of its effective control. Evidence for Akkadian rule over the western Zagros region, where Naram Sîn sets his victory of the Lullubi on his stele, is scant, and Akkad's grip on regions beyond the mid-Diyala area was loose at best. Niqqum—probably near the modern town of Khanaquin—was ruled by a certain Karšum, who called himself "governor of Niqqum, his [Naram-Sîn's] servant," in an inscription on a mace-head (Frayne 1993:167–178, E2.1.4.2005, E2.1.4.2006). What is clear, however, is that the Akkadian military forays into distant regions resulted in the acquisition of new knowledge of distant people and landscapes, which are represented on the Naram Sîn stele. The Naram Sîn stele was originally displayed at the Mesopotamian city of Sippar, and its primary target audience would have been a local, Mesopotamian one, in particular, other elite competitors that needed to be persuaded of Naram Sîn's new role as divine sovereign. The knowledge of a particular alien landscape and people in this sense forms part of the costliness of the signal of military and political strength being conveyed, one that underscores Naram Sîn's expansive territorial aspirations as the "King of the Four Quarters" (Gelb and Kineast 1990:NSin3, C1, C4, C5).

Monumental display in the landscape in the form of reliefs carved on the living rock at locations that hold political, economic, and symbolic significance first emerge in the western Zagros region probably during the late third millennium, but flourish as a means of political contest in the early second millennium B.C. Beyond the geographical link that exists between the scene depicted on the Naram Sîn stele and the region where landscape monuments first emerge, there is also a clear thematic connection in the depiction of the triumphant royal hero. Traditionally, this has been interpreted as lowland Mesopotamian cultural and artistic influence extending into the Zagros. The reliefs of Zagros rulers have tended to be assessed according to how successful the purported Mesopotamian prototype(s) is/are imitated (e.g., Börker-Klähn 1982:44, 138; Westenholz 2000:108–110). Derivations from what is considered the (Mesopotamian) aesthetic ideal are described as "wooden and lifeless" (Edmonds 1928:162) or *"provinziell-rustikal"* (Hrouda 1976 cf. Börker-Klähn 1982:139) and thought to be indicative of a local stonemason unfamiliar with the standard conventions and techniques of Mesopotamian sculpture and inscription (Postagte and Roaf 1997:149). Whether or not the Naram Sîn stele inspired the Zagros monuments or whether Darband-i Gawra may in fact predate it are questions that are, without further evidence, impossible to answer. What we can say about them is that both types of monuments were born out of historically specific lowland-highland relationships on the one hand as well as competitive political climates in each of the two regions on the other. This interaction expanded the mental and political geographies of Akkadian rulers. Akkadian, and later Mesopotamian, military forays into the western Zagros and brief episodes of lowland control over parts of the region, local responses to this external threat, as well as intraregional political competition, are the geopolitical backdrop against which we see the emergence of monuments that claim hegemony over the very landscapes which they transform.

The geographical area defined by the Zagros reliefs measures about 20,000 km^2, a size equivalent to modern Slovenia or Israel, and a rather small region when compared to the over 100,000 km^2 interaction sphere encircled by the majority of Late Bronze Age landscape monuments in central Anatolia or the even larger Neo-Assyrian interaction sphere. In comparison to the traditional territories of Mesopotamian city-states, which range around 3,000 km^2 (e.g. Yoffee 2005:57), however, the sphere of interaction defined by the Zagros monuments is rather large. Although it is evident from accompanying inscriptions and the repeated placement of monuments by local rulers near those of their competitors that the Zagros reliefs formed part of an ongoing regional contest of local potentates, their standard depictive theme and Akkadian inscriptions would have made them easily comprehensible to a potentially hostile lowland audience interested in expanding their control over the Khorasan highway and into the fertile Sharezor and Rania plains. Following this spatial logic though, we would expect to see at least some Akkadian landscape monuments, given the expanded geographical sphere of their military and political interaction. A lack of natural rock faces onto which images and inscriptions could be carved is one persuasive reason. But it would seem that rather than concerned with external competition, monument construction was part of an internal

Mesopotamian discourse of manifesting and legitimizing, in the case of Akkadian rulers especially, a new centralized state and divine kingship, among its own elite and the formerly independent city-states.

There is a significant overlap in the themes depicted, image composition, and iconographic detail (see Postgate and Roaf 1997:Fig. 10 for a comparative summary), as well as the content and style of accompanying inscriptions (Shaffer et al. 2003:Table 1) among the western Zagros reliefs. This suggests that landscape monuments were a well-established and successful, that is, long-lived, practice of communication among the rulers of the western Zagros and their southern neighbors.

Differences in iconographic detail suggest the participation of several different Zagros rulers, each depicted with signs of subtle cultural differences and temporary fashions, such as a bracelet or necklace, a beard or clean-shaven, the depiction and/or mention of a deity or divine force. The presence or absence of accompanying inscriptions, as well as the skill displayed by the stonemasons who carved the monuments, moreover, point to differential access to knowledge and skilled craftsmen by different monument patrons. While precise dating remains difficult to reconstruct, it is likely that we are dealing with several generations of Zagros rulers who engaged in monument construction. The four adjacent carvings at Sar-e Pol-e Zohab further support this assumption. The adding of reliefs to already significant places with existing monuments attests to several episodes of monument construction, each drawing further on the cultural and symbolic significance of an already highly significant place as well as a historic consciousness of those making their marks on adjacent rock faces. Curse formulae directed toward anyone who damages a monument conclude most accompanying inscriptions. The often lengthy lists of misfortunes that would befall anyone who dared to erase the image would suggest that active, if undesired, engagement with such monuments was to be expected or at least a distinct possibility. Recent suggestions to bring the reliefs of Bitwata and Sar-e Pol-e Zohab in close chronological association and evidence for a partial overlap of Iddi(n)-Sîn of Simurrum and Anubanini of Lulubum (Ahmed 2012:258; Frayne 1990; Shaffer 2003:21–22, 49–50) point to an apogee of monument construction toward the end of the Ur III and the early Old Babylonian period, when pressure from the south gradually ebbed off and local polities entered into intensive conflict and competition with each other.

Many of the landscape monuments are not especially large in size nor are they necessarily carved in highly visible locations above, for instance, important communication routes (although some are). It is possible that some or all reliefs were painted in bright colors to enhance their visibility, such as in the case of Neo-Assyrian or Achaemenid reliefs (e.g., Ambers and Simpson 2005; Verri et al. 2009). High visibility, however, to passers-by may or may not have been an important variable in monument function. Monument production events are highly visible occasions, often accompanied by work parties and ceremonies, which would have ensured the creation of common memories of the monument and its patron (e.g., Harmanşah 2007; Shaffer 2007) and the subsequent spread of its news. It is such practice of place that would have ensured that elite competitors were aware of the monument and its message of territorial hegemony.

In recent discourse, the distribution of rock reliefs and stele has been used to define political borders. Drawing on later Neo-Assyrian practices, the Zagros rock reliefs have recently been proposed to represent the end points of military campaigns and mark out the territory of particularly Simurrum (Altaweel et al. 2012), or at least the region over which its king(s) claimed hegemony (Shaffer et al. 2003:28). With monuments the media in an ongoing political contest, the latter scenario is more likely to be the case. Darband-i Gawra, the reliefs of the king(s) of Simurrum, their competitor Anubanini of Lullubum, and that of Shaikhan represent claims over strategic, and therefore contested, landscapes, which may have changed political hands frequently. The reliefs, therefore, define only in very general terms and in the case of each monument for a limited period of time only, the course of political boundaries.

CONCLUSION

In this chapter, I have argued that an expanded geographical sphere of military and political interaction leads to a heightened awareness of distant landscapes and people on the one hand, and the engagement in strategies of political (re)production, such as monument construction, on an enlarged spatial scale of interaction on the other. The origins of both landscape representations and monumental display in landscape settings first developed in the late third and early second millennium B.C. in Mesopotamia and the western Zagros region. The historical contexts of these developments were an unprecedented centralization and territorial expansion that transformed the political landscape of southern Mesopotamia and brought the western Zagros into a more intensive military and political relationship with the lowland plains. An expanded mental geography is evident from Akkadian artistic engagement with landscape, especially distant, undomesticated landscapes outside the Mesopotamian realm that are used in an internal, urban, lowland discourse of authority and legitimacy. The rock reliefs of the Zagros region, on the other hand, attest to a primarily intraregional political contest over strategic boundaries and communication routes in which several generations of Zagros rulers took part and which was at least partially influenced by lowland pressures and oscillating control over the region.

ACKNOWLEDGEMENTS

I would like to thank James Osborne for inviting me to a most interesting workshop on monumentality, which provided fertile ground for the development of this paper. I am also indebted to Stephanie Langin-Hooper for her insightful suggestions concerning the dating of some of the Zagros reliefs. All errors are of course my own.

NOTE

1.   I would like to thank Stephanie Langin-Hooper for pointing out this possibility (personal communication 2012).

References Cited

Adams, Robert McC., and Hans J. Nissen 1972 *The Uruk Countryside. The Natural Setting of Urban Societies.* University of Chicago Press, Chicago.

Ahmed, Kozad M. 2012 *The Beginnings of Ancient Kurdistan (c. 2500–1500 BC): A Historical and Cultural Synthesis.* PhD thesis, Leiden University, Leiden.

Albenda, Pauline 1983 A Mediterranean Seascape from Khorsabad. *Assur* 3(3). Undena, Malibu.

Al-Fouadi, Abdul-Hadi 1978 Inscriptions and reliefs from Bitwata. *Sumer* 34:122–129.

Ambers, Janet C., and St. John Simpson 2005 Some Pigment Identifications for Objects from Persepolis. Arta2005.002:1–13. (http://www.achemenet.com/ressources/enligne/arta/pdf/2005.002-Ambers-Simpson.pdf last accessed 14 September 2012).

Altaweel, Mark, Anke Marsh, Simone Mühl, Olivier Nieuwenhuyse, Karen Radner, Kamal Rasheed, and Saber Ahmed Saber 2012 New Investigations in the Iraqi Hilly Flanks: Environment, Archaeology, and History of the Shahrizor Iraq (forthcoming).

Bahrani, Zainab 2003 *The Graven Image: Representation in Babylonia and Assyria.* University of Pennsylvania Press, Philadelphia.

Bahrani, Zainab 2008 *Rituals of War: The Body and Violence in Mesopotamia.* Zone Books, New York.

Bliege Bird, Rebecca, and Eric A. Smith 2005 Signaling Theory, Strategic Interaction, and Symbolic Capital. *Current Anthropology* 46(2):221–248.

Boese, Johannes 1973 Zur stilistischen und historischen Einordnung des Felsreliefs von Darband-i-Gaur. *Studia Iranica* 2:3–48.

Börker-Klähn, J. 1982. *Altvorderasiatische Bildstelen und vergleichbare Felsreliefs.* Band I-II. Baghdader Forschungen 4. Philip von Zabern, Mainz.

Cooper, Jerrold 1990 Mesopotamian Historical Consciousness and the Production of Monumental Art in the Third Millennium B.C. In *Investigating Artistic Environments in the Ancient Near East*, edited by Anne Gunter, pp. 39–51. Smithsonian Institution Press, Washington D.C.

Edmonds, Cecil J. 1928 Two More Ancient Monuments in Southern Kurdistan. *Geographical Journal* 72:162–163.

Faber, Walter 1975 Zur Datierung der Felsinschrift von Šaih-Han. *Archäologische Mitteilungen aus Iran* NF 8:47–50.

Fincke, Jeanette 1993 *Die Orts- und Gewässernamen der Nuzi-Texte.* Répertoire géographique des textes cuneiforms 10. Reichert, Wiesbaden.

Foster, Benjamin, A. 1985. The Sargonic Victory Stele from Telloh. *Iraq* 47:15–30.

Foucault, Michel 1978 *The History of Sexuality, Vol. 1 An Introduction.* Translated by Robert Hurley. Penguin, London.

Foucault, Michel 1980 Truth and Power. *Power/Knowledge.* Harvester, Brighton, Sussex.

Frayne, Douglas, R. 1990 *Old Babylonian Period (2003–1595 BC).* The Royal Inscriptions of Mesopotamia: Early Periods 4. University of Toronto Press, Toronto.

Frayne, Douglas, R. 1993 *Sargonic and Gutian Periods (2334–2113 BC).* The Royal Inscriptions of Mesopotamia: Early Periods 2. University of Toronto Press, Toronto.

Frayne, Douglas, R. 1997 On the Location of Simurrum. In *Crossing Boundaries and Linking Horizons: Studies in Honor of Michael C. Astour*, edited by Gordon D. Young, Mark W. Chavalas, and Richard E. Averbeck, pp. 243–269. CDL Press, Bethesda.

Frayne, Douglas, R. 2011 Simurrum. *Reallexikon der Assyriologie und vorderasiatischen Archäologie* 12(7–8):508–511.

Gelb, Ignace J., and Burkhart Kienast 1990 *Die altakkadischen Königsinschriften des dritten Jahrtausends v. Chr.* Freiburger altorientalische Studien 7. Steiner, Stuttgart.

Glatz, Claudia, and Aimée Plourde 2011 Landscape Monuments and Political Competition in Late Bronze Age Anatolia: An Investigation of Costly Signaling Theory. *Bulletin of the American Schools of Oriental Research* 361:33–66.

Hansen, Donald P. 2003 Art of the Akkadian Dynasty. In *Art of the First Cities. The Third Millennium B.C. from the Mediterranean to the Indus,* edited by Joan Aruz and Ronald Wallenfels, pp. 189–233. Metropolitan Museum of Art and Yale University Press, New York and New Haven.

Harmanşah, Ömur 2007 "Source of the Tigris." Event, place, and performance in the Assyrian landscapes of the Early Iron Age. *Archaeological Dialogues* 14(2):179–204.

Harmanşah, Ömur 2012 Beyond Aššur: New Cities and the Assyrian Politics of Landscape. *Bulletin of the American Schools of Oriental Research* 365:53–77.

Herzfeld, Ernst E. 1968 *The Persian Empire: Studies in the Geography and Ethnography of the Ancient Near East.* Steiner, Wiesbaden.

Hrouda, Barthel, and Leo Trümpelmann 1976 *Iranische Denkmäler, Lieferung 7 C. Sarpol-i Zohab. Die Felsreliefs I–IV, Das Parthische Felsrelief.* Reimer, Berlin.

Huot, Jean-Louis 2004 *Une archéologie des peuples du Proche-Orient,* vol. 1. Paris: Errance.

Kantor, Helen J. 1966. Landscape in Akkadian Art. *Journal of Near Eastern Studies* 25(3):145–152.

Kuhrt, Amélie 1995. *The Ancient Near East ca. 3000–330 BC.* Volume 1. Routledge, London.

Lefebvre, Henri 1991 *The Production of Space.* Translated by Donald Nicholson-Smith. Blackwell, Oxford.

McLuhan, Marshall 1964 *Understanding Media: The Extensions of Man.* McGraw-Hill, New York.

Meek, Theophile J. 1935 *Old Akkadian, Sumerian and Cappadocian Texts from Nuzi.* Excavations at Nuzi 3. Harvard University Press, Cambridge.

Mitchell, W. J. T. 2002. Imperial Landscape. In *Landscape and Power,* edited by W. J. T. Mitchell, pp. 5–34. University of Chicago Press, Chicago.

Morrison, Kathleen D., and Mark Lycett 1994. Central Power, Centralized Authority? Ideological Claims and Archaeological Patterns. *Asian Perspectives* 33:327–350.

Neiman, Fraser 1997 Conspicuous Consumption as Wasteful Advertising: A Darwinian Perspective on Spatial Patterns in Classic Maya Terminal Monument Dates. *Archeological Papers of the American Anthropological Association* 7:267–90.

Pollinger Forstner, K. 1998. Gardens of Eden: Exotic Flora and Fauna in the Ancient Near East. In *Transformations of Middle Eastern Environments: Legacies and Lessons,* edited by Jeff Albert, Magnus Bernhardsson, and Roger Kenna, pp. 320–329. Bulletin of the Yale School of Forestry and Environmental Studies 103. New Haven.

Pollock, Susan 1999 *Ancient Mesopotamia: The Eden that Never Was.* Cambridge University Press, Cambridge.

Postgate, J. Nicholas, and Michael D. Roaf 1997 The Shaikhan Relief. *Al-Rafidan* 18:143–156.

Potts, Daniel 1999 *The Archaeology of Elam. Formation and Transformation of an Ancient Iranian State.* Cambridge University Press, Cambridge.

Ristvet, Lauren 2007 The Third Millennium City Wall at Tell Leilan, Syria: Identity, Authority, and Urbanism. In *Power and Architecture: Monumental Public Architecture in the Bronze Age Near East and Aegean,* edited by Joachim Bretschneider, Jan Driessen, and Karel V. Lerberghe, pp. 183–211. Peeters, Leuven.

Said, Edward 1978 *Orientalism.* Vintage Books, New York.

Sallaberger, Walther 1999 Ur III-Zeit. In *Mesopotamien: Akkade und Ur III-Zeit*, edited by Walther Sallaberger and Aage Westenholz, pp. 121–390. Orbus Biblicus et Oriemtalis 160/3. Universitätsverlag, Vandenhoeck and Ruprecht, Fribourg and Göttingen.

Shafer, Ann 2007 Assyrian Royal Monuments on the Periphery: Ritual and the Making of Imperial Space. In *Ancient Near Eastern Art in Context. Studies in Honor of Irene J. Winter by Her Students*, edited by Jack Cheng and Marian H. Feldman, pp. 133–153. Brill, Leiden.

Shaffer, Aaron, Nathan Wasserman, and Ursula Seidl 2003 Iddi(n)-Sîn, King of Simurrum. A New Rock-Relief Inscription and a Reverential Seal. *Zeitschrift für Assyriologie und Vorderasiatische Archäologie* 93:1–52.

Seidl, Ursula 1986 *Die elamischen Felsreliefs von Kurangun und Naqs-e Rustam*. Iranische Denkmaler, II 12. Reichert, Berlin.

Smith, Adam T. 2003 *The Political Landscape. Constellations of Authority in Early Complex Polities*. University of California Press, Berkeley.

Stone, Elisabeth 1995 The Development of Cities in Ancient Mesopotamia. In *Civilisations of the Ancient Near East*, edited by Jack Sassson, pp. 235–248. Scribners, New York.

Strommenger, Eva 1962 *Fünf Jahrtausende Mesopotamien: die Kunst von den Anfängen um 5000 v. Chr. bis zu Alexander dem Grossen*. Hirmer, München.

Strommenger, Eva 1963 Das Relief von Darband-i Gawr. *Baghdader Mitteilungen* 2:83–88.

Stronach, David 1990 The Garden as Political Statement: Some Case Studies from the Near East in the First Millennium BC. *Bulletin of the Asia Institute* 4:171–180.

Thomason, Allison K. 2001 Representations of the North Syrian Landscape in Neo-Assyrian Art. *Bulletin of the American Schools of Oriental Research* 323:63–96.

Trigger, Bruce 1990 Monumental Architecture: A Thermodynamic Explanation of Symbolic Behaviour. *World Archaeology* 22: 119–132.

Walker, Marcie F. 1985 *The Tigris Frontier from Sargon to Hammurabi. A Philologic and Historical Synthesis*. Unpublished PhD thesis. Yale University, New Haven.

Westenholz, Aage 1999 The Old Akkadian Period, History and Culture. In *Mesopotamian, Akkade-Zeit und UrIII-Zeit*, edited by Walther Sallaberger and Aage Westenholz, pp. 17–117. Orbus Biblicus et Oriemtalis 160/3. Universitätsverlag, Vandenhoeck and Ruprecht, Fribourg and Göttingen.

Westenholz, Joan 2000 The King, the Emperor, and the Empire. Continuity and Discontinuity of Royal Representation in Text and Image. In *The Heirs of Assyria. Proceedings of the Opening Symposium of the Assyrian and Babylonian Intellectual Heritage Project. Held in Tvärminne, Finland, October 8–11, 1998*, edited by Sanno Aro and R. M. Whiting, pp. 99–125. The Neo-Assyrian Text Corpus Project 2000, Helsinki. Publisher: http://www.helsinki.fi/science/saa/ (last accessed 12 September 2012).

Wiseman, Donald J. 1983 Mesopotamian Gardens. *Anatolian Studies* 33:137–144.

Winter, Irene J. 1985 After the Battle is Over: The Stele of the Vultures and the Beginning of Historical Narrative in the Art of the Ancient Near East. In *Pictorial Narrative in Antiquity and the Middle Ages*, edited by Herbert Kessler and Marianna Shreve Simpson, pp. 11–32. National Gallery of Art, Washington, D.C.

Winter, Irene J. 1999. Tree(s) on the Mountain: Landscape and Territory on the Victory Stele of Naram-Sîn n of Agade. In *Landscapes: Territories, Frontiers, and Horizons in the Ancient Near East, Papers Presented to the XLIVe Rencontre Assyriologique Internationale, Venezia 7–11 July 1997*, edited by L. Milano, S. de Martina, T.M. Fales, and G.B. Lafranchi, pp. 63–72. Sargon, Padua.

Verri, Giovanni, Paul Collins, Janet Ambers, Tracey Sweek, and St. John Simpson 2009 Assyrian Colours: Pigments on a Neo-Assyrian Relief of a Parade Horse. *The British Museum Technical Research Bulletin* 3:57–62.

Yoffee, Norman 2005 The Myth of the Archaic State. Evolution of the Earliest Cities, States, and Civilisations. Cambridge University Press, Cambridge.

CHAPTER SEVEN

Roman Soliloquies

Monumental Interventions in the Vacant Landscape
in the Late Republic and Early Empire

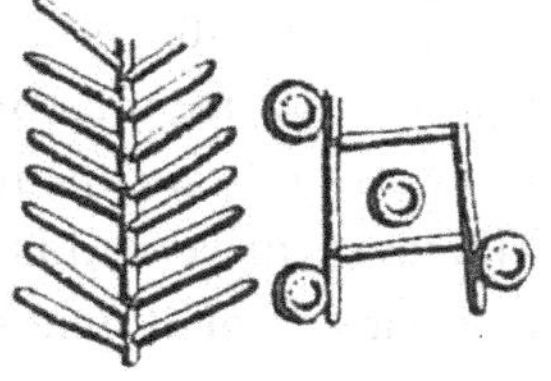

Álvaro Ibarra

Abstract *Roman monuments are laden with symbolic importance. They manipulated both the landscape and its inhabitants. We can decipher the transactions between powerful patrons and audiences in a place such as ancient Rome. But what is the function of a marginally Roman monument in the provinces? And, more important, what purpose does a monument erected in the vacant provincial landscape fulfill? This chapter examines Roman trophy monuments as examples of commemorative structures virtually devoid of an audience. There were no urban centers of significant population at or near these structures and the limited number of provincials that did behold the trophies could not decode the monuments' meaning beyond the most overt message, that of Rome's dominance. Moreover, the styles and narratives found on provincial trophies are fragmentary representations of Roman ideals, such that Romans from the capital would also be hard-pressed to read the trophy successfully. Rather than critique the trophies for falling short of some centralized Roman standard or celebrate the hybrid structure as a monument to provincial negotiation, I suggest that trophies are at once the manifestation of the convergence of utopian visions and the disruption of the utopian fantasy. In this way, provincial trophy monuments are radical performance pieces that expose the imaginary community invoked by its outward Roman appearance.*

ALL MONUMENTS ARE SIGNS

The modern and postmodern debates concerning monuments and public art largely consider the changing value placed on certain architectonic forms and the rituals and traditions associated with these constructions. The various arguments about the production and reception of monuments can be summarized by acknowledging that all monuments are—first and foremost—signs. They are proxies for an intangible referent. In the context of Roman studies, the referent is an extinct civilization, or at least the idea of that civilization, that lingers in the existence of the various signage that survives today. Ideas, like civilizations, are fleeting, transient, and prone to change. Knowing the geographical and historical specificity of Rome helps to crystallize ancient referents to the modern viewer, especially when considering monuments in the capital. However, Roman provincial art and architecture presents deviant signs, invoking countless versions and visions of Rome.

Predictably, scholars analyzing new archaeological and epigraphic evidence and applying recent postcolonial ethnocultural theories produce divergent, yet valid, interpretations of Rome in the provinces. This recent scholarly trend proposes a negotiation between Romans and non-Romans, one that uses material culture as a significant mediator in the process of acculturation (Hales and Hodos 2010). Moreover, newer studies consider both the Romanization of provincials as well as the "nativization" of Romans. Manifestations of Rome in the provinces are limitless and the readings of any given Roman monument are manifold. Although I retain the conviction that Roman provincial artworks indeed served as vehicles for cultural exchange, I also believe that the initial motivation for certain works was singular—the product of highly specified signs constructed by Roman elites for Roman elites. One such example is the Roman trophy monument.

The Romans and Greeks erected battlefield trophies that consisted of an upright stake, log, or even a tall tree stump, anthropomorphized with a helmet, cuirass, grieves, and weapons of the victor. A pile of enemy armor helped secure the armored scarecrow in place (Charles-Picard 1957; Hölscher 2006; Pritchett 1974) (Figure 7.1). The Romans perpetuated this temporary symbol of victory by constructing stone versions of the battlefield trophy placed atop large stone structures. The structure served to elevate the battlefield trophy over the provincial landscape using various architectural forms, including drums, rectilinear bases, columns, and arches. Its elaborate façade contained inscriptions and images that communicated the monument's commemorative intent.

Both temporary and permanent trophies marked the spot of a Roman triumph, often at the very place where the tide turned in Rome's favor. They also identified the location where hundreds or thousands of soldiers fell in a given battle. In this way, the trophy was at once triumphal and funerary. It is likely that the raising of a temporary battlefield trophy was a common practice throughout the Republican and early Imperial Age given the ubiquity of representations in Roman sculpture, architecture, and coins. But the Romans did not commemorate every victory with a permanent trophy monument. Despite the tremendous amount of information concerning Rome's military exploits and references to honorific structures, there are only nine commemorations that called for trophy monuments mentioned in ancient accounts and only five verified through archaeological remains.

The earliest was dedicated by Cn. Domitius Ahenobarbus and Fabius Quintus Amelianus in Aquitania in 121 B.C. for conquering the Arveni and Allobrogi (Strab. 4.1.11).

FIGURE 7.1 Typical battlefield trophy construction (drawing: Álvaro Ibarra).

Sulla erected two monuments at Chaeroneia in 86 B.C. after defeating Mithridates's wily general, Archelaus (App. *Mith.* 45; Paus. 9.40.7–8; Plut. *Sull.* 19). Pompey raised two trophies at Panissars in 71 B.C. for his double victory over rioting tribes in southern Gaul and Sertorius in Spain (DioCass. 41.24; Pliny. *Nat.* 3.3.18; Sal. *Hist.* 3.89; Strab. 3.4.1). Caesar built a monumental trophy at Zela in 47 B.C. after defeating the Pontic king, Pharnakes (DioCass. 42.48). Octavian constructed a massive trophy complex at Nikopolis in 29 B.C. overlooking the Actian Bay (DioCass. 51.1–3). Two trophy monuments are associated with Augustus's Alpine Wars (16–9 B.C.). Drusus raised trophies in northern Germany on the banks of the Elbe around 9 B.C. (DioCass. 55.1.2–5). Augustus dedicated his Alpine Trophy in present-day La Turbie at the conclusion of the Alpine Wars between 7 and 5 B.C. (Plin. *Nat.* 3.136–138). Trajan erected the last known trophy in present-day Adamklissi in A.D. 109 in honor of winning the Dacian Wars, fought between A.D. 101–102 and 105–106. There is no ancient account describing the Adamklissi monument structure as a *tropaeum*; the attribution is based on the formal qualities of the monument and its dedicatory inscription.

Only five of these survive in various states of ruin: those at Chaeroneia, Panissars, Nikopolis, La Turbie, and Adamklissi.

The formal qualities of early trophy monuments were not static. Builders used any number of architectural forms to elevate the petrified battlefield trophy. Ultimately, only ancient texts can definitively distinguish a trophy or *tropaeum* from other monuments such as arches, altars, columns, or cenotaphs. It is the ancient Greek and Roman historian that also provides the necessary signifiers that help us understand the commemorative intent of the trophy—one that originates in the actions and desires of a conquering general or emperor. Inscriptions are also helpful for interpreting the intended message, but no surviving dedication contains the word *tropaeum*.

Various ancient sources relate the criteria for *tropaia,* commonalities shared by almost all eight trophies (Pritchett 1974:252–262).[1] First, victors raised trophies at the conclusion of a successful campaign or even after a significant battle, oftentimes overlooking battlefields. They were appropriate for battles punctuated by a significant loss of life. The locations were often boundaries, liminal areas between one province and another, land and sea, life and death. The trophy commemorated victory, memorialized fallen soldiers, and honored the gods. Once built, the trophy was inviolable regardless of its patron. In one famous example, Caesar built larger trophies adjacent to those previously erected by Mithridates at Zela rather than destroy them (Cass.Dio. 42.48).

Tropaeia were a provincial phenomenon. No trophy monuments were ever erected in Rome, although representations of battlefield trophies abound in friezes and architectural sculptures decorating buildings throughout the city. They were stamped on the coinage that circulated in the capital and likely painted on the frescoed walls of elite homes. However, ancient writers fail to name any structure decorated with petrified trophies as a *tropaeum*. In Rome, these remain arches, columns, fora, basilicas, et cetera. The same commemorative intent that transforms a structure into a *tropaeum* in the provincial landscape makes a trophy monument inappropriate in Rome.

Many scholars surmise that *tropaia* were straightforward, overt statements of power and dominance (Hölscher 2006:34–37). They were visual warnings against further rebellion sent by the conquerors to the conquered. The depictions of graphic violence on the Adamklissi monument, for example, surely communicated conquest and served to dissuade would-be rebels (Figure 7.2). However, the remaining visual and textual program on this and other trophies eluded the local population, one that did not read Latin and did not subscribe to Roman iconography. If anything, the patchwork presentation relayed an arbitrary sense of historical circumstance for locals, not a deterministic sense of fated *imperium*. The more specialized and specific messages on trophies, such as representations of Roman generals and textual dedications to Roman gods, were largely meaningful to the structures' elite patrons.

Roman trophies were fanciful constructions, manifestations of a fictitious conceit of Rome's imperial legacy (Forster 1998:18–35).[2] Close examination of imperial narratives reveals Roman patriarchs' concern for establishing continuity for Roman prominence. It is a history that begins with the Trojan War and the near-eradication of Rome at its

FIGURE 7.2 Metope 25, *Tropaeum Traiani* (photo: Álvaro Ibarra).

very inception. Luckily, Aeneas escaped the sacking of Troy and went on to establish the regal bloodline of Romulus, Remus, and all Romans. Rome's rise to prominence was a self-fulfilling prophecy. In particular, the conquest of Greece was justified as revenge for the Trojan War. During his visit to Troy in A.D. 18, the younger Drusus spoke to Hektor as an avenging heir, a statement that implies his direct lineage (*Ant.Lat.* 708). Drusus and the rest of the Julio-Claudians have direct, even genealogical, connections to these Homeric heroes, more so than any other Roman. The legacy of empire stretched from the past through the Republican and Imperial Age into the unknown future. The concept of *imperium sine fine* (Verg. *Aen.* 1.278), "empire without end," was temporal as well as territorial (Nicolet 1991:29).

In the provinces, elite Roman patrons spoke to each other in the past, present, and future through their actions and their monuments. This is evidenced, in part, in the Roman practice of the grand tour, a more elaborate form of pilgrimage practiced by the Julio-Claudian family. While Rome's ambition was infinite, her history was finite. Early Republican elites spoke to their perceived ancestors such as Aeneas and compared themselves to venerated historical figures like Alexander the Great. During the Republic, Romans such as Lucius Aemilius Paullus visited the oracle of Delphi and even modified a local Macedonian monument to communicate Roman victory after the Battle of Pydna in 168 B.C. (Plut. *Aem.* 28). Similarly, Sulla saw the Pythian oracle before his victory over Mithridates at Chaeroneia in 86 B.C. (Plut. *Sull.* 12). Both pilgrimages led to Roman victories that were recognized by the gods, a celestial sanctioning of Rome's destiny. In turn, Julius Caesar and Augustus manipulated foreign exaltations of Roman dominance into personal symbols of their absolute authority (Zanker 1990).

After defeating Marc Antony and Cleopatra at the Battle of Actium, Augustus (then called Octavian) took a four-year grand tour of his empire between 31 and 27 B.C. Octavian famously visited Alexander the Great's tomb in Alexandria, echoing Alexander's own visit to the tomb of Achilles (DioCass. 51.16). Octavian populated Troy with veterans after the Battle of Philippi in 42 B.C. and finally visited in 20 B.C., in imitation of his adoptive father's own pilgrimage in 48 B.C. (Luc. 9.954–999).

The young emperor also viewed the Mausoleum of Halicarnassus, deemed one of the seven wonders of the ancient world by Antipater of Sidon (*Anth.Pal.* 9.58). Antipater's poem was in circulation in the late second century B.C. and would have been known to as erudite an individual as Octavian. This designation would make it worth drawing Octavian to the tomb of a relatively unimportant Persian satrap.

Alexander's and Mausolus's tombs both influenced the design for Augustus's own mausoleum in Rome (Nicolet 1991:16). Octavian made sure his achievements would be compared to those of Caesar, Alexander, Aeneas, and Achilles via pilgrimage, achievements perpetuated through the monuments he left in Troy (Ilium) and Nikopolis, and, finally, eloquently reformulated in the monumental tomb raised in the Campus Martius (Tac. *Ann.* 2.54). The Mausoleum of Augustus communicated the emperor's autocratic role to fellow patricians and introduced hereditary succession for this new office in Roman politics (Davies 2001:49–74).

The Augustan mausoleum became the model for imperial trophies, specifically the Alpine Trophy at La Turbie and the Adamklissi Monument in Romania. All three multitiered structures possess a stepped base, a drum, and a conical roof that serve to elevate the armored mannequin to great heights. All three are massive constructions designed to dwarf onlookers. All three speak to Julio-Claudian formulations of imperial legacy—evidence of the changing referent.

By comparison, Republican monuments to Roman conquest in the provinces are inconsistent. Conquerors had a myriad of architectural choices for communicating Roman triumph, one of which incorporated the commemorative concept of the *tropaeum*. In considering the archaeological remains of the earliest surviving Republican trophy, the Sullan structure near Chaeroneia, one finds a stepped rectangular base and a vertical platform containing sculpted friezes representing weapons and a dedication naming Sulla (Kountouri 2004).[4] This structure elevated the petrified battlefield trophy to more prominent heights, a small feat in the low-lying areas surrounding the structure's placement on the shores of Lake Copais (Camp, Ierardi, McInerney, Morgan, and Umholz 1992).[5]

Pompey's monument at Panissars is poorly preserved. Only the foundations and a few lower courses of stonework of the building survive (Castellvi, Nolla, and Rodà 1995). The archeological remains suggest either a singular monument bifurcated by a road or two roadside structures. I contend that the structure was an arch surmounted by two battlefield trophies, an elegant solution to ancient authors' use of both singular *tropaeum* and plural *tropaia* to describe Pompey's commemorations (Plin. *Nat.* 3.3.18; Strab. 3.4.1, 3.4.7, and 4.1.3). Although archeologists unearthed no decorative elements, primary accounts relate that the dedication listed the 876 towns Pompey subjugated in Gaul en route to Spain in 75 B.C. (Plin. *Nat.* 7.26.96). Little more is clear.

The most radical trophy monument of the Republican era belongs to Octavian. Caesar's heir commissioned an enormous multitiered structure surmounted by Greek-style *stoa* overlooking Nikopolis and the Bay of Actium (Murray and Petsas 1989; Zachos 2003). The courtyard on the upper tier featured an altar and two monumental statues. Octavian's memorial contained numerous physical trophies that included martial spoils housed in the *stoa* and the 35 bronze *rostra* displayed on the front façade. The commemorative inscription dedicates the monument to Neptune and Mars on behalf of the son of the divine Julius (Murray and Petsas 1989:76).

As noted above, the architectonic forms, decorative embellishments, and Latin inscriptions make the structure recognizably Roman—evidence of Rome's intervention in the alien landscape. The placement of a petrified battlefield trophy atop one of these structures arguably identified the structure as a trophy monument. Republican generals needed little beyond this simple formula. By far, a trophy's location was more important than its specific message.

Republican trophies were all located in prominent places. Sulla's trophies were raised in close proximity to the famous battlefield of Chaeroneia near the city of Thebes, a city that played a significant role in Rome's imaginary history similar to the one played by Troy (Braund 2006). Pompey erected his trophies atop a busy Roman road, the *Via*

Domicia/Augusta. This road cut through the Pyrenees Mountains and connected the provinces of Iberia and Narbonesis, the two areas directly affected by Pompey's victories. Octavian built his *stoa* overlooking his newly founded Nikopolis, a victory city populated through the forced migration of local Greeks. These trophy monuments spoke to a local population in a fairly unsophisticated fashion. Soldiers made locals participate in rituals for state holidays in the shadow of the memorial structure, reiterating the simple yet potent message: *Roma invicta* (Campbell 1994:127–131).

Trophies rarely spoke to other elite Romans, those few that happened upon them in the provinces. On these occasions, the trophy spoke about the developing Republican concept of *imperium.* Although the inscription named the conquering general, the structure ultimately celebrated the greatness of Rome as proven through victory in battle. As ambitious as Sulla, Pompey, and Caesar may have been, victorious generals only served as agents of Rome as communicated in their use of Republican triumphal iconography. For the educated Roman aristocrat, the Republic-era trophy monument was a sign of Roman dominion rather than a sign of one Roman's domination; the referent was a complex conflation of ideas that included the fleeting victorious moment and the perpetual influence of Rome over the world.

Up until the end of the Republic, patrons placed trophy monuments in the most visible locations available, despite the unlikely chance one of their elite Roman compatriots would ever come across the structure. They used various architectonic forms to elevate the panoply. And it communicated only the simplest message of Roman dominance to locals as it simultaneously developed a utopian narrative of Roman *imperium* on the edges of the world. This narrative changed with the ascension of Augustus.

TRANSFORMING TROPHIES IN THE AGE OF AUGUSTUS

Perhaps Augustus's greatest and most lasting achievement was in the realm of propaganda. Specifically, Augustus managed to insert himself into the Roman concept of *imperium.* He blurred the boundary between ruler and empire (a notion echoed seventeen centuries later by Louis XIV when he famously said, "*L'état c'est moi.*") Augustan monuments are not merely commemorations of the emperor's achievements on behalf of Rome; they are testaments to an *imperium* directly achieved through the actions of Augustus. One cannot exist without the other. The Augustus from Primaporta is a prime example of the new regime's combination of ruler, rule, and empire. The statue promises perpetual victory under Augustus's leadership. More specifically, the cuirass presents Augustus's rule as the dawn of a new age marked by Roman superiority that extends from Rome to the provinces and to every corner of the world (Galinsky 1996:156–162; Zanker 1990:188–192). As the founder of this golden age, Augustus conflates *imperium sine fine* and *imperator perpetuus.*

Once he established his autocratic rule, the emperor needed to secure the continuation of the newly created office. As Augustus was not immortal, the perpetuation of the new autocratic position of power also fell to his heirs. Augustus's own concern for continuity is evidenced in the completion of his divine father's works around Rome, actions that connected Augustus to Caesar in a concrete fashion. In securing his place for his heirs, we can cite the presence of the imperial family upon the friezes of the Ara Pacis, the carved likenesses on the *Gemma Augustea,* and—more significantly—the construction of the mausoleum in the Campus Martius, a tomb designed as a glorious receptacle for Augustus and his successors.

However, it was not enough to introduce the concept of hereditary succession in the capital. The Augustan regime also needed to imbed itself in the physical landscape of the empire. One strategy of continuity was to have members of the imperial family behave like Augustus throughout the empire and not merely look like him in official imperial portraiture. This would certainly include their roles as successful generals that helped expand and consolidate Rome's territories. Another significant, but lesser-known, role brings us back to the concept of the Roman grand tour. Male members of the imperial family visited famous sites throughout the empire, locations that were increasingly associated with Caesar and Augustus by chroniclers back in Rome. Pilgrimages by Tiberius, Drusus, and Germanicus occurred in a specific imperial Roman context.

In particular, Germanicus's tour of the eastern Mediterranean in A.D. 18 included Nikopolis, reiterating the importance of the Battle of Actium and hence Augustus's importance. On that same journey, he visited Troy only after stopping in Athens first. Tacitus relates that the Athenians treated Germanicus with great respect in acknowledgment of Rome's greatness. In Troy, Germanicus served as witness to an ancient vengeance that finally came to pass a millennium after the Trojan War, as noted above (Tac. *Ann.* 2.53–54). As a member of the Julio-Claudian family, Germanicus was a direct descendent of Hektor and Aeneas and a particularly appropriate Roman to carry out such a dedication. His pilgrimage was as much to ancient Troy as to the Roman Ilium restored by Augustus in 20 B.C.

After Augustus, Roman pilgrims no longer needed foreign figures, gods, or events as a means to gauge the greatness of Rome. Imperial pilgrims either sought to construct continuity through references to earlier accomplishments by Caesar and/or Augustus or they looked to correct Rome's rare shortcomings around the empire. Two corrected shortcomings included Tiberius recovering the military standards from the Parthians and Drusus erecting a heroic tumulus for those that fell in the Teutoburgian forest.

In addition, the pilgrims' observations abroad functioned to correct misconceptions about the greatness of famous locations that always paled in comparison to Rome. According to Livy, Aemilius Paullus found little to justify Romans' perception of the greatness of Greece based on monuments left behind (Liv. 45.27.5). Monuments in the provinces served as proof of Rome's greatness for future Romans, testaments that the empire would continue its dominance for all time (Woodman 2012).[7] And Rome's greatness was increasingly tied to Julio-Claudian success: *not* leaving glorious monuments would have risked calling doubt upon Rome's greatness in the future.

Similarly, many Julio-Claudian monuments erected in the provinces contain distinctly Julio-Claudian stories—records of family achievements that became difficult to distinguish from narratives of Roman glory. Notably, Drusus the Younger restored a canal built by Drusus the Elder in the Rhineland, a structure destroyed by barbarians in an effort to impede Roman troop movement (Suet. *Claud.* 1.2). The reconstruction served as a powerful manifestation of order restored to a province by a Julio-Claudian, the restoration of dominion first established by a member of the imperial family. As patrons of such monuments, members of the imperial family became the exclusive guardians of the empire at the end of the first century B.C. In this way, all triumphal works in the provinces from this era contain Julio-Claudian narratives—soliloquies that increasingly had little to nothing to do with locals.

One telling example is the triumphal Arch at Orange. The friezes depict various scenes of war, including a naval battle. Although the arch dates to the reign of Augustus, scholars debate whether these friezes reference the Battle of Actium or some other local skirmish (Gros 1979). The latter arguments rely on the insistence that provincial Roman monuments speak to locals in more than just the most overt fashion. But locals only read the significance of yet another Roman structure in their midst, an indication of Rome's permanent presence in Transalpine Gaul. As a Julio-Claudian soliloquy, the Arch at Orange is there to secure the Julio-Claudian legacy in perpetuity.

Tiberius likely restored the arch between A.D. 26 and 27 (Bromwich 1993:181–186). He may also be responsible for having added the Actian scene. The restoration at Orange was part of a rebuilding initiative carried out in a colony founded by Octavian in 35 B.C., at least four years prior to the Battle of Actium. Like Tiberius, future members of Augustus's dynasty could also use Orange as a pilgrimage site and yet another vehicle for directly concretizing Julio-Claudian autocracy back in Rome. Additionally, the Battle of Actium did not need to be known or understood in southern Gaul in the early first century A.D.; future dynasts and the fully Romanized inhabitants of Gallia Narbonensis would eventually come to venerate *imperium* and *imperator* in a not-so-distant future.

The Roman trophy monument also becomes exclusively Julio-Claudian in form as well as content. The Alpine Trophy at La Turbie and possibly the lost trophies erected by Drusus on the banks of the Elbe were purposefully modeled on the Mausoleum of Augustus in an effort to reserve yet another visual cue of Roman dominion for the Julio-Claudians. Unfortunately, the victory monuments raised by Drusus on Rome's German frontier do not survive.[8] The ancient sources relating this construction mention neither the size and shape of the trophies, nor do they have descriptions of decorative or textual elements. I hazard that they were tumlus-style structures possessing Julio-Claudian narratives of power and legacy.

It is worth exploring the chosen location of this commission, a piece of information roughly estimated by ancient historians. Drusus built his trophies far away from the sites of major battles during the Alpine Wars and a great distance from the peoples directly affected by the Alpine Wars. His foray into Germania Superior (on the occasion he built these memorials) was not a proper military campaign as much as an adventurous expedition, one that echoed Caesar's own Rhine crossing in 54 B.C. (Caes. *Gal.* 4.16–19). Both were also imitating Alexander the Great's ventures into unknown lands and his subsequent erection of Greek-style altars in new lands. To a greater extent than the Arch of Orange, Drusus's actions and monuments in Germania were Julio-Claudian soliloquies meant to speak to aristocratic Romans back in the political theater of Rome.

As symbols of Roman dominance in the provincial landscapes, the trophies were likely torn down by locals in a region that remained highly contested for centuries.

A third trophy related to the Alpine Wars did survive through the centuries (Figure 7.3). The Alpine Trophy remains on a cliff overlooking the Mediterranean in the modern mountainside town of La Turbie, France. It was completed sometime between 9 and 7 B.C. The basic components of the trophy itself consist of a rectangular base approximately 15 m tall and 47 m wide and a colonnaded drum with a twelve-stepped conical roof, topped by a battlefield trophy—making it a total of 49 m high. The base is undecorated except for the victory trophies and personified victories that flank the dedicatory text. The inscription contains a list of the 44 tribes vanquished by the Romans during the

FIGURE 7.3 Alpine Trophy at La Turbie, France, 7–5 B.C. (photo: Álvaro Ibarra).

Alpine War preceded by the dedication. The patrons, Drusus and Tiberius, dedicated the monument to Augustus, son of the divine Caesar, rather than to any deity on behalf of the emperor (Plin. *Nat.* 3.136–138).

The drum contains the most lavish decorations, which included a Doric frieze and 24 Tuscan columns. Between each of the drum's columns stood statues set into niches built onto the interior wall of the drum; the only one that survives is a statue of Drusus. The rest may have been representations of Tiberius, Polibius Silius (who also led troops in the Alpine War), Augustus, other members of the imperial family, and/or the gods. However, there is no textual or material evidence for this hypothesis.

Yet again, the location of the Alpine Trophy displays a deviation from Republican antecedents. It does not speak to locals because its location has little or nothing to do with the battles of the Alpine Wars. Corroborating Cassius Dio's account about the Alpine War, the tribes came exclusively from throughout Alps, spanning hundreds of miles of difficult terrain (DioCass 54.20–55.1). Dio's text situates the most difficult and bloody fighting on the other side of the Danube, including the largest battle of the entire campaign against an allied barbarian force led by the Rhaetian tribe. However, he relates that this last and greatest battle occurred at the northernmost part of the Alpine mountain chain—quite far away from La Turbie. Interestingly, the tribes in this last clash mentioned by the ancient author are not recognized on the Alpine Trophy. Moreover, the material remains do not indicate any kind of permanent habitation of the area until the Middle Ages. The earliest known settlement of La Turbie dates to the twelfth or thirteenth century, when warlords representing the Republic of Genoa transformed the pagan remains into a castle (Lamboglia 1976:18–19). The nearest Roman settlement was in present-day Nice and the Greek-Massilote Monoikos, also known as the Port of Hercules (Ebel 1976:28). These facts compel us to question why the Romans chose to build a monument to a war in a locale that witnessed little or no direct conflict, in a landscape largely devoid of population.

The Alpine Trophy and Drusus's trophies in Germania continue speaking of a Julio-Claudian dynasty and to Julio-Claudian dynasts of an imminent future yet realized. At least the trophy implies that such a future was imminent. In the cases of these particular memorials, their locations provide a blank slate for future expressions of power that are not compromised by Eastern kings or Republican generals.

After Augustus, the Romans erected no more trophy monuments until the reign of Trajan. Too much of that visual vocabulary directly invoked Julio-Claudian accomplishments, especially for rulers looking for forge their own dynastic legacies. Moreover, the trophy monument spoke only to those present and future Romans that prescribed to the primacy of Augustus and his heirs within the empire once its appearance was codified. The absence of such structures suggests that the Julio-Claudians were successful in making the trophy speak on their behalf to rivals and followers alike, even in their physical absence.

The Flavians built no trophies in the provinces, despite their monumental victory in Judea. Instead, Domitian raised a Republican-style arch in Rome to commemorate his brother's victory over the Jews and over death itself. The aversion to erecting trophies under the Flavian regime is understandable. The Flavians certainly made efforts to distance themselves from Nero, but not the office of emperor as formulated by Augustus. Attacks directed at the Julio-Claudians largely portrayed Nero as an aberration in the succession of emperors. Vespasian and his new dynasty represent the restoration of just rulership. At the same time, Flavian propagandists take cues from Augustus.

The Flavians' seizure of power brought peace and prosperity back to Rome in much the same way Octavian's defeating Marc Antony ushered in the *pax Romana*. However, Vespasian's own *republica restituta* needed to be distinct. Invoking Augustus too frequently or too directly could undermine the Flavians' own dynastic ambitions. The biggest distinction came in the way of using arenas as symbols of Flavian power. The amphitheater was a native invention that housed homegrown rituals, in contrast to the mausoleum, which incorporated Eastern forms and concepts. Vespasian and Titus constructed arenas in Rome, Pozzuoli, and Pula, buildings that served as direct testaments to their magnanimity. The Flavians needed no complex visual vocabulary to communicate their distinction from Nero; the Colosseum allowed them to directly show their generosity and greatness to the people of Rome (Gunderson 2003). Building the Flavian amphitheater on the grounds of Nero's Golden House was no subtle statement of distinction.

It was only Trajan, the first Roman emperor from the provinces, who resurrected the trophy monument from potential obscurity and prompted its demise. Once again, the key to understanding the commemorative intent of the *Tropaeum Traiani* lies in text rather than material culture.

Compared to Domitian, Trajan made open and overt appeals to Julio-Claudian concepts of empire, as opposed to the Republican fantasy that ultimately failed under Domitian. And the provinces (as opposed to Rome) became the proving ground for this comparison. Trajan succeeded in Dacia where Domitian failed. The great success of the Dacian Wars called for a monument that could revive the concept of *imperium sine fine*. Like Augustus, such messages helped Trajan secure his position as *princeps*. After all, Trajan was not only a new emperor, he was an emperor from the provinces.

Like the Alpine Trophy at La Turbie, the *Tropaeum Traiani* is a Roman soliloquy that speaks to the ghosts of Rome's past, to Roman elites in the present, and to future Ulpian dynasts (Figure 7.4). Trajan commissioned his trophy to commemorate his victories in Dacia, but placed the triumphal monument in northeastern Moesia. The modern village of Adamklissi is located in the Danube basin of present-day southeastern Romania, 65 km west of the Black Sea coast and 10 km south of the Danube River in the Roman province of Moesia.

In its original form the *Tropaeum Traiani* measured 30 m in diameter and stood 40 m high. It sits on a nine-stepped base and consisted of a solid masonry drum and a conical roof topped by a hexagonal pedestal carrying a Roman battlefield trophy. Seven layers of decorated stonework covered the massive drum base (Florescu 1965). The bottommost decorative registers on the drum featured six courses of faux blocks—decorative applications applied to the façade. A continuous band with a foliage motif frieze surrounds the drum immediately above the blocks. This scroll frieze is below a register of triglyph-like forms and metopes. Above the metopes, a viewer finds another continuous

FIGURE 7.4 *Tropaeum Traiani* at Adamklissi, Romania, A.D. 109 (photo: Álvaro Ibarra).

decorative band depicting alternating palmette patterns topped by a small rope-patterned register. The uppermost register contains sculpted panels as well as freestanding sculpture. Vertical rectangles containing renditions of captives interrupt a rectangular band of geometric patterns. Lastly, statues of lions positioned at the rim of the top register act as water spouts.

Scholars posit that modern-day Adamklissi was the site of a battle related to Trajan's Dacian Wars, perhaps the rearguard action carried out by the Roxolani cavalry in the second Dacian War (Rossi 1971:146–148). There is no archaeological evidence to prove any battle took place in the plains outside Adamklissi to date. Moreover, there is no textual or epigraphic evidence to suggest that this area of Moesia held any kind of symbolic or martial significance for the Romans. The closest Roman military installations were Troesmis and Durostorum, 100 and 25 km away respectively.

To be succinct, the Romans constructed the *Tropaeum Traiani* in the middle of nowhere. Its most significant purpose was to serve as a visible contrast or even a replacement to an earlier *tropaeum* raised by Domitian at the same site. A. S. Stefan makes a case for identifying earlier Roman foundations at Adamklissi as the remains of a Domitianic trophy, one destroyed by Trajan prior to the erection of the *Tropaeum Traiani*. Domitian's *damnatio* may have countered the understanding of the trophy as sacrosanct. (Stefan 2005:437–444). Trajan's motivation was political and symbolic, on the level of a Julio-Claudian eclipsing a rival's monument without any consideration of native perspectives. Just as the Flavians sought to distance themselves from the last Julio-Claudian, Nero, so too did Trajan seek to distinguish himself from the last Flavian, Domitian. One possible choice was a return to privileging Julio-Claudian behavior, styles, and even monuments. In this case, Trajan acted to reclaim the *tropaeum*.

From the outset, Trajan established a pattern of behavior that invoked the Julio-Claudians, particularly Augustus. He accepted the title of *pontifex maximus* in A.D. 98 after the death of Nerva. However, Trajan repeatedly refused the title of *Pater Patriae,* purportedly out of humility and out of respect for figures such as Cicero, Caesar, and Augustus. Unlike the practice of automatically bestowing new emperors with various titles in the early principate, these late Republican heroes earned their honors through heroic deeds (Bennett 1997:51). Such a refusal echoes Caesar repeatedly declining the civic crown in an example of false modesty to modern audiences (Plut. *Caes.* 61.5–6).

Trajan also took a grand tour of the western provinces before returning to Rome to take office, a gesture that copied Augustus's own journey after the Battle of Actium. The new emperor's year-long delay was due to his desire to secure the Danubian frontier personally. Pliny describes Trajan's eventual arrival in Rome in a manner reminiscent of a triumphal parade, although the senate awarded Trajan no triumph at this point in his career (Plin. *Pan.* 22). Pliny assures us that Trajan would use his position to return peace to the empire, much in the way Augustus delivered the *pax Romana* (Plin. *Pan.* 63.2). Trajan was like Augustus in various other ways. He displayed restraint in every facet of his life, from his political and military actions to his own moderate lifestyle. Trajan's portraiture quoted early Julio-Claudian coiffures. Such overt comparisons positioned Trajan as a new Augustus, the founder of a new dynasty of rulers that would produce a new golden age. However, unlike Augustus, Trajan had no need to invoke the deeds of Achilles, Perikles, or Achilles. Trajan's propagandists promoted the restoration of absolute autocracy solely through direct references to Roman precedents.

It is not surprising that Trajan adopted Augustan practices in the provinces as well. The *Tropaeum Traiani* functioned like the Alpine Trophy and the Arch at Orange in referencing the importance of Julio-Claudian-style autocracy to a Rome devoid of Julio-Claudian rivals. News and descriptions of the Adamklissi monument created yet another useful connection to Augustus, the erection of a massive structure that so closely resembled the Mausoleum of Augustus. Like those frontier populations along the Elbe, future inhabitants of rural Moesia would come to understand the significance of the *Tropaeum Traiani* and value the importance of the Ulpian dynasty.

FAILING ROME

Unfortunately for Trajan, his adopted son Hadrian had different opinions about the future of the empire. Back in Rome, the Ulpian soliloquy fell on deaf ears once Trajanic supporters ceased spreading the deceased emperor's particular referent of *imperium* and *imperator*. After Trajan, no other emperor raised another provincial trophy monument in the history of the Roman Empire. Battlefield trophies are rare in the iconography applied to multiple media in the post-Trajanic era. This may also indicate that Roman soldiers raised fewer trophies in battlefields. Ultimately, more functional and less symbolic structures such as amphitheaters and baths and aqueducts replaced trophies as monumental statements of Roman power.

The *tropaeum* became obsolete as a monument and as a symbol, largely due to the triumph of Julio-Claudian propaganda. After more than a millennium of martial tradition surrounding the battlefield trophy, one man's ambitions singlehandedly transformed the trophy into a politically toxic symbol. Beyond being "too Julio-Claudian," Imperial trophy monuments invoked aborted beginnings and the failure to deliver on the promise of *imperium sine fine*. The Romans would never conquer the land and the people beyond the Elbe as Drusus intended. The Romans tenuously held Dacia for 161 years (A.D. 109–270). Neither the Dacians nor the Germans embraced Roman culture, remaining enemies of Rome for centuries. Later Roman dynasts disassociated themselves from a monument whose referent was lamented in Rome and uselessly manifold in the provinces. The Imperial trophy monument became a Roman soliloquy delivered in an empty theater.

NOTES

1. I modify Pritchett's original criteria, changes that rely on closer scrutiny of the trophies in question.
2. Although Forster is referring to the modern phenomenon of restoring ancient buildings to an original state that never truly existed, Roman patrons are producing provincial monuments in a similar fashion.
3. Nicolet shows that, for the Romans, the empire existed within a verifiable geographic context. I believe the empire existed in both space and time, and the world's greatest historical figures were gauged against those that came before and those yet to be born.
4. My formal analysis is based on Kountouri's published reconstruction and my own viewing of the remains in present-day Pyrgos and Orchomenos on July 29, 2005.
5. The authors found a fragment of what may be another Sullan trophy related to the Battle of Chaeroneia on Thourion Hill in 1990. The discovery does not challenge Kountouri's own Sullan trophy, as Plutarch relates that Sulla built two trophies at Chaeroneia (Plut. *Sull.* 19).
6. A third-century military calendar found in Dura Europos contains the same holidays as those celebrated in Rome, particularly imperial holidays such as emperors' birthdays, military victories, and ascension to power and holidays for traditional Roman deities such

as Jupiter, Mars, Juno, Minerva, and Neptune. The prescribed sacrifice accompanied each holy day listed.

7.   I extend my most profound thanks to Dr. Woodman for his close examination of textual evidence of Julio-Claudian propaganda. The specific examples from Tacitus and Livy on the monumentalizing of Germanicus in the provinces come directly from his lecture.

8.   Some believe the so-called *Drususstein* in Mainz, Germany, to be one of the trophies mentioned by Cassius Dio (55.1.2–5). However, Mainz is quite some distance from the River Elbe and there is no certain proof that the monument is, in fact, Julio-Claudian.

REFERENCES CITED

Bennett, Julian 1997 *Trajan: Optimus Princeps.* Indiana University, Bloomington.

Braund, Susanna 2006 A Tale of Two Cities: Statius, Thebes, and Rome. *Phoenix* 60.3–4:259–273.

Bromwich, James 1993 *The Roman Remains of Southern France.* Routledge, London.

Camp, John, M. Ierardi, J. McInerney, K. Morgan, and G. Umholtz 1992 A Trophy from the Battle of Chaeroneia of 86 B.C. *American Journal of Archaeology* 96.3:443–455.

Campbell, Brian 1994 *The Roman Army 31B.C.–A.D. 337: A Sourcebook.* Routledge, London.

Castellvi, Georges, J. M. Nolla, and I. Rodà 1995 La identificación de los trofeos de Pompeyo en el Pirineo *Journal of Roman Archaeology* 8:6–11.

Charles-Picard, Gilbert 1957 *Les trophées romains.* E. de Boccard, Paris.

Davies, Penelope J. E. 2001 *Death and the Emperor.* Cambridge University Press, Cambridge.

Ebel, Charles 1976 *Transalpine Gaul: The Emergence of a Roman Province.* Studies of the Dutch Archaeological and Historical Society, Leiden.

Florescu, Florea B. 1965 *Das Siegesdenkmal von Adamklissi Tropaeum Traiani.* University of Bucharest, Bucharest.

Forster, Kurt W. 1998 Monument/Memory and the Mortality of Architecture. *Oppositions Reader,* edited by K. M. Hays. Princeton Architectural, New York:8–35.

Galinsky, Karl 1996 *Augustan Culture.* Princeton University Press, Princeton.

Gros, Pierre 1979 Pour une chronologie des arcs de triomphe de Gaule narbonnaise. *Gallia* 37: 55–87.

Gunderson, Eric 2003 The Flavian Amphitheatre: All the World as Stage. In *Flavian Rome: Image, Culture, and Text,* edited by A. J. Boyle and W. J. Dominik, 637–658. Brill, Leiden.

Hales, Shelley, and T. Hodos, eds. 2009 *Material Culture and Social Identities in the Ancient World.* Cambridge University Press, Cambridge.

Hölscher, Tonio 2006 The Transformation of Victory into Power. In *Representations of Warfare in Ancient Rome,* edited by Sheila Dillon and K. E. Welch, 27–48. Cambridge University Press, Cambridge.

Kountouri, Eleni 2004 Ενημέρωση για αρχαιολογικό εύρημα. Press release. December. Athens.

Lamboglia, Nino 1976 *Le Trophée d'Auguste a La Turbie.* Institut International d'Étude Ligures, Bordighera.

Murray, William, and P. Petsas 1989 Octavian's Campsite Memorial for the Actian War. *Transactions of the American Philosophical Society* 79.4.

Nicolet, Claude. 1991 *Space, Geography, and Politics in the Early Roman Empire.* University of Michigan Press, Ann Arbor.

Pritchett, William K. 1974 *The Greek State at War,* Vol. 2. University of California Press, Berkeley.

Rossi, Lino 1971 *Trajan's Column and the Dacian Wars.* Translated by J. M. C. Toynbee. Thames and Hudson, New York.

Stefan, Alexandre S. 2005 *Les guerres daciques de Domitien et de Trajan: Architecture militaire, topographie, images et histoire.* École Français de Rome, Rome.

Woodman, Anthony J. 2012 Tacitus and Germanicus: Monuments and Models. *History,Poetry, and War: Basil Gildersleeve's Past and Present.* Paper presented at the Classical Charleston Lecture Series. 21 February. Charleston.

Zachos, Konstantinos L. 2003 The *tropaeum* of the Sea-Battle of Actium at Nikopolis: Interim Report. *Journal of Roman Archaeology* 16:65–92.

Zanker, Paul 1990 *The Power of Images in the Age of Augustus.* Translated by Alan Shapiro. University of Michigan Press, Ann Arbor.

Chapter Eight

Monumentality among the Mediterranean Isles

Michael J. Kolb

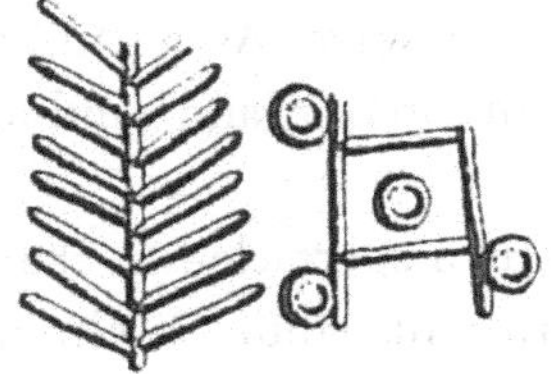

Abstract *The Mediterranean islands are home to some of the world's most impressive monuments. These include the colossal tombs, temples, and palaces present on Menorca, Sardinia, Pantelleria, Malta/Gozo, Crete, and Cyprus. Although substantial differences exist in their chronology, construction style, and function, these monuments also share a number of key similarities. First, the origins of these monuments may be traced to two specific social fabrics of "place." Second, those who built and used them made logical choices for negotiating social competition and consensus. Finally, environmental productive circumscription may also have served to stimulate a divergence in the way these monuments were utilized in the East versus the West.*

Introduction

Monuments and other forms of architecture are imbued with cultural value and meaning. As human modified objects they share a history just about as old as humanity, helping us negotiate the world around us and structure the operation of the human mind. As Colin Renfrew has consistently argued, objects externalize, amplify, and distribute the ways in which individuals and societies represent reality (c.f. Renfrew 2007; Renfrew, Firth, and Malafouris 2008; Renfrew and Scarre 1998).

For the purposes of this chapter, the concept of monumentality pertains to large architectural structures such as palaces, fortifications, tombs, and temples (Kolb 1994, 2004, 2012; Smith 2007; Trigger 1990). Monuments are usually buildings that are formally placed, large-scale, and require greater energy investment than the simple construction of houses or other structures. Unlike most other forms of material culture that archaeologists study, a monument is an example of a culturally constructed *place*, a permanent and visible space upon the physical landscape that mediates human experience and memory (see the formative works of Bourdieu 1977; Lefebvre 1991; Relph 1976; Tuan 1977; and the recent archaeological treatises of Hendon 2007; Lightfoot et al. 1998; Meskell 2003; Rubertone 2008; Whitridge 2004). Yet how is a physical space transformed into social place? Simply stated, people build and alter a space in ways that demarcate and personalize their life experiences. Place making is a ubiquitous social and cognitive process that is cumulative; over time a space becomes associated with a vast network of experiences and memories as people reoccupy, reuse, and recreate places. Each place therefore becomes a mediator of social experiences, possessing a horizon of meaning that is discernible at many difference levels and in many different ways. As repetitive place-making practices become habitualized over time they begin altering and guiding the ways in which people respond and act to place.

What sets large-scale monuments apart from other places is their spectacle-like character, which evokes collective social identities and values (Osborne this volume). Group histories cling to old stones as enduring residues of human experience, much in the way that a family heirloom informs us about an ancestor. But such histories are mental constructions only; memories, imaginations, and knowledge that are highly personal as well as collectively shared. A monument provides both material and psychological structure and form to society, giving social meanings precise and explicit spatial definition and helping to direct human activity. Monumental palaces, forts, temples, or tombs offer commentary about society; they cast social ideals and principles as being naturally true within the landscape in which they stand, and transform private actions and behaviors into movements of the collective public. In this way, a monument represents an emergent nexus of collective mental representations, embodied behavioral practices, and material things (Alcock 2002; Nelson and Olin 2003).

Although immutable and immobile, a monument also mediates spatial practice by directing how people move through and interact together in space (see Fisher, this volume; Turnbull 2002). It is an assembled spatial story that creates collective narrative through the process of journeying. A pilgrimage, a ritual, a procession—all orient and demarcate real and imagined boundaries that enable people to "make sense" of things. Three types of spatial movements associated with monuments exist (Figure 8.1): (1) encoding; (2) performance; and (3) way finding. Encoding is the act of physical construction that captures and records a history. It is the rendering of meanings into stone, the construction of walls and other architectural elements that formalize movement in a durable fashion. The building of a monument casts social ideals and principles as being naturally true because they become physically codified upon the landscape in which they stand. Encoding employs space in a very unique way to forge the consciousness and movements of the collective public. The more complex the architectural plan, the larger the effort to devise a collective vision and encode symbolism.

The second type of movement associated with monuments is performance. Performance includes the actions of public spectacle; the funeral processions, sacrificial ritu-

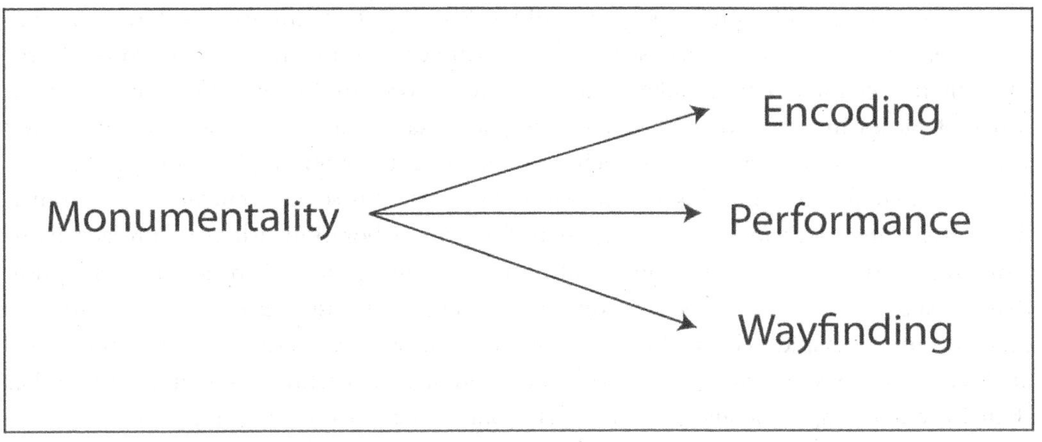

FIGURE 8.1 Spatial movements involving monumentality.

als, and commemorative ceremonies that reconstruct spatial and social history. It is the movement through and the use of different portions of a codified monument that enact shared social practices to broadly forge relationships, ideas, and values among people (Gilibert 2011; Inomata and Coben 2006). The durable architecture and design continuity of a monument conveys a sense of permanence in the phenomenology of everyday life not found in other places (Connerton 1989; Halbwachs 1980; Joyce 2005; Tringham 2000:131). Because of the interactive and collective nature of monumental performance, monuments have been referred to as "theaters of knowledge" or "theaters of memory" as they merge place, art, and collective social action (Turnbull 2002; Watkins 2004a, 2004b, 2012). However, as a theatrical focal point of social action, performance movements are never static or fixed over time. The physical alteration of monuments may cause selective forgetting or revision of performance, while iconoclasm or destruction permanently defies or denies the intentions of the original builders (Bradley 2003; Papalexandrou 2003). The older the monument becomes, the more likely future generations retrospectively develop new and alternative interpretations and understandings for it (Bender 1998).

The third type of movement associated with monuments is way finding. Way finding is movement that uses spatial information to orient and navigate the individual within and between places (see Turnbull 2002). It proceeds along paths of observation and integrates knowledge laterally rather than vertically, constructing spatial stories and forms of narrative understanding that proceed from a part to a whole (Ingold 2000:229; Lefebvre 1991:225; Tilley 1994:28). Way finding includes such social actions as pilgrimages, journeying, and other motions in and around a monument, movements that convey meanings by crossing thresholds, experiencing geometric principles, or mapping relationships. Way finding engages fundamentally different meanings of the social collective than other sorts of movement. It creates textures rather than text, generating spatial anchors rather than spatial networks, and conveying meanings that are acted out and experienced rather than read.

The way finding itself becomes a sequence of localities to which attention is drawn through movement. But how do we make sense of the nature of monumentality outlined thus far?

In this chapter, I undertake a comparative analysis of Mediterranean island monumental places in order to understand how place making and movement are associated with the other important factors, such as island circumscription (Carneiro 1970; Earle 1991:10–11), and the differing competition and consensus social strategies (see Feinman 2012) associated with monumental construction and elaboration. Islands represent excellent study areas because of the additional degree of geographic and social circumscription that is usually present, and because some of the most impressive examples of monumentality occur on islands (Kolb 2012). I have chosen six Mediterranean case studies for analysis, each representing the apex of monumental construction for that island (rather than fully contemporaneous examples). This was done because they represent the most monumental form in terms of scale and elaboration and therefore represent a fully developed trajectory of monumentality rather than just a portion of it.

The six case studies are: (1) the *talayot* towers of Menorca (Balearic Islands); (2) the *nuragi* towers of Sardinia; (3) the *sesi* tombs of Pantelleria; (4) the temple and funerary complexes of Malta and Gozo; (5) the palaces of Minoan Crete; and (6) the court complexes of Cyprus (Figure 8.2). The goal with this data set is to obtain a more precise understanding of how Mediterranean monuments were employed. Three questions become predominant: (1) How and why do certain types of social and ritual elaboration assume monumental proportions? (2) What are the functional and morphological similarities and differences of these monument types? And (3) what was the basis of power associated with the construction of these monuments?

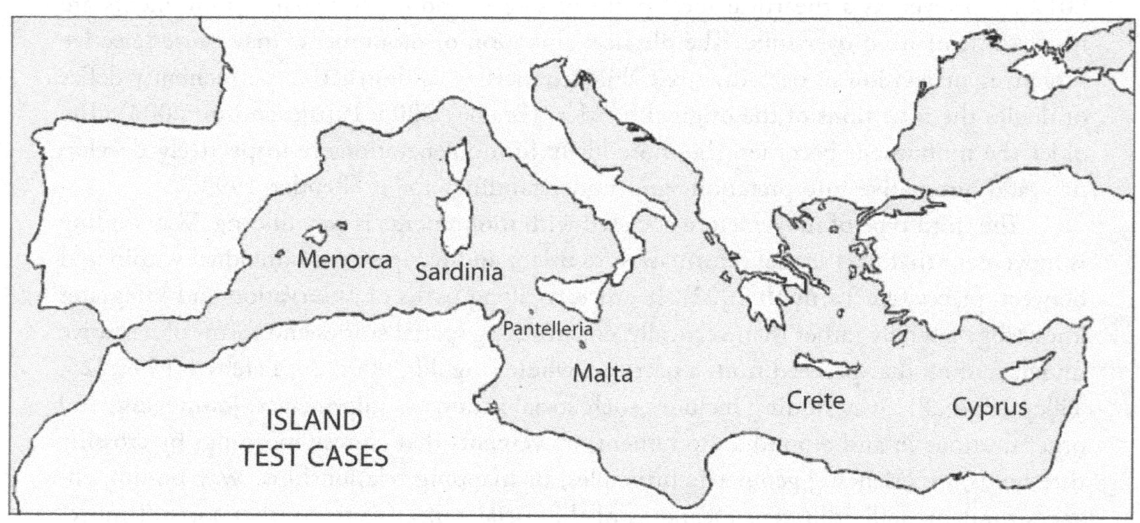

FIGURE 8.2 The various Mediterranean island test cases.

Menorca

The monumental phase of Menorca (area of 623 km²) in the Balearic Islands spans the Bronze and Iron Ages (the Talayotic Period 1700–123 B.C.). Less work has been done on these monuments than on those from other island groups, but a number of important syntheses do exist (Bellard 1995; Calvo Trias et al. 2001; Gasull et al. 1984; Patton 1996; Plantalamor and Rita 1984; Rita 1988; Waldren 1982, 1992). The *talayot*, a tower-like structure similar to the Sardinian nuragic towers (Waldren 1982), is the predominant monument feature of the island (although others exist, such as the *naveta* burial tomb and *taula* sanctuary). A *talayot* may be square, round, oval, or stepped in form, averaging 12–20 m in diameter and containing a massive central roof pillar (Figure 8.3). The *talayot* tower is usually found at the center of a settlement, or built adjacent to defensive walls. Some settlements have more than one *talayot*. More than 300 of the structures are still preserved on Menorca.

The *talayot* monuments trace their origins to the megalithic chamber tombs, fortified enclosures, and standing menhir stones of the Pretalayotic Period (Bellard 1995; Rita 1988). Settlements from the Pretalayotic Period, such as Ferrandell-Oleza on Mallorca, often incorporate central tower-like structures (Waldren 1982), facilitating spatial movements of encoded social relations and territoriality. Material culture indicates a clear link with the Iberian mainland, and includes such things as metal and Bell-Beaker pottery (Chapman 1985:145). The circular *talayot* style was developed earliest and eventually evolved into the square and stepped forms (Waldren 1982). The functions of *talayot* are unclear, but they may have served as defensive structures, community storage areas, or possibly as loci for social movements of performance involving ceremonial community

FIGURE 8.3 Planview and isometric reconstruction of the Menorcan *talayot* of Son Fornes.

feasting (see Gasull et al. 1984). The chronology of these monuments is still somewhat imprecise given the paucity of modern systematic excavations, but we do know all three monument types were built in the late Bronze Age, between 1400 and 800 B.C. and were used simultaneously. The *talayot* does bear a resemblance to the towers of Sardinia and Corsica even though the Balearic Islands are clearly linked to the Iberian mainland (Patton 1996:94).

SARDINIA

The Mediterranean megalithic tomb was also the architectural precursor to Bronze Age monumental structures (ca. 1750–900 B.C.) on the island of Sardinia (area of 23,949 km^2). These structures are called *nuraghe,* which means "heap" or "hollow," and are truncated conical or sub-rectangular towers built using large basalt or granite rocks (Balmuth 1992; Balmuth and Rowlands 1982; Blake 1998, 2001; Lilliu 1982; Tore 1984; Webster 1991, 1996). More than 7,000 remain today (Figure 8.4), and the typical *nuraghe* is between 11 and 16 m in diameter and 18 m in height, with 1 m thick walls built

FIGURE 8.4 A *nuraghi* of Sardinia (http://commons.wikimedia.org/wiki/File:Nuraghi_Nuradeo_Sardinia.jpg; photo: Mihai Sorin Sirbu).

with dry-laid stone stacked either into concentric rows or cyclopean style. A lintel-style doorway, often facing south, opens to a short entrance passage that in turn leads to a central chamber. A small window may be present above the lintel. The central chamber averages 4 m in diameter, has a corbelled roof, and has several niches set into the walls. The entrance passage usually has a niche to the right of the doorway, and if a second story floor or rooftop balcony is present, a circular stairway leads upward to the left of the door. The conical *nuraghi* usually have more than one story, while the sub-rectangular towers have flat roofs and a central corridor with radiating side chambers.

Most *nuraghi* served as fortified residences, though their size suggests some sort of role for community defense, and movements of both encoding and way-finding territorial relations. Clusters of adjacent *nuraghi* were built as "fortified villages" or "proto-castles," perhaps signifying and spatially encoding interclan feuding or regional elites, although the labor needed to build a *nuraghe* was modest (averaging 3,600 person-days for a single tower), suggesting that there was no need for feudal elites, social specialization, or political centralization (see Balmuth 1992 and Webster 1996).

However, as culturally constructed places these *nuraghi* were important spaces, contemporary phenomena of significant social changes, including an influx of eastern Mediterranean trade goods, more intensive agriculture, and flourishing craft production, particularly copper working (See Giardino 1992:307; c.f. Lo Schiavo et al. 1985). Other *nuraghi* served as tombs (called giant's tombs), sacred wells, and megaron-temples (Balmuth 1992), and would have facilitated movements of performance, centered upon large upright stones placed within the enclosed corridor chamber. This semi-subterranean chamber averages 10 m² (5 by 2 m). A carved stone slab is placed at one end, usually before a crescent forecourt defined by more upright stones. Up to 60 individuals were collectively interred in these tombs, along with ample grave goods. The sacred wells were paved and benched constructions built around springs and used for ritual activities. The megaron-temples were rectangular *nuraghi* with multiple chambers and large caches of bronze items. Although the apex of nuragic construction was over by 900 B.C., many continued to be modified and occupied until medieval times.

Pantelleria

On the central Mediterranean island of Pantelleria (area of 92 km²) more than fifty communal tombs called *sesi* were constructed during the first half of the second millennium B.C. (Tusa et. al. 1992). These *sesi* were constructed along the perimeter of the hamlet at Mursia, an insular Bronze Age community not materially linked to other islands in the region (Ardesia et. al. 2006). Mursia sat upon a basalt terrace overlooking the western coast of the island complete with a small harbor and natural spring. The hamlet of about 20 longitudinal stone huts was reinforced on the landward side with a large dry-laid perimeter wall, approximately 200 m long, 10 m wide, and 7 m tall. The chronology of Mursia spans the Bronze Age (c. 1700–1100 B.C.), and its villagers pursued a diverse subsistence regime typical of the time period: fishing, shellfish collecting, herding, hunting, and agriculture.

Each *sesi* was constructed using stacked lava rock and ground-level passages that led to vaulted chambers, used by the villagers as tombs; some chambers were discovered with the disturbed remains of inhumation burials with offerings. Most *sesi* average 10 m in diameter, however the prestigious *sesi grande* was 20 m in diameter and had 12 passage chambers (Figure 8.5). As tombs the *sesi* would have been intimately involved with all three types of movements—their construction, placement upon the landscape, and use serving to mediate social practice evolving ancestry and the afterlife.

MALTA

The earliest monumental design among the test cases is a variety of temple and funerary structures constructed during the Copper Age (c. 3600–2500 B.C.) on the islands of Malta and Gozo (combined area of 383 km^2). Little is known about the builders of these structures. The original inhabitants of the Maltese Islands had clear affinities to the Neolithic Stentinello culture of Sicily (ca. 5000–4500 B.C.), and were farmers who grew cereal crops and raised domestic livestock. A number of syntheses exist regarding the

FIGURE 8.5 The *sesi grande* at Mursia, Pantelleria.

Maltese temples and their chronology (Bonanno et al. 1990; Evans 1984; Lewis 1977; Patton 1996; Stoddart 1999; Stoddart et al. 1993; Trump 1972, 2002).

About forty temples are distributed on Malta and Gozo, often in complexes. The seven largest complexes had a perimeter wall that encircled two or more adjacent temples. Megalithic upright stones were used to construct an apse, a curved hemispheric room that is broad at the base but tapered towardthe top. The typical apse averaged 6 m in diameter with a post-and-lintel trilithon arch entryway and a suspended roof made of wooded rafter covered in thatch, wattle and daub, or animal hides. The Malta structures were built with multiple apses, usually laid out in paired or trefoil (clover leaf–shape) groups, ranging from three to six apses per temple.

The largest and best preserved of the Malta complexes is Ggantija (or giantess' tower; see Figure 8.6). Two neighboring temples were constructed using undressed coralline

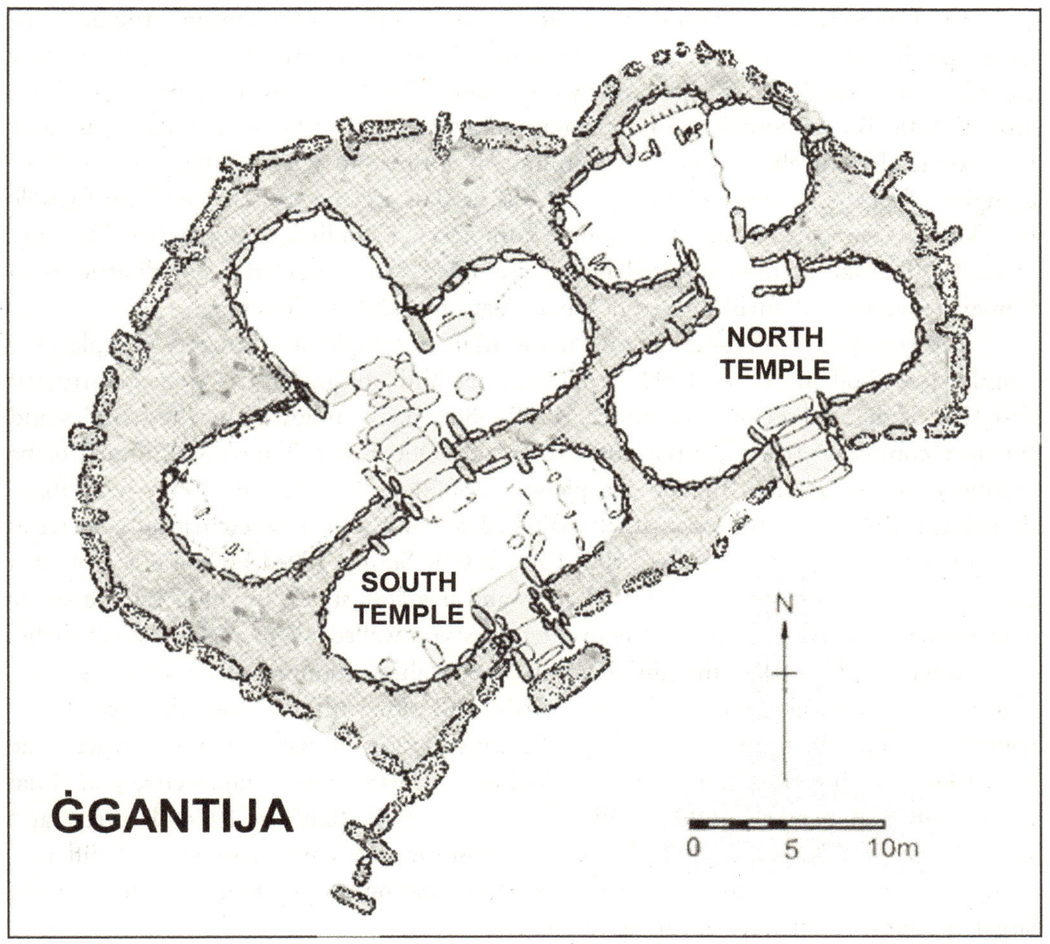

FIGURE 8.6 Plan view map of Ggantija on the island of Malta.

limestone boulders 6 m tall. The rough interior surfaces of these stones were originally coated with clay and lime plaster. The southern temple is 25 m long with five large chambers and was constructed about 3700 B.C. The northern temple is 19 m long with four chambers and was built around 3200 B.C. A massive curvilinear perimeter surrounds both temples, constructed of limestone slabs up to 6 m long. The space between the temple walls and the perimeter wall are filled with earth and rubble. The most elaborate temple complex is at Tarxien (pronounced *Tar-sheen*), built after 3300 B.C. A large central six-apse temple was built last. The remains of an older abandoned temple lie nearby. The Tarxien temples contained significant numbers of "cult" objects found in the innermost apses. These include major concentrations of pottery, carved female figurines, and animal bones. These same apses had doorjambs and holes used to restrict access. A number of statues and spiral wall carvings were also present, the best-known statue being an oversized female torso.

Two large funerary complexes were also associated with the Maltese temples. Both are below ground carved-rock *hypogea,* following the same modular design as the temples. The Hal Saflieni Hypogeum at Tarxien is an expansive subterranean structure with large uprights of coralline limestone. It remains the most extensively excavated funerary complex, and was built in three successive phases. The first was a simple tomb built around 3000 B.C., about 2 m in diameter and averaging 2 m below ground. This space was extended both above and below ground over time, to where it became the most complex of all the Maltese monuments. It was used as a cemetery. The Brochtorff Circle on Gozo is centered between two temple complexes, including Ggantija (see Bonanno et al. 1990). One of the excavated niches was filled with articulated and disarticulated human remains, and small terracotta female figurines and statuettes.

The chronology of construction for the Maltese temple and funerary complexes is lengthy (see Stoddart et al. 1993). Small shrines and upright stones were constructed first (the Skoba and Zebbug phases ca. 4500–3800 B.C.), followed by the temples and funerary complexes (the Ggantija phase ca. 3600–3000 B.C.). Temples continued to be expanded and elaborated (the Tarxien phase ca. 3000–2500 B.C.) until they were abandoned at a time when funerary rituals switched to the use of new cremation cemeteries (the Tarxien Cemetery phase ca. 2500–1500 B.C.). Simple lobed apses built around a central court were replaced with trefoil apses and five-apse styles. By 3000 B.C., a single apse in many of the five- and three-apse temples was walled off to make a small niche.

Much as the earlier megalithic tomb, the Maltese monuments were places that blended the physical cosmos of stone, earth, and sky with the Neolithic social and spiritual cosmos. In terms of encoding, the construction of the structures suggests the rise of an emerging elite class who controlled and mediated sacred knowledge and ritual practice (Bonanno et al. 1990; Meillassoux 1964, 1967; Renfrew 1974; Renfrew and Level 1979; Stoddart et al. 1993:17, 1999). However, the construction of 40 different structures suggests a decentralized network of competing groups that built successively larger monuments in response to social rivalry.

Movements of performance would have been elaborate, and oriented along a direct axis from the entrance to the innermost apse. The process of entry would have been a very dramatic and sacred experience as participants crossed the threshold from lighted exterior to darkened interior, perhaps symbolic of a transition from life to afterlife or from profane to sacred. As progression was made toward the interior, sanctified thresholds would be crossed as one passed by apses with carved stones and female-statues that led to the sanctum sanctorum. Rituals that included animal sacrifice may have also been performed. The experience would have been similar to entering the threshold of a megalithic tomb, only more structured and ornate.

As physical landmarks, the Maltese temples were important geographic and social places that created an island network of cognitive space. Way finding toward a temple and perceiving the surrounding landscape as a spiritual "place" would give rise to social contemplation and reflection. Way finding between temples would have been a socially shared skill that resulted in the socialization of the landscape.

As places, the Maltese temples sustained Neolithic social order as places of collective memory and rearranged time. They emphasized community and collectivism in both real and ancestral time, becoming arenas for revealing the spirit world upon gaining entrance to a semi-subterranean timeless place of megalithic apses. However, they fell into disuse after 2500 B.C.; although Tarxien continued to be used as a cremation cemetery with imported metal status burial goods (see Bonanno et al. 1990; Stoddart et al. 1993; Trump 1977). Perhaps this represents a migration of new peoples to the islands, or perhaps a change in religious expression. Whatever the reason, the Maltese religious elite may have found their power slowly waning in the wake of a broadening Mediterranean world that offered better access to trade goods for everyone.

CRETE

Another example of Mediterranean monumental elaboration are the labyrinthine structures of Middle to Late Bronze Age Crete (ca. 2200–1200 B.C., island area of 8,336 km^2). Much has been written about the Minoan culture and its "palaces" of Homeric legend (e.g. Driessen et al. 2002; Graham 1987; Hägg and Marinatos 1987; Hamilakis 2002; Kolb 2004; Letesson and Vansteenhuyse 2006; Manning 1994; Patton 1996; Rehak and Younger 1998; Renfrew 1972; Schoep 2006, 2010; Watrous 1994; Watrous et al. 2004), even though their true function is debatable. The Minoans are regarded as the Mediterranean's first large complex society, replete with political centralization, organized government, record keeping, specialization of labor, and mass-produced trade goods.

Four labyrinthine palaces were constructed on Crete by 1900 B.C. at the sites of Knossos (13,000 m^2), Mallia (7,600 m^2), Phaistos (6,500 m^2), and Zakros (2,800 m^2). The precursor of these palaces was the monumental tomb of the Pre-Palatial Period (e.g., Branigan 1970, 1993; Goodison 2001; Watrous 1994:715). Tombs were either rectangular in design averaging over 1,000 m^2, or circular *tholos* tombs often built with adjacent enclosed courts and an annex of auxiliary rooms built against the circular wall near the entrance. They would have been used to spatially encode territoriality. Sacrificial and ritual activity in some of the adjacent room annexes suggests movements of performance that involved worship tied to the dead (Murphy 1998). Perhaps these tombs served as inspiration for a burgeoning Minoan elite class, who, after being bolstered economically by trade contacts with Egypt and Mesopotamia (see Schoep 2006), were inspired to spatially encode a series of administrative and religious "palaces" that followed their own culturally distinctive design.

Cretan palaces were built using ashlar masonry and recessed façades, embellished with decorated engravings, painted stucco, veneering, and clay ornamentation (Figure 8.7). Each palace was a multistory building consisting of a series of recessed and projecting rectilinear architectural units, giving the entire structure an irregular shape. Vertical pillars included a startling variety of forms, often clustered in particular combinations. Palaces were located at places thought to have religious significance and/or provide easy access to the sea.

All palaces contain certain key architectural features including public spaces, clusters of similar room and hall units, and storage magazines and grain silos affiliated with sunken cult rooms. The most prominent feature is a rectangular central court, oriented slightly east of a north-south axis with dimensions that are 2:1 in size proportion. This orientation dictated the general layout of the entire structure, important for optimal

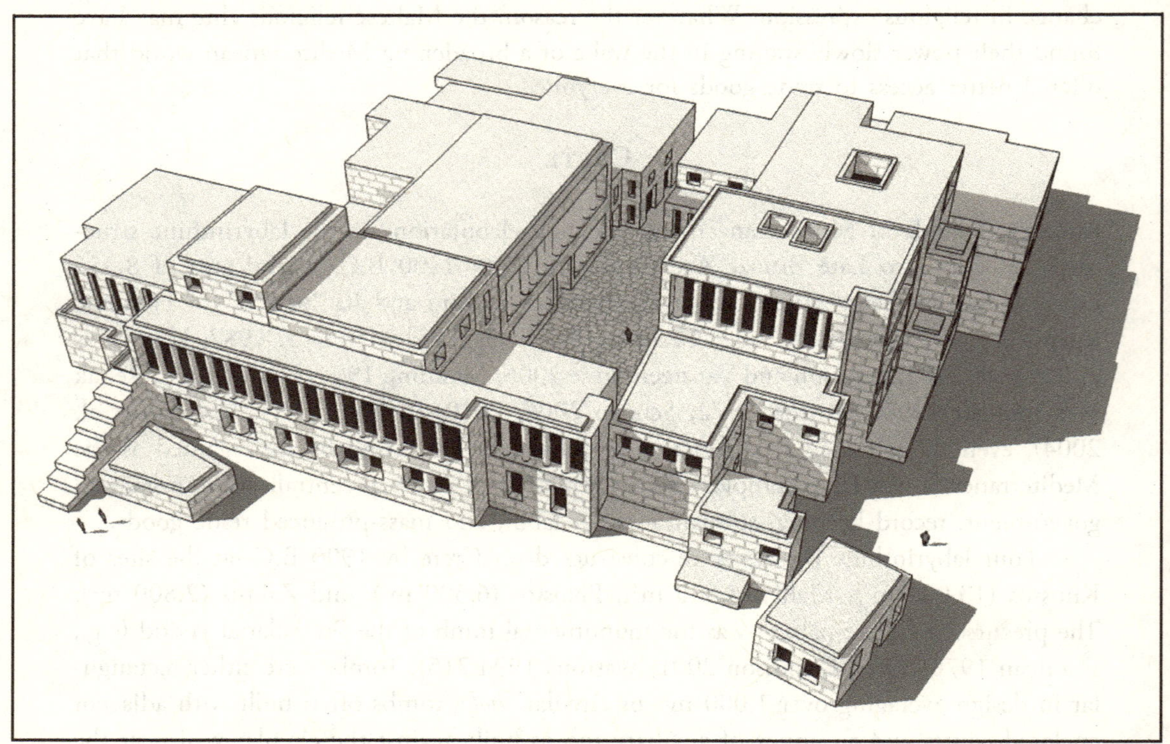

FIGURE 8.7 Planview and isometric reconstruction of the palace at Knossos (after Evans 1921).

sunlight exposure, recognizing sacred mountains and caves, or exposing certain rooms to the rising sun (Shaw 1973). Minoan art and frescoes suggest a variety of performance movements that involved court rituals such as bull leaping and group dancing (Davis 1987; Sipahi 2001; Younger 1995), but other possibilities include feasting, astronomical observation, and ceremonial displays. The central court at Knossos held as many as 5,435 people (Gesell 1987), the equivalent of one-quarter of the estimated total population of Neopalatial Knossos (Whitelaw 2001:27). Additional public spaces include a plaza entryway at Knossos, Mallia, and Phaistos (see Davis 1987; Marinatos 1987; cf. Driessen et al. 2002), a second-story reception hall at all the palaces, and small auditoriums at Knossos and Phaistos. Possible activities for these secondary public spaces may have also involved other spatial movements of performance—such things as political assemblies, religious gatherings, sporting events, or entertainment.

In contrast to public spaces, the private room/hall units give each palace its maze-like appearance (see Graham 1987). These units, dubbed "Minoan halls," consist of two unequally sized rectangular rooms separated by a row of pillars and piers where a retractable door was set for permitting or restricting the access of movement, air, or light. Some halls also include a third, more private room that contains a short flight of doglegged stairs leading to a toilet and a decorated "lustral basin." This third room may have been used for simple bathing or ritual initiation/purification/rite-of-passage. In sum, each unit probably served a multifunctional role as living/meeting/ceremonial spaces. A stairway fresco at Knossos and the presence of tablets or sealing archives suggest that these rooms may have been used as a meeting place for bureaucratic record keepers.

A large amount of palatial space was devoted to storage magazines. These long and narrow rooms were located to the west and north, and commonly contained *pithoi,* large clay storage jars often several feet tall (see Christakis 1999). Storage items probably included grain, wine, olive oil, textiles, and smaller pottery vessels. Large cylindrical semi-subterranean grain silos are also present. At the three largest palaces these silos were placed in prominent locations outside the west façade in or near the west plaza. Cult rooms known as "pillar crypts" with single or double pillars (see Graham 1987) are closely associated with the storage magazines. The pillars frequently bear carved mason insignias, particularly the prominent Minoan cult symbol of the double-axe. Some also contain pyramidal stone stands for mounting double-axes or other cult emblems.

The construction chronology of Minoan palaces is long and complex. The palaces were first constructed during the Protopalatial Period (ca. 1900–1720 B.C.) and were rebuilt or modified during the Neopalatial (ca. 1720–1470 B.C.), and declined and then were abandoned after the violent eruption of Thera ca. 1470 B.C. (cf. Driessen and. Macdonald 1997). Discussions of palatial emergence have emphasized local social, economic, and political factors (e.g., Cherry 1983, 1986; Graham 1987; Hägg and Marinatos 1987; Hamilakis 1999; Hansen 1988; Knappett and Schoep 2000; Manning 1994; Renfrew 1972; Sherratt 1981). The general consensus is that the palaces helped an emerging elite class accumulate and redistribute vital resources such as food and specialized craft items, although specific economic and social motivations are debatable and may include forced specialization, environmental instability, economic control, or trade monopolization.

CYPRUS

Monumental elaboration occurred on the island of Cyprus (area of 9,234 km²) during the Late Bronze Age (Late Cypriot Period 1650–1100 B.C.). Cyprus at this time made an important transition from a village-based society with incipient social differentiation to an urbanized and socially stratified civilization (Fisher 2009a, 2009b; Knapp, 2008:131–280; Knapp et al. 1994:224–229; Steel, 2004:149–186). Cyprus became an important producer of copper at this time, an essential component of bronze, exporting metal and ceramics throughout the eastern Mediterranean. Cyprus was mentioned in Egyptian royal texts, and the principal coastal centers of Enkomi and Kition displayed a high degree of prosperity as evidenced by its employment of an indigenous writing system, the importation of exotic goods, the construction of city walls and large houses, and lavish mortuary rituals (see Fisher this volume).

The basic Cypriot monument is classified as a "sanctuary" and was a court complex used for ritual purposes and spatial movements associated with performance. Identification of these monuments has been problematic (Fisher 2007; Knapp 2009; Webb 1999; Wright 1992), but approximately 13 to 38 of these structures have been definitively identified (depending upon which scholar one cites), usually within town centers. The typical Late Bronze Age monument averaged 963 m² in size and consisted of a rectangular ashlar-constructed structure or building complex located within or next to an unroofed courtyard. The building complex was usually a roofed two-room structure building, and probably served multiple functions as public meeting hall, secular gathering place, or administrative/industrial space (Fisher in press; Knapp 2008:211–33). Some of these monumental buildings served as performance ritual space, discerned by material finds associated with feasting (animal sacrificial debris or imported drinking kraters) or "cult" objects such as altars, bronze or terracotta cult images, offering stands, and horns of consecration (Steel 1998). Secular monumental space has been identified by the presence of luxury goods such as bronze or gold implements and jewelry, table vessels, metal hoards, storage areas, wells, and bathrooms.

For example, the Sanctuary of the Horned God (Level IIIB of the monumental "Ashlar" Building) at Enkomi (896 m²), contained a combination of public ritual space (Room 45), a more private sanctum sanctorum (Room 10), and other spaces used for food preparation (Room 37). The "Ashlar Building" at Alassa Paliotaverna (Figure 8.8) was built at the highest point of the settlement using huge cut-stone blocks, some almost 5 m long. It represents one of the largest court complexes (1,400 m²), complete with public ritual space, rooms for ceremonial purposes, and a storage area capable of holding enough foodstuffs for hundreds of people. Storage vessels were sealed with stamps suggesting important spatially encoded elite bureaucratic activities.

COMPARISONS

Table 8.1 presents eleven general descriptive measures used for comparing the six island test cases and their monumental sequences. In regard to measures of island geography, easterly location is measured by longitude, and varies between 4.23° E (Menorca) and

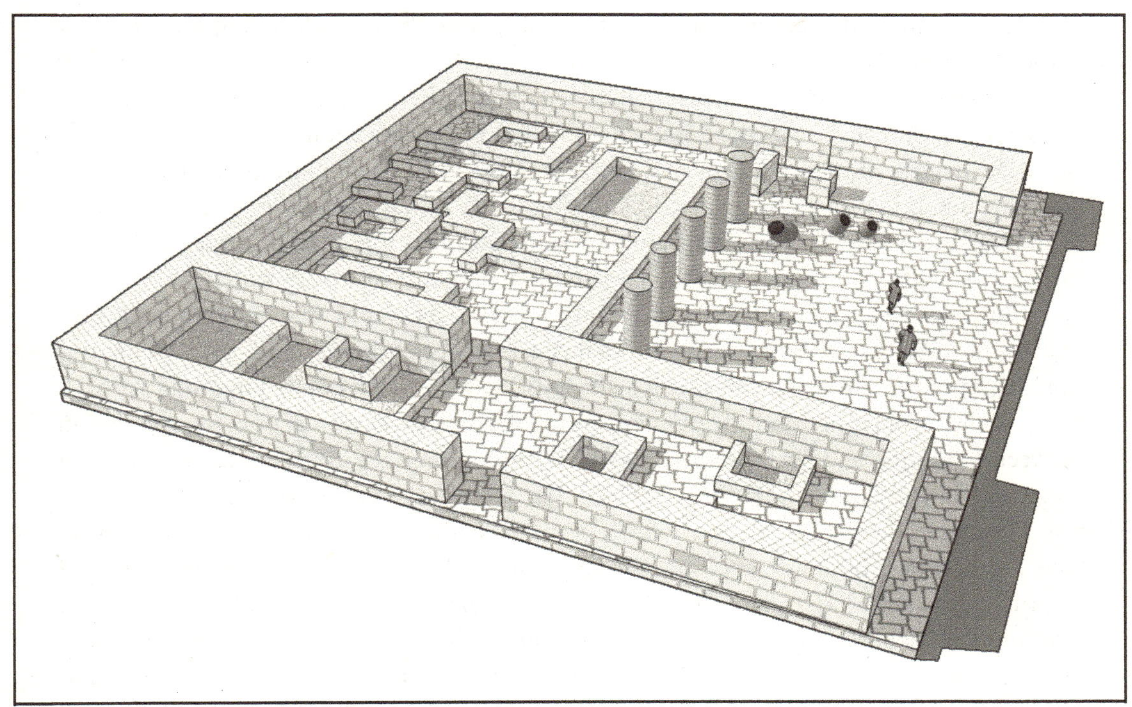

FIGURE 8.8 Planview and isometric reconstruction of Building II at Alassa Paleo-taverna, Cyprus (after Sophocles Hadjisavas in Knappet 2009).

33.61° E (Cyprus). Island area ranges from 92 km² (Pantelleria) to almost 24,000 km² (Sardinia), and averages around 7,000 m². The variation between islands as measured by Isolation Index is minimal, ranging between 27 (Cyprus) to 35 (Malta and Menorca). The average Isolation Index is 31. The Mediterranean islands, relatively speaking, are not very isolated and possess easy to moderate access to neighboring landforms (none are more than 250 kilometers from another land form), particularly in comparison to many of the Pacific islands that have an indices well over 100 (see Kolb 2012). Island annual rainfall is relatively consistent throughout the Mediterranean, varying between 447 mm (Crete) and 600 mm (Menorca), averaging 506 mm. The variation in arable land is much higher, ranging from 14 percent (Cyprus, approximately 1,293 km²) to 33 percent (Sardinia, approximately 7,903 km²). The average arable land value is 24 percent.

In regard to measures of monumental elaboration among the Mediterranean, the number of monumental structures varies between 8 (Crete) and 7,000 (Sardinia), with the median amount of structures being 45. The average size varies highly as well, between 79 m² (Pantelleria) and 5,652 (Crete). The median monument size is 250.5 m². The total area devoted to monuments is the sum of the areas of all individual monuments and represents an approximation of the overall space utilized for collective social activities. Island variation in total area is high as well, varying between 0.4 ha (Pantelleria) and 100.1 ha (Sardinia), with the median value of the island total monumental area being 4.5 ha.

Two additional measures document the dispersal of monumental space; the first is the density of island monuments as measured by the number of monuments divided by the overall island area as square kilometers, and the area density of monuments as measured by the total area of monuments divided by square kilometers of island arable land. The density of monuments varies between 0.001 monuments/km^2 (Crete) and 0.543 monuments/km^2 (Pantelleria), the median being 0.198 monuments/km^2. The area density of monuments varies between 0.002 monuments/km^2 of arable land (Cyprus) and 0.028 (Menorca), with the median being 0.015 monuments/km^2 of arable land.

Both visually and statistically, the data on island geography and monumental elaboration in Table 8.1 reveals a general distinction between the east and west Mediterranean. Spearman's ranked correlation coefficients (r_s, η = 6) of island longitude with all other island geographic and monumental variables reveals a strong positive correlation between longitude and average area (r_s = 0.71), and strong negative correlations between longitude and isolation index (r_s = –0.75). The longitude and arable land (%) correlation is statistically significant (r_s = –0.94, p < 0.01); the central and western islands all have a percentage of arable land at 25% or greater, while the eastern isles of Crete and Cyprus has values of less than 19%. This east-west distinction is also visible in terms of monumental elaboration: a pattern of bifurcation is highly visible in the two measures of monumental dispersal, the number of monuments per square kilometer (η/ km^2), and the number of total hectares of all monuments divided by the arable land as measured in square kilometers (ha/arable km^2). Both are strongly negative correlated with longitude (r_s = –0.77 for both). Likewise, the average monument area is positively correlated with longitude (r_s = 0.71), and the correlation between longitude and the number of monuments is negatively correlated at a statistically significant level (r_s = –0.87, p < 0.02). Although local processes of social and ritual elaboration for each of these six test cases were undoubtedly important, I argue that three interrelated variables—productive circumscription, traditions of place, and social competition—influenced the rise and use of each of the six monumental trajectories.

PRODUCTIVE CIRCUMSCRIPTION

Islands, more than most other type of landforms, are highly susceptible to geographic circumscription. Circumscription (Carneiro 1970) occurs when social distress peaks as increasing populations become stymied because no new suitable locations are available for economic expansion. This leads to either increased conflict or hierarchical formations that regulate existing resources. Productive circumscription is a product of how concentrated or controllable resources are in any given environment (Earle 1991:10–11), and thus predicts social complexity, especially for early agrarian societies that focus on staple production. Among the six test cases, both island isolation indices and the amounts of annual rainfall are relatively similar, and so a poor correlation exists between these measures and the total area of monumental construction (Table 8.1). No matter how small, every island was close enough to the mainland to allow food resources to remain stable over time.

TABLE 8.1
DESCRIPTIVE DATA OF ISLANDS AND THEIR MONUMENTS

	Menorca	Sardinia	Pantelleria	Malta/Gozo	Crete	Cyprus	Correlation Coefficients (r_s) [E]
Geography							Longitude to:
Longitude *(°East)*	4.23	9	11.95	14.52	24.91	33.61	—
Area *(km²)*	693	23,949	92	383	8,336	9,234	0.14, $p > 0.79$
Isolation Index[A]	35	32	29	35	28	27	–0.75, $p > 0.08$
Rainfall *(mm)*	600	473	460	560	447	498	–0.37, $p > 0.47$
Arable Land *(km²)*	27	33	26	25	19	14	0.09, $p > 0.87$
Arable Land (%)	187	7903	24	96	1584	1293	***–0.94, p < 0.01***
Monuments							
Number (η)	300	7,000	50	40	4	20	***–0.87, p < 0.02***
Average Area *(m²)*	177	143	79	324	7,475	1,439	0.71, $p > 0.11$
Total Area *(ha)*[B]	5.3	100.1	0.4	1.3	3.0	2.9	0.31, $p > 0.54$
Density							
$(\eta/ km²)$[C]	0.433	0.292	0.543	0.104	0.000	0.002	–0.77, $p > 0.07$
(ha /arable km²)[D]	0.028	0.013	0.017	0.014	0.002	0.002	–0.77, $p > 0.07$

[A] The index of island isolation is calculated by totaling the square roots of the distances to the nearest equivalent or larger island, the nearest island group or archipelago, and the nearest continent. As presented by the United Nations Environmental Programme: http://islands.unep.ch).

[B] The total monumental area is the sum of the areas of all individual monuments in hectares; it represents an approximation of the overall space utilized for collective social activities.

[C] The density of monuments is the number of monuments divided by the island area; it is a measure of the dispersal of monumental space.

[D] The arable density of monument is calculated by taking the total monumental area in hectares and dividing by the arable land in square kilometers. This is a measure of the dispersal of monumental space.

[E] Spearman's ranked correlation coefficient calculations for longitude versus all other variables for all islands $(\eta = 6)$.

However, the total percentage of arable land reveals that there is a dramatic decrease in arable land among the east Mediterranean islands (see Figure 8.9, Table 8.1). Arable land, of course may represent a proxy measure of environmental circumscription and therefore agro-economic potential. Farming became an important subsistence regime over time and therefore could have easily created conditions of productive circumscription and sustainability as populations increased. Although all if not most of the Mediterranean islands remained self-sustainable throughout antiquity, Crete and Cyprus were perhaps less sustainable in the long term given their smaller ratio of available arable land.

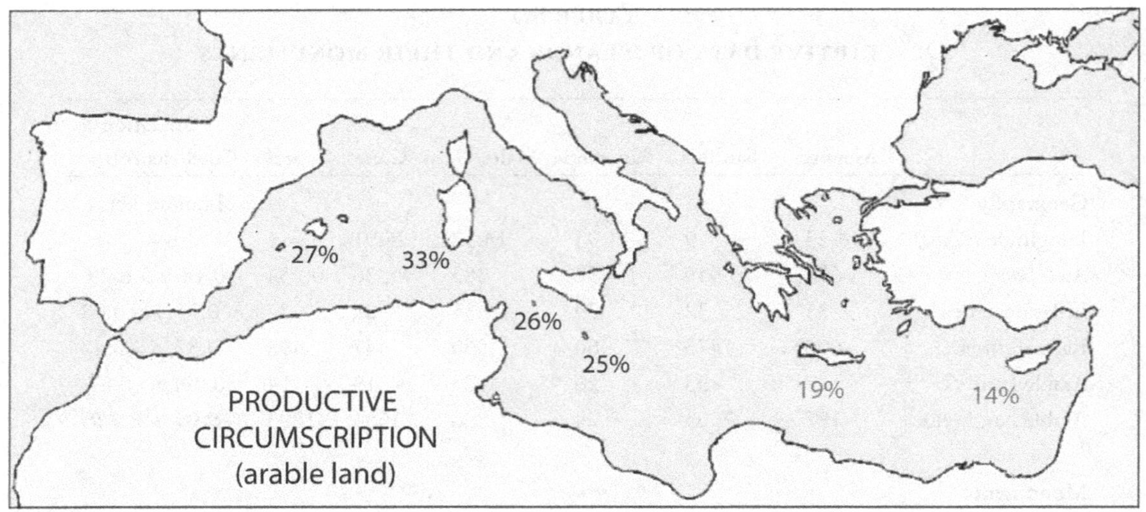

FIGURE 8.9 The percentage of arable land by island. This percentage is negatively correlated to longitude at a statistically significant level using Spearman's Ranked Correlation Coefficient (η = 6, r_s = –0.94, p < 0.01).

PAN-REGIONAL TRADITIONS OF PLACE

While environment may have played a key role in monumental elaboration, the variation that existed among the east and west Mediterranean monuments is also linked to the rise of two pan-regional traditions of "place." The first is the megalithic and cut-stone tomb tradition that developed by the fifth millennium B.C. along the coasts of Spain, France, Italy, Corsica, and Sardinia (Burenhult 2001; Grisnell 1975; c.f. Hoskin 2001), and the second is the court complex design that developed during the Bronze Age in Crete and Cyprus (see Lettesson and Vabsteenhuyse 2006; Schoep 2006; Shaw 1994). These concepts of ritual place may in fact represent a broader cultural distinction, between Europe and the Near East.

The megalithic tomb tradition was similar to Atlantic and continental European tombs, which were regionally diverse in style and included passage graves, gallery graves, cist graves, dolmens, hypogea, and beehive tombs (Figure 8.10). All were circular or squared stone chambers often covered by earth or stone mounds and marked with large upright monoliths called *menhir* stones. Most tombs were single chambered but some had entry areas used for ritual. Burial practices associated with megalithic tombs were varied, and included inhumation, secondary bundles of long bones, cremation, or excarnated remains from funeral pyres. Grave goods were uncommon. The rise of megalithic tombs coincided with distinctive Mediterranean-wide changes, including rising populations, larger villages, plow agriculture, and sheep/cattle herding that produced wool,

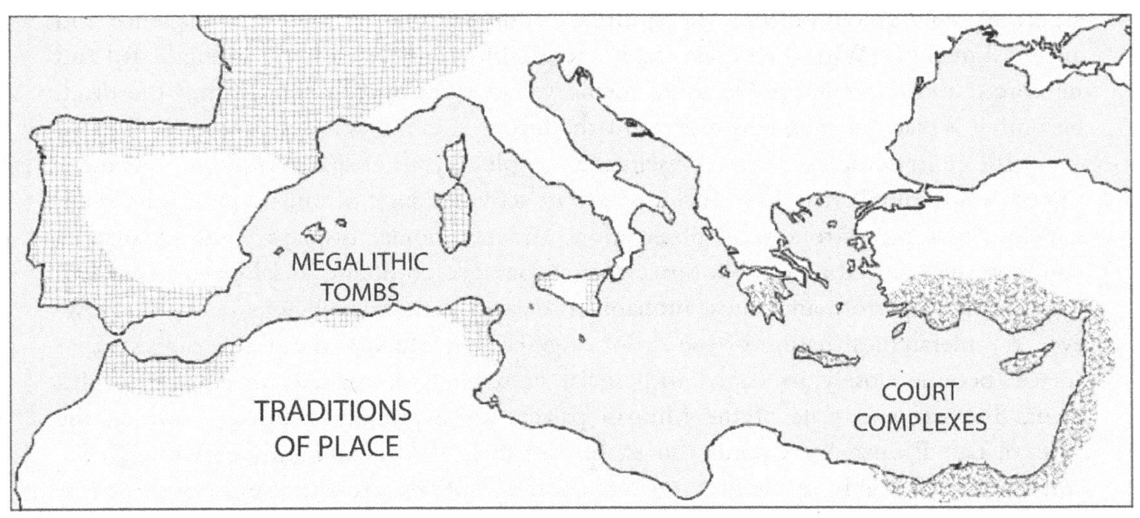

FIGURE 8.10 The distribution of megalithic tombs and the eastern Mediterranean court complexes.

leather, and milk (Sherratt 1983). Megalithic tombs continued as collective burials in parts of the western Mediterranean through the third millennium even though they were slowly supplanted by smaller collective graves or single tombs in Atlantic Europe. About this same time, megalithic chamber tombs and beehive tombs with vaulted roofs were first employed on the island of Crete in Greece, perhaps erected as artificial burial caves (Branigan 1970, 1993). Many were constructed with antechambers.

The third millennium also saw the rise of the court complex tradition in Crete and Cyprus (see Lettesson and Vabsteenhuyse 2006; Schoep 2006; Shaw 1994). This tradition derived from the court-style palaces and temple buildings of the Near East and Egypt (see Figure 8.10). A court complex included an arrangement of circular or square stone structures laid out around an open rectangular courtyard and that sometimes contained a series of pillars or colonnades. The courts provided access to many of the surrounding buildings and probably served as public meeting spaces for social occasions. The function of these court complexes was highly variable and is still debatable for certain sites; most represented cult sanctuaries, large temples, elite palaces, or a combination thereof.

Despite the variability of monuments in the Mediterranean, a number of observations may be made regarding pan-regional designs of place. Much, of course, has been written regarding the meaning and function of the megalithic tomb (see Cooney 2000), but as a culturally constructed place, these tombs helped the living cope with the concept and meaning of the afterlife. Each tomb, though unique in its layout and local topography, conceptually blended the physical world with the Neolithic spiritual realm. The physical world was one of earth and sky, the natural elements that permeated every aspect of daily Neolithic life. The spiritual realm was one of deadly permanence and ancestral memory. With their exaggerated monolithic stones, each tomb strengthened and reinforced the concepts of Neolithic memory and time by commemorating the dead, becoming a place of temporal order and rhythm.

The court complexes also represented a complex layout of spatial meanings. As mentioned, court rituals may have included group activities such as bull leaping (in Crete), dancing, feasting, astronomical observation, and ceremonial displays. Used as such, a court complex served as a public space that encouraged corporate social engagement and movements of performance most probably associated with cult religious practices. However, the hierarchical nature of the Bronze Age eastern Mediterranean also suggests that "place" became closely associated with social status and the capacity to employ surplus labor. The size and scale of the Minoan palaces are a primary example; however, the elites of Late Bronze Age Cyprus also established their identity and authority through the construction of highly visible monumental court complexes across the landscape. The fact that an unroofed court was often surrounded or spatially contained by elite structures suggests that access was routinely restricted so that only certain social strata or segments of society were permitted access to the court ceremonies carried out in them (see Kolb 1994 for an analogous example in ancient Hawai'i).

Social Competition

Social competition is also important to monumental elaboration. Certainly one of the most perplexing facets of island monumentality is the fact that the caloric and economic investments required for monumental construction seem counterproductive in more circumscribed environments. The construction of significantly larger monuments in the eastern Mediterranean is a case in point. Obviously, monuments become an important form of currency for social conflict or competition that results in channeling and controlling a set of limited productive resources.

One way to examine the relationship between monumental elaboration and conflict or competition is through the continuum of corporate and exclusionary strategies of social organization (see Feinman 2012). Corporate strategies are political relations that emphasize collective unity rather than personal aggrandizement, suppressing economic differentiation and deemphasizing personal wealth (Blanton 1998; Blanton et al. 1996; Feinman 1995; Feinman et al. 2000). Corporate organization is linked with local economic production, shared political power, and architecture emphasizing cooperative religious rituals, food production, and boundary maintenance (see Kolb 1997). Exclusionary or networked organization is linked with long-distance economic networks, more centralized/individualized rule, higher degrees of social inequity, and buildings such as the enclosed courtyards of the East that employed exclusionary strategies of elite aggrandizement.

The dispersed nature, horizontal differentiation, and centrality of the monumental landscape are important measures for assessing the nature of social competition. Interestingly, the two density measures of (1) monument density/dispersal (per square kilometer), and (2) the total hectares of sacred space/total square kilometers of arable land (see Figure 8.11), are both relatively constant except for the eastern islands of Crete and Cyprus. Both isles have a monument density at least 100 times less than all other islands. This suggests that corporate competition, as measured by monumental dispersal, intensified on islands that are more environmentally or socially circumscribed. A dispersed monumental landscape suggests greater island-wide political participation (and therefore competition), as well as less centralized control over productive resources. Viewing island monuments as territorial markers (Kolb 1994, 2012; Renfrew 1976), or as levers for negotiating religious or ideological activities in exchange for food or economic resources (Rainbird 2007; Stoddart et al. 1993), are two arguments that may explain this type of monumental functionality.

The Sardinian, Menorcan, Pantellerian, and Maltese monuments are good examples of the use of corporate social power. All are smaller-scale structures equally distributed across the landscape. They hosted important group-oriented rituals that allowed various social groups to exercise political, spiritual, and economic control. As these monuments became more architecturally complex over time, they served as markers for expressing territorial conflagrations and social dissent between social groups. It is unclear whether power became centralized under one or more elites/social groups over time, but it appears that social friction was on the rise. The eventual shift to cremation burials on Malta indicates a subsequent breakdown of corporate power, where leadership became more authoritative in order to access external metal exchange and maintain elite power (see Stoddart et al. 1993).

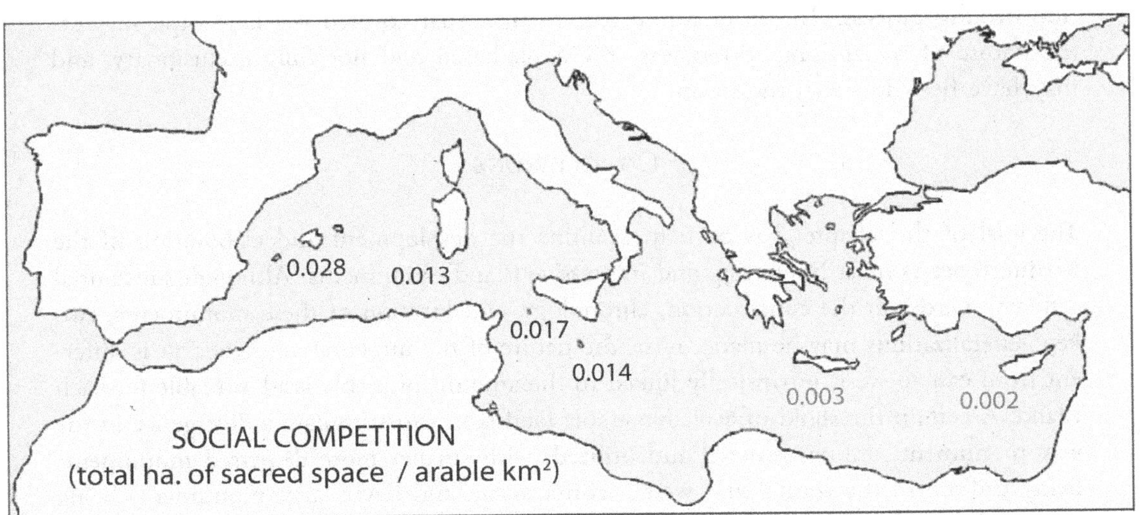

FIGURE 8.11 The total hectares of sacred space by the number of square kilometers of arable land for each island.

The Cypriot court complexes reveal a more mixed pattern of corporate and exclusionary social competition. Their moderate size and dispersal pattern suggest some form of corporate group competition, perhaps coinciding with a period of political tension when it was important to encourage and control social allegiances. As urbanization intensified in a few centers, their function appears to be associated with maintaining territorial control and social consensus within a broader exclusionary network of elite centralization.

The Minoan palaces represent the most drastic departure from the corporate strategy of social competition. On Crete, long-distance trade of prestige goods fostered more exclusionary social control, where palaces with their magnificent frescos served as centralizing nodes of organizational development, enhancing the social and ideological stature of local elites. Undoubtedly the rapid changes experienced in the eastern Mediterranean during the second millennium (e.g., increasing population, more intensive farming, Near Eastern contact, rise of metallurgy) stressed more exclusionary forms of ritual practice and leadership by enhancing social distinctions among individuals. On the other hand, a diverse set of palatial functions seem to indicate the expression of corporate relationships control, even if it were a vestige of the past. These include the public spaces and processional ways, the decentralized use of apartment spaces, and the lack of elite spaces.

The Sardinian *nuraghi* towers represent perhaps the most fascinating test case, demonstrating an interesting amalgam of corporate and exclusionary monumental elaboration. In one sense they represent clear indicators of corporate expression: single structures commissioned and built by individual families probably with the clan support. Their multifunctional nature denotes horizontal differentiation of social control and competition. Unfortunately, better chronological control of the sequence of construction is needed. However, the arrangement of many large *nuraghi* into clusters or protocastle formations may be indicative of exclusionary social competition with a centralized decision-making process. The sheer number of *nuraghi* that covered the landscape suggests the nature of social competition was still staple-based and not fully exclusionary, and may have been in social transition.

CONCLUSIONS

The goal of this chapter has been to examine the development and elaboration of the Mediterranean's most interesting and impressive island monuments. Although substantial differences exist in the construction, chronology, and location of these monuments, two key generalizations may be made. First, the nature of monumental construction is different from east to west, intrinsically linked to the amount of arable land available for each island. A certain threshold of available arable land seems to stimulate a divergence in the way monuments are constructed and utilized, with smaller more dispersed monuments being utilized in the central and west Mediterranean and fewer large monuments being used in the east Mediterranean. Second, those who built and used these monuments made logical choices for undertaking social competition and negotiating social consensus. As social inequality and economic intensification increased over time, island communities struggled with ways to maintain their collective unity in the face of emerging elites.

These monuments represent a variety of expressions for economically and ideologically enhancing long-term authority. In those cases where political and territorial cohesion could be maintained (such as on Crete and Cyprus), very tangible economic benefits emerged for elites. The pattern of monumental use in island societies has significance for the development of complex societies throughout the world, where the processes of political formation and ritualized ideology can be interwoven with architectonic and economic questions when discussing historical or archaeological change.

References Cited

Alcock, S. E. 2002 *Archaeologies of the Greek Past: Landscape, Monuments, and Memories.* Cambridge University Press, Cambridge.

Ardesia, V., Maurizio Cattani, Massimiliano Marazzi, Fabrizio Nicoletti, Manuela Secondo, Sebastiano Tusa 2006 Gli scavi nell'abitato dell'età del Bronzo di Mursia, Pantelleria (TP). Relazione preliminare delle campagne 2001–2005. *Rivista di scienze preistoriche* 56:293–367.

Balmuth, M. S. 1992 Archaeology in Sardinia. *American Journal of Archaeology* 96:663–687.

Balmuth, M. S., and R. J. Rowlands, eds. 1984 *Studies in Sardinian Archaeology.* University of Michigan Press, Ann Arbor.

Bellard, C. G. 1995 The First Colonization of Ibiza and Formentera (Balearic Islands, Spain): Some More Islands out of the Stream? *World Archaeology* (26):442–445.

Bender, B. 1998 *Stonehenge: Making Space.* Berg, Oxford.

Blake, E. 1998 Sardinia's Nuraghi: Four Millennia of Becoming. *World Archaeology* 30:59–71.

Blake, E. 2001 Constructing a Nuragic Locale: The Spatial Relationship between Tombs and Towers in Bronze Age Sardinia. *American Journal of Archaeology* 105:145–162.

Blanton, R. 1998 Beyond Centralization: Steps toward a Theory of Egalitarian Behavior. In *Archaic States,* edited by G. M. Feinman, and J. Marcus, pp. 135–172. School of American Research Press, Santa Fe.

Blanton, R. E., Gary M. Feinman, Stephen A. Kowalewski, and Peter N. Peregrine 1996 A Dual-Processual Theory for the Evolution of Mesoamerican Civilization. *Current Anthropology* 37:1–86.

Bonanno, A., Tancred Gouder, Caroline Malone, and Simon Stoddart 1990 Monuments in an Island Society: The Maltese Context. *World Archaeology* 22: 90–205.

Bourdieu, P. 1977 *Outline of a Theory of Practice.* Cambridge University Press, London.

Bradley, R. 2003 Archaeologies of Remembrance: Death and Memory in Past Societies. *Cambridge Archaeological Journal* 3 (2):298–299.

Branigan, K. 1970 *The Tombs of Mesara: A Study of Funerary Architecture and Ritual in Southern Crete 2800–1700 B.C.* Duckworth, London.

Branigan, K. 1993 *Dancing with Death: Life and Death in Southern Crete c. 3000–2000 B.C.* Adolf M. Hakkert, Amsterdam.

Burenhult, G. 2001 Long-Distance Cultural Interaction in Megalithic Europe: Carrowmore and the Irish Megalithic Tradition in a Western European and Mediterranean Context. In *Cultural Interactions in Europe and the Eastern Mediterranean During the Bronze Age (3000–500 BC): Papers from a Session Held at the European Association of Archaeologists Sixth Annual Meeting in Lisbon, 2000,* edited by B. Wyszomirska-Werbart, pp. 47–66: British Archaeological Reports 985.

Calvo Trias, M., V. M. Guerrero Ayuso, and B. Salvà Simonet 2001 *Arquitectura Ciclópea del Bronce Balear. El Tall del Temps 37*. El Tall, Mallorca.

Carneiro, R. L. 1970 A Theory of the Origin of the State. *Science* 169:733–738.

Chapman, R. W. 1985 The Later Prehistory of Western Mediterranean Europe: Recent Advances. In *Advances in World Archaeology*, edited by F. Wendorf and A. Close, pp. 115–187. Academic Press. New York.

Cherry, J. F. 1983 Evolution, Revolution, and the Origins of Complex Society in Minoan Crete. In *Minoan Society*, edited by O. Krzyszkowska and L. Nixon, pp. 33–45. Bristol Classical Press, Bristol.

Cherry, J. F. 1986 Polities and Palaces: Some Problems in Minoan State Formation. In *Peer Polity Interaction and Socio-political Change*, edited by A. C. Renfrew, and J. F. Cherry, pp. 19–45. Cambridge University Press, Cambridge.

Christakis, K. S. 1999 Pithoi and Food Storage in Neopalatial Crete: A Domestic Perspective. *World Archaeology* 31:1–20.

Connerton, P. 1989 *How Societies Remember*. Cambridge University Press, Cambridge.

Cooney, G. 2000 *Landscapes of Neolithic Ireland*. Routledge, London.

Davis, E. N. 1987 The Knossos Miniature Frescoes and the Function of the Central Courts. In *The Function of the Minoan Palaces*, edited by R. Hägg, and N. Marinatos, pp. 157–161. Svenska Institutet i Athen, Stockholm.

Driessen, J., and C. Macdonald 1997 *The Troubled Island. Minoan Crete before and after the Santorini Eruption*. Aegaeum 17. Université de Liège, Liège.

Driessen, J., I. Schoep, and R. Laffineur, eds. 2002 *Monuments of Minos: Rethinking the Minoan Palaces*. Aegaeum 23. Université de Liège, Liège.

Earle, T. 1991 The Evolution of Chiefdoms. In *Chiefdoms: Power, Economy, and Ideology*, edited by T. Earle, pp. 1–15. Cambridge University Press, Cambridge.

Evans, A. 1921 *The Palace of Minos*. Macmillan, London.

Evans, J. D. 1984 Maltese Prehistory: A Reappraisal. In *The Deyà Conference of Prehistory. Early Settlement in the West Mediterranean Islands and the Peripheral Areas*, edited by W. H. Waldren, R. Chapman, R. L. Lewthwaite, and R. C. Kennard, pp. 489–497. British Archaeological Reports, Oxford.

Feinman, G. M. 1995 The Emergence of Inequality: A Focus on Strategies and Processes. In *Foundations of Social Inequality*, edited by T. D. Price and G. M. Feinman, pp. 255–280. Plenum Press, New York.

Feinman, G. M. 2012 Comparative Frames for the Diachronic Analysis of Complex Societies. In *The Comparative Archaeology of Complex Societies*, edited by M. E. Smith, pp. 21–43. Cambridge University Press, Cambridge.

Feinman, G. M., Kent G. Lightfoot, and Steadman Upham 2000 Political Hierarchies and Organizational Strategies in the Puebloan Southwest. *American Antiquity*:65.

Fisher, K. D. 2007 Building Power: Monumental Architecture, Place, and Social Interaction in Late Bronze Age Cyprus. PhD thesis. University of Toronto.

Fisher, K. D. 2009a Elite Place-Making and Social Interaction in the Late Cypriot Bronze Age. *Journal of Mediterranean Archaeology* 22(2):183–209.

Fisher, K. D. 2009b Placing Social Interaction: An Integrative Approach to Analyzing Past Built Environments. *Journal of Anthropological Archaeology* 28:439–457.

Fisher, K. D. In press. Rethinking the Late Cypriot Built Environment: Households and Communities as Places of Social Transformation. In *The Cambridge Prehistory of the Bronze and*

Iron Age Mediterranean World, edited by A. B. Knapp and P. van Dommelen. Cambridge University Press, Cambridge.

Gasull, P., V. Lull et al. 1984 *Son Fornes I: La Fase Talayotica. Ensayo de Reconstruccion Socio-Economica de una Comunidad Prehisorica de la Isla de Mallorca.* British Archaeological Reports, International Series, no. 209, Oxford.

Giardino, C. 1992 Nuragic Sardinia and the Mediterranean: Metallurgy and Maritime Traffic. In *Sardinia in the Mediterranean: A Footprint in the Sea,* edited by S. R. H. Tykot, and T. K. Andrews, pp. 304–316. Sheffield Academic Press, Sheffield.

Gilibert, A. 2011 *Syro-Hittite Monumental Art and the Archaeology of Performance.* Walter de Gruyter, Berlin.

Goodison, L. 2001 From Tholos Tomb to Throne Room: Perceptions of the Sun in Minoan Ritual. In Potnia. Deities and Religion in the Aegean Bronze Age. In *Aegaeum,* ed.ited by R. L. a. R. Hägg, pp. 77–88. University of Liège, Liège.

Graham, J. W. 1987 *The Palaces of Crete.* Princeton University Press, Princeton.

Grinsell, L. V. 1975 *Barrow, Pyramid, and Tomb: Ancient Burial Customs in Egypt, the Mediterranean, and the British Isles.* Thames and Hudson, London.

Hägg, R., and Nanno Marinatos, eds. 1987 *The Function of Minoan Palaces. Proceedings of the Fourth International Symposium at the Swedish Institute at Athens.* Paul Åströms Förlag Göteborg.

Halbwachs, M. 1980 [1925]. *The Collective Memory.* Harper and Row, New York.

Hamilakis, Y. 1999 Food Technologies/Technologies of the Body: The Social Context of Wine and Oil Production and Consumption in Bronze Age Crete. *World Archaeology* 31:38–54.

Hamilakis, Y., ed. 2002 *Labyrinth Revisited: Rethinking Minoan Archaeology.* Oxbow Books, Oxford.

Hansen, J. M. 1988 Agriculture in the Pre-Historic Aegean: Data versus Speculation. *American Journal of Archaeology* 92:39–52.

Hendon, J. A. 2007 Production as Social Process. *Archeological Papers of the American Anthropological Association* 17(1):163–168.

Hoskin, M. A. 2001 *Tombs, Temples, and Their Orientations: A New Perspective on Mediterranean Prehistory.* Ocarina, Bognor Regis.

Ingold, T. 2000 *Perception of the Environment: Essays in Livelihood, Dwelling, and Skill.* Routledge, London.

Inomata, T., and L. S. Coben, eds. 2006 *Archaeology of Performance: Theaters of Power, Community, and Politics.* Altamira, Lanham, Maryland.

Joyce, R. A. 2005 Archaeology of the Body. *Annual Review of Anthropology* 34:139–158.

Knapp, A. B. 2008 Prehistoric and Protohistoric Cyprus: Identity, Insularity, and Connectivity. Oxford University Press, Oxford.

Knapp, A. B. 2009 Monumental Architecture, Identity and Memory. In *Proceedings of the Symposium: Bronze Age Architectural Traditions in the East Mediterranean: Diffusion and Diversity,* pp. 47–59. Verein zur Förderung der Aufarbeitung der Hellenischen Geschichte, Weilheim.

Knapp, A. B., S. O. Held, and S. W. Manning. 1994 The Prehistory of Cyprus: Problems and Prospects. *Journal of World Prehistory* 8:377–453.

Knappett, C., and Ille Schoep 2000 Continuity and Change in Minoan Palatial Power. *Antiquity* 74:365–371.

Kolb, M. J. 1994 Monumentality and the Rise of Religious Authority in Precontact Hawai'i. *Current Anthropology* 35:521–547.

Kolb, M. J. 1997 Labor, Ethnohistory, and the Archaeology of Community in Hawai'i. *Journal of Archeological Method and Theory* 4:265–286.

Kolb, M. J. 2004 The Genesis of Monuments among the Mediterranean Islands. In *The Prehistoric Archaeology of the Mediterranean*, edited by B. A. Knapp and E. Blake, pp. 156–179. Blackwell, London.

Kolb, M. J. 2012 The Genesis of Monuments in Island Societies. In *The Comparative Archaeology of Complex Societies*, edited by M. E. Smith, pp. 138–164. Cambridge University Press, Cambridge.

Lefebvre, H. 1991 *The Production of Space*. Basil Blackwell, Oxford.

Letesson, Q., and Klaas Vansteenhuyse 2006 Towards an Archaeology of Perception: "Looking" at the Minoan Palaces. *Journal of Mediterranean Archaeology* 19(1):91–119.

Lewis, H. 1977 *Ancient Malta; A Study of Its Antiquities*. Smythe, Gerrards Cross.

Lightfoot, K. G., Antoinette Martinez, and Ann M. Schiff. 1998 Daily Practice and Material Culture in Pluralistic Social Settings: An Archaeological Study of Culture Change and Persistence from Fort Ross, California. *American Antiquity* 63:199–222.

Lilliu, G. 1982 *La civiltà nuragica*. Sassari: Carlo Delfino.

Lo Schiavo, F., Ellen Macnamara, and Lucia Vagnetti 1985 Late Cypriot Imports to Italy and their Influence on Local Bronzework. *Papers of the British School at Rome* 53:1–71.

Manning, S. W. 1994 The Emergence of Divergence: Development and Decline on Bronze Age Crete and the Cyclades. In *Development and Decline in the Mediterranean Bronze Age*, edited by C. Mathers and S. Stoddart, pp. 221–270. J. Collis, Sheffield.

Marinatos, N. 1987 Public Festivals in the West Courts of the Palaces. In *The Function of the Minoan Palaces*, edited by R. Hägg and N. Marinatos, pp. 135–143. Svenska Institutet i Athen, Stockholm.

Meillassoux, C. 1964 *Anthropologie Économique des Gouro de Côte d'Ivoire; de l'économie de Subsistance à l'agriculture Commerciale*. Mouton, Den Haag.

Meillassoux, C. 1967 Récherche d'un niveau de détermination dans la société Cynégétrique. *L'Homme et la Société* 6:24–36.

Meskell, L. 2003 Memory's Materiality: Ancestral Presence, Commemorative Practice and Disjunctive Locales. In *Archaeologies of Memory*, edited by R. M. Van Dyke, and Susan E. Alcock, pp. 34–55. Blackwell, London.

Murphy, J. 1998 The Nearness of You—Proximity and Distance in Early Minoan Funerary Landscapes. In *Cemetery and Society in the Aegean Bronze Age*, edited by K. Branigan, pp. 27–40. Sheffield Academic Press, Sheffield.

Nelson, R. S., and M. R. Olin 2003 *Monuments and Memory, Made and Unmade*. University of Chicago Press, Chicago.

Papalexandrou, A. 2003 Memory Tattered and Torn: Spolia in the Heartland of Byzantine Hellenism. In *Archaeologies of Memory*, edited by R. M. Van Dyke and Susan E. Alcock. Blackwell, London.

Patton, M. 1996 *Islands in Time: Island Sociogeography and Mediterranean Prehistory*. Routledge, London.

Plantalamor, L., and M. C. Rita 1984 Formas de poblacion durante el segundo y primero milenio BC en Menorca: Son Merver de Baix, transicion entre la cultura Pretalayotica y Talayotica. In *The Deyà Conference of Prehistory. Early Settlement in the West Mediterranean Islands and the Peripheral areas*, edited by W. H. Waldren, R. Chapman, R.J. Lewthwaite, and R.C. Kennard, pp. 797–826. British Archaeological Reports, Oxford.

Rainbird, P. 2007 *The Archaeology of Islands*. Cambridge University Press, Cambridge.

Rehak, P. a. J. G. Y. 1998 Review of Aegean Prehistory VII: Neopalatial, Final Palatial, and Postpalatial Crete. *American Journal of Archaeology* 102:91–173.

Relph, E. 1976 *Place and Placelessness*. Pion, London.

Renfrew, A. C. 1972 *The Emergence of Civilisation*. Methuen, London.

Renfrew, A. C. 1974 Beyond a Subsistence Economy. In *Reconstructing Complex Societies,* ed. C. B. Moore, pp. 69–96. Supplement to the Bulletin of American School of Prehistoric Research, Cambridge, Massachusetts.

Renfrew, A. C. 1976 Megaliths, Territories, and Populations. In *Acculturation and Continuity in Atlantic Europe,* edited by S. DeLaet, pp. 198–220. Dissertationes Archaeologicae Gandenses, Ghent.

Renfrew, A. C. 2007 *Prehistory: The Making of the Human Mind*. Random House, London.

Renfrew, A. C., and E. V. Level 1979 Exploring Dominance: Predicting Polities from Centers. In *Transformations: Mathematical Approaches to Culture Change,* edited by A. C. Renfrew and K. L. Cooke, pp. 145–167. Academic Press, New York.

Renfrew, C., Chris Firth, and Lambros Malafouris 2008 The Sapient Mind: Archaeology Meets Neuroscience. *Philosophical Transactions of the Royal Society B* 363:1935–1938.

Renfrew, C., and Christopher Scarre, eds. 1998 *Cognition and Material Culture: The Archaeology of Symbolic Storage*. McDonald Institute for Archaeological Research, Cambridge.

Rita, C. 1988 The Evolution of the Minorcan Pretalayotic Culture as Evidenced by the Sites of Morellet and Son Mercer de Baix. *Proceedings of the Prehistoric Society* 54:241–247.

Rubertone, P. E., ed. 2008 *Archaeologies of Placemaking: Monuments, Memories, and Engagement in Native North America*. Left Coast Press, Walnut Creek, California.

Schoep, I. 2006 Looking beyond the First Palaces: Elites and the Agency of Power in EM III–MM II Crete. *American Journal of Archaeology* 110(1):37–64.

Schoep, I. 2010 The Minoan "Palace-Temple" Reconsidered: A Critical Assessment of the Spatial Concentration of Political, Religious and Economic Power in Bronze Age Crete. *Journal of Mediterranean Archaeology* 23(2):219–244.

Shaw, J. W. 1973 The Orientation of the Minoan Palaces. *Antichità Cretesi Studi in onore di Doro Levi* 2: 47–59.

Sherratt, A. 1981 Plough and Pastorialism: Aspects of the Secondary Products Revolution. In *Pattern of the Past: Studies in Honour of David Clark,* edited by I. Hodder, and N. Hammond, pp. 261–305. Cambridge University Press, Cambridge.

Sherratt, A. 1983 The Secondary Exploitation of Animals in the Old World. *World Archaeology* 15:90–104.

Steel, L. 1998 The Social Impact of Mycenaean Imported Pottery in Cyprus. *Annual of the British School at Athens* 93:285–296.

Steel, L. 2004 *Cyprus before History: From the Earliest Settlers to the End of the Bronze Age*. Gerald Duckworth, London.

Stoddart, S. 1999 Long-Term Dynamics of an Island Community; Malta 5500 BC–2000 AD. In *Social Dynamics of Prehistoric Central Mediterranean,* edited by R. H. Tykot, J. Morter, and J. E. Robb, pp. 137–147. Accordia Research Institute, University of London, London.

Stoddart, S., A. Bonanno et al. 1993 Cult in an Island Society: Prehistoric Malta in the Tarxien Period. *Cambridge Archaeological Journal* 3:3–19.

Tilley, C. Y. 1994 *A Phenomenology of Landscape: Places, Paths, and Monuments*. Berg, Oxford.

Tore, G. 1984 Per una rilettura del complesso Nuragico di S'Uraki, Loc. Su Pardu, S. Vero Milis, Oristano (Sardegna). In *The Deyà Conference of Prehistory. Early Settlement in the West Mediterranean Islands and the Peripheral Areas,* edited by T. W. H. Waldren, R. Chapman, R. J. Lewthwaite, and R.C. Kennard, pp. 703–723. British Archaeological Reports S229, Oxford.

Trigger, B. G. 1990 Monumental Architecture: A Thermodynamic Explanation of Symbolic Behavior. *World Archaeology* 22(2):119–132.

Tringham, R. 2000 The Continuous House: A View from the Deep Past. In *Beyond Kinship, Social and Material Reproduction in House Societies,* editd by R. A. Joyce and S. D. Gillespie, pp. 115–134. University of Pennsylvania Press, Philadelphia.

Trump, D. H. 1972 *Malta: An Archaeological Guide.* Faber and Faber, London.

Trump, D. H. 1977 The Collapse of the Maltese Temples. In *Problems in Economic and Social Archaeology,* edited by G. d. G. Sieveking, I. H. Longworth, and K. E. Wilson, pp. 605–609. Westview, Boulder.

Trump, D. H. 2002 *Malta: Prehistory and Temples.* Midsea Books, Valetta, Malta.

Tuan, Y.-F. 1977 *Space and Place: The Perspective of Experience.* Edward Arnold, London.

Turnbull, D. 2002 Performance and Narrative, Bodies and Movement in the Construction of Places and Objects, Spaces, and Knowledges. *Theory, Culture and Society* 19(5/6):125–143.

Tusa, S., G. Foderà Serio et al. 1992 Orientations of the Sesi of Pantelleria. *Journal for the History of Astronomy, Archaeoastronomy Supplement* 23:S15–20.

Waldren, W. H. 1982 *Balearic Prehistoric Ecology and Culture.* British Archaeological Reports S149, Oxford.

Waldren, W. H. 1992 Radiocarbon and Other Isotopic Age Determinations from the Balearic Islands: A Comprehensive Inventory. In *Deyà Archaeolocial Museum and Research Centre.* Deyà Archaeological Museum and Research Centre, Deyà, Mallorca.

Watkins, T. 2004a Architecture and Theatres of Memory in the Neolithic of Southwest Asia. In *Rethinking Materiality: The Engagement of Mind with the Material World,* edited by C. Renfrew, E. DeMarrais, and C. Gosden, pp. 97–106. McDonald Institute for Archaeological Research, Cambridge.

Watkins, T. 2004b Building Houses, Framing Concept, Constructing Worlds. *Paléorient* 30(1):5–24.

Watkins, T. 2012 Household, Community, and Social Landscape: Building and Maintaining Social Memory in the Early Neolithic of Southwest Asia. In *As Time Goes By, Monuments, Landscapes, and the Temporal Perspective. Socio-Environmental Dynamics over the Last 12,000 Years,* edited by M. Furholt, M. Hinz, and D. Mischka Kiel, pp. 23–44. Rudolf Habelt, Bonn.

Watrous, L. V. 1994 Review of Aegean Prehistory III: Crete from Earliest Prehistory through the Protopalatial Period. *American Journal of Archaeology* 98:695–753.

Watrous, L., V. Despoina Chatzåe-Vallianou et al. 2004 *The Plain of Phaistos: Cycles of Social Complexity in the Mesara Region of Crete.* Cotsen Institute of Archaeology, Los Angeles.

Webb, J. M. 1999 *Ritual Architecture, Iconography, and Practice in the Late Cypriote Bronze Age. Studies in Mediterranean Archaeology and Literature, Pocket-book 75.* P. Åström's Förlag, Jonsered.

Webster, G. S. 1991 Monuments, Mobilization, and Nuragic Organization. *Antiquity* 65:840–856.

Webster, G. S. 1996 Social Archaeology and the Irrational. *Current Anthropology* 37:609–627.

Whitridge, P. 2004 Landscapes, Houses, Bodies, Things: "Place" and the Archaeology of Inuit Imaginaries. *Journal of Archaeological Method and Theory* 11(2):213–250.

Wright, G. R. H. 1992 *Ancient Building in Cyprus. Handbuch der Orientalistik 7. Abteilung, Kunst und Archaeologie. I Band, Der Alte Vordere Orient 2B/7/1 and 2B/7/2.* Brill, Leiden, Köln.

CHAPTER NINE

4100–2700 B.C.

Monuments and Ideologies in the Neolithic Landscape

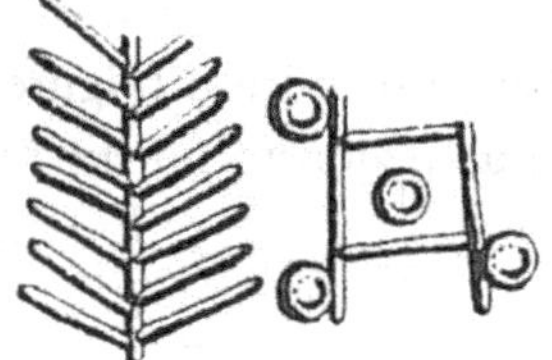

Johannes Müller

Abstract *In northern central Europe and southern Scandinavia thousands of megalithic monuments were constructed ca. 3600–3200 B.C. Which societies erected them, and why? Were different ideologies responsible for different patterns of social space, reflected in monumental constructions? Beside different types of megalithic burial sites, causewayed enclosures were very important for the earliest agriculturalists of northern Europe. They were placed in a landscape that went through dramatic environmental changes. Within European society collective and cooperative behavior changed through time into a pronunciation of individual differences. Different architecture was used for the display of different social roles, and in this sense megalithic constructions are a reflection of the need to express stability in the relation between individuals and society, humans and nature. As a consequence, the Neolithic mobility of ideas led to the formation of reorganized space during the Funnel Beaker, or "TRB" (Trichterbecher), age, a reorganized space that—as a social space—utilized the position of the ancestors for the positioning of the living.*

INTRODUCTION

One of the main questions of social anthropology concerns how social relations within societies are created and confirmed. Within nonliterate societies these processes were linked to other means than in literate societies: the creation and reconstruction of memories, social memories, was related to a variety of mechanisms in which material culture played an important role as a medium of knowledge transformation. Within many

European Neolithic societies such constitutions are linked to the construction of visible monuments, which function for ancestor worship or as gathering places. Within the social space created by such monuments, the reconfirmation of rules of individual behavior and group activities could have taken place, as well as the introduction of new ideas.

A monument of this type found in numerous regions in western, central, and northern Europe is the so-called megalith, in most cases megalithic tombs consisting of uprights and capstones. It can be extrapolated from the current state of documentation that in southern Scandinavia and northern central Europe approximately 15,000 more or less well-preserved megalithic tombs are in existence, although originally almost a half-million megalithic tombs probably were erected.

Apart from the distribution of megalithic tombs along the western Mediterranean they can also be principally found along the so-called Atlantic Facade as well as in northern central Europe and southern Scandinavia (Fischer 1979). Their distribution (Figures 9.1 and 9.2) stretches from Portugal to Galicia and from the Basque region to northwest

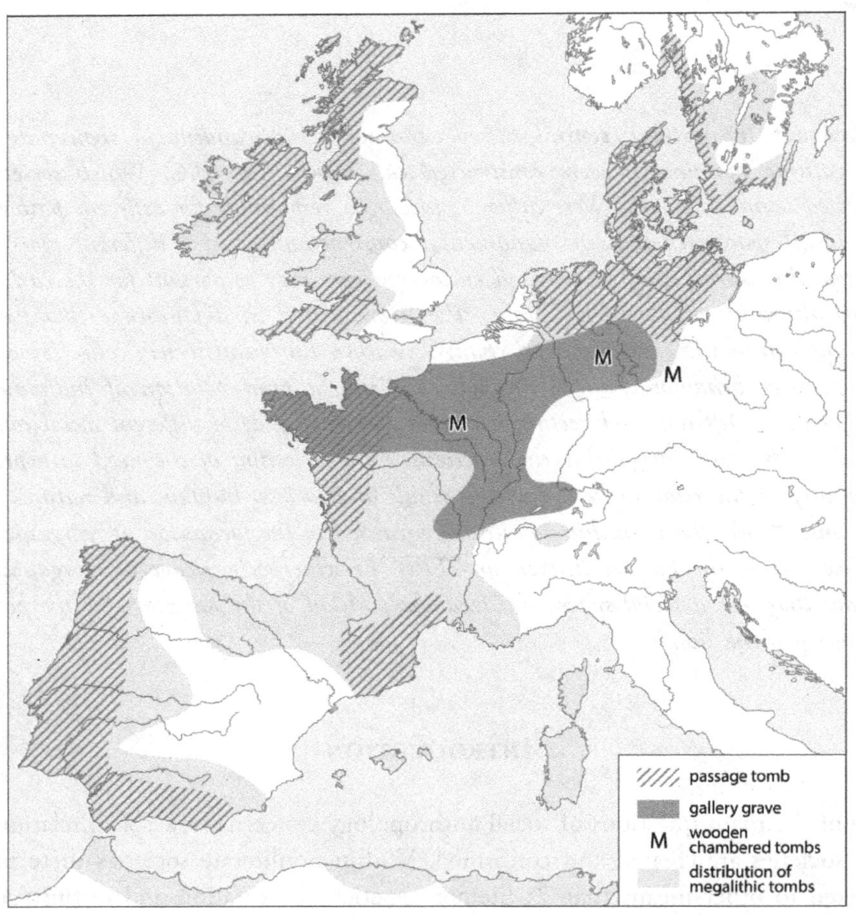

FIGURE 9.1 The distribution of megaliths in western, central, and northern Europe (after Müller 2006; graphic: Holger Dieterich).

FIGURE 9.2 The distribution of megaliths in northern central Europe and southern Scandinavia. Important sites mentioned in the article are marked. 1 Barkaer, 2 Vroue Heide, 3 Bygholm, 4 Dragsholm, 5 Sarup, 6 Frälsegården, 7 Saxtorp, 8 Dagstorp, 9 Almhov, 10 Trolasten, 11 Tinnum, 12 Schwesing, 13 Büdelsdorf-Borgstedt, 14 Rastorf, 15 Flintbek, 16 Albersdorf-Dieksknöll, 17 Albersdorf-Brutkamp, 18 Oldenburg, 19 Wangels, 20 Bad Oldesloe-Wolkenwehe, 21 Triwalk, 22 Ostorf, 23 Parchim-Löddigsee, 24 Flögeln, 25 Himmelpforten, 26 Hunte 1, 27 Kassel-Calden, 28 Lüdelsen, 29 Haldensleben, 30 Hundisburg-Olbetal, 31 Halle-Dölauer Heide.

France, from southern England and Ireland to the North Atlantic Shetland Islands, and from Drenthe in the Netherlands to Pomerania and central Sweden. Even though they are difficult to date, the oldest are to be found in the Vendée and on the Armorican Peninsula. Radiometric dating and Chasséen pottery from the earliest grave chambers indicate a construction phase beginning ca. 4700 B.C. (Cassen et al. 2009; Laporte 2005; Müller 1997). The Breton development appears to be a reaction to different influences.

We know that at approximately the same time nonmegalithic long barrows of the Passy type in the Blique/Epi-Rössen tradition were erected in the Paris Basin and the concept of trapezoidal-rectangular long barrows coming from the east reached the area on the northwest coast of France (Chambon and Thomas 2010). At the same time stone cists and early passage graves, whose polygonal form appears similar to Epi-Cardial and Cerny grave traditions farther to the south, are to be found in these and other mounds. From a mixture of a variety of influences—surely based on an indigenous substratum and in connection with the development of agriculture—the oldest preserved monuments in Europe emerged. These monuments leave their imprint on the landscape and, for example, in the Gulf of Morbihan they cluster to ritual centers of transregional significance. In cists within nonmegalithic long barrows interred humans were richly furnished with alpine jadeite axes (Cassen et al. 2010), while menhirs as tall as 21 m were ceremoniously broken and used as capstones, for example at the famous facility Table des Marchand (Cassen 2009). In Brittany and Normandy, a centuries-long tradition of the construction of megalithic tombs develops until ca. 3200 B.C., during which dolmen, passage graves, gallery graves, and menhirs were built (Boujot and Cassen 1993).

Not all megalithic facilities in Europe are as old as those in northwestern France. In the Mediterranean region, for example on Corsica and Sardinia (see Kolb, this volume), simple dolmen appear first as of 4200 B.C., whereas on the British Isles they first emerge as of approximately 4000 B.C. and in the north central Europe and southern Scandinavia regions, which are to be the center of attention here, they exist only as early as 3650 B.C. (Leandri et al. 2007; Müller 2009; A. Whittle et al. 2011). In fact, according to the current state of research we cannot state with certainty how much the high mobility of Neolithic society promoted a diffusion of the idea of laying large stones while using them for collective graves, or whether we must assume convergent architectural developments in different regions from the outset. Although it is relatively clear that the *allées couvertes* and gallery graves both developed as of 3600 B.C. in inland settings from Brittany over the Paris Basin to central Germany, the northern central European-Scandinavian area appears to have undergone a spatially and culturally autonomous development separate from the west, though naturally accompanied by the reception of outside innovations.

These preliminary considerations lead us to the primary questions of the present chapter: (1) Why, and from which date, were megalithic graves built in the northern central European lowlands and in southern Scandinavia? (2) How can the different phases of monumental development be explained for the area under investigation? and (3) Why did this tradition cease after its 500-year existence?

FUNNEL BEAKERS AND MONUMENTS

When speaking of megalithic graves in northern central Europe and southern Scandinavia one is simultaneously taking Funnel Beaker societies into account as well (Figure 9.3). Since the early nineteenth century we have known that megalithic graves in the Netherlands and northern Germany as well as in Denmark and Sweden are associated with a specific form of ceramics, the so-called Funnel Beaker pottery. Defined recurring features of material culture characterize Funnel Beaker societies (TRB or *Trichterbecher*)

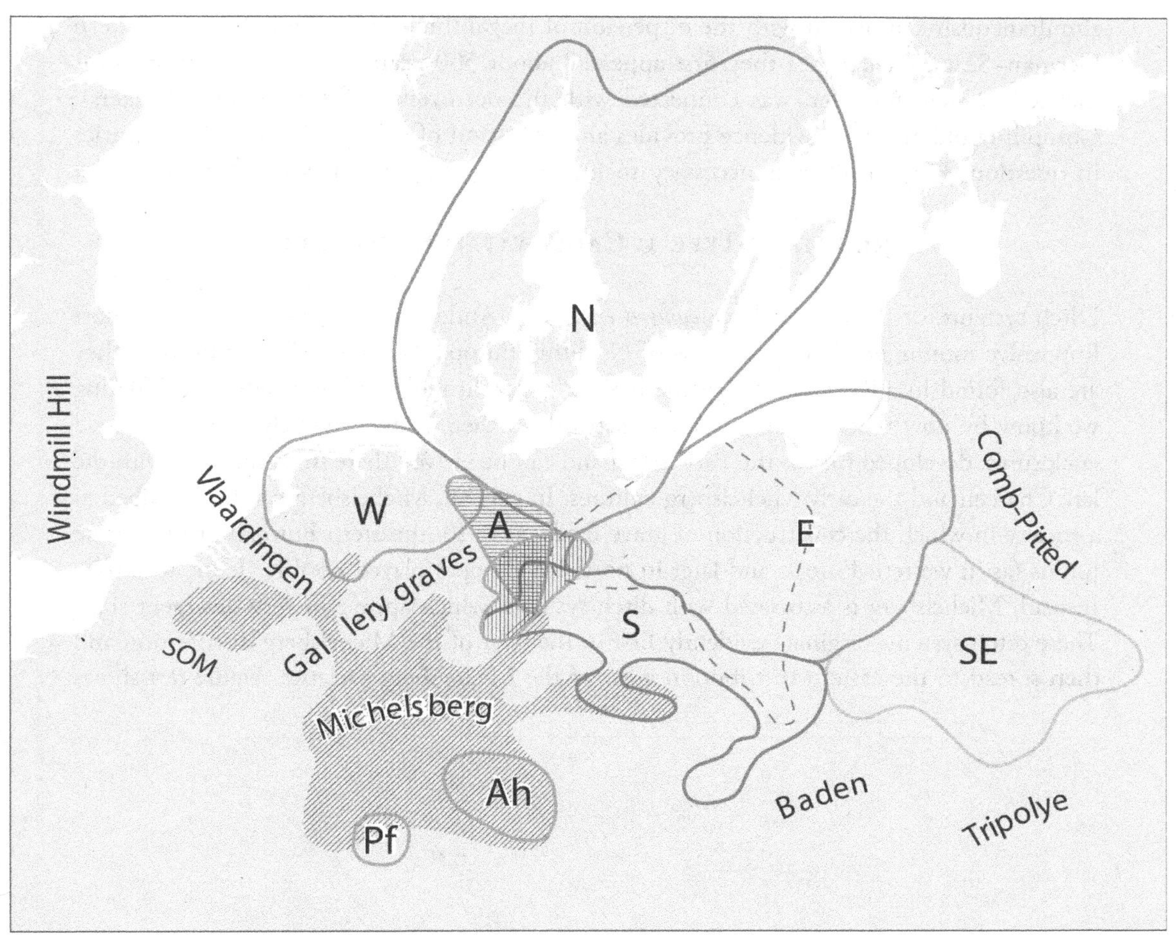

FIGURE 9.3 Regional groups of the TRB culture (after Bakker 1979, Figure 1; graphic: Andrzej Link). W = West Group, N = North Group, E = East Group, S = South Group, SE = Southeast Group, Ah = Altheim Group or Culture, Pf = Pfyn Group, A and horizontally hatched = Altmark Group, vertically hatched = Walternienburg-Bernburg Group. The broken line indicates the occurrence of the Luboń decoration of three-strand cord impressions. Diagonal hatching indicates the related Michelsberg culture. SOM = the Seine-Oise-Marne Culture.

and set them apart from other Neolithic societies to the south and to the west (see, e.g., Bakker 1979; M. Midgley 1992). Precisely this autonomy of the material culture of TRB societies will occupy us in the following investigation. The development of monumentality is closely related to other aspects of TRB societies and the key to understanding the phenomenon of megalithic tombs lies in deciphering the social conditions and ritual practices of these societies.

It is clear that the area under discussion here possesses a different dynamic than that in Britain and northwestern France since neolithization in the latter regions was simultaneously connected with the dispersion of megalithic tombs, while in the northern German–Scandinavian area they first appeared about 500 years after neolithization commenced (which, however, was connected with the occurrence of early Funnel Beakers). Compiling old and new evidence provides an impression of the dynamics of the centuries in question. First of all, it is necessary to identify the three main types of monuments.

MONUMENT TYPE 1: CAUSEWAYED ENCLOSURES

Ditch systems, or the so-called *causewayed enclosures* (Andersen 1997), are among the most impressive monumental constructions of Neolithic Europe. Scattered all over Europe, they are also found in TRB regions. On the basis of typo-chronological and radiometric dating we know by now that the typical enclosures with earthen bridges, namely, the causewayed enclosures, developed first in the Paris Basin and can be viewed there in connection with the late Chaséen and the early Michelsberg cultures. In general, Michelsberg can be described as a society in which the construction of grave fields (as in southeastern Europe) or megalithic tombs (as in western Europe and later in northern Europe) played no role (Jeunesse 2010). Instead, Michelsberg is associated with ditch systems, which appear in very divergent sizes. These ditch systems originate evidently first in the west of the Michelsberg distribution and then spread to the eastern distribution areas of the Michelsberg societies. Figure 9.4 shows

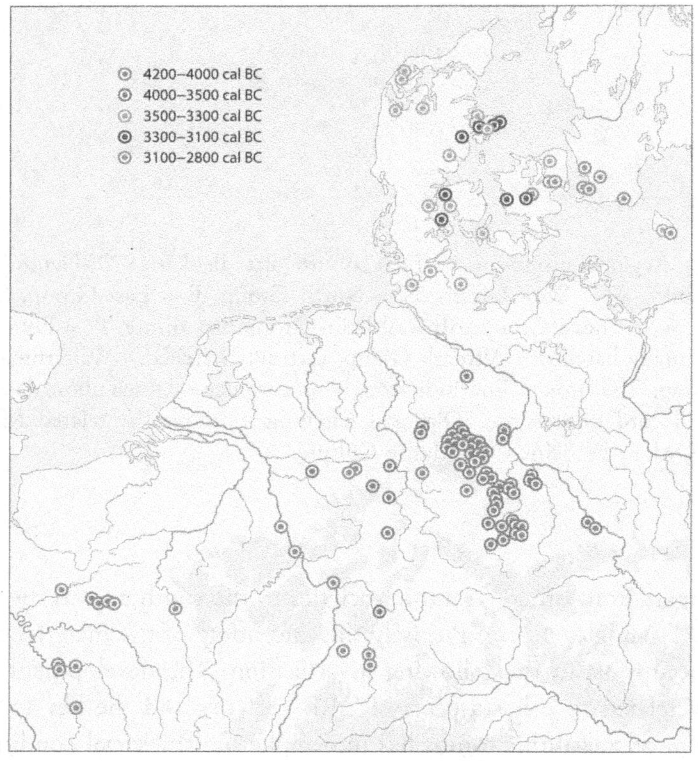

FIGURE 9.4 Distribution and dating of causewayed enclosures (after Müller 2010; graphic: Holger Dieterich).

this chronological trend. The central German region (Baalberg) also acquired the idea of building ditch systems around 3800 B.C. at the latest. Consequently, we observe a large territory during the entire fourth millennium in which such ditch systems appear in quite different forms after the idea of building them was adopted in a west to east movement like a weather front.

The emergence of causewayed enclosures represents societal transformations. Investigations of most ditch systems have shown that causewayed enclosures are comprised of a succession of elongated single pits that were possibly dug collectively by individual small groups such as families (Figure 9.5). While no causewayed enclosures have been found in the western, southeastern, and eastern TRB groups, enclosures are known in the Middle

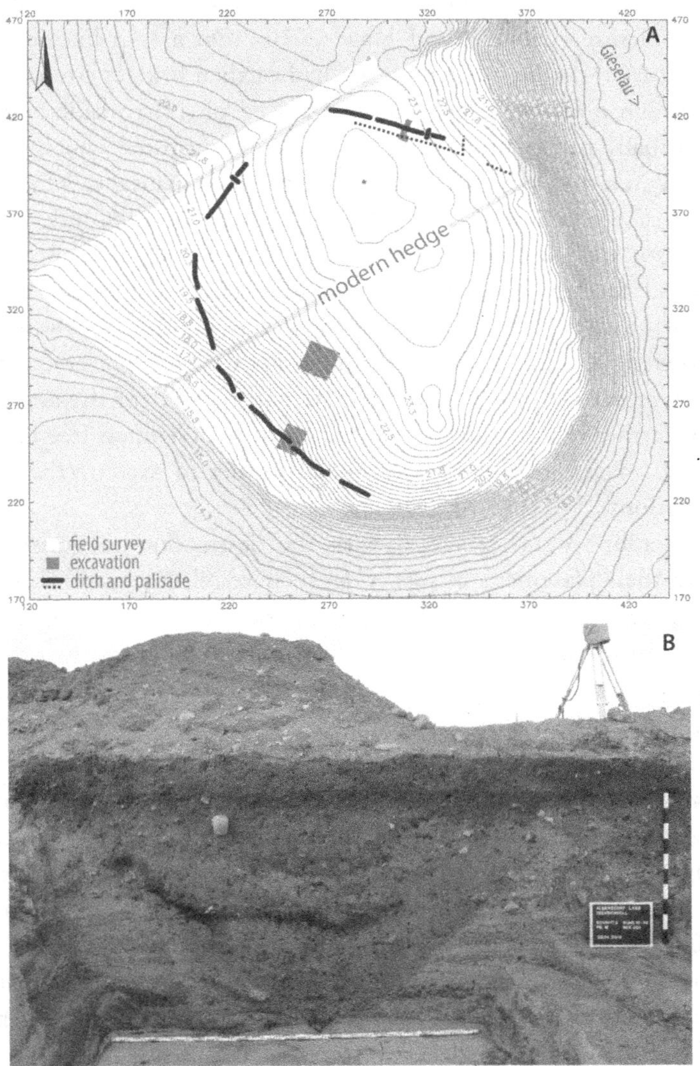

FIGURE 9.5 The causewayed enclosure Albersdorf-Dieksknöll and the profile of a ditch with signs of re-cuttings and in-fillings (after Hauke Dibbern and Franziska Hage).

Elbe-Saale region as well as in eastern Lower Saxony in connection with Michelsberg or Baalberg pottery. They are then attested in the TRB North group, though with a certain temporal and spatial gap: in 3600 B.C. at the earliest, 16 enclosures are located here (Klatt 2009). Büdelsdorf in Schleswig-Holstein and Sarup on Fune are among the earliest excavated enclosures here (Andersen 1997). For the latter site Niels Andersen was not only able to work out two different phases with a larger and a downscaled enclosure at the end of the development, he also clarified the function of the construction. Again, we are dealing with elongated pits, which, in connection with a complex palisade system and depositions of artifacts, served ritual purposes. Burying and renewed digging in the ditches, which could be followed across a number of phases, played an important role in this context and was also attested in the pits within the interior of the enclosure.

The site Albersdorf-Dieksknöll (Figure 9.5) is a newly excavated ditch system which reveals a similar picture (Dibbern and Hage 2010). On a spur-like setting protruding into a wetland area, pit ditches were dug that had earthen bridges connecting a supposed entranceway through a further deep, crosswise-placed pit. The inside of the causewayed enclosure was virtually free of findings and architectural features, which pedological analysis indicates can in no way be attributed to erosion. A palisade, which is continuous even in the area of the openings, can be found within the enclosure. It either became a victim of a fire or was purposefully set on fire around 3500 B.C. According to radiometric datings and the few archeological finds, the actual ditches can be placed within the time span of ca. 3650 and 3300 B.C. Eight burying and renewed digging phases can be reconstructed for this period. Accordingly, approximately every second generation such processes were carried out on the ditch system. In light of the assumed settlement pattern in single farmyard compounds or at the most small hamlets (see below) we assume that at intervals farmyard inhabitants convened in order to reassure their cooperation at particular celebrations.

These celebrations were associated with the destruction of vessels (perhaps used for libation) and their placement in pits. One such vessel, for example, was broken and deposited in both parts of the northern and southern ends of the ditch. Due to its heavy wood posts it was obviously covered up in a tent-like fashion and was reserved for other special purposes, still connected to re-cuttings and in-fillings. The activities that we attribute to the ditch system correspond surely to temporary gatherings. The quantity of archeological finds is meager and is completely different from contemporary domestic sites. The deposition of clay dishes and Funnel Beakers verifies from my point of view that only temporary activities such as feasts took place there. The archaeobotanical results show that gathered and not cultivated plants played a role in these rituals (Kirleis and Klooß in press). Furthermore, it is interesting that the pits were repeatedly dug out perhaps until around 3300 B.C. However, afterward a phase began in which the ritual was no longer maintained. The renewed pit diggings around 2800 B.C. verify however, that knowledge of the assumed activities was still present over the centuries, and that at the end of the TRB societies and the beginning of Single Grave societies it was briefly practiced once again.

Taking the causewayed enclosure Albersdorf-Dieksknöll as an example of ritual gatherings that primarily took place among neighboring communities, including "strange" activities within the palisade and pit ditch area in the phase between 3600 and 3300 B.C., we can compare it to other causewayed enclosures where productive activities took place in connection with the ditch systems. The production of adzes directly on-site next to the pits at Sarup, Büdelsdorf, and also in Rastorf can be mentioned here (Andersen 1997; Hassmann 2000; Steffens 2009). In Rastorf, for example, the production led to the development of a 40 cm thick "occupation layer." The production of flint adzes within the enclosures was conceivably integrated into distribution mechanisms of flint planks that were traded as valuable goods across the entire territory and were distributed from the west to the east coast. At different ditch systems ritual activities were likely interconnected with processes of specialized craft production.

In the area of the TRB Northern Group causewayed enclosures are always accompanied by other monuments: the megalithic tombs. It is therefore intensively documented for Sarup that in the area of the fjord-like bay approximately 110 megalithic tombs can be found near to the enclosure (Andersen 2008). In Albersdorf-Dieksknöll, groups of megalithic tombs can also be found near the enclosure and in Büdelsdorf a group of megalithic tombs is closely connected to the enclosure. In fact, the analyses in Albersdorf and in Büdelsdorf have shown that the construction of the first megalithic tombs took place simultaneously with the construction of the ditch system. The extended dolmen in Albersdorf-Brutkamp was constructed around 3650 B.C. as well, which exhibits in turn an occupancy history that suggests the use of the landmark over many centuries. Also in the case of Borgstedt near Büdelsdorf it is clear that the facility of the megalithic tombs which proceed in a radial form toward the ditch system was used at the same time as the ditch system. Rastorf is one of the few cases in which a causewayed enclosure as well as a settlement and megalithic tombs are found. The megalithic tombs are situated near the settlement, not near the causewayed enclosure. In principle, the population of these separate hamlets, which are associated not only with their houses, but also single megaliths, needed places to gather communally. Therefore, the role of causewayed enclosures in the northern area of TRB appears quite clear: they constituted ritual foci in spatial planning, which embraces local entities of the area at temporary gatherings.

Causewayed enclosures did not all have the same function. A glance at the Brunswick Land suggests that the frequency of ditch systems plays a very different role in this area located in the northwestern edge of the densely populated central German region (Geschwinde and Raetzel-Fabian 2009). New excavations on the southern edge of the TRB domain also show how ditch systems can function differently (Fritsch et al. 2010). At the enclosure of Hundisburg-Olbetal the depth of the V-shaped ditches increases as one proceeds from inside to outside. This is likely playing a defensive role in order to delimit the internal area. In contrast to Dieksknöll, this causewayed enclosure is filled inside with numerous concurrent pits so that they do not feature any re-cuttings or in-fillings and are quite clearly settlement remnants. Respectively, we are dealing here with a fortified settlement of the southern TRB group. This causewayed enclosure also is connected to megalithic tombs, the graveyard of Haldensleben with probably 90 megalithic tombs. The division of the Loess Zone of the south and the northern moraine landscape occurs here, as well as the division of Tiefstich and Bernburg styles and most likely also different modes of spatial planning. A contrast is surely evident in a southern direction in that, for example, in Halle-Dölauer Heide massed V-shaped ditches appear there in the enclosure where the terrain is rather flat (Behrens and Schröter 1980).

Monument Type 2: Megaliths

The construction of causewayed enclosures within the TRB North group is accompanied by the construction of megaliths. As has already been stated, a very high number of megalithic tombs must have been built in northern Europe and southern Scandinavia. It is a rather simple concept to collect matching boulders to form a corridor covered with a capstone and—in contrast to the earlier stone cists—to leave an access open and thus form a chamber that may be reentered recurrently. In the northern European and southern Scandinavian area we find *dolmen* and passage graves: simple *("Ur-")dolmen* with closely arranged upright slabstones and a flat capstone, extended *dolmen* with two or three case bays of opposing orthostats and an axial, sometimes slanting marked access (Figure 9.6),

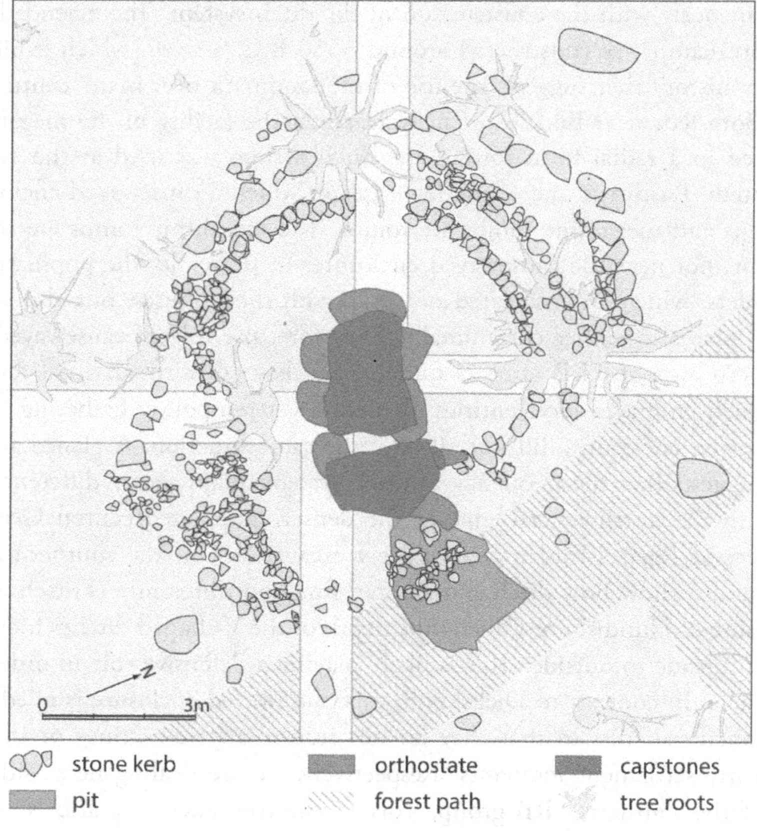

FIGURE 9.6 The elongated dolmen of Lüdelsen 3 (Denis Demnick; graphic: Denis Demnick).

and finally passage graves featuring passages of different lengths and an entrance that is placed either along one side of a polygonal chamber or—when dealing with an oval or rectangular chamber—aligned laterally. Since corbelling remains unknown in the north, the span of the chambers is limited due to the technical obstacles and the static qualities of the stone material. In order to gain space, it is necessary to either create a more oblong shape from the start or to later add lateral cubicles to the chamber. Thus, the typological sequence of the northern central European-southern Scandinavian megaliths might be explained in the following way: small dolmen gave way to extended dolmen and to those with a marked access, and finally we find passage graves with passages of varying lengths and large chambers. Within the west group of the TRB phenomenon the elongation of the chamber is most impressively documented by the Wechte chamber type, whereas the Limfjord region and northwestern Zealand possess other techniques to enlarge the chambers, such as two graves in one mound or lateral cubicles.

The construction of a megalith, which relies solely on slabstones and dry masonry walls, needs a supportive mound which may also serve as a ramp during the building process. Megaliths might be found in rectangular, oblong, or trapezoidal barrows, in round barrows, sometimes even in square barrows. They often comprise different construction phases or further mounds.

Apart from the burial rite, which is connected to other related transitory/transitional rites, we find a multitude of constructional changes at megalithic graves. The recently excavated and rather simple large dolmen of Lüdelsen 3, situated in the Altmark, serves as a good example (Demnick et al. 2008). The excavation revealed that around 3650 B.C. a clearing was created in which the megalithic tomb was built. The surrounding area revealed a few extraction pits and the slabstones were arranged to form a chamber with three bays and an axial side entrance. Even at that time, a flat entrance pit, which contained several sherds of smashed funnel beakers, was placed directly in front of the entrance and the grave itself already held the first burials together with three funnel beakers ornamented with cannelures. Meanwhile, the pits from which the mound soil was taken were filled with fluvial sediments carried from at least as far away as 250 m from the nearby valley of the *Hartau*. The entrance pit was partially covered by the external stone kerb (with a diameter of 9.6 m) that also delineates the outer boundary of the mound. The existence of pottery from the phase Haldensleben 2 found in the chamber itself, around the entrance, and in the excavation trenches of the outer stone kerb reveals that further actions and burials had to have taken place. We see these finds as ritual depositions and manipulations at the mound, at which time the capstone and entrance were the only visible parts of the stone construction.

The pottery of the Globular Amphora must have been deposited around 3000 B.C. in the upper part of the chamber and around the menhir, which had been erected near the entrance to the chamber. These finds point to a particularly high intensity of activities near the grave. All this took place when the grave had already been largely covered by trees, a process that must have already started shortly after the construction of the megalith. Thus, the grave had been intentionally kept from any economic activity whatsoever, a characteristic that can also be ascribed to the four other graves near Lüdelsen.

We find the nearest settlements at the above mentioned Hartau and near the forest mire of Betzendorf, where the settlement of Tangeln has left but little trace of any settlement activity. A palynological analysis reveals deforestation in the surroundings of the TRB settlements and an increase in the founding of settlements during the phase of the Single Grave culture. At Lüdelsen 3, which remained largely untouched after 3000 B.C., the Single Grave culture left its mark around 2400 B.C., when an individual lying in the right crouched position was buried there. This process might be connected to a second aggradation of the mound. Above layers that still contained TRB sherds that could be refitted to those of the chamber, and which must have been cleared out of the grave, a mound with a diameter of 30 m was built, thus camouflaging the megalithic tomb as a plain Single Grave mound. Apart from the use of the mound as a landmark in Late Bronze Age we cannot account for any further manipulations around the megalithic tomb of Lüdelsen 3.

However, other monuments were manipulated in a similar way: At Rastorf, for example, one megalith features a secondary grave chamber and a mound with a diameter of around 10 m, which had been built above a few flat graves, and by adding a partial extension created an oval mound already at the end of the Early Neolithic (Steffens 2009). This process took place as several other flat graves appeared around the megalithic tomb, until finally the whole mound had been turned into a long barrow with a façade made up of a dry stone wall. As before, we can make out two construction phases. In Rastorf, a fairly average-sized megalithic tomb had thus been turned into a far larger monument. A certain significance may be ascribed to the integration of single graves into the mound.

The megalithic site of Flintbek shows a similar development (Mischka 2010). Especially the long barrow LA3 consists of a line of several nonmegalithic grave mounds turned into a long barrow with dolmens inside. Similar to the development in Barkaer, northeast Jutland (Liversage 1992), we seem to observe a change from simple wooden constructions to simple dolmen. According to the very accurate radiometric dating method this transition took place at around 3500 B.C.

The appearance of the megalithic tombs takes on various forms, and so we find that at Lüdelsen 6, situated very near Lüdelsen 3, at least one nonmegalithic grave has been transformed into a megalithic construction featuring a rectangular long barrow front and a passage grave. The excavation of the long barrow could not yet confirm that the interpretation as a grave is correct, but the construction itself dates back to around 3700 B.C. according to radiometric dating, whereas the passage grave was built around 3300 B.C. We know for certain that at least two nonmegalithic mound phases had existed before the first changes took place and before the megalithic component was ultimately integrated. In contrast to the fairly small amount of ceramic finds uncovered at the entrance of the dolmen of Lüdelsen 3, a large quantity of sherds and other finds were found at Lüdelsen 6, pointing to an intentional smashing of the items at the side of the entrance. These actions can be interpreted as ritual offerings accompanying the worship of ancestors. There seems to be a striking difference between megaliths that were frequently revisited and formed central places with a high amount of vessel finds in front of or near the entrance and those with only few such finds. At Lüdelsen 6 we see the end of these activities, when the dry stone wall filling between the slab stones was literally ripped out, maybe in connection with the appearance of pottery from the Globular Amphora culture found here.

Related activities at the end of the TRB culture and in the following Neolithic stages might be found at other grave sites as well. The extended dolmen of Albersdorf-Brutkamp, around 3 km away from the ditch system described above, is a good example (Dibbern/ Hage 2010): excavations near the entrance revealed that the monument was built around the same time as the causewayed enclosure was constructed. The grave was used until approximately 3100 B.C. and destroyed around 2300 B.C. during the phase of the Late Neolithic 1: a cup-marked stone which originally formed the lid of the entrance was taken down and the whole chamber was cleared out.

I would like to emphasize that only by looking at the architecture are we able to trace different regions in the western Baltic that might be considered core regions of the TRB development. Besides the obvious demographic hotspots, such as the Olden-burg Graben, eastern Holstein or southwestern Fune, there are densely populated areas in which wealth and power are expressed by a special type of architecture. The above mentioned double chambers of passage graves or passage graves with lateral cubicles seem to be limited to the region of the Limfjord and northwestern Zealand (Midgley 1992). The exploitation of flint might be seen as a material base for this area. It seems conspicuous that the following periods during the Younger and Late Neolithic are also set apart by an architectural specialty, which might be interpreted as a similar indicator of might or power.

Until now, we have mainly focused on the architecture of megaliths. As for the finds, there is no case where it is possible to ascribe a grave good to an individual, par-tially because of the bad preservation conditions due to acidic soils, among other things. We see different forms of depositions in or in front of the grave chamber as part of the burial rite. Some megaliths display a rather sparse spectrum of finds, whereas other megaliths hold an immense number of vessels deposited near the entrance. Lüdelsen 3, with few finds, held no more than six vessels and three flint blades, whereas in Lüdelsen 6 a count of around 50 partially deposited vessels has been reached to date, and that only at the entrance. There are other southern Scandinavian examples for this tradition such as Trollasten dolmen in Scania (Malmer 2002) and graves in northwestern central Europe, but there the sherds were not found primarily at the entrance but in the grave chamber. Apart from this phenomenon, we also encounter the whole inventory of the TRB development that has survived in the ground, namely flint artifacts, adzes, and amber finds. There is evidence of artifacts that were produced with the sole intention of giving them to the dead. The thick-butted flint axes in northern Frisian graves are always longer than 18 cm in contrast to the actual tools that show traces of edging or use wear (Hinrichsen 2006).

Therefore, we are able to discern between graves that have obviously had a long tradition of being a focal point for deposition rites, maybe even for the duration of several generations, and those which had a rather low significance after the actual burial had taken place. Ritual foci emerge that are often placed in the center of a regional cluster of megalithic graves. They emphasize the high effort that has been invested within a small region or even at a single place, setting them apart from places where only few megaliths were found, even though the preservation conditions were the same.

The acidic soils and the poorly preserved bone remains do not allow for the exact reconstruction of the burial rites at megalithic sites. In many cases, the better preserved bones belong not to the TRB culture, but to the Late Neolithic (compare, e.g., Andersen 2008). Therefore, considerations of probable ritual scenarios often depended on analogies taken from southern realms. Boulders are mainly limited to the southernmost spread of the last ice age glaciers and for lack of other construction materials the people living to the south of this boundary followed the idea of a collective burial rite by building chambered graves made of stone or wood. Furthermore, we know gallery graves from the northern part of the Central Lower Mountain Range which might also be considered a parallel to the megaliths of northern Europe, even though their conception is based on a totally different approach (Günther 1997; Hinz 2007; D. Raetzel-Fabian 2000). These graves hold up to 300 individuals, some of them disarticulated at random whereas later ones are often more "in order." The anthropological analysis of the skeletal remains of Odagsen suggests that the way the bones are found is consistent with "normal" decomposition processes (Grupe 1989), so we may also assume a deposition and clearing away of skeletal remains. The collective burials were therefore not depositions of disarticulated bones or only partial burials. Instead, the skeletons were usually deposited as a whole. As long as we do not have similar analyses in a megalithic grave, we must be careful with the assumption that only partial burials were placed in the chamber. This is also the case for the northeastern German megalithic tombs. Some are characterized by a compartmentalization of the chamber (Schuldt 1972). The accumulation of bones in these separations has often led to the conclusion that the individuals were only partially buried there. The trait of dividing the chambers links the northeast of Germany to Scania.

In contrast to the northern central European and Danish areas, the preservation of bones of TRB origin in some sites of southern and central Sweden is considerably better and therefore enables us to reconstruct the burial rite of the passage graves. The best example is the passage grave at Frälsegården in Falbygden (Sjögren 2010). Like others, the grave evidences the burying of individuals as a whole. Isotope analyses in Falbygden lead to the discovery that the buried individuals came from the surrounding region. The animal bones, however, show that the different animals came from areas farther away. On the whole, we might state that the graves of the TRB North group either hold full-body burials that were kept untouched if they lay in a less frequented tomb, or gave way to later burials and were put to the side if they lay in one of the greater, central tombs.

MONUMENT TYPE 3: NONMEGALITHS

Describing the TRB burial rite as full-body collective burial does not account for the multifarious burial ceremonies attested in the TRB area. Throughout the TRB age, people were buried in flat graves which were either situated alone or clustered in small groups or even small grave fields (Kossian 2005).

TRB flat graves outside the settlements are rare during the start of the Early Neolithic (4100–3800 calB.C., partially until 3500 calB.C.). The whole TRB North group features fewer than 10 burials that date to the Early Neolithic, for example, the burial of Dragsholm of a 20-year-old male interred with a very early ceramic vessel, lying in a straight position on his back (Figure 9.7). The number of single burials then increases during the Early Neolithic II. They are often placed in grave groups with the usual

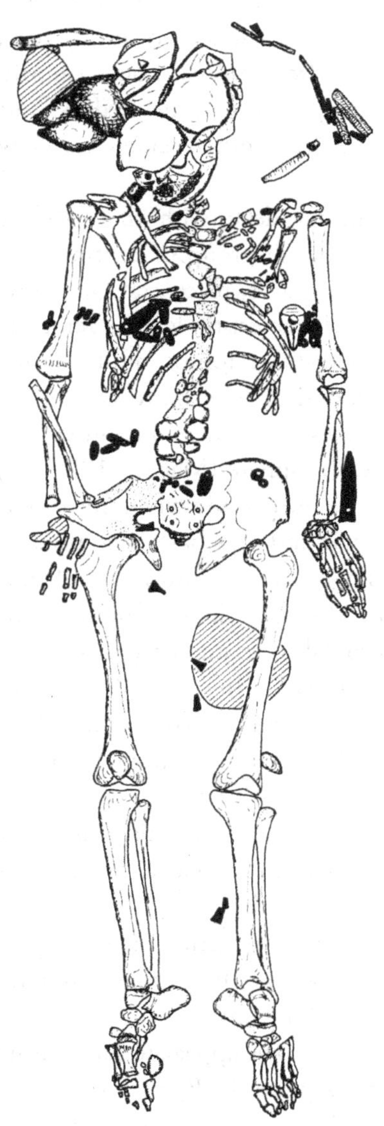

FIGURE 9.7 Dragsholm, grave II.—Scale 1:10 (after Brinch Petersen and Egeberg 2009, Figure 3). One of the earliest TRB single burials recorded from Zealand.

furnishing of grave goods, such as, for example, one vessel and a flint axe or the like. Rastorf and also Vroue Heide are excellent examples for flat graves connected to megalithic tombs: they prove that single burials may have been placed outside the chambers (Jörgensen 1977; Steffens 2009). The inventory of a flat grave could be as rich as the effort of construction could be high. The grave at Konsens Høj features two thick oak beams and an oblong stone packing between them, suggesting that trouble had been taken to create this burial. The finds of a golden ring in Schwesing, Holstein, and Himmelpforten also prove the relevance of single flat graves within the TRB development.

Ostorf is another fine example of a typical TRB cemetery, this time on an island in the lake of Schwerin. The cemetery was used during the phases MN II/III–IV which has been evidenced by ^{14}C-dates from animal bones (mostly dating to 3100 until 2900 B.C.). Men in this grave field are distinctly marked as "hunter" or "warrior," as is also known in a more gradual form from other cemeteries between Elbe and Oder (Lübke et al. 2009; Meyer 2009).

The description has thus far dealt with the TRB North and West groups but applies in a similar way to the South group of central Germany and the eastern group in Poland. We frequently see flat graves, in central Germany often single graves, beneath round barrows, which are also characteristic for the remaining TRB regions. Besides the common flat graves and the megalithic tombs, another category of graves can therefore be identified: nonmegalithic round or long barrows.

Nonmegalithic long barrows are a phenomenon closely connected to the heartland of the TRB as well as to the wider sphere (Madsen 1979; Midgley 1985; Midgley 2005). They are often earlier than the megalithic phenomenon throughout northern central Europe and southern Scandinavia and may have been used for a very long period of time. The long barrows often are single burials furnished with flint axes and TRB vessels. We know different categories, and the most famous examples are the Kujavian graves of the Sarnowo type: they are trapezoidal to triangular barrows whose longitudinal axis radially points to some important landmark. They usually hold the burial of an older male. Aerial photography and recent excavations have extended the geographic distribution of long barrows: they did not only exist in southern Scandinavia, but may also be found in northern central Europe and central Germany. Some are even known from southwest Germany and on the British Isles. Thus, the distribution of TRB long barrows ranges from southern England to southern Scandinavia, from northeastern Germany to eastern Germany, and Great and Little Poland.

It is important to state that the construction of long barrows dates back to as early as 3800 B.C. and that neither the megalithic tombs nor the causewayed enclosures are the oldest relics of the TRB development.

These nonmegalithic long barrows appear to have been multiphase structures where a variety of ritual sequences took place. In Bygholm, for example, a palisade was erected on the short side with various pits containing bone depositions. We also observe wooden mound kerbs, the burial itself, and finally the whole structure was covered by earth. In later times the long barrows seem to serve as burial sites with a richer inventory, as we see in Sylt-Tinnum (Hinrichsen 2006). There are also several cases where single mounds were integrated into one long barrow as in Flintbek (Mischka 2010). Nonmegalithic round barrows may be explained in a similar way: they mark individual burials in the landscape.

The similarity between the long barrows of Britain and those of southern Scandinavia, both of which appeared around 3800 B.C., was always very obvious (Madsen 1979). The extreme resemblance of these structures will not be part of our discussion, but it is all the same very surprising that there should be only sparse evidence of any exchange of material culture whatsoever. The flint adzes from the TRB age identified within the realm of the definite British long barrows might be an exception to this (Walker 2010). The confirmation of this conformity could evidence relations surpassing the ritual similarities. The actual exchange could only have taken place along the coastal lines, namely, the coast of the North Sea crossing the Thames corridor, but surprisingly just there—between Calais and Hamburg—not one nonmegalithic long barrow has been discovered so far.

Many researchers argue that long barrows derived from the long houses of the Linear Pottery culture and their successors. This might be an option when considering the long barrow of Passy, but for the long barrows of the Sarnowo type or the very early barrow of Bygholm, not to mention the late Tinnum, the chronological gap is far too wide.

But there is another possible explanation: the use of late Mesolithic shell middens remains common during the Early Neolithic but then ceases at the time the long barrows appear, marking the societal turn to TRB monuments. Since shell middens had served as burial sites all along, the step of constructing a long barrow seems like a logical development.

In conclusion, we demonstrated that the TRB societies not only featured rich ceramic inventories, they also displayed a great variety of monumental ensembles and burial sites, all of which lay outside the settlements. In the following, we will see that burials may also be found within a settlement.

DOMESTIC SITES, DEPOSITIONS, AND THE ORGANIZATION OF SPACE

For a long time, the absence of information about TRB settlements in northern central Europe and southern Scandinavia was one of the most prominent problems in European archaeology. During the last two decades, however, great linear construction projects as well as large excavations have provided us with knowledge about a number of TRB settlements. Today, we are aware of at least around 200 ground plans of houses, allowing us to paint a fairly accurate picture of what life was like. Local studies of the distribution of sites give us an idea on which behavioral principles TRB societies enacted when organizing their environment and social space.

With regard to houses and huts, distinct patterns through time and space of the TRB phenomenon can be identified (Artursson/Linderoth/Nilsson/Svensson 2003): Not taking into account local or functional variations, the master plan of the TRB house shows a two-naved rectangular (Limesgard/ Dagstorp 2 type) or slightly rounded ground plan (Mossby type), the latter of which seems to belong to the Early and beginning Middle Neolithic. The Dagstorp type is predominant during the Younger Early Neolithic and the

Middle Neolithic. The houses are usually between 4 and 7 m wide and range from 8 to 20 m in length. The outer walls are made up of closely spaced planks or wattle-and-daub walls. The interior did not have separate rooms. All TRB stages also feature round huts.

A particularly well-excavated site is Dagstorp in Scania (Figure 9.8) where various forms of houses and huts were documented (Andersson 2004). We observe large houses in the Early Neolithic 1 and smaller houses and huts from the Early Neolithic 2 until the Middle Neolithic II, which are partially aligned. Occupational debris layers were, not unlike on sites of the Linear pottery, uncovered in front of the houses outlining the former courtyard of the farm. The ceramic remains make it possible to determine that in

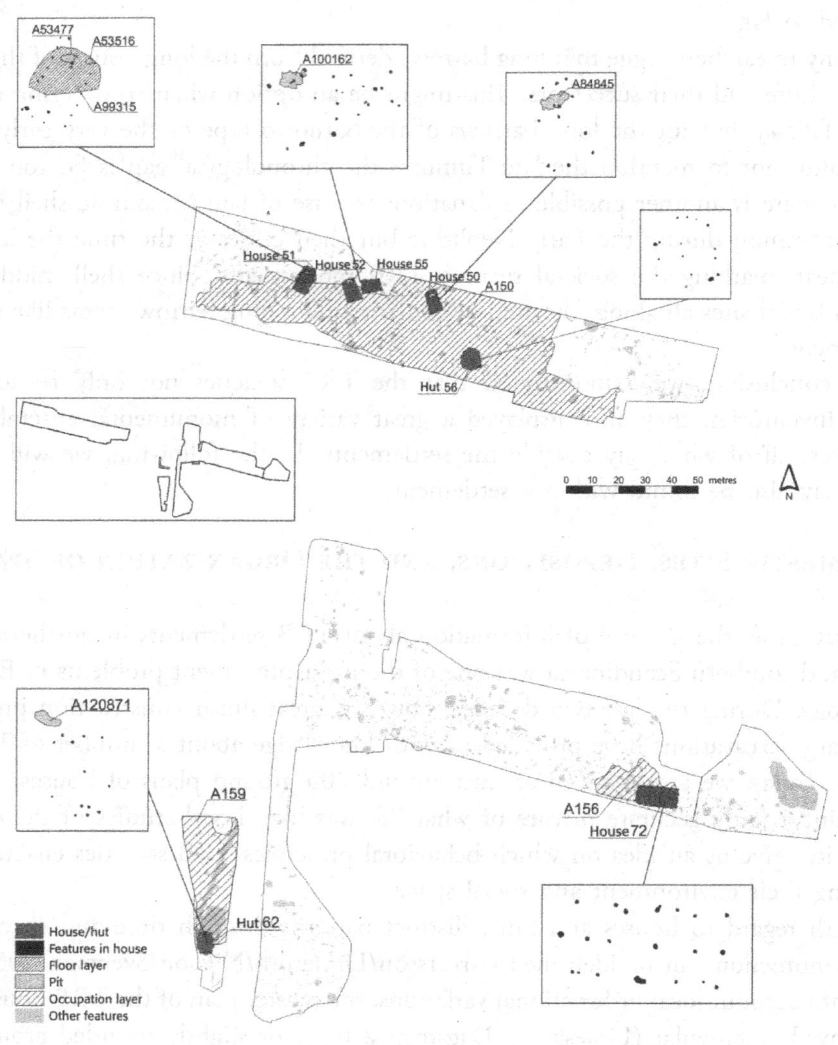

FIGURE 9.8 The settlement of Dagstorp 19, Scania (after Andersson 2004). Beside houses a cultural layer exists.

Dagstorp 19 two houses coexisted at any given time, so the settlement must have been a single farmyard. The entrances to the house were most probably placed on one or both long sides and usually there were no separate rooms, whereas the house of Flögeln gives evidence that separations did exist, since it features a division into two rooms. At the site of Saxtorp 23 burials were discovered approximately 100 m away from the houses and huts. Very often the floor of a TRB house was pitted, a property described by the term "sunken floors." These pits could have been used as work station fire pits, thus providing the inhabitants with a certain functional division inside the house.

Crucial discoveries about TRB housing mainly came from Sweden during the last decade, but most recently this information is supplemented by research in the more southern areas. In Wolkenwehe, situated in the Trave valley in East Holstein, several small rectangular houses with rounded corners could be reconstructed (Brozio 2010, 2011) (Figure 9.9). The overlapping of some of the post-holes suggests that no more than three houses existed simultaneously. The reexamination of the Hunte village of Hunte 1 by Kossian (Kossian 2007) shows further examples of equally sized houses which date from the Middle to Younger Neolithic transition. Furthermore the site of Rastorf in East Holstein

FIGURE 9.9 The reconstruction of houses in Bad Oldesloe-Wolkenwehe (after Brozio 2011). Probably 2–3 houses existed contemporaneously.

features a house of the Dagstorp type in front of which lay pits, a burial, and plough marks: a classical example of a single farmstead with associated fields (Steffens 2009).

The general setting of TRB settlements during the fourth millennium therefore seems to comprise single farmsteads or small hamlets. The occasional two or three neighboring farms seem to always have kept a certain distance from one another.

If we look more closely at two of the settlements, however, the interpretation of the uncovered features becomes more complex and we have to concede that the only explanation lies in the reconstruction of spatial concepts on a local scale.

Looking at Bad Oldesloe-Wolkenwehe, we observe an insular situation within a wetland area (Mischka et al. 2003/2004 [2007]). The settlement is placed more or less directly in the former Middle Trave lowland. The palynological and sedimentological analyses show that the settlement must have been deserted during the winter and spring floods. The activities of the settlement seem to have evolved around the production of flint tools, including adzes. There is no trace of any agricultural activity, whereas the slaughter of domestic and wild mammals is accounted for in various areas of the settlement. A patchy ditch system and high charcoal quantities cannot be explained but may reflect some special local production. Maybe these finds are associated with the exploitation of the nearby saline springs and thereby with a form of salt production, although there is no archaeological evidence for this. Overall, Wolkenwehe seemed to be a very special kind of settlement in the wetland, closely linked to permanent settlements in the vicinity. The distribution of sites in the Middle Trave Valley reveals a specific pattern: we see megalithic tombs in the hinterland, permanent settlements on the middle river bench, and temporary specialized insular settlements in the lowland.

Almhov in southwest Scania near Malmö is another example of a temporary settlement (Rudebeck 2009). The excavation uncovered Early Neolithic I circular structures with a diameter of 200 m made up of pairs of thick posts with double pits in front of each pair. It must have been a circular cluster of tents, perhaps used for a feast of some kind. Food waste was discovered in the pits. Later, the place featured a long barrow and two regular long houses. Other temporary situations are known, such as Alvastra, where a wooden platform with planked pathways in a wetland might be interpreted as a temporary pasture of some kind (Malmer 2002).

The treatment of death within the settlement is most clearly revealed at the site of Oldenburg, a permanent TRB settlement located on a former island of the Oldenburg Fjord and mainly dating to the Middle Neolithic II (Brozio 2011). The mineral soil of the site preserved the remains of several houses, some of which featured sunken floors. Evidence of tool production, grinding stones, ceramic inventories, and bone tools accounts for the various everyday activities dominating the life of the few families that must have lived there.

A part of the settlement lay at the edge of the fjord bank, which today marks the beginning of bog land and must have once demarcated a zone of brackish water. Various wooden posts could have belonged to the fortification of the embankment, behind which waste and other depositions were found under waterlogged conditions. The settlement was used between 3400 and 2900/2800 B.C. according to radiometric dating. The area of the fjord bank held human remains—several bones and a cranium—which were deposited together with some broken objects on the border between dry and wetland. At first glance there seems to be no difference between the treatment of these bones and the treatment of animal bones.

In the center of the settlement, a pit also revealed how death could be dealt with: The pit held skeletal remains of an approximately 40-year-old female who had been arranged in a straight position on her back, with the neck and upper body apparently following the curve of the pit's upper profile (Figure 9.10). The skeleton lacked the left femur, and traces of another pit indicated a secondary, intentional manipulation of the burial. Taking the bone (or maybe trying to get to the object placed on the upper limb) out of the joint capsule resulted in a slight elevation of the skeleton. Later the remaining disturbance was filled with soil again. Two m away, a well, 2.3 m deep and 1.3 m wide, confirms that the brackish water was not drinkable. The fill within the well revealed several funnel beakers, depositions of grinding and whetstones, as well as a high quantity of settlement waste and, last but not least, the missing femur from the nearby burial (Figure 9.11). The latter may either be seen as an intentional, perhaps ritual deposition or as a profane disposal.

Apart from these more obscure details the general pattern of the distribution of TRB settlements in the Oldenburg Graben is relatively clear. Botanic and geological analyses allow for the reconstruction of the ancient coastline, so the fjord also provided maritime resources for subsistence. Around 3200 B.C., an alignment of several settlements along the fjord bank, on islands, and in the lowland can be made out (Hoika 1986). Similar to the situation in the Trave valley, the megalithic sites are limited to the hinterland, thus narrowing the land used as pasture or cropland by the TRB societies in the area.

FIGURE 9.10 A burial from the domestic site Oldenburg. The 40-year-old woman was placed in a pit, and later—during a secondary manipulation—the left *femur* was removed.

FIGURE 9.11 The well from the domestic site Oldenburg (after Brozio 2011). Besides many archaeological objects, the *femur* from the nearby burial was also found.

The settlement on the island in the Oldenburg Fjord must have had farmland in the dry areas cultivated by the families belonging to the site. Such insular sites already existed during the earliest TRB phase: the site of Wangels represents such an early settlement (Grohmann 2010), with Oldenburg coming later.

The ritual deposition of objects is another very important find category that characterizes the TRB world, apart from burials, enclosures, and settlements. Besides depositions within settlements (Oldenburg) and around or in front of megalithic tombs, a number of sacrifices were made in dry and wetland areas (e.g., Rech 1975). The TRB North group leaves most of these obviously ritual depositions during the Early Neolithic II and Middle Neolithic Ia, between 3600 and 3300 B.C. The abundant depositions of amber chains and pendants or the like, the laying down of vessels, hammer axes, and various adzes take place at the same time as enclosures and megaliths are built, and the pottery is richly ornamented. In the Swedish region of Falbygden a visibility analysis between megaliths, settlements, and lowlands with a history of depositions has led to the discovery that the deposition sites usually lie in areas that are clearly set apart by environmental conditions and constitute their own entity within the landscape (Sjögren 2003).

The idea of *landscape* in TRB times can nearly be felt here, but we have to deal with a multitude of different approaches to understand it. However, we now know for a fact that the TRB people did pay attention to demarcations in the Neolithic landscape. We see this in the above described settlement patterns of the Oldenburg Fjord or the Trave valley, as well as through the visibility analyses of the Altmark that show that settlements and burial sites were clearly set apart. The economic and demographic developments behind these concepts have yet to be brought to light.

Ecology and Subsistence Economy

Within the northern central European and southern Scandinavian area the TRB development is closely related to the introduction of a new subsistence strategy: the cultivation of cereals and livestock farming.

New economies result in marked changes of ideological attitudes that also have an impact on the lifestyle and outward expressions of human habits. A survey of the overall pattern that accompanied the spread of these new economies accentuates strong similarities between the neolithization of the British Isles and Ireland on the one hand and southern Scandinavia and the northern European plains on the other, but also of the circum-Alpine regions. Around the same time (after 4100 B.C.), large parts of the non-loess areas were subjected to the spread of farming and breeding. But if we compare TRB regions with the British Isles, we discern clear differences: the latter is characterized by cereal cultivation, pottery, and the custom of building megalithic tombs *before* non-megalithic long barrows and finally enclosures "infiltrate" the landscape of the British isles around 3750 B.C. (Whittle et al. 2011). In northern central Europe and southern Scandinavia, on the other hand, the development followed another schedule: causewayed enclosures and megalithic tombs appeared around 3600 B.C., long after nonmegalithic long barrows were known. A structural comparison allows for a careful explanation: At the outset, Western Baltic areas were inhabited by Endmesolithic Ertebölle groups. They largely relied on hunting and gathering and the exploitation of aquatic resources, thus enabling them to, at least to a certain extent, live a sedentary life and use pottery as early as 4800 B.C. On the British Isles, Mesolithic groups never produced ceramics or reached such a degree of sedenterism.

The "hard" evidence of a Neolithic lifestyle is represented by low proportions of domestic animals at the beginning of the Early Neolithic (Steffens 2005). Between 4100 and 3800 B.C. the shares of domestic bones within zoological inventories range from 14.5 percent in Danish Svaleklint, to 22.6 percent in Basedow/Mecklenburg, only 6 percent in Scanic Lödelsborg and 25.8 percent in Bebensee, whereas Wangels displays a percentage of 64 percent of domestic animals. The following Early Neolithic Ib is characterized by values of more than 60 percent, for example Siggeneben-Süd features 67 percent. With the EN II and MN the values typically level off at over 90 percent. We have to concede, therefore, that the adoption of a Neolithic lifestyle took place gradually, beginning in the Early Neolithic and ended a few centuries later.

The evidence of cereals or cereal-related weeds paints a similar picture (Kirleis et al. 2012, 2011; Sjögren 2006). Between 4100 and 3800 B.C. we do not have a single grain of cereal from a settlement (though cereal impressions on pottery do exist). Not until the Early Neolithic IB, after 3800 B.C., do we get cereal samples from multiple different sites. The Early Neolithic I must be seen as a transitional phase during which foraging was gradually substituted by relying on livestock and farming. Other indicators of the new economic foundation such as grinding stones and sickle glance were not common before 3600 B.C., when the intensive agricultural production process had finally set in.

Palynology supports these results in principal (e.g., Nelle and Dörfler 2008). The decrease of tree pollen in pollen profiles confirms the opening of the landscape in the southern part of the Cimbric peninsula around 3600/3500 B.C. in the Early Neolithic II. There are no earlier significant changes recorded. After 3800 B.C., a continuous percentage of *Plantago Lanceolata* marks the beginning of an intensive livestock feeding in the forests, related to the appearance of the *Hude* forest. The opening of the landscape commences later on the Jutland Peninsula, the Danish isles and southern Sweden. This chronological offset is also reflected in average percentages of bones from domestic animals, which decrease from south to north and therefore document the loss of significance of stock herding in the north.

The development of agricultural techniques has to be considered as well. The opening of the landscape was likely connected to the introduction of the crooked plough, marks of which are found under and near megalithic graves and houses since the Early Neolithic II in northern central Europe and southern Scandinavia. (Hübner 2005; Steffens 2009).

Wheat and barley are seconded by related weeds, and poppy and other garden plants such as fennel also appear. The cultivation of gardens augments the opening of the landscape and the increase of shrubs in pollen profiles suggests the existence of hedges. Grinding stones and sickles become common finds within most settlement types. The appearance of sickle glance serves as another indicator for a chronological offset from south to north: the percentages of sickle glance are higher in southern settlements. In Sarup, the deforestation is evidenced as late as 3300 B.C., accompanied by a simultaneous rise of sickle evidence within the settlement (Jensen 1994).

Stable agriculture has surely existed since 3600/3500 B.C. but what about the time before? Certain palynological evidence, for example from the Belau Lake, reports an increase of ashes and coal between 4100 and 3700 B.C. (Kirleis et al. 2011). The first half of the fourth millennium is characterized by a distinct increase of colluvial depositions in Schleswig-Holstein, followed by a decrease (Dreibrodt et al. 2010). Both discoveries may be seen as indicators of the slash-and-burn farming method in which small forest areas were burned down and the ground was then fertilized by wood ("Brandfeldbau"; Schier 2009). This method led to very good harvesting results and may have opened up the non-loess areas and the northern central European and south Scandinavian region to cereal cultivation long before the invention of the crooked plough could consolidate the new economy.

The significance of hunting and gathering remained stable. Throughout the different societal spheres herbal products were used and deposited in various, sometimes markedly different ways which are reflected in the variety of find scenarios.

Cereals, namely einkorn and barley, predominate in the settlement of Oldenburg, whereas the site of the megalithic tomb of Albersdorf-Brutkamp is mainly characterized by noncultivated gathering fruits such as, among others, hazel (Kirleis and Klooß in press). The same applies to the causewayed enclosure of Albersdorf-Dieksknöll, where the proportion of cereals remains even lower. It cannot be said with certainty whether shrubs such as hazel or species of fruit trees were promoted by a special kind of forest management.

Temporary TRB settlements or camps were built for different purposes but some of them were clearly engaged in hunting activities, as we have already stated for Bad Oldesloe-Wolkenwehe, with a high percentage of game in the Early as well as the Middle Neolithic. A straightforward example of a hunting camp is the temporary station in Parchim-Löddigsee from which no domestic animal remains are known (Becker and Benecke 2002). There is evidence that the settlement was used to carry out a specialized hunting of wild horses at the end of the Middle Neolithic.

As for animals in this context, the cart tracks of Flintbek were recently dated to 3400 B.C. and confirm the use of cattle as a working animal (Mischka 2010). The appearance of double burials of animals, especially of cattle, in wide areas of Europe is a very powerful indicator for the increasing significance of animals. For example, we find antipodic double burials of cattle that were placed by analogy with human burials in a crouched position alongside common grave goods.

A recent study revealed that cattle teeth were the sole remains found in the double burials aligned in front of the megalithic tomb of Vroue Heide (Johannsen and Laursen 2010). The position of the finds suggests that the burials could well have been double burials of cattle that had been buried together with a cart or carts. This is another strong indication for the importance of animals.

We have as yet not mentioned fishing and the exploit of maritime resources, which remained common during the whole time, as many finds of seal and fish bones, fishing hooks, and weights from fishing nets confirm. In Bad Oldesloe-Wolkenwehe, seal bones were found and indicate that these animals were an important resource even inland.

Some areas were reforested after 3100 B.C., while in other areas we observe an increase of pasture land. The transition to an Early Neolithic economy with a strong bias toward animal husbandry also characterizes the end of the TRB development, which seems as diverse as the beginning.

BEYOND SUBSISTENCE

There seems to be no monocausal approach to explain the neolithization of northern Europe, and it is necessary to concede that other factors apart from subsistence economy helped form the TRB society. The use and production of amber which has been traded far to the south is one such factor, but flint and flint production is significantly more important. Flint was produced by coastal and surface mining, processed, and finally exchanged (Midgley 1992). Large flint mines existed in the Limfjord region, with a highly specialized production, and especially on the south Cimbric coast of the North Sea we have flint-related workplaces that demonstrate the sheer mass of available material. The resulting distribution maps allow us to identify the network of exchange relations.

Another characteristic trait is the use of copper. Since around 3500 B.C. the TRB North group conducted its own copper technology, using not only local but also foreign copper which had originally come to the north as an import (Klassen 2004). The copper daggers in the deposition of Bygholm and from the single grave of Aspenstedt indicate a new social evaluation of societal roles.

A highly specialized stone mining industry ("Montanindustrie") and new construction methods supported the building of aboveground monuments. The manipulation of large capstones requires a high amount of planning and skill. Not only manual skills are needed, but also the ability to mobilize a certain number of fellow people at a certain time is essential. It is a process highly reliant on demographic and social relations—relations we would like to reconstruct for the TRB age.

Demography and Social Formations

Social reconstructions first require knowledge about the size of social groups. Demography is a limiting factor to the size of a social group, as is economic ability. A simple model analysis therefore helps to emphasize that demography and economy are imperative for the reconstruction of social formations and social reorganization.

The demographic problem might be solved by extrapolating from certain kinds of excavated data. We could use palynological evidence of human impact as a proxy for a general evaluation of demographic development. The amount of ^{14}C-dates reflects the amount of archaeological features left behind, and by carefully discussing and evaluating the circumstances under which a deposition took place we might even be able to add to our knowledge of demographic development (Müller 2010).

Both methods result in the discovery that there was a marked increase of population in the southern TRB area, mainly during the Early Neolithic II and at the beginning of the Middle Neolithic. The late TRB development was most likely characterized by a decrease of population.

To get a more accurate picture of these tendencies, a test region was defined in which we tried to summarize all relevant archaeological data in order to gain more solid knowledge about what the demographic and social development looked like (Müller 2010).

The nearly complete survey of megalithic tombs and other archaeological finds and features on the North Friesian islands provided us with the ideal sample region and could be used as basis for further observations. There are 94 megalithic tombs densely packed around a small area, at least in comparison to other areas.

The reconstruction of the minimum population size draws upon simple calculations: The average area of a TRB single grave (of around 1 m²) represents one individual. Summing up all areas of the recorded grave sites (megalithic tombs, flat graves, and other grave types) that are known to have been in use at the same time on the islands would result in a minimum individual count, assuming that all the chambers contained burials. The calculation is more difficult than it seems at first because some corrections have to be made, as, for example, the loss rate of megalithic tombs. This rate has to be derived from similar calculations for other regions where old maps and thorough excavation and survey techniques in small areas provide a fairly good idea of how many megaliths must have disappeared over the centuries.

In flat grave cemeteries the proportion between burials with and without burial items should give us another correction value, as flat graves without any such items might never be detected. We also have to consider how long the grave structures were used, but in the case of the North Friesian islands we may only draw upon typo-chronological considerations to reconstruct probable periods of utilization.

If we take all of the above factors into account, the North Frisian islands, today encompassing ca. 202 km², were inhabited by 200–400 people at the beginning of the Early Neolithic II, 500–1,500 during the Middle Neolithic I and 350–550 people in the Middle Neolithic IV.

If a TRB farmstead was inhabited by the average of 10 people, between 20 and 150 farms would have existed simultaneously during any of the above mentioned stages. More or less 100 megalithic tombs are known to us today and the assumption that there is a 1:1 proportion between farmstead and megalithic tomb might well be correct.

We could then conclude that the density of population must have amounted to between one and seven person(s)/km² which reflects a considerable increase of the island population during the Early Neolithic II. Calculations based on other, quite different data sets in southwest Fune rendered similar numbers.

Our model calculation also indicated a decrease of population during the Late Neolithic, but this could also be due to a miscalculation based on unreliable data. Still, the pollen analyses of southern Jutland and the compilation of the relevant ¹⁴C-dates indeed show a similar dropoff.

Such models give us a rough idea of the population density and of the number of people having been buried in the archaeologically confirmed graves of at least the TRB North group.

The Single Grave culture is known for its quantity of possibly 50,000 southern Scandinavian grave mounds. Still, only about 100 burials per year could have been placed inside them (summary in Hübner 2005). In contrast, 50,000 megalithic tombs would have had a capacity to house 10,000 burials per year within the same area. If we consider the average life expectancy and death rate of Neolithic times, the area of study could have been the home of around 500,000 TRB people.

All in all, the Early and Middle Neolithic was characterized by single farmsteads and hamlets, likely associated with exogamic procreation strategies and therefore making people reliant on a cooperative way of life.

SOCIAL ORGANIZATION AND IDEOLOGIES

The outline of demographic development described above, notwithstanding distinct regional differences, is not only reflected in relation to technological improvements regarding, for example, the subsistence economy, but also in a change of character in material culture.

There are four principal phases featuring different material assemblages that might be linked to social differences:

A (4100–3800 B.C.):   farms and single graves, continuous use of shell middens in the north;

B (3800–3500 B.C.):   farms and single graves, nonmegalithic long barrows;

C (3600–3100 B.C.):   farms and causewayed enclosures; single graves, dolmen, non-megalithic long barrows, and as of 3400 B.C., passage graves; depositions;

D (3100–2800 B.C.):   farms, single graves, continued use of causewayed enclosures and passage graves, and, as of 2900 B.C., palisade structures in southern Scandinavia.

An attempt to interpret this leads to the conclusion that step by step the early centuries of the northern TRB development must have undergone ideological changes without giving any indication of a marked social differentiation.

The multifaceted ornamentation of the early stages of some of the TRB groups outlined above can be seen as indicating distinct social demarcations of neighboring groups that catalyzed the formation of dense communication areas that covered the size of approximately one day's walk.

Around 3800 B.C., nonmegalithic long barrows mark these areas and are also connected to ritual activities and the burials of socially outstanding individuals. After 3600 B.C. the societal change becomes more noticeable: the landscape is opened and new production technologies are introduced. Furthermore, there are burials of obviously very special individuals in nonmegalithic structures and in dolmen, and last but not least we witness the construction of large cooperative monuments—the causewayed enclosures.

These only temporarily used and visited "areas of festivities, distribution, and partially also of production" represent the heart of a cooperative enterprise. The construction of enclosures and the act of depositing and thereby destroying goods in isolated parts of the landscape dominates the cooperative ideology of the late Early and beginning Middle Neolithic. The conformity of the Fuchsberg-style pottery, which is spread across a wide area, could also symbolize the concept of a cooperative life style.

These general changes are related to a marked growth of population, which—after several generations—leads to an increase of internal conflicts. After 3200 B.C., existing enclosures remain in use but there is no evidence that the construction of new ones has been carried out. Burials in passage graves now predominate, and consume a high amount of energy. The idea of collective burials prevails in most areas of northern central Europe and southern Scandinavia. The term *collectivity* contradicts all other visible social tendencies: The proportion of items that might have been used as weapons rises, a tendency also observable in other areas, for example in central Germany (Figure 9.12). Pottery ornamentation lessens and there is a renewed regionalization of ornamentation and vessel forms.

It is impossible to grasp the reasons for this social diversification within the TRB groups but we are able to identify special, socially relevant components: animals, especially cattle, are associated with wealth, and the significance of the male individual is emphasized in single grave burials. A social separation evolves, and new symbols predominate material culture, pointing to the position of a new group of distinct individuals within the social network.

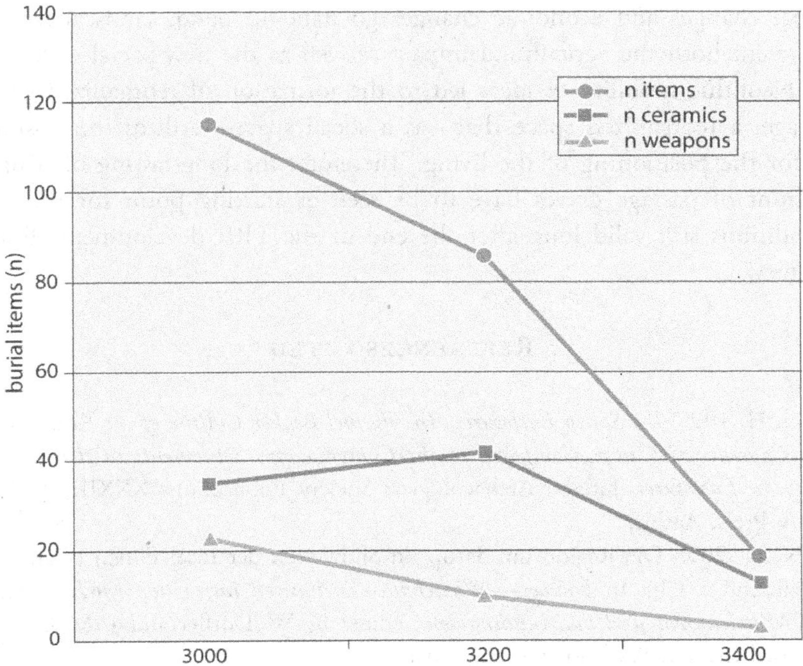

FIGURE 9.12 The distribution of goods in graves on the North Frisian Islands according to time period. Represented are the total number of grave items in three phases and the proportion of artifacts, which could be used as weapons, and ceramics, which are interpreted as consumptive commodities (Müller 2010, Figure 6).

After 2800 B.C., a new society develops in all TRB areas, which has not yet been sufficiently explained: the Single Grave culture with its selective burial tradition of individuals and an apparently strong focus on livestock husbandry.

OUTLOOK

Generally speaking, all TRB groups remain quite heterogeneous despite their strong similarities regarding material culture. These differences might be seen as a reaction of the indigenous hunter groups to influences coming to them from various directions, which were then translated into inner-societal changes. The partial substitution of the hunter-gatherer concept by a subsistence based on agriculture is associated with the construction of the first graves above ground. The prevalence of the new economy does not further the "clearing" of the landscape and of social relations before 3600 B.C.: only from then on are the areas covered with numerous boulders cleared and the largest stones used to build grave structures above ground. The idea is simple and might stem from northwestern France, an area to which social groups had a certain inclination at that time. Ritual changes and economic changes go hand in hand: landscapes are formed, which represent both the agricultural impact as well as the new social order.

The Neolithic mobility of ideas led to the formation of reorganized space during the TRB age, a reorganized space that—as a social space—utilizes the position of the ancestors for the positioning of the living. Therefore, the long-lasting offerings of TRB in or in front of passage graves have to be seen as starting point for the creation of societal traditions still valid long after the end of the TRB development. But that is a different story.

REFERENCES CITED

Andersen, N. H. 1997 *The Sarup Enclosures. The Funnel Beaker Culture of the Sarup Site Including Two Causewayed Camps Compared to the Contemporary Settlements in the Area and Other European Enclosures.* Jutland Archaeological Society Publications XXXIII, 1, Aarhus University Press, Aarhus.

Andersen, N. H. 2008 Die Region um Sarup im Südwesten der Insel Fünen (Dänemark) im 3. Jahrtausend v. Chr. In *Umwelt—Wirtschaft—Siedlungen im dritten vorchristlichen Jahrtausend Mitteleuropas und Südskandinaviens,* edited by W. Dörfler and J. Müller, pp. 35–48. Offa-Beihefte 84, Wachholtz Verlag, Kiel.

Andersson, M. 2004 *Making Place in the Landscape: Early and Middle Neolithic Societies in Two West Scanian Valleys.* National Heritage Board, Skånska spår, Lund.

Artursson, M., T. Linderoth, M.-L. Nilsson, M. Svensson 2003 Byggnadskultur i södra & mellersta Skandinavien. In *I det Neolitiska rummet,* edited by M. Svensson, pp. 40–171. Riksantikvarieämbetet, Skånska spår, Lund.

Bakker, J. A. 1979 *The TRB West Group: Studies in the Chronology and Geography of the Makers of Hunebeds and Tiefstich Pottery.* Cingula 5. Albert Egges van Giffen Instituut voor Prae- en Protohistorie, Amsterdam.

Becker, D., and N. Benecke 2002 *Die neolithische Inselsiedlung am Löddigsee bei Parchim. Archäologische und archäozoologische Untersuchungen.* Beiträge zur Ur- und Frühgeschichte Mecklenburg-Vorpommerns 40. Archäologisches Landesmuseum Mecklenburg-Vorpommern, Lübsdorf.

Behrens, H., and E. Schröter 1980 *Siedlungen und Gräber der Trichterbecherkultur und Schnurkeramik bei Halle.* VEB Deutscher Verlag der Wissenschaften, Berlin.

Bollongino, R. 2006 *Die Herkunft der Hausrinder in Europa. Eine aDNA-Studie an neolithischen Knochenfunden.* Universitätsforschungen zur Prähistorischen Archäologie 130. R. Habelt, Bonn.

Boujot, C., and S.Cassen 1993 A Pattern of Evolution for the Neolithic Funerary Structures of the West of France. *Antiquity* 67:477–491.

Brinch Petersen, E., and T. Egeberg 2009 Between Dragshom I and II. *Bericht der Römisch-Germanischen Kommission* 88 (2007):447–467.

Brozio, J. P. 2010 Neue Untersuchungen zu trichterbecherzeitlichen Organisationsformen in Ostholstein. *Archäologischen Nachrichten aus Schleswig-Holstein* 16:30–33.

Brozio, J. P. 2011 Von Siedlungen und Grabenwerken der Trichterbecher-Gemeinschaften. *Archäologie in Deutschland* 2:24–25.

Cassen, S., ed. 2009 *Autour de Table. Explorations archéologiques et discours savants sur des architectures néolithiques á Lochmariaquer, Morbihan (Table des Marchands et Grand Menhirs).* Actes du colloque international, Vannes (Morbihan), 5–7 octobre 2007. Université de Nantes, Nantes.

Cassen, S., P. Lanos, P. Dufresne, C. Oberlin, E. Delqué-Kolic, and M. Le Goffic 2009 Datations sur site (Table des Marchands, alignement du Grand Menhir, Er Grah) et modélisation chonologique du Néolithique morbihannais. In *Autour de Table. Explorations archéologiques et discours savants sur des architectures néolithiques á Lochmariaquer, Morbihan (Table des Marchands et Grand Menhirs)*, edited by S. Cassen, pp. 737–768. Actes du colloque international, Vannes (Morbihan), 5–7 octobre 2007. Université de Nantes, Nantes.

Cassen, S., P. Pétrequin, C. Boujot, S. Domínguez-Bella, M. Guiavarc'h, and G. Querré 2010 Measuring Distinction in the Megalithic Architecture of the Carnac Region: From Sign to Material. In *Megaliths and Identities: Early Monuments and Neolithic Societies from the Atlantic to the Baltic*, edited by Martin Furholt, Friedrich Lüth, and Johannes Müller, pp. 225–248. Dr. Rudolf Habelt GmbH, Bonn.

Chambon, P., and A. Thomas 2010 The First Monumental Cemeteries of Western Europe: The "Passy type" Necropolis in the Paris Basin around 4500 BC. www.jungsteinsite.de 2010, version 19.0.2010.

Demnick, D., S. Diers, H.-R. Bork, B. Fritsch, J. Müller 2008 Der Großdolmen Lüdelsen 3 in der westlichen Altmark (Sachsen-Anhalt)— Baugeschichte, Rituale und Landschaftsrekonstruktion. Mit Beiträgen von Arno Beyer, Jan-Piet Brozio, Ercan Erkul, Helmut Kroll. und Edeltraud Tafel. www.jungsteinzeit.de 92, 2008.

Dibbern, H., and F. Hage 2010 Erdwerk und Megalithgräber in der Region Albersdorf-Vorbericht zu den Grabungskampagnen am Dieksknöll und Brutkamp. *Archäologischen Nachrichten aus Schleswig-Holstein*:34–37.

Dreibrodt, S., C. Lubos, B. Terhorst, B. Damm, H.-R. Bork 2010 Historical Soil Erosion by Water in Germany: Scales and Archives, Chronology, Research Perspectives. *Quaternary International* 222:80–95.

Fritsch, B., M. Lindemann, J. Müller, C. Rinne 2010 Entstehung, Funktion und Landschaftsbezug von Großsteingräbern, Erdwerken und Siedlungen der Trichterbecherkulturen in der Region Haldensleben-Hundisburg. Vorarbeiten und erste Ergebnisse. *Archäologie in Sachsen-Anhalt Sonderband* 13:39–46.

Geschwinde, M., and D. Raetzel-Fabian 2009 *Eine Fallstudie zu den jungneolithischen Erdwerken am Nordrand der Mittelgebirge.* Verlag Marie Leidorf, Rahden.

Grohmann, I. M. 2010 Die Ertebölle- und frühtrichterbecherzeitliche Keramik aus Wangels, Kr. Ostholstein. In *Die Neolithisierung Mitteleuropas*, edited by D. Gronenborn and J. Petrasch, pp. 407–422. Verlag des Römisch-Germanischen Zentralmuseums, Mainz.

Grupe, G. 1989 Die Skelettreste aus dem neolithischen Kollektivgrab von Odagsen, ldkr. Northeim. In *Paläanthropologie im Mittelelbe-Saale-Werra-Gebiet. Beiträge zur Rekonstruktion der biologischen Situation ur- und frühgeschichtlicher Bevölkerungen. Weimarer Monographien zur Ur- und Frühgeschichte 23*, edited by H. Bach and A. Bach, pp 80–93. Museum für Ur- und Frühgeschichte Thüringens, Weimar.

Günther, K. 1997 *Die Kollektivgräber-Nekropole Warburg I–V.* Bodenaltertümer Westfalens 34. von Zabern, Mainz.

Hassmann, H. 2000 *Die Steinartefakte der befestigten neolithischen Siedlung von Büdelsdorf, Kreis Rendsburg-Eckernförde.* Universitätsforschungen zur Prähistorischen Archäologie 62. In Kommission bei R. Habelt, Bonn.

Hinrichsen, C. 2006 *Das Neolithikum auf den Nordfriesischen Inseln.* Universitätsforschungen zur Prähistorischen Archäologie 133. Verlag Dr. Rudolf Habelt, Bonn.

Hinz, M. 2007 Territoriale und soziale Strukturen. Modelle zur Kollektivgrabsitte der Wartberg-Gruppe. www.jungsteinsite.de article 15/12/2007.

Hoika, J. 1986 Die Bedeutung des Oldenburger Grabens für Besiedlung und Verkehr im Neolithikum. *Offa* 43:185–208.

Hübner, E. 2005 *Jungneolithische Gräber auf der Jütischen Halbinsel. Typologische und chronologische Studien zur Einzelgrabkultur.* Nordiske Fortidsminder B24. Der Kongelige Nordiske oldskirftselskab, København.

Jensen, H. J. 1994 *Flint Tools and Plant Working: Hidden Traces of Stone Age Technology; A Use Wear Study of some Danish Mesolithic and TRB Implements.* Aarhus University Press, Aarhus.

Jeunesse, C. 2010 Die Michelsberger Kultur. In *Jungsteinzeit im Umbruch. Die "Michelsberger Kultur" und Mitteleuropa im Umbruch vor 6000 Jahren,* edited by: C. Lichter, pp. 46–55. Badisches Landesmuseum, Karlsruhe.

Johannsen, N., and S. Laursen 2010 Routes and Wheeled Transport in Late 4th–Early 3rd Millennium Funerary Customs of the Jutland Peninsula: Regional Evidence and European Context. *Prähistorische Zeitschrift* 85:15–58.

Jörgensen, E. 1977 *Hagebrogard—Vroue—Koldkur. Neolithische Gräberfelder aus Nordwestjütland.* Akademisk Forlag, Kopenhagen.

Kirleis, W., I. Feeser, and S. Klooß 2011 Umwelt und Ökonomie. *Archäologie in Deutschland* 2:34–37. In Press Food Production and Beyond: Social Context of Plant Use in the Northern German Neolithic. In *Plants and People. Choices and Diversity through Time,* edited by A. Chevalier, M. Elena, and P. Leonor.

Kirleis, W., S. Klooß, H. Kroll, and J. Müller 2012 Crop Growing and Gathering in the Northern German Neolithic: A Review Supplemented by New Results. *Vegetation History and Archaeobotany* 21:221–242.

Klassen, L. 2004 *Klassen, Jade und Kupfer. Untersuchungen zum Neolithisierungsprozess im westlichen Ostseeraum unter besonderer Berücksichtigung der Kulturentwicklung Europas 5500–3500 BC.* Jutland Archaeological Society, Moesgård.

Klatt, S. 2009 Die neolithischen Einhegungen im westlichen Ostseeraum. Forschungsstand und Forschungsperspektiven. In *Neue Forschungen zum Neolithikum im Ostseeraum,* edited by T. Terberger, pp. 7–134. Verlag Marie Leidorf, Rahden/Westf.

Kossian, R. 2005 *Nichtmegalithische Grabanlagen der Trichterbecherkultur in Deutschland und den Niederlanden.* Veröffentlichungen des Landesamtes für Denkmalpflege und Archäologie Sachsen-Anhalt–Landesmuseum für Vorgeschichte 58. Landesmuseum für Vorgeschichte, Halle.

Kossian, R. 2007 *Hunte 1: Ein mittel- bis spätneolithischer und frühbronzezeitlicher Siedlungsplatz am Dümmer, Ldkr. Diepholz (Niedersachsen). Die Ergebnisse der Ausgrabungen des Reichsamtes für Vorgeschichte in den Jahren 1938 bis 1940.* Veröffentlichungen der archäologischen Sammlungen des Landesmuseums Hannover 52. Niedersächsisches Landesmuseum, Hannover.

Laporte, L. 2005 Néolithisation de la façade atlantique du Centre-Ouest de la France. Actes des journées SPF de Nantes. In *Unité et diversité des processus de néolithisation. Actes du colloque de Nantes, Mémoire XXXVI de la Société Préhistorique Française,* pp. 99–125. Société Préhistorique Française, Paris.

Leandri, F., C. Gilabert, and F. Demouche 2007 Les chambers funéraires des Ve et IV millénaires av. J-C.: le cas de las Corsica. In *Les cistes de Chamblandes et la place des coffres dans les pratiques funéraires du Néolithique moyen occidental. Actes du colloque de Lausanne, 12 et 13 mai 2006,* edited by P. Moinat and P. Chambon, pp. 41–61. Société Préhistorique Française, Paris.

Liversage, D. 1992 *Barkær. Long Barrows and Settlements.* Akademisk forlag, Kopenhagen.

Lübke, H., F. Lüth, and T. Terberger 2009 Fishers or Farmers? The Archaeology of the Ostorf Cemetery and Related Neolithic Finds in the Light of New Data. *Bericht der Römisch-Germanischen Kommission* 88 (2007):307–338.

Madsen, T. 1979 Earthen Long Barrows and Timber Structures: Aspects of the Early Neolithic Mortuary Practice in Denmark. *Proc. Prehist. Soc.* 45:301–320.

Malmer, M. P. 2002 *The Neolithic of South Sweden: TRB, GRK. and STR.* Royal Swedish Academy of Letters, History and Antiquities, Stockholm.

Meyer, M. 2009 Neolithische Flachgräberfelder zwischen Elbe und Oder. *Bericht der Römisch-Germanischen Kommission* 88 (2007):429–446.

Midgley, M. 1992 *TRB Culture: The First Farmers of the North European Plain.* Edinburgh University Press, Edinburgh.

Midgley, M. 2005 *The Monumental Cemeteries of Prehistoric Europe.* Tempus, Gloucestershire.

Midgley, M. 2009 *Antiquarians at the Megaliths.* Archaeopress, Oxford.

Mischka, D. 2010 Flintbek LA 3, Biography of a Monument. www.jungsteinsite.de article from 20/12/2010.

Mischka, D., W. Dörfler, P. Grootes, D. Heinrich, J. Müller, and O. Nelle 2007 Die neolithische Feuchtbodensiedlung Bad Oldesloe-Wolkenwehe: Vorbericht zu den Untersuchungen 2006. *Offa* 59/60(2003/2004):25–64.

Müller, J. 1997 Zur absolutchronologischen Datierung der europäischen Megalithik. In *Tradition und Innovation. Prähistorische Archäologie als historische Wissenschaft. Festschrift für Christian Strahm,* edited by B. Fritsch, M. Maute, I. Matuschik, J. Müller, and C. Wolf, pp. 63–105. Verlaf Marie Leidorf, Rahden.

Müller, J. 2006 Die altmärkischen Großsteingräber im europäischen Kontext. In *Großsteingräber der Altmark,* edited by H. Bock, B. Fritsch, and L. Mittag, pp. 17–45. Theiss-Verlag, Stuttgart.

Müller, J. 2009a, Neolithische Monumente und neolithische Gesellschaften. In *Neolithische Monumnete und neolithische Gesellschaften,* Varia neolithica 6, edited by H.-J. Beier, E. Claßen, T. Doppler, and B. Ramminger, pp. 7–16. Verlag Beier & Beran, Langenweissbach.

Müller, J. 2009b Monumente und Gesellschaft. *Archäologische Nachrichten aus Schleswig-Holstein*:30–33.

Müller, J. 2010a Dorfanlagen, Siedlungssysteme—Die europäische Perspektive: Südosteuropa und Mitteleuropa. In *Aufbruch in eine neue Zeit: Europas Mitte um 4000 v. Chr.,* edited by C. Lichter, pp. 250–257. Ausstellungskatalog. Primus Verlag Karlsruhe, Karlsruhe.

Müller, J. 2010b Ritual Cooperation and Ritual Collectivity: The Social Structure of the Middle and Younger Funnel Beaker North Group (3500–2800 B.C.). www.jungsteinsite.de (Artikel vom 29.10.2010).

Nelle, O., and W. Dörfler 2008 A Summary of the Late- and Post-Glacial Vegetation History of Schleswig-Holstein. In *Flora, Vegetation, and Nature Conservation from Schleswig-Holstein to South America—Festschrift for Klaus Dierßen on Occasion of his 60th Birthday,* edited by: J. Dengler, C. Dolnik, and M. Trepel, pp. 45–68. Arbeitsgemeinschaft Geobotanik in Schleswig-Holstein und Hamburg, Kiel.

Raetzel-Fabian, D. 2000 Calden. *Erdwerk und Bestattungsplatz des Jungneolithikums.* Universitätsforschungen zur prähistorischen Archäologie 70. Habelt, Bonn.

Rech, M. 1975 *Stein- und bronzezeitliche Depotfunde im westlichen Norddeutschland.* S.I., Schleswig.

Rudebeck, E. 2009 I trästodernas skugga—monumentala möten i neolitiseringens tid. In *Arkeologiska och förhistoriska världar,* edited by B. Nilsson and E. Rudebeck, pp. 83–252. Malmö museer, Malmö.

Schier, W. 2009 Extensiver Brandfeldbau und die Ausbreitung der neolithischen Wirtschaftsweise in Mitteleuropa und Südskandinavien am Ende des 5. Jahrtausends v. Chr. *Prähistorische Zeitschrift* 84:15–43.

Schuldt, E. 1972 *Die mecklenburgischen Megalithgräber*. Beitr. Ur- Frühgesch. Bezirke Rostock, Schwerin u. Neubrandenburg 6. Deutscher Verl. d. Wissenschaften, Berlin.

Sjögren, K.-G. 2003 *Mêangfalldige uhrminnes grafvar: megalitgravar och samhèalle i Vèastsverige*. GOTARC. Series B, Gothenburg Archaeological Theses 27. Coast-to-Coast Books, Göteborg.

Sjögren, K.-G. 2006 *Ecology and Economy in Stone Age and Bronze Age Scania*. National Heritage Board, Lund. 2010 Megaliths, Landscapes, and Identities: the case of Falbygden, Sweden. www.jungsteinsite.de article from 29/10/2010.

Steffens, J. 2005 Die Bedeutung der Jagd in der Trichterbecherkultur. www.jungsteinsite.de 2005, article 15/2/2005.

Steffens, J. 2009 *Die neolithischen Fundplätze von Rastorf, Kreis Plön. Eine Fallstudie zur Trichterbecherkultur im nördlichen Mitteleuropa am Beispiel eines Siedlungsraumes*. Universitätsforschungen zur prähistorischen Archäologie. R. Habelt, Bonn.

Walker, K. 2010 Landscapes, Seascapes, and Sandbanks: Neolithic Exchange and a North Sea Network. In *Landscapes and Human Development: The Contribution of European Archaeology*, edited by Kiel Graduate School "Human Development in Landscapes," pp. 159–169. In Kommission bei Dr. Rudolf Habelt GmbH, Bonn.

Whittle, A., F. Healy, and A. Bayliss 2011 *Gathering Time: Dating the Early Neolithic Enclosures of Southern Britain and Ireland*. Oxbow Books, Oxford.

PART III

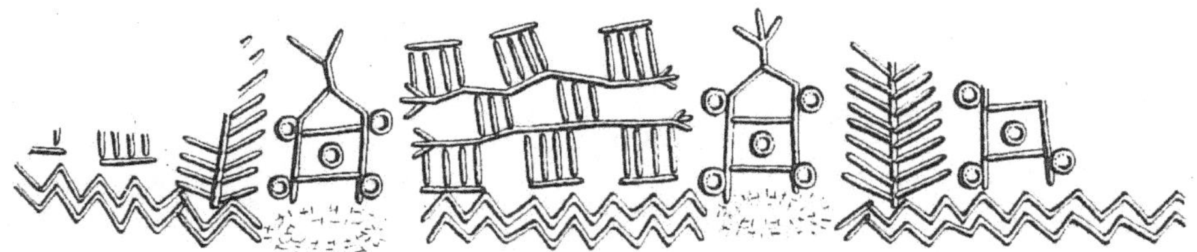

Monuments and Memory Work

CHAPTER TEN

Planning for the Past in Neolithic Central Europe

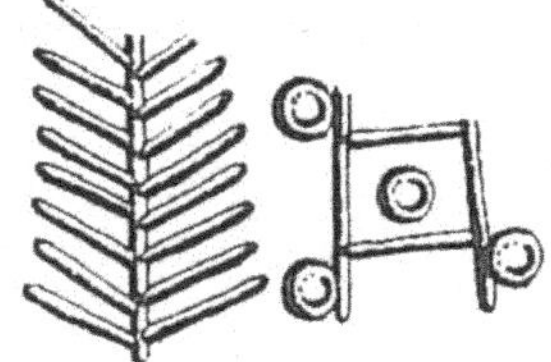

Peter Bogucki

Abstract *Longhouses and enclosures notwithstanding, the earlier Neolithic societies in central Europe (ca. 5500–4000 B.C.) at first glance appear to have a decidedly nonmonumental character. If, however, we view monuments as facilitating the persistence of memory, we can identify several practices that have monumental character at a micro scale. The first of these is the practice of making deposits/caches/hoards of ground and chipped stone tools, which exhibits considerable variability from one region to the next. Moreover, earlier Neolithic deposits do not have the character of offerings that we find in later Neolithic societies, but contain the same items common in burials. The second is the emergence during the fifth millennium B.C. of "micro-cemeteries" in household clusters such as those of the Brześć Kujawski Group. The graves in these clusters must have been marked in some way, and they also juxtaposed the mortuary and residential aspects of Neolithic life to perhaps pave the way for later monumental expressions.*

INTRODUCTION

The title of this chapter takes its inspiration from the line addressed by Amanda Wingfield to her son Tom in Scene 5 of the play *The Glass Menagerie* by Tennessee Williams (1999[1945]): "You are the only young man that I know of who ignores the fact that the future becomes the present, the present becomes the past, and the past turns into everlasting regret if you don't plan for it!" *The Glass Menagerie*, as Williams notes in his Production Notes (1945), is a "memory play," and it brings forth several of the key themes of this chapter. The construction of memory not only has a backward-looking aspect but also a forward-looking one, in which people in the present imagine how a past will appear to themselves, their contemporaries, and their descendants in the future. As such, it has the power to integrate generations vertically: the living, the dead, and the yet-unborn.

This chapter explores the topic of "memory work" (Mills and Walker 2008) among the earliest farmers of central Europe. The evidence on which is it based, deposits of stone artifacts and clusters of burials in settlements, are small and found below the ground surface, echoing Osborne's observation (this volume) that an object need not be immense to be monumental. Yet, these features and their content certainly conform to Osborne's criterion that they have "an agreed-upon special meaning to a community of people." The goal of this chapter is to enlarge the discussion of monumentality to include less obvious instances of memory work and to argue that the impulse for the maintenance of social memory across generations can occur on a small and personal scale rather than exclusively on a grand scale.

The Danubian World

This chapter is far removed in time and space from St. Louis during the 1930s. To quote Tom Wingfield, "Time is the longest distance between two places." It deals with the first farming societies of interior central Europe between 5500 and 4000 B.C. V. Gordon Childe's term for these farmers, the "Danubians" (Childe 1929), describes their close association with the riverine corridor from central Hungary to southern Germany, although many of the localities that I will mention are outside the Danube drainage (Figure 10.1). Nonetheless, we can speak of a "Danubian World" during this period, in which there are clear connections across time and space between the first farming communities of the Linear Pottery culture and their later congeners, such as Rössen and Lengyel, and the late borderland manifestations such as the Brześć Kujawski Group in northern Poland and Villeneuve-Saint-Germain in northwestern France.

Research in western Hungary has pointed to a fusion between late Mesolithic communities north of Lake Balaton and farming communities on the northern fringe of the Balkan Starčevo culture as the deepest root of the Linear Pottery culture (Oross and Bánffy 2009). From there, a complex process of diaspora (perhaps abetted by free-range cattle grazing) of farming communities, along with the entrainment of indigenous foragers in this process, resulted in several spurts of farming dispersal across central Europe. Subsequently, farming communities in many different regions attempted to copy their ancestral practices and values in their own ways, resulting in a number of regional creoles. Further mini-diasporas and creolizations occurred during the fifth millennium B.C. Brześć Kujawski and Villeneuve-Saint-Gemain represent two late Danubian creole societies along the borderlands with the late Mesolithic world of the Baltic and the Atlantic fringe.

Although it is common to characterize the first farming societies of central Europe as initially having been unusually homogeneous in their material culture and economy (e.g., Bogucki 2000), emerging evidence for regional and temporal variability in many different cultural practices confirms the appropriateness of Modderman's (1988) characterization of the Linear Pottery culture as "diversity in uniformity," which becomes even

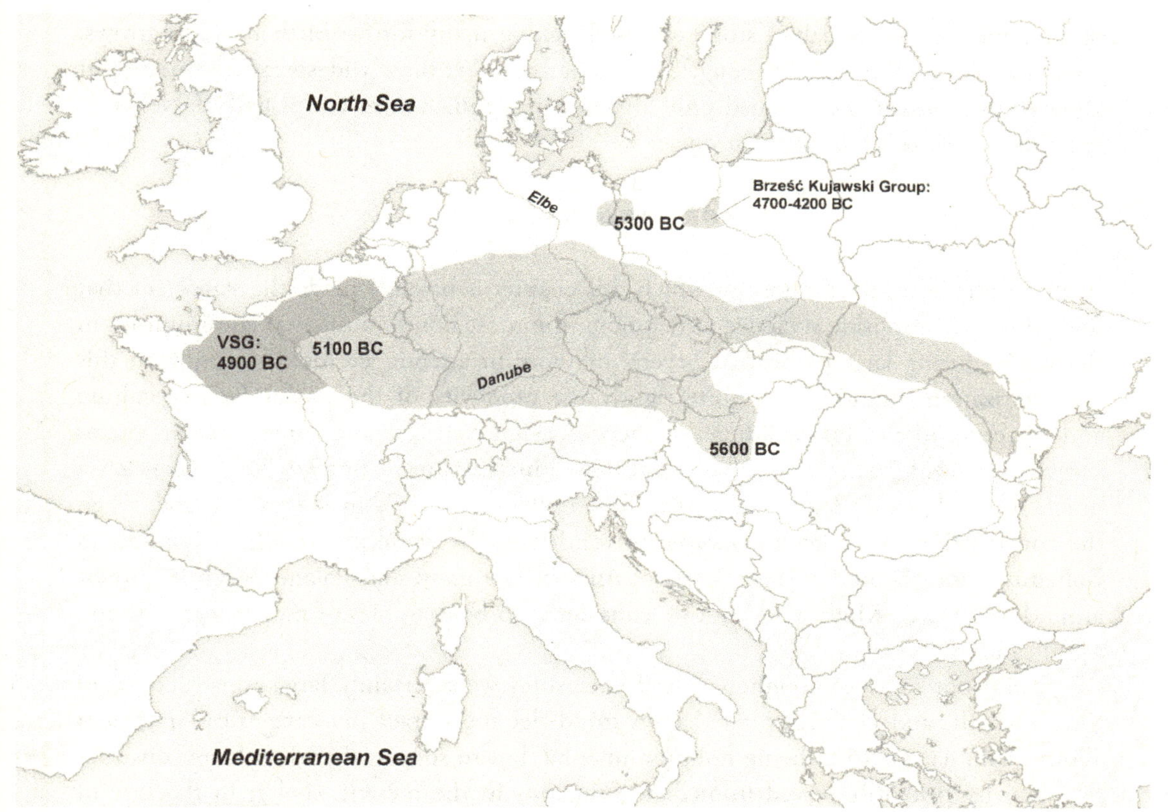

FIGURE 10.1 Distribution of early farming societies in Central Europe, showing core area of the Linear Pottery culture, its exclaves on the North European Plain in the late sixth millennium B.C., the westward extension of the Villeneuve-Saint-Germain Group in the early fifth millennium B.C., and the area settled by the Brześć Kujawski Group in the mid-fifth millennium B.C.

more pronounced in the following centuries. In addition to differentiation in ceramic styles toward the end of the sixth millennium B.C. and then more markedly during the fifth millennium B.C., we see many regional traits that do not occur over the entire Danubian world. For example, ceramic sieves probably used in dairy production are ubiquitous at Linear Pottery sites on the North European Plain but are found only sporadically elsewhere in central Europe (Bogucki 1984). The more we think we know about the first farmers of central Europe, the more questions arise, and the more questions we decide are worth asking.

It is also clear that toward the end of the fifth millennium B.C. there was another great transformation throughout temperate Europe. The foragers of the Atlantic façade and northern Europe adopted agriculture very rapidly, and the farming societies of central Europe also changed dramatically (for example, in their settlement patterns). In both areas, clear and widespread traditions of large-scale monumental construction in earth, timber, and (where available) stone emerged, taking many forms: earthen long barrows, causewayed camps, megaliths, henges, round barrows. Yet these widespread and persistent monumental practices developed only after about a millennium and a half of Neolithic settlement in interior central Europe.

MEMORY AND ITS PLANNING

In the conference presentation on which this chapter is based, I made the statement that the Danubian Neolithic societies were among the most nonmonumental communities in the world during later prehistory. Several of those in attendance took exception to this characterization, pointing out quite rightly the proclivity of the Linear Pottery culture and its descendants for building longhouses (Figure 10.2), and large circular enclosures (e.g., Biehl 2012). These first appear in Linear Pottery contexts but then reach a much more elaborate form during the fifth millennium B.C. in central Europe, when the construction of *Kreisgrabenanlagen* or rondels in the western Carpathian foothills of Bohemia, Moravia, and adjacent parts of Austria, Germany, and Poland began in earnest around 4800 B.C. Might these not be considered to be examples of monumentality, and significant ones at that?

I am not so sure. Longhouses and enclosures were certainly large constructions of timber, earth, and clay. Keeping that in mind, let me retract my categorical statement about Danubian societies being nonmonumental, but to suggest that their large construction activity primarily served immediate functions in the present: shelter in the case of longhouses, fortification in the case of enclosed settlements, and ceremonialism in the case of *Kreisgrabenanlagen*. Of course, these functional purposes were fraught with meaning, and I do not mean to dismiss the symbolic roles of such massive constructions. However, I do not see them as being involved in the deliberate construction of memories across generations. Instead, they were visible markers of previous activity upon the landscape in their decayed state (Bradley 1998:44–46), sites of memories in their abandonment, thus memories by default.

As Halbwachs (1980[1950]:140) reminds us, memory unfolds within a spatial framework. For the Danubian farmers of central Europe, settlements consisting of several household clusters arranged around longhouses were the principal anchor points of their spatial framework. In most areas, many of these household clusters persisted across several generations. In many regions, cemeteries were located apart from the settlements, whereas elsewhere burials on settlements were common. The rest of the landscape was relatively unstructured except for gardens and small fields adjacent to the houses and trails leading through the surrounding forest.

Danubian memories, then, were largely created at their settlements. We can situate them in the realm of what scholars such as Halbwachs (1980[1950]), Assmann (1995), and Misztal (2003) refer to as "cultural memory," "collective memory," or "social memory,"[1] particularly among the members of individual households and hamlets, as contrasted with the personal memories of individuals. There is a large body of literature on how social memory functions in theory and practice, and my purpose here is not to review

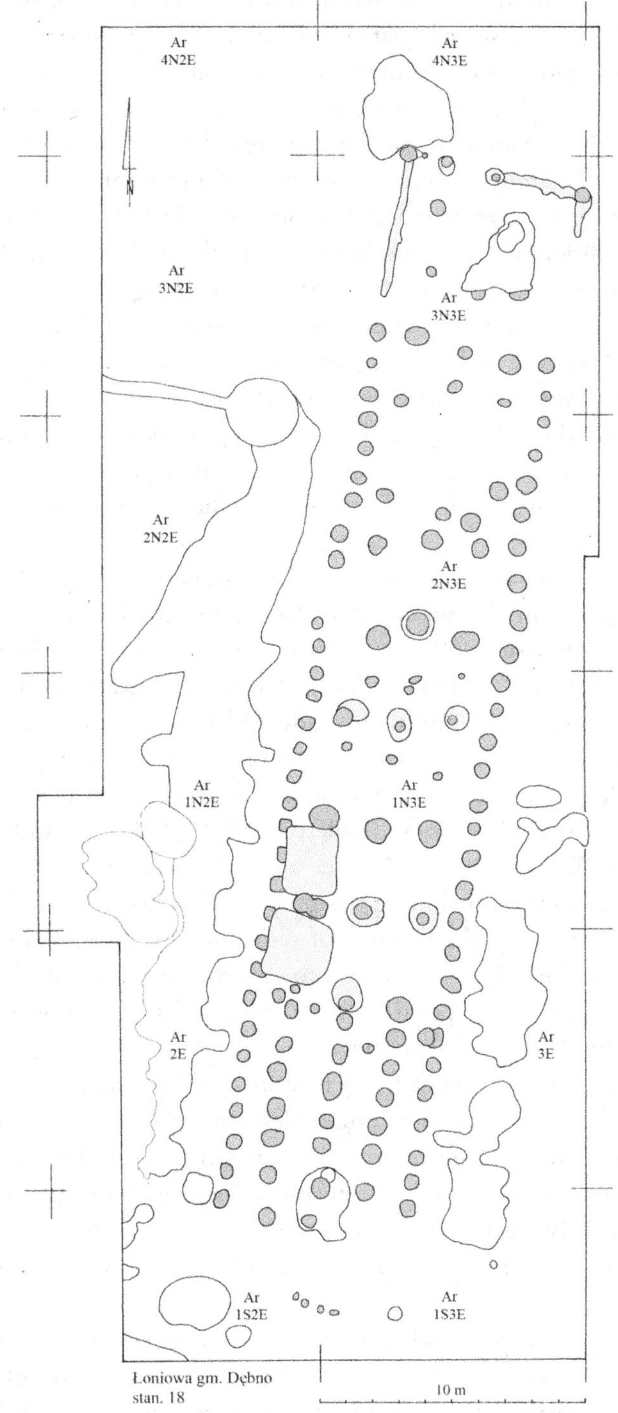

FIGURE 10.2 Linear Pottery longhouse at Łoniowa, southern Poland (from Val-de-Nowak 2009, used with permission).

it exhaustively. Several common ideas stand out, however (summarized in Schwake and Iannone 2012:332–334). A strong spatial referent is often involved, possibly associated with ritual behavior and objects. Objects that mediate social memory are situated in standardized locations, and there is consensus among members of the group as to where these locations are to be found or can be expected. Moreover, objects or constructions that might be called "memory prompts" are durable and lasting.

Many authors emphasize that the function of collective or social memory is the conservation of tradition or the representation of the past as a means of expressing identity in the present (e.g., Misztal 2003:25). As Alcock (2002:1) notes, "People derive identity from shared remembrance—from social memory—which in turn provides them with an image of their past and a design for their future." My argument is instead that Danubian memories were made to express something about the present to be *read* in the future, by which time the present had become the past. This is not just a way of "complicating" the argument, as college freshmen are taught to do in their writing courses. Rather, it calls for the construction of memories to have a forward-looking as well as a backward-looking aspect.

Unbeknownst to me when I was invited to speak at the IEMA conference, there is a very rich literature on the theme of collective or social memory in archaeological interpretation (see Chapman 2009 for a review, as well as many of the papers in Kienlin and Zimmermann 2012). A common theme of these discussions is how ancient people used artifacts, buildings, burials, and their modified landscapes to construct their social or collective memories and that these were purposive activities rather than passive byproducts of surviving. Capturing this concept succinctly for the purposes of the discussion here is the expression "memory work" (Gillespie 2010; Hoffmann and Bickle 2011:196; Mills and Walker 2008), which encompasses a range of activities related to shaping and transmitting social memories, including the purposeful construction of material remains. Credit for first characterizing the practice of remembering as a form of work might be given to Rowlands (1993:144), who goes on to say that "it is inseparable from the motive to memorialize." He made this point in the context of a discussion of durable objects and how they "assert their own memories."

The notion that memory work has a forward-looking aspect is echoed by Gillespie (2010:401–402), who also notes that certain elements or recollections are selected to be commemorated by a "technology of memory" in which everyday objects and features provide "non-textual *aides-mémoires*" to transmit collective memory. Ancient people who engaged in such memory work would have been acutely aware of the passage of time and that it was necessary to plan for the past by actively creating memories for subsequent generations.

When thinking about cultural transmission and social memory in the Danubian Neolithic, we need to take into account the relatively brief duration of each generation. Rather than 20 or 25 years, Kilmurray (2009) has persuasively argued that a more accurate length of Neolithic generations would be on the order of 15 years, with relatively few people surviving beyond 30 or 35. Based on the skeletal sample from Osłonki and Brześć Kujawski (Lorkiewicz 2012:55), I would suggest that 40 is a more reasonable threshold for becoming a scarce elderly person in the Neolithic, for the average age at death of males at these sites was 35.8 and females 33.2, but this does not change the main point. Short Neolithic generations have two important implications for the current analysis. First, it means that the most significant social actors, the adults in charge of households who made key decisions within the Neolithic hamlet, would have been young by our standards, many in their late teens or twenties. Second, it means that grandchildren did not know their grandparents very long, if at all. Active young adults of each generation bore the burden of doing the memory work for the next rather than a large group of elders, and most would not live to see their grandchildren reach adulthood.

It might also be helpful here to differentiate between fine-scale memories and grand-scale memories (Claassen 2010:218). Grand-scale memories might be considered to be those that resulted in major transformations of the built environment, visible and evocative beyond the local community and a short time horizon. Most of the monuments that are the focus of this volume would fit this category. Among the Danubian societies of the sixth and fifth millennium B.C., however, we are in the realm of fine-scale memories, small activities that prompted the memories of individuals and households. As we will see below, the practices that I discuss are local and domestic, constrained in both time and space. They are thus quite unmonumental in their expression, although by their contrast with the grand-scale monumental activities discussed in the other chapters in this volume, perhaps it might be possible to clarify their motivations.

We know that social life in the Danubian World was precarious. On one hand, we have an impression of diligent peasants pursuing their happy farming lives around their longhouses, surrounded by their livestock and crops. On the other hand, these lives could end suddenly and grimly, with whole communities apparently wiped out as at Talheim (Wahl and Trautmann 2012) and corpses used for unfathomable ritual activities as at the Linear Pottery enclosure at Herxheim (Orscheidt and Haidle 2012). A pervasive sense of transience in the present may have motivated the urge to prompt memories in the future.

Neolithic Memory Creation

The first farmers of central Europe probably had many different ways of creating memories for future generations. In this chapter, I focus on two practices that I believe have particular significance in this regard. The first is the practice of making deposits of ground and chipped stone tools, while the second is the practice of creating small groups of graves at settlement sites. Both of these, in my view, qualify as "memory work."

Deposits (Caches, Hoards)

A recent PhD dissertation by Marta Kaflińska in Kraków (Kaflińska 2011) has drawn together much of what we know about Neolithic deposits in central Europe. Following Kaflińska, the neutral term *deposit* is used rather than a more functional term such as *cache* or *hoard,* since as Kaflińska's work shows, it is possible to debate the function of these features from first principles. In North America, such deposits would be called "caches," although this designation implies that the objects they contain are meant to be retrieved, while elsewhere in the literature they are called "hoards" on the assumption that the objects have an intrinsic value.

Danubian stone tool deposits consist either of ground stone tools, including the famous "shoe-last celts" (Figure 10.3), or chipped stone tools or blanks. Many are unused, but some have been reworked. In the case of celts, there are instances of apparent attempts to arrange them in the pit, some vertically, others stacked. In some cases, large pieces of broken pottery were placed over the stone tools as a cover.

Many Danubian stone tool deposits, unlike those of later Neolithic periods, are found in settlement contexts: small pits or other shallow depressions. Others are found as accidental finds, but in habitable locations suggesting a settlement was not too far away. This has led to their attribution to an economic or safekeeping purpose of some sort, involving the storage or hiding of tools or raw materials that for some reason were not recovered before the abandonment of the settlement (Vencl 1975:61–62, discussed by Kaflińska 2011:57–58). While plausible, it leads to the question of why it was necessary to hide items that were in general use. If adzes had biographies, then perhaps

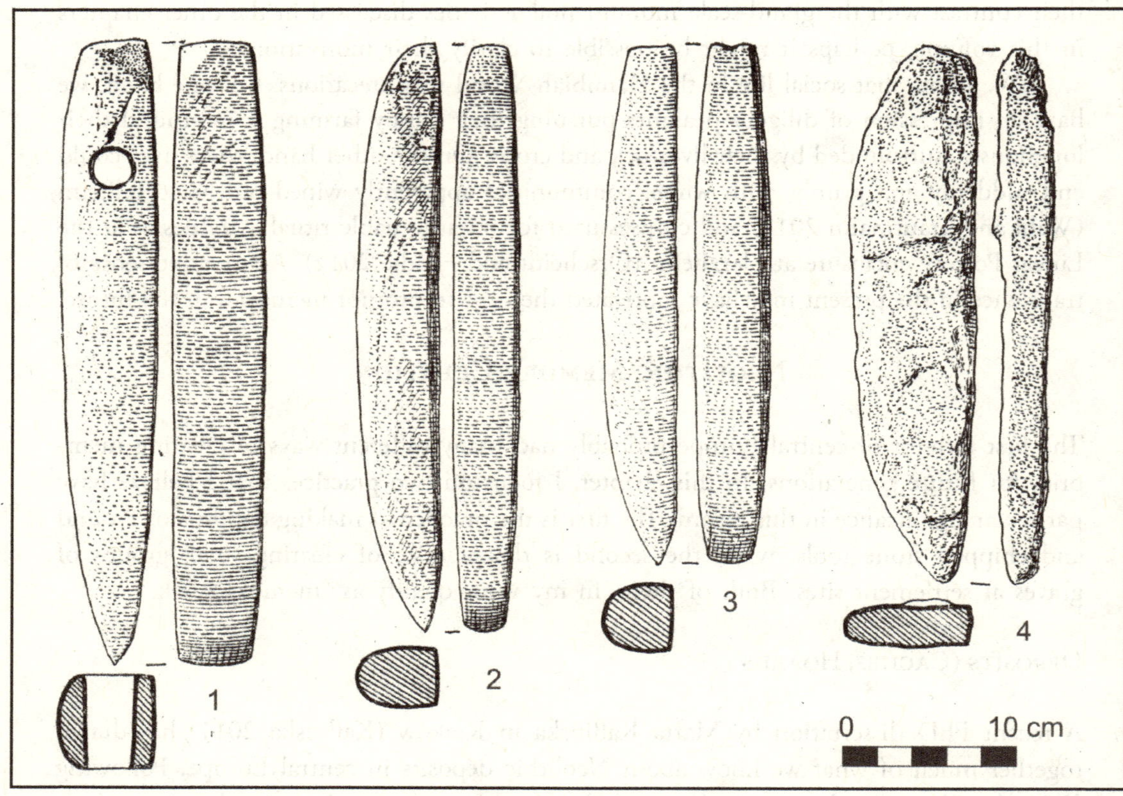

FIGURE 10.3 Deposit of ground stone tools from Stary Zamek, SW Poland (after Kaflińska 2011, used with permission).

some circumstances required them to be treated in this way, and it is also possible that keeping them out of sight would minimize requests to borrow them. For example, among the villagers of Gapun in Papua New Guinea, personal assets such as tools are closely guarded lest someone ask to borrow them, for the owner has a social obligation to lend and risk having them broken (Kulick 1992).

While it is conceivable that these deposits have a simple prosaic explanation, let me introduce a consideration of them as memory work.

Interestingly, the practice of making such deposits is not geographically uniform, and if there was a functional purpose behind them, one might expect that to apply more widely across the Danubian world. Dense concentrations of Danubian deposits with finished and unfinished ground stone tools are found near the Elbe-Saale confluence of central Germany and in central Bohemia. In other parts of central Europe, the distribution of deposits containing objects datable to the sixth and fifth millennia B.C. is more dispersed, and in some places they have not been documented at all. Some regions, however, display specific characteristics. For example, deposits of the fifth millennium B.C. from the Vistula valley contain almost exclusively chipped flint tools.

Thus, different forms of Danubian deposits seem to be geographically and temporally variable. This poses a challenge for our concept of earlier Danubian society, which we are often tempted to view as having been initially a single ethnolinguistic entity which then fragmented into regional variants at the end of the sixth millennium B.C. In fact, the practice of making deposits seems to be scarce or absent in large parts of the Danubian World, such as in southern Germany. Regional variation in behavior is at odds with the traditional view of the homogeneous Linear Pottery culture but consistent with the regional variation mentioned above. By the start of the fifth millennium B.C., more regional variability would be expected, despite the shared Danubian lineage, but it is still very clear that the practice of making deposits has a very regional, even local, character.

Clearly, something more is going on here, undermining our perception of widely uniform Danubian approaches to social practice. Daniela Hofmann and Penny Bickle (2011:196), writing with specific reference to Linear Pottery mortuary practices, note similar local variability and make the observation that even broad cultural entities such as Linear Pottery, Stroke-Ornamented Pottery, and the other Danubian groups that appear so homogenous at first glance are fundamentally local entities. As with mortuary practices, the creation of deposits of ground stone or chipped stone tools seems to have been a local or regional choice from a broad repertoire of Danubian cultural practices. Thus, it seems likely that Danubian memory work is based in daily experience and represents individual and small-group choices from a pool of widely held ideas.

The attribution of Danubian deposits to memory work rather than as ritual or caching behavior is echoed by observations of Pollard (2008) at Neolithic sites in southern Britain. At sites such as Etton, concentrations of animal bone, human bone, and stone axes are found in different parts of segmented enclosure ditches. Pollard even suggests that some of the deposits were intended to make reference to others, a sort of "depositional citation" (Pollard 2008:58), and such linkage across time would add another consideration to the notion of deposits as memory work rather than regarding each as a "one-off" event. In any event, it seems clear that Neolithic deposits require much more careful consideration and do not allow themselves to be easily explained as caches or offerings.

MICRO-CEMETERIES

A second category of memory-making observed at some Danubian sites is the construction of what might be called "micro-cemeteries."[2] These are clusters of graves within settlements. Sometimes they take the form of concentrations of burials without much apparent arrangement, while elsewhere they consist of several burials aligned in a row side by side. Although it may be possible to point to examples from different parts of the Danubian world, I would like to focus on two specific areas. The first is on settlements of the Brześć Kujawski Group, a late Danubian society on the lowlands of northern Poland (Bogucki 2003; Grygiel 2008) that I have studied along with my Polish collaborators for nearly four decades. The other is on settlements of the late Linear Pottery of the Paris Basin and the Villeneuve-Saint-Germain Group (VSG) found in the Paris Basin and its surrounding areas, including Normandy to the edge of the Breton Massif (Bedault 2009; Vander Linden 2011). In both cases, the micro-cemeteries are composed of distinct individual grave pits rather than large continuous collective interments.

Osłonki is a large settlement of the Brześć Kujawski Group in north-central Poland that we have been studying for more than two decades. Among its longhouses are dozens of burials. Upon closer examination, many form small groups, often in rows (Figure 10.4). We first noticed this at Osłonki, but going back to the plans of other large settlements, we found such alignments there as well.

FIGURE 10.4 Microcemetery at Osłonki, Poland, with three male skeletons (from Grygiel 2008:979; used with permission).

The micro-cemeteries are important because they are clear recognition of the multigenerational character of these settlements and that it was anticipated that these settlements would persist across generations by intent rather than by accident. It is common for the graves to be of varying depths and to have differences in their furnishings, suggesting that they do not represent multiple concurrent deaths. (When several presumably related people died or were killed at the same time, we usually find them in the same grave.)

In order to create such micro-cemeteries, it would have been necessary to have some sort of aboveground indication of where earlier burials could be found. We have no idea what these markers might have been: a small mound, perhaps a wooden post, or a slab of stone? Earlier graves, containing ornaments of shell and especially of copper, do not appear to have been disturbed by later graves during later phases of the Brześć Kujawski Group occupation, suggesting that these burial areas were spatially discrete and known as burial plots (a number of graves at Brześć Kujawski and Osłonki were probably disturbed by Iron Age habitation several millennia later).

At sites of the Brześć Kujawski Group, the micro-cemeteries are particularly characteristic of the "classic" phase of occupation between 4500 and 4300 B.C., in which burials were consistently flexed, with heads pointed toward the south or southeast, with males on their right side and females on their left. Toward the end of the occupation, the discipline of the burial rite unravels, perhaps reflecting other signs of stress and crisis seen in other remains, with the dead finding their way into rubbish pits and other contexts. For some reason, the past for which the classic-phase inhabitants of Brześć Kujawski had prepared was not appreciated by their descendants.

At the late Linear Pottery and VSG sites of the Paris Basin and eastern France, the small groups of settlement burials do not usually form the same neat rows as they do in the Brześć Kujawski Group. At the same time, they do not interfere with each other, suggesting that the diggers of new graves knew how not to disturb earlier ones. A good example is from the site of Bucy-le-Long "La Fosselle" (Hachem et al. 1998), in which late Linear Pottery and early Villeneuve-Saint-Germain burials form small groupings of up to three or four graves (perhaps up to seven if two adjacent groups are considered together). As in the Brześć Kujawski Group, these burials are richly ornamented, including one with a tiara of animal teeth (Bonnardin 2003). Other nice examples of micro-cemeteries are seen at Marainville-sur-Madon (Jeunesse 1997) and Menneville "Derrière le Village" (Farrugia, Guichard, and Hachem 1996).

An interesting convergence of settlement burial and deposit is found at the VSG site of Buthiers-Boulancourt in central France south of Paris (Gosselin and Samzun 2008). Burial 269 is part of a cluster of three burials. Set somewhat apart from the skeleton of a woman is a deposit consisting of four flint scrapers, one burin, and several flakes along with a whole turtle carapace (*Emys orbicularis*). Flint tools are rare in VSG burials, while the turtle shell find is unique. The tools are unused. Unlike the close association between the body and the ceramics and schist bracelets that typically characterize VSG burials, the separation between the body and the flint tools, plus the unusual turtle shell, in Burial 269 presents a highly structured deposit that appears to combine the motivations between the creation of micro-cemeteries and the placing of deposits to construct an object of memory.

Returning to Poland, in Grave 56 at Osłonki, we also find a combination of burial and deposit (Grygiel 2008:954). A double burial of two males, in itself an unusual event, is followed by a deposit of flint flakes and nodules about 50 centimeters above one of the individuals (Figure 10.5). It does not appear to have been an accidental juxtaposition. Whether it was made at the same time as the burials or later is unclear. The vertical separation between the flints and the skeleton would seem to parallel the horizontal separation seen in Burial 269 at Buthiers-Boulancourt and remove these items from the category of grave good. Instead, some sort of "memory work" again appears to have been going on.

WHY NO DANUBIAN MONUMENTS?

As I noted earlier, I am skeptical of the idea that Danubian longhouses and enclosures, while certainly large-scale constructions, could actually be considered true monuments, given that they served their primary purpose in the present. The theme of this chapter is about memory as the motivation for monument building, and I do not believe that the construction of longhouses and enclosures was *primarily* motivated by memory-work. This may be too constrained a view of the concept of a monument, and it seems clear from the other papers delivered at the conference that the other participants had a more inclusive view of what constitutes monumentality.

FIGURE 10.5 Grave 56 at Osłonki, Poland, showing deposit of flint blades and flint pebbles (arrow) in burial fill above skeletons (from Grygiel 2008:954; used with permission).

In a subsequent conversation at the conference, David Anthony, who was in the audience, suggested a possible reconciliation between these views on the basis of Claassen's distinction between fine-scale and grand-scale memory.[3] Perhaps longhouses and enclosures provided grand-scale collective memory but over a short duration, while the deposits and microcemeteries constituted fine-scale memories deliberately constructed to persist over a longer time. In light of the other views of monumentality advanced at the conference, Anthony's view is very reasonable, although I would still argue that the motivations behind the construction of longhouses and enclosures on one hand and the structured deposition of deposits and micro-cemeteries on the other were different.

In their decayed state, longhouse settlements and enclosures certainly would have prompted memories, and perhaps that is one reason why the early farmers in central Europe did not supplement them with additional grand constructions such as large barrows. It is possible that as colonists, and then later creoles, the Danubian farmers may not yet have made a priority of creating a grand collective history on a regional or transregional scale. Their multigenerational settlements may have been sufficient monuments in their own right simply by existing and eventually decaying, communicating to the future about their presence and containing enough material reminders about their past occupants. Abandoned settlements (and enclosures), as Magdalena Midgley (2005) has noted, would have been persistent landscape features standing in silent testimony to earlier human presence, and it may not have been necessary to overemphasize a shared past with additional grand monuments.

Instead, the inhabitants of Danubian hamlets chose to perpetuate memories on a fine scale for their descendants, largely within the precincts of settlements that they knew would remain visible points and provide the foci of later habitation. Different regions developed these local practices to different degrees, accounting for the geographical heterogeneity in making deposits and practicing settlement burial. Rather than making a grand statement for all to see far and wide, the ultimate purpose of such activity was to foster long-term vertical integration across generations within the hamlet, a big theme in the Danubian world.

Messages to the Future for the Past

Danubian settlements with their deposits and settlement burials included tangible, structured, material reminders of their past occupants left there with conscious foresight to plan for the memories of future inhabitants. People chose how to send these messages to the future in different ways in different places. In some parts of the Danubian World, memory work may not have been seen as important, or perhaps it took forms that we have not yet detected, while in some of the times and places that I have mentioned it was considered to be crucial. Such variability presages the variation in monumental construction seen later in central Europe. The shift to large public monuments during the second half of the fifth millennium B.C. coincides with a de-nucleation of settlements, perhaps a dispersal of households to situate themselves optimally among their fields and pastures. The settlement ceased to be the focus of memory work, and deposits came to be found primarily in extramural areas, often in bogs and other wet localities. Eventually, the practice of making deposits virtually disappeared, overtaken by tumuli and other mortuary and ceremonial monuments.

Small-scale memory-making practices on the Danubian settlements of interior central Europe, including deposits and micro-cemeteries, were expressions of the same instincts and motivations that led later Neolithic societies to build monuments. The practice of remembering was just as strong among the first farmers of central Europe as among monument builders elsewhere. They simply planned for the past in a less grand way.

NOTES

1.   Very useful reviews of approaches to collective or social memory are also provided by Schwake and Iannone (2010) with specific reference to Mayan examples from Belize and by Wilson (2010) with reference to Moundville in Alabama.
2.   Chris Scarre (2004) used the term *micro-nécropoles* in a review of Chambon and LeClerc (2003), and I have applied a translation of this term in this discussion.
3.   I am grateful to David Anthony for permission to quote his personal comment.

REFERENCES CITED

Alcock, S. 2002 *Archaeologies of the Greek Past: Landscape, Monuments, and Memories.* Cambridge University Press, Cambridge.

Assmann, J. 1995 Collective Memory and Cultural Identity. *New German Critique* (65):125–133.

Bedault, L. 2009 First Reflections on the Exploitation of Animals in Villeneuve-Saint-Germain Society at the End of the Early Neolithic in the Paris Basin (France). In *Creating Communities: New Advances in Central European Neolithic Research,* edited by D. Hofmann and P. Bickle, pp. 111–131. Oxbow Books, Oxford.

Biehl, P. F. 2012 Meanings and Functions of Enclosed Places in the European Neolithic: A Contextual Approach to Cult, Ritual, and Religion. *Archeological Papers of the American Anthropological Association* 21(1):130–146.

Bogucki, P. 1984 Ceramic Sieves of the Linear Pottery Culture and Their Economic Implications. *Oxford Journal of Archaeology* 3(1):15–30.

Bogucki, P. 2000 How Agriculture Came to North-Central Europe. In *Europe's First Farmers,* edited by T. D. Price, pp. 197–218. Cambridge University Press, Cambridge.

Bogucki, P. 2003 A Neolithic Tribal Society in Northern Poland. In *The Archaeology of Tribal Societies,* edited by W. A. Parkinson, pp. 372–383. International Monographs in Prehistory, Ann Arbor.

Bonnardin, S. 2003 La parure funéraire des 6e et 5e millénaires avant J.-C. dans le Bassin parisien et la plaine du Rhin supérieur: traces d'usure, fonctionnement et fonction des objets de parure. In *Les pratiques funéraires néolithiques avant 3500 av. J.-C. en France et dans les régions limitrophes: Table ronde SPF, Saint-Germain-en-Laye, 15–17 juin 2001,* edited by P. Chambon and J. Leclerc, pp. 99–113. Mémoires de la Société Préhistorique Française. vol. 33. Société Préhistorique Française, Paris.

Bradley, R. 1998 *The Significance of Monuments: On the Shaping of Human Experience in Neolithic and Bronze Age Europe.* Routledge, London.

Chambon, P., and J. Leclerc 2003 *Les pratiques funéraires néolithiques avant 3500 av. J.-C. en France et dans les régions limitrophes: Table ronde SPF, Saint-Germain-en-Laye, 15–17 juin 2001*. Mémoires de la Société Préhistorique Française. Société Préhistorique Française, Paris.

Chapman, J. 2009 Notes on Memory-Work and Materiality. In *Materializing Memory. Archaeological Material Culture and the Semantics of the Past*, edited by I. Barbiera, A. M. Choyke, and J. A. Rasson, pp. 7–16. BAR International Series. Archaeopress, Oxford.

Childe, V. G. 1929 *The Danube in Prehistory*. Oxford University Press, Oxford.

Claassen, C. 2010 *Feasting with Shellfish in the Southern Ohio Valley: Archaic Sacred Sites and Rituals*. University of Tennessee Press, Knoxville.

Farrugia, J.-P., Y. Guichard, and L. Hachem 1996 Les ensembles funéraires rubanés de Menneville "Derrière le Village" (Aisne) In *La Bourgogne entre les Bassins rhénan, rhodanien et parisien: Carrefour ou frontier? Actes du 18e colloque interregional sur le Néolithique*, Dijon, 1991 pp. 119–174. Revue archéologique de l'Est, quatorzième supplement.

Gillespie, S. D. 2010 Maya Memory Work. *Ancient Mesoamerica* 21(02):401–414.

Gosselin, R., and A. Samzun 2008 Un dépôt associé à une sépulture de la fin du Néolithique ancien à Buthiers-Boulancourt (Seine-et-Marne, France). Approche tracéologique et techno-fonctionnelle du mobilier lithique. *Préhistoires Méditerranéennes* (14):91–104.

Grygiel, R. 2008 *Neolit i Początki Epoki Brązu w Rejonie Brześcia Kujawskiego i Osłonek (The Neolithic and Early Bronze Age in the Brześć Kujawski and Osłonki Region), Volume II*. Konrad Jażdżewski Foundation for Archaeological Research, Museum of Archaeology and Ethnography, Łódź.

Hachem, L., P. Allard, C. Constantin, J. P. Farruggia, Y. Guichard, and M. Ilett 1998 Le site néolithique de Bucy-le-Long "La Fosselle" (Aisne). *Actes des Journées Internéo* (2):17–22.

Halbwachs, M. 1980[1950] *The Collective Memory*. Harper and Row, New York.

Hofmann, D., and P. Bickle 2011 Culture, Tradition, and the Settlement Burials of the *Linearbandkeramik* (LBK) Culture. In *Investigating Archaeological Cultures: Material Culture, Variability, and Transmission*, edited by B. W. Roberts and M. Vander Linden, pp. 183–200. Springer, New York.

Jeunesse, C. 1997 *Pratiques funéraires au néolithique ancien: sépultures et nécropoles des sociétés danubiennes (5500–4900 av. J.-C.)*. Editions Errance, Paris.

Kaflińska, M. 2011 *Społeczno-Rytualny i Gospodarczy Kontekst Depozytów Neolitycznych w Europie Środkowej*. Unpublished PhD dissertation, Institute of Archaeology, Jagiellonian University, Kraków, Poland.

Kienlin, T. L., and A. Zimmermann, eds. 2012 *Beyond Elites: Alternatives to Hierarchical Systems in Modelling Social Formations*. R. Habelt, Bonn.

Kilmurray, L. 2009 The Re-generation of the Neolithic Social Memory, Monuments and Generations. In *Materializing Memory. Archaeological Material Culture and the Semantics of the Past*, edited by I. Barbiera, A. M. Choyke, and J. A. Rasson, pp. 41–51. BAR International Series. vol. 1977. Archaeopress, Oxford.

Kulick, D. 1992 *Language Shift and Cultural Reproduction: Socialization, Self, and Syncretism in a Papua New Guinean Village*. Cambridge University Press, Cambridge.

Lorkiewicz, W. 2012 Skeletal Trauma and Violence among the Early Farmers of the North European Plain: Evidence from Neolithic Settlements of the Lengyel Culture in Kuyavia, North-Central Poland. In *Sticks, Stones, and Broken Bones: Neolithic Violence in a European Perspective*, edited by R. Schulting and L. Fibiger, pp. 51–76. Oxford University Press, Oxford.

Midgley, M. S. 2005 *The Monumental Cemeteries of Prehistoric Europe*. Tempus, Stroud.

Mills, B. J., and W. H. Walker, eds. 2008 *Memory Work: Archaeologies of Material Practices*. School for Advanced Research Press, Santa Fe.

Misztal, B. A. 2003 *Theories of Social Remembering*. Open University Press, Maidenhead, Berkshire, UK.

Modderman, P. J. R. 1988 The Linear Pottery Culture: Diversity in Uniformity. *Berichten van de Rijksdienst voor het Oudheidkundig Bodemonderzoek* 38:63–139.

Oross, K., and E. Bánffy 2009 Three Successive Waves of Neolithisation: LBK Development in Transdanubia. *Documenta Praehistorica* 36:175–189.

Orschiedt, J., and M. N. Haidle 2012 Violence against the Living, Violence against the Dead on the Human Remains from Herxheim, Germany. Evidence of a Crisis and Mass Cannibalism? In *Sticks, Stones, and Broken Bones: Neolithic Violence in a European Perspective*, edited by R. Schulting and L. Fibiger, pp. 121–137. Oxford University Press, Oxford.

Pollard, J. 2008 Deposition and Material Agency in the Early Neolithic of Southern Britain. In *Memory Work: Archaeologies of Material Practices*, edited by B. J. Mills and W. H. Walker. School for Advanced Research Press, Santa Fe.

Rowlands, M. 1993 The Role of Memory in the Transmission of Culture. *World Archaeology* 25(2):141–151.

Scarre, C. 2004 Review of *Les pratiques funéraires néolithiques avant 3500 av. J.-C. en France et dans les régions limitrophes. Table ronde SPF, Saint-Germain-en-Laye 15–17 juin 2001*, edited by Philippe Chambon and Jean LeClerc, Mémoire XXXIII de la Société Préhistorique Française. Société Préhistorique Française, Paris, 2003. Book Reviews, The Prehistoric Society, http://www.ucl.ac.uk/prehistoric/reviews/04_04_scarre.htm.

Schwake, S. A., and G. Iannone 2010 Ritual Remains and Collective Memory: Maya Examples from West Central Belize. *Ancient Mesoamerica* 21(02):331–339.

Valde-Nowak, P. 2009 Early Farming Adaptation in the Wiśnicz Foothills in the Carpathians. Settlements at Łoniowa and Żerków. *Recherches Archéologiques (Kraków)* 1:15–35.

Vander Linden, M. 2011 To Tame a Land: Archaeological Cultures and the Spread of the Neolithic in Western Europe. In *Investigating Archaeological Cultures: Material Culture, Variability, and Transmission*, edited by B. W. Roberts and M. Vander Linden, pp. 289–319. Springer, New York.

Vencl, S. 1975 Hromadné nálezy neolitické broušené industrie z Čech. *Památky Archeologické* 66(1):12–73.

Wahl, J., and I. Trautmann 2012 The Neolithic Massacre at Talheim: A Pivotal Find in Conflict Archaeology. In *Sticks, Stones, and Broken Bones: Neolithic Violence in a European Perspective*, edited by R. Schulting and L. Fibiger, pp. 77–100. Oxford University Press, Oxford.

Williams, T. 1945 Production notes. In *The Glass Menagerie*. New Directions, New York.

Williams T. 1999 [1945] *The Glass Menagerie*. New Directions, New York.

Wilson, G. D. 2010 Community, Identity, and Social Memory at Moundville. *American Antiquity* 75(1):3–18.

CHAPTER ELEVEN

Death and the City

Asiatic Columnar Sarcophagi in Context

(In memory of Crawford H. Greenewalt)

Annetta Alexandridis

Abstract *This chapter examines a type of Graeco-Roman funerary monument, the so-called Asiatic columnar sarcophagi, with particular emphasis on form and iconography. Produced in the second and third centuries A.D. for members of the highest elite, these marble containers consist of a box and a lid showing a couple reclining as if for a banquet. The high reliefs decorating the chest on all four sides replicate public civic architecture in miniature. Human figures within this architecture represent (statues of) mythological figures or honorable citizens. Seen within the "local" framework of Asia Minor, these monuments convey civic pride and prestige. In the broader "global" context of the Roman Empire they testify to the broad acceptance and reputation of Greek culture and education (paideia), but seen, canonized, and simultaneously recreated through Roman eyes. This revival of the past as a "past in the present" becomes particularly poignant in the funerary monuments with their ambivalent distinction between living and dead, flesh and marble, transience and immortalization. The play between different scales and realities in the sarcophagi's overall design and decoration turns the funerary containers into "other" spaces and gives them their monumental quality.*

TOWARD A DEFINITION

Acontemporary visitor to the ancient necropoleis of Asia Minor such as Assos or Hierapolis might not find the individual broken funerary containers lying next to the streets particularly appealing. Strolling in between hundreds of sarcophagi, however, this same person might be overwhelmed seeing their sheer number against the city walls or a spectacular landscape with mountains or the sea in the background. The single, unappealing sarcophagus would consequently acquire a monumental quality, literally or metaphorically, in this person's mind. An ancient visitor, on the other hand, could have been drawn toward a single piece destined for a family member, anxious about its execution and display. The necropolis as a whole was not of interest, or only insofar as single burials spurred competitive comparison. At a larger event, however, with a procession leading into the city, the necropolis as a whole could have been an object of local civic pride, where a stranger might have been appalled by the amount of ostentatious expenditure.

I start with this sketch as a reminder of the many various elements that can impact the experience of "monumentality" in a given time and place—elements that usually escape the archaeological record, but that deserve to be considered in a definition of the phenomenon (Ingold 2011; Thomas 2007:207–220). Derived from the Latin *monumentum* and *monere,* monumentality, one could argue from a simple grammatical point of view, designates the ideal quality or qualities we ascribe to a monument, namely that it commemorates and/or admonishes (Thomas 2007:168–170, 179–203). Or so it seems. But the term has a history beyond its Latin origin. Often based on the ancient meaning of monument, it has been adapted and appropriated for different cultural contexts. For Wu Hung, for example, in his study of early Chinese art and architecture, monumentality "denotes memory, continuity, and political, ethical, or religious obligations to a tradition." Monumentality is the quality that sustains the functions of a monument, their relationship being equivalent to that between content and form (Wu 1995:4).[1] But monumentality is not self-explanatory, nor is meaning. It is generated in a "relationship between . . . monuments and those experiencing" them, as James Osborne points out in his introduction. Many elements and agents will shape such an experience, from the material qualities of monuments and the specific contexts of their display to the sensations and memories they evoke in their beholder. The higher the number of agents and the more complex their relationship, the more urgent it is to insist on the historical contingency of monumentality. And yet, I still believe that there is a "gap" unaccounted for in any definition; a gap that might be best described by the effect it causes: an almost visceral reaction of awe, which some would call "presence." This "presence" might result from or in what Osborne calls the "active force" of a monument. What exactly constitutes this force, however, can only be described and analyzed in retrospect, when "a community has agreed upon a monument's meaning(s)" (Osborne, this volume). In other words: a monument can be planned, monumentality cannot (Riegl 1903; see also Fisher and Pauketat, this volume).[2] Whether conceived as a primarily spatial or temporal, formal (visual and aural) or material phenomenon, monumentality is both historically contingent and yet able to transcend this contingency, that is to say, to overcome the constraints of time and space. How do we deal with such phenomena as scholars, with this certain something that we cannot capture but seemingly only experience? We are faced with a methodological blind spot: there is an element that detracts itself from analysis. I take this as monumentality's paradoxical and universal aspect: experiencing something that transcends human experience and that results in a constant shifting between the particular and the universal, the ephemeral and the eternal, absence and presence.

Asiatic Columnar Sarcophagi

Monumentality cannot be planned; it happens. Yet, that does not mean that people did not try to make it happen by providing all the "ingredients" deemed necessary in a particular time and situation. These "ingredients" can be studied. They can include—as the contributions in this volume exemplify—setting, scale, human and material resources; but also form, images, spectacle, rituals and performances, and so on. In the following pages[3] I examine a particular group of funerary monuments in Roman Asia Minor,[3] the so-called Asiatic columnar sarcophagi, from the second and third centuries A.D. (for a general introduction on funerary containers from Asia Minor, see Koch 2011, and Koch and Sichtermann 1982:476–557; for columnar sarcophagi from Dokimeion, see Koch and Sichtermann 1982:503–509; Lawrence 1958; Morey 1924; Thomas 2010; Waelkens 1982:68–101; Wiegartz 1965). As their primary function was to commemorate, meaning to presence the absent, the sarcophagi lend themselves to a discussion of the above-mentioned paradoxical aspects of monumentality. Unfortunately, these sarcophagi have mostly survived as single "masterpieces," often chopped up into single reliefs held in different locations. Highly sought after by looters and collectors on the art market, the fragments' precise find spots, let alone original contexts of display, most often remain unknown.

I start by sketching out possible settings. However, the framework in which I want to situate the sarcophagi is less their specific archaeological context than their broader cultural milieu, looking primarily at their material and conditions of production, their structure, and their iconography. These aspects might ultimately not explain the containers' monumentality. But they make it very clear that these were objects of conspicuous consumption, as well as why and how they were conceived as monuments in a highly sophisticated, multilayered way. The sarcophagi did not only commemorate their deceased owners, but in a very self-conscious fashion also referenced the culture to which they—sarcophagi and their users alike—belonged and which is generally subsumed under the term *Second Sophistic* (for recent contributions see Borg 2004; Cordovana and Galli 2007; Goldhill 2001; Whitmarsh 2005, 2010). In the second and third centuries A.D., Greek education and culture (*paideia*) enjoyed wide acceptance and dissemination among the elites (and others) across the Roman Empire. Simultaneously, we witness a sort of global or homogeneous Roman imprint in public architecture and the visual arts next to older local traditions (Macready and Thompson 1987). The sarcophagi referenced this cultural milieu in the architectural and figural decoration of their exterior. Mythological figures and famous works of art from the heydays of Greek culture were resuscitated to appear in new contexts and arrangements. The strategy was indicative of the particular historical situation in which these sarcophagi were produced. But it also follows more general mechanisms of memory work (Galli 2007:8–10), according to which memory is not only a storage space, but an active agent that shapes its own content (on both types of memory see Assmann 1999:133–142, 249–250). The dynamics are not dissimilar from those that result in how we experience monumentality and meaning, namely in constantly negotiating, reaffirming, and actualizing a relationship between thing and person (see Osborne, this volume). Finally, both the sarcophagi's structure and iconography, as I hope to show, materialized the "heterotopic" (Cormack 2004:46–49, 106–107; Ewald 2008:624–625; Foucault 1986) status of these objects and their content in a more universal way. Rather than only their physical dimensions, form or material, then, it was these combined qualities that let the Asiatic columnar sarcophagi eventually appear monumental.

THE SETTING: ANCIENT CITIES OF THE DEAD

Heterotopias, according to Foucault, are "counter-sites," juxtaposing in a single real space different spaces, sites, and times that are in reality incompatible, such as the mirror that presences the absent (Foucault 1986:24). Cemeteries are heterotopias par excellence (Foucault 1986:25). In Graeco-Roman culture, tombs as *mnēmeia* or *monumenta* had a commemorative function. In addition, they served as the house (*oikos, domus*) of the deceased—but also for the families, who regularly convened in such places to remember the departed with ritual offerings such as libations, or in communal banquets.[4] The setting of the tombs additionally materialized their liminal or shifting status: located outside, but next to, settlements or cities, the dead, although they were not part of life in the city anymore, enclosed or framed it. Simultaneously there was a constant movement of the living—the future dead—between the two spheres that ensured various forms of connection and that kept the memory of the departed alive, at least for a while (Cormack 2004:105–107, 116–122; Morris 1992:8–30). The Greek tradition of heroizing the dead and the ensuing cult crossed another line, that between mortals and immortals (e.g., Cormack 2004:109–112).

Cemeteries in Asia Minor showed a broad spectrum of monuments. Sarcophagi, for example, could be erected right next to the streets leading into the city, they could be installed on little podia or on high pedestals, displayed in larger, often two-storied tomb structures together with others or as a single monument, or they could be hidden in underground chambers (e.g., Cormack 2004; Equini Schneider 1971–73:103–110; Köse 2005). As Cormack emphasizes (2004:112–116), the tombs' hierarchical organization, restricting or facilitating access to the burials, was a characteristic feature. This clearly impacted their potential monumentality, but in ambiguous ways. A sarcophagus deposited in an underground chamber could be inconspicuously "tucked away" or staged as the stunning final destination of an exclusive visit.

A spectacular example of such a hierarchical display is the recently discovered, two-storied funerary house at Perge. The farther away a funerary container had been manufactured, the more conspicuous its display. Sarcophagi made of local marble were set up in the courtyard. Two rooms in the first floor, decorated with mosaics similar to banquet rooms, each housed a Prokonnesian and an Asiatic sarcophagus. Finally, the top floor was reserved for the "pinnacle," a huge Attic sarcophagus. This import from overseas was proudly installed in the center of the room (Abbasoğlu 2006:298–301, Figure 10), the couple on the lid reclining as if ready to preside at a banquet and receiving guests.

The few records we have about specifically Asiatic columnar sarcophagi within their funerary setting reflect this variety to a certain extent. The sarcophagus of Claudia Antonia

Sabina from Sardis (Figures 11.1 and 11.2), according to Charles Morey's reconstruction, was put up in the front porch of her tomb (today destroyed). Installed next to that of her husband, it was visible to passers-by (Morey 1924:5). Another such sarcophagus from Sardis, which recently came to light much closer to the city center in a rescue excavation, seems to have been put up in the corner of a narrow brick chamber. This does not suggest a display for easy viewing. Another Asiatic sarcophagus, this time from Aizanoi, was sitting in a vaulted stone chamber, clearly exhibited in a central axis from the entrance (Türktüzün 1993; Wulf 1993:527–531).[5] All these examples present different options for regulating access, each of them impacting the viewing experience and an eventual staging of monumentality, in different, if not opposite ways as explained above. Without further evidence of how their surroundings were configured, the experience of the sarcophagi is impossible for us to assess. But it is important to recall that in all cases there was clear concern with providing an individual setting for each piece, as all the sarcophagi were displayed in larger tomb structures and not just parked next to the street like other bulk commodities. This status is confirmed by their material and production.

THE MARBLE: MATERIAL AND PRODUCTION

It makes sense to look at the Asiatic columnar sarcophagi as a homogenous group, even if each of them had a different destination and fate, since they all come from the same quarries. They are made of a particular marble with bluish-purple veins that has been identified as coming from Dokimeion (modern İscehisar) in Phrygia in Western Anato-

FIGURE 11.1 Sarcophagus of Claudia Antonia Sabina from Sardis; now Istanbul, Archaeological Museum; reconstructive drawing; reproduced from Morey (1924:frontispiece).

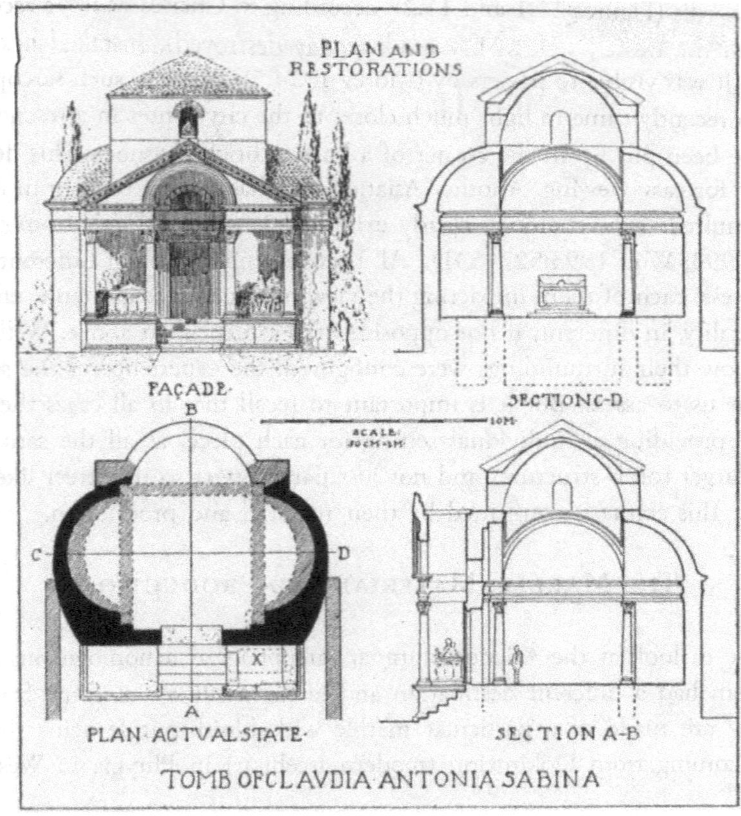

FIGURE 11.2 Tomb of Claudia Antonia Sabina; reconstruction; reproduced from Morey (1924:Figure 2).

lia.[6] Administered by the Roman emperor, these quarries were—besides Prokonnesos—the most exploited in Asia Minor at the time. Architectural pieces, sarcophagi, or other funerary containers, statues, and decorative pieces were extracted from here (Fant 1985, 1989; Filges 1999b:419–423; Pensabene 2011:40–49; Röder 1971; Waelkens 1982, 1985). The workshops seem to have been situated in or near the quarries. They exported the pieces to numerous places in Asia Minor, but also to the western part of the Roman Empire and, though less often in the case of the sarcophagi, to the Levant. Expenditures for material and transportation already suggest that only the very rich could afford such a coffin. Dokimeion's landlocked location complicated transport. Unlike at Prokonnesos, for example, which is situated in the sea of Marmara, the products had to be transported by land and water (via the Maeander River) to get shipped to their final destination (Hirt 2010:27–28).

The prestige these coffins brought with them is confirmed by several texts. Roman sources identify the quarries with "Synnada," where their administrative center was located, or "Phrygia." But as Strabo tells us the locals called the stone Dokimeian (*lithos dokimites* or *dokimaios*). In this area, that is, the marble itself had a name (Strab. *Geogr.* 12.8.14). The sarcophagi in particular seem to have been something like a brand: inscriptions from different places mention sarcophagi or generally marbles from Dokimeion (*soroi dokimenai; ta dokimeia*) that a tomb owner had erected (Ferrari 1966:90–92; Pensabene 2011:43). The coffins themselves in these cases have not always survived so that we cannot know whether they were really produced in Dokimeion and made public as such to the passersby. That this could have been more an aspirational statement is suggested by the situation at Hierapolis, where most of the city's marble sarcophagi come from Aphrodisias, even though the epigraphic evidence for Dokimeion is higher than for any other quarry (Equini Schneider 1971–73:117).

The reputation of Dokimeian workshops gets further support by the observation that the Asiatic columnar sarcophagi always seem to have left the quarries as finished products, suggesting that the customer also desired and paid for the craftsmanship, and not simply the raw material.[7] Inscriptions confirm that sculptors from Dokimeion were renowned: they proudly advertised their workshop when itinerant or settling down in other areas of Anatolia and possibly even Rome (Hall and Waelkens 1982; Koch 2011:13; Pensabene 2011:40–49).

Finally, the sarcophagi themselves occasionally make it explicit that they had been acquired by the highest elite, namely, people of senatorial or consular rank. Claudia Antonia Sabina from Sardis, whom we have already encountered, had her name inscribed on the rim of her sarcophagus lid mentioning her as *hupatikē,* wife of a consul (ΚΛ. ΑΝΤ. ΣΑΒΕΙΝΗΣ ΥΠΑΤΙΚΗΣ; Morey 1924:14–16; Raepsaet-Charlier 1987:203–204).[8]

FORM

Material and various expenditures turned the sarcophagus already into a "monumental" purchase. Furthermore, the social rank of its owners as stated in inscriptions marked it explicitly as an outstanding object. How, then, did the container's form contribute to its monumentality?

The known Asiatic columnar sarcophagi reach dimensions from 2.325 m to 3.135 m in length and 1.65 to 3.81 m in height, the larger ones being a later development (Morey 1924:6, 34, 40). They consist of a chest and a lid. All four sides of the chest were carved in relief. Unlike sarcophagi from Roman workshops, which were usually displayed in niches and had only their front decorated in full relief, the Asiatic sarcophagi stood as independent monuments, inviting viewers to surround them, even though the actual setting (see above) did not always bring this to bear. The lid was flat. It represented a couple reclining on a mattress in round sculpture. Whereas lids of sarcophagi from Rome or Prokonnesos were usually shaped like a roof, the entire container appearing as a house, the general shape of the Asiatic sarcophagi did not imitate domestic or any other type of architecture. Nevertheless, to better understand their symbolic meaning, it is worth considering these sarcophagi as—heterotopic—structures in their own right. The iconography of the reliefs on the chest proves to be key.

THE ARCHITECTURE

On all four sides the chests of Asiatic columnar sarcophagi displayed a variety of figures, framed by columns (even if only at the corners), by arcades or, most conspicuously, by a more elaborate architecture. This "microarchitecture" (Thomas 2010; Ertuğ and Smith 2001:274) was a hallmark of the series. Usually, a number of columns or arcades running around the chest suggested a portico or an intricate architecture with shell niches and protruding and receding entablature. In between the columns or in front of them we see various male and female figures (e.g., Figures 11.1, 11.4). Often the left short side featured a closed door in front of which a couple, usually a man and a woman or two sacrificial servants (Wiegartz 1965:72–73) perform a sacrifice (e.g., Figure 11.5).[9] This last element in particular has suggested to scholars that the sarcophagus represented a tomb for a deified human, a *heröon* (Thomas 2010:393; Wiegartz 1965:22–24). However, as Thomas has definitively shown (Thomas 2010:409–420), the columnar architecture reflected contemporaneous civic architecture, most notably stage houses of theaters (de Bernardi Ferrero 1974; Gros 2011:285–305), the facades of fountain houses (*nymphaia*) (Gros 2011:418–444), the interior of baths (Figure 11.3) (Gros 2011:397–417), of other civic buildings such as gates (e.g., Strocka 1981), basilicas (Gros 2011:244–260), or libraries (Gros 2011:362–275; Strocka 2003, 2009), or colonnaded streets (Bejor 1999;

FIGURE 11.3 Sardis, Bath-Gymnasium, Marble Court (photo: author).

FIGURE 11.4 Asiatic sarcophagus from Konya, front; Konya Museum 1990.38.1 (photo: Ramazan Özgan).

FIGURE 11.5 Asiatic sarcophagus from Konya, side; Konya Museum 1990.38.1 (photo: Ramazan Özgan).

Heinzelmann 2003), and also temples (Gros 2011:140–206; Lyttelton 1987; Thomas 2007:46–49). The sarcophagi therefore evoked monumental public spaces in miniature. They did so in a way that reminded one of the contemporaneous "global" and local environments alike, for some of these spaces and their splendid architecture could be considered "standard equipment" of a Roman city in general, such as theaters or baths, while others were more characteristic of urban culture in the Graeco-Roman East specifically, such as bath-gymnasia (Farrington 1987; Yegül 1982) or lavish fountain facades (Dorl-Klingenschmid 2001:48–60; Gros 2011:418–444).[10] In addition, moldings of the entablature adhered to local, micro-Asiatic traditions, like their models in large-scale architecture (Lyttelton 1987:47–48). This "micro-architecture" of the sarcophagi, in other words, was also a microcosm. It referenced the city, but also the empire as a cultural community (*koinē*).

What did that mean for the sarcophagus as container of a body? Was it supposed to represent a civic building and suggest that the deceased was actually buried not beside a road outside the gates but rather in the city center? This was an honor only granted to outstanding benefactors (e.g., Berns 2013; Cormack 2004:44–49), such as the acclaimed Tiberius Iulius Celsus Polemaeanus, consul of 92 and Proconsul of Asia in A.D. 106–107. He was buried in a half-finished garland sarcophagus in the library at Ephesus (Koch and Sichtermann 1982:520, 522, Figure 506), the erection of which had been accomplished by his son. The building stood next to a small square at a connecting point between the main street (*embolos*) and the commercial agora of the city. Its facade proudly displayed the same type of architecture that Asiatic sarcophagi refer to (Strocka 2003, 2009).[11]

A claim to similar fame, albeit unfulfilled, might have been made by the above-mentioned Claudia Antonia Sabina from Sardis. An inscription lists her as one of the sponsors of the so-called bath-gymnasium complex, more specifically of the marble courtyard, which was dedicated to the emperor Caracalla (Yegül 1986:48, 170). The courtyard's spiral columns in *giallo antico* marble, imported from the imperial quarries at Simitthus (Chemtou) in North Africa, found a nice counterpart in the spiral columns of their donor's Asiatic sarcophagus (Figures 11.1, 11.3) (Yegül 1986:55, 136). Did Sabina hope to be buried in this area as a major benefactress of the city? There is not the slightest evidence for such a desire on her part, but ancient viewers, when seeing her funerary container, might have made the personal and visual connection between her tomb and the imposing structure in the city.[12] Both, in any case, commemorated its owner as a citizen of the empire and of the city of Sardis alike.

Yet, I do not think the sarcophagus was imagined as a building, even if the doors we sometimes see on the left side suggest otherwise (see Thomas 2010:389). While theater stages, facades of *nymphaia*, interiors of baths, and other buildings usually displayed at least two, and often three, registers of columnar architecture with niches, the sarcophagi confront us with a single one. Was this supposed to be just the first register, that is, a representation of civic architecture on eye level? Or did it refer more specifically to temples whose interior facades consist of only one register? The altar in front of the door on the left short side next to which a couple is performing a sacrifice might confirm the idea that the sarcophagus imitated a temple or rather an open enclosure for a temple or *heröon* (e.g., Cormack 2004:166–168, 297–300; Thomas 2007:186, Figure 152; Thomas 2010:393–394), a place where the deceased would receive divine/heroic honors. But the referent is less clear than we might think. Whereas temples, like theaters or baths, were decorated with this sort of architecture in their inside (*pace* Thomas 2012:389), here it adorned the outside of the chest.[13] The architecture on the reliefs does therefore not represent a specific type of building. I suggest instead that the sarcophagus was a coherent "other" structure in its own right. Because it was a heterotopic space, it did not follow the rules for ordinary buildings. Reversing inside and outside seems key here. As a box, the sarcophagus contained a body, similar to a *heröon* or temple enclosing a burial or shrine. But the reliefs on the outside of the chest suggested that this box had to be imagined as a structure turned inside-out (at least on three sides, if one assumes the sacrifice in front of the door is already being performed outside the structure).

The Figures

The same uncertainty about the relationship to real models is conveyed by the figures in the intercolumnia representing mythological and nonmythological men and women. None of the Asiatic columnar sarcophagi exactly repeat each other in design, which suggested to Strocka (1984), no doubt influenced by interpretations of mythological sarcophagi from the city of Rome (Amedick 1991; Zanker and Ewald 2004), that they were special commissions, each conveying an individualized, sometimes even eschatological meaning reflective of the biography of the deceased. However, although some mythological figures were more specific, the general repertoire consisted of a rather limited number of generic types of men, women, and children, combined in numerous variations. Moreover, it is unclear how particular wishes of the customers would have been communicated to the workshops: through middlemen, pattern books, or both? While Strocka is certainly right in pointing out that the figures are not merely meaningless decoration, the consistent decorative variations they display was a substantial part of the message: they replicated or imitated the kinds of works of art that filled urban public architecture (e.g., Manderscheid 1981:43–45, 86–100 plates 25–34; Slavazzi 2007; various contributions in D'Andria and Romeo 2011).

The figures are depicted as standing or sitting in front of arcades, sometimes on pedestals. Among the mythological figures we count the Dioskouroi Castor and Pollux, shown as nude riders with horses (Wiegartz 1965:73–80 plate 19a.b), Heracles performing his twelve labors (Özgan 2003:plate 18), or famous Homeric heroes such as Odysseus and Diomedes, who stole the Palladion from the acropolis of Troy (Wiegartz 1965:plate 18f), or Achilles who is approached by his mother with his helmet (Figure 11.6). Sometimes the figures interact; at least they seem to look at each other. Otherwise, there is not much narrative in the scenes. Quite to the contrary, the figures are separated by columns. Rather than representations of Greek heroes, they are representations of statues of these heroes. This is obvious, when they stand on pedestals (Thomas 2010:401 Figure 12.4). Moreover, they rely on famous or widely used models or types from (over) life-size sculpture that stylistically belong to the Classical and Hellenistic periods. In this

FIGURE 11.6 Asiatic sarcophagus from Konya with representation of Thetis; Karaman Museum A 2179 (photo: Ramazan Özgan).

way, the sarcophagus figures showcased—again in miniature—the predominant form of artistic practice in the Roman Empire: copying, in the broadest sense.[14] The repertoire covered the whole span from close reproductions, only reduced in scale, to looser variations. Among the former is the so-called Penelope type, a statue so famous that a replica, if not the original, made it even to Persepolis (Figures 11.7 and 11.8) (Hölscher 2011; Kader 2006). Another very popular type is depicted in the center of the front of Melfi sarcophagus' front: a female figure writing on a shield.[15] The type, the so-called Aphrodite from Capua, underwent numerous transformations in Roman times. It can appear with a naked torso (Bieber 1977:plates 19–22; Kousser 2007:674), or completely covered as on the Melfi sarcophagus (Kousser 2007:676, 679; Thomas 2010:414 Figure 12.11), as an image of the goddess Venus/Aphrodite, or as portrait statue. The addition of wings turned the figure into Victory, well known from the central panel of the column of Trajan (Hölscher 1970; Kousser 2008:81–100). Repeated in different sizes (from over-life size to miniature), forms (sculpture in the round, relief, engraving), and materials (marble, bronze, gemstones, clay), the type was an enormously popular image across the Roman Empire.

Many of the nude heroic figures standing between the columns in contrast had no precise model, but they clearly followed and confirmed Classical or Hellenistic tradition (Wiegartz 1965:81–99, 119–139). In content (myth) and form (statue types, if not works of art), these figures displayed a sort of "classical heritage," the "musts" or "best of," as it were, of what was considered Greek culture at the time.[16]

The unidentified, richly draped men and women (Figures 11.1, 11.4, 11.5), who stand or sit in between the statues of heroic or divine figures, could to a certain extent be seen in a similar vein. They are usually too generic to be understood as representations of

FIGURE 11.7 Fragment of Asiatic sarcophagus with "Penelope" figure, Afyon Museum 1991 (photo: Ramazan Özgan).

the deceased, as some scholars propose (Cormack 2004:75; Thomas 2007:197; Wiegartz 1965:119–130).[17] By replicating postures or statue types known from public honorific portraiture or from tomb reliefs, they personified the civic part of urban life. But if the mythological figures and miniature works of art represented the global side of this Greek

FIGURE 11.8 Roman copy of statue of "Penelope"; Vatican, Galleria delle statue 754; courtesy of the German Archaeological Institute, Rome; D-DAI-ROM-97VAT395B (photo: Karl Anger).

culture, that is, the form in which it shaped aesthetics and education in the whole of the Roman Empire, then these nonmythological figures emphasized its more local aspects.

Similar to the mythological figures on the sarcophagi, these miniature statues referred to a range of models, from closely replicated types to looser adaptations. A standard type for men, for example, showed them wrapped in a Greek mantle (*himation*) with the right arm hanging in the cloth in front of their chest (cf. Bieber 1977:plates 104–106; Filges 1999a; Smith 2006:nos. 48–49 plates 42–43, 158; Wiegartz 1965:plate 16a). Some displayed a more complicated arrangement of the drapery, as it was also known from honorary statues (Figure 11.5; 11.9) (cf. Smith 2006:nos. 45, 50, 51 plates 35, 44, 46; Wiegartz 1965:plate 16d). A preference for Greek-style costume is clear, unlike in the ideal figures. Wiegartz (1965:119) lists only one example for a man in distinctively Roman dress, the toga. Men were also shown seated as philosophers. Another widespread form of self-representation in East and West, such life-size commemorative statues and their respective miniature versions on the sarcophagi visualized learnedness (Ewald 1999:54–134; Smith 2006:37–38 nos. 46, 47, 52; Zanker 1995:90–145, 226–233, 267–284).

Female figures replicated types such as the Large or Small Herculaneum women, which were the most widely distributed types for honorary statues in the Roman Empire and particularly popular in the Greek East (Daehner 2007; Trimble 2000, 2011; Wiegartz 1965:plate 20a.b). Other models are less easy to pin down, but they emulated and rearranged motives from types well represented in life-size statuary (e.g., Figure 11.4) (Alexandridis 2004:235–238; Bieber 1977:nos. 827–828, 872–874 plates 126–128, 141, 150; Schneider 1999:plates 6, 29–34; cf. Wiegand 1965:plates 20f.h, 21a.b.d). Again, emphasis seems to have been more on local, Eastern traditions, for female figures in the scheme of the so-called Ceres type (Bieber 1977:plates 123–125; Wiegartz 1965:plate 20c) or the so-called Pudicitia, which were at the time more popular for portrait statues in the Roman West (Alexandridis 2004:57–63, 229–231, 261–265; 2010), did not appear very often among the figures on Asiatic sarcophagi.

In sum, these mythological and nonmythological figures represented a selection of Greek myth, art, and civic life, mostly in the visual language of the Classical and Hellenistic age. Conceived and perceived by inhabitants of the Greek East that had at this time been part of the Roman Empire for several generations, this Greek cultural heritage was by no means an ossified past, but rather a "past in the present." It was not only reconstructed or staged as bygone glory, but lived, constantly performed and put in new contexts, and this way renewed (e.g., von Hesberg 2007; Zeitlin 2001:207–233). The Asiatic columnar sarcophagi themselves can count as a prime example of this practice, as they placed Greek statue types in ever-new arrangements in Roman architecture.

At the same time, both mythological and "civic" figures in the reliefs featured a heterotopic quality as their referent seemed to be of a shifting or uncertain nature. Their gestures and gazes suggested that some of them were conversing among each other. Were the figures meant to be living heroes or citizens standing among statues? Were citizens and heroes, mortals and immortals acting in the same sphere?

FIGURE 11.9 Man in *himation* from Aphrodisias; courtesy of the NYU excavations at Aphrodisias; 95.328.3.

What did this do to the sarcophagus as a structure? Thomas points to the ancient tradition to parallelize the human body to columns. The figures or miniature statues, from this point of view, would be a supporting part of the architecture, rather than just its filling. But in some cases, they outgrew the *aediculae* and entablature (Figures 11.4–11.6), further diminishing the built environment while at the same time monumentalizing the human figure.[18] Moreover, the status of all these figures deliberately shifted between living being and lifelike statue, between life and artifice, presence and representation. The oscillation of lifelikeness and highest artificiality was a particular aesthetic concern of the Second Sophistic (e.g., Schade 2007). But in the context of a funerary container this move could gain additional meaning. It was, I would argue, a sophisticated way to render the equally unclear status of the deceased: a mortal, who might have received heroic honors and whose absence was commemorated with the sarcophagus, the dimension, form, and decoration of which suggested that the body it housed was still present and intact.

THE LID

But this is not the whole story. The architecture of the marble box that we might by now consider monumental was dwarfed by the sarcophagus lid.[19] As mentioned earlier, the latter did not represent a roof, but a mattress on which a couple, usually a man and woman, appeared reclining as if for a banquet. Unlike the vertical, standing figures on the chest, the horizontal, reclining couple had life-size or slightly greater than life-size dimensions (Strocka 1971). The juxtaposing of the different human scales, however, made the bodies on the lid look much larger, "monumental" as it were. Moreover, portrait heads individualized the couple on the lid, while the small figures on the chest remained generic.

The image of the reclining couple also combined several traditions or layers of cultural memory. First of all, it recalled a widely disseminated form of funerary representation of the Hellenistic age, the so-called *Totenmahlreliefs* that rendered the deceased reclining at a banquet (Fabricius 1999). Women, however, would usually not recline or share a couch (*klinē*) with their husband, but be seated. The reclining couple was instead prominent in Etruscan funerary culture. From there it seems to have been adapted for funerary monuments in Rome (Wrede 1977), and subsequently found its way to the East, stimulating a reanimation and reformulation of older local traditions.

But the lid did not only petrify another facet of a complicated cultural history. It belonged again to an "other" space. What the lid represented reversed the rules: massive architecture supported not a roof, but a mattress and two reclining banqueters. Finally, towering above the architecture, it completed the idea of a built structure turned inside out. Elevated from below, as it were, the figures on the lid revealed and monumentalized what the chest contained: the most ephemeral and still central part of its main function, the human body.

CONCLUSION

In the immediate experience of losing a loved one, any attempt to commemorate the deceased and to symbolically overcome transience might appear monumental. In Asia

Minor during the second and third centuries A.D. most people chose to bury their dead in stone sarcophagi outside of the settlements. They were granted a cult, men even heroic honors. Commemorating the dead institutionalized, as it were, the overcoming of the constraints of time and space, as it involved the constant crossing of the line between the dead and the living in ritual and symbolically also in topography. The interest in overcoming the constraints of time and space, however, at the time also characterized civic life beyond the cemetery. During the Second Sophistic, people in the Greek East in particular, were intensely concerned with their own place within the empire and with reviving the memory of their history. Commemorating their past meant to experience and simultaneously shape their own culture as a monument (cf. Assmann 2011). Mechanisms of memory work were at stake here that also played a role in commemorating the dead. The Asiatic columnar sarcophagi as a product of this particular cultural milieu exemplify the ensuing, sometimes paradoxical relationship between a historically contingent and a universal desire to overcome transience.

This way, they offer various avenues into monumentality, a phenomenon equally oscillating between historically specific and universal experiences. As imposing physical objects, as materialization of memory work and as durable containers of ephemeral objects, namely, dead bodies, the sarcophagi resulted from and potentially initiated multiple relationships between themselves and different people. Individual solutions for the sarcophagi's display, albeit varying in the degree of accessibility or hierarchization of space, always seem to have staged them as particularly precious and prestigious objects. Material, form, and iconography aggrandized the boxes as structures, for they referenced contemporary architecture and figural decoration of public spaces, including honorary statues and works of art. The models defined such spaces as pertaining both to the Roman Empire and to the local communities of Asia Minor with their Greek traditions. Consequently, the sarcophagi's micro-architecture and miniature figures encapsulated a microcosmos. Moreover, they materialized and reformulated Greek cultural heritage and education (*paideia*), which had acquired empire-wide recognition. Material, form, and iconography symbolically concentrated the empire in one place or projected the urban environment of a particular region unto other locales by mixing global and local traditions. In addition, they revived the past in the present similar to their large-scale models.

The same mechanisms and "ingredients," however, that guided this memory work also served to overcome the constraints of time and space in another way, for the sarcophagi did not only imitate, but they also reversed their models. The chest turned the building types it referenced inside-out. Moreover, it overturned the rules of proportionality: columns supported a mattress; aggrandized human figures reclined on top of miniaturized architecture. What disappeared inside the sarcophagus, namely the flesh of the dead human body, was revealed and made present in stone by lifelike portrait statues. In these reversals, the sarcophagi materialized their status as countersites or heterotopic places.

Each of these mechanisms and "ingredients," whether repeating, reaffirming, or reversing the sarcophagi's large-scale models, but also their paradoxical relationship itself, could contribute to letting monumentality happen.

Acknowledgments

I would like to thank the organizers and all participants of this stimulating conference as well as the anonymous readers for their questions and comments. James Osborne's thoughtful suggestions and patient, careful editing proved to be most helpful. My thanks also go to the Archaeological Exploration of Sardis and its director Nicholas D. Cahill. He and the late Crawford H. Greenewalt got me started on the Asiatic sarcophagi. Julia Lenaghan, Christine Bruns-Özgan, Ramazan Özgan, and Volker Michael Strocka generously provided me with photographs. I am particularly grateful to Michael D. Morris for important comments and criticism.

Notes

1. Wu Hung thus emphasizes the manmade, ideological, and historically specific aspects of monumentality.

2. Alois Riegl's notion of an unintentional (*"ungewollt"*) monument, as opposed to intentional (*"gewollt"*) or "historical" (Riegl 1903), explicitly rejected by Wu Hung (1995:1–3), points in a similar direction, albeit not from a phenomenological point of view.

3. I use the term *Asia Minor* for Western Anatolia, when it coincides with the Roman province of *Asia*.

4. Latin inscriptions even talk about the *domus aeterna* (eternal house). Tombs or sarcophagi can be shaped like a house. But "house" does not only describe an architectural entity. *Oikos* and *domus* also refer to the living house, i.e., the family. Grave terraces in ancient Greece, for example, united tombs of several generations of a family.

5. This sarcophagus, on display in the museum of Kütahya, does not belong to the columnar sarcophagi I am discussing here in the strict sense, as it mixes Attic and Asiatic traditions.

6. The color spectrum reaches from pure white to light grey-blue with dark purple veins (*pavonazzetto*) (see Röder 1971:255–256 plate 2). The purple dye had royal or imperial connotations (Thomas 2007:209). For doubts about the localization see Koch 2011.

7. Only the portraits on the lids were finished at the final destination (see Wiegartz 1974, mostly on Attic sarcophagi). Waelkens (1982, 1986) argues for a specialization of the workshops according to object groups (i.e., architecture; statues; sarcophagi). This high significance of the craftsmanship sets these quarry products, similarly to the Attic ones, clearly apart from the so-called Prokonnesian *Halbfabrikate* (half-finished sarcophagi), another type of funerary chest also very popular among elite clientele.

8. Other high elite owners of such sarcophagi are mentioned by Thomas (2010:392, 400, 418 with notes 30, 79). Unlike sarcophagi from the city of Rome or others from workshops in Asia Minor, the Asiatic columnar sarcophagi usually provide no space (such as a *tabula ansata*) for an inscription to indicate the name/s of the person/s buried within. Maybe it was assumed that the coffin would have been installed in a bigger architecture that would have provided an opportunity to promote the names of the deceased in a more ostentatious way.

9. Sometimes we see an altar with or without a bull, e.g., Özgan (2003:plate 6.2). Some sarcophagi have no sacrificial scene at all. In later examples in particular, the architecture

is overlaid or replaced by a landscape with hunters, see, e.g., Özgan 2003:plate 15.3, 32.2.

10. See, for a more nuanced chronological account Thomas (2010), who stresses the Roman aspect of this architecture. I would nevertheless point out that within this "global" standardized architecture there were local preferences; see also Thomas 2007:81–90.

11. Another esteemed citizen of Ephesos, the orator T. Claudius Flavianus Dionysios was buried right across the library (Cormack 2004:223). The donor of the library of Nysa also found his eternal rest in the building he gave to the city (Strocka 2011). On intramural buildings in general: Cormack 2004:35–49.

12. Morey (1924:5) suggests the sarcophagus was displayed outside of a tomb structure (Figure 11.2). Compare the case of asiarch Euethius Pyrrhon, whose sarcophagus would have recalled the buildings financed by his owner (Thomas 2010:418).

13. Temples did, of course, have rows on columns on the outside, but not the niches or the protruding and receding entablature we mostly find on the Asiatic sarcophagi.

14. Scholarship on the topic of Roman copies and their relation to Greek models is huge and diverse; for newer varying approaches see, e.g., Alexandridis 2010; Gazda 2002; Hallett 2005; Junker and Stähli 2008; Landwehr 1998; Marvin 2008; Perry 2005; Trimble 2011; Zanker 1974. The modern dichotomy between "copy" and "original" is misleading. Copying should rather be understood as a traditional, multifaceted, and dynamic practice.

15. The correct reconstruction is due to Thomas 2010:413–414 Figure 12.11.

16. Ewald (2004) shows that the same cultural climate was responsible for the rather restricted repertoire of mythological subjects represented on Attic sarcophagi. Myths that were easily and canonically labeled as "Greek" (and which constituted simultaneously the greatest moments in Greek "history") formed the core, such as the Sack of Troy or the Amazonomachy. No identification with mythological figures took place, unlike in Rome; see Zanker and Ewald 2004.

17. Sometimes, however, the sarcophagus owners could make that link explicit. The inscriptions on a recently discovered sarcophagus at Sardis, for example, are placed on the bottom rim of the chest underneath the center figures, the male name underneath a seated philosopher, the woman's name underneath the female figure standing next to him.

18. Thomas (2010:409–420) sees size as part of a chronological and stylistic development.

19. See also Thomas 2010:393 for the architecture.

REFERENCES CITED

Abbasoğlu, Haluk 2006 Perge. In *Stadtgrabungen und Stadtforschung im westlichen Kleinasien. Geplantes und Erreichtes,* edited by Wolfgang Radt, pp. 289–302. Internationales Symposion 6/7. August 2004 in Bergama (Türkei). Ege Yayınları, İstanbul.

Alexandridis, Annetta 2004 *Die Frauen des römischen Kaiserhauses. Eine Untersuchung ihrer bildlichen Darstellung von Livia bis Iulia Domna.* Philip von Zabern, Mainz.

Alexandridis, Annetta 2010 Neutral bodies? Female Portrait Statue Types from the Late Republic to the Second Century. In *Material Culture and Social Identities in the Ancient World,* edited by: Shelley Hales and Tamar Hodos, pp. 252–279. Cambridge University Press, Cambridge, New York.

Amedick, Rita 1991 *Die Sarkophage mit Darstellungen aus dem Menschenleben.* Mann, Berlin.

Assmann, Aleida 1999 *Erinnerungsräume. Form und Wandlungen des kulturellen Gedächtnisses.* C. H. Beck, Munich.

Assmann, Jan 2011 *Cultural Memory and Early Civilization. Writing, Remembrance, and Political Imagination.* Cambridge University Press, New York, Cambridge (German orig. 1992).

Bejor, Giorgio 1999 *Vie colonnate. Paesaggi urbani del mondo antico.* Giorgio Bretschneider, Rome.

de Bernardi Ferrero, Daria 1974 *Teatri classici in Asia Minore IV.* L'Erma di Bretschneider, Rome.

Berns, Christof 2013 The Tomb as a Node of Public Representation. Intramurial Burials in Roman Imperial Asia Minor. In *Le mort dans la ville. Pratiques, contextes et impacts des inhumations intra-muros en Anatolie, du début de l'Age du Bronze à l'époque romaine,* edited by Olivier Henry, pp. 231–242. 2èmes rencontres d'archéologie de l'IFEA Istanbul 2011. IFEA-Ege Yayınları, Istanbul.

Bieber, Margarete 1977 *Ancient Copies. Contributions to the History of Greek and Roman Art.* New York University Press, New York.

Borg, Barbara E., ed. 2004 *Paideia. The World of the Second Sophistic.* de Gruyter, Berlin and New York.

Cordovana, Orietta D., and Marco Galli, eds. 2007 *Arte e memoria culturale nell'età della Seconda Sofistica.* Edizioni del Prisma, Catania.

Cormack, Sarah H. 2004 *The Space of Death in Roman Asia Minor.* Phoibos, Vienna.

Daehner, Jens, ed. 2007 *The Herculaneum Women. History, Context, Identities.* J. Paul Getty Museum, Los Angeles.

D'Andria, Francesco, and Ilaria Romeo, eds. 2011 *Roman Sculpture in Asia minor.* JRA, Portsmouth, Rhode Island.

Equini Schneider, Eugenia 1971–73 La necropoli di Hierapolis di Frigia. Contributi allo studio dell'architettura funeraria di età romana in Asia Minore. *Monumenti antichi, Serie miscellanea* 1:95–138.

Ertuğ, Ahmet, and Roland R. R. Smith 2001 *Sculptured for Eternity. Treasures of Hellenistic, Roman and Byzantine Art from Istanbul Archaeological Museum.* Ertug and Kocabiyik, Istanbul.

Ewald, Björn C. 1999 *Der Philosoph als Leitbild. Ikonographische Untersuchungen an römischen Sarkophagreliefs.* Zabern, Mainz.

Ewald, Björn C. 2004 Men, Muscle, and Myth. Attic Sarcophagi in the Cultural Context of the Second Sophistic. In Borg 2004, pp. 229–275.

Ewald, Björn C. 2008 The Tomb as Heterotopia (Foucault's "hétérotopies"): Heroization, Ritual, and Funerary Art in Roman Asia Minor (review of Cormack 2004). *JRA* 21:624–634.

Fabricius, Johanna 1999 *Die hellenistischen Totenmahlreliefs. Grabrepräsentation und Wertvorstellungen in ostgriechischen Städten.* Pfeil, Munich.

Fant, J. Clayton 1985 Four Unfinished Sarcophagus Lids at Docimium and the Roman Imperial Quarry System in Phrygia. *AJA* 89:665–662.

Fant, J. Clayton 1989 *Cavum antrum Phrygiae: The Organization and Operations of the Roman Imperial Marble Quarries in Phrygia.* B.A.R., Oxford.

Farrington, Andrew 1987 Imperial Bath-Buildings in South-West Asia Minor. In Macready and Thompson 1987, pp. 50–59.

Ferrari, Gloria 1966 *Il commercio dei sarcofagi asiatici.* L'Erma di Bretschneider, Rome.

Filges, Axel 1999a Himationträger, Palliaten und Togaten: Der männliche Mantel-Normaltypus und seine regionalen Varianten in Rundplastik und Relief. In *Munus. Festschrift für Hans Wiegartz,* edited by Dieter Korol and Torsten Mattern, pp. 95–109. Scriptorium, Münster.

Filges, Axel 1999b Marmorstatuetten aus Kleinasien. Zu Ikonographie, Funktion und Produktion antoninischer, severischer und späterer Idealplastik. *IstMitt* 49:377–430.

Foucault, Michel 1986 Of Other Spaces. *Diacritics* 16.1:22–27.

Galli, Marco 2007 Processi della memoria nell'età della Seconda Sofistica. In Cordovana and Galli 2007, pp. 7–14.

Gazda, Elaine, ed. 2002 *The Ancient Art of Emulation. Studies in Artistic Originality and Tradition from the Present to Classical Antiquity.* University of Michigan Press Ann Arbor.

Goldhill, Simon, ed. 2001 *Being Greek under Rome. Cultural Identity, the Second Sophistic, and the Development of Empire.* Cambridge University Press, Cambridge.

Gros, Pierre 2011 *L'architecture romaine. Du début du IIIe siècle av. J.-C. à la fin du Haut-Empire. Vol. 1: Les monuments publics.* Picard, Paris.

Hall, Alan, and Marc Waelkens 1982 Two Dokimeian Sculptors in Iconium. *Anatolian Studies* 32:151–155.

Hallett, Christopher H. 2005 Emulation versus Replication: Redefining Roman Copying. *JRA* 18:419–435.

Heinzelmann, Michael 2003 Städtekonkurrenz und kommunaler Bürgersinn. Die Säulenstrasse von Perge als Beispiel monumentaler Stadtgestaltung durch kollektiven Euergetismus. *AA*:197–220.

Hesberg, Henner von 2007 Stützfiguren im 2. und 3. Jh. n.Chr. Spiele mit der Tradition. In Cordovana and Galli 2007, pp. 67–77.

Hirt, Alfred M. 2010. *Imperial Mines and Quarries in the Roman World. Organizational Aspects 27 BCE–AD 235.* Oxford University Press, Oxford.

Hölscher, Tonio 1970 Die Victoria von Brescia. *Antike Plastik* 10:67–80.

Hölscher, Tonio 2011 Penelope für Persepolis. Oder: Wie man einen Krieg gegen den Erzfeind beendet. *JDAI* 126:33–76.

Ingold, Tim 2011 *Being Alive. Essays on Movement, Knowledge, and Description.* Routledge, London, New York.

Junker, Klaus, and Adrian Stähli, eds. 2008 *Original und Kopie: Formen und Konzepte der Nachahmung in der antiken Kunst.* Reichert, Wiesbaden.

Kader, Inge 2006 *Penelope rekonstruiert. Geschichte und Deutung einer Frauenfigur.* Museum für Abgüsse klassischer Bildwerke, Munich.

Koch, Guntram 2011 Sarcofagi di età imperiale romana in Asia Minore: una sintesi. In D'Andria and Romeo 2011, pp. 9–29.

Koch, Guntram, and Hellmut Sichtermann 1982 *Römische Sarkophage.* C. H. Beck, Munich.

Köse, Veli 2005 *Nekropolen und Grabdenkmäler von Sagalassos in Pisidien in hellenistischer und römischer Zeit.* Brepols, Turnhout.

Kousser, Rachel M. 2007 Mythological Group Portraits in Antonine Rome: The Performance of Myth. *AJA* 111(4):673–691.

Kousser, Rachel M. 2008 *Hellenistic and Roman Ideal Sculpture. The Allure of the Classical.* Cambridge University Press, Cambridge, New York.

Landwehr, Christa 1998 Konzeptfiguren: Ein neuer Zugang zur römischen Idealplastik. *JDAI* 113:139–194.

Lawrence, Marion 1958 Season Sarcophagi of Architectural Type. *AJA* 62:273–295.

Lyttelton, Margaret 1987 The Design and Planning of Temples and Sanctuaries in Asia Minor in the Roman Imperial Period. In Macready and Thompson 1987, pp. 38–59.

Macready, Sarah, and F. H. Thompson, eds. 1987 *Roman Architecture in the Greek World.* Society of Antiquaries, London.

Manderscheid, Hubertus 1981 *Die Skulpturenausstattung der kaiserzeitlichen Thermenanlagen.* Mann, Berlin.

Marvin, Miranda 2008 *The Language of the Muses. The Dialogue between Roman and Greek Sculpture*. J. Paul Getty Museum, Los Angeles.

Morey, Charles R. 1924 *The Sarcophagus of Claudia Antonia Sabina and the Asiatic Sarcophagi*. Sardis: Publications of the American Society for the Excavations of Sardis. 5. Roman and Christian sculpture 1. Princeton University Press, Princeton.

Morris, Ian 1992 *Death-Ritual and Social Structure in Classical Antiquity*. Cambridge University Press, Cambridge.

Özgan, Ramazan 2003 *Die kaiserzeitlichen Sarkophage in Konya und Umgebung*. Habelt, Bonn.

Pensabene, Patrizio 2011 Su alcuni aspetti produttivi delle "scuole" di scultura di Docimio, Afrodisia e Nicomedia. In D'Andria and Rome 2011, pp. 37–61.

Perry, Ellen 2005 *The Aesthetics of Emulation in the Visual Arts of Ancient Rome*. Cambridge University Press, Cambridge.

Raepsaet-Charlier, Marie-Thérèse 1987 *Prosopographie des femmes de l'ordre sénatorial (Ie-IIe siècles)*. Peeters, Leuven.

Riegl, Alois 1903 *Der moderne Denkmalkultus. Sein Wesen und seine Entstehung*. Braumüller, Vienna, Leipzig.

Röder, Josef 1971 Marmor Phrygium. Die antiken Marmorbrüche von İscehisar in Westanatolien. *JDAI* 86:253–312.

Schade, Kathrin 2007 Ein Paragone der Künste. Betrachtungen zur Idealplastik der mittleren Kaiserzeit. *JDAI* 122:163–200.

Schneider, Carsten 1999 *Die Musengruppe von Milet*. Zabern, Mainz.

Slavazzi, Fabrizio 2007 Uso dei modelli e recupero del passato nei programmi scultorei ufficiali di età antonina in Asia Minore. In Cordovana and Galli 2007, pp. 123–136.

Smith, Roland R. R. 2006 *Roman Portrait Statuary from Aphrodisias*. Zabern, Mainz.

Strocka, Volker M. 1971 Kleinasiatische Klinensarkophagdeckel. *AA* 1971:62–86.

Strocka, Volker M. 1981 *Das Markttor von Milet*. de Gruyter, Berlin.

Strocka, Volker M. 1984 Sepulkral-Allegorien auf dokimeischen Sarkophagen. *Marburger Winckelmannprogramm* 1984:197–241.

Strocka, Volker M. 2003 The Celsus Library in Ephesos.In *Ancient Libraries in Anatolia,* pp. 44–43. Middle East Technical University, Ankara.

Strocka, Volker M. 2009 *Die Celsusbibliothek als Ehrengrab am Embolos*. Verlag der ÖAW, Vienna.

Strocka, Volker M. 2011 Der Stifter-Sarkophag der Bibliothek von Nysa am Mäander. In D'Andria and Romeo 2011, pp. 269–278.

Thomas, Edmund V. 2007 *Monumentality and the Roman Empire. Architecture in the Antonine Age*. Oxford University Press, Oxford.

Thomas, Edmund V. 2010 Houses of the Dead? Columnar Sarcophagi as "Micro-architecture." In *Life, Death, and Representation. Some New Work on Roman Sarcophagi,* edited by Jaś Elsner and Janet Huskinson, pp.387–435. de Gruyter, Berlin, New York.

Trimble, Jennifer 2000 Replicating the Body Politic. The Herculaneum Women Statue Types in Early Imperial Italy. *JRA* 13:41–68.

Trimble, Jennifer 2011 *Women and Visual replication in Roman Imperial Art and Culture. Visual Replication and Urban Elites*. Cambridge University Press, Cambridge.

Türktüzün, Metin 1993 Zwei Säulensarkophage aus der Südwestnekrople von Aizanoi. *AA*:517–526.

Waelkens, Marc 1982 *Dokimeion. Die Werkstatt der repräsentativen kleinasiatischen Sarkophage. Chronologie und Typologie ihrer Produktion*. Mann, Berlin.

Waelkens, Marc 1985 From a Phrygian Quarry. The Provenance of the Statues of the Dacian Prisoners in Trajan's Forum at Rome. *AJA* 89:641–653.

Waelkens, Marc 1986 *Die kleinasiatischen Türsteine. Typologische und epigraphische Untersuchungen der kleinasiatischen Grabreliefs mit Scheintür.* Zabern, Mainz.

Whitmarsh, Tim 2005 *The Second Sophistic.* Oxford University Press, Oxford.

Whitmarsh, Tim, ed. 2010 *Local Knowledge and Microidentities in the Imperial Greek World.* Cambridge University Press, Cambridge.

Wiegartz, Hans 1965 *Kleinasiatische Säulensarkophage. Untersuchungen zum Sarkophagtypus und zu den figürlichen Darstellungen. IstForsch 65.* Mann, Berlin.

Wiegartz, Hans 1974 Marmorhandel, Sarkophagherstellung und die Lokalisierung der kleinasiatischen Säulensarkophage. In *Mansel'e armağan. Mélanges Mansel*, pp. 345–383. Türk Tarih Kurumu, Ankara.

Wrede, Henning 1977 Stadtrömische Monumente, Urnen und Sarkophage des Klinentypus der beiden ersten Jahrhunderte n. Chr. *AA*:395–431.

Wu Hung 1995 *Monumentality in Early Chinese Art and Architecture.* Stanford University Press, Stanford.

Wulf, Ulrike 1993 Zwei Grabbauten in der Südwestnekropole von Aizanoi. *AA*:527–541.

Yegül, Fikret 1982 A Study in Architectural Iconography: Kaisersaal and the Imperial Cult. *ArtBull* 64:7–31.

Yegül, Fikret 1986 *The Bath-Gymnasium Complex at Sardis.* Harvard University Press, Cambridge.

Zanker, Paul 1974 *Klassizistische Statuen. Studien zur Veränderung des Kunstgeschmacks in der römischen Kaiserzeit.* Philipp von Zabern, Mainz.

Zanker, Paul 1995 *The Mask of Socrates. The Image of the Intellectual in Antiquity.* University of California Press, Berkeley (German orig. 1995).

Zanker, Paul, and Björn C. Ewald 2004 *Mit Mythen leben. Die Bilderwelt der römischen Sarkophage.* Hirmer, Munich.

Zeitlin, Froma 2001 Visions and Revisions of Homer. In Goldhill 2001, pp. 195–266.

CHAPTER TWELVE

Function and Impact of Monumental Grave Vases in the Eighth Century B.C.

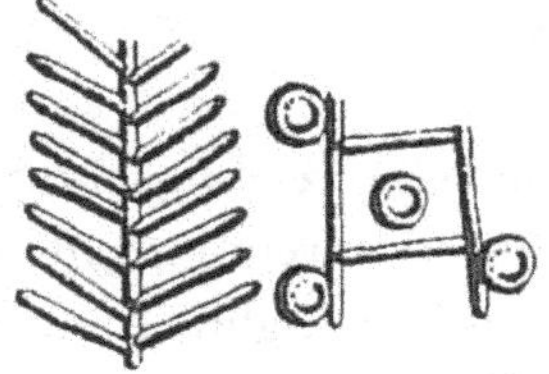

Dietrich Boschung

Abstract *Attic funerary vases underwent a significant change in terms of their monumentalization during the eighth century B.C. Marking graves with amphorae and kraters above ground was a centuries-old tradition. The mid-eighth century saw vases not only of larger scale but also with new figured drawings mainly reflecting values of a warrior aristocracy: The vases show bloody and vicissitudinous battles on the one hand, and a deceased man laid upon a bier and surrounded by mourners on the other. Both scenes illustrate the outstanding social status of the deceased and their families. These new and splendid grave monuments were specially produced by Attic potters for a small elite group emphasizing therewith its precedence over contemporaries. It is evident by the huge size of the amphorae and kraters that they were not meant for daily use. Military exploits as well as a decisive moment of the funeral ritual were recorded in vase-paintings, and remained therefore permanently present.*

INTRODUCTION

The Latin word *monumentum* means an object reminiscent of something, whether a situation, an event, or a person. It is derived from the verb *moneo,* "to remind someone of something." The range of meanings of the Latin word *monumentum* includes a victory monument, a tomb, a memento, a document. Thus, "monumentality" is the capability of an object to activate remembrance. To this purpose, an object must be perceived intensely; this means it must be conspicuous in its presentation and design.[1] But of course, recollection is neither objective nor constant. Memory can be produced, formed, strengthened, and stabilized. Collective memories of events, experiences, and persons shape a society and can weld it together. The role of monuments and thus also of objects of remembrance in this process is obvious and has been much investigated in recent years (e.g., Hölkeskamp 2012).

My second preliminary note deals with my personal interest in the topic. I am concerned with the problem of how archaeological objects can substantiate epistemic concepts and bring them into a concrete form that can be apprehended by the senses. At the same time, I investigate what these concrete forms can achieve in different media and how they impact the ideas that they represent.[2] Monumentality has the capacity to play an important role in these processes.

GEOMETRIC NECROPOLEIS IN ATHENS

In this chapter, I investigate this general problem using the necropoleis of eighth-century Athens as a case study. Similar to the *agora* and sanctuaries, cemeteries were present in the public spaces of Greek cities since the Geometric Period (tenth to eighth century B.C.) (Hölkeskamp 2003; Hölscher 1998:26–27). The best evidence comes from the necropoleis of Athens (Kalaitzoglou 2010:52; Kraiker 1961; Kübler 1954). Here, big vessels serving as receptacles for offerings to the dead had been standing on the graves from the tenth century onward. Some graves had additionally been marked by coarsely worked boulders. This phenomenon was not a universal one, but apparently concentrated on just a few cemeteries of limited size.

During his excavations in the Kerameikos cemetery, Karl Kübler found thirteen graves of the Geometric Period marked with amphorae and kraters (Figure 12.1, Table 12.1) (Kraiker 1961:108–110; Kübler 1954:7–19, 33–36). One of the earliest examples is a nearly complete amphora placed over a tenth-century grave. Tombs of the tenth and early ninth centuries lay immediately adjacent to each other. Two had been marked by amphorae, two others with kraters.

In the late ninth and the first half of the eighth century, big vessels as grave markers were more frequent. In this phase, kraters clearly prevailed; only a single grave of the eighth century was marked by an amphora. Only a few vessels displayed isolated figures such as a horse or a mourning person (Kübler 1954:227 nr. 26 pl. 23; 238 nr. 43 pl 22). Frequently, the bases of these vessels were perforated so that funeral offerings could get through the vessels into the graves (Kübler 1954:237).

For the mid-eighth century, features observed in excavations (Figure 12.2) on the western fringe of the Eleftheria Square in 1891, northeast of the Dipylon Gate, provide the clearest picture (Brueckner and Pernice 1893; Coldstream 2008:349–351; Grunwald 1983:197–198; Morris 1987: 64–65). Grave III of the mid-eighth century contained a bronze urn with cremated human bones and five pottery vessels as grave goods (Figure 12.3). The tomb's grave shaft, which was only partly refilled, contained a krater 1.1 m tall and halfway projecting above the ground surface (Ahlberg 1971[b]:nr. 20; Huber 2001:216 nr. 26; Kahane 1940:477 pl. 25). The circumferential frieze of the krater's han-

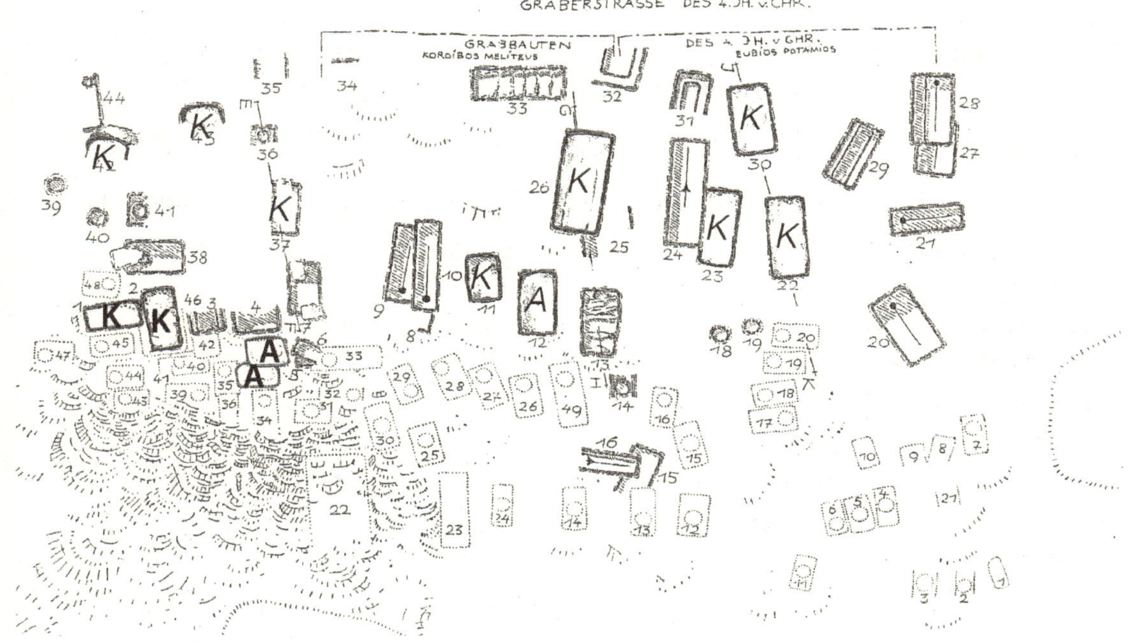

FIGURE 12.1 Athens, Kerameikos cemetery; kraters (K) and amphorae (A) over tombs of tenth and early ninth century (**bold**) and of the ninth and eighth century (*italic*) (after Kübler 1954:Beilage 2).

dle zone only survives in fragments: it showed mourning men on one side and chariots and warriors on the other.

The neighboring grave II, some three meters away, was marked by the so-called Dipylon Amphora, with a height of 1.55 m (Brueckner and Pernice 1893:104; Grunwald 1983:200). Between its handles, lined by ornamental bands, there is the central picture of the laying-out of a dead woman (Figure 12.4). The deceased is extended on her back on a *kline,* a reclining couch with headboard and footboard. To her left and right and facing the dead, there are groups of almost identical figures. Two of them are touching the checkered shroud and raising the other hand to their own head. These gestures characterize all bystanders as mourners. On the far left, there are two mourners wearing swords around their hips, indicating that they are armed males. A considerably smaller person immediately to the right of the *kline* grabs the piece of furniture with one hand. Like the deceased, she wears a skirt and is thus identified as a girl. Between the legs of the bed, the painter added another four figures: to the right, two persons sitting on plain chairs; to the left two kneeling women with long skirts. The painter made quite clear that an entire family is mourning here: children and adults, men and women.

What is represented in this scene is the *prothesis,* the laying-out of the dead, which formed part of the Greek funeral ritual: a deceased person was laid out in the house after the corpse had been washed, anointed, dressed, and garlanded, with a shroud covering

TABLE 12.1
GEOMETRIC PERIOD GRAVES IN THE KERAMEIKOS CEMETERY
MARKED BY AMPHORAE AND KRATERS

10th century	amphora, over tomb of a female (Kübler 1940:2, 4, 38–39 nr. 37)
	amphora and boulder, over a female's tomb (Kübler 1940:2, 4, 38–39 nr. 38)
3rd quarter of the 10th century	krater and boulder, over tomb of a male (Kübler 1954:26, 209–210 nr. 1 pl. 1. 16)
1st half of the 9th century	krater with perforated base and boulder, over tomb of a warrior (Kübler 1954:210–211 nr. 2 pl. 1. 17)
Last quarter of the 9th century	krater with perforated base, depicting a horse; over tomb of a male (Kübler 1954:222 nr. 22 pl. 3. 20. 21)
	krater and boulder, over tomb of a male (Kübler 1954:233 nr. 37 pl. 2. 19)
	krater with perforated base, over tomb of a male (Kübler 1954:236–237 nr. 42 pl. 1. 18)
	krater depicting a horse and a figure mourning; base perforated. Dating after Coldstream 2008:20 note 7 (Kübler 1954: 238 nr. 43 pl. 22)
1st quarter of the 8th century	krater and boulder, over tomb of a male (Kübler 1954:216–217 nr. 11 pl. 2. 21)
	amphora with perforated base and boulder, over a female's tomb containing spindle whorls and iron needles (Kübler 1954:216–217 nr. 12 pl. 1. 147)
	krater with perforated base, over tomb of a warrior containing a lance (Kübler 1954:224–225 nr. 23 pl. 4. 18)
	krater, over tomb of a male (Kübler 1954:229 nr. 30 pl. 2. 19)
3rd quarter of the 8th century	krater with painting of deers and horses; base perforated. Dating after Coldstream 2008:34, 39–40 (Kübler 1954:227 nr. 26 pl. 23)

the body (Andronikos 1968). Here, relatives and friends assembled in order to bemoan the deceased. This was done by loud lamentation and dirges, invocation of the dead, striking one's chest, scratching one's cheeks, and tearing one's clothes. The next day, the dead body was carried to the grave and inhumed.

Just two meters south of grave II was another amphora, this time 1.75 m tall. It was placed above grave I and carried the image of an *ekphora,* or funeral procession, and a frieze of mourners (Ahlfeld 1971[b]:nr. 53 Figure 53; Brueckner and Pernice 1893:91; Korou 2002:85–88 pl. 102–105; Moore 2007:9–23). The vase scene shows the *kline* with the deceased and the shroud folded back on top of a cart drawn by two horses. Here, too, the *kline* is in the center and the mourners are facing it. On top of grave IV there was also a large grave vessel of which, however, only fragments were found (Brueckner and Pernice 1893:106–107).

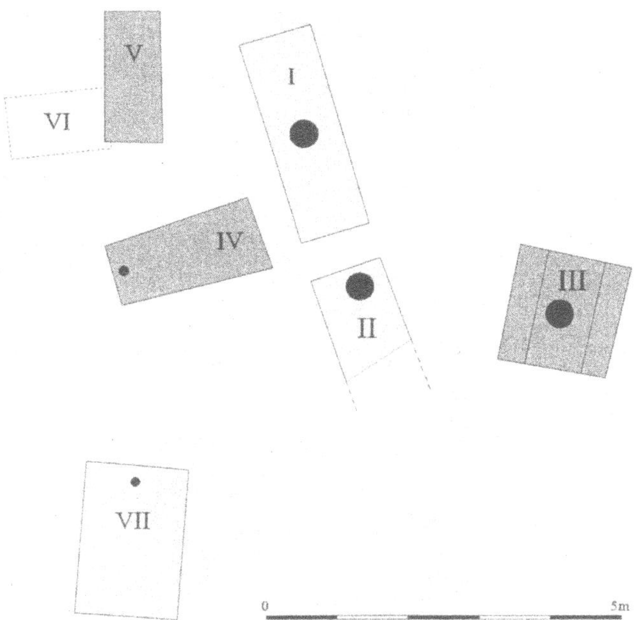

FIGURE 12.2 Athens, eighth-century necropolis near Eleftheria Square (excavated in 1891) (from Boschung 2003:Figure 4).

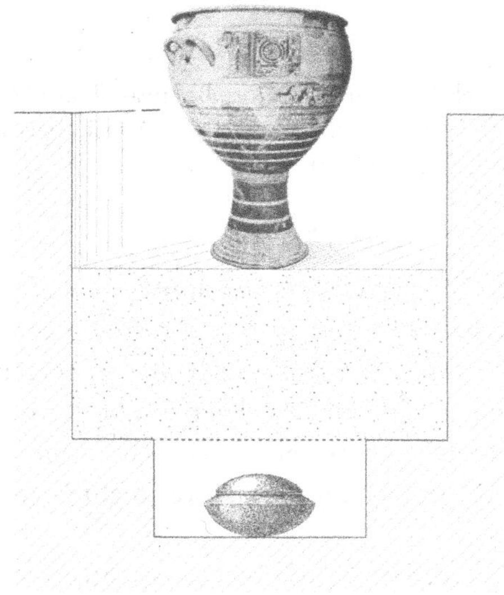

FIGURE 12.3 Athens, eighth-century necropolis near Eleftheria Square; tomb III (from Boschung 2003:Figure 5).

FIGURE 12.4 Athens, eighth-century necropolis near Eleftheria Square; "Dipylon Amphora" from tomb II (Athens, NM 804) (from Archäologisches Institut der Universität zu Köln, Photothek Nr. 9815).

This sketch (Figure 12.5) reconstructs the appearance of the cemetery around 750 B.C.[3] The monumental vessels were set up a few meters from one another, with their lower parts being hidden in the grave shafts such that kraters and amphorae with their pictures seemed to grow out of the earth. At this place both men (Brueckner and Pernice 1893:tombs III, IV, V) and women (tombs I, II, VII) were buried, and infant graves (tombs IX, X) also existed in the vicinity; thus, we might be dealing with the cemetery of a noble clan.

In 1871, part of the Geometric necropolis was uncovered during excavations in adjacent terrain to the east (Coldstream 2008:350. Grunwald 1983:197–198). For these excavations only vague reports exist, but it is certain that numerous monumental vessels of the mid-eighth century B.C. were found here. Among them is an amphora now in the museum in Sèvres (Ahlberg 1971[b]:25 nr. 3 Figure 3). It very much resembles the so-called Dipylon Amphora and is contemporaneous to it. Its main picture shows the *prothesis* of a deceased woman. This amphora in Sèvres also was a grave vessel originally marking a tomb. But among the finds from this necropolis there are also numerous

FIGURE 12.5 Athens, eighth-century necropolis near Eleftheria Square; with tombs I–III (from Boschung 2003:pl. 4).

fragments of large kraters with images of war dating into the mid-eighth century B.C. (Ahlberg 1971[b]:nr. 4, 5, 7, 10, 11, 13, 15, 16, 54; Grunwald 1983:159–180 nr. A-I). Their exact location and context remain unknown, but a dense arrangement of vessels must be assumed. According to the scarce excavation notes, many males had been buried here with their weapons (Coldstream 2008:350; Grunwald 1983:197–198; Hirschfeld 1872:135–136, 142–153 pl. 39–40).

The pictures on the kraters display the *prothesis,* too, but also warriors: marching or driving men under arms, more rarely fighting scenes proper. On a fragmentary krater (Figure 12.6) of the mid-eighth century, now in Paris, both topics can be found (Ahlberg 1971[a]:12 A5, 15–17 Figures 6–8; Grunwald 1983:160–161 nr. A Figures 4–5; Coldstream 1991:49–52 Figure 17). In the lower frieze there are marching warriors with their shields; at the left breaking edge of the fragment it can be recognized that fighting scenes followed as a second motif.[4] The upper frieze also shows images of war. Here, the battle is split up into three groups of figures of which the central one comprises two combatants, the two lateral ones three persons each. In all three groups there is an archer on the left, next to him a warrior wearing a cuirass.[5] The first of these loricate men is grabbing his opponent by the crest of the helmet, pulling him to the ground and threatening him with his sword. In the central duel, the mail-clad warrior is succumbing and dying. His head is pierced by an arrow; lethally wounded he falls backward to the ground. In the right engagement the armored warrior is victorious once more: he is grabbing his adversary, who is dropping from an elevated platform onto a dead body, by the crest of the helmet. This dying soldier is larger than any other and it is only on him that the artist painted the eye, while the heads of all other figures are executed as silhouettes.

The battle scene is enclosed on both sides by heaps of corpses: behind the falling warrior there are at least two extended dead bodies, perhaps even three or more. On the other side there are six corpses, some lying on their back, the others lying face down.

FIGURE 12.6 Paris; fragments of a krater from tomb of the eighth century (excavated in 1871) (from Grunwald 1983:Figure 4).

In some of them, arms and legs are twisted or dislocated; in all of them, the heads are hanging down atonicly.

The krater in Paris with its detailed fighting scenes was not a unique specimen: this is made quite clear by fragments of other vessels of this kind from the same find spot (Grunwald 1983:159–180 nr. B-I). They, too, show collapsing warriors, bodies pierced by spears and arrows, men trying to pull the lethal projectile out of their body with their last ounce of strength. A variation of the topic occurs on the fragmentarily surviving krater in Athens and Brussels also dating into the mid-eighth century (Ahlberg 1971[a]:89 Figure 89; Ducrey 1985:183 Figure 127; Grunwald 1983:168 nr. 19 Figure 21; Junker 2012:6 Figure 6). In its upper frieze there are marching soldiers; in the lower frieze attention is immediately attracted by a large rowing boat and its crew (Figure 12.7). Above the ship there are dead bodies, once more with their heads falling back. The painter's endeavor to capture combat action in a detailed and precise way is particularly obvious in the figure at the stern: here, the head and the upper part of the body of a kneeling man are falling forward. He is still propping himself on one of his arms; but this arm slides off to the fore and will soon buckle. The lower part of the body is pierced by a spear that penetrated the body with great vehemence and came out at the front; with his last bit of strength the tumbled man tries to pull the projectile out of his body.

THE MONUMENTALITY OF THE VESSELS AND THEIR IMPACT

The vessels of the mid-eighth century, of which we have seen some examples, represent a new category of monumental artifacts. They are clearly distinct from earlier grave markers. But this raises a number of questions: What constitutes the new monumentality of these

FIGURE 12.7 Athens/Brussels; fragments of a krater from tomb of the eighth century; excavated in 1871 (from Grunwald 1983:Figure 22).

vessels; How did they create and shape remembrance; and What led to the genesis of this monumentality and what was it caused by?

The first factor is their unusually large size. The Dipylon Amphora, for example, is more than twice as big as the grave amphora of the late tenth century. This made them visible for a long way; already from a great distance they were perceivable as indications of a sumptuous grave. Additional arguments are their high quality, the precision of the potter's work, and the richness of detail in their painting.

At the same time, their shape was not chosen haphazardly. Rather, the vessels had a twofold signaling effect: they marked the exact location of a grave and denoted where the offering to the dead was to be made. Additionally, their shape revealed the sex of the deceased to the viewer, even from afar, with amphorae marking women's graves and kraters standing on men's tombs (Coldstream 2008:350; Osborne 44–48).

It is also critical to recall the function of these two types of vessels in non-funerary contexts. A krater was used for the preparation of wine during a symposium, the convivial drinking of men (Kaeser 1990:194–196; Scheibler 1995:18). When placed on tombs, the krater evoked the role of the dead as the host of his *hetairoi*, his equals in social standing, and, by its size, stressed the host's generosity toward his guests (Kistler 1998:85–146; Kistler and Ulf 2005:273–277). The amphorae that were the inspiration for the vessels above female graves, however, served for the storage of provisions of different kind in the house (Scheibler 1995:16–17). Thus, the role of the dead woman as a caretaker of the house is alluded to, by which she had made great contributions to the *oikos* and earned the appreciation of her family (Wickert-Micknat 1982:50–65).

As we have seen before, the differentiation of grave vessels according to the sex of the dead goes back to the tenth century and thus was already traditional at the time the graves in the Eleftheria Square were deposited. What was new, however, was the increase of dimensions. It is in this enlarged scale that such wealth of provisions and munificence toward guests were symbolized, exceeding earlier generations.

On the other hand, the monumentality of grave vessels also consisted in the consequent use of a new medium, namely, figurative painting. Earlier grave vessels had been decorated almost exclusively with ornaments; now figurative scenes are shown at particularly prominent spots. At the same time, the topics themselves are not new. Prior to the scenes, there had already been images of individual mourners painted in a rather concealed manner, for example next to the handles (Junker 2012:10 Figure 3; Kübler 1954:238 nr. 43 pl 22). But now, figures are arranged into scenes and combined into long rows. In doing so, the symmetry stresses the importance of the centrally placed dead. The pictures thus created are set in particularly striking zones and occupy the center of the decoration.

War images, too, had existed earlier. Thus, a skyphos from Eleusis with two war scenes was probably made already in the years after 800 B.C. (Figures 12.8, 12.9). Thus, it is at least one generation older than the kraters in Paris and Brussels (Blome 1982:91; Coldstream 2008:26–28; Giuliani 2003:67–69; Pandou 1988:62–63). The picture on one of its sides shows two opposed archers. Between them there are two soldiers killed in action, and other figures have been added: on the lefthand side there is a warrior with lance and sword; to the right there is another one swinging his spear. The reverse displays a second fighting scene: one figure with a bow and arrow is standing on a warship, toward which two warriors with lances and shields are turned. Another figure is busy with the rudder. The figures are arranged symmetrically, but they are not clearly relating to each other.

The krater in the Louvre has a similar subject, but it presents it in a different way. The picture surface is much larger and allowed a detailed illustration. This enlargement resulted from the vessel format on the one hand, but also from the repression of ornaments. Additionally, the figurative scenes have been placed at the most conspicuous points of the vessels. A second difference consists in the fact that the chronologically younger painter unmistakably referred the opponents to each other: The swordsmen grab their tumbling antagonists by the crest of the helmet and the central archer is correlated to a hit enemy; victory and death are immediately connected.

The representations of *prothesis* and *ekphora* are obviously related to the function of the vessels as grave markers. Each of these pictures shows the person to be buried in the focus of an elaborate funeral ceremony. They concentrate on the moment of laying-out of the dead and, at the most, include the transfer of the deceased to the cemetery. This preference for *prothesis* images can be explained by the fact that they not only place the dead in the center of attention but, at the same time, are able to show the entire clan

FIGURES 12.8 AND 12.9 Skyphos from Eleusis; early eighth century (from Grunwald 1983:Figures 1–2).

mourning the deceased. Pictures at men's graves also preserved the bloody fights in which courage and strength of the warrior had stood their test. The participation in such battles had constituted his splendor and rank and was now to be documented forever. Everlasting glory, of which even future generations will know, is the hero's reward for death in battle in the *Iliad*. When the deceased was characterized as a warrior by equipping him with his weaponry in the ephemeral burial rite, the friezes of the grave kraters visualized the deeds of heroes undaunted by death.

Thus, the two main topics of grave vessels—war and funeral ritual—are closely connected to each other. Martial glory was the basis for the honorable position (*timé*) of a nobleman and his closest relatives, which found its spectacular expression in the *prothesis* and *ekphora* by the participation of social equals and the family. Shape, size, and decoration of the grave vessel stressed the social position of the deceased by complementary statements and praised his exemplary fulfillment of the aristocratic code of conduct at war and at home (Boschung 2003).

The monumental nature of these vessels, or rather their ability to generate and perpetuate remembrance, was augmented by a third factor: it was at these objects that the sacrifices to the dead were offered (Andronikos 1968:93–97). Thus, they stood in the center of the funeral ritual. This directed the attention of the community assembled at the grave to their shape and pictures, and this provided for their being perceived intensely.

What was the cause for this sudden monumentalization? All these sumptuous grave vessels were made within a few years and they were set up together in a confined space. Their concentration at one place and over a short period is all the more striking since the vessels also form a close stylistic entity and were almost exclusively produced in a single workshop, the workshop of the so-called Dipylon painter (Coldstream 2008:29–41). This can only be explained by close coordination between a circle of sophisticated customers and a high-quality workshop.

Ian Morris has demonstrated that funeral customs changed in many Greek landscapes in the mid-eighth century (Morris 1995:61–73). In Attica, for example, the number of graves increased by four times (Kistler 1998:11–15). If sumptuous burials had previously been the prerogative of a relatively small elite, tombs as a means for social representation were now obviously used by a much larger group (Junker 2012:5). If this is true, it offers an explanation for the eye-catching and rapid monumentalization of Athenian graves: the large grave vessels elaborately painted with figurative pictures originated because the Athenian warrior aristocracy wished to justify its social prominence by new means. Therefore, its members availed themselves of the virtuosity of Athenian potters and vase painters. The customers desired images rich in figures, as detailed as possible and of a realistic nature of the dramatic battles and the sumptuous funeral ceremonies that had established and illustrated their status. The Attic craftsmen were absolutely equal to this challenge: In order to perpetuate the elaborate and spectacular funeral ritual, which had made the glory of the deceased obvious to the entire city, with as many details as possible, the Dipylon painter created a new picture type by using preexisting motifs. In a similar way, he developed the battle scenes created by earlier vase painters: they now become very rich in figures, fill large zones of the vessel surface, and display a surprising wealth of details.

We do not know whether Athenian aristocrats achieved their original goal with their lavish and novel grave images; in any case they started a process they cannot have intended. With the pictures of these grave vessels, a continuous development of European painting over many centuries began (Boschung 2003; Coldstream 1991; Junker 2012:9–12).

Text translated by Dr. Janine Fries-Knoblach

NOTES

1.   See the introduction to this volume by James Osborne.
2.   This is the research topic of the Center for Advanced Studies Morphomata at the University of Cologne, which I lead together with Günter Blamberger, a specialist in German studies. Blamberger and Boschung 2011.
3.   The draft is based on the publication of Brueckner and Pernice 1893:91–92 Figure 4, 104–105 pl. 7.

4. The scene is often interpreted as a mythological fight against Aktorione-Molione; see, e.g., Fittschen 1969:68–73; Giuliani 2003:56–58; and Grunwald 1983:160 argue against a mythological interpretation.

5. The object is explained as a square shield by Ahlberg 1971(a):15–17, 48; Coldstream 1991:50; Grunwald 1983:160. However, its position directly in front of the chest and the missing decoration chararactestic of square shields (Tölle 1964:Beil. IV 21–32) indicate a cuirass; Catling 1977:116–118; Courbin 1957:340–356 pl. 1–3; Snodgrass 1964:72–90.

References Cited

Ahlberg, Gudrun 1971a *Fighting on Land and Sea*. Svenska Institutet i Athen, Stockholm.

Ahlberg, Gudrun 1971b *Prothesis and Ekphora in Greek Geometric Art*. Paul Åströms Förlag, Göteborg.

Andronikos, Manolis 1968 *Totenkult*. In *Archaeologia Homerica* III, edited by Friedrich Matz and Hans-Günter Buchholz. W. Vandenbeck & Ruprecht, Göttingen.

Blamberger, Günter, and Dietrich Boschung, eds. 2011 *Morphomata. Genese, Dynamik und Medialität kultureller Figurationen*. Fink Verlag, München.

Blome, Peter 1982 *Die figürliche Bilderwelt Kretas in der geometrischen und früharchaischen Periode*. Verlag Philipp von Zabern, Mainz.

Boschung, Dietrich 2003 Wie das Bild entstand. Kunstfertigkeit, Ruhmsucht und die Entwicklung der attischen Vasenmalerei im 8. Jahrhundert v. Chr. In *Medien in der Antike*, edited by H. von Hesberg, pp. 17–49. Lehr- und Forschungszentrum für die antiken Kulturen des Mittelmeerraums, Köln.

Brueckner, Alfred, and Erich Pernice 1893 *Ein attischer Friedhof*. In *Mitteilungen des kaiserlichen Deutschen Archäologischen Institut, Athenische Abteilung 18*, pp. 6–191. Verlag von Karl Wilberg, Athen.

Catling, Hector W. 1977 Panzer. In Hans-Günter Buchholz and Joseph Wiesner, *Kriegswesen 1*. Archaeologia Homerica I E 1, pp. 74–118. Vandenbeck & Ruprecht, Göttingen.

Coldstream, J. N. 1991 *The Geometric Style: Birth of the Picture*. In *Looking at Greek Vases*, edited by Tom Rasmussen and Nigel Spivey, pp. 37–56. Cambridge University Press, Cambridge.

Coldstream, J. N. 2008 *Greek Geometric Pottery. A Survey of Ten Local Styles and Their Chronology*. 2nd ed. Bristol Phoenix Press, Exeter.

Courbin, Paul 1957 Une tombe géométrique d'Argos. In *Bulletin de Correspondance Hellénique* 81. Ecole française d' Athènes, Athens.

Ducrey, Pierre 1985 *Guerre et guerriers dans la Grèce antique*. Office du Livre, Fribourg.

Fittschen, Klaus 1969 *Untersuchungen zum Beginn der Sagendarstellungen bei den Griechen*. Verlag Bruno Hessling, Berlin.

Giuliani, Luca 2003 *Bild und Mythos. Geschichte der Bilderzählung in der griechischen Kunst*. Verlag C. H. Beck, München.

Grunwald, Christiane 1983 Frühe attische Kampfdarstellungen. In *Acta Praehistorica et Archaeologica* 15, pp. 155–203. Verlag Volker Spiess, Berlin.

Hirschfeld, Gustav 1872 Vasi arcaici ateniesi. In *Annali dell'Istituto di Corrispondenza Archeologica* 44, 131–153; Monumenti dell' Instituto IX pl. 39–40.

Hölkeskamp, Karl-Joachim 2003 Institutionalisierung durch Verortung. Die Entstehung der Öffentlichkeit im frühen Griechenland. In *Sinn (in) der Antike. Orientierungssysteme, Leitbilder und Wertkonzepte im Altertum,* edited by Karl-Joachim Hölkeskamp, Jörn Rüsen, Elke Stein-Hölkeskamp, and Heinrich Th. Grütter. Verlag Philipp von Zabern, Mainz.

Hölkeskamp, Karl-Joachim 2012 Im Gewebe der Geschichte(n). Memoria, Monumente und ihre mythhistorische Vernetzung. In *Klio,* pp. 380–414. Beiträge zur Alten Geschichte 94 Akademie-Verlag, Berlin.

Hölscher, Tonio 1988 *Aus der Frühzeit der Griechen. Räume, Körper, Mythen.* Lectio Teubneriana 7. Verlag K. G. Saur, München.

Huber, Ingeborg 2001 *Die Ikonographie der Trauer in der Griechischen Kunst.* Bibliopolis, Mannheim und Möhnsee.

Junker, Klaus 2012 Zur Entstehung von Bildlichkeit im frühen Griechenland. In *Kunst und Kommunikation. Zentralisierungsprozesse in Gesellschaften des europäischen Barbaricums im 1. Jahrtausend v. Chr.,* edited by Christoph Pare, pp. 1–16. Verlag der Römisch-Germanischen Zentralmuseums, Mainz.

Kaeser, Bert 1990 Tradition durch dunkle Zeiten. In *Kunst der Schale—Kultur des Trinkens,* edited by Klaus Vierneisel and Bert Kaeser, pp. 194–196. Staatliche Antikensammlungen und Glyptothek, München.

Kahane, Peter 1940 Die Entwicklungslinien der attisch-geometrischen Keramik. *American Journal of Archaeology* 44: 464–482.

Kalaitzoglou, Georg 2010 Adelsgräber des 9. Jhs. v.Chr. in Athen und Attika. In *Attika. Archäologie einer "zentralen" Kulturlandschaft,* edited by Hans Lohmann and Thorsten Mattern, pp. 47–72. Harrassowitz Verlag, Wiesbaden.

Kistler, Erich 1998 *Die "Opferrinne-Zeremonie." Bankettideologie am Grab, Orientalisierung und Formierung einer Adelsgesellschaft in Athen.* Franz Steiner Verlag, Stuttgart.

Kistler, Erich, and Christoph Ulf 2005 Athenische "Big Men"—ein "Chief" in Lefkandi? Zum Verhältnis von historischen und archäologischen Aussagen vor dem Hintergrund der Bedeutung anthropologischer Modelle. In *Synergesia. Festschrift für Friedrich Krinzinger,* edited by Barbara Brandt, Verena Gassner, and Sabine Ladstätter, pp. 271–277. Phobos Verlag, Wien.

Korou, Nota 2002 *Attic and Atticizising Amphorae of the Protogeometric and Geometric Periods,* Corpus Vasorum Antiquorum Greece 8, Athens National Museum 5. Academy of Athens.

Kraiker, Wilhelm 1961 Die Anfänge der Bildkunst in der attischen Malerei des 8. Jahrhunderts vor Christus. In *Bonner Jahrbücher des Rheinischen Landesmuseums in Bonn 161,* pp. 108–120. Verlag Butzon & Bercker Kevelaer, Rhld.

Kübler, Karl 1940 *Neufunde aus der Nekropole des 11. und 10. Jhs.,* Kerameikos IV. Walter de Gruyter, Berlin.

Kübler, Karl 1954 *Die Nekropole des 10. bis 8. Jhs.,* Kerameikos V. Walter de Gruyter, Berlin.

Moore, Marie B. 2007 Athens 803 and the Ekphora. *Antike Kunst* 50:9–23.

Morris, Ian 1987 *Burial and Ancient Society. The Rise of the Greek City-State.* Cambridge University Press, Cambridge.

Morris, Ian 1995 Burning the Dead in Archaic Athens: Animals, Men, and Heroes. In *Culture and Cité. L' avènement d' Athènes à l' époque archaïque,* edited by Annie Verbanck-Piérard and Didier Viviers. De Boccard, Bruxelles.

Osborne, Robin 2004 *Monumentality and Ritual in Archaic Greece.* In *Greek Ritual Poetics,* edited by Dimitrios Yatromanolakis and Panagiotis Roilos. Harvard University Press, Cambridge.

Pandou, Mary 1988 Clay Skyphos. In *The Human Figure in Early Greek Art.* National Gallery of Art, Washington, D.C.

Scheibler, Ingeborg 1995 *Griechische Töpferkunst. Herstellung, Handel und Gebrauch der antiken Tongefäße.* 2nd ed. Verlag C. H. Beck, München.

Snodgrass, Antony 1964 *Early Greek Armour and Weapons from the End of the Bronze Age to 600 b.c.* University Press, Edinburgh.

Tölle, Renate 1964 *Frühgriechische Reigentänze.* Stiftland-Verlag, Waldsassen.

Wickert-Micknat, Gisela 1982 Die Frau. In *Archaeologia Homerica III,* edited by Friedrich Matz and Hans-Günter Buchholz. R. Vandenhoeck & Ruprecht, Göttingen.

CHAPTER THIRTEEN

Mobile Monumentality

The Case of Obelisks

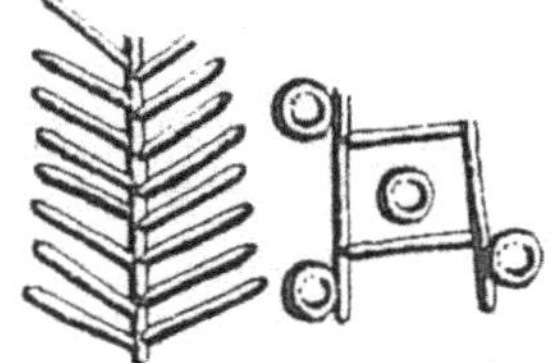

Grant Parker

Abstract *Obelisks may seem in many ways memory-objects par excellence, and thus easily qualify for the category of "monument." However, Roman textual sources (especially Pliny the elder, Ammianus Marcellinus, and various inscriptions) suggest that it was their mobility that informed their monumental status in Roman eyes. Their size, bulk, and the attendant engineering challenges ensured that Romans marveled at the details of their transportation no less than they did at the monoliths themselves. The obelisk now in the Hippodrome in Istanbul presents a case study, particularly since there is a rich dossier of evidence concerning its transportation. This evidence brings to light the dynamics of exchange that the obelisk's movement set in motion, even before it began its northward journey from Egypt. It also raises questions about how to understand the intentions that were responsible for the various feats of engineering that informed its life history, and ultimately point to a definition of monumentality that brings intentions into focus, in relation to the life history of an artifact.*

EGYPT AND ROME

The obelisk still standing at Heliopolis goes back to the time of Senusret I (1956–1911 B.C., Twelfth Dynasty), known to the Greeks as Sesostris (Figure 13.1). Today it cuts a lonely figure. Since the establishment of Cairo in the tenth century A.D., building materials from this ancient religious center have been despoiled, hence the very limited archaeological context. In one sense the Heliopolis obelisk looks back to the smaller, composite, obelisk-shaped structures that were placed in pairs in front of tomb

FIGURE 13.1 (1) Obelisk of Senusret I (Twelfth Dynasty), Heliopolis, Egypt (Wikimedia Commons).

chapels. An example from Heliopolis itself is the fragment of an obelisk of King Teti of the Sixth Dynasty, but there is evidence that the practice goes back to the earliest pharaonic times (Habachi 2000). In another sense, Senusret's obelisk also looks forward to the heyday of obelisks, namely the New Kingdom, and in particular the Eighteenth and Nineteenth Dynasties. It was during the New Kingdom that obelisks were erected in the Karnak and Luxor temple complexes at Thebes. Rameses II (1279–1213 B.C., Nineteenth Dynasty) was one of the main figures involved, and his name is inscribed in Middle Egyptian hieroglyphs on the flanks of several obelisks in Egypt and elsewhere. A number of monoliths are still standing *in situ*, whereas others exist in fragmentary form or have since been transported out of Egypt. The gargantuan unfinished obelisk at Aswan, probably dating also from the Eighteenth Dynasty, is today a valuable source of information on the quarrying of such monoliths (Aston et al. 2000:7). In ancient

Egypt, obelisks were linked to cults of the sun, in which respect the pyramidion on top was important (Curran et al. 2009:13–33; Iversen 1968:11–18).[1]

In terms of contemporary location, the obelisks at Heliopolis, Thebes, and Aswan are exceptions that prove the rule. For Egypt's own obelisks are today outnumbered by those standing in the city of Rome, not to mention additional examples around the world. It was with Augustus that Rome's passion for Egyptian obelisks began in 10 B.C., when monoliths were brought to two sites that were central to his ambitious building program, namely, the Campus Martius and the Circus Maximus. Those obelisks are today at the Piazza di Montecitorio and the Piazza del Popolo, respectively, having been subjected to transposition, excavation, alteration, and re-erection within the city of Rome, over a period of nearly two millennia (Iversen 1968:142–160, 65–75; Schneider 2004). By the fourth century, when the seat of political power was moved to Constantinople, Rome had apparently become home to several dozen obelisks, not only the larger and conspicuous ones more than 20 m high, but also a number of smaller ones that were placed in the Iseum Campense, the shrine of Isis on the Campus Martius. When Theodosius I transported an obelisk belonging originally to Thutmose III (r. 1479–1425 B.C.) to the Hippodrome of Constantinople in A.D. 390, this was a highly visible symbol that the new Rome on the Bosporus had surpassed and superseded the old one on the Tiber. In fact, much recycling of decorative marble columns and capitals took place in the building of Constantinople (Ward-Perkins 2012).

The history of appropriating obelisks does not end in late-fourth-century Constantinople. Within the city of Rome, there was a great deal of activity around obelisks in the early modern period: Pope Sixtus V (1585–1590) was responsible for excavating, moving, and re-erecting four of the city's most prominent obelisks. Several other popes followed suit. The longevity of obelisks in Rome has led to a high degree of adaptation. In the nineteenth century, obelisks were exported from Egypt to Paris (1836), London (1877–1878), and New York (1880–1881). A *longue durée* is thus already apparent in obelisk histories but even this says nothing of a much more widespread phenomenon, namely the use of the obelisk form in monuments and a vast range of media, large and small. In such cases, obelisks have been restored, relocated, and redeployed (Curran et al. 2009; Sorek 2010).

From this broad overview, a hypothesis emerges for consideration, if we are to concentrate on the ancient Roman lives of Egyptian obelisks: that the monumentality of obelisks at Rome was constituted by, or at the very least located in, a number of "re"s: restoration, relocation, and redeployment. This would suggest that there is a deeply belated quality to be explored in Rome's negotiations with ancient Egypt, via its objects. While size is obviously a visible feature of obelisks, it is in the current analysis epiphenomenal to their monumental qualities (Osborne, this volume)—even if it brings those qualities into sharper relief.

In this chapter, I shall be focusing on the ancient Roman uses of these granite monoliths, in the hope of identifying elements that might usefully be considered monumental. Given that obelisks have recently attracted much scholarly attention (most notably Curran et al. 2009), it is important to point out that these comments come from a Romanist rather than an Egyptologist or early modernist, since scholars from those backgrounds would likely produce entirely different interpretations. After a brief glance at the main literary sources we turn to the obelisk of Thutmose III now in Istanbul, both because it has an unusual object history in general and because its Roman recontextualization is uncommonly visible.

From the point of view of their Egyptian origins and their ongoing careers, obelisks have extraordinary stories to tell. These are basically stories about appropriation. Some of the factors for their desirability might have been as follows: symbolism of the notion of Rome as a long-lived universal empire; the distinctive design of the obelisk form in promoting that notion; and the openness of the obelisk to adaptation via additional features, including additions on the top or the bottom, both material and inscribed. Such considerations are addressed here only briefly, but would be central to a fuller account of the obelisks' monumental qualities.

The relative variety of the obelisks in Rome is hardly covered by the few texts that give any clue as to how they were understood in Roman antiquity. It is tempting to draw inspiration from texts linked to the later movements of obelisks, such as Cleopatra's Needle in Manhattan's Central Park; Filippo Napoletano's engineering fantasy of a trans-Mediterranean obelisk raft (1615–1629) (Figure 13.2); or the Luxor Obelisk at the Place de la Concorde. Arguably a monument to a failed enterprise, namely Napoleon's expedition of 1798–1801, this obelisk constitutes a particularly strong link between

FIGURE 13.2 Filippo Napoletano (early seventeenth century), seaborne transport of an obelisk, on a raft with sail. British Museum 1946-7-13-769, recto, Gernsheim Photographic Corpus of Drawings.

ancient and modern histories. Inscribed originally for Rameses II, it was placed in the square where the guillotine had been used during the French Revolution (Curran et al. 2009:251). Only in the 1990s did President Mitterand formally renounce France's claim to an additional obelisk granted it in 1829 by the Ottoman leader Mehmet Ali. The nineteenth-century engraving on the pedestal commemorates the engineering feat used when it was installed in Paris (in which respect, as we shall see, it recalls the Hippodrome obelisk); its mate remains at the Luxor Temple, the loss of symmetry a telling reminder of the removal.

Against this modern background, the ancient Roman evidence for obelisks and their movement is limited. Nonetheless, a quick survey of the ancient evidence is needed, for it is here that we have our best hope of grasping the monumental qualities of obelisks.

PLINY AND AMMIANUS

The Elder Pliny's treatment of obelisks comes up in the 36th book of his encyclopedia, the *Natural History,* within an extended discussion of marble in all its possible variants. The work was written before Pliny's death in A.D. 79, and lays out as many aspects as possible of all-provident *Natura* (Beagon 1992). It does so, as Pliny remarks in the prologue, in view of Rome's conquest of the extended Mediterranean, and in fact the work is dedicated to the future emperor Titus.

Even though Pliny's immediate context is the material, namely marble, he reveals particular interest in the engineering involved. Its transportation would turn out to be, for Pliny, even more spectacular than its original preparation in the quarry:

> It proved to be a greater achievement to carry it down the river [to Alexandria] than to have quarried it. (36.67)

Later, he comments in greater depth on the process of transportation:

> Above all, there came also the difficult task of transporting obelisks to Rome by sea. The ships used attracted much attention from sightseers. (36.70)

Indeed, the ships involved have received much attention, and have fueled modern speculation about the technology used (e.g., Wirsching 2007). The scale involved is such that moving any such object would be a major feat today, too. Pliny makes much of numbers in this passage of the *Natural History,* mostly with regard to measuring, which for him is linked to the competitive element involved when rulers erect obelisks.

Ammianus Marcellinus's history starts its narrative in the year A.D. 96, but the parts surviving today cover only the later fourth century (A.D. 353–378). The immediate pretext of his discussion of obelisks is the transportation by the emperor Constantius of an obelisk to the city of Rome around the year A.D. 357. The obelisk in question still stands today, having been moved outside the Piazza di San Giovanni Laterano. Once brought to Rome, the monolith was stood on a base that contained a Latin inscription, now lost (discussed below; cf. Iversen 1968:57–58).

A native speaker of Greek, Ammianus wrote in Latin, in a style revealing some of the flavor of Herodotus's *Histories,* with their digressions of a scientific or even folkloristic nature:

> Obelisks were hewn by early kings out of veins of stone for which they ransacked mountains at the ends of the earth, and dedicated them to the gods of heaven to commemorate the defeat of a foreign race or some other successful achievement. (17.4.2)

Ammianus shows more interest than Pliny had done in the writing on the flanks of the obelisks.

> By carving many kinds of birds and beasts . . . men left a record of the vows which the kings promised or performed in order that the memory of their exploits might be widely preserved among generations to come. (17.4.9)

Ammianus proceeds to quote a Greek translation of the hieroglyphic inscription, and he attributes that translation to a certain Hermapion, who is otherwise unknown. It is interesting that Ammianus chooses to keep the obelisk inscription in the Greek translation rather than further translating it into Latin. Why this should be so is unclear, but it is at least possible that Ammianus is adhering to Greek scholarly tradition that is expressed in a roughly contemporary text, the *Hieroglyphics* attributed to Horapollo (Boas 1993). In the Roman Empire Greek was the preeminent language for the study of Egypt (Hartog 2001:41–77). Ammianus's discussion of obelisks is a complex and subtle passage, which appears to downplay the significance of Constantinople in favor of the old Rome as metropolis (Kelly 2003:603–606).

It is Pliny's text that brings the title of the current essay into sharper relief: it is here we come closest to the counterintuitive but telling point that the monumental aspect of Rome's obelisks is closely entwined with their mobility. Their meaning for Roman viewers was tied to the power of those emperors who could take credit for having them transported. In this respect, inscriptions played a substantial role: in several cases a Latin inscription would be carved on the base of the obelisk, as for example in Augustus's two obelisks. Given that most obelisks came to Rome already inscribed on their flanks in honor of the pharaohs, these inscriptions on the bases were essentially belated in the lives of individual obelisks—all the more so if we bear in mind that most of the larger obelisks came to Rome, having long since been inscribed in honor of the pharaohs (Ciampini 2004). Yet these late inscriptions were also a focal point of the processes by which obelisks were appropriated by emperors, as we discuss below.[2]

THE HIPPODROME OBELISK AND ITS BASE

It is necessary to move from Rome on the Tiber to the second Rome on the Bosporus. The city of Constantinople, now Istanbul, was built in the 320s at the behest of the emperor Constantine, Rome's first ruler to convert to Christianity. The obelisk now standing in the Hippodrome, or Atmeidan, was, as we know from its flanks, quarried and inscribed for Thutmose III of the Eighteenth Dynasty (fifteenth century B.C.) (Figure 13.3). It seems to have attracted the attention of both Constantine and Constantius, but it was Theodosius (A.D. 379–395) who had it brought to Constantinople. On the way, around one-third of the monolith became detached, so its original height would have been as much as 30 m (Curran et al. 2009:54–58). An elaborate pedestal depicts the emperor offering the crown of victory in chariot races, framed by Corinthian columns, with musicians and others in attendance; another side shows the submission of barbarians, marked as such by their clothing. It is intriguing to imagine spectators at the Hippodrome in the 390s—at least those with good eyesight—watching a statue of the emperor watching them (Safran 1993).

The base of the obelisk also contains inscriptions in both Greek and Latin. The Latin version may be translated as follows:

> Formerly reluctant, I was ordered to obey the serene lords and carry the palm of the extinct tyrants. Everything yields to Theodosius and his everlasting offspring. So, conquered and vanquished in thirty days, I was raised to the lofty sky while Proclus was judge.

This constitutes a *titulus loquens,* a "speaking inscription," in that, by the use of the first person, the monument itself seems to address viewers. The Greek version carries the same

FIGURE 13.3 Obelisk erected in Hippodrome, Istanbul, in A.D. 390 by Emperor Theodosius; originally erected by Thutmose III (Eighteenth Dynasty) at the great temple of Karnak (Wikimedia Commons).

gist but differs in a few details, for instance, 32 days and the use of the third person rather than the first. In both Greek and Latin inscriptions, credit for the erection of the obelisk is given to Proclus, prefect of Constantinople (A.D. 388–392). In keeping with court intrigues of the time he was executed by Rufinus, a rival, through trickery, but posthumously rehabilitated by the new emperor Arcadius in 395. These changing fortunes are reflected in the visible erasure and subsequent reinsertion of Proclus's name (Iversen 1972:14).

The base also depicts the obelisk horizontally, in the process of being transported and erected in the Hippodrome (Figure 13.4) (Effenberger 2007). This would appear to be a late ancient equivalent to Domenico Fontana's detailed illustrated account of the erection of the obelisk now in St. Peter's Square (Fontana 1590). Roman viewers would thus see the obelisk itself, together with its new Roman context, complete with emperor, entourage, and spectators at the Hippodrome, and the means by which it was put in place. Another side of the base also contains scenes from the chariot race and subsequent prize giving. Many of the figures are severely damaged (Iversen 1972:15–16; Safran 1993). The process of moving the obelisk has thus become folded into the product and, as a representation, predicts the later work of Fontana.

FIGURE 13.4 Hippodrome obelisk, detail showing marble base, which depicts the erection of the obelisk in its current location (Wikimedia Commons).

An Obelisk Please: Julian's Letter to the Alexandrians

It so happens that the literary evidence on obelisks contains a back story concerning the Hippodrome obelisk and its arrival in Constantinople (Curran et al. 2009:55–56; Kelly 2003:597). Its existence adds a different level of evidence to an investigation of this obelisk. In early A.D. 362 or 363, in a letter written at Antioch, the emperor Julian makes an immodest proposal to the people of Alexandria:

> I am informed that there is in your neighbourhood a granite obelisk, which, when it stood erect, reached a considerable height, but has been thrown down and lies on the beach as though it were something entirely worthless. For this obelisk Constantius of blessed memory had a freight-boat built, because he intended to convey it to my native place, Constantinople. But since by the will of heaven he has departed from this life to the next on that journey to which we are fated [Plato, *Phaedo* 117C], the city claims this monument from me because it is the place of my birth and more closely connected with me than with the late emperor. For though he loved the place as a sister I love it as my mother. I was in fact born there and brought up in the place, and I cannot ignore its claims. (trans. Wright 1913:153)

Julian is here competing with his predecessor Constantius. Alexandria will receive, as a compensatory measure, the permission to erect a colossal statue:

> Well then, since I love you also, no less than my native city, I grant to you also permission to set up the bronze statue in your city. A statue has lately been made of colossal size. If you set this up you will have, instead of a stone monument, a bronze statue of a man whom you say you love and long for, and a human shape instead of a triangular[3] block of granite with Egyptian characters on it.

Whom, we ask today, does this statue represent? This is not specified, but it is reasonably assumed that it is a statue of Julian himself rather than Constantius. Nonetheless, Julian, with a hint of special pleading, assures the Alexandrians that they have a special reason to make the exchange: the obelisk has become the scene of superstitious and licentious practices, which deserve to be stamped out. Trans-Mediterranean reciprocity, Julian admonishes, should spur the Alexandrians to provide this obelisk willingly to Constantinople.

> Therefore, for this very reason it is the more proper for you to assist in this business and to send it to my native city, which always receives you hospitably when you sail into the Black Sea, and to contribute to its external adornment, even as you contribute to its sustenance. It cannot fail to give you pleasure to have something that has belonged to you standing in their city, and as you sail towards that city you will delight in gazing at it.

This letter offers insights into the monumental intentions of one ruler, and tantalizing clues about what is at stake in the putative exchange of artifacts. While there is no certainty about the outcome of this conversation, it is possible that it involves the same monolith transported by Theodosius, which became the Hippodrome obelisk. One might argue that Julian dissimulates the power dynamic, in trying to give the impression of equal exchange, whereas the parties are not equal. The inequalities are expressed in terms of political power (emperor and subjects) and economic power (the grain supply received by Constantinople from Egypt, via Alexandria).[4]

MONUMENTALITY

It is time to step back a little so as to ask the question: By what criteria, in this account, might obelisks be considered monumental? Three elements, not quite parallel, come to the fore and will be considered in turn.

MOBILITY

It is already clear that mobility defined the lives of many obelisks. Now we have to recognize its improbability, given their enormous scale. Mobile monumentality might seem like a paradox, but here the concept might be deployed quite pointedly to highlight a feature that is prominent in several aspects we have seen already: the literary accounts of Pliny and Ammianus, as well as the reliefs on the base of the Hippodrome obelisk. It is useful to turn first to the inscription on the base of the two obelisks Augustus had moved in 10 B.C.:

> When emperor for the twelfth, consul for the eleventh, and tribune of the people for the fourteenth time, the emperor Augustus, son of the deified Caesar, dedicated this gift to the Sun, once Egypt had been restored to the power of the Roman people.[5]

Here, there is no reference to the fact that the obelisk had been brought to Rome: yet Egypt's conquered status certainly is more pointed when the obelisk stands in Rome. One might in fact argue that movement is implied in Augustus's "dedication" of the obelisk.

If this was the first obelisk to be moved from Egypt to Rome, then the theme of movement is explicit in the last obelisk that came to Rome on the Tiber, namely that now located outside San Giovanni Laterano and discussed by Ammianus Marcellinus (17.4). An inscription, now lost, on the base of the obelisk gives credit for the obelisk—and not least its transportation—to Constantius. The emperor's glory comes in part from the emphasis on the failed effort of his father, Constantine, who had intended that it be moved to Constantinople:

> His father, wishing this monument to adorn the city named after him, hewed it from the rock at Thebes, but a greater worry troubled the sanctified emperor, in that far-spread rumour warned that the mass of Caucasian proportions could not be moved by an ingenuity or physical effort. But Constantius, lord of the world, confident that everything yields to excellence, gave orders that the sizeable slice of mountain should roll over the land and entrusted it to the swelling sea, and (had it carried) to the shores of Italy while the calm waves wondered at the (huge?) boat. (Courtney 1995:56)

Monumentality may be considered memory-work that is realized in a particular place, as several contributors to this volume remark. This is clearly a productive line of inquiry for the urban landscape of Rome or Constantinople. In a different but overlapping sense, it is also a matter of the production of space, since it evokes the geographical range of empire, a reminder of Rome's conquest of Egypt, and therewith the symbolic conquest of an entire world empire.

In a colonial context, physical transportation is accompanied by symbolic appropriation: in other words, new meanings are conferred in keeping with the dynamics of colonial power. When Pliny claimed that "an obelisk is a symbolic representation of the sun's rays, and this is the meaning of the Egyptian word for it" (*Natural History* 36.64), this is in itself a Roman imposition of meaning on a foreign object. Pliny's comment appears to be in keeping with ancient Egyptian ideas, according to Egyptologists (Curran et al. 2009:14–15), yet it is Pliny himself that has been influential on later scholars. The Latin language has had a more or less continuous tradition in Western scholarship, unlike Middle Egyptian. This process of colonial resignification is thus very clear with regard to obelisks, and the linguistic difference between pharaonic Egypt and imperial Rome has been of lasting significance.[6] When it comes to the ancient meaning of obelisks, readers will encounter Pliny's comment more often than they will the relevant Middle Egyptian vocabulary. Egyptian texts are not explicit about the meaning of obelisks, hence the regular use of Latin texts in making historical reconstructions.

EXCHANGE

Second, we come to the dynamics of exchange and distribution. Julian's letter contains fascinating snippets of a conversation about both the political and the economic value of memory-objects. The transaction he suggests is the trading of an obelisk and a bronze statue between two of the main cities of the eastern Mediterranean, Alexandria and Constantinople. It is a transaction of complex meaning, given that the proposed bronze statue has a closer link with Julian, being his likeness (presumably), than the obelisk has with even Constantius. When Julian mentions the prospect that Alexandrians might one day sail into the harbor at Constantinople and feel at home, he points to collective memory in the form of metropolitan pride, and the exchange is presented as a kind of two cities (cf. Grig and Kelly 2012). It is in this broader sense that exchange should be interpreted, as the phenomenon of bringing together different kinds of capital (Morley 2007). A monument is, by this reckoning, a commodity, an object that is liable for exchange; it is also marker of value, the kind of value that can be converted between different media. At the same time, the obelisk has considerable evocative capacity, part of the source of its value.

The monumentality that Julian envisages in Constantinople stands in direct relation to something more mundane yet of the utmost significance: the grain supply. Indeed, with only a few exceptions, the grain supply is seldom represented in Roman artistic productions despite its fundamental importance to the Roman state. At the time when Augustus had the two obelisks imported to Rome on the Tiber in 10 B.C., that city was deeply dependent on the Egyptian grain supply. In this context, the obelisk carries a range of meanings, explicit and implicit. Such meanings may, in the more explicit sense, be gleaned from the inscriptions on the base and from Pliny's references to them;

in more implicit senses, they should be considered in light also of the economic ties between Rome and Egypt (Scheidel et al. 2007). What makes Julian's letter particularly interesting is that it reveals awareness of a range of meanings, and shows a negotiation of value that is underway.

Such negotiations continue to be politically charged in the present day. To take the famous case of an artifact that is known as an obelisk only in a popular sense, the Axum stele that Mussolini had brought to Rome in 1937 was subject to intense international debate before it was returned to Ethiopia in 2005, where it was re-erected in 2008 (Croce 2009). (Italy had in fact agreed to its repatriation as far back as 1947, but a number of factors intervened.) Mussolini's obeliscomania, though an extreme case, would suggest that the use of obelisks by modern colonial powers is a direct response to Roman practices rather than the original Egyptian ones.

To take another example, the obelisk now in New York's Central Park, the so-called Cleopatra's Needle, was subject to a muted claim for its repatriation in January 2011 by Dr. Zahi Hawass, then Egypt's Minister of Antiquities. Hawass claimed that in New York City the obelisk was prone to damage stemming from harsh weather conditions, and especially drew attention to the deterioration of the inscription on the flanks.[7] The collapse of the Mubarak government a few weeks later put paid to that discussion, or so, at least, it seemed at the time of writing. Nonetheless, both Ethiopian and Egyptian claims resonated with debates over cultural property or heritage, and both were finally determined in a context of asymmetrical international relations.

INTENTIONS

Julian's letter presents the intentions of first Constantine and then his son Constantius with regard to the monument. In fact, the letter is motivated by Julian's own intentions of obtaining an obelisk, while at the same time monumentalizing himself. Julian is by this reckoning the third in a line of emperors attempting to appropriate the obelisk. In each case, the emperor's obelizing intentions were defeated by premature death—premature, at least, from the obelisk's point of view.

Indeed, intentions are fundamental to any consideration of these obelisks as monuments. This much is clear from Pliny and Ammianus, and is true also of inscriptions on the obelisk bases, to the degree we have been able to glimpse them. Yet those intentions need to be considered against the life histories of obelisks, with their many turns, many of which have in practice thwarted intentions (Parker 2003).

The longevity of the monuments has created a recurring paradox: the longer an artifact survives, the greater the opportunities that it will be appropriated in ways not foreseen or even wished by the person setting it up, the author of the monument, as it were. To trace the object biography of any obelisk is to see a variety of renegotiated relationships between object and persons over time (cf. Osborne, this volume).

The obelisk now at Piazza Navona was originally inscribed in hieroglyphs, and perhaps originally carved, for the emperor Domitian (A.D. 81–96). This fact is extraordinary, but it would be hard to imagine that Piazza Navona's many tourists dwell on it. Indeed, the question about the failure of monuments is apt here. How would Domitian have felt that, after breaking into several parts in its subsequent location along the Via Appia, it would later be placed atop one of Bernini's most virtuosic confections, the Fountain of Four Rivers, around 1652? We never will know, though I suspect he particularly might have enjoyed all the attention. And equally, how might Theodosius have felt that the Hippodrome obelisk, where he himself is so strongly represented on the base, visually and verbally, now forms an axis with the minarets of the Blue Mosque? The reason to ask such absurd questions is to be reminded that intentions are indeed inherent in monuments, but there are multiple intentions among which origins can easily be eclipsed. Theodosius is merely one of several who have used the obelisks with the express goal of manipulating collective memory; Thutmose III is another.

In the broader reception history of obelisks there seems a deep paradox that is in itself very characteristic of the ancient Romans as well. Several later cities, including Sydney and Washington, D.C., have used obelisks to assert metropolitan status and legitimacy. Such appeals to Rome in fact do memory work at several levels. Not only do they evoke Rome itself, but in effect they simultaneously invoke Rome's own receptivity toward an older and grander civilization: Egypt (Schneider 2004). From this point of view, the obelisks are a sign not merely of Roman pride, but on the contrary of, first, Rome's need to prove a point about its own antiquity and legitimacy. Mobility, it would seem, mark obelisks as preeminent monuments of belatedness.

NOTES

1. The definitive discussion of obelisks is still Iversen (1968–1972); for more up-to-date accounts see also D'Onofrio (1992) and now Curran et al. (2009). The overview by Sorek (2010) is very general.
2. It should also be pointed out that obelisks display a wide variety of epigraphic habits: some were left uninscribed, others were even inscribed by Roman emperors on their flanks in Middle Egyptian hieroglyphs, notably the obelisk now at Piazza Navona in Rome (on which, see further Parker 2003).
3. The Greek text unambiguously states "triangular" at this point, which does not make sense: it appears that "quadrangular" was meant instead. It is unlikely that the pyramidion at the top of the obelisk is meant.
4. Kehoe even speculates that the transportation of such large items, given the huge costs involved, negatively affected economic growth (2007:550).
5. *Corpus Inscriptionum Latinarum* VI 701 = 702; cf. Iversen 1968:65.
6. Compare Mignolo's apt concept of the "colonization of language" (2003:29–123).
7. Comparison with the deterioration of the obelisk now at Kingston Lacy, a lavish, Italianate country house in Dorset, UK, emphasizes the real dangers of rain and humidity. Cf. Iversen 1972:85.

REFERENCES CITED

Aston, Barbara G., James A. Harrell, and Ian Shaw 2000 Stone. In Nicholson and Shaw 2000, pp. 5–77.

Beagon, Mary 1992 *Roman Nature: The Thought of Pliny the Elder.* Clarendon Press, Oxford.

Boas, George, trans. and ed. 1993 *The Hieroglyphics of Horapollo.* 2nd ed. Princeton University Press, Princeton.

Ciampini, Emanuele Marcello 2004 *Gli obelischi iscritti di Roma.* Libreria dello Stato, Rome.

Courtney, E. 1995 *Musa Lapidaria: A Selection of Latin Verse Inscriptions.* Scholars Press, Atlanta.

Croce, Giorgio 2009 From Italy to Ethiopia: the Dismantling, Transportation, and Re-erection of the Axum Obelisk. *Museum International* 61(1–2):61–67.

Curran, Brian A., Anthony Grafton, Pamela O. Long, and Benjamin Weiss 2009 *Obelisk: A History.* MIT Press, Cambridge.

D'Onofrio, Cesare 1992 *Gli obelischi di Roma: storia e urbanistica di una città dall'età antica al XX secolo.* Romana società editrice, Rome.

Effenberger, Arne 2007 Nochmals zur Aufstellung des Theodosius-Obelisken im Hippodrom von Konstantinopel. *Gymnasium* 114(6):587–598.

FitzGibbon, Kate, ed. 2005 *Who Owns the Past? Cultural Policy, Cultural Property, and the Law.* Rutgers University Press, New Brunswick, New Jersey.

Fontana, Domenico 1590 *Della trasportatione dell'obelisco Vaticano e delle fabriche di Sisto V.* Domenico Baso, Rome.

Grig, Lucy, and Gavin Kelly, eds. 2012 *Two Romes: Rome and Constantinople in Late Antiquity.* Oxford University Press, Oxford.

Habachi, Labib 2000 *Die unsterblichen Obelisken Ägyptens.* 2nd ed. Edited by Carola Vogel. Verlag Philipp von Zabern: Mainz.

Hartog, François 2001 *Memories of Odysseus: Frontier Tales from Ancient Greece.* Translated by Janet Lloyd. University of Chicago Press, Chicago.

Iversen, Erik 1968–1972 *Obelisks in Exile.* 2 vols. Gad, Copenhagen.

Kehoe, Dennis P. 2007 The Early Roman Empire: Production. In Scheidel et al. 2007, pp. 543–569.

Kelly, Gavin 2003 The New Rome and the Old: Ammianus Marcellinus' Silences on Constantinople. *Classical Quarterly* 53(2):588–607.

Mignolo, Walter 2003 *The Darker Side of the Renaissance.* 2nd ed. University of Michigan Press, Ann Arbor.

Morley, Neville 2007 The Early Roman Empire: Distribution. In Scheidel et al. 3007, pp. 570–591.

Nicholson, Paul T., and Ian Shaw, eds. 2000 *Ancient Egyptian Materials and Technology.* Cambridge University Press, Cambridge.

Parker, Grant 2003 Narrating Monumentality: The Piazza Navona Obelisk. *Journal of Mediterranean Archaeology* 16(2):193–215.

Parker, Grant 2007 Obelisks Still in Exile: Monuments Made to Measure? In *Nile into Tiber: Egypt in the Roman World. Proceedings of the Third International Conference of Isis Studies, Leiden, May 11–14 2005,* edited by Miguel John Versluys, Paul Meyboom, and Laurent Bricault, pp. 209–222. Religions in the Graeco-Roman World v. 159. Brill, Leiden.

Parkinson, Richard 1999 *Cracking Codes: The Rosetta Stone and Decipherment.* University of California Press, Berkeley.

Safran, Linda 1993 Points of View: The Theodosian Obelisk Base in Context. *Greek, Roman and Byzantine Studies* 34(4):409–435.

Scheidel, Walter, Ian Morris, and Richard Saller, eds. 2007 *The Cambridge Economic History of the Greco-Roman World.* Cambridge University Press, Cambridge.

Schneider, Rolf Michael 2004 Nicht mehr Ägypten, sondern Rom: Der neue Lebensraum der Obelisken. *Städel Jahrbuch,* Neue Folge 19:155–179.

Schneider, Rolf Michael 2005 Römische Bilder ägyptischer Obelisken (Kat. 335–343). In *Ägypten Griechenland Rom: Abwehr und Berührung, Städelsches Kunstinstitut und Städtische Galerie, Ausstellung vom 26. November 2005 bis 26. Februar 2006,* pp. 416–425 and 721–728. Ernst Wasmuth, Tübingen.

Sorek, Susan 2010 *The Emperor's Needles: Egyptian Obelisks and Rome.* Bristol Phoenix Press, Exeter.

Swetnam-Burland, Molly 2010 Aegyptus Redacta: The Egyptian Obelisk in the Augustan Campus Martius. *Art Bulletin* 112(2):135–153.

Ward-Perkins, Bryan 2012 Old and New Rome Compared: the Rise of Constantinople. In Grig and Kelly 2012, pp. 53–78.

Wirsching, Armin 2010 *Obelisken transportieren und aufrichten in Ägypten und in Rom.* 2nd ed. Books on Demand, Norderstedt.

PART IV

Monuments, Settlements, and Cities

CHAPTER FOURTEEN

Citadels in Spectacle-scapes in Bronze Age Anatolia

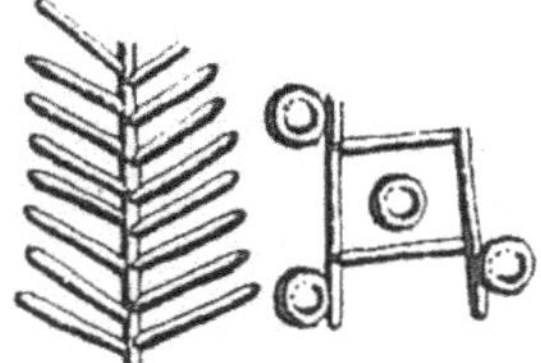

Christoph Bachhuber

Abstract *The relationship between violence, social memory, and monumentality has been underconsidered in the archaeological literature. In this chapter, I approach a particular archaeological phenomenon—the cyclical construction, violent destruction, and reconstruction of Bronze Age citadels on top of settlement mounds in Anatolia—to consider whether the settlement mound was a "historically" significant place to build upon in an unstable social milieu. I focus my analysis on Bronze Age Troy to distinguish two kinds of memory work that can assist in understanding settlement mounds as places of return: one related to spectacles of consumption in and around citadels, and one related to spectacles of catastrophic violence. Both kinds of events have the potential to politicize social memory, necessarily heightening the salience of settlement mounds as places to build upon during the Bronze Age.*

The past within the past is a dominant concern in archaeological approaches to monumentality (see Osborne this volume, and chapters 10–13 this volume). Settlement mounds are an ambiguous category of place from this perspective. They are not constructed things, like the visually analogous tumulus built in one event; rather, they are the composition of thousands upon thousands of constructed things, representing thousands upon thousands of construction and destruction events over hundreds or thousands of years. If a tumulus was inscribed in the landscape by the people who built it, then this chapter explores the ways in which the accumulated settlement debris of a mound may have existed as a "historically" meaningful feature in the Bronze Age landscape of Anatolia (Figure 14.1), for the people who built on top of it. To what extent can the temporal and taphonomic depth of a settlement mound equate with "memory work"?

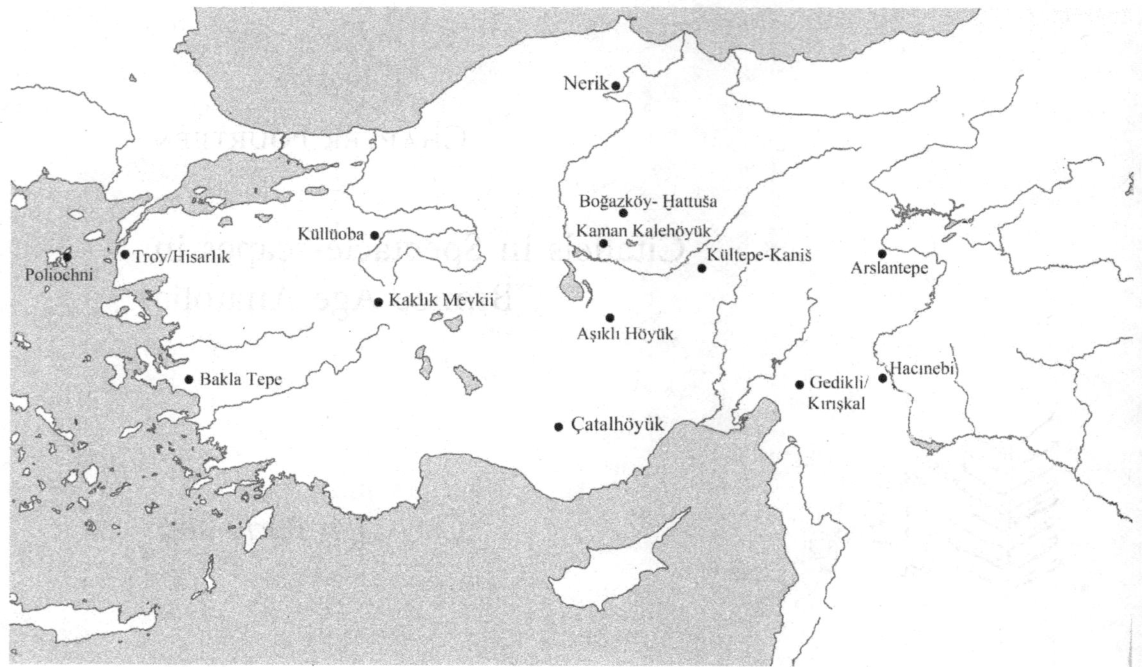

FIGURE 14.1 Sites and places mentioned in the text.

The broadest distinction that can be made between a settlement mound and a flat settlement is that the former creates path dependency: "Once they are in place . . . they will continue to be reoccupied, thereby continuing to structure the landscape" (Wilkinson 2003:108). Settlement mounds emerged as focal and prominent places in the alluvial plains of Anatolia, elevating its inhabitants onto a dry, defensive, and commanding vantage above the plains. This feature was appreciated by Neolithic, Chalcolithic, and Bronze Age societies alike.

The interpretive significance of the settlement mound has been considered from perspectives that emphasize its spatial and, by extension, social continuity through time, in particular as an ancestral place of return and a "nexus of stored meaning" in the landscape (for the Balkans see Chapman 1990:52; see also 1997:39–40). A similar interpretation has been offered for Neolithic settlements on the Anatolian Plateau at places such as Çatalhöyük and Aşıklı Höyük, where mounds had begun to form over the course of long durations of superimposed and similar (or replicated) settlement and building plans, characterized by nonviolent destruction and reconstruction activities. Hodder (2005:185–186) suggests that this continuity and replication may have stemmed from two kinds of memory work: one related to the routinization or habituation of everyday activities and the transmission of this behavior from one generation to the next, and the other related to a mythical and/or historical engagement with the previous inhabitants of the settlement mound as a form of commemorative memory.

The reasons to build on top of or otherwise inhabit a settlement mound are socially and historically contingent and defy generalization. One obvious contrast can be made between the construction and destruction activities of Neolithic settlements compared with the Bronze Age. The palimpsest of Bronze Age settlement plans in mounds is inconsistent from one level to the next (for Troy, see Ünlusöy 2010: plan 1), often punctuated by violent and catastrophic destructions. If a stratigraphic and architectural sequence can be any guide to interpreting evidence for a "historical" consciousness in settlement mounds, then the memory work of the Bronze Age inhabitants of these places differed from their Neolithic predecessors. In this chapter, I suggest that the path dependency created by settlement mounds is related to social memory during both the Neolithic and the Bronze Age, although the social contexts and necessarily the reasons to build on top of previously inhabited places were wholly divergent between the two periods.

During the Bronze Age, most of the accumulation of a settlement mound was the result of the construction, violent destruction, and reconstruction of fortified citadels and palaces. These elevated and enclosed places mobilize the potential for two kinds of memory making (see Bradley 1998; Connerton 1989; Rowlands 1993): one that is inscribed (or representational) in the architectural edifice, and one that is embodied in a ritual panoply that was performed in and around these structures by exclusive and self-aggrandizing social groups.

For similar reasons citadels or palaces were highly contested places and regular targets of violence. My understanding of the cycles of violence and reconstruction during the Bronze Age is informed by recent work on the relationship between violence and memory (Argenti and Schramm 2010). Catastrophic destruction events were a form of embodied spectacle that should not be too clearly distinguished from the spectacle and memory work of ritual and ceremony. The cyclical eruptions of violence at these places would have created certain "time marks" in their locales (see Chapman 1997, the temporal equivalent of "landmarks").

If the taphonomic process of mound accumulation was the unintended consequence of construction, destruction, and reconstruction activities over centuries (for partially analagous Mississippian mound building over centuries in the prehistoric U.S., see Osborne, this volume; Paukekat 2000), I nevertheless suggest that the burnt detritus of catastrophic events accumulated in a repository of social memory. This repository—the settlement mound—increased the commemorative or monumental aspect of Bronze Age architecture. I bring similar considerations to bear on the most well-known and extensively excavated settlement mound in Bronze Age Anatolia, the site of Troy.

Settlement Mounds and Hittite Social Memory

Social memory is elusive in research on Bronze Age societies in Anatolia. This problem has been explicitly formulated in a study of Hittite royal elites (Gilan 2008), in particular the shallow historical consciousness of the kings of the Hittite Old Kingdom (ca. 1650–1400 B.C.). The historical introduction to the "Proclamation of Telipinu" (ca. 1525–1500

B.C.) records a remarkably short royal genealogy: six generations. Gilan (2008:11) suggests that the Hittite elite compensated for this shallow social memory by incorporating Mesopotamian (in particular Akkadian, ca. 2350–2150 B.C.) historical-literary traditions as their own. One, titled "the King of Battle," recounts an Anatolian campaign of the Akkadian king Sargon; the other, titled "the Great Revolt," describes a rebellion including Anatolian kingdoms against his grandson Naram-Sin. The Hittite elite drew upon the history of their Mesopotamian neighbors, much like the Romans incorporated Troy in their own narratives of ethno-genesis, to fill in a largely empty past (Gilan 2008:112).

It goes without saying that the past of the Anatolian Plateau was not empty. In the centuries preceding the Hittite Old Kingdom, the Anatolian Plateau was a thriving and urbanizing place. Archaeologists and historians label this the "Assyrian Trading Colony" period, which I refer to as the Middle Bronze Age (MBA, Table 14.1). The MBA is best known for the textually documented inhabitants of the lower towns of palace polities, including Assyrians and other foreign (Hurrian) merchants (for recent overview, see Bachhuber 2012). Assyrian language archives recovered from the houses of lower towns have overshadowed research on the palaces themselves. For the purposes of this chapter, palaces were invariably built on top of settlement mounds that had been accumulating for hundreds or thousands of years.

By most measures the Anatolian Plateau was an unstable place to do business during the MBA. Political unrest was a regular concern among the Assyrian traders, as was the safety of their caravans (Veenhof 2008:99–101). At the best-known palace of Kültepe-Kaniš in Cappadoccia, the first Old Palace was destroyed in a catastrophic fire together with the lower town of Level II. Within a couple of generations, the subsequent Late Palace was constructed, retaining very little of the architectural plan of its predecessor. The foundations of the ramparts of the "Late Palace" also destroyed much of the architectural integrity of the "Old Palace" (Özgüç 1999:136), revealing a disregard or even callousness toward the earlier complex. This may be usefully contrasted with contemporary (Old Babylonian) palace construction activities in Syria at Tell Leilan, where the catastrophic destruction of Building Level 3 of the Eastern Lower Town Palace was followed by a rebuilding of the Level 2 palace to nearly the same alignment and plan, including the reuse of several walls and floors (Weiss and Ristvet 2010:xxi–xxii).

The violent destruction of the Late Palace (terminating both the MBA and the enterprise of the Assyrian merchants) was mirrored by similar events on every known MBA citadel on the Anatolian Plateau. The most graphic illustration of this region-wide catastrophe has been recorded at the palace of Kaman-Kalehöyük, where the destruction of Stratum IIIc preserved a casualty who was shot through with a spear, and a group of 11 individuals (including many small children) who perished in the burning collapse of a building (Omura 2005:33).

A different kind of instability may be noted in the architectural plans of MBA palaces and their citadels on the Anatolian Plateau, which were varied across time and space (Bachhuber 2012:587). Palace construction did not follow a local, time-honored architectural tradition on the Anatolian Plateau, such as buildings that drew upon earlier (Early Bronze Age, hereafter EBA) traditions. Thus, the extent to which palatial architecture embodied a revered and universal institution of kingship should similarly be doubted. This seeming lack of ideological cohesion during the MBA—at least in terms of the architecture of power—may go some way toward understanding the shallow social memory of the later Hittite elites.

Following the catastrophic destructions of the MBA palaces, most settlement mounds were not built on again during the Late Bronze Age (LBA, Hittite period), terminating hundreds if not thousands of years of settlement at these places. Glatz (2009:132) has interpreted the abandonment of the settlement mounds as a strong symbolic message, related to the shift of power from a local palatial authority during the MBA to a spatially more extensive, integrated polity during the LBA—i.e., the Hittite Empire. Such a strategy may also help explain the shallow social memory of the early Hittite rulers, and warrants more careful consideration with regard to the relationship between settlement mounds, previously destroyed citadels, and social memory during the LBA.

At least one Hittite king recognized an ancient place in the landscape as a nexus of stored meaning. In a text from the annals of a later imperial Hittite king (Hattusili III, ca. 1260–1230 B.C.) titled the "Apology of Hattusili III," he records campaigning into the enemy territory of the Kaska to the north and encountering a "ruin-heap of a town" (Sumerian logogram URU DU$_6$ = Hittite *pupulli* = "ruin-heap of a town"; see Otten 1981:11; Weeden 2012:195–196). The place was called Nerik, which Hattusili III believed was the ruins of a city built by a much earlier Hittite king Hattusili I (ca. 1650–1620 B.C.). Hattusili III rebuilt this "ruin-heap of a town," which is to say he built on top of this ruin-heap; and by doing so he laid claim to a Hittite past in enemy (Kaska) territory, a past that could have been real or imagined. To Hattusili III, the "ruin-heap of a town" of Nerik existed as a place to commemorate much earlier Hittite achievements, and as a place to demonstrate his own imperial worth by reclaiming it.

The Apology of Hattusili III is a clear illustration of the relationship between an ancient place in the landscape (a "ruin-heap of a town") and historical consciousness. Did similar kinds of ancient places exist for those who built citadels and palaces on top of settlement mounds during the EBA (3000–2200 B.C.) and the MBA (ca. 2000–1600 B.C.)? There are no annals or myths or commemorative inscriptions with which to examine the problem. The absence of relevant epigraphic material also denies the ruling elites of these earlier periods a potential strategy to preserve social memory. This is not to say that literacy is the only recourse to social memory, but it clearly helps to maintain it, particularly during periods of profound social instability.

Ruin-Heaps of Towns in Prehistory?

The equation of social, ideological, and spatial continuity in Neolithic settlements and settlement mounds cannot be maintained for the Bronze Age in Anatolia. A comparison of EBA plans from Troy in Figure 14.2 (plan of Troy IIc-e) with Figure 14.3 (the plan of the subsequent Troy IIf-III) shows a total disregard for buildings of the earlier period. This inconsistency from one building phase to the next is evident in every architectural level at Early Bronze Age Troy (Ünlusöy 2010:plan 1)—catastrophic destructions punctuated this

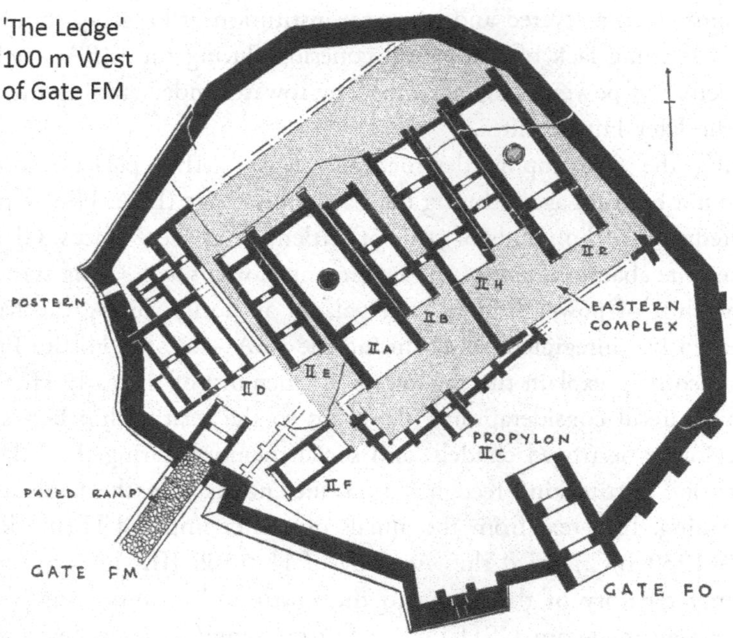

FIGURE 14.2 Showing a plan of Troy IIc-e (modified from Mellaart 1959: Figure 6, courtesy of the British Institute at Ankara/Anatolian Studies, with text added).

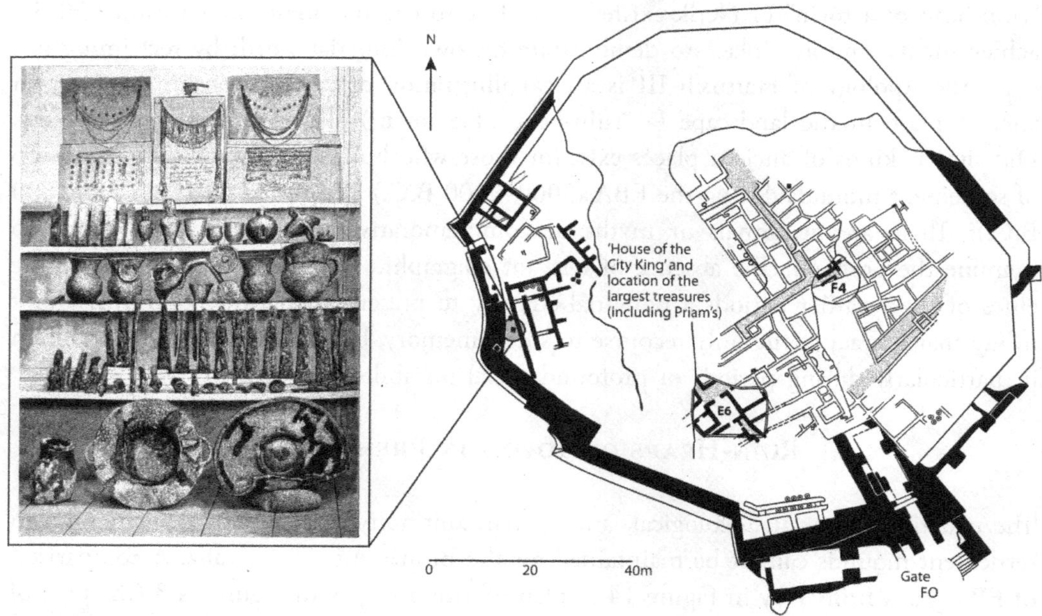

FIGURE 14.3 Showing a plan of Troy IIf–III, and the location of the largest treasure, "Priam's," or Treasure A (drawing by Xavier Droux).

sequence in four events (terminal Troy I, IIb, IIe, III: Table 14.1). This sequential instability in the building plans of Bronze Age settlement mounds continued right through the MBA (as above at Kültepe-Kaniš). Clearly, another approach is needed that can account for settlement mounds as places of return in this particular Bronze Age milieu.

The least ambiguous context to study a settlement mound as an ideologically meaningful place of return is when it has been abandoned as a settlement, and subsequently returned to not as a place to permanently inhabit, but rather as a focus of commemorative activity. This happens with some frequency during the EBA, in particular in the form of burials. Mortuary contexts quickly replace abandoned settlement contexts (probably within a generation) at the mounds of Arslantepe (Frangipane 2001), Hacınebi (Stein 1998), Gedikli Höyük (Duru 2006), Kaklik Mevkii (Topbaş et al. 1998), and Bakla Tepe (Erkanal 2008; Şahoğlu 2008). Other commemorative activity on settlement mounds can be inferred from pits filled with feasting equipment on top of the abandoned Phase IV citadel of Küllüoba (Efe 2006; Fidan 2012:26; Türkteki 2012:Figure 5), and in corbel-vaulted tunneling into abandoned settlement mounds at Gedikli Höyük and

TABLE 14.1

**CHRONOLOGICAL CHART EMPHASIZING EPISODIC VIOLENCE
AND INSTABILITY AT TROY DURING THE BRONZE AGE**

Year (B.C.)	Anatolia	Troy
500	Iron Age	Homer
1000	**Region-wide catastrophe** Late Bronze Age 'Hittite'	Troy VII **violent destruction** Troy VI **violent destruction**
1500		Troy V (no large-scale violence)
	Region-wide catastrophe Middle Bronze Age 'Assyrian Trading Colony'	
2000		Troy IV (no large-scale violence)
	Region-wide catastrophe	terminal Troy III **violent destruction** Troy IIe **violent destruction**
2500	Early Bronze Age	Troy IIb **violent destruction** terminal Troy I **violent destruction**
3000		Troy I (no large-scale violence)

neighboring Kırışkal Höyük (Duru 2006). As a focus of commemoration, settlement mounds in these contexts clearly reveal inscribed and embodied memory practices that probably relate to the earlier inhabitants of the mound. As a mortuary context, the settlement mound may have been perceived and used within an ancestral ritual panoply (see further for EBA mortuary practices, Bachhuber in press:ch. 4). The dead may have mediated cosmological relationships between the living and the earlier inhabitants of the settlement mound.

Inscribed or embodied memory work is more difficult to study when the Bronze Age settlement mound was the focus of a sequence of building activities, one immediately following the other, seemingly not adhering to any time-honored spatial logic, and often punctuated by catastrophic destructions. In an unbroken sequence of construction (and violent destruction) events, there is no a priori reason to assume that a settlement mound existed as a mytho-historical place to the people who claimed it, and to those who reappropriated it.

In the following analysis, I focus on two kinds of spectacle that may have mobilized embodied forms of memory making in this particular social context: one manifest in the display and consumption of wealth on citadels built on top of settlement mounds, and the other manifest in the eruptions of violence that were targeted at these same citadels. I suggest that settlement mounds had become places of a particular form of history making (or memory work) precisely when they had become places of sumptuary and violent spectacle, both of which can be interpreted as commemorative acts with potential to prolong social memory.

TROY AS A TARGET OF VIOLENCE

The following analysis broadly agrees with Osborne's (this volume) dichotomy between form/monument (this section) and meaning/monumentality (the following sections). In this section I describe what was built, and violently destroyed, and rebuilt. In the following sections I address why it was built, and violently destroyed, and rebuilt. I focus on the best-known settlement mound in Bronze Age Anatolia: Hisarlık, the place widely associated with Troy from the Homeric epics.

My choice of Troy requires some justification. As an archaeological site, Hisarlık/Troy is enmeshed in the deepest—or most ancient—social memory of violence in the Western imagination. Because of its longstanding literary associations, Troy holds much potential to cloud the judgment of archaeologists who try to understand it. However, four large-scale excavation campaigns over a 140-year period have revealed a Bronze Age sequence in the settlement mound like no other site in Anatolia or in the Aegean region. For example, no other settlement mound could so clearly illustrate the radical architectural transformation from one building phase (Troy IIe: Figure 14.2) to the next (Troy IIf: Figure 14.3).

The two most violent periods in the Bronze Age sequence of Troy were also the most architecturally formidable: during the EBA with a peak of violence during Troy II–III (Table 14.1), and during the LBA with catastrophic events terminating the Troy VI and

VII phase (Table 14.1). Here, I focus on the EBA, in large part because the archaeology of the earlier citadels is better able to inform the sumptuary spectacle that underlies my discussion of embodied memory practice. Similar kinds of spectacles would have likely been performed in and around the LBA citadel, although they are less archaeologically accessible.

The most iconic architecture of EBA Troy (Troy IIc-e, Figure 14.2) was built on top of a settlement mound that had been accumulating for about 500 years. Much of the monumentality of the citadel was derived from the way it transformed this long-established place of settlement into a fortified edifice. The stone glacis best represents how this transformation was achieved (Figure 14.4). The glacis was used to encase and stabilize the loose mound of mudbrick detritus and construction fill upon which most known settlements in Bronze Age Anatolia were built. It also provided structural support for the erection of a mudbrick circuit wall and/or rampart. At Troy II, the glacis was built up as a towering, neatly finished, and formidable façade (Figure 14.4), analogous with the curtain wall of a medieval castle.

The glacis at Troy is monumental in two related respects: (1) as a representation of space; (2) as evidence for a corporate investment in an architectural program. A glacis transforms the landscape in which it is built by encasing in stone the accumulated debris of a settlement mound. It ordered the landscape with a construction program that transcended the basic architectonic needs of the edifice, and the basic safety needs of its inhabitants (Trigger 1990). It was part of a "representation of space" (Lefebvre 1991:38–39), or a conceptual "blueprint" held by those with the power to define what space is. The glacis existed as a potent signifier of exterior and interior to people who were permitted access to this place, and to people who were not. It encoded information related to the permanence, solidity, and strength of the edifice and, ultimately, the power of the people who quarried, transported, finished, and set the many thousands of tons of stone invested in the façade (see Fisher 2009:192). In this way the construction of the glacis also ordered social relationships, defined by who commissioned and mobilized the labor and who supplied it. The monumental significance of the glacis in Bronze Age Anatolia is preserved on the façade of the LBA citadel of the capital of the Hittite Empire Boğazköy-Hattusa (Schirmer 2002:Figures 7–8), where a glacis served no architectonic function whatsoever, covering the slope of a mountain that would have been visible for miles on the main southern approach to the city.

The glacis was just one feature on the façade of the Troy citadel that increased the stability of the edifice, heightened its defensibility, and signified the power of its builders and inhabitants. The gateways were the most vulnerable points in the powerful presentation of this façade and were secured architecturally and militarily (Figure 14.3). The gatehouses of Gate FM and FO were part of an innovative building program that characterizes the whole of the Troy IIc citadel (following the catastrophic destruction of Troy IIb). Like the gatehouse of any castle or walled city, these features heightened the posture and impressiveness of the citadel façade at its most vulnerable points.

Gates FM and FO were different from one another in the duration of their use, in the scale of elaboration, and in their spatial relationship with the central buildings of

FIGURE 14.4 (a) View looking west on the south-facing glacis of the Troy II–III citadel from Schliemann's excavations (unpublished photo D-DAI-IST-R 26.896, from the Troy archives at the Deutsches Archäologisches Institut-İstanbul, courtesy of the Deutsches Archäologisches Institut-İstanbul; (b) Showing height of the south-facing glacis and buttressing of the Troy II–III citadel from Schliemann's excavations (unpublished photo D-DAI-ATH Troja-227, from the Troy archives at the DAI Athens, courtesy of the Deutsches Archäologisches Institut-Athens).

the citadel. They may also have served different functions. Gate FO was the more robust of the two and was used for a longer period. Gate FO continued in use into Troy III, whereas Gate FM had been abandoned by the end of Troy II (Sazcı 2005:58). On the other hand, Gate FM was the focus of greater architectural elaboration: namely a large stone-paved ramp that represents the most iconic architectural feature from Bronze Age Troy. I have suggested that Gate FM served a more commemorative function than its FO counterpart. The most archaeologically obvious function included joining activities in the central buildings of the citadel to an extramural cult-depositional feature located 100 m west of Gate FM (Bachhuber 2009:4–5): the so-called Ledge (see below).

The spatial and social logic of the Troy IIc-e citadel can be reconstructed in three tiers of exclusivity. The first tier was formed by the façade of the citadel and the gates, ramp, and gatehouses that pass through it (Figure 14.2). The entrant through Gate FO crossed over a gravel-paved court area and was confronted with a rectilinear enclosure wall (forming the second tier of exclusivity). Passage into the central court area and Megaron IIA required entering another gatehouse-like structure (Propylon IIc). Conversely, the entrant through Gate FM was granted direct access to the court area and central buildings. The third tier of exclusivity was formed by the porticoes of the central longhouse buildings, in particular the portico to Megaron IIA with access to a large, central hearth.

This citadel was destroyed utterly and catastrophically in an event that terminated the Troy IIe phase. Schliemann (1880:76–88) commented on the vitrified state of the burnt mudbrick of all buildings. One victim of the catastrophe was identified in the court area of the central complex (Schliemann 1880:270–2; Götze 1902:342). Construction activities immediately following this event included replacing the singular plan of Troy IIc-e (Figure 14.2), with a plan that was more sprawling and fragmented in Troy IIf (Figure 14.3). The rectilinear enclosure and all the buildings from the Troy IIc-e were burned, leveled, and not rebuilt; Gate FM was sealed and the stone-paved ramp abandoned; the large central hearth of Megaron IIA was not reconstructed; indeed large central hearths do not feature in any of the buildings from the later Troy IIf–III. This reappropriation and remodeling of the Troy citadel immediately following the destruction of Troy IIf is all the more remarkable as most other categories of material culture remained unchanged in the transition.

What happened in the Troad? The construction sequence at EBA Troy warrants considering evolutionary studies that prioritize the role of monumental building during the initial stages of political and economic consolidation (Kolb 1994:521–552). The Troy IIc-e citadel represents the peak of architectural elaboration, sophistication, and scale during the EBA. The building of this citadel was perhaps effective in consolidating social groups in the Troad through ideological and commemorative means rather than via more overtly oppressive political and militaristic ones (see Bradley 1984:73). These kinds of construction projects tend to emphasize the social collective in both endeavor and ideological observance, suppressing (though not eliminating) both socioeconomic differentiation and opportunities for individual aggrandizement (Knapp 2008:206; Kolb 2005:174; see also Osborne this volume, discussion in "Form and Monument").

Nevertheless, efforts of political centralization at Troy may not have been as consensual as this outline would suggest. If political unification did occur in the Troad in the Troy IIc-e period, its hold was tenuous and probably not that expansive, judging from the bolstering of the citadel's fortifications in Troy IIc, and the extreme violence that was targeted at the citadel in Troy IIe. Tensions may have existed between those who commissioned the construction projects of the Troy IIc-e citadel, and other social groups in the region who may not have enjoyed all the privileges of the citadel and who did not fully succumb to the will of the elite of Troy IIc-e.

The transition between Troy IIe and Troy IIf is the most dramatic and best illustrated on the settlement mound. However, the citadel was also the target of large-scale violence in the transitions from Troy I to IIa, IIb to IIc, and in a final catastrophic event in Troy III that terminated the EBA in the Troad (Table 14.1). Each of these destruction events was followed by construction activities where no attempt was made to rebuild destroyed structures. It is worth reemphasizing a contrast with violently destroyed citadels/palaces that were rebuilt to plan, for example, at MBA Tell Leilan in northern Syria as above. From the perspective of monumentality and social memory, how does one reconcile continuity of place, continuity in most categories of material culture, with so much violence, instability, and architectural erasure? Is social memory even an appropriate concept with which to approach this problem on the settlement mound of Troy?

The discussion needs to consider why the citadel was contested in the first place. Who were the victims and who were the perpetrators of this violence? The victims are the easier of the two to identify: they were the inhabitants of the citadel. Some of their activities on the citadel are archaeologically accessible, and can begin to address the problem. I consider some implications for the conspicuous consumption of wealth that was performed in a ritual panoply at EBA Troy.

Ritual Spectacle and Embodied Social Memory

What was a citadel to the people who built the edifice? What was a citadel to the people who attacked and destroyed it? Select inhabitants of EBA citadels consolidated social and political power by naturalizing their roles as ritual specialists, in large part through the conspicuous consumption of wealth. At Troy, the two most accessible activities include the use of controlled flame in different contexts of ritual burning, and the votive-like deposition of wealth. The former can be observed in the dedication of burned meat/animals (one form of wealth) in the so-called Ledge basin of Troy IIc 100 m west of the citadel and overlooking the sea (Blegen et al. 1950:270–77), the use of the monumental hearth in Megaron IIA (Troy IIc-f), and in cremation rites that were likely performed in or near the EBA citadel (for cremation burials in the citadel see Schliemann 1874:107–108; 1880:39). The votive deposition of wealth can be observed in the so-called treasures of Troy IIf–III (Bachhuber 2009). Both activities created a spectacle that secured the attention of participants and cosmological entities alike (Renfrew 1994:51), effectively defining a boundary between the two realms. In fire rites such as the sacrificial dedication of animals/meat or in cremation spectacles, smoke was a primary channel of communication with the cosmos. The ascending smoke and aromas from burnt meat/animal sacrifice in the ritual panoply of several ancient religions (for example, in the Sumerian and Greek religions, and Judaism) was a propitiatory gesture to gods who desired the same meat that humans desired (Fuller and Rowlands 2011:45). Some cosmological entity was similarly looked after at the Troy IIc Ledge. The burned offerings of animals/meat in this large, rock-cut basin on a cliff edge overlooking the sea was performed in rites that included the deposition of great volumes of pottery in the same basin, and other objects such as stone idols. The cult context is clear, as is the evocation of feasting.

Ritual maintenance of monumental hearths on citadels is a more ambiguous channel of communication with the cosmological realm. Its symbolic power was clearly derived from their fulfillment of basal household needs of warmth and nourishment. It was essential furniture in the atmosphere of hospitality and conviviality that was created in these buildings, and is analogous with, if not predecessor to, the hearth-*wanax* ideological panoply of Mycenaean palaces (Wright 1994). But monumental hearths probably did not create smoke spectacles (in enclosed spaces) by the burning of sacrificial flesh. Here, the heat of the flame held greater ideological significance. A hearth cult on EBA citadels related to the regeneration or well-being of ruling households—and by extension of political economies—is a more likely interpretation. An animate hearth in Hittite palace construction ritual texts expresses pleasure in its ability to gather all members of the royal household around it, and in the future biological reproduction of the royal household (see Schwartz 1947:§44–47).

The ideological significance of both the Ledge where burnt offerings were made and the monumental hearth of Megaron IIA can be glimpsed in their abandonment, and the abandonment also of the commemorative Gate FM that joined the citadel to the Ledge. Originally, all of these features helped encode the ritual authority, prosperity, and permanence of the builders of the earlier citadel. Subsequently, they became targets for destruction and erasure during an episode of profound instability in the Troad. Another fire spectacle—the total razing of the Troy IIe citadel—defines the end of this particular ritual cycle at Troy and its associated authority.

The transition from Troy IIe to Troy IIf included a dramatic transformation of the ritual panoply on the citadel. Spectacles were now created with the votive dedication of metal objects and other valued materials (see further Bachhuber in press:ch. 8). As arenas for ritual performance and cult sacrifice, the contexts of votive deposition of treasures may be usefully contrasted with the open-air fire and smoke spectacles at the Troy IIc Ledge. Both included the prestige-enhancing sacrifice of different forms of wealth (livestock/meat in the one, and mostly metal objects in the other), but the later votive depositions were performed in enclosed and restricted spaces. The restricted context is clearly illustrated in a reconstruction of a contemporary context of treasures deposition at Poliochni Yellow (on the island of Lemnos in the north Aegean west of Troy), where a cache of gold jewelry was located in a kind of shrine attached to a large building (Figure 14.5; see Cultraro 1999). The "shrine" could only be accessed via descending some stairs. The spatial/architectural context for the Troy treasures is less well understood, although many of them appear to have been located beneath the floors of the "house of the city king," including probably in an auxiliary room or "shrine." These were not "public" spaces that could accommodate large audiences; rather, they show the withdrawal of ritual spectacle into exclusive quarters.

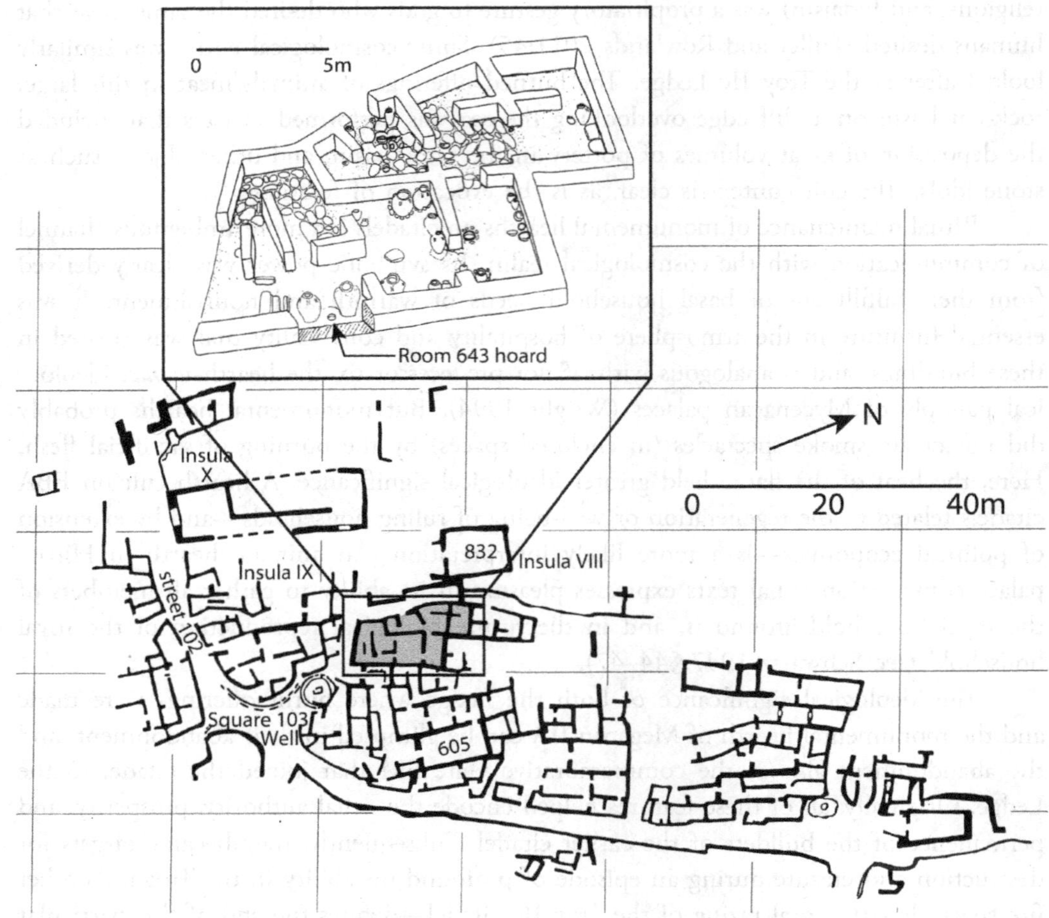

FIGURE 14.5 Detailed reconstruction of the find context of the Poliochni Yellow hoard in Room 643 in Insula VII (drawing by Xavier Droux, modified from Cultraro 1999:Figure 4).

This ritual panoply was not public or socially integrative. The votive dedication of metal on citadels was performed in an esoteric setting for a closely circumscribed group of peers. It was made to enhance an elite reputation among people who mattered more than the subaltern farming populations of the Troad or on Lemnos (see Baines 2006:291 for ancient Egypt). The withdrawal of ostentatious ritual spectacle into "shrines" or other interior spaces attached to buildings at Poliochni Yellow and Troy IIf–III, from the public spectacles in and around the Troy IIc-e citadel, agrees with evolutionary studies on the life cycles of early states. In the later stages of the cycle, ruler personages tend to invest less in corporate projects of monumental construction and the collective observance of these monuments, and more in person-focused activities of display and consumption (Kolb 1994:531).

If fire and smoke created the attention-grabbing spectacle in the sacrifice of animals/meat, then the reflective surfaces and clamor of metal objects captured the attention of a human and cosmological audience in esoteric settings of votive sacrifice on EB III citadels. The gesture of sacrifice, like wearing or using these objects, communicated information about gender, age, group membership, or social position to both audiences. They were a powerful signifier of social position and political power in contexts of display and deposition (see DeMarrais et al. 1996:18). The ritual consumption of all these objects on citadels created a vivid visual experience of an elite ideology, which included gestures of piety that would have been incomprehensible for people living in the hinterland of citadels, further magnifying the degree of separation between those who inhabited or could access citadels, and those who could not.

The ritual panoply of such events in and around the Troy citadel, whether public burned sacrifice or esoteric votive deposition, mobilized embodied forms of social memory. Here, an event is not simply something that happened; rather, it needs to have resonated through and ultimately to have transformed a chain of social relationships—and/or structures (Sewell 2005:227; Bolender 2010). As parts of spectacles on the Troy citadel, the animals that were sacrificed and burned at the Troy IIc ledge and the objects sacrificed in the Troy IIf-III treasures "serve(d) as repositories of narrative" (Inomata and Coben 2006:31) that foregrounded the role of a few people on the Troy citadel as exclusive initiators and mediators with the sacred realm. The things that were consumed in these events were "made monumental" (Osborne this volume) in the spectacle of their consumption. Such ritual activity and events likely impressed time marks in the Troad (see Chapman 1997), and across a larger region, increasing the historical or commemorative salience of this place. Such activities also heightened the citadel's profile as a target of violence.

VIOLENT SPECTACLE AND EMBODIED MEMORY

Citadels at EBA Troy were catastrophically destroyed four times in a ca. 400-year period. The place was likely attacked several more times when a total destruction was not the end result. Two scenarios can account for the perpetrators of this violence at Troy: those who were engaged in acquisitive raids and retributive attacks; and those who held rival claims to the citadel. The two scenarios need not be mutually exclusive, although the latter motivation perhaps better explains the total erasure of the previous signifiers of ritual authority on the citadel, most evident in the reappropriation of the citadel in the transition between Troy IIe and Troy IIf: Figures 14.3 and 14.4.

Mikhail Yampolsky's understanding of the iconoclastic treatment of monuments in Soviet and post-Soviet Europe is instructive here:

> Destruction and construction can be understood, in a certain context, as two equally valid procedures of immortalization. Destruction affirms the power of the victor to the same extent as the erection of a monument to victory. A tradition has developed historically to build a new monument precisely on the site of the old one, as though accumulating in one place two commemorative gestures: vandalism and the erection of a new idol. (Yampolsky 1995:100)

Replace "vandalism" with "targeted violence" and "idol" with "citadel" and Yampolsky's formulation of iconoclasm assists in my understanding of the cyclical destruction and construction events at Bronze Age Troy. Targeted violence—which included a pyrotechnic spectacle—was a commemorative act that served not to erase social memory, but actually to prolong it (see Forty 1999:12). As a recurring target of violence, the settlement mound of Troy was part of a "traumascape" in the Troad during the Bronze Age (see Tumarkin 2005). Here, the regular eruptions of violence on top of and around the settlement mound were a form of embodied spectacle that should not be too clearly distinguished from the spectacles of ritual and ceremony.

> Yet if one considers the impact of violence on people's cultural and political identities . . . it becomes clear that embodied memory is not only relevant in terms of social stability, but perhaps even more so as an indicator of social disruption. (Argenti and Schramm 2010:8)

As spectacles that included large-scale injury and destruction, these cataclysmic events at Bronze Age Troy may have become politicized memories with potential to spur future action (Argenti and Schramm 2010:18). In a spectacle-scape, the citadels that were destroyed in pyrotechnic events, rebuilt, and destroyed again accumulated in the settlement mound as a nexus of stored meaning. Troy existed in the landscape as a contested place, and a focus for ritual-like cycles of warfare where a memory of past violence may have spurred future violence during the EBA, and during the LBA also.

Concluding Thoughts

> The association between the fall of Troy and the faculty of memory has become so conventional throughout cultural history that it is almost as if Troy existed only to the extent to which it was remembered. (Bellamy 1992:56)

Few "places" are more monumental than Troy in the Western canon by virtue of the epic violence that was described "there." This paper is neither a defense nor a critique of the historicity of a Late Bronze Age Trojan War, but a rather straightforward distinction needs to be made between the original cataclysmic events and the ways that they are remembered (Argenti and Schramm 2010:19). During the Bronze Age, I have suggested that the place of Troy was remembered through two kinds of archaeologically accessible spectacle: one related to a ritual panoply of conspicuous consumption increasing the potential for conflict; and one manifest in cataclysmic pyrotechnic events and attendant destruction and injury. Both can result in embodied forms of memory work, replayed in cycles of consumption and warfare alike. "Memory" of these Bronze Age spectacles likely reverberated into the Archaic Period of western Anatolia (and into the mind of one or more Homers). Similar kinds of events and activities were nevertheless performed and witnessed during the violent and unstable Archaic Period (Gottschall 2008). The spectacles from both periods likely informed the poetry of Homer.

As a monument in the Western imagination, the violent destruction of Troy has fulfilled the role of a ruin on top of which new political structures (Athenian, Roman, etc.) may be built (Yampolsky 1995). Similarly the "ruin-heap of a town" that the Hittite king Hattusili III encountered in enemy territory was an appropriate place to reassert Hittite authority in that region. There is good cause to believe that similar narratives surrounded memory-making events of large-scale construction, sumptuary spectacle, and cataclysmic destruction on settlement mounds across Bronze Age Anatolia and in contemporary and adjacent regions.

Acknowledgments

My warmest thanks to James Osborne for inviting me to participate in the monumentality forum at IEMA, University of Buffalo, and for his thoughtful edit of the paper. The ideas in this paper benefited from a one-year fellowship in the Joukowsky Institute for Archaeology and the Ancient World at Brown University, and in particular from conversations with Felipe Rojas and Ömür Harmanşah. Thanks also to Mark Weeden for pointing me to relevant Hittite material, and to Elizabeth Frood for comments on a draft.

References Cited

Argenti, Nicolas, and Katharina Schramm 2010 Introduction: Remembering Violence: Anthropological Perspectives on Intergenerational Transmission. In *Remembering Violence: Anthropological Perspectives on Intergenerational Transmission,* edited by Nicolas Argenti and Katharina Schramm, pp. 1–39. Berghan Books, New York.

Argenti, Nicolas, and Katharina Schramm, eds. 2010 *Remembering Violence: Anthropological Perspectives on Intergenerational Transmission.* Berghan Books, New York.

Bachhuber, Christoph 2009 The Treasure Deposits of Troy: Rethinking Crisis and Agency on the Early Bronze Age Citadel. *Anatolian Studies* 59:1–18.

Bachhuber, Christoph 2012 Bronze Age Cities of the Plains and the Highlands: the Anatolian Plateau. In *Companion to the Archaeology of the Ancient Near East,* edited by Daniel Potts, pp. 575–595. Wiley-Blackwell, Oxford.

In Press *Citadel and Cemetery in Early Bronze Age Anatolia.* Monographs in Mediterranean Archaeology, vol. 15. Equinox, London.

Baines, John 2006 Public Ceremonial Performance in Ancient Egypt: Exclusion and Integration. In *Archaeology of Performance: Theaters of Power, Community and Politics,* edited by T. Inomata and L. S. Coben, pp. 261–302. Altamira, Lanham.

Bellamy, Elizabeth J. 1992 *Translations of Power: Narcissism and the Unconscious in Epic History.* Cornell University Press, Ithaca.

Blanton, Richard, Gary M. Feinman, Stephen A. Kowalewski, and Peter N. Peregrine 1996 A Dual-Processual Theory for the Evolution of Mesoamerican Civilization. *Current Anthropology* 37(1):1–14.

Blegen, Carl W., John Caskey, Marioni Rawson, and Jerome Sperling 1950 *Troy: The First and Second Settlements.* Princeton University Press, Princeton.

Bolender, Douglas J. 2010 Introduction: Towards an Eventful Archaeology. In *Eventful Archaeologies: New Approaches to Social Transformation in the Archaeological Record,* edited by Douglas J. Bolender, pp. 3–16. State University of New York Press, Albany.

Bradley, Richard 1984 *The Social Foundations of Prehistoric Britain: Themes and Variations in the Archaeology of Power.* Longman, London.

Bradley, Richard 1998 *The Significance of Monuments: On the Shaping of Human Experience in Neolithic and Bronze Age Europe.* Routledge, London.

Chapman, John 1990 Social Inequality on Bulgarian Tells and the Varna Problem. In *The Social Archaeology of Houses,* edited by Ross Samson, pp. 49–92. Edinburgh University Press, Edinburgh.

Chapman, John 1997 Places as Time Marks—the Social Construction of Landscapes in Eastern Hungary. In *Semiotics of Landscape: Archaeology of Mind,* edited by George Nash, 137–162. Archaeopress, Oxford.

Connerton, Paul 1989 *How Societies Remember.* Cambridge University Press, Cambridge.

Cultraro, Massimo 1999 Non è tutt'oro quel che luce: per una rilettura del repostiglio di oreficerie di Poliochni. In *Simposio italiano di Studi Egei: dedicato a Luigi Bernabò Brea e Giovanni Pugiliese Carratelli,* edited by V. La Rosa. D. P. Palermo, and L. Vagnetti, pp. 41–52. Scoula Archeologica Italiana di Atene, Rome.

DeMarrais Elizabeth, Luis Jamie Castillo, and Timothy Earle 1996 Ideology, Materialization, and Power Strategies. *Current Anthropology* 37(1):15–31..

Duru, Refik 2006 *Gedikli Karahöyük: Prof. Dr. U. Bahadır Alkım'in yönetiminde 1964–1967 yıllarında yapılan kazıların sonuçları.* Türk Tarih Kurumu Yayınları, Ankara.

Efe, Turan 2006 Report on the 2006 Season of the Küllüoba Excavations. Electronic document, http://kulluobakazisi.bilecik.edu.tr/Dosya/Arsiv/kulluoba%20REPORT,2006.pdf, accessed September 16, 2012.

Erkanal, Hayat 2008 Die neuen Forschungen in Bakla Tepe bei İzmir. In *The Aegean in the Neolithic, Chalcolithic, and the Early Bronze Age, Proceedings of the International Symposium in Urla, October 13th–19th 1997,* edited by Hayat Erkanal, Harald Hauptmann, Vasıf Şahoğlu and Rıza Tuncel, pp. 165–177. Ankara University Press, Ankara.

Fidan, Erkan 2012 Küllüoba İlk Tunç Çağı Mimarisi. *MASROP/ E-Dergi* 7:1–44.

Fisher, Kevin D. 2009 Elite place-Making and Social Interaction in the Late Cypriot Bronze Age. *Journal of Mediterranean Archaeology* 22(2):183–209.

Forty, Adrian 1999 Introduction. In *The Art of Forgetting,* edited by Adrian Forty and Susanne Küchler, pp. 1–18. Berg, New York.

Frangipane, Marcella 2001 The Transition Between Two Opposing Forms of Power at Arslantepe (Malatya) at the Beginning of the Third Millennium. *Türkiye Bilimler Akademisi* 4:1–24.

Fuller, Dorian Q. and Michael Rowlands 2011 Ingestion and Food Technologies: Maintaining Differences over the Long-Term. In *Interweaving Worlds: Systemic Interactions In Eurasia, 7th to 1st Millennia BC,* edited by T. Wilkinson, S. Sherratt, and J. Bennet, pp. 37–60. Oxbow, Oxford.

Gilan, Amir 2008 Hittite Ethnicity? Constructions of Identity in Hittite Literature. In *Hittites, Greeks, and their Neighbours. Proceedings of an International Conference on Cross-Cultural Interaction, September 17–19, Emory University, Atlanta, GA,* edited by Billie Jean Collins, Maria R. Bachvarova, and Ian C. Rutherford, pp. 107–116. Oxbow, Oxford.

Glatz, Claudia 2009 Empire as Network: Spheres of Material Interaction in Late Bronze Age Anatolia. *Journal of Anthropological Archaeology* 28:127–141.

Gottschall, Jonathan 2008 *The Rape of Troy: Evolution, Violence, and the World of Homer.* Cambridge University Press, Cambridge.

Götze, Alfred 1902 Die Kleingeräte aus Metall, Stein, Thon und ähnliche Stoffen. In *Troia und Ilion: Ergebnisse der Ausgrabungen in den vorhistorischen und historischen Schichten von Ilion,* edited by Wilhelm Dörpfeld, pp. 320–343. Beck and Barth, Athens.

Hodder, Ian 2005 Memory. In *Çatalhöyük Perspectives: Reports from the 1995–99 Seasons,* edited by Ian Hodder, pp. 183–195. British Institute at Ankara, Cambridge: McDonald Institute Monographs, London.

Inomata, Takeshi, and Lawrence S. Coben 2006 Overture: An Invitation to the Archaeological Theater. In *Archaeology of Performance: Theaters of Power, Community, and Politics,* edited by Takeshi Inomata and Lawrence S. Coben, 11–44. AltaMira, Lanham.

Kolb, Michael J. 1994 Monumentality and the Rise of Religious Authority on Precontact Hawai'i. *Current Anthropology* 34:521–547.

Kolb, Michael J. 2005 The Genesis of Monuments among the Mediterranean Islands. In *The Archaeology of Mediterranean Prehistory,* edited by Emma Blake and A. Bernard Knapp, 77–106. Blackwell, Oxford.

Knapp, A. Bernard 2008 *Prehistoric and Protohistoric Cyprus: Identity, Insularity and Connectivity.* Oxford University Press, Oxford.

Korfmann, Manfred 2001 Troia als Drehschiebe des Handels im 2. und 3. vorchristlichen Jahrtausend. In *Troia: Traum und Wirklichkeit,* edited by Joachim Latcaz, Peter Blome, Jochen Luckhard, Horst Brunner, and Manfred Korfmann, pp. 355–372. Theiss, Stuttgart.

Lefebvre, Henri 1991 *The Production of Space.* Translated by D. Nicholson-Smith. Blackwell Oxford.

Omura, Sachihiro 2005 Preliminary Report on the 19th Excavation at Kaman-Kalehöyük. *Anatolian Archaeological Studies: Kaman-Kalehöyük* 14:1–36.

Otten, Heinrich 1981 *Die Apologie Hattusilis III. Das Bild der Überlieferung.* Harrasowitz, Wiesbaden.

Özgüç, Tahsin 1999 *Kültepe Kaniš/Neša Sarayları ve Mabetleri/The Palaces and Temples of Kültepe-Kaniš/Neša.* Türk Tarih Kurumu Basımevi, Ankara.

Pauketat, Timothy 2000 The Tragedy of the Commoners. In *Agency in Archaeology,* edited by M.-A. Dobres and J. Robb, pp. 113–129. Routledge, London, New York.

Renfrew, Colin 1994 The Archaeology of Religion. In *The Ancient Mind: Elements of Cognitive Archaeology,* edited by C. Renfrew and E. B. W. Zubrow, pp. 47–54. Cambridge University Press, Cambridge.

Rowlands, Michael 1993 The Role of Memory in the Transmission of Culture. *World Archaeology* 25(2):141–51.

Sazcı, Göksel 2005 Troia I–III, die Maritime Troia-Kultur und Troia IV–V, die Anatolische Troia-Kultur: eine Untersuchung der Funde und Befunde im Mittleren Schliemanngraben. *Studia Troica* 15:35–98.

Schirmer, Wulf 2002 Stadt, Palast, Tempel: Charakteristika hethitischer Architeketur im 2. Und 1.Jahrtausend v. Chr. In *Die Hethiter und ihr Reich: das Volk der 1000 Götter,* edited by Tahsin Özgüç, Jutta Frings, Helga Willinghöfer, Uta Hasekamp, and Ayse Baykal-Seeher, pp. 204–217. Theiss, Stuttgart.

Schliemann, Heinrich 1874 *Trojanische Alterthümer, Bericht über die Ausgrabungen in Troja.* F. A. Brockhaus, Leipzig. 1880 *Ilios: The City and Country of the Trojans.* J. Murray, London.

Schwartz, Benjamin 1947 A Hittite Ritual Text *(KUB 29.1 = 1780/c). Orientalia* 16:23–55.

Sewell, William H. 2005 *Logics of History: Social Theory and Social Transformation.* University of Chicago Press, Chicago.

Stein, Gil 1998 1996 Excavations at Hacınebi Tepe. *Kazı Sonuçları Toplantısı* 20(1):179–208.

Şahoğlu, Vasıf 2008 New Evidence for the Relations between the Izmir Region, the Cyclades, and the Greek Mainland during the Third Millennium BC. In *The Aegean in the Neolithic, Chalcolithic, and the Early Bronze Age, Proceedings of the International Symposium in Urla,*

October 13th–19th 1997, edited by H. Erkanal, H. Hauptmann, V. Şahoğlu and R. Tuncel, pp. 483–502. Ankara University Press, Ankara.

Topbaş, Ahmet, Turan Efe, and Ahmet İlaslı 1998 Salvage Excavations of the Afyon Archaeaological Museum *Anatolia Antiqua*: 6:21–94.

Treister, Mikhail 1996 The Trojan Treasures: Description, Chronology, Historical Context. In *The Gold of Troy: Searching for Homer's Fabled City,* edited by Irina Antonova, Vladimir Tolstikov, Mikhail Treister, and Donald Easton, pp. 197–234. H. N. Abrams, New York.

Trigger, Bruce 1990 Monumental Architecture: A Thermodynamic Explanation of Symbolic Behaviour. *World Archaeology* 22:119–131.

Tumarkin, Maria 2005 *Traumascapes.* Melbourne University Press, Melbourne.

Türkteki, Murat 2012 Batı ve Orta Anadolu'da Çark Yapımı Çanak Çömleğin Ortaya Çıkışı ve Yayılımı. *MASROP/E-Dergi* 7:45–111.

Ünlüsoy, Sinan 2010 *Die Stratigraphie der Burg von Troia II.* PhD dissertation, University of Tübingen, published online at: http://tobias-lib.uni-tuebingen.de/volltexte/2010/4509/.

Veenhof, Klaas.R. 2008 The Old Assyrian Period. In *Mesopotamia: The Old Assyrian Period,* edited by M. Wäfler, pp. 13–266. Academic Press, Fribourg.

Weeden, Mark 2012 *Hittite Logograms and Hittite Scholarship.* Studien zu den Boğazköy Texten 54. Harrasowitz Verlag, Wiesbaden.

Weiss, H., and L. Ristvet 2010 Introduction. In *The Royal Archives from Tell Leilan: Old Babylonian Letters and Treaties from the Eastern Lower Town Palace,* authored by Jesper Eidem, pp. xi–xlvii. Yale University Press, New Haven.

Wilkinson, Tony J. 2003 *Archaeological Landscapes of the Near East.* University of Arizona Press, Tucson.

Yampolsky, Mikhail 1995 In the Shadow of Monuments: Notes on Iconoclasm and Time. *Soviet Hieroglyphics: Visual Culture in Late Twentieth Century Russia,* edited by Nancy Condee, pp. 93–112. Indiana University Press, Bloomington.

Zimmermann, Thomas 2006 Bottles and Netbags. Some Additional Notes on the Article About "Syrian Bottles" in *Anatolica* 31, 2005. *Anatolica* 32:229–232.

CHAPTER FIFTEEN

The Phenomenon of Residential Cities and City Foundations in the Ancient Near East

Common Idea or Individual Cases?

Mirko Novák

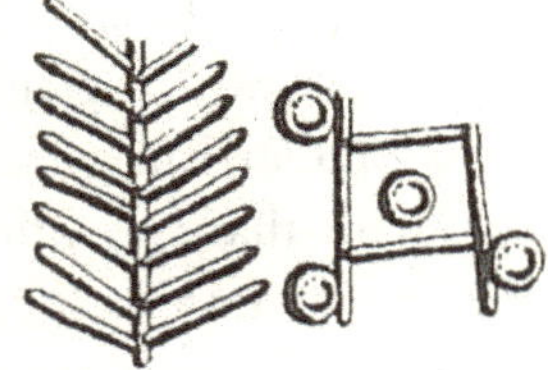

Abstract *In the history of the Ancient Near East a considerable number of residential cities were built, either as a foundation ex nihilo on virgin soil or as the result of a massive transformation of an already existing town. Created as the center of an empire, every residential city constituted a symbol of political, economic, and ideological power. Several periods of ambitious building programs of residential cities can be identified: one certain peak was the Late Bronze Age (ca. 1550–1200 B.C.) with almost contemporary foundations in Babylonia, Assyria, Elam, Mittani, Hatti, and Egypt. Another peak took place in the Iron Age (ca. 1200–600 B.C.), with that period's shift of the region's political center of the Assyrian Empire. But the phenomenon of major urban building projects in the Near East continued even until the medieval Islamic period. Determining the factors that inspired these urban projects and their ideological backgrounds is not easy: each case has to be examined on an individual basis. It seems that the Late Bronze Age examples were the result of competition between territorial empires, whereas the Iron Age examples were an expression of exclusivity and claim for universal power.*

If one approaches the question of what monumentality is and how it finds its physical expression, there is hardly any doubt that the foundation of a new or the recreation of an already existing city requires a huge effort in labor and acquisition of enormous economic resources and thus produces a monument, "an object that is generally huge in size, that commemorates or memorializes, that is historically significant, and that has longevity" (Osborne *infra*). All people involved in a project such as building or reforming a complete city—either as workmen, architects, and artisans, or as subjects who were obliged to pay for the labor, or as attending visitors of foreign citizenship—recognized that the political will of the ruling system was able to plan, organize, and conduct it. Hence, the building process and its result were easily recognizable as a symbol of political, social, and economic power. If we follow Osborne's introductory remarks on the relationship of monument and monumentality as similar to form and meaning, we have to reconsider the perception of this newly built city as a monument by its contemporary and later inhabitants: Did it function as a (cosmological or any other kind of) symbol? Did it inhere and transpond a social memory? Did it fulfill all the other possible criteria for monumentality?

Let us start with a very obvious and simple matter: the name of the city. In almost all cases under discussion here we deal with politically chosen toponyms, which guaranteed either the remembrance of the city's founder (as in the cases of Dūr-Kurigalzu, Āl-Untaš-napirīša, Pi-Ramesses, Dūr-Šarrukēn) or of a religious program that was promoted (as in the cases of Akhet-Aten or Tarḫuntašša). This was the case at least as long as the city did exist and was not renamed (Novák 1999:381–384).[1] However, expressing and transmitting a certain political or social message by a city works even on a much higher and more sophisticated level than just its toponym: by the spatial organization of the city, its layout, its outer shape, and its inner structure.

Every urban settlement is a reflection on the society that created it (Novák 1999; Pezzoli-Olgiati 2002; Harmanşah 2013; Liverani 2013; Wirth 2000). The outer shape may follow either the morphology of the natural landscape or any geometrical patterns. The latter could be the reflection of a cosmological idea, a symbol of the image of the world. This is the case with some historical circular or rectangular cities, which were supposed to represent the *axis mundi*.[2] The alignment of the streets, their breadth and decoration were not only the result of traffic requirements but also of political or religious expressions, being manifested by ceremonies or processions. The position of the main architectural elements of the city, either palaces or temples or other features within the urban organism, reflected the ideological system, maintained by their visibility or hiddenness for every visitor or inhabitant moving inside the city. Was the temple in the center of the city or at its periphery? Was the street system oriented toward a temple, a citadel, or a palace? What was the building that was the focus of the perception of the urban inhabitants in their daily life? A medieval European town, for example, was centered on the main church or cathedral. In contrast, the baroque city, founded in the spirit of absolutism, was centered on the royal palace. Whether the layout of the city is the result of a long-time evolution or of a punctual foundation process, it is always a symbol of a political and socioeconomic system. Social dynamics may transform the original layout and structures and thus also the original semiotic message. However, this process takes a long time and huge efforts.[3]

Following these thoughts, we can conclude that both the building process of a city and the final monument itself constitute political messages that perpetuated after the generation of the founders, irrespective of all later modifications. Hence, we can ascribe to each foundation of a city an inherent monumentality, either a performative one, lasting only during the building activities, or a perceptional one in the time of the city's existence.

This is especially the case with so-called residential cities, a phenomenon that has appeared frequently in human history all over the world. Creating a residential city, including the building activities involved, demonstrates in the highest degree the will and ability of a ruling class to initiate and fulfill such a huge project. The residential city is thus a "monument of power" and also the reflection of a certain ideology. Hence, there is hardly any need to discuss *whether* a residential city represents and expresses monumentality. Instead, research questions should address *how* it did it: What were the reasons for the creation of specific cities? Which ideology was expressed? Was there a general idea behind the concept of all residential cities, or does each known example indeed require individual explanations?

This is not the place to deal with all the examples attested in ancient history. Instead, we will focus on the Ancient Near East, where the first creations of residential cities are attested. Two periods are of particular interest here. First, the Late Bronze Age (ca. 1500–1200 B.C.), in which residential cities appear almost contemporary and suddenly in every major territorial state of that time, namely, Babylonia, Elam, Assyria, Mittani, the Hittite Empire, and Egypt. And second, the Iron Age (ca. 1200–600 B.C.), in which this phenomenon is almost exclusively restricted to Assyria, with only very few exceptions outside of this region. Both periods will be examined briefly to get an impression on how the crucial question—common idea or individual causes?—might be answered. But first we have to determine how a residential city can be defined.

Capital and Residential Cities

The distinction between a capital and a residential city is difficult and, of course, somewhat artificial: almost every capital city hosts the residence of a ruler or government, and a residential city could easily, and sometimes also quickly, be transformed into a real capital. The crucial difference between both types of cities is its primary function, as function is the basis of urban classifications; although every city fulfils a number of purposes, this defines its attribution to a special "ideal type" of a city (Novák 1999:52–57). Whereas a true capital represents the economic, administrative, political, religious, and cultural center of its political entity, the main characteristic of a residential city is the domination of the representational, administrative, and political functions (Liverani 2013; Novák 1999:56f.). Moreover, the economic dependency of all inhabitants of a residential city is decisive: the palace forms the economic basis of nearly all of its inhabitants, while alternative factors and autonomous structures do not exist on any larger scale (Braunfels 1976:155). Thus, there are always cities with important economic or religious, most often also cultural, functions existing apart from the residential cities, and in many cases (but not necessarily) they are identical with the capital. However, we have to keep in mind that the type of the "residential city" is still a subjective construction, since the distinguishing features between it and a "capital" are fluid.

The arrangement of any urban settlement depends on socioecological factors, climatic conditions, geomorphological assumptions about the site, and local building traditions. Furthermore, political concepts influence the external shape and internal structure of a city. This last factor is disproportionately present in the formation of a residential city because of its special economic background and its function as a symbol of the ruling system.

This type of city can only be founded in a social context characterized by the strong ideological and economic position of the king (or his substitutes) as an institution. In almost all cases, a residential city is either a creation ex nihilo or, at least, a large-scaled transformation of an existing (but in most cases rather unimportant) town into the residence of the king. A basic prerequisite for its existence is the significant economic power of the responsible institution. Such economic might can only be generated by a large territorial state, hardly ever by a small entity such as a city-state or a moderate principality. Hence, the construction and the existence of a residential city can be seen as a physical expression of the ideologically based and economically manifested power and self-understanding of a king, a ruling class, or a specific political system (even if it has a democratic constitution). Well-known examples in history are Constantinople, Versailles, Potsdam, or Washington, D.C. Some of them gained the position of a real capital, while others remained residential cities, or were abandoned, or suffered substantially from the collapse and change of the political system. Due to the efforts undertaken to construct a residential city, the labor required and the dimensions created, there is no question whether it did express monumentality or not; it is a monument par excellence.

THE FIRST RESIDENTIAL CITY IN THE THIRD MILLENNIUM B.C.

Hardly anything is known of the earliest intentionally built residential city of the Near East: Agade. It was the center of the first so-called "world empire" of the Akkadian dynasty (around 2200–2050 B.C.; Sallaberger and Westenholz 1999). Both empire and city were founded by the charismatic king Sargon, a *homo novus* who subjugated the Sumerian city-states in the southern and Semitic polities in Upper Mesopotamia (Sallaberger 2004, 2012). He raided the northern Levant, southern Anatolia, and western Iran. His successors even expanded the empire to the southern Gulf region and far into the countries on the Anatolian and Iranian plateaus.

The designation of Agade as residential city follows the premise that the economic base of this city type is exclusively the royal court. Since the city did not exist before Sargon, it was obviously his foundation; and since it continued to exist long after the collapse of the Akkad Empire, but never again gained any economic or political significance, it was obviously lacking any independent economic resources. Thus, its glorious period was exclusively the result of the political will and economic power of an empire, which made it its political seat. The religious center of Babylonia, however, remained even during the Akkad dynasty in Nippur.

The reasons for the foundation of Agade are obscure. Unfortunately, the city has never been excavated or even identified. Nevertheless, there are indications concerning its approximate location. Several scholars have argued that the city must have been situated along the middle Tigris Valley, somewhere upstream of Baghdad (Wall-Romana 1990). J. Reade (2002) has furthermore argued that it is most probably buried under the Abbasid residential city of Samarra, halfway between Baghdad and Ashur.

Since we know that the city already existed before the empire was established, when Sargon was still struggling with other Sumerian city-states, it was at the beginning not the result or expression of imperial power. It seems much more likely that it owed its existence to the circumstances under which Sargon and his people gained power. There is evidence that the "Akkadians," or at least their troops, had a nomadic or semi-nomadic background. As depictions on monuments and cylinder seals indicate, their warfare tactics differed completely from those of the soldiers of the Sumerian city-states: contrary to the (urban) tactic of heavy phalanx infantry equipped with long spears and big shields, the Akkadians fought in light and more mobile infantries with bow and arrow (Sallaberger and Westenholz 1999:65–68). This tactic was presumably developed and preferred by rural or nomadic populations. Hence, the area in which Sargon could most successfully establish his power was outside the urban landscapes of the alluvial plain of Babylonia with its huge cities. The core of Akkadian territory seems to have been farther upstream the Tigris, outside the dry farming belt of Upper Mesopotamia but also outside the alluvium, where the narrow river valley cuts deeply into the Northern Mesopotamian plateau. Here, no huge urban entity could grow, depending only on the resources of its agricultural hinterland. Only small towns existed in the river valley and the plateau was populated by nomadic and semi-nomadic tribes and pastoralists.

Although Sargon adopted the prestigious and historic title "King of Kiš," named after the traditional urban center of northern Babylonia, he decided to keep his seat at Agade and not to move it to Kiš or any other major city. Instead, he transformed Agade into a flourishing metropolis, where the resources to run the city, obtained by receiving tribute and booty, were concentrated: "He moored the ships of Meluhha [Indus valley], Magan [Oman and/or Baluchistan] and Dilmun [Bahrain] at the quay of Agade" (Frayne 1993:28; Sargon E2.1.1.11, 9–13). Thus, the city must have been considerably wealthy. Contemporary and later inscriptions suggest the city was fortified, had a palace built by Sargon himself, and two major temples, dedicated to the tutelary goddess Ištar and Abā respectively (for the summary, see Novák 1999:83–84).

Agade, which was the political center of an empire for three generations and continued as the center of a reduced political entity for two more, came to an unfortunate end. It was seized and raided first by the Gutians and finally by the Elamites under their king Kutik-Inšušinak. Although the city was not abandoned completely—it is still attested in written sources in the first millennium B.C.—it never regained any larger political importance than a purely symbolic one (McEwan 1980). This again indicates that Agade did not have a rich natural hinterland, which allowed for independent prosperity without being supported by a large political power.

The experience of a newly founded residential city was not repeated in Mesopotamia until the middle of the second millennium B.C.[4] Hence, the "project" of Agade was exceptional and did not create a pattern for the following dynasties.

The Second Millennium B.C.: Competing Empires and Residential Cities

The Late Bronze Age was a period of competing empires, whose relationships were characterized by military conflicts, political tensions, intensive diplomatic correspondences and economic exchange, friendly relationships, and dynastic marriages (Liverani 2001). For the first time, a close international network existed, covering the entire Near East from Egypt to Iran, and Anatolia to Mesopotamia. The political landscape saw the dominating powers Egypt (New Kingdom), Hatti, Mittani, Assyria, Babylonia, and Elam, and a number of vassal kingdoms in between (Figure 15.1). In the context of this situation, the foundation of several residential cities took place, starting in Mesopotamia by two newly established dynasties (Figure 15.2).

The Fifteenth Century B.C.: Kassite Babylonia (Dūr-Kurigalzu) and the Mittani Empire (Waššukanni and Tā'idu)

The foundation of the earliest examples of residential cities in the second millennium B.C. in the Near East is closely connected with two dynasties that both derived from mercenaries: the Kassites and the Mittani.

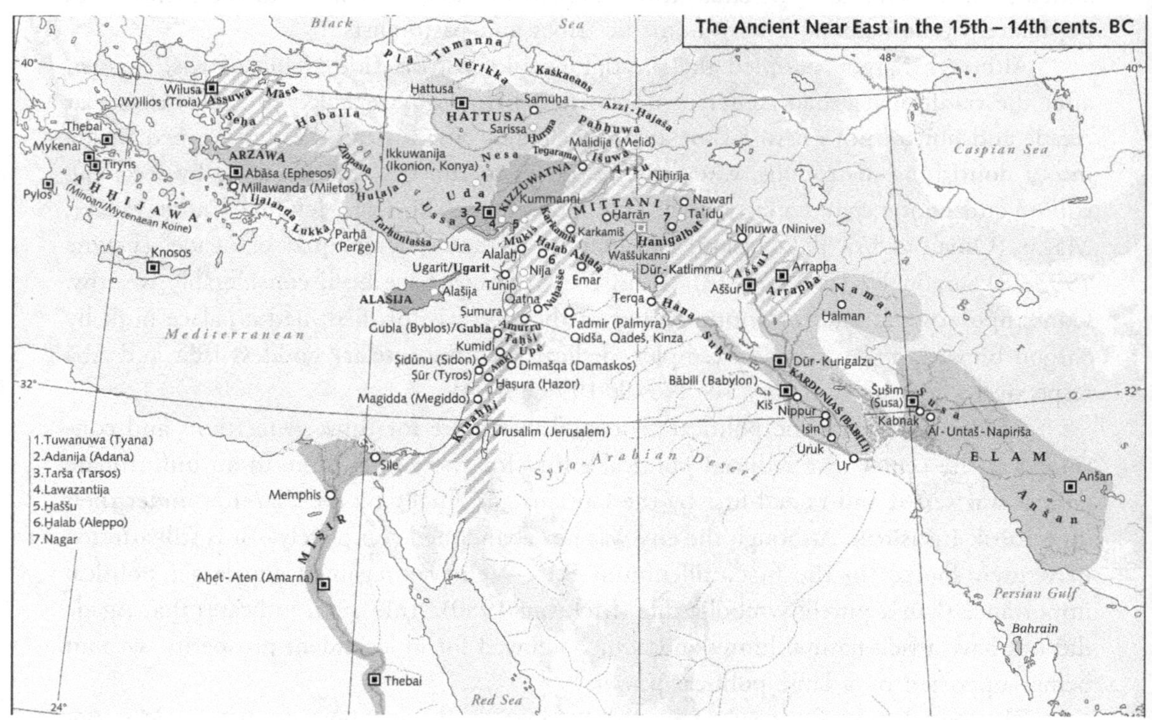

FIGURE 15.1 Map showing the political situation in the Late Bronze Age (from: A. Wittke et al., eds., "Historical Atlas of the Ancient World" (Leiden: 2009), originally "Historischer Atlas der Antiken Welt," Supplement of "Der Neue Pauly."

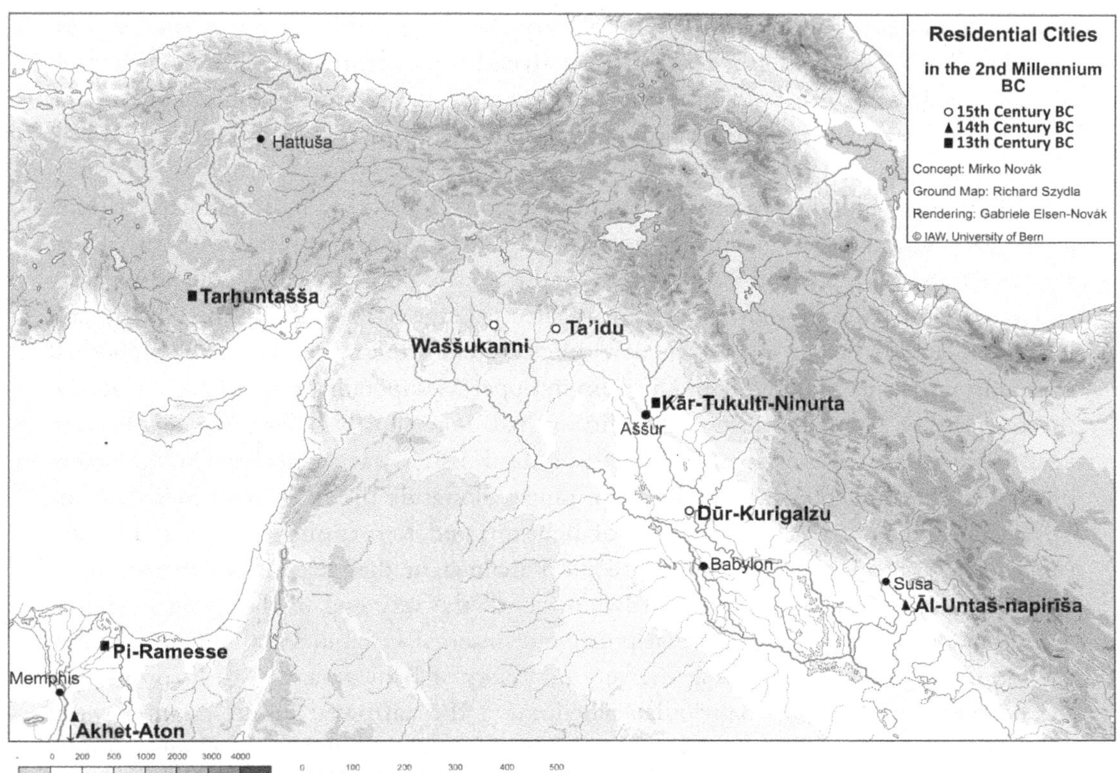

FIGURE 15.2 Map showing the Late Bronze Age residential cities in the Near East.

The origin of the Kassite dynasty goes back to the Old Babylonian Period when mercenaries, coming from the Zagros ranges or beyond, were taken into the service of the kings of the First Dynasty of Babylon (von Koppen 2010). Kassite soldiers from several tribes infiltrated Babylonia, either summoned by the rulers of the Babylonian kingdom themselves or attracted by the success and income of their tribesmen in Babylonia. After building a strong position in the Babylonian military during the last generations of the Old Babylonian period, they were the benefiters of the Hittite raid that led to the sack of Babylon in 1522 B.C. (date after Mebert 2010) and thus terminated Hammurapi's ruling dynasty. The role of the Kassites at this crucial point of Babylonian history is still unclear. Either they were not able to protect their overlords against the Hittites or they were not willing to do so. Probably they are even to be seen as secret supporters of the Hittites. Eventually, they gained power in Babylon after the retreat of the aggressors. For the coming four centuries, a Kassite dynasty ruled over Babylonia.

There are many indications that support identifying of Babylon as the continuing and unchallenged cultural and economic capital of Babylonia. Even more, there was an ongoing and irreversible shift of the religious center of the country from Nippur, seat of Ellil, to Babylon, seat of the new national god Marduk, during the Kassite period. Nonetheless, a new city was founded by king Kurigalzu I in the last decade of the fifteenth century B.C., approximately one century after his predecessor Agum took control over Babylonia and established the Kassite dynasty. He named the city after himself "Dūr-Kurigalzu" ("stronghold of Kurigalzu"). Due to the enormous dimensions of the city and the main palace, it was a prominent, if not the primary, seat of kingship (Novák 1999:85–91; Clayden in print).

To understand the reasons for the foundation of the city, it is necessary to look at the geopolitical situation during the early reign of the Kassites: The southern part of Babylonia up to Nippur had long been under the control of the so-called Sealand Dynasty and was conquered only shortly before Kurigalzu I. Large parts of the country might still have been latently hostile toward the new ruling caste. Furthermore, the newly established and constantly expanding Mittani kingdom in upper Mesopotamia might have threatened the integrity of Babylonia just as the Hittites had done shortly before. We also have to keep in mind that the original homeland of the Kassites was somewhere in the region of, or even beyond, the Zagros Mountain ranges alongside the main road following the Diyala river upstream in the direction of Behistun and Kermanshah (Fuchs 2011:236). Obviously, large numbers of Kassite people remained in that region, which continued to be under the control of Kassite Babylonia until the very end of the dynasty. Hence, a combination of aspects of external policy and internal instabilities might have caused the foundation of a stronghold at the very periphery of Babylonia: due to its position at the northern fringe of the Babylonian alluvium, at the narrowest funnel point between Tigris and Euphrates, Dūr-Kurigalzu was both a watchtower and a launching point of quick raids to the north against Mittani. In case of internal rebellions within Babylonia there was a short distance to the Kassite homeland in the Zagros, either to escape or to get reinforcements. The foundation may thus have been a result of relative regional instability, paired with the wish to express power and offensive abilities by the new rulers. Religious reasons may also have played a role: at the time in which Marduk's move to the top of the pantheon was still fresh and ongoing, the new city was dedicated to Ellil, probably to offer a kind of compromise.

The huge city stretched alongside a canal system—probably a watercourse connecting the Euphrates and Tigris rivers—and was situated on top of a limestone ridge. This caused a relatively narrow (less than 2 km) and extremely long (more than 5 km) shape of the overall urban layout. The monumentality of the city itself and its public buildings, the central temple area (Figure 15.3) with the ziqqurat (Figure 15.4) and the huge royal palace in particular, illustrated in impressive manner the Kassite claim of power in Babylonia.

Almost contemporary to the Kassites in Babylonia, the Mittani dynasty gained power in upper Mesopotamia (van Koppen 2004). They were most likely descendants of mercenaries and deportees brought from the Zagros region or western Iran to upper Mesopotamia by the Assyrians already in the seventeenth century B.C. Shortly after they established an independent kingdom, which existed from the late sixteenth until the middle of the fourteenth century B.C. and expanded from the Mediterranean coast and the northern Levant in the west to the Zagros Mountain ranges in the east. Since

FIGURE 15.3 Reconstructed temples in the center of Dūr-Kurigalzu (photo by the author).

FIGURE 15.4 Remains of the *ziqqurat* of Dūr-Kurigalzu (photo by the author).

the majority of their subjects were Hurrians, their Hittite opponents designated them as "Kings of the Hurrians" (Wilhelm 1982:29ff.). Whether or not the Mittani dynasty itself was of Hurrian or Indo-Aryan origin (as their throne-names seem to indicate) cannot be decided and is probably not important, since their members were almost completely "Hurrianized." In the early time of their reign, the heartland of the kingdom was widely de-urbanized, with the exception of their two residential cities, Waššukanni and Tāʾidu, and a moderate number of smaller towns (Novák 2013). It is remarkable that neither Waššukanni nor Tāʾidu was of any significant political importance during the preceding Old Babylonian period. Both cities were clearly overshadowed by neighboring—and at that time already vanished—cities such as, for example, Šeḫna/Šubat-Enlil. Why the new dynasty chose two less important towns for their main residences cannot be determined so far. However, it may have been the political decision of a foreign military caste, which ruled over a heterogeneous and presumably at least partly hostile population.

Little is known about the layout of the first residential city, Waššukanni. Even its precise location is not yet defined beyond doubt, although there are good reasons to identify it with modern Tall Faharīya at the source of the Ḫābūr river (Novák 2013:346). As in the case of Agade, it was of moderate significance before and again after the period of the Mittani Empire, hence indicating a strong economic dependency of the city's fate from the royal court. The other residential city, Tāʾidu, is identical with modern Tall al-Ḥamidīya. The site covered an area of 250 ha *intra muros,* if the reconstruction of the excavators is correct (Kaelin 2013; Wäfler 2003). The nearly oval city was divided into two parts by the course of the Ġaġġaġ, the main tributary of the Ḫābūr (Figure 15.5). The old settlement mound, located slightly south of the city center, was transformed into a 20 ha large citadel with the main buildings placed upon an artificial terrace (Figure 15.6). The central part of the citadel was occupied by a five-step mudbrick-terrace with a monumental staircase, reaching from the lowest terrace to the uppermost one. Only small portions of the building, which had once stood on top of the terrace, have survived. Contrary to the excavators' assumption that the building was the "Central Palace," it rather represents the remains of the main temple of the city, constructed as a *ziqqurat,* thus following a clear southern Mesopotamian pattern (Novák 2013:353). The neighboring "Southwestern Palace" was most likely the main palace.

Summing up the information available, it seems as if the foundations of the earliest residential cities of the second half of the second millennium B.C. in Babylonia and upper Mesopotamia were initiated by two new dynasties, both of them offspring of former mercenaries, who came to power under obscure circumstances. Military and strategic aspects may have been the dominant factors leading to the foundation of these new residences, reflecting both a still-fragile internal and an unsecure external situation. However, these initial considerations surely became obsolete within a short period of time after the foundation of the cities, leaving the notion of a residential city as an expression and demonstration of political power. This idea even emerged far beyond the limits of Mesopotamia proper.

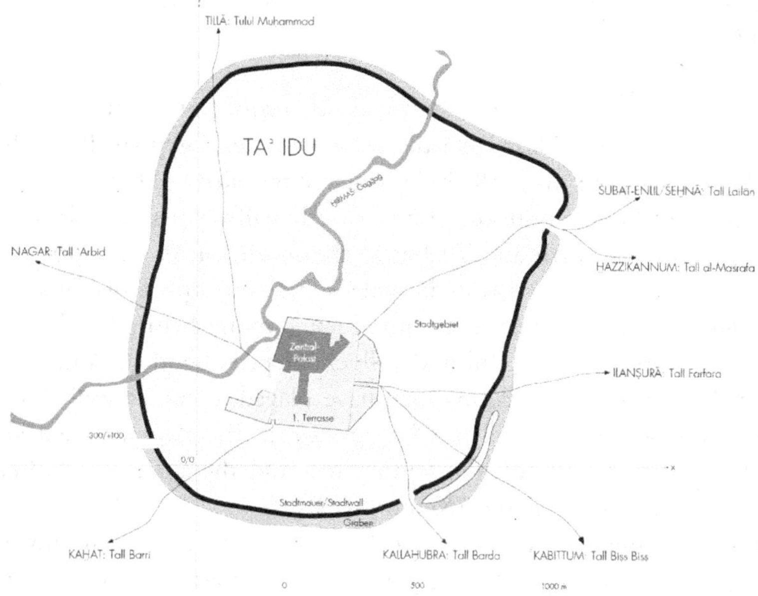

FIGURE 15.5 City plan of Ta'idu (from Kaelin 2013:185, Fig. 3).

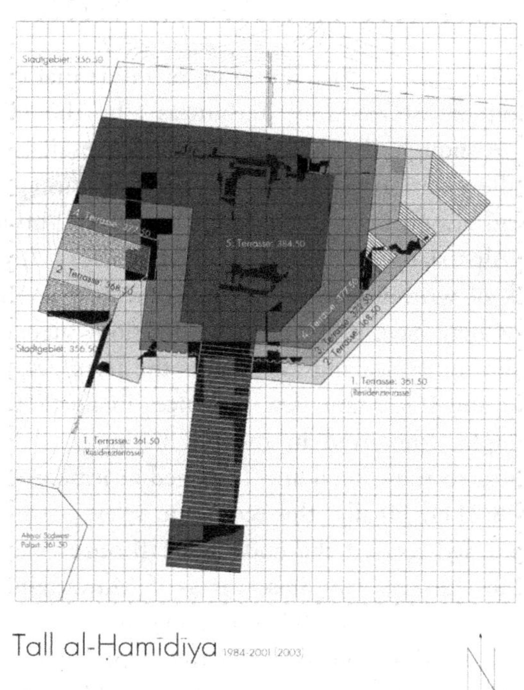

FIGURE 15.6 Ta'idu, Central Building (from Kaelin 2013:187, Fig. 4).

THE FOURTEENTH CENTURY B.C.: ELAM (ĀL-UNTAŠ-NAPIRIŠA) AND EGYPT (AKHETATON)

Within a relatively short period in the fourteenth century, two more residential cities were founded in the Ancient Near East: the New Kingdom Egyptian Pharaoh Akhenaten (Eighteenth Dynasty, ca. 1356–1339) built a new city called "Akhetaten" ("The Horizon of the [Sun-God] Aten") on virgin soil, almost exactly halfway between the two traditional capitals, Memphis in the north and Thebes in the south. In his inscriptions, Akhenaten states that the new foundation was dedicated to the worship of his favorite god Aten. This is considered an early attempt at introducing monotheism by the pharaoh, but also as a way to escape the powerful and influential priesthood of Amun-Râ at Thebes (Kemp 2012). However, other reasons may have played a role as well, for instance, to restore the balance between Upper and Lower Egypt. The city extended alongside the right bank of the Nile River, with the temple area and the adjacent administrative and representational palaces in its center (Kemp 2012).

Almost contemporary to Akhetaten, another residential city was founded in Elam by king Untaš-napiriša (ca. 1340–1300 B.C.), who named it after himself Āl-Untaš-napiriša ("City of Untaš-napiriša") (cf. Potts this volume).

THE THIRTEENTH CENTURY B.C.: HATTI (TARḪUNTAŠŠA), EGYPT (PI-RAMESSES), AND ASSYRIA (KĀR-TUKULTĪ-NINURTA)

The thirteenth century B.C. saw further founding of residential cities. The first of them was Tarḫuntašša ("[City] of [Storm-God] Tarḫunzas") by the Hittite king Muwattalli II (1295–1272 B.C.). Although the Hittite kings had residences in several cities of the Hittite heartland, the position of Hattuša as the religious, political, and economic capital of the empire had always been unchallenged until the foundation of Tarḫuntašša (Doğan-Alparslan and Alparslan 2011). The motivations for Muwattalli's move remain obscure due to the lack of written sources on the subject. It seems as if a combination of several considerations may have influenced the decision, such as the rapid expansion of the empire toward the south, leaving Hattuša at the northern periphery and situated far from the prosperous and important new provinces in northern Syria. Moreover, the tribes of the Kaška people, who lived in the mountainous regions north of Hattuša, caused a permanent threat to the capital and managed at least twice to plunder it (Bryce 2005:223; Klengel 1998:211). Finally, the economic relevance of Hattuša and its hinterland may have diminished toward the end of the Bronze Age. Since all the gods of the old capital moved to the new city, it seems as if Muwattalli planned a permanent and irreversible shift of the capital to the south. Hattuša was left in the hands of his younger brother Hattušili II (III) as governor of the "Upper Lands." It was the death of Muwattalli and Hattušili's coup d'état against his nephew, Muwattalli's son and legitimate heir Urhi-Teššup, that enabled the reestablishment of Hattuša as capital. Tarḫuntašša has not yet been located. Hence, nothing is known about its layout and urban structure. Even its precise location can only approximately be determined.

Slightly better known is Pi-Ramesses ("House of Ramesses"), the residential city of Muwattalli's counterpart in the famous battle of Qadesh, Ramesses II (1279–13 B.C.). It is situated near Avaris, the former capital of the Hyksos, at the eastern fringe of Lower Egypt, that is to say, the Nile Delta (Pusch 2004). It is obvious that strategic considerations stood behind the pharaoh's decision to move the court here. The city was still situated within Egypt proper, but very close to the main road to the Near Eastern provinces of the Egyptians, which were threatened by the Hittites.

The "last actor in the concert of main powers" was Assyria. Dominated by Mittani and Babylonia during the sixteenth, fifteenth, and early fourteenth centuries, it gained independence in the middle of the fourteenth century under king Assur–uballit I (1353–1318 B.C.). Within the time span of a few generations it not only expanded its territory drastically, but also incorporated the Mittani heartland and replaced it as the dominant power in Upper Mesopotamia. Moreover, the Assyrians could defeat the Hittites in the battle of Nihriya as well as the Babylonians under the Kassite king Kaštiliaš IV. This enemy was caught alive by the Assyrian king Tukulti-Ninurta I (1233–1197 B.C.), an enormously prestigious success. It is thus not surprising that this victory was celebrated in many ways, including the composition of an epic about Tukulti-Ninurta. Masses of Kassites were deported and settled in Assyria. For a short period—and for the first time in history—Babylonia was ruled by an Assyrian king. At the peak of its power, Assyria had to realize that it was the only main power in this international concert lacking a really representative capital. Ashur, the birthplace and religious heart of the kingdom, seat of the national god and home of the Assyrian elite, was a small and moderate town compared to even second-class cities in Babylonia, Elam, or Egypt. Its position on the western bank of the Tigris River close to the borderline of the dry-farming region of upper Mesopotamia made urban expansion almost impossible. Furthermore, within the city the king was only the high priest and physical substitute of the tutelary god, who was considered the real king of the city. All this led the victorious Tukulti-Ninurta, now the most powerful king of the Near East, to found a new residential city as the seat of his kingdom and expression of power. The city was built slightly north of Ashur on the opposite bank of the Tigris River and named after him, "Kār-Tukulti-Ninurta," the "Harbor of Tukulti-Ninurta" (Gilibert 2008).

Its layout comprised elements of the city of Ashur, but combined them with some urban innovations, including a fortified citadel. Hence, Kār-Tukulti-Ninurta marked a new step in the development of Assyrian town planning (Novák 2004). However, its size and the monumentality of its public buildings enabled it to compete with the residential cities of the other Near Eastern powers.

Late Bronze Age Residential Cities: An Expression of Competition?

As demonstrated above, the phenomenon of newly founded residential cities appeared during the period of the fifteenth to the thirteenth centuries B.C. in all empires of the Ancient Near East. In contrast, we lack any attestation for such foundations in smaller kingdoms or vassal states, making it a clear characteristic trait of large-scale territorial dominions.

A detailed analysis of each case demonstrates that internal particular motivations for the creation of residential cities existed, they be military (Dūr-Kurigalzu), strategic (Tarḫuntašša), or religious (Akhetaton) in nature, or as a result of topographic conditions (Kār-Tukultī-Ninurta). In most cases, it was likely a combination of several factors.

Nevertheless, residential cities were such a characteristic feature of all the existing territorial powers that it is too striking a similarity to be coincidental. On the contrary, it is very likely that the phenomenon was actually part of a region-wide political concept, an expression of power in a time of competing territorial empires.

In the political ideology of almost all of the major powers, the claim for universal rule over the entire world existed, as can easily be recognized in the royal inscriptions. But the political reality looked completely different: none of them was actually able to overwhelm its rivals (with the exception of Mittani, which was first defeated and later completely erased by the Hittites and Assyrians in the late fourteenth century B.C.). This tension between ideology and reality resulted in a competition of the empires not only for economic, political, and military dominance, but also for ideological supremacy. The addressees of the growing battle of propaganda—which influenced, for example the style of inscriptions or royal images on monuments—were the rivals (and their representatives), their own subjects and vassals, and, of course, the gods.

A perfect expression of economic and ideological power, therefore, was the foundation of new residential cities. The diffusion of this idea, which was originally born out of strategic necessities, was made possible by the frequent exchange of correspondence, goods, and personages between the courts (Liverani 2001). Once this scheme was recognized by the competing rivals, it was adapted and reinterpreted within their own cultural syntax. Thus, although the layout, the structure, and even the individual motivation for the foundation of the specific residential cities differed substantially from case to case, the idea behind it was a common one.

THE FIRST MILLENNIUM B.C.:
RESIDENTIAL CITIES AS AN EXPRESSION OF CLAIMS OF WORLD RULE

The Late Bronze Age sociopolitical system collapsed in the twelfth century as a result of severe political, social, and economic changes. Some political entities vanished completely, such as the Hittite Empire, while others were only temporarily reduced to unimportance, like Egypt. The system of competing equal territorial powers was replaced by a strongly fragmented structure of small principalities, some of them hardly more than city-states. Ethnic changes as the result of movements and several processes of ethnogenesis created a colorful map of mixed Luwian, Aramaean, Phoenician, and Hebrew entities in the Levant, as well as the foundation of the Phrygian and the Urartaean kingdoms in Anatolia (cf. the maps and explanations in Wittke et al. 2007:32f., 38f., 40f., 42f.). In Assyria, Babylonia, and Elam the former territorial states survived, although reduced in territorial extent.

It was primarily Assyria that managed to keep its infrastructure. Although it too lost most of its territory and was reduced to its original heartland along the middle of the Tigris River, Assyria's political, economic, and military institutions survived. For this reason, it was able to recover after a period of weakness. It had also been put under pressure by Aramaean tribes, who established small kingdoms up to the Habur triangle and along the Middle Euphrates. From the tenth century B.C. onward, Assyria started to reconquer its former territories. The policy of incorporating the troops of the defeated enemies and vassals (Fuchs 2005) let Assyria's army grow rapidly and brought an enormous advantage against all rivals. Already in the ninth century only a few other powers were left in the Near East, none of them really capable of challenging Assyria's power. Only Phrygia (for less than two generations), Urartu, and Elam were able to maintain their independence and flourished as independent territorial empires (a special case was Babylonia, which was treated in a special way by the Assyrian kings).

The foundation of new cities was still well known in most of the countries, however (Mazzoni 1994). The Aramaeans built new capital cities beside the old and mostly depopulated or ruined urban settlements from the second millennium. The Urartians had to urbanize their country, which hitherto did not have any urban infrastructure at all. They began a tradition of building castles, which in turn became the core of urban sites (Salvini 1995:122–126). In Elam, it seems as if some new residential cities, such as Madaktu, were founded beside the traditional capitals Susa and Anšan, probably for security reasons. The Babylonians, after having established the Late Babylonian Empire following the destruction of Assyria, decided to rebuild Babylon, the cultural, economic, religious, and political center of the country. Babylon thus regained its traditional position and became the unchallenged capital of Babylonia again (Novák 1999:91–104).

Assyria was thus the only empire that took up the idea of the newly founded residential city as a political statement (Figure 15.7).

Neo-Assyrian Residential Cities

The first Assyrian residential city built in the first millennium B.C. was Kalḫu (Oates and Oates 2001). In the ninth century, the ruins of this once (in the thirteenth century) flourishing city were chosen by Ashurnasirpal II (883–859 B.C.) as the new seat of his royalty. Kalḫu was situated close to the confluence of the Tigris and Greater Zab rivers in between the two major cities Ashur and Nineveh. The city was surrounded by extra-urban royal gardens and a "zoo," in which plants and animals from conquered countries were settled, representing the conquered parts of the world. The same holds true for the inhabitants of the city itself, in which deportees from all countries subjugated to the Assyrian king were living. All public buildings were situated on top of a citadel on the edge of the city. The temples and the palace formed a close spatial connection, higher in elevation than the dwelling quarters. Since the citadel was physically connected with the lower city walls, the public buildings were visible from the outside and perceived as "riding" on top of the fortification. During the reign of Shalmaneser III (858–824), a second citadel was added on top of an artificial terrace near the southeastern city corner (Novák 1999:129–140; Novák 2004).

This urban layout was copied 150 years later by king Sargon II (721–705 B.C.) when he founded the next residential city Dūr-Šarru-ukīn on virgin ground, not far

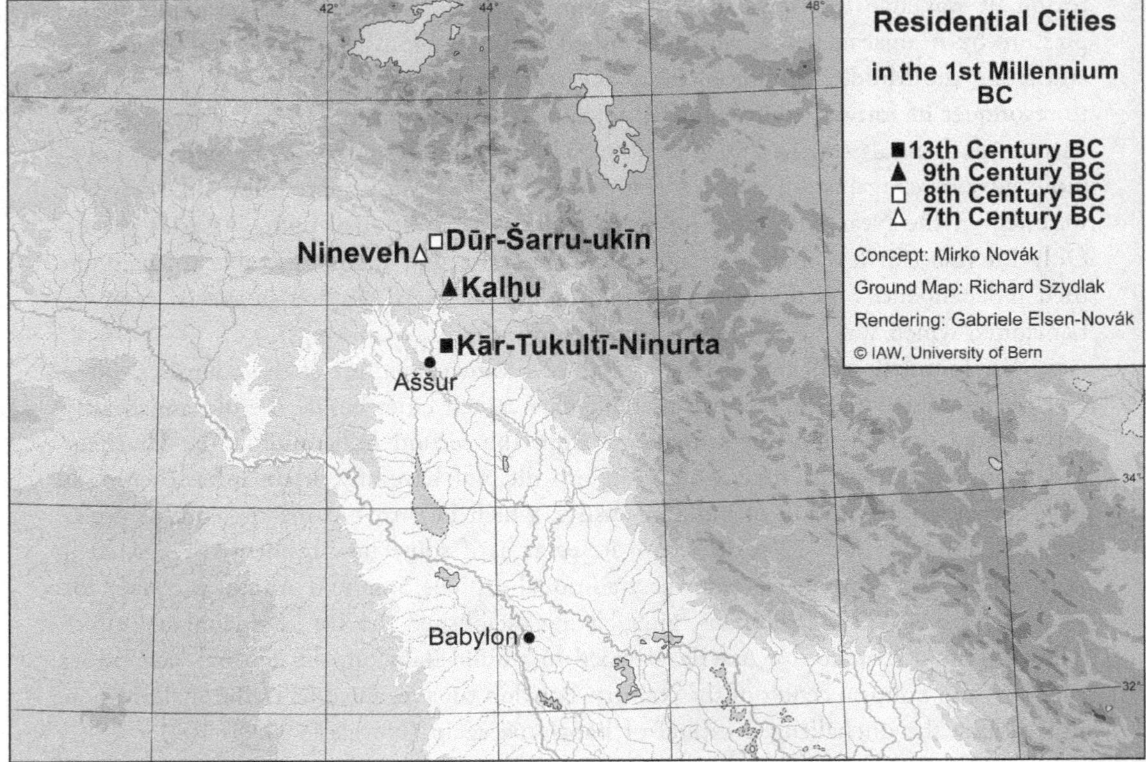

FIGURE 15.7 Map showing the Neo-Assyrian residential cities.

away from Nineveh. Here, an almost square layout was chosen for the city (Figures 15.8 and 15.9).

The last Assyrian residential city was Nineveh, an already existing city, which was rebuilt and significantly enlarged by Sargon's son Sennacherib (704–681 B.C.). As before, the environment was transformed into artificial landscape parks and gardens (cf. the contributions in Collon and George 2005). Two citadels dominated the skyline of the city: the larger one (Kuyunjik) was the main citadel, while the smaller one (Nebi Yunus) was the secondary one. On top of the main citadel and close to its edges, the palaces of Sennacherib and Ashurbanipal were erected, while temples occupied the area in between them. Since the palace of Sennacherib lay close to the western slope of the citadel, it overlooked the riverside and the gardens, just as the palaces of his predecessors had (Novák 2004).

While the old capital Ashur remained the religious and ceremonial center of the country, the residential cities were the seats and manifestations of power, created artificially by the king.

The position, environment, layout, and structure of the Assyrian residential cities illustrated the ideology of Assyrian kingship and claim of universal power. Some of them were built on virgin ground, others the result of enormous re-creations, thus demonstrating the ability of the Assyrian king to transform desert land into a fertile landscape and

FIGURE 15.8 City plan of Dūr-Šarru-ukīn (from Loud and Altman, OIP 40, 1938, Pl. 69).

ruins into prosperous cities. This was accomplished by imposing horticultural activities, including landscape parks, botanical gardens, and "zoos" with plants and animals from all conquered countries. The residential cities had a more or less rectangular outline with two citadels at the periphery, the larger one being the location of the royal palaces and main temples. The visual communication between the public buildings (palaces and temples altogether) on top of the citadel and the dwelling quarters in the lower town, on the one hand, and the distance and different elevation between both, on the other hand, created the perception of the nearly supernatural position of the king, living in the sphere of the gods and dominating the world of his subjects.

The Neo-Assyrian city, with its mixed "international" inhabitants and artificial parks and gardens, is to be seen as a microcosm, that is, a symbol of the empire and its order (Novák 1999:385–387).

RESIDENTIAL CITIES AS EXPRESSIONS OF EXCLUSIVITY

The foundation of residential cities during period of the ninth to seventh centuries B.C. followed different concepts than those of the Late Bronze Age. There was only one dominating power left in the Near East—Assyria. The few other entities, such as

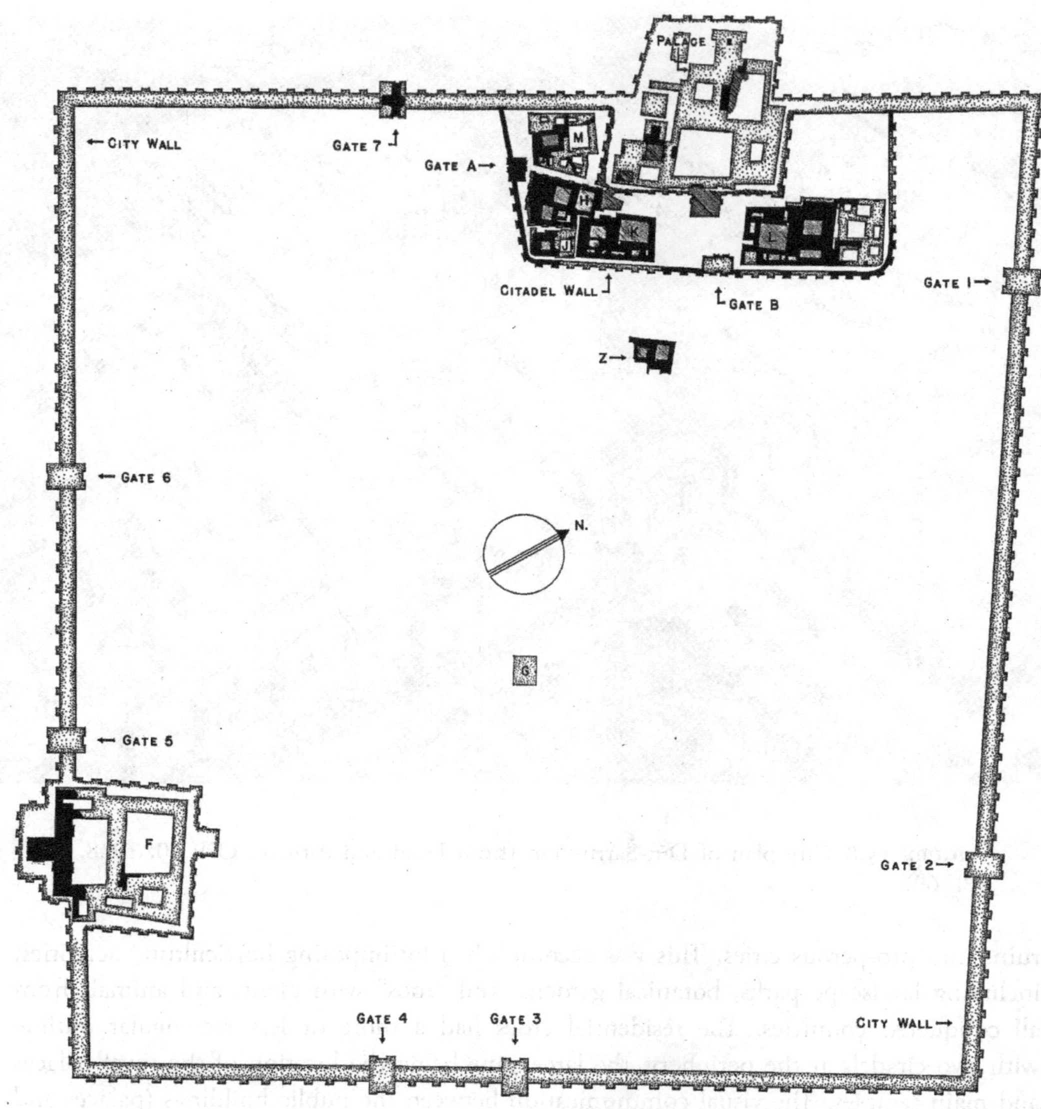

FIGURE 15.9 Reconstruction of the citadel of Dūr-Šarru-ukīn (from Loud and Altman, OIP 40, 1938, Pl. 1).

Urartu or Elam, were in a defensive position most of the time. Hence, the city-building
programs outside Assyria had different backgrounds: in Urartu it was part of a general
urbanization program of a former nonurbanized country; in the Luwo-Aramaean entities
it was the attempt to reconsolidate urban societies after the crisis years that followed the
Late Bronze Age collapse.

In Assyria, city building was an instrument of imperial claim: residential cities were created to represent the empire and universe (which in ideology were the same), and to structure the position of the Assyrian king as the representative of the gods on earth. Ashur, home of the national god, kept its position as the religious and spiritual heart of the empire, but the "city of the kingship" was a symbol of unchallenged royal power. This idea of the residential city survived the collapse and final destruction of Assyria and its cities by far: Not only was Babylon re-embellished during the Late Babylonian period as an *axis mundi*—a combination of capital and residential city—the dynasties of the Achaemenids, Seleucids, Arsacids, Sasanians, and even the Muslim Abbasids founded residential cities in a comparable way: the ruins of Pasargadae, Persepolis, Seleucia on the Tigris, Ctesiphon, Firuzabad, Baghdad, or Samarra are witnesses of these enterprises (Novák 1999:385–398).

CONCLUSION

Doubtless, the foundation of a new residential city is always to be seen as a monument with a clear political message. It bears testimony to the will and power of a political system to create something important and transfer state institutions from their original location into it. This is the main purpose for such an act and the main function of a residential city.

However, there are a lot of reasons that may initiate such a building program. We thus always have to analyze each individual case to get a better understanding of the specific political, economic, or social circumstances leading to such a move. Nevertheless, general comparisons can be made as well, mostly when it is recognizable that the creation of residential cities took place almost contemporaneously in different regions, or, on the other hand, only in one region, but several times within a relatively short period of time.

Two such situations were examined above. It seems that the different political constellations in the Near East during the Late Bronze and Iron ages caused similar results due to very different factors and causes: the foundation of residential cities.

ACKNOWLEDGMENTS

I thank the organizers of the conference, and James Osborne in particular, for inviting me to the very stimulating and informative meeting, and Alexander Ahrens (Bern) for improving the manuscript.

NOTES

1. As long as you live in a city named Leningrad you hardly can avoid remembering a person called Lenin, even if you still remember that it once was called St. Petersburg.
2. One of the most prominent and expressive examples is the Abbasid foundation Madīnat as-Salām "City of Peace" (modern Baġdād), a circular image of the Islamic universe, with

the palace and the main mosque in its center and paradise-gardens surrounding it (Novák 2012).

3.   Even nowadays, after several changes of the political system in Germany and the social structure of its inhabitants, Berlin still commemorates its Prussian and military character in many respects, such as the broad processional streets and the straight view axis from the original gates to the original place of the vanished (and now to be rebuilt) palace of the Prussian king.

4.   On the possible excaption of Šeḥnâ, a town in Upper Mesopotamia, which was refounded by Assyrian king Šamšī-Adad and renamed as Šubat-Enlil, cf. Novák 1999:115–120.

REFERENCES CITED

Braunfels, W. 1976 *Abendländische Stadtbaukunst. Herrschaftsform und Baugestalt.* DuMont Schauberg, Köln.

Bryce, T. 2005 *The Kingdom of the Hittites.* New Edition. Oxford University Press, Oxford.

Clayden, T. In Print Dūr-Kurigalzu. New Perspectives. In *Karduniaš: Babylonien in der Kassitenzeit,* edited by K. Sternitzke, A. Bartelmus, and M. Roaf. Institut für Vorderasiatische Archäologie der Ludwig-Maximilians-Universität München, Munich.

Collon, D., and A. George, eds. 2005 *Nineveh. Papers on the XLIXe Rencontre Assyriologique Internationale, London, 7–11 July 2003.* The British School of Archaeology in Iraq, London.

Dogan-Alparslan, M., and M. Alparslan 2011 Wohnsitze und Hauptstädte der hethitischen Könige, *Istanbuler Mitteilungen* 61:85–103.

Fuchs, A. 2005 War das Neuassyrische Reich ein Militärstaat? In *Krieg, Gesellschaft, Institutionen: Beiträge zu einer vergleichenden Kriegsgeschichte,* edited by B. Meißner et al., pp. 35–60. Akademie Verlag, Berlin.

Fuchs, A. 2011 Das Osttigrisgebiet von Agum II. bis zu Darius I. (ca. 1500 bis 500 v. Chr.). In *Between the Cultures. The Central Tigris Region from the 3rd to the 1st Millennium BC,* edited by P. A. Miglus and S. Mühl, pp. 229–320. *Heidelberger Studien zum Alten Orient* 14. Heidelberger Orientverlag, Heidelberg.

Gilibert, A. 2008 On Kār-Tukultī-Ninurta: Chronology and Politics of a Middle Assyrian Ville Neuve. In *Fundstellen. Gesammelte Schriften zur Archäologie und Geschichte Altvorderasiens ad honorem Hartmut Kühne,* edited by D. Bonatz, R. Czichon, and J. Kreppner, 177–188. Harrassowitz, Wiesbaden.

Harmanşah, Ö. 2013 *Cities and the Shaping of Memory in the Ancient Near East.* Cambridge University Press, Cambridge.

Kaelin, O. 2013 Tall al-Ḥamidīya/Tā'idu (?), Residenzstadt des Mitanni-Reiches. In *100 Jahre archäologische Feldforschungen in Nordost-Syrien—eine Bilanz, Schriften der Max Freiherr von Oppenheim-Stiftung,* edited by D. Bonatz and L. Martin, pp. 181–192. Harrassowitz Verlag, Wiesbaden.

Kemp, B. 2012 *The City of Akhenaten and Nefertiti: Amarna and its People.* Thames & Hudson, London.

Klengel, H. 1998 *Geschichte des Hethitischen reiches. Handbuch der Orientalistik I/34.* Brill, Leiden.

van Koppen, F. 2004 The Geography of Slave Trade and Northern Mesopotamia in the Late Old Babylonian Period. In *Mesopotamian Dark Ages Revisited, Österreichische Akademie der Wissenschaften, Denkschriften der Gesamtakademie* 32, edited by H. Hunger and R. Pruzsinsky, pp. 9–33. Verlag der Österreichischen Akademie der Wissenschaften, Wien.

van Koppen, F. 2010 The Old to Middle Babylonian Transition: History and Chronology of the Mesopotamian Dark Age. *Ägypten & Levante* XX:453–463.

Liverani, M. 2001 *International Relations in the Ancient Near East 1660–1100 BC.* Palgrave, Houndmills.

Liverani, M. 2013 *Immaginare Babele. Due secoli di studi sulla città orientale antica.* Laterza, Roma-Bari.

Mazzoni, St. 1994 Aramaean and Luwian New Foundations. In *Nuove Fondazioni nel vicino oriente antico: Realità e ideologia, Seminari di Orientalistica* 4, edited by St. Mazzoni, pp. 319–340. Giardini, Pisa.

McEwan, J. P. G. 1980 Agade after the Gutian Destruction: The Afterlife of a Mesopotamian City. *Archiv für Orientforschung Beiheft* 19:8–15.

Mebert, J. 2010 *Die Venustafeln des Ammī-ṣaduqa und ihre Bedeutung für die astronomische Datierung der altbabylonischen Zeit. Archiv für Orientforschung Beiheft* 31. Institut für Orientalistik der Universität Wien, Wien.

Oates, D., and J. Oates 2001 *Nimrud. An Assyrian Imperial City Revealed.* British School of Archaeology in Iraq, London.

Novák, M. 1999 *Herrschaftsform und Stadtbaukunst. Programmatik im mesopotamischen residenzstadtbau von Agade bis Surra man ra'ā.* SDV, Saarbrücker, Saarbrücken.

Novák, M. 2004 From Ashur to Nineveh: The Assyrian Town-Planning Programme. *Iraq* LXVI:177–186.

Novák, M. 2012 The Change of Caliphate Ideology in the Light of Early Islamic City Planning. In *Stories a Long Ago. Festschrift für Michael D. Roaf. AOAT 397,* edited by H. D. Baker, K. Kaniuth, and A. Otto, pp. 385–404. Ugarit-Verlag, Münster.

Novák, M. 2013 Upper Mesopotamia in the Mittani Period. In *Archéologie et Histoire en Syrie I, Schriften zur Vorderasiatischen Archäologie,* edited by W. Orthmann, pp. 345–356. Harrassowitz Verlag, Wiesbaden.

Pezzoli-Olgiati, D. 2002 *Immagini urbane. Interpretazioni religiose della città antica.* OBO, Universitätsverlag; Vandenhoeck & Ruprecht, Fribourg-Göttingen.

Pusch, E. B. 2004 Piramesse-Qantir. In *Pharao siegt immer. Krieg und Frieden im Alten Ägypten. Katalog zur Ausstellung Gustav-Lübcke-Museum, Hamm,* edited by S. Petschel and M. von Falk, pp. 240–263. Kettler, Bönen.

Reade, J. 2002 Early Monuments in Gulf Stone at the British Museum, with Observations on Some Gudea Statues and the Location of Agade. *Zeitschrift für Assyriologie* 92:258–295.

Sallaberger, W. 2004 Relative Chronologie von der späten Frühdynastischen bis zur Altbabylonischen Zeit. In *2000 v.Chr. Politische, wirtschaftliche und kulturelle Entwicklung im Zeichen einer Jahrtausendwende, Colloquium der Deutschen Orient-Gesellschaft* 3, edited by J.-W. Meyer and W. Sommerfeld, pp. 15–43. In Kommission bei SDV, Saarbrücker Druckerei und Verlag, Saarbrücken.

Sallaberger, W. 2012 History and Philology, edited by M. Lebeau. *ARCANE Vol. I: Jezirah,* pp. 327–342. Brepols, Turnhout.

Sallaberger, W., and A. Westenholz 1999 *Annäherungen 3. Mesopotamien, Akkad-Zeit und Ur III-Zeit. OBO 160/3.* Universitätsverlag; Vandenhoeck & Ruprecht, Fribourg-Göttingen.

Salvini, M. 1995 *Geschichte und Kultur der Urartäer.* Wissenschaftliche Buchgesellschaft, Darmstadt.

Wäfler, M. 2003 *Tall al-Ḥamidīya 4, OBO Series Archaeologica 21.* Universitätsverlag; Vandenhoeck & Ruprecht, Fribourg.

Wall-Romana, C. 1990 An Areal Location of Agade. *Journal of Cuneiform Studies* 49:205–245.

Wilhelm, G. 1982 *Grundzüge der Geschichte und Kultur der Hurriter.* Wissenschaftliche Buchgesellschaft, Darmstadt.

Wirth, E. 2000 *Die orientalische Stadt im islamischen Vorderasien und Nordafrika.* P. von Zabern, Mainz.

Wittke, A., E. Olshausen, and R. Szydlak 2007 *Historischer Atlas der Antiken Welt. Der Neue Pauly Supplement 3.* Metzler, Stuttgart

Chapter Sixteen

Modern Monumentality

European Experiences

Göran Therborn

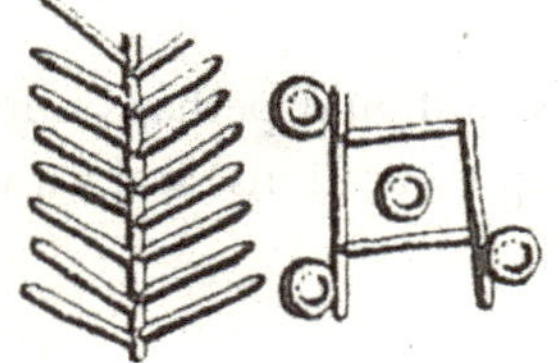

Abstract *Political power needs symbolic representation, of which monumentality is an important part. This chapter presents a general analytical framework for an understanding of representations of power and of its problems, of execution as well as of interpretation, with a focus on urban forms of representation. Then a wide-ranging overview of national and popular monumentality in Europe, east and west, from the rise of nation-states until today is given, comparing forms and contexts and relating them to constellations of power and kinds of political conflict. Finally, the chapter deals with new challenges to national monumentality, from globalization and from the European Union, finding that the former is still significant in Europe, and in some parts of increasing salience.*

In his introduction, James Osborne asked the fundamental question of this volume, "What is the social and political significance of monumentality as it is manifested in particular ways around the world?" The modern European answer of this chapter is that it has been of central importance to the establishment of nation-states. Furthermore, monumentality, in the meaning of symbolic representation, is an intrinsic dimension of exercises of political power. Within the nation-state framework, there is also a potential space for a popular monumentality, which has been of particular strength and significance in Europe, the historical world center of the working-class and the labor movement.

Monumentality is under challenge, with its communities of meaning seemingly eroding, and has been at least since the time of Lewis Mumford. However, the European experiences call for some caution here. The Latin inscriptions of many nineteenth-century monuments, kept in London's Admiralty Arch of 1901, clearly spoke only to small communities. Nor was the frequent allegorical iconography likely to be widely understood.

Contemporary Europe offers hard evidence of the continuous significance of monumentality, in its recent civic and political conflicts about it, in western as well as eastern Europe. Lewis Mumford's statement, noncommittally quoted by Osborne, "If it is a monument, it is not modern, and if it is modern, it cannot be a monument," comes out, not as a statement of modernity, but of the late 1930s.

This chapter is part of a long ongoing global research project on *Cites of Power,* already leaving some traces (on Europe alone, see Therborn 2002, 2006, 2008), and it will deal with a specific variant of monumentality, that of European nation-states, as manifested in their capital cities. Much of the evidence below comes from extensive field observations.

Before diving into the historical record, as a social scientist I should perhaps offer some general analytical reflections on power's need of symbolic representations, and some generalizations about the monumental challenges of nation-states.

Representations of Power

Political power needs representations at least for two crucial reasons, and often for a third:

1. To instill respect, something which may be given variable accents, admiration, awe, fear, pride, identification;

2. To emphasize its legitimacy, which may be religious, dynastic, imperial, national, popular, or global, as major examples;

3. To give direction, conveying the worldview and the intentions of the ruler.

The representational needs often have to operate under a security constraint, which may limit the visibility/accessibility of the ruler.

To the ruler, as well as to his subjects (or citizenry/electorate) and, not the least, to latter-day scholars trying to decode the representations, there are some intrinsic problems of power representation of which we had better be aware.

Problems of Power

Will and Context. There are constraints of context even to the most resourceful and ruthless of wills. For instance, Stalin never managed to build the megalomaniac Palace of Soviets in Moscow, mainly because of its geological unviability on the Moscow riverbanks (see further Coulton 1995:ch. 4 and 365ff).

Principal-Agent Relations. There are the principal-agent relations, never to be assumed simple and frictionless, between the ruler and his architects, artists, master-builders. The intrinsic problem has been spotted in economic and organizational theory, but there seems to be little empirical research into it by historians of art and architecture.

Multivalence of Form. Thirdly, there is the often intrinsic multivalence of symbolic forms, which does not necessarily guarantee that the ruler's choice, or his artist's, is exactly on the target intended. In the traditional European repertoire of architectural styles, the Gothic, for instance, is of French origin, but is also claimed as "*echt deutsch*" (genuinely German) from Goethe onward, as English (in the commissioning of the Houses of Parliament), and Flemish (by designers of the Vienna City Hall).

Problems of Interpretation, to Contemporary Participants as Well as to Latter-Day Scholars

Multiple Ways of Seeing and Reading Any Given Object. Transparency, for instance, is currently interpreted as a feature of democratic government, and therefore of democratic architecture. However, a famous example of Italian Fascist modernism, the *Casa del Fascio* in Como by Giuseppe Terragini, is a light four-story structure with large glass doors to the piazza and big windows, intended to convey the transparency of Fascism, as a "glass-house" with "no obstacle between the political leaders and the people" (Kirk 2005:98).

Time-Lags between Decisions and Realizations. Most cities are overlayered by different, coexisting historical cultural strata. In general, contemporary cities have to be approached through a perspective of cultural geology.

Tradeoffs between Identification on the One Hand, and Respect and Awe on the Other. Heroes may be respected, but not always identified with.

Urban Forms of Power Representation

My research has so far come down to six key variables of urban representations of power, of which only the first five, and in particular 2–4, will be touched upon in this archeological context.

1. Urban Spatial Layout, Including Social Uses of Topography

Topographies of high versus low cities are often used to demarcate political-ecclesiastical from economic power. This, with the ruler and the main church in the high city, is a pattern found in Brussels, in Budapest, in Kyiv, and in Prague. Lisbon, on the other hand, built its political center, particularly before the 1755 earthquake, in the low city by the river. Also frequent in Europe is an east-west class differential, maybe deriving from the predominant westerly winds. Upper-class west and lower-class east is very established in London, Paris, Berlin, and Vienna, although recent eastern developments qualify the judgment, especially in London. Cities on rivers have usually developed on one bank, but have by now spilled well over onto the other side, into a "young" or "new" city. This pattern is most clear in eastern Europe, in Warsaw, Prague, Bratislava, Budapest, in Belgrade, but noticeable also in London. The significance of the division, although present, is more blurred in Paris, which developed out of an island in the river.

2. The Clustering of Buildings of Different Kinds

The somewhat a-centric and relative modesty of Buckingham Palace indicates the British monarchy's long financial dependence on the tightly held purse of Parliament, and contrasts with the central baroque *Stadtschloss* in Berlin. That the new nineteenth-century nation-state of Belgium was a constitutional but not really a parliamentary monarchy is visible from the more imposing size of the coeval royal palace compared to the parliament nearby. The fact that the somewhat later *Palais de Justice* is by far the biggest building of Belgium, at the time second in Europe, after St. Peter's in Rome, points to another dimension of predemocratic Belgian politics, the Liberal veneration of law.

State and church buildings prevailed over private ones in the centers of modern European capitals. In Berlin's Wilhelmstrasse and surroundings, for instance, aristocratic palaces were bought by the new Reich government and enlarged for ministerial offices (Wilderotter 1998). But from the second half of the nineteenth century, some capitals built challenging city halls. Most powerful is the Siena-inspired Copenhagen City Hall, whose City Hall Square (*Rådhuspladsen*) constitutes the heart of the city. Ambitious, if not predominant city halls were built in Vienna, Stockholm, and Oslo, and Brussels had one before the national buildings.

The military had a unique presence in Absolutist St Petersburg, with the huge General Staff building in front of the Tsar's Winter Palace and the Admiralty Spire providing the city's central point of orientation. In the Vienna *Ringstrasse,* the monumental ring around the city center built in the third quarter of the nineteenth century, the Ministry of War was located in the back part.

3. Architecture, the Meaning of the Style of Which Has to Be Treated as Historically Path-Dependent, While Paying Attention to What Has Been Called the Architectural Grammar of Power (See Further Below)

4. Monumentality, in the Narrow Sense of Specific Commemorating Structures, Statues, Columns/Obelisks, Commemoratives Ensembles, Musea of Commemoration

The Renaissance monarchies and Baroque Papal Rome, for example, had rediscovered and revived imperial Roman monumentality, which thus came to provide the iconographic background for the later emerging nation-states.

5. Toponymy, the Naming of Streets, Places, Institutions

As a political practice, and not just a reference of orientation—indicating, for example, a profession of artisans, the house of somebody, some geographical feature of the area—urban naming is a post-medieval phenomenon. In Paris, it goes back to Henri IV, late-sixteenth–early-seventeenth century, who laid out and named three royal squares

(Jones 2004:159ff.). But street names became official only in the eighteenth century, and a hot political topic only from the Revolution on (Favier 1997:124ff.).

6. The Allocation of Public Amenities, Such as Parks, and Public Services, from Garbage Collection, Sewage and Electricity, and Postal Services to Child and Health Care, and Schools.

Architecture of Power

The meaning of architectural styles is path-dependent. Late-eighteenth and early-nineteenth-century neoclassicism, for instance, is imperial in Russia and France, but Republican in the United States. However, architecture may have a language of power, to which a Norwegian academic architect, (Thiis-Evensen 1998) has given us a very valuable brief guide. According to him, architecture aimed at manifesting (overtowering) power tends to have the following characteristics: (1) (Big) Size; (2) (Heavy) Weight; (3) (High) Verticality; (4) Closure; (5) Distance; and (6) Symmetry.

Thiis-Evensen's list is largely validated by the broad German post-1945 discussion of, search for, and attempts at democratic, nonauthoritarian building (cf. Flagge and Stock 1992). German "democratic architecture" is perhaps best illustrated by the chancellor's bungalow in Bonn, a small, one-story building with big windows, visible to the public, situated in a parkland and separated from the street only by a low hedge. This attention to democratic monumentality was also very much present in the construction of the governmental quarter in Berlin after 1990, although the scale had then been altered upward (Wise 1998:69ff.). The new chancellor's office is actually huge, but hidden behind a light glass façade.

On the whole, the European monumental tradition is less exuberant than those of the rich civilizations of Asia and Egypt, but more so than those of Indo-America. In size, in ancient and imperial China and Moghul India more concentration of power and resources was gathered and expressed than in Europe. The Vatican comprises 110 acs, about 445,000 m^2, and the Moscow Kremlin 68 acs or 275,000 m^2. The *chateau* of Versailles has 63,000 m^2 (ww.chateauversailles.fr), or almost 16 acs, but the gardens around it comprise almost 2,000 acs This may be compared with 255 acs of the Delhi Red Fort, 720,000 m^2 or about 175 acs for the Beijing Forbidden City, and with the 1,200 acs of the 200 B.C. Weiyang or Er fang palace complex of Chang'an, built for the commissioner of the Great Wall, Emperor Qin Shi Huangli, the main building of which comprised 75,000 m^2 (Cotterell 2008:32; other size data are taken from Wikipedia: http//:en.wikipedia.org). St Peter's in Rome is much larger than the Main Temple of the Aztecs in Tenochtitlán, 20,000 (www.santpetersbasilica.org) to 8,000 m^2, and much larger still than the Inca Temple of the Sun in Cuzco.

Verticality was above all a religious striving until the twentieth-century corporate skyscrapers. The medieval Lincoln Cathedral (of 1311) and a few sixteenth-century churches matched and surpassed the Great Giza pyramid (2500 B.C.), at 146 m, but most of their spires were short-lived. The seventeenth-century Strasbourg Cathedral with its 142 m was more stable.

Alongside Taj Mahal (the mausoleum of a non-reigning queen), the Lenin mausoleum looks very modest. Even the Roman Vittoriano or "Altar of the Fatherland," the most bombastic tomb of modern Europe, appears not only ugly, but minor in a long intercontinental comparison. National power, however dictatorial or authoritarian, is less concentrated than monarchical power of the premodern empires.

Transparency is an opposite of closure, and a current keyword of EU (Parliament) as well as of German public building. Norman Foster's glass cupola on the *Reichstag* is part of the same program, making it possible for visitors to look down at the people's representatives through a glass floor. Despite recent security concerns, the area between the German parliament and the new chancellor's office is open to the public. Here, the contrast is primarily with Africa, where presidential palaces are often hidden from view, and where photographing governmental buildings is in principle prohibited.

Symmetry, the sixth element in Thiis-Evensen's grammar of power, clearly indicates a quest for order, but its representation of assertive power hardly appears quite convincing.

KINDS OF POWER AND THEIR HISTORICAL DEVELOPMENT

As already indicated above, my work is primarily focused on representations of political power, but in order to grasp that adequately we need to be aware of sources of power other than the one deriving from control of a polity. Following the historical sociologist Michael Mann (1986) we may then distinguish between political, economic, ideological, and military (sources of) power. Although in many polities two or all of them may de facto be fused, keeping the analytical distinction in mind can sharpen understanding and analysis.

Power may not only spring from different sources. It is also subject to historical change and development. "Modern" monumentality in this chapter has a specific meaning, referring to modern political power. Modern political power, I have argued (Therborn 2011:54ff), is best understood as power claiming to derive from, to represent, a nation, in other words a nation-state. Nation-states were the outcome of the late-eighteenth-century Atlantic revolutions, the American and the French, and became the central political agenda of nineteenth-century Europe and Americas, of Asia from the late nineteenth on, and in Africa from the mid-twentieth century.

Modern political monumentality, then, is nations—as conceived by their rulers—representing and commemorating themselves.

Before the nation-states, there were the prince-states, usually dynastic, governed by divine right or mandate from Heaven and/or by legitimate descent, and oligarchic city-states ruled by *"regimentsfähigen Familien."* Princely palaces and, in postmedieval Europe, princely statues (inspired by imperial Rome) were the typical form of prenational political representation. Powerful cities had their own manifestations of splendor, such as the Doge palace of Venice, the *Palazzo Vecchio* of Florence, grand city halls, as in Augsburg, Lübeck, and Amsterdam. In the Brussels *Grande Place,* the city Hall overshadowed the palace of the representative of the Habsburg King/Emperor. City gates were often built to monumental proportions, the Holstein Gate in the Hansa capital Lübeck perhaps the most magnificent.

Occasionally, as in Viking Iceland and in the medieval Swiss *Urkantone,* power was dispersed among the propertied farmer-patriarchs, and as such largely lacked symbolic representation.

The economic power of capital manifested itself early in the western European cityscape. Most strongly in London, where it has for long been concentrated in a legally separate city, the City (with a capital c) of London, distinct from the governmental and ecclesiastical power in the City of Westminster. London is the old name of the urban settlement on the Thames, true, but it is not without significance that since the end of the Middle Ages it has been the City of capital and not the city of government that designates the whole conurbation. On the continent, the Norwegian political scientist Stein Rokkan (1973) pointed to a late medieval and early modern "City Belt," of strong commercial cities, early general urbanization, and a relative weakness of princely and landed power, running up through Italy, Switzerland, the Rhineland and the Low Countries. The enduring outcome of it is a polycentric city system, often with a separation of political and economic capitals, Rome and Milan, Berne and Zürich, Bonn and Frankfurt in the West German republic, the Hague and Amsterdam.

The guilds were often competing with architectural grandeur, the Drapers' Hall (*Lakenhal)* in Ghent being one of the most remarkable manifestations. The historical competition can still be seen in buildings around the Brussels *Grande Place* (restored in the nineteenth century).

Ideological power in premodern Europe was vested in the Christian churches, the Gothic cathedrals being the skyscrapers of the age, and the Orthodox ones shining with their golden cupolas.

Prenational Europe was almost constantly at war, but in comparison with the national era, or with the Roman model, there was rather little commemoration of wars and battle victories. Louis XIV's Parisian *Place des Victoires* and *Place des Conquêtes*) (Favier 1997:194f) were exceptional. The royal equestrian statues tended to give monarchical power a clearly martial accent, however.

Forms of National Representation

In national monumentality, respect and legitimacy have specific functions. Respect has to express collective national self-respect: national pride, the community of the nation. Legitimacy has to provide identification with the power, as representing the nation, its experiences, its strivings and aspirations. This can be done, and has been done, in a wide variety of ways.

National representation first emerged, gradually, during the eighteenth century in the form of public sculptural homages to nonroyal members of the nation. In London, the Poets' Corner in Westminster Abbey then developed into a literary Parnassus of the country (Bradley and Pevsner 2003:165ff), and was consecrated in St Paul's Cathedral in 1795, when three distinguished citizens were given statues, the prison reformer John Howard, the lexicographer Samuel Johnson, and the painter Joshua Reynolds (Weinreb and Hibbert 1993:782). At the very end of the French *ancien régime* something similar was being planned for the Louvre (Hargrove 1986:244). In the German archipelago of dynastic states, non-princely representations seem to have become common only in the second third of the nineteenth century, although public statues of Martin Luther began to appear in Protestant cities from the first decade of the century (Chaix 2001:15).

The French Revolution tore down the royal statues of Paris, and the Napoleonic Wars spread the new nationalism across the continent. The latter were crucial to the national iconography of London, with its Waterloo Bridge, its Trafalgar Square, originally intended as King William Square (Hood 2005:35ff), with its Nelson Column, and its equestrian statues and monumental St Paul's tomb of the Duke of Wellington. Even Tsarist Russia paid tribute to its nonroyal commanders, Kutuzov and Barclay de Tolly, with full-size statues outside the Kazan Cathedral of St. Petersburg. Only Habsburg Vienna, the center of the counterrevolutionary Holy Alliance, paid no national attention until a half-century after Waterloo.

The nation was amply represented in allegoric forms and symbolic language, most often by female figures, both abstract—as Liberty, the Nation, the Republic—and more ethno-national, as French Marianne, German Germania, Mother Russia, Britannia (cf. v. Plessen 1995). Architects and their nationalist commissioners went searching for national architectural languages. For most of the nineteenth century, the searchlight was focused on the inherited repertoire of European architecture. The British opted for neo-Gothic, in the Houses of Parliament first of all, as best representing freeborn Englishmen. The national empires, from Britain via France to Russia had a predilection for neoclassicism, as the style of the Roman Empire. Greek Athens, under its German and Danish architects, naturally adopted it as ancient Greek.

In the last third or quarter of the nineteenth century, the European tradition of architecture was burst open. The Austrian Secession or the French Art Nouveau did not have anything intrinsically national about them. But their new architectural language provided a particular inspiration to emergent nations, their rising bourgeoisies, and their architects. Orientalist ornamentalism was adopted by the avant-garde of Magyar Budapest. After using neo-Renaissance construction with folkloric iconography for their national theatre, Czech nationalist Prague turned increasingly to Secessionism in the decades around 1900. Known as *Jugendstil* in Germany and northern Europe, the new florid architecture became an expression of the Latvian bourgeoisie in Riga (Krastins 2006), and, as Art Nouveau of the Belgian in Brussels.

Financed by *arrivés* Catalan industrialists and under the label of *modernisme,* the new style of building reached its curvaceous climax in Barcelona in the decade before World War I (see further Montaner 1997). Poor and austere but recently nationally aroused Finland developed its own national emancipation from academic architecture, usually referred to as National Romanticism, characterized by its reliance on rough-hewn grey granite.

Representations of national power have in Europe emphasized two kinds of the new legitimacy of power. One is the majesty of new *institutions* of national government.

The British Houses of Parliament is the model example. In some nation-states, the rule of law, instead of will of the prince, was placed as the central institution of the new power, above representative government. The gigantic Brussels *Palais de Justice* is here the prime manifestation.

By contrast, Europe's first national capital, Paris, has no center of a national institution. What it has instead, are a set of places, still foci of public rallies, commemorating constitutive *events* of national power, the places de la Bastille, de la République, de la Nation—ex-Throne Square—de l'Étoile, with their monuments of the July Revolution, the Third Republic, the Nation, and the Triumphal Arch of the Grand Army, respectively. Furthermore, public space in Paris is historically divided, until and including today. To the east are the rallying points of the national-popular Left, la Bastille, where the Socialists celebrated their recent presidential victory, la République, la Nation, usually in the May Day circuit. To the west are those of the national Right, the Champs Elysées and l'Étoile (now place Général de Gaulle), where the Fourteenth of July is celebrated, where the Gaullists had their massive manifestation against the May 1968 rebellion, and les Invalides, where Napoleon is buried, and in front of which the anti-same-sex marriage demonstrations congregated in 2013.

National legitimacy may also be fostered by highlighting prenational tyranny. Balkan national literature and historiography talked a lot about the "Ottoman yoke," but it did not get prominence in Balkan national monumentality. More typical were the Bucharest Triumphal Arch commemorating the (Russian-assisted) victory against the Ottomans, and the Bulgarian central statue in honor of the (Russian) Tsar Liberator. The 1989–1991 wave of nationalism paid much more attention to national oppression and suffering.

The twentieth century saw the emergence of a monumentality of national mourning. On a large scale it developed after the hecatomb of World War I. Burial monuments to the Unknown Soldier, huge war cemeteries, institutional plaques listing the fallen of the institution—e.g. the railway center, the university, school alumni, or the employees of the London Zoo (Baker 2004:111)—overwhelmed monuments of victory (Kosellek and Jeismann 1994; Winter 1995).

In Western Europe this tradition was largely continued after World War II. In contrast to the case in the United States, there was not a single major World War II victory monument in Western Europe. Oblique references there were—featuring Churchill or de Gaulle, for instance—and minor ones, including a London bust of Arthur Harris, chief of the British Bomber Command, whom many people today would regard as a war criminal. The Soviets, on the other hand, were very keen on celebrating monumentally the heroism of the Red Army, sometimes starting preparing even before the war had ended.[1] But in contrast to the monumentality within the Soviet Union itself, their East-Central European motifs were generally not victory but the Soviet sacrifices for Europe's liberation from fascism. The Soviet monumental complex on Gellert Hill in Buda is actually dominated by a statue of Liberty.

West Germany, in its last stage, pioneered a monumentality of atonement for the crimes of Nazism. In reunified Berlin, it is expressed, above all (but far from only), in an abstract commemoration of the "Murdered Jews of Europe," a field of concrete slabs of varying size, in the classical center of the city, close to Brandenburger Tor. Near to it in a corner of the Tiergarten Park there is a more discreet memorial to the persecution of Sinti and Roma, and, in another corner, still more discreet, to that of homosexuals. Well placed in Berlin is further a big monument-museum to the whole spectrum of Nazi oppression, the Topography of Terror. To designate monuments of horror, the German language has developed a distinction between two kinds of monument, the conventional *Denkmal* and the *Mahnmal,* warning against repeating past terror.

National monumentality everywhere had to assert itself against previously prevailing religious, princely, or other power representations. Doing so, it had to find an adequate symbolic language—at the same time novel and intelligible—that might be taken from the national past, a regional cultural tradition, or imported. Europe had a strong regional symbolic tradition which the new nations made ample use of, deriving from Greco-Roman Antiquity. But, particularly in more peripheral nations, vernacular symbolic languages were also dug up or invented.

SPECIFIC ISSUES OF NATIONAL MONUMENTALITY—AND ITS LIMIT

The first and foremost issue of national monumentality concerns the self-conception of the nation whose power is to be represented. This chapter will only look at European nations, but any general approach to representations of national power should be aware of the existence of other types of nations than the European ones (cf. Therborn 2011:69ff).

European nations all rose in opposition to princely power, but in different ways. A very important difference has been between a ruptural path of revolution, of which France is the prototype, and a gradual, negotiated process, of which Scandinavia is the purest case, and Britain—in spite of its seventeenth-century civil war and "Glorious Revolution"—is the most important.

A ruptural path of historical development also means a rupture of political iconography. The French Revolution destroyed the royal statues of Paris, and the post-Waterloo Restoration restored (many of them), while stopping the unfinished Napoleonic constructions, such as the Triumphal Arch. Then came the July Monarchy paying respect to Napoleon, the short-lived 1848 Republic, the Second Empire, and the final Republican settlement of the Third Republic, which launched a massive iconographic drive in Paris, and in the rest of country, celebrating the national-popular victories of the people-nation against the monarchies and aristocracies.

The city center of Oslo is dominated by the Royal Castle on a low hill, built after 1814 for the representative of the Swedish King, and its main street, running from below the hill, is Karl Johan, named after the first Swedish king, who overthrow the brief Norwegian independence of 1814. This is the most telling urban expression of a peacefully negotiated nation-state (in 1905) in Europe. The castle is now inhabited by the (parliamentarily powerless) King of Norway, whereas political power is centered in a dignified but nonimposing *Storting* (parliament) farther down Karl Johan street. In Czechoslovakia, on the other hand, anything Habsburg was taken down, by popular force and/or by decree (Demetz: 1997:339–340; Miháilová:306–315). In independent Polish Warsaw, the Russian Orthodox Cathedral was officially dynamited.

The British path to a post-dynastical nation-state had more instances of violence than the Norwegian, but London too demonstrates a politics of posthumous inclusion. In Trafalgar Square, you find not only the imperial admirals and generals but also the once beheaded Charles I, and after World War I, the first successful anti-imperial rebel, George Washington. By Parliament you find the regicide of Charles I, Oliver Cromwell. In contrast to Paris, there is no important place commemorating any internal political conflicts, not even the so-called Glorious Revolution in 1688.[2]

The term *national* should be further specified. We ought to make at least four distinctions. One is *national tout court,* referring to a nation rising against a foreign prince (or other power), such as Balkan nations against the Ottomans, the Czecho-Slovaks and the Yugoslavs against the Habsburgs, the Irish against the British, the Norwegians against the Swedish king. Or it may indicate a nation asserting itself above and beyond a set of princedoms, as in Italy. German unification was more ambiguous, not issuing into a full nation-state, rather, into dynastic state, proclaimed in the Versailles Hall of Mirrors, using a nationalist rhetoric. The new German *Reichstag* was meant to be dedicated "To the German People," but it took two decades for it to overcome the emperor's preference for "German Unity" (Wise 1998:125). The square in front of it was named King's Square, with the *Siegessäule,* the Victory Column celebrating the Prussian victories over Denmark, Austria, and France. From the square through the Tiergarten park led a new monumental construction. The Victory Avenue (*Siegesallee*), commemorating the exploits of the Hohenzollern dynasty (see further Lehnert 1998).

The Balkan nation-states were delivered by Russia and other foreign anti-Ottoman powers. But only in Sofia is this remembered in the national monumentality, with a central statue and avenue dedicated to the Russian Tsar Liberator.

Another form of the national we may name is the *national-popular,* in which the people of the nation are rising against the domestic prince and his aristocratic and high clergy supporters. The French Revolution is the model, although the process could also be gradual and negotiated, as in Scandinavia. Italian unification, although finally brought about by the Kingdom of Piemonte, had more in common with the French Revolution than with the Prussian Empire. It had a much more important popular component, in Rome taking an antipapal edge. Garibaldi is towering over the Vatican on horseback on the Gianicolo Hill, and in the Campo dei Fiori, where the Inquisition once burned him as a heretic, Giordano Bruno was resurrected. The city's innumerable churches were left in peace by the new nation-state, but the *Quirinale,* the former summer palace of the pope, became the royal, and later presidential, palace, and the Chamber of Deputies was housed in the *Montecitorio,* former headquarters of the papal police. Liberal-national anticlericalism and a political volatility that made long-term construction plans difficult resulted in the Spanish and Portuguese national parliaments both being located in deconsecrated monasteries.

Napoleonic France also provided the model of, or the causal shock for, a third version of the national, the *national-imperial.* The Parisian Triumphal Arch, dedicated to Napoleon's *Grande Armée,* and celebrating its victories in central and eastern Europe and in Egypt, is the pioneering example of national-imperial monumentality. Parisian street names are full of victorious Napoleonic battlefields, Iéna, Friedland, Austerlitz, Pyramides,

Aboukir, Ulm, etc. The London Trafalgar Square is another key example, commemorating the British naval victory in the Franco-British imperial world war, and later adding a roster of imperial generals. Napoleon's armies also triggered imperial nationalisms in Russia and Prussia.

Finally, we have the *popular*, in which it is meaningful to distinguish from the national-popular, although the popular is also vested in a nation-state. In the popular perspective, the suffering, the struggles, the victories, and the achievements of the nation as a whole are not in focus, but those of the common people, the popular classes, of women, or of other suppressed subjects of the nation, such as ethnic groups, which in Europe have played a smaller role than in other parts of the world. Below we shall touch upon a dimension of the popular of particular importance in modern European history.

The nation-state is still with us, but in the age of globalization there is a possibility of national monumentality being overtaken by a global one, or being eclipsed by some form of post-monumentality. The former could take at least two different paths. One would be the erection of global symbolic signifiers. The first enduringly successful one was the Paris Eiffel Tower, put up at the centenary of the Revolution in 1889, but for its World Exhibition and celebrating world industrial technology. About a century later, I. M. Pei, commissioned by President Mitterand, added another global signifier to Paris, the glass pyramid in the main courtyard of the Louvre. In reunified Berlin, the new construction of the *Potsdamer Platz* area included two different transnational concepts, a European part designed by the Italian Renzo Piano and financed by Daimler-Benz, and a more American part, drawn up by the German-American architect Helmut Jahn, and largely financed by Japanese Sony. However, the Parisian and the Berlin examples both demonstrate the possible compatibility and coexistence of national and transnational monumentality.

Another, more zero-sum game possibility would be assertions of transnational economic power overtaking public national monumentality. This alternative is much more recent, manifested in corporate "iconic buildings," without any attempt at conveying any shared public meaning, only the wealth, power, and the taste of the owner, in a new fusion of economics and architecture, often, but far from always, with tourism industry interests in mind (cf. Jencks 2005). In this respect, London is the showcase of Europe, building upon the inherited economic power of the City. The City itself has erected a set of spectacular architectural monuments to the power of capital, most attractively Norman Foster's "Gherkin," originally for the insurance company Swiss Re, while its off-center Canary Wharf offshoot looks more like a standard North American "Central Business District" (CBD). It is characteristic of the contemporary cityscape of London that a corporate tower financed by Qatari capital and designed by Renzo Piano is allowed to overtower St. Paul's Cathedral opposite it, on the north bank of the Thames.

The rule among European capitals so far, however, has been to keep corporate power representation at bay, regulating the location of skyscrapers, for instance. After the late 1950s *Tour de Montparnasse*, Paris banished them to the outskirts of *La Défense*, and skyscraper plans for central Berlin (Alexanderplatz) have been shelved. Only in postcommunist Warsaw is an American-type CBD under construction, around the Stalinist Palace of Culture, which has finally become non-demolishable and instead is to be overshadowed by a circle of business buildings, according to the new rulers. In the conclusion, we shall return to the question whether monumentality is being rendered meaningless in the fragmented societies of the twenty-first century.

Finally, in Europe the EU might be seen as a limit to the national, adding a third form of the postnational to the two just mentioned. In terms of monumentality this has clearly not happened, thereby manifesting the enduring political dominance of the nation-states in the Union. EU monumentality is mainly concentrated in three cities, the three capitals of the Union, Brussels, Luxemburg, and Strasbourg, and concentrated in buildings, rather than specific monumental ensembles. Frankfurt is soon to be added, with an expensive but hardly iconic skyscraper of the European Central Bank, alongside other bank towers. In all three, competitive Union capital ambitions have generated a kind of new supranational cities within or on the outskirts of the national ones. In Brussels, which has most of the EU capital functions, a new, third city center is emerging, inside modern city boundaries, but east of the prenational Low City around the *Grande Place* and City Hall, and of the national High City, with the official Royal Palace, Parliament, and the Palace of Justice. The big complex of the European Parliament, accentuating its transparency and accessibility, the upscale convention center of the European Council (representing the member-states), and the more functionalist headquarters of the commission constitute the core.

In Luxemburg, a new European quarter has been built on a hill outside the small historical capital of a small country. Its most important institutional building, with clear iconic ambitions, is the European Court of Justice, but *Kirchberg* hill also houses cultural architecture of star quality. The French contender for EU capital status, Strasbourg, is actually a medium-size provincial city with a great cultural history and a historical center of Franco-German conflict. The EU Parliament has a grand pied-à-terre here, traveling down from Brussels every month, and there is also another, non-EU European institution, the Council of Europe and its Court of Human Rights. Europe is obviously very important to the city of Strasbourg, and the French nation-state is a vigilant supporter of city interests, which represent no challenge to the nation.

Working-Class Europe and the Popular Moment of Monumentality

The Popular Moment in European monumentality was above all that of the working-class and the labor movement. The century from the Paris Commune (of 1870–1871), the fear of which inspired the German welfare state (Vogel 1951), until about 1980 was the working-class century in social history, recognized as such even by enemies of the socialist labor movement, such as Pope Leo XIII in his 1891 Encyclica *Rerum novarum* (On New Things) or the racist nationalist who led to power in Germany the "National Socialist German Workers' Party." The working-class century was Eurocentric, centered on, if not confined to, European trade unions, labor parties, and working-class cultural and leisure organizations. Through the Comintern, in particular, European labor inspired workers, intellectuals, and peasants around the world, first of all in China and Vietnam.

What, if any, monumental traces did this working-class popular moment leave in Europe? They can be tracked along two main paths. One follows Western European Social Democracy, the other Russian and Russian-imposed or -inspired Eastern Europe.[3]

Least known outside the tribe of specialists is the ideologically very self-conscious municipal socialism of Western European big cities, in Amsterdam and Vienna in particular. It is a very particular kind of monumentality "of beautiful workers' dwellings" as "monuments to [the working-class] struggle," as the Dutch housing campaigner Ary Kepler put it in 1912 (Searing 1978:230). After World War I, this program was implemented in Amsterdam, under the alderman for housing, the left-wing Social Democrat Wiebaut, with the help of the modernist Amsterdam School of architecture (Searing 1978).

The most monumental program of working-class housing was implemented in Vienna, where radical Social Democracy governed alone, in contrast to the perennial coalition politics of Amsterdam. In both cities, a working-class monumentality was seen as focused on high quality, aesthetic housing for the working class, combined with an extensive collective infrastructure, most developed in Vienna, of kindergartens, schools, libraries, laundries, shops, leisure facilities of various kinds, and in Vienna also programs of public health (Blau 1999).

The peak of this class-conscious working-class monumentality was the big Viennese housing estate *Karl Marxhof*, built in the last years of the 1920s and still standing, although a battlefield in 1934 between Austrofascism and the labor movement. A huge modernist brick complex of apartments, with a monumental entrance, a large courtyard, and ample collective residential resources, with a name that signifies social defiance, and with masts for red banners hoisted on working-class holidays.

The Social Democratic housing programs in Amsterdam and Vienna got their monumental edge and meaning from the particularly ideologically charged and divided character of interwar Dutch and Austrian politics, ultimately peacefully coexisting in the former case, running into violent confrontations in the latter. The modernist housing and suburban planning pushed by the Swedish Social Democrats in the 1930s and 1940s attracted a great deal of postwar interest, but was presented and perceived as generally "progressive" and not as monuments to the working-class struggle.

The labor movement also built for itself, for the *Arbeitervereine* in Germany and Austria (in Austria, in particular), what were seen by its leaders as "houses of struggle," "fortresses of solidarity" (Blau 1999:228f). In Belgium and France they had a less militant accent, and went under the name of *Maisons du Peuple* (Houses of the People), a concept prominent also in Scandinavia. Most of these buildings were functional halls for meetings and socialization, sometimes including some residential apartments, without monumental ambitions. But a few had higher aspirations, such as the Art Nouveau Maison du Peuple built by Victor Horta in Brussels and the *Arbeiterheim* in the Viennese neighborhood *Favoriten*.

The heyday of working-class monumentalism in Western Europe was the period from the 1890s to the 1930s, before the labor movement had national power to shape the general symbolic landscape. After World War I, social democratic ministers and leaders could achieve some forms of public commemoration, usually modest and peripheral, detectable in London but virtually absent from Paris or Rome. Three Western European labor monuments, apart from the above-mentioned buildings, should be noted. One is the statuesque ensemble that the Belgian sculptor Cionstantin Meunier worked on for many years. In spite of its lack of any reference to the labor movement, and its dedication only to the dignity of manual labor, it could never be put up in his lifetime. Not until 1930 was his Monument to Labour, with a rural sower as the central figure, erected in the then-peripheral northwest of Brussels, where today it looks quite abandoned.

In the main O'Connell Street of Dublin stands, since 1979, the only central labor monument in Western Europe, a huge statue commemorating the radical trade union leader Jim Larkin, a key figure in the struggle for union rights in the Dublin Lockout of 1913–1914, in oratorical pose. The statue was commissioned by the Irish trade unions, but it was inaugurated by the President of the Republic, never a polity with a particularly strong working-class influence. But in spite of becoming a communist in the United States in the 1920s, before becoming more mainstream labor Left in the mid-1930s upon his return to Ireland, Larkin occupies a place in the nationalist Irish canon.

On a wooded hill in Helsinki, not far from the Olympic Stadium, visible only to those who know where to search, is a third remarkable Western European working-class monument: a rough, slightly folded, torn, and damaged-looking concrete wall, with sculptured reliefs of harrowed humans on one side, and a poetic dedication to "heroes' graves" on the other. It was put up in 1970, after a symbolic reconciliation of Red and White Finland under President Kekkonen, and it commemorates the Reds who fell in the civil war of 1918 or who died in the prison camps afterward.

The twentieth-century monumental experience of Eastern and East Central Europe is, of course, different. The Russian Revolution initiated an iconoclasm similar to the French, including the latter's qualifications: "Monuments erected in honour of the tsars and of their servants and that do not present interest either from a historical or from an artistic viewpoint are to be dismantled and taken off the squares and streets," the Bolshevik government decreed in April 1918. At about the same time, Lenin launched an extensive monumental program of cultural and political pedagogy, of which the Third French Republic could also have been proud. Figures to be immediately monumentalized included not only the obvious Marx and Engels but a whole lineage of rebels and revolutionaries, from Spartacus to Robespierre, Garibaldi, Bakunin, and Kropotkin, a long roster of radical thinkers and writers including Voltaire, Byron, Heine, Lermontov, and Gogol, and a string of painters and composers, Rublev, Cézanne, Chopin, Skryabin, and Rimsky-Korsakov among them (Bowlt 1978:186ff).

Another characteristic moment of Eastern and East Central European popular monumentality took place in Budapest on May Day 1945, when the crowd of May First demonstrators toppled the statue of Istvan Werböczy and attached a note "To the memory of Gyrögy Dósza" (Sinkó 1978:73), who was later given a prominent statue. Dósza led a big (finally crushed) peasant uprising in the early-sixteenth century, whereas Werböczy was a leading statesman of the period, and the codifier of the landed rights of the gentry and the magnates. Most emblematic of communist popular iconography is, arguably, the double statue of Industrial Worker and Kolkhoz Peasant Woman, made by Vera Mukhina for the Soviet Pavilion at the World Exhibition in Paris in 1937, later put up on Soviet exhibition ground in Moscow.

Actually existing communism added another dimension of monumentality, much more akin to imperial Rome, with its emperors considered to be divine, than to anything popular, the personality cult. It was the invention of Stalin and the Stalinist leadership of the USSR after Lenin, which first developed as a cult of the dead Lenin—who while alive would have abhorred it—and then from the mid-1930s the living Stalin. After World War II the cult was imported into East Central Europe by eager local zealots, with colossal statues in Budapest and Prague, and the grand Stalin Allee of East Berlin. (Sensitivities regarding proper location and form delayed the achievement of a complete area coverage by statues, until Khrushchev put an end to the cult in early 1956.) Hitler and Mussolini, although officially adored and consecrated as Leaders (*Führer/Duce*), never inflated themselves to the same degree of monumentality as "comrade" Stalin.

ENVOI

Europe has a long monumental tradition, going back to Greco-Roman Antiquity, evolving across centuries, adding new elements, from medieval Church Gothic to twentieth-century International Style modernism and occasional postmodernism. The modern era of nation-states has seen the nation become the focus, overtaking the monarch and the palaces of the aristocracy, the church, and the cities with their city halls and gates, and with their guild buildings. The national was not of one piece, but may be better specified in the national-*tout court,* the national-imperial, the national-popular, and the popular. Since modern Europe has a social history in which the working class and the labor movement have played a uniquely important part, working-class monumentality is significant to European experience. We have also looked at the boundaries of the national, the supplementary aspect of the European, and the possible, but so far limited, coming of the global.

National monumentality was revived in postcommunist Eastern Europe. It played a direct role in the implosion of communism, most concretely in Croatia, where the demand for the return to the central city square of Bán Jellacic—an able Croat Habsburg commander, whose monument the communists removed because of his counterrevolutionary part in crushing the Hungarian revolution of 1848—started the public anticommunist movement in Croatia (Rihtman-Augustin 2004:187ff). Attacks on Lenin statues were often the first symbolic victories of the anticommunists in the Baltics, in western Ukraine, and in the Caucasus. In Ukraine, the disappearance or survival of Lenin is still an important characteristic of the political landscape. West of the Dniepr he has been taken down or cut to pieces; east of the river he is still standing tall. In Kyiv, where local opinion is predominantly anticommunist but which as the capital for some time had to bridge the west and the east of the country, Lenin was standing until December 2013, when militants of the far right Svoboda party brought him down, as part of the ongoing movement to topple the government. Postcommunist Warsaw is full of recent monuments to Polish national martyrdom, but also includes a new column celebrating a millennium of victorious Polish cavalry. Moscow returned to its national-imperial past, with a huge statue and monumental complex commemorating Peter the Great. In Budapest, the current right-wing government is busy restoring the iconography of the central city to its shape during the counterrevolutionary, semi-fascist regime of Admiral Horthy, in 1920–1944. The Macedonian government is frantically trying to make Skopje a city of historical national monuments, while the Greeks are preventing them from officially calling its main equestrian statue Alexander the Great.

Monumentality is still on the European agenda, and not only in the East. Berlin, as we have seen above, has been much preoccupied with anti-Nazi monuments of atonement, and is now planning to make something bigger out of anticommunism, than the old Cold War rhetoric of West Berlin. At the same time, there have been fierce political fights about whether anything of the political iconography of East Berlin would be allowed to survive. Marx and Engels were never seriously threatened, it seems, and the Social Democrats finally found that they could live with Rosa Luxemburg. That the Communist Party leader Ernst Thälmann, in a militant pose by a late Soviet modernist sculptor, survived was apparently more accidental and due to right-wing exhaustion in the iconographic war in Berlin. It helped, of course, that Thälmann, although never popular outside party ranks, had been jailed and finally murdered by the Nazis.

Although far from the "statuemania" of the Third Republic, France and Paris have not abandoned monumental politics. A very controversial decision was President Chirac's decision to honor the *harkis,* the Algerian colonial troops who fought with the French against Algerian independence. Even in globalized London, debates have been going on in recent years about what or whom to place on the fourth plinth in Trafalgar Square. Democratic, post-Franco Madrid erected an abstract monument, on the grand thoroughfare Paseo Castellana, to Spain's democratic Constitution of 1978. Devolution in Britain has spawned a new national monumentality vested in the new Scottish and Welsh parliaments.

Monumentality is an important part of urban European experience. Political and cultural elites are today much more divided in their appreciation than a century ago. However, the historical change of popular attention and concern is much more difficult to gauge. The anticommunist iconoclasm of 1989–1991 stands up very well, both to the monumental demolitions of the French Revolution and to those of the local communists. In the Ukraine of 2013–14, monumental issues reached a pitch that was only decided by force.

The era of national monumentality in Europe may be ending, but it is certainly not finished yet.

NOTES

1.   In January 1945, the Fourth Ukrainian Front of the Red Army launched an architectural competition for a monument to its coming liberation of Vienna (on April 13, 1945).

With its dedication to "the eternal fame of the solders of the Soviet Army who fell in the combat against the Fascist German occupiers," the colonnaded hemicycle was inaugurated in the Vienna Schwarzenbergplatz on August 19, 1945 (Klein 2004:105ff).

2.   There is, however, a rather discreet homage to the suffragettes in Victoria Street in Westminster, in the form of an upright bronze scroll.

3.   This is not the full story. After World War II, the big communist parties of France and Italy did leave an iconographic legacy in regions and areas of strength. Today it is most discernible in toponomies in the areas of Paris and Rome, where Stalingrad, Lenin, and Togliatti et al. may still be found.

REFERENCES CITED

Baker, M. 2002 *Discovering London Statues and Monuments*. Shire, London.

Blau, E. 1999 *The Architecture of Red Vienna, 1919–1934*. MIT Press, Cambridge.

Bowlt, J. 1978 Russian Sculpture and Lenin's Plan of Monumental Propaganda. In *Art and Architecture in the Service of Politics*, edited by H. Millon and L. Nochlin, pp. 182–193. MIT Press, Cambridge.

Bradley, S. and N. Pevsner 2003 *London & Westminster*. Yale University Press, New Haven and London.

Chaix, G. 2001 Die Reformation. In *Deutsche Erinnerungsorte*, edited by F. Schulze, pp. 9–27. C. H. Beck, Munich.

Colton, T. 1995 *Moscow*. The Belknap Press, Cambridge, Massachusetts.

Cotterell, A. 2008. *The Imperial Capitals of China*. Pimlico, London.

Demetz, P. 1997. *Prague in Black and Gold*. Allen Lane Penguin, London.

Favier, J. 1997. *Paris. Deux mille ans d'histoire*. Fayard, Paris.

Flagge, I., and W. J. Stock, eds. 1992 *Architektur und Demokratie*. Hatje, Stuttgart.

Hargrove, J. 1986 Les statues de Paris. In *Les lieux de mémoire*, II, edited by P. Nora, pp. 243–282. Gallimard, Paris.

Hood, J. 2005 *Trafalgar Square*. Batsford, London.

Jencks, C. 2005. *Iconic Building*. Frances Lincoln, London.

Jones, C. 2006. *Paris. Biography of a City*. Penguin, London.

Kirk, T. 2005 *The Architecture of Modern Italy vol 2*. Princeton Architectural Press, New York.

Klein, E. 2004 *Denkwürdiges Wien*. Falter, Vienna.

Kosellek, R., and M. Jeismann 1994 *Der Politische Totenkult*. Wilhelm Fink, Munich.

Krastins, J. 2006 Architecture and Urban Development of Art Nouveau-Metropolis Riga. *International Review of Sociology* 16(2):395–425.

Lehnert, U. 1998 *Der Kaiser und die Siegesallee: réclame royale*. Reimer, Berlin.

Mann. M. 1986 *The Sources of Social Power vol. 1*. Cambridge University Press, Cambridge.

Miháilová, S. 2006 The Making of the Capital of Slovakia. *International Review of Sociology* 16(2):309–328.

Montaner, J. M. 1997 *Barcelona. Stadt und Architektur*. Taschen, Köln.

Plessen, M-L., ed. 1995 *Marianne und Germania, 1789–1889*. Argon, Berlin.

Rihtman-Augustin, D. 2004 The Monument in the Main City Square. In *Balkan Identities*, edited by M. Todorova, pp. 180–196. Hurst and Company, London.

Rokkan, S. 1973 Cities, States and Nations: A Dimensional Model for the Study of Contrasts in Development. In *Building States and Nations, vol. I*, edited by S. N. Eisenstadt and S. Rokkan. Sage, London.

Searing, H. 1978 With Red Flags Flying: Housing in Amsterdam, 1915–1923. In *Art and Architecture in the Service of Politics,* edited by H. Millon and L. Nochlin, pp. 230–269. MIT Press, Cambridge.

Sinkó, K. 1992 Political Rituals: The Raising and Demolition of Monuments. In *Art and Society in the Age of Stalin,* edited by P. György and H. Turai, pp. 73–86. Corvina, Budapest.

Therborn, G. 2002 Monumental Europe: The National Years. On the Iconography of European Capital Cities. *Housing, Theory and Society* 19(1):26–47. 2006 Eastern Drama. Capitals of Eastern Europe, 1830s–2006: An Introductory Overview. *International Review of Sociology* 16(2):209–242.

Therborn, G. 2008 Identity and Capital Cities: European Nations and the European Union. In *The Search for a European Identity: Values, Policies, and Legitimacy of the European Union,* edited by F. Cerutti and S. Lucarelli. Routledge, London. 2011 *The World.* Polity, Cambridge.

Thiis-Evensen, T. 1998 Arkitekturens maktgrammatik. In *Maktens korridorer,* edited by C. Kullberg Christophersen, pp. 5–14. Norsk Form, Oslo.

Vogel, W. 1951 *Bismarcks Arbeiterversicherung: ihre Entstehung im Kräftespiel der Zeit.* G. Westermann, Braunschweig.

Weinreb, B., and C. Hibbert, eds. 1993 *The London Encyclopedia* Rev. ed. Macmillan, London.

Wilderotter, H. 1998 *Alltag der Macht. Berlin Wilhelmstrasse.* Jovis, Berlin.

Winther, J. 1995 *Sites of Memory, Sites of Mourning.* Cambridge University Press, Cambridge.

Wise, M. 1998 *Capital Dilemma.* Princeton Architectural Press, New York.

PART V

The Experience of Monuments

Chapter Seventeen

The Creation and Experience of Monumentality on Protohistoric Cyprus

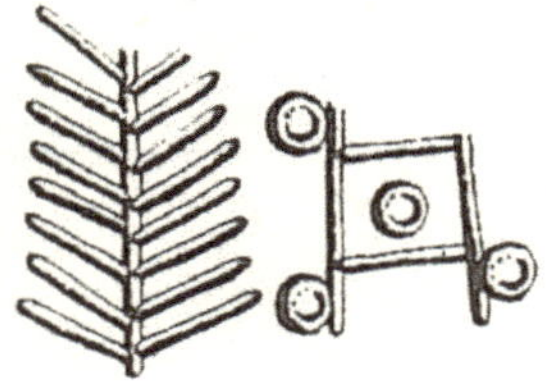

Kevin D. Fisher

Abstract *The Protohistoric Bronze Age (c. 1700–1100 B.C.) was a period of revolutionary social change on the island of Cyprus. I argue that the creation and experience of monumental architecture played a central and active role in these developments. To examine this dynamic interrelationship, I take an integrative approach that acknowledges the agency of both social actors and the material world they inhabit. Monumentality was created in acts of place making by many individuals and groups on Protohistoric Cyprus. It was materialized and experienced at various scales, from the orthogonal street plans and cyclopean fortifications of new cityscapes, to the impressive buildings that served as centers of elite power, and the individual spaces within them. Protohistoric built environments were a fundamentally different experience from the Prehistoric Bronze Age villages that preceded them, creating new patterns of interaction and daily practice that generated social change. More than mere symbols of elite control over material and human resources, monumental constructions became the primary arena in which sociopolitical dynamics were enacted.*

Cyprus lagged well behind its Near Eastern neighbors, as well as other Mediterranean islands (Kolb this volume), in the development of monumental construction. Its earliest expressions of monumentality do not appear until the Protohistoric Bronze Age (or ProBA; Middle Cypriot III through Late Cypriot IIIA, c. 1700–1100 B.C.), when wholesale changes to the island's built environment occur that included new forms of domestic and mortuary architecture and, eventually, the first cities (Figure 17.1). At the same time, we see revolutionary societal changes, including the development and institutionalization of hierarchical and heterarchical social structures associated with the emergence of what was likely some form of state-level sociopolitical organization. I have argued elsewhere that, rather than serving merely as an indicator or product of this transformation, the new built environments played an active and integral role in how and why it occurred (Fisher 2009a, 2014a). Indeed, the Protohistoric built environments were a fundamentally different experience from those of the Prehistoric Bronze Age that preceded it, providing new patterns of movement, surveillance, interaction, and daily practice that generated social change. As acts of place making, monumental constructions were a central facet of these developments.

In what follows, I attempt to address some of themes raised in this volume's introduction (Osborne this volume) by first outlining an integrative approach to investigating past built environments that considers the agency of both builder and building through

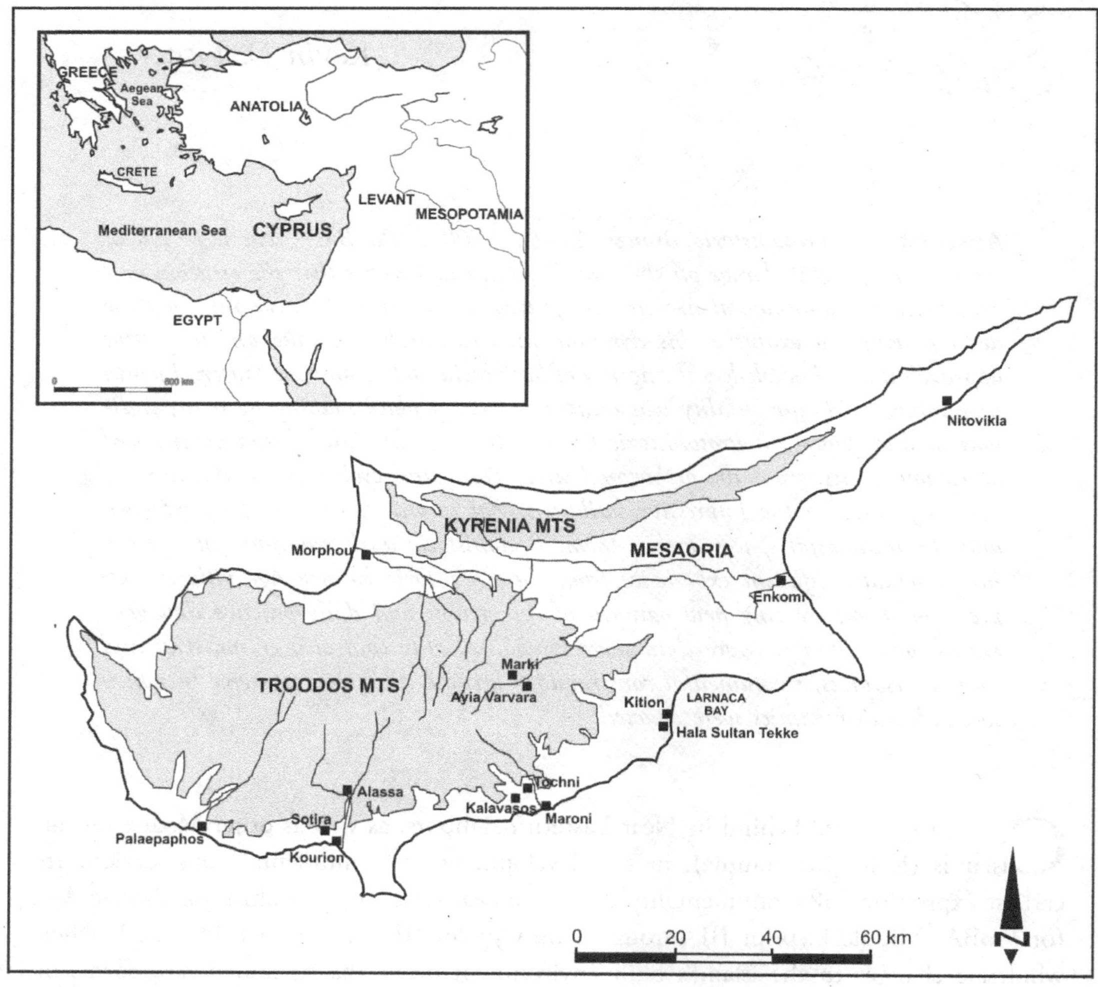

FIGURE 17.1 Map of Cyprus showing locations of sites mentioned in text (drawn by K. Fisher).

the relationship between built environments and social interaction. I focus particularly on the materiality of ashlar (cut stone) masonry, which became one of the defining features of both monumental buildings and the identities of the people who made them. Drawing on specific examples from a number of sites, I then apply this approach in examining some aspects of how Protohistoric Cypriotes created and experienced monumentality at multiple scales, from the cityscape through to individual buildings and their constituent spaces.

APPROACHING MONUMENTALITY: HUMAN AND MATERIAL AGENCIES

Large size and elaborate construction are characteristics that typify many traditional views of what makes something monumental. Yet, as Osborne makes clear in the introduction to this volume, monumentality arises only in part from the inherent properties of a structure or object. It is constituted, rather, in the ever-changing and historically contingent interplay of human and material agencies. This relational definition of monumentality rightly recognizes that things *become* monumental and may not necessarily have been intended as such from their initial construction (e.g., Joyce 2004; Thompson and Andrus 2011). Erecting a building, however, is always an intentional act, and I would argue that ProBA elites envisioned the structures discussed here as monuments from the outset of their design. Other social actors were also involved in this process and, indeed, these monuments were the products of the actions of many agents (a point I return to below). Influenced by the work of Bourdieu (1977), Giddens (1984) and other social theorists who have attempted to bridge the gap between individual and society, the idea of past humans as active, perhaps even knowledgeable agents who in some way shaped the social worlds they lived in, has gained currency among archaeologists—even if there remain methodological and epistemological issues regarding its use in archaeological inquiry (Dobres and Robb 2000; Dornan 2002; Gardner 2007). The agency of things, however, is a concept that archaeologists have typically been slower to accept.

This is now changing in the wake of recent studies of materiality, which highlight the vital and recursive role that things play in social reproduction and begin to blur distinctions between human/subject and material/object (Demarrais et al. 2004; Gosden 2005; Meskell 2005; Miller 2005). Hodder (2012), who has long recognized the role of the material world in constituting the social one, has recently argued that previous approaches to materiality do not go far enough in acknowledging the ways in which the physicality or "material objectness" of things entraps people into particular *entanglements*: sets of interlinked dependencies between humans and things (see also Knappett 2012; Latour 2005; Webmoor and Whitmore 2008). Following Ingold (2010), he challenges assumptions regarding the inanimate nature of things, suggesting rather that things are imbued with life as characterized by the flow of matter, energy, and information. Indeed, by moving beyond an anthropocentric conception of agency based on consciousness and intention, we can now speak of material agency (Knappett and Malafouris 2008).

This agency extends to the built environment. Perhaps more than most material actors, the sheer size and near-omnipresent nature of buildings makes their physicality nearly impossible to ignore. As much as they are products or embodiments of human agency, buildings at the same time divide and order space, structuring and routinizing the movements and social interactions of daily practice, and therefore play a direct and active role in social reproduction. While size is not a prerequisite for monumentality, often the sheer mass of monumental buildings or complexes means that even people who might never set foot inside such buildings are affected by the gravity of their presence. Buildings, especially monumental ones, can also enable patterns of movement and surveillance that are implicated in the exercise of power (Foucault 1977; Leone et al. 2005). Their agency is not based solely in their formal qualities, however, as monumental built environments also materialize ideologies (DeMarrais et al. 1996). On one level, they are powerful symbols of the conspicuous consumption of energy and control over material and human resources by their creators (Trigger 1990), yet they also encode and communicate meanings, often aimed at particular audiences, regarding the appropriation of space, the organization and materialization of social relationships and boundaries, and the legitimation of sociopolitical inequalities.

In many respects, the agency of buildings is encapsulated in the idea of place. If space is the passive, neutral, physical location of social action, then place is "lived space" imbued with meanings, identities, and memories that actively shape, and are shaped by, the daily practice and experiences of its inhabitants and historically contingent social processes (de Certeau 1998; Low and Lawrence-Zúñiga 2003; Preucel and Meskell 2004; Pred 1990; Rodman 1992; Tuan 1978). The distinction between material and human actors is thus blurred in the mutually constituting human-environment relationship embodied in places. It is further undermined by the affective relationships that people often develop with the places in which they live. The importance of *place attachment* to well-being and identity formation has long been recognized by environmental psychologists (Altman and Low 1992; Marcus 1995; Russell and Snodgrass 1987). Like other human and material actors, buildings develop unique life histories or "biographies" (Kopytoff 1986) constituted in the meanings accumulated over the duration of their use life, which are a product of the historically contingent actions, experiences, and memories of their human occupants (Pred 1990; Tringham 1995; see also Düring 2005; Hendon 2004:276).

Pred (1984:279) argues that the creation of place "always involves an appropriation and transformation of space and nature that is inseparable from the reproduction and transformation of society in time and space." In ProBA Cyprus, the scale of spatial appropriation and transformation that underlies monumental construction makes its initial creation an act of elite place making. These monumental built environments were intended to be visually impressive symbols of the power of their creators, but it was in the experience of social interactions and occasions performed in and around these structures that the social dynamics of power were enacted, negotiated, and reproduced. ProBA monumental buildings have long been recognized as symbols of the emergence and power of elites, but only recently have scholars begun to examine these built environments as places that had a vital role in identity formation and social reproduction (Bolger 2003; Knapp 2008:201–248, 2009; Manning 1998). Even these approaches, however, have not gone far enough in considering how the creation and experience of specific monumental contexts actively influenced these processes (cf. Kearns 2011). Such an investigation, given the limited remains of Late Bronze Age built environments, presents a significant challenge.

I have developed an approach that analyzes how buildings affect movement and interaction while also examining how they encode and communicate meanings to occupants and visitors. I discuss this in detail elsewhere and provide only a brief outline here (see Fisher 2007, 2009b). It begins with the use of access analysis, which can determine likely patterns of movement and encounter based on the topological properties of a building's spaces (Hillier and Hanson 1984). To get a more complete picture of social interaction, however, it is necessary to combine this with a detailed study of how a building influences human behavior and interaction through the nonverbal communication of meanings. These meanings are encoded or materialized in fixed-feature elements such as walls and floors, semifixed-feature elements such as furnishings and other artifacts, and nonfixed-feature elements including the physical and verbal expressions of the building's occupants and users (Rapoport 1990:87–101). Rapoport (1988) suggests that encoded meanings may be high-level, representing cosmological principles; mid-level, relating to status, power and identity; or low-level, which are mnemonic cues indicating the intended uses of a setting. In reality, most meanings defy easy categorization and often cut across these levels.

While humans perceive meanings or cues as they experience built environments using an array of sensory stimuli (Frieman and Gillings 2007), vision remains one that can be analyzed most easily with the architectural remains left to us. We can analyze visibility using isovists, or the set of all points visible from a single point in space (Benedikt 1979:47); isovist fields, which indicate everything that can be seen from anywhere in a particular room; and viewsheds, which represent what is visible from the perspective of the viewer facing a particular direction (see Fisher 2009b:448–451; e.g., see Figures 7 and 8). Such an analysis reduces a 3D phenomenon to 2D polygons, but it can at least begin to give some sense of the visual experience of a space. There is clearly potential for computer-based 3D modeling to further develop these analyses (e.g., Wendrich this volume). To this we can add insights gained from environmental psychology. Hall's (1966) research on proxemics, the study of people's use of space as an aspect of culture, is especially useful in illuminating the relationship between interpersonal spacing and human sensory perception during social interaction, suggesting a range of distances at which certain types of social interaction might take place (Fisher 2009b:Table 1).

This integrative approach (see Lawrence and Low 1990:482–491) allows one to determine the likely locations for particular types of social interactions, including fleeting encounters while moving through a space, and social occasions, which are more intensive interactions and range from some of the more routine aspects of daily life (e.g., the regular preparation and consumption of a meal) to more formally defined events in terms of time, space, and participants (Giddens 1984:64–73; Goffman 1963:18–24). The new monumental buildings of the Protohistoric Bronze Age were typically designed around contexts for what I have termed public-inclusive social occasions, which bring together visitors and inhabitants in large, architecturally elaborate, and relatively accessible spaces.

It was during such interactions that social statuses, roles, and identities were negotiated and reproduced. In order to better understand how this dynamic process worked, it is necessary to examine how people created and experienced monumental built environments at various scales.

CREATING MONUMENTALITY

As I noted in the introduction, the earliest monumental architecture on Cyprus dates to the seventeenth century B.C., when it appears as part of a suite of changes to the island's built environment. While the Prehistoric Bronze Age that came before it is better known from its burial evidence, excavations at settlements such as Sotira-*Kaminoudhia* and Marki-*Alonia* have revealed villages with agglomerative domestic architecture that displays little evidence of planning or social differentiation (Frankel and Webb 2006; Swiny et al. 2003:Figure 1). Indeed, most aspects of Cypriot society were revolutionized during the ProBA, which witnessed the widespread rise and institutionalization of social inequalities, the emergence and integration of specialized systems of production and exchange, and the engagement of the island into the wider politico-economic system of the Near East and eastern Mediterranean. Control over the production and export of the island's abundant copper resources was a key element underpinning the economic power of emerging ProBA elites (Knapp 2008:159–172). Whether the island was ruled as a unified entity or through a more heterarchical system of regional polities, or vacillated between these forms of political organization, is the subject of much debate (e.g., Knapp 2008:298–340; Peltenburg 2012).

It is not surprising, perhaps, that the first monumental buildings are a series of so-called forts, which appear in the central and northeastern part of the island at the beginning of the ProBA (Fisher 2007:287–298) and may have been built in order to control routes from the copper-bearing pillow lavas of the Troodos Mountains to the newly emerging urban centers on the north and east coasts (Fortin 1981; Peltenburg 1996). The Fortress building at the new east coast settlement of Enkomi is the best known example (see Dikaios 1969–1971:16–21) and was designed to restrict physical and visual access to the copper production facilities inside it (Fisher 2007:199–204). The forts were by far the largest structures that had been built on the island up to that point, marking an unprecedented appropriation of space and investment in construction. Their often prominent locations were probably as much to enhance their prominence on the ProBA landscape as they were for defensive purposes. We know frustratingly little about the settlements that appear at this time, during what I have called the "Proto-urban" phase of the ProBA (Fisher 2007:287–289). Limited exposures in the settlement to the south of the Fortress at Enkomi reveal evidence for a series of large court-centered compounds in the location of the later Ashlar Building (Dikaios 1969–1971:plates 267–271; Figure 4). These buildings and the Fortress itself were separated from other structures by open spaces in which chamber tombs were located. Intramural tombs were a vital part of these Proto-urban built environments, marking a distinct break from thousands of years of burial in extramural cemeteries (Keswani 2004). Their visibility and continued reuse throughout this Proto-urban period likely indicates that they were the primary means of status display among competing groups (Keswani 2004) and used in the negotiation and demarcation of both physical and social boundaries between them.

The fourteenth century B.C. marked the beginning of a fully urban period in which some new centers were founded, while other previously occupied settlements were urbanized and monumentalized. While these cities exhibit differing patterns of urbanization and internal structure (Iavovou 2007; Keswani 1996), they do share evidence for at least some degree of urban planning, a point I discuss further below (see Fisher 2014b). Something else that nearly all of these centers have in common is the presence of monumental buildings. In spite of attempts to assign specific labels (e.g., "sanctuary" or "public") and functions to these new buildings, my analysis of an admittedly incomplete dataset suggests that they tended to serve multiple social, administrative, economic, and domestic purposes. Whatever other functions we might assign to these complexes, I have argued that they were designed largely around the provision of spaces for social occasions that brought occupants and visitors together, replacing the funerary realm as the primary arena in which ProBA social dynamics were enacted (Fisher 2007, 2009a). In general, ProBA monumental buildings were usually quite large, at least by Cypriot standards (c. 1400 m² for the largest such structure, Building II at Alassa-*Paliotaverna*, compared with c. 65–200 m² for typical domestic structures) and they tended to have a large, often central, court that was a focal point of such activities. Perhaps their most distinguishing feature, however, is the use of ashlar masonry, which I discuss in greater detail below. In spite of these general similarities, however, each building exhibited significant variation in how these elements were arranged, with the result that each was experienced differently and developed its own distinct biography through use and renovation.

The creation of ProBA monumental places involved the interplay of material agencies and human actions. People's experience of these buildings began with the initial planning and construction, a process of materialization that transformed ideas and values into physical reality. DeMarrais et al. (1996:16) emphasize that this was an ongoing process of creation and "that to materialize culture is to participate in the active, ongoing process of creating and negotiating meaning." Building a monumental structure was undoubtedly a complex and long-term undertaking that involved the participation of a number of stakeholders from the elites who commissioned the building, through architects, various trained craftspeople, and numerous laborers, all of whom would have contributed to the building's biography and encoded meanings (Allison 1999:4; Fisher 2009a:189; Locock 1994:5; Markus 1993:23). In trying to imbue places with meanings that conveyed their power and identity, while at the same time facilitating desired behaviors in those who used these places, and providing opportunities for themselves to engage in or avoid social interaction, elites faced a number of choices regarding building layout and materials. These choices were influenced to some degree by the nature of the building site, particularly whether or not there was extant architecture that needed to be incorporated into the design (or removed), as well as by the ability to procure various material and human resources.

These choices were further constrained by what Rapoport (1990:87–122 Figure 17) refers to as the culturally determined "palette of elements" (height, size, color, orientation, materials, etc.) and the "display rules" by which these elements could be combined to encode meanings. For ProBA elites, there was also the potential to draw upon the longer-established traditions of monumental construction of neighboring cultures with which they had regular diplomatic and economic contacts. Hitchcock (2009) suggests that the so-called "international style" seen in prestige goods that circulated among Late Bronze Age elites in this region, characterized by artistic motifs that reflect the hybridization of Near Eastern, Egyptian, and Aegean influences (Feldman 2006), may have extended to elite architecture as well (also Knapp 2008:160–162).

Beyond their role in configuring space, the characteristics of walls, including the materials with which they were made and the use of elaboration or decoration, were an essential aspect of monumental place making. Stone was a key material in this regard, serving as the foundations for all ProBA architecture, both nonelite and monumental. As I alluded to above, recent considerations of materiality have criticized the (over)emphasis of the role of things in facilitating the social lives of humans, while often failing to consider the physicality of the things themselves—their material properties and how these affect our engagement with the material world and create networks that link people and things (Hodder 2012; Ingold 2007; Knappett 2011). My own work on ProBA monumental architecture, while considering at some length the vital role of ashlar masonry in the nonverbal communication of meaning and the formation of elite identity, has only briefly touched on the materiality of the stone itself (Fisher 2009a:192–193). I reconsider it here, drawing on recent approaches that look at stone as both a physical and symbolic material, while attempting to outline some elements of the *chaîne opératoire,* or the steps that unfold in the technological sequence of turning raw stone into ashlar blocks (see Knappett 2012:196–201).

THE MATERIALITY OF ASHLAR MASONRY

The use of stone construction on Cyprus dates back at least to the Pre-Pottery Neolithic (PPN) B (c. 9100–8500 cal B.C.), or even the PPNA (c. 9100–8500 cal B.C.) if we consider the carving of pits and postholes into bedrock seen at the site of Ayia Varvara-*Asprokremnos* (Manning et al. 2010). Field stone rubble construction would continue to be used for building foundations until modern times. Yet it was not until the beginning of the ProBA that ashlar masonry is first seen on the island, where blocks with drafted margins were used for jambs and coigning in the otherwise rubble walls of the possibly Late Cypriot I fort at Nitovikla, one of the island's earliest monumental buildings (Wright 1992:410). By the fourteenth or thirteenth centuries B.C., this type of masonry was generally used to replace (at least partially) the field stone rubble component of walls in monumental construction. In most situations the ashlar masonry would have extended up to 1.5 m or more above the floor level and was then topped by a superstructure of plastered and painted mudbrick. The Cypriotes developed a number of types of ashlar masonry, ranging from the most elaborate with a large projecting plinth of blocks with drafted margins surmounted by orthostats, to simpler solid or shell walls of small square or rectangular blocks (Fisher 2007:102–103 Figure 5.2; Hult 1983:5). The technical expertise and expense in material and labor required by this form of construction were such that it tended to be applied strategically, with the more elaborate forms of masonry deployed where it was most likely to be seen or in spaces were high-level social interactions took place. Only Building II at Alassa-*Paliotaverna* makes extensive use of the most elaborate form of ashlar masonry (Hadjisavvas 2000).

It is perhaps not surprising that Cypriot elites would use cut stone in monumental construction, since ashlar masonry was a clear symbol of elite ability to control both material and human resources. Given that stone is one of the most difficult materials to work, the extent of its use provides some indication of the investment in monumental construction (Trigger 2003:567). We know more about the material resources than the human participants in these "projects of stone" (Richards 2010:57), but they undoubtedly involved the long-term engagement of large numbers of skilled and general laborers, overseers, and support workers at various resource extraction sites and the construction site itself, creating a web of human-material entanglements that would have implications beyond the spatial extent and temporal duration of a single project.

The long-term survival of stone allows us some insight into the *chaîne opératoire* of ashlar production. In addition to having desired aesthetic qualities, stone sources for ashlar construction had to be able to yield adequate block sizes (one ashlar block from Building II at Alassa-*Paliotaverna*, for example, was nearly 5 m long x 0.75 m wide), while being free of any minerals that might cause chemical decomposition or be affected by weather conditions (Philokyprou 2011:40). Ashlar sources were typically sedimentary formations found within a site's hinterland, although the stone still had to be quarried some distance away and transported to the construction site. The centers of Kalavasos-*Ayios Dhimitrios*, Maroni-*Vournes* and *Tsaroukkas*, Alassa-*Paliotaverna* and Palaepaphos used high quality calcareous sandstone from the Pachna geological formation (Philokyprou 2011:40; Wright 1992:364). At Kalavasos, this stone was likely obtained from a quarry at Tochni, c. 4 km to the east, which is still in use today (South 1989:320). In an example of material agency, or the *affordances* offered by a particular source material (Gibson 1986), Philokyprou (2011:40) notes that, in some cases, discontinuities in the Pachna formation create a "rectangular grid" that facilitates the easy removal of rectangular pieces of stone. These kinds of natural breaks in the source material might account for the irregular sizes of most ashlar blocks.

Ashlar construction at Kition illustrates that there was a gradation of stone use from three different sources (Philokyprou 2011:40–42 Figure 7; Xenophontos 1985; Wright 1992:365). A lower quality (due to its porosity) calcareous sandstone from the Nicosia and Athalassa formations (c. 4 km away) was used for "utilitarian" purposes such as blocks in the towers of the city wall, and is also used in ashlar construction in lower-order elite houses at the nearby urban center of Hala Sultan Tekke. Meanwhile, the monumental orthostats of the Temple 1 building at Kition were constructed using a visually striking whitish-colored reef limestone from the Koronia formation, located across Larnaca Bay, approximately 20 km away by sea. The impressive nature of these orthostats drew attention away from the fact that they were supported by a plinth of ashlars made from a conglomerate available on site (Figure 17.2). Other types of cut stone were also used in

FIGURE 17.2 Kition, Temple 1 showing ashlar orthostats on interior of north wall (photo by K. Fisher).

construction, including fine-grained chalk from the Lefkara formation, which could be cut into thin slabs and used as a veneer (Philokyprou 2011:42), as in the famous Basin Room in House A at Hala Sultan Tekke (Hult 1981:17). Gypsum was fairly abundant in Cyprus and could also be cut into thin slabs.

Other than the ashlar blocks themselves, there is little direct evidence for the process of quarrying on the island from the ProBA and no quarries have been identified as definitively from this period. What evidence there is from ProBA tools and ancient quarries of indeterminate date on the island suggests that once a suitable rock face was exposed and the block shape marked, circumferential trenches were cut down to the desired depth (perhaps determined by an existing fracture plane) using tools such as bronze axes, chisels, hammers, and perhaps saws. Metal or wooden wedges were then inserted into notches cut under the block and struck with hammers to split the block loose so that it could then be pried up using levers (Philokyprou 2011:43; Wright 1992:363). Initial dressing, especially for larger blocks, likely took place at or near the quarry site and involved cutting the block back with bronze or stone tools to reveal a protruding lug or lifting boss that could be used to help secure ropes to move the stone.

Whether transported overland, perhaps by ox-drawn cart (undoubtedly an impressive sight), or by sea, the remains of ashlar "debitage" used to level some floors in the central part of the Ashlar Building at Enkomi suggest that the blocks likely underwent their final dressing on site (Dikaios 1969–1971:172). Based on the evidence of Aegean and Egyptian ashlar construction, Nelson (2003) suggests that this took place *in situ* and that the blocks were laid with extra material on their upper surfaces to permit an entire course to be leveled and cut back using only one measurement across an entire wall surface. A number of blocks were fashioned with mortises or rabbets, indicating that wooden structural components were also an important part of monumental construction.

Most ashlar walls were of shell construction with rubble-packed centers, allowing the blocks to be finished only on surfaces that would be seen. In more elaborate ProBA ashlar walls, the exposed surfaces of blocks were only cut back and dressed along their margins, leaving a raised boss. While these drafted margins were used to correctly align blocks with their neighbors, it is clear that they became an important stylistic element of Cypriot ashlar construction. There was a great deal of variation among (and even within) sites as to how this was executed. In some cases, such as the exterior wall of Temple 1 at Kition, the drafted margins on the orthostats are barely visible and the central boss has been fully dressed. In others, such as the west wall of Building X at Kalavasos-*Ayios Dhimitrios*, the margins were fully dressed while the central boss was left rough, with obvious tool marks (Figure 17.3). The lifting bosses were also often left in place, despite having fulfilled their practical purpose, and even if they were wholly or partially cut back, their locations often remained obvious. While Wright (1992:370–371) attributes this to an "aesthetics of economy," he admits that it would have been a simple matter for even an apprentice mason to dress away the remainder of the block. I would suggest, rather, that these features were left deliberately as mnemonic devices symbolizing the process of monumental construction (and hence elite control of that process)—powerful reminders of the place from which these blocks came, the labor that was required to quarry and move them to the site, and the technical and managerial expertise needed to create a building with them. They are perhaps something akin to the "cut-away" images of vehicles used today by manufacturers to show the impressive engineering rarely seen beneath the polished exteriors. In a similar vein, we might also read these features as embodying the domestication of stone. In her study of the Inka use of stone, Dean (2010:76) suggests that to build with stone was to put it into order, essentially taming it. Thus, "[d]ressed and fitted stone might well be thought of as the most thoroughly domesticated of all rock" (Dean 2010:76).

Ashlar masonry contributed to the solidity and stability of monumental buildings, qualities that were instrumental in convincing people of the reality of the power through which the structures were built (Wilson 1988:179). In a culture where sundried mudbrick was the primary building material, stone symbolized permanence—not only of the building itself, but also of the social structure and underlying inequalities that facilitated its construction. Yet the significance of ashlar masonry went beyond merely symbolizing

FIGURE 17.3 Kalavasos-*Ayios Dhimitrios*, Building X showing detail of ashlar masonry on interior of west wall of the Pithos Hall (photo by K. Fisher).

elite power. The process of creating ashlar buildings outlined above points to an intimate knowledge of the physical properties of stone, obtained through embodied experience, by at least some of the participants. Stone was experienced in daily practice through an interlinked combination of sensorial characteristics that included visual, acoustic, and tactile properties (Tilley 2004). It is also implicated in the formation of identities and notions of personhood (Bukach 2003; Kirk 2006). In many past and ethnographically attested cultures, stones were not merely things, but were considered sacred, if not animate, active beings or even ancestors (Dean 2010; O'Connor and Cooney 2010:xxiii; Parker Pearson and Ramilsonina 1998; Scarre 2010:10–11; Taçon 1991; Tilley 2004). Given the importance of stones in human-environment interactions on ProBA Cyprus, we should acknowledge the possibility that they were not only active agents as argued above, but may have been perceived as such by the people who encountered them in daily practice. In any case, stones, and ashlar masonry in particular, played a vital role in ProBA place making, shaping social interactions while forming an integral part of the identity of urban inhabitants. As O'Connor and Cooney (2010:xxii–xxiii) argue,

> [its] enduring character means that stone is inextricably linked to notions of monumentality and remembrance, and formed an active medium in the creation of identities and memory life in a range of social contexts and practices. . . .[T]he material presence and physical character of stone objects and monuments are not only actively harnessed in these encounters but are also the very stuff from which social relations are derived, perceived and thought through.

This materiality was experienced at multiple scales from cityscapes through particular buildings and their spaces.

EXPERIENCING MONUMENTALITY

CITYSCAPES, MONUMENTALITY, AND INTERACTION

I noted above that by the fourteenth century B.C. there were a number of urban centers on the island (Figure 17.1). While excavations have been conducted at all of them, the rather limited exposures provide only glimpses of their layouts. In spite of variation in the way it was executed, these cityscapes consistently exhibit varying degrees of top-down urban planning, presumably initiated by local ruling elites. Such planning was undoubtedly closely coordinated with the placement of major monumental buildings. The sites of Enkomi and Kalavasos-*Ayios Dhimitrios* give us the best indication of what a nucleated ProBA city looked like. These settlements' extant plans suggest that they were characterized by the architectural definition and enclosure of the vast majority of urban space through the contiguous placement of building walls and streets. This contrasts with what (little) we know of centers such as Maroni and perhaps Palaepaphos, which, while apparently larger, may represent a lower density form of urbanism spread across multiple nuclei (Iacovou 2007:3–6).

Excavations at Enkomi have revealed nearly 20 percent of the city's urban plan, although difficulties in sorting out the site's complex chronology make a detailed assessment of its urban development difficult (see Fisher 2007:120–122 Figure 17.4). The city was rebuilt on a grand scale c. 1200 B.C. (start of the ProBA 3; LC IIIA) using what Smith (2007:12–21) would call a modular orthogonal plan (Courtois et al. 1986; Dikaios 1969–1971). The grid, oriented to about 7° west of north, consists of a single, central north-south artery dissected by nine evenly spaced, east-west running streets, forming 20 blocks.

Covering about 14 ha, Enkomi was surrounded by a fortification wall and towers made with a base of cyclopean masonry (massive, roughly shaped boulders), undoubtedly

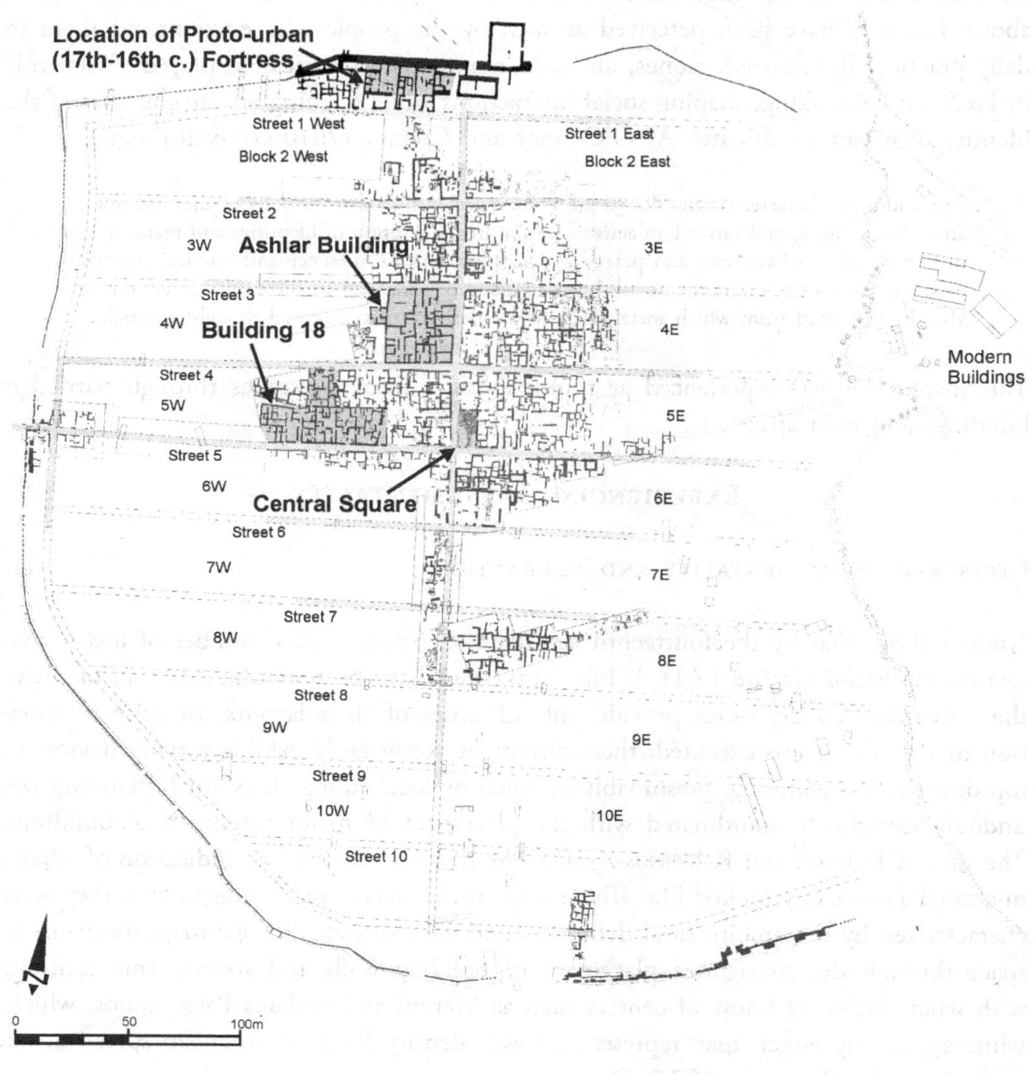

FIGURE 17.4 Schematic plan of Enkomi, c. 1200 B.C. (adapted by K. Fisher from Courtois et al. 1986:Figure 1; and Schaeffer 1971:Plan IV).

one of its most impressive monumental constructions. The city contained a variety of contiguously placed structures, including a number of monumental buildings built using ashlar masonry. The most architecturally elaborate of these, Building 18 (actually not a single building, but series of interconnecting units) and the Ashlar Building, had ashlar facades that could not have failed to make an impression on passersby. Building 18's façade of massive orthostats stretched more than 40 m along the north side of Street 5 West. Both structures were located on one of the major streets running between the city's gates. The Ashlar Building (Dikaios 1969–1971:171–190; Fisher 2007:115–198) is substantially larger than any other structure in the city, but it appears to have been an elite residence, lacking compelling evidence for administrative activities. The same might be said of the Building 18 complex (Schaeffer 1952:239–369). The lack of a single obvious administrative center, together with the generally widespread distribution of the highest status goods among elite graves throughout the city has led Keswani (1996, 2004:115) to suggest that there was no single focus of administrative power at Enkomi and that the site was therefore characterized by a heterarchical sociopolitical organization with power dispersed among multiple nodes (also Manning 1998:53).

The situation was different at sites such as Kalavasos-*Ayios Dhimitrios*, Maroni, and Alassa, each of which has a single monumental complex that likely served as its administrative center, suggesting a more hierarchical distribution of power with a paramount ruling individual or group (Keswani 1996). Kalavasos is the best-known of these cities. In addition to data acquired from previous excavations in four separate areas (South 1980, 1997), research has recently been reinitiated with a new program of geophysical survey and test excavations by the Kalavassos and Maroni Built Environments Project (Fisher et al. 2011–12). This work has revealed roads and buildings that are generally oriented to 25° west of north, indicating that the city was laid out on a preconceived plan (Figure 17.5). No fortification wall has yet been found, but the distribution of surface finds and architectural remains suggests that the site was about 11.5 ha in size. The plan is characterized by what is likely an orthogonal grid with at least one major "north-south" street and one or more transverse "east-west" streets (Wright 1992:115). The north-south street, roughly 3.8 m wide, extends at least 150 m through three separate excavation areas, ending in the Northeast Area at Building X. This monumental building, built partially with ashlar masonry, is the largest structure found so far at the site and has revealed evidence for economic production, storage, and administration. South (1988:223) suggests that a large wall excavated along the north and east sides of Building X may have enclosed the entire Northeast Area. It is likely, therefore, that some form of zoning may have been imposed at the site in which the monumental administrative buildings were in the northeast, while other official buildings and higher-status residences, some of which also contained industrial facilities, were found in the eastern and central parts of the city, and smaller, nonelite dwellings were on the western outskirts (Wright 1992:115). The alignment of some buildings on opposite sides of the street suggests the possible existence of "lots," which in some cases were demarcated by long stretches of wall (South 1995:192).

The ProBA cities were, on one level, materializations of elite place making writ large. While nonelite city dwellers also engaged in place making at the neighborhood and

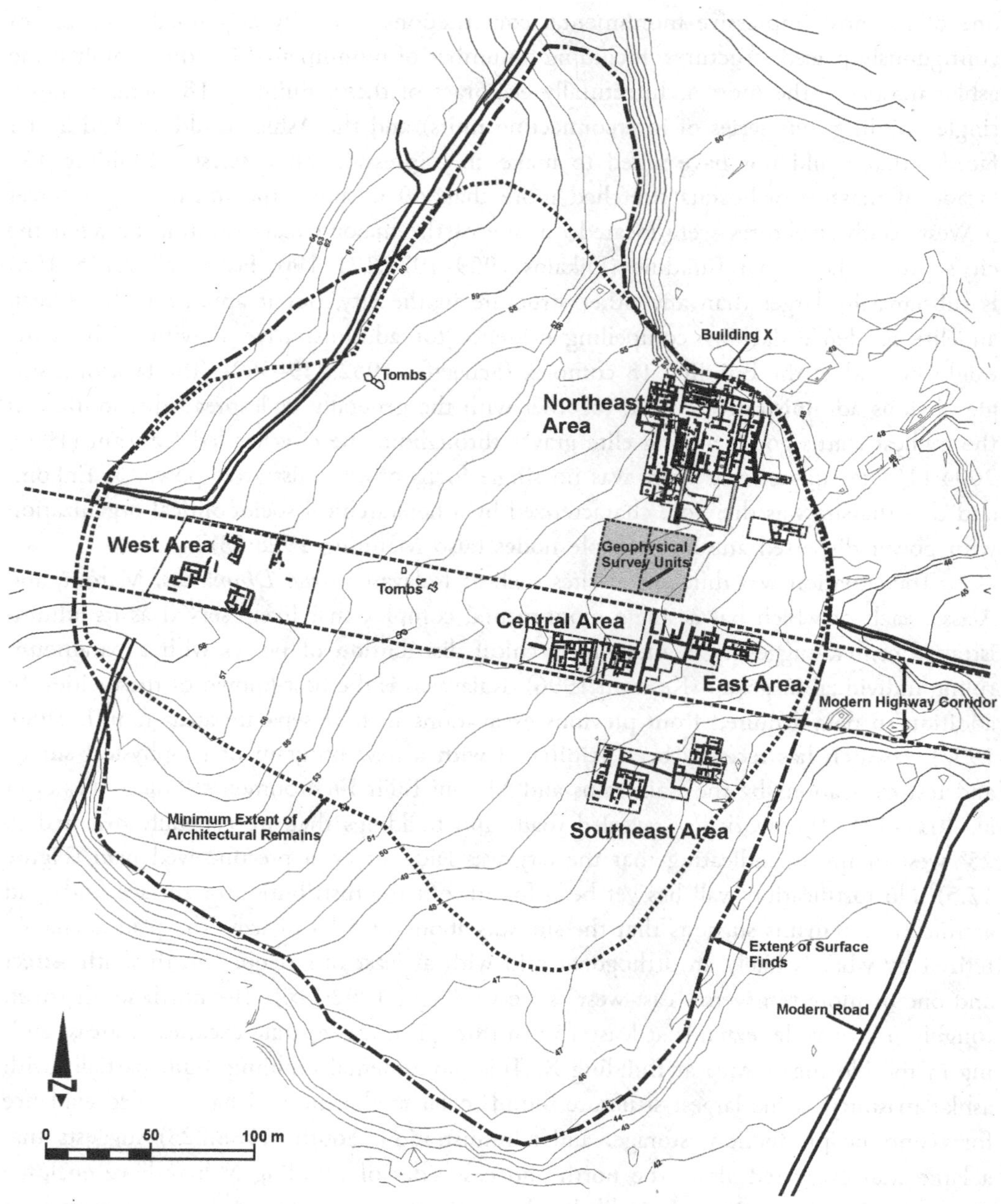

FIGURE 17.5 Schematic plan of Kalavasos-*Ayios Dhimitrios* showing excavation areas (drawn by K. Fisher from data provided by A. South).

household scales, sometimes in ways that ran counter to top-down attempts to impose order (see Fisher 2014b), it is clear that urban planning facilitated the appropriation of space on an unprecedented scale and the creation of ordered and, what Kevin Lynch would call *imageable,* built environments. Lynch (1960:9) defines *imageability* as "that quality in a physical object which gives it a high probability of evoking a strong image in any given observer. It is that shape, color, or arrangement which facilitates the making of vividly identified, powerfully structured, highly useful mental images of the environment." This was materialized in some of the new cities in part through monumental construction, whether buildings, tombs, or massive fortifications, and the use of the orthogonal grid, which has been recognized as a tool of dominance in societies engaged in centralizing authority (e.g., Grant 2001; Love 1999; Smith 2007). These ordered environments were a profoundly different experience from the winding alleys and undifferentiated architecture of Prehistoric Bronze Age villages and undoubtedly contributed to the formation of new urban-based identities for their residents. Proshansky (1978:161) argues that an urban identity arises from the physical characteristics and requirements of life in urban contexts that socialize individuals to move, think, feel, play social roles, and solve problems in ways that are uniquely urban.

Another significant feature of ProBA urban environments is the limited number of publicly accessible open spaces (other than the streets themselves) where spontaneous gatherings or planned public-inclusive social occasions among a city's inhabitants and visitors could take place. One of the only such spaces, the central square at Enkomi, was relatively small, but could hold roughly 380 standing people (based on modern architectural conventions [see Fisher 2009b:444], and not including the adjoining road space). Yet, the general lack of such spaces (bearing in mind the very incomplete plans we have to work with) suggests this was perhaps an effort by those who planned the infrastructure of cities to limit the occurrence of large-scale, uncontrolled social gatherings. The preference was instead to create monumental places with venues for staging social occasions that could be more easily controlled in terms of timing, the participants involved, and their proxemic relations.

INTERACTION IN AND AROUND MONUMENTAL BUILDINGS

One such place was in the Northeast Area of Kalavasos-*Ayios Dhimitrios*. We are uncertain where the main north-south street begins in the southern part of the city, but it ran in a direct line for at least some 150 m before "ending" at the southwest corner of Building X, at which point it narrows to an alleyway and runs up the west side of the building. Archaeological evidence from both past and current excavations combined with ongoing ground-penetrating radar survey suggests that, as people moved north along this road, they would have reached some kind of structure in the road that may have controlled access to the Northeast Area (Fisher et al. 2011–12; Figure 17.6). Beyond this point, the road widens from nearly 4 m to 6 m, creating a large space more than 30 m long that may have functioned as a processional or ceremonial way or similar monumental performative space. The street was bounded on the east by the largely robbed-out ashlar façade of Building XII, which may have been a large columned hall (South 1991:136–137), and ended at the southwest corner of Building X. This building was undoubtedly two stories in height and, while the south façade is not well preserved, it was likely a continuation of the building's impressive west façade, the base of which was made with

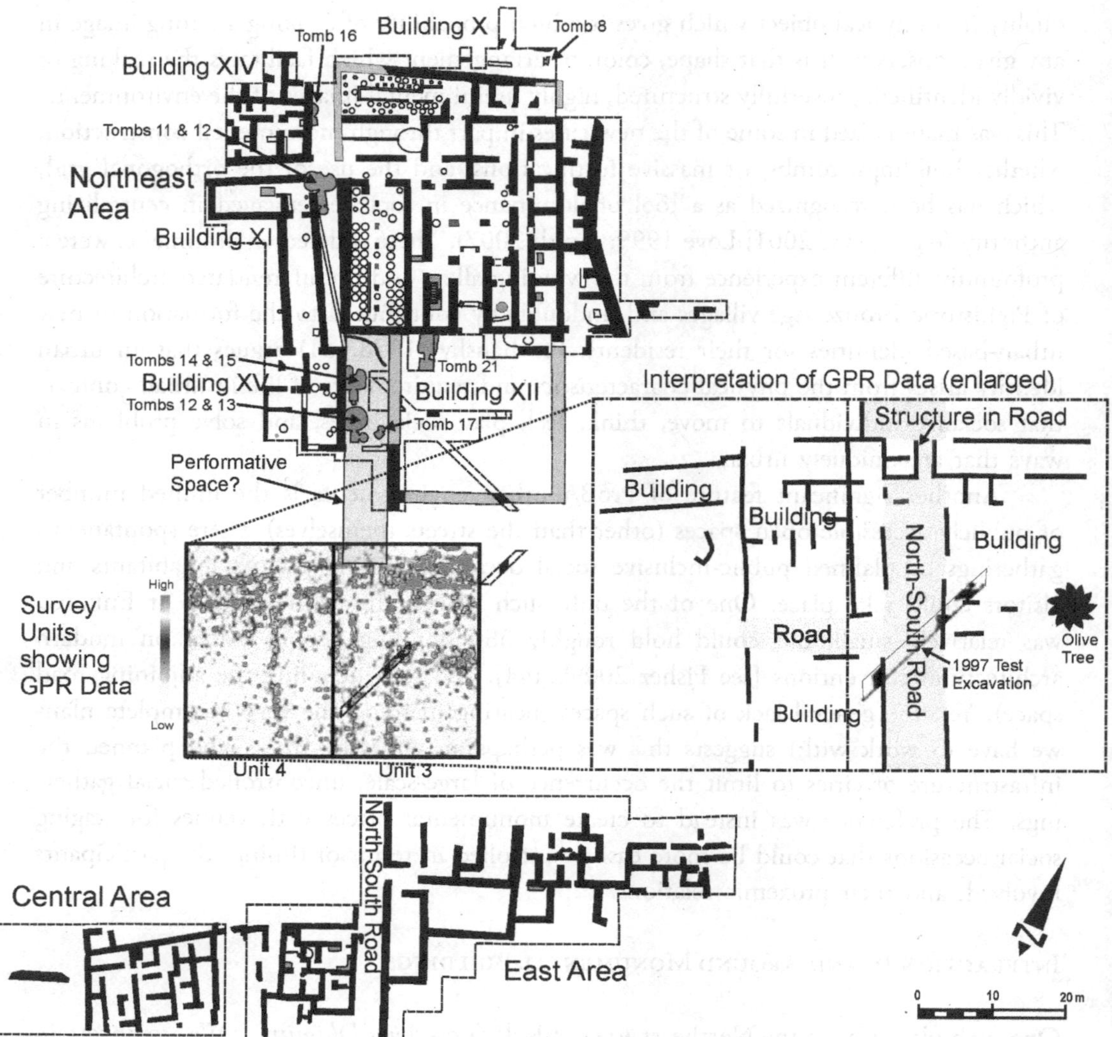

FIGURE 17.6 Kalavasos-*Ayios Dhimitrios,* detail of Northeast, Central, and East excavation areas, including results of 2010 ground penetrating radar survey (see Fisher et al. 2011–12 for details; adapted by K. Fisher from plan provided by A. South).

a plinth of monumental ashlar blocks with drafted margins and rough-hewn central bosses, topped by an orthostat of large blocks, also with drafted margins and lifting bosses (South 1984:19). In addition to the role of these various features in symbolizing the process of monumental construction as I suggested above, they also drew visual attention to the surface, highlighting the textures of the stone and the tool marks on the central bosses in the play of changing light and shadow. The use of a plinth with slightly inset orthostats also created additional visible contrast in the wall surface, while producing lines that emphasized the horizontal extent of the building. As Tuan (1977:108) observes, "Spatial dimensions such as vertical and horizontal, mass and volume are experiences known intimately to the body. . . . But the meaning of these spatial dimensions gains immeasurably in power and clarity when they can be seen in monumental architecture."

This effect was enhanced by the presence of earlier elite tombs (Tombs 12, 13, and 14), which would have been visible along the west side of the street, their entrances monumentalized with vertically placed stones and possibly posts (South 1997:170–171). These tombs predate the final phase of Building X and their continuity of use suggests a deliberate attempt to lay claim to these ancestors, whether the relationship was one of real or fictive kinship. This contrasts with the situation at nearby Maroni-*Vournes,* where the Ashlar Building was deliberately built on top of earlier tombs and elite architecture, essentially destroying them while announcing the ascendancy of these new ruling elites over the previous social order (Manning 1998). In either case, the memory of the earlier built environment still had great sociopolitical potency, which needed to be appropriated by either incorporation or effacement, and no doubt contributed to the efficacy of these places as monumental venues for social interaction. The space at the end of the north-south road at Kalavasos undoubtedly provided a highly imageable context for social occasions that took place there. There is no direct evidence for what these occasions were, but they likely included the arrival or departure of Building X's elite inhabitants (perhaps in procession), as well as the arrival of visitors who were permitted access to this part of the city, perhaps as participants in the social occasions that occasionally took place within Buildings X and XII.

As important as the exteriors of monumental buildings were in communicating messages regarding the identity and social position of their builders, it was during the interactions that took place inside them that social relations of power were negotiated and enacted. I have argued elsewhere that interactions focused on ceremonial feasting, in addition to other ritual activities, were of particular importance in this regard (Fisher 2007, 2009a). Feasts were not only important arenas for display and competition for resources and power among various individuals and groups. These events also gave hosts the opportunity to either emphasize or downplay social distance depending on their sociopolitical objectives (see various papers in Bray 2003; Dietler and Hayden 2001; Wright 2004). ProBA monumental buildings were typically constructed with multiple venues to accommodate both public-inclusive and private-exclusive interactions, allowing for events that could be tailored to groups of various sizes and social statuses. The central court (Room 157) in Building X at Kalavasos was one such space (Figure 17.7). This architecturally elaborate room was constructed with ashlar masonry, at least along its north, east, and west walls, and had two large central columns, perhaps also of ashlar (only one base remains *in situ*), suggesting that this space was partially roofed. As an outdoor space it had a pebble floor, in contrast to the plaster floors elsewhere in the building (South 1984:22). Its main entrance, which appears to have been only accessible through Building XII, was an elaborate entry hall, with a series of thresholds of inset ashlar slabs that clearly marked the significance of movement into (or out of) the court. They also served as nonverbal cues for the movement of visitors forward, funneling view-

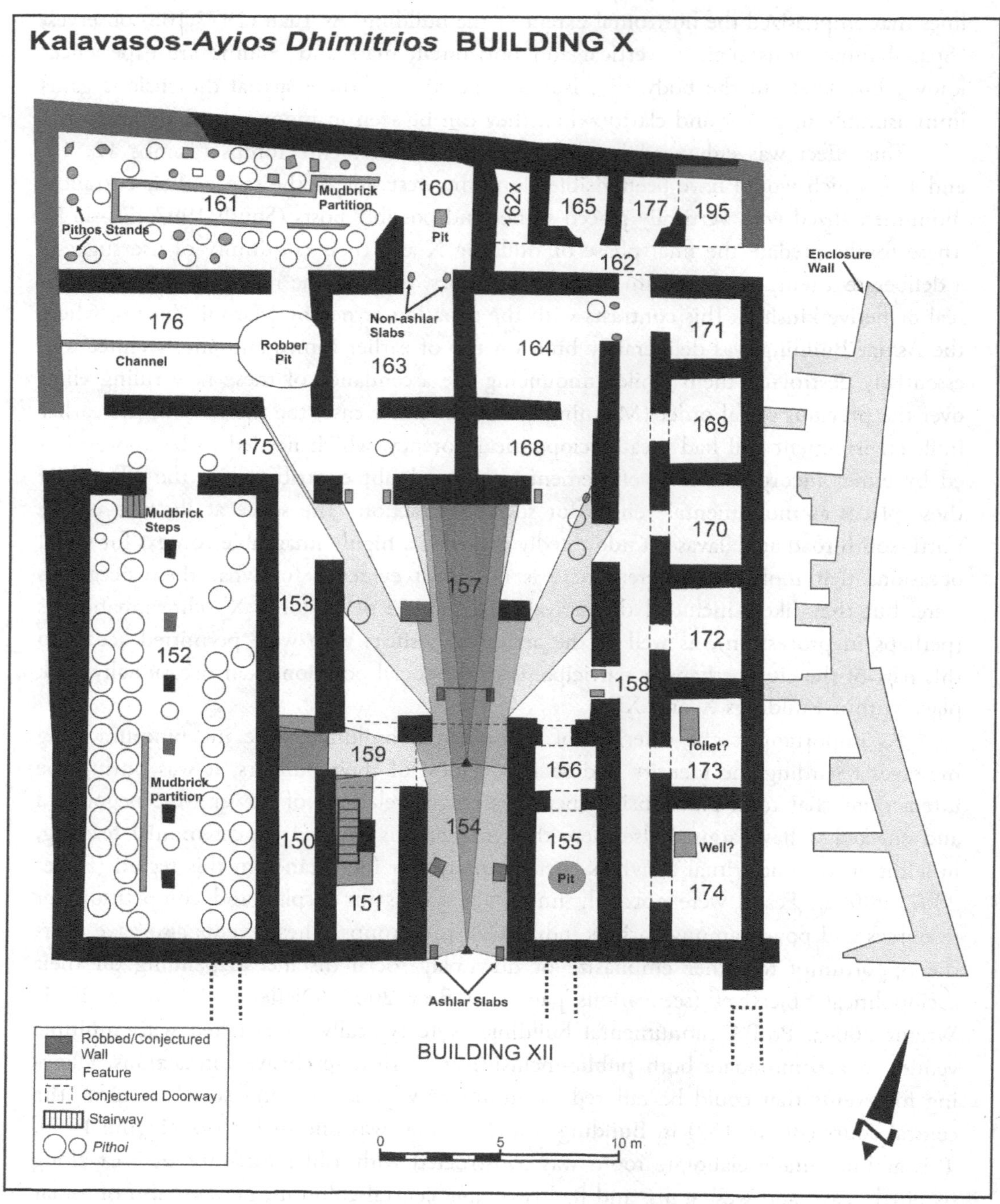

FIGURE 17.7. Kalavasos-*Ayios Dhimitrios*, schematic plan of Building X showing view-sheds from two points as one moves toward central court (Room 157) from the main entrance (Room 154). A viewshed represents what a person can see looking forward, with the lighter shaded area indicating the full 200° range of peripheral vision and the smaller darker shaded area indicating the 10° range of detailed (macular and foeval) vision (drawn by K. Fisher).

sheds into the impressive court and gradually revealing this monumental space as one moved forward. A deposit from a shaft in Room 173 (likely a latrine) contained 4.4 kg of animal bones in association with some 85 ceramic vessels, many of them Mycenaean imports, which appear to have been purposefully broken in an act of conspicuous consumption that must have ended a large feasting event (Fisher 2007:224–225; South and Russell 1993:304–306; South 2008). I have suggested that such an event would have likely taken place in the central court, although a larger, less exclusive feast could have been accommodated in Building XII.

Equally impressive are Building X's facilities for the production and storage of olive oil. The centerpiece of this is the "Pithos Hall" (Room 152), which was the largest and most architecturally elaborate room in the building, with its south and west walls constructed of the most elaborate type of ashlar masonry and a roof supported by six ashlar columns carved from single blocks. The room contained the remains of more than 50 massive ceramic storage jars (*pithoi*), 1.5 to 2 m in height, with a total capacity exceeding 33,000 l and which analyses suggest would have likely held olive oil (South 1989:321). I suggest that these *pithoi* were monumental objects in their own right and expressions of elite identity, symbolizing control over both the highly specialized labor behind their production as well as their economically important contents. It is no coincidence that they are often displayed in prominent places, such as the central court, where they could be easily recognized.

A similar sociospatial dynamic is evident in the Ashlar Building at Enkomi, although it was materialized rather differently (Fisher 2009b:451–455 Figure 17.8). There, the highest-level social occasions were held in a central hall (Room 14) constructed mainly of the most elaborate type of ashlar masonry, and focused around a monumental central hearth, possibly surrounded by up to four wooden posts. This arrangement created a context for interaction that corresponds quite closely to Hall's "personal" proxemic distance within which participants are within or just outside of touching distance (Hall 1966). At this distance, participants are close enough to perceive facial details and expressions, as well as what Goffman (1963:25) refers to as one's personal front: details in clothing, hair, jewelry, and other nonfixed-feature elements that nonverbally communicate gender, rank, office, and other aspects of individual and group identity. Sense of smell is also important at this distance and likely played a significant role in the context of preparing and consuming food and drink, as suggested by the ceramic assemblage recovered in this room (Dikaios 1969–1971:314–315). The Ashlar Building had two other such halls (Rooms 45 and 46), but made of rubble masonry, allowing the hosts to "filter" visitors according to their social status, and providing multiple venues for ceremonial or competitive feasts during which the elite occupants could, depending on the occasion and context, either build social ties with guests or create and reinforce social distance and distinction.

CONCLUSIONS: BECOMING MONUMENTAL

The Ashlar Building at Enkomi was destroyed in the early twelfth century B.C. and rebuilt shortly thereafter. Tellingly, perhaps, the new occupants broke up the impressive central hall into smaller rooms and built a staircase directly over its hearth, obliterating

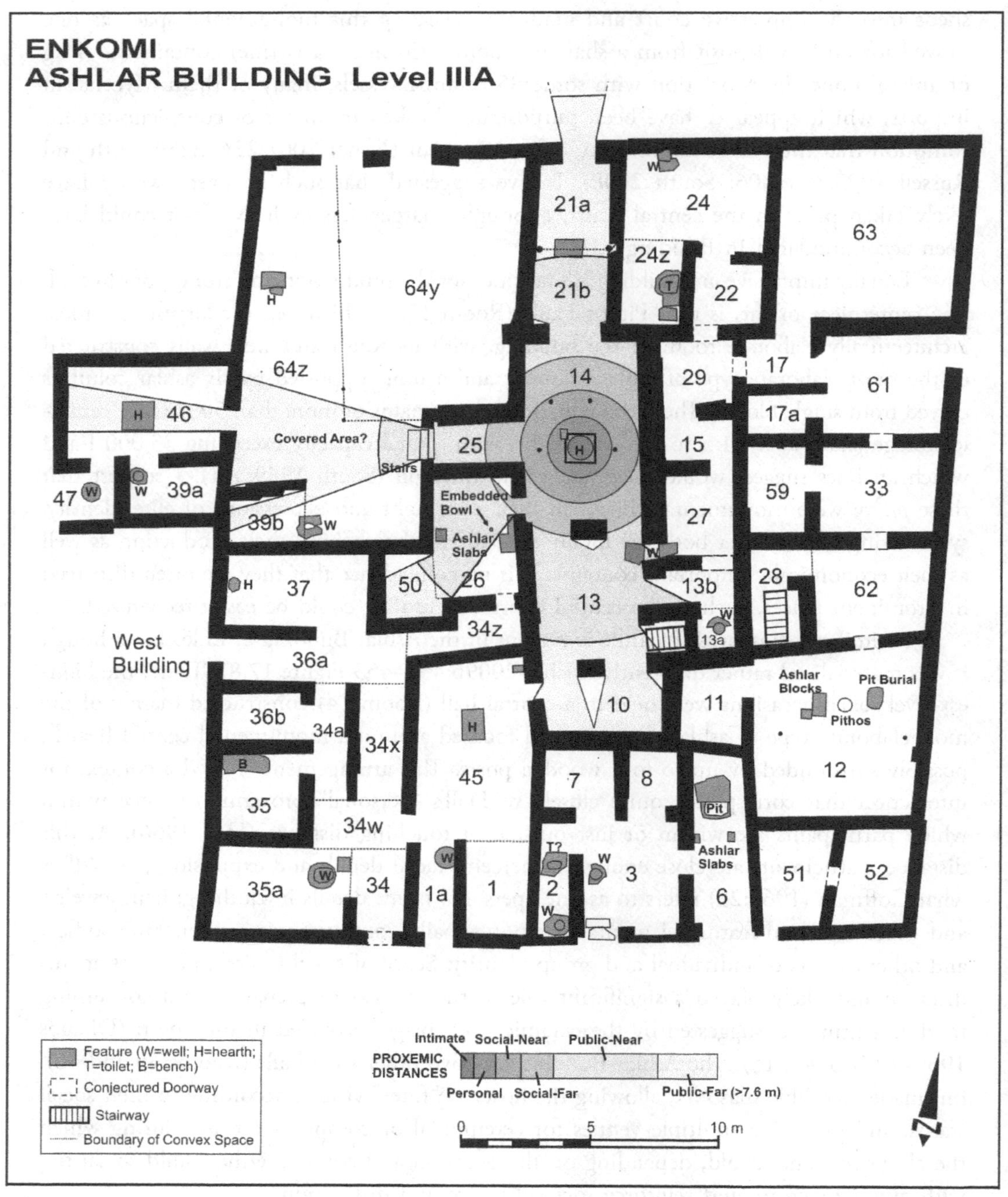

FIGURE 17.8 Enkomi Ashlar Building Level IIIA schematic plan with isovist field for Room 14 showing proxemic distances from central hearth (drawn by K. Fisher).

the remains of the monumental core of the original building. Its ashlar blocks were reused or repositioned to materialize completely new messages of power and identity and structure new patterns of movement and interaction. This illustrates the seemingly contradictory qualities of permanence and mutability that are essential characteristics of monumentality. The enduring materials of which many monuments are made appear to make permanent the ideologies that underlie their creation. Yet this same enduring quality makes monuments primary targets for appropriation, alteration, or even destruction by those who come after, seeking to manipulate social memory for their own purposes (van Dyke and Alcock 2003; Zerubavel 2003:41). The discovery of ProBA monuments by archaeologists has once again engaged these places in the island's sociopolitical dynamics as they become implicated in the construction of identity in a contested present (e.g., Knapp and Antoniadou 1998; Leriou 2002). Monumentality is thus a process rather than a state and we should view the Ashlar Building and its contemporaries as always in a process of becoming monumental.

In their initial construction and use, ProBA monumental buildings were symbols of conspicuous consumption, marking the efforts of powerful elites to demonstrate their control over human and material resources. As I have tried to demonstrate, however, this only tells part of the story of what makes something monumental. Monumentality was the product of acts of place making, expressed and experienced at various spatial and temporal scales. Indeed, it was through the dynamic interplay of people and things in the context of daily practice and ritual performance that monumental places were imbued with meanings and memories that contributed to their unique biographies. As Osborne illustrates in this volume's introduction, any attempt to define monumentality must acknowledge this codependent and mutually constituting relationship.

Acknowledgments

I would like to thank James Osborne and the Institute for European and Mediterranean Archaeology for their kind invitation to participate in the *Approaching Monumentality* conference. This chapter has benefited from the stimulating presentations and insightful discussions of my fellow participants and James Osborne's judicious editing. My research and fieldwork with the Kalavasos and Maroni Built Environments (KAMBE) Project is supported by the National Science Foundation (Awards # BCS-0917732 and 0917734), the Social Sciences and Humanities Research Council (Canada), Cornell University, Ithaca College, and the University of Arkansas. My heartfelt thanks go to the KAMBE Project staff and students for their tireless efforts. I am grateful to the Department of Antiquities Cyprus and its director, Dr. Maria Hadjicosti, for permission to conduct our work, and Alison South for her ongoing support and encouragement of our efforts. Any errors or omissions are my own.

References Cited

Allison, Penelope M. 1999 Introduction. In *The Archaeology of Household Activities,* edited by P. M. Allison, pp. 1–18. Routledge, London, New York.

Altman, Irwin, and Setha M. Low, eds. 1992 *Place Attachment.* Plenum Press, New York.

Benedikt, Michael L. 1979 To Take Hold of Space: Isovists and Isovist Fields. *Environment and Planning B: Planning and Design* 6:47–65.

Bolger, Diane R. 2003 *Gender in Ancient Cyprus: Narratives of Social Change on a Mediterranean Island.* AltaMira Press, Walnut Creek, California.

Bourdieu, Pierre 1977 *Outline of a Theory of Practice.* Translated by R. Nice. Cambridge University Press, Cambridge.

Bray, Tamara. L., ed. 2003 *The Archaeology and Politics of Food and Feasting in Early States and Empires.* Kluwer Academic/Plenum, New York.

Bukach, D. 2003 Exploring Identity and Place: An Analysis of the Provenance of Passage Grave Stones on Guernsey and Jersey in the Middle Neolithic. *Oxford Journal of Archaeology* 22:23–33.

de Certeau, Michael 1998 *The Practice of Everyday Life, Volume 2: Living and Cooking,* edited by Luce Giard, translated by Timothy J. Tomasik. University of Minnesota Press, Minneapolis.

Courtois, J., J. Lagarce, and E. Lagarce 1986 *Enkomi et le Bronze Récent à Chypre.* Impr. Zavallis, Nicosia, Cyprus.

Dean, Carolyn 2010 *A Culture of Stone: Inka Perspectives on Rock.* Duke University Press, Durham.

DeMarrais, E., L. J. Castillo, and Timothy K. Earle 1996 Ideology, materialization, and power strategies. *Current Anthropology* 37(1):15–31.

DeMarrais, E., Chris Gosden, and Colin Renfrew, eds. 2004 *Rethinking Materiality.* McDonald Archaeological Institute, Cambridge.

Dietler, Michael, and Brian Hayden, eds. 2001 *Feasts: Archaeological and Ethnographic Perspectives on Food, Politics, and Power.* Smithsonian Institution Press, Washington, D.C.

Dikaios, Porphyrios 1969–1971 *Enkomi: Excavations 1948–1958.* Ph. von Zabern, Mainz.

Dobres, Marcia-Anne, and John E. Robb 2000 Agency in Archaeology: Paradigm or Platitude? In *Agency in Archaeology,* edited by Marcia-Anne Dobres and John E. Robb, pp. 3–17. Routledge, Oxon, New York.

Dornan, Jennifer L. 2002 Archaeology and Agency: Past, Present, and Future Directions. *Journal of Archaeological Method and Theory* 9:303–329.

Düring, Bleda S. 2005 Building Continuity in the Central Anatolian Neolithic: Exploring the Meaning of Buildings at Aşıklı Höyük and Çatalhöyük. *Journal of Mediterranean Archaeology* 18(1):3–29.

Feldman, Marian H. 2006 *Diplomacy by Design: Luxury Arts and an "International Style" in the Ancient Near East, 1400–1200 BCE.* University of Chicago Press, Chicago.

Fisher, Kevin D. 2007 Building Power: Monumental Architecture, Place and Social Interaction in Late Bronze Age Cyprus. Unpublished PhD dissertation, Department of Anthropology, University of Toronto.

Fisher, Kevin D. 2009a Elite Place-Making and Social Interaction in the Late Cypriot Bronze Age. *Journal of Mediterranean Archaeology* 22(2):183–209. 2009b Placing Social Interaction: An Integrative Approach to Analyzing Past Built Environments. *Journal of Anthropological Archaeology* 28:439–457.

Fisher, Kevin D. 2014a (in press) Rethinking the Late Cypriot Built Environment: Households and Communities as Places of Social Transformation. In *The Cambridge Prehistory of the Bronze and Iron Age Mediterranean,* edited by A. B. Knapp and P. van Dommelen. Cambridge University Press, Cambridge.

Fisher, Kevin D. 2014b Making the First Cities on Cyprus: Urbanism and Social Change in the Late Bronze Age. In *Making Ancient Cities: Space and Place in Early Urban Societies,* edited by A. Creekmore and K. D. Fisher, 181–219. Cambridge University Press, Cambridge.

Fisher, Kevin D., Jeffrey F. Leon, Sturt W. Manning, Michael Rogers, and David Sewell 2011–12 (in press) The Kalavasos and Maroni Built Environments Project: Introduction and Preliminary Report on the 2008 and 2010 Field Seasons. *Report of the Department of Antiquities, Cyprus.*

Fortin, Michel 1981 Military Architecture in Cyprus during the Second Millennium BC. Unpublished PhD Dissertation, Institute of Archaeology, University of London.

Foucault, Michel 1977 *Discipline and Punish: The Birth of the Prison.* Pantheon Books, New York.

Frankel, David, and Jennifer M. Webb 2006 *Marki Alonia: An Early and Middle Bronze Age Town in Cyprus: Excavations 1995–2000.* P. Åströms Förlag, Sävedalen, Sweden.

Frieman, Catherine, and Mark Gillings 2007 Seeing is Perceiving? *World Archaeology* 39(1):4–16.

Gardner, Andrew 2007 Introduction: Social Agency, Power, and Being Human. In *Agency Uncovered. Archaeological Perspectives on Social Agency, Power, and Being Human,* edited by Andrew Gardner, pp. 1–18. Left Coast Press, Walnut Creek, California.

Gibson, James J. 1986 *The Ecological Approach to Visual Perception.* Lawrence Erlbaum, Hillsdale, New Jersey.

Giddens, Anthony 1984 *The Constitution of Society: Introduction of the Theory of Structuration.* University of California Press, Berkeley.

Goffman, Erving 1963 *Behavior in Public Places: Notes on the Social Organization of Gatherings.* Free Press of Glencoe, New York.

Gosden, Chris 2005 What do Objects Want? *Journal of Archaeological Method and Theory* 12(3):193–211.

Grant, Jill 2001 The Dark Side of the Grid: Power and Urban Design. *Planning Perspectives* 16(3):219–241.

Hadjisavvas, Sophocles 2000 Ashlar Buildings and Their Role in Late Bronze Age Cyprus. In *Acts of the Third International Congress of Cypriot Studies, 16–20 April 1996, Nicosia,* edited by G. K. Ioannides and S. A. Hadjistyllis, pp. 387–398. Society of Cypriot Studies, Nicosia.

Hall, Edward T. 1966 *The Hidden Dimension.* Doubleday, Garden City, New York.

Hendon, Julia A. 2004 Living and Working at Home: The Social Archaeology of Household Production and Social Relations. In *A Companion to Social Archaeology,* edited by L. Meskell and R. W. Preucel, pp. 272–286. Blackwell, Malden, Massachusetts.

Hillier, Bill, and Julienne Hanson 1984 *The Social Logic of Space.* Cambridge University Press, Cambridge.

Hitchcock, Louise 2009 Building Identities: Fluid Borders and an "International Style" of Monumental Architecture in the Bronze Age. In *Crossing Cultures: Conflict, Migration, and Convergence, Proceedings of the 32nd International Conference of Art History (CIHA), University of Melbourne, 13–18 January 2008,* edited by J. Anderson, pp. 165–171. The Miegunyah Press, Melbourne.

Hodder, Ian 2012 *Entangled: An Archaeology of the Relationships between Humans and Things.* Wiley-Blackwell, Malden, Massachusetts.

Hult, Gunnel 1981 *Hala Sultan Tekke 7,* Studies in Mediterranean Archaeology. Paul Åströms Förlag, Göteborg.

Hult, Gunnel 1983 *Bronze Age Ashlar Masonry in the Eastern Mediterranean: Cyprus, Ugarit, and Neighbouring Regions.* SIMA Vol. 66. Paul Åströms Förlag, Göteborg.

Iacovou, Maria 2007 Site Size Estimates and the Diversity Factor in Late Cypriot Settlement Histories. *Bulletin of the American Schools of Oriental Research* 348:1–23.

Ingold, T. 2007 Materials against Materiality. *Archaeological Dialogues* 14(1):1–16.

Ingold, T. 2010 Bringing Things Back to Life: Creative Entanglements in a World of Materials. *ESRC National Center for Research Methods. Working Paper Series 05/10.* http://eprints.ncrm. ac.uk/1306/, accessed September 15, 2012.

Joyce, Rosemary A. 2004 Unintended Consequences? Monumentality as a Novel Experience in Formative Mesoamerica. *Journal of Archaeological Method and Theory* 11(1):5–29.

Kearns, Catherine 2011 Building Social Boundaries at the Hybridizing First-Millennium BCE Complex of Vouni (Cyprus). *Journal of Mediterranean Archaeology* 24(2):147–170.

Keswani, Priscilla 1996 Hierarchies, Heterarchies, and Urbanization Processes: The View from Bronze Age Cyprus. *Journal of Mediterranean Archaeology* 9(2):211–250.

Keswani, Priscilla 2004 *Mortuary Ritual and Society in Bronze Age Cyprus.* Equinox, London.

Kirk, T. 2006 Materiality, Personhood, and Monumentality in Early Neolithic Britain. *Cambridge Archaeological Journal* 16:333–347.

Knapp, A. Bernard 2008 *Prehistoric and Protohistoric Cyprus: Identity, Insularity, and Connectivity.* Oxford University Press, Oxford, New York.

Knapp, A. Bernard 2009 Monumental Architecture, Memory and Identity. In *Proceedings of the Symposium: Bronze Age Architectural Traditions in the East Mediterranean: Diffusion and Diversity (Gasteig, Munich, 7–8 May, 2008),* edited by A. Kyriatsoulis, pp. 47–59. Verein zur Förderung der Aufarbeitung der Hellenischen Geschichte e.V, Weilheim.

Knapp, A. B., and S. Antoniadou 1998 Archaeology, Politics, and the Cultural Heritage of Cyprus. In *Archaeology Under Fire: Nationalism, Politics and Heritage in the Eastern Mediterranean and Middle East,* edited by L. Meskell, pp. 13–43. Routledge, New York.

Knappett, Carl 2011 Networks of Objects, Meshworks of Things. In *Redrawing Anthropology: Materials, Movements, Lines,* edited by T. Ingold, pp. 45–63. Anthropological Studies of Creativity and Perception, Ashgate.

Knappett, Carl 2012 Materiality. In *Archaeological Theory Today,* 2nd Edition, edited by I. Hodder, pp. 188–207. Polity Press, Cambridge.

Knappett, Carl, and L. Malafouris 2008 Material and Non-Human Agency: An Introduction. In *Material Agency: Towards a Non-Anthropocentric Approach,* edited by C. Knappett and L. Malafouris, pp. ix–xviii. Springer, New York.

Kopytoff, Igor 1986 The Cultural Biography of Things: Commoditization as Process. In *The Social Life of Things: Commodities in Cultural Perspective,* edited by A. Appadurai, pp. 64–94. Cambridge University Press, Cambridge.

Latour, Bruno 2005 *Reassembling the Social: An Introduction to Actor Network Theory.* Oxford University Press, Oxford.

Lawrence, Denise L., and Setha M. Low 1990 The Built Environment and Spatial Form. *Annual Review of Anthropology* 19:453–505.

Leone, Mark P., James M. Harmon, Jessica L. Neuwirth 2005 Perspective and Surveillance in Eighteenth-Century Maryland Gardens, Including William Paca's Garden on Wye Island. *Historical Archaeology* 39:138–158.

Leriou, Anastasia 2002 The Mycenaean Colonisation of Cyprus under the Magnifying Glass: Emblematic Indica versus Defining Criteria at Palaepaphos. In *SOMA 2001: Symposium on Mediterranean Archaeology. Proceedings of the Fifth Annual Meeting of Postgraduate Researchers, University of Liverpool, 23–25 February 2001,* edited by G. Muskett, A. Koltsida, and

M. Georgiadis, pp. 169–177. British Archaeological Reports: International Series 1040. Archeopress, Oxford.

Locock, Martin 1994 Meaningful Architecture. In *Meaningful Architecture: Social Interpretations of Buildings,* edited by M. Locock, pp. 1–13. Avebury/Ashgate, Aldershot, UK.

Love, Michael 1999 Ideology, Material Culture, and Daily Practice in Pre-Classic Mesoamerica: A Pacific Coast Perspective. In *Social Patterns in Pre-Classic Mesoamerica: a Symposium at Dumbarton Oaks, 9 and 10 October 1993,* edited by D. C. Grove and R. A. Joyce, pp. 127–153. Dumbarton Oaks, Washington, D.C.

Low, Setha M., and Denise Lawrence-Zúñiga, eds. 2003 *The Anthropology of Space and Place: Locating Culture.* Blackwell, Malden, Massachusetts.

Lynch, Kevin 1960 *The Image of the City.* M.I.T. Press, Cambridge.

Manning, Sturt W. 1998 Changing pasts and socio-political cognition in Late Bronze Age Cyprus. *World Archaeology* 30(1):39–58.

Manning, Sturt W., Carole McCartney, B. Kromer, and Sarah T. Stewart 2010 The Earlier Neolithic in Cyprus: Recognition and Dating of a Pre-Pottery Neolithic A Occupation. *Antiquity* 84:693–706.

Marcus, Clare C. 1995 *House as a Mirror of Self: Exploring the Deeper Meaning of Home.* Conari Press, Berkeley.

Markus, T. C. 1993 *Buildings and Power: Freedom and Control in the Origin of Modern Building Types.* Routledge, London.

Meskell, L., ed. 2005 *Archaeologies of Materiality.* Wiley-Blackwell, Oxford.

Miller, D., ed. 2005 *Materiality.* Duke University Press, Durham.

Nelson, M. C. 2003 Leveling Ashlar Walls. In *METRON: Measuring the Aegean Bronze Age (Aegaeum 24),* edited by K. P. Foster and R. Laffineur, pp. 269–274. Université de Liège, Liège.

Parker Pearson, M., and Ramilsonina 1998 Stonehenge for the Ancestors: The Stones Pass on the Message. *Antiquity* 72:308–326.

O'Connor, Blaze, and Gabriel Cooney 2010 Introduction: Materialitas and the Significance of Stone. In *Materialitas: Working Stone, Carving Identity,* edited by Blaze O'Connor, Gabriel Cooney and J. Chapman, pp. xxi–xxv. Prehistoric Society Research Papers, Oxbow Books, Oxford.

Peltenburg, Edgar J. 1996 From Isolation to State Formation in Cyprus, c. 3500–1500 BCE In *The Development of the Cypriot Economy: from the Prehistoric Period to the Present Day,* edited by V. Karageorghis and D. Michaelides, pp. 17–44. University of Cyprus and Bank of Cyprus, Nicosia.

Peltenburg, Edgar J. 2012 Text Meets Material Culture in Late Bronze Age Cyprus. In *Cyprus: An Island Culture. Society and Social Relations from the Bronze Age to the Venetian Period,* edited by A. Georgiou, pp. 1–23. Oxbow Books, Oxford.

Philokyprou, Maria 2011 The Initial Appearance of Ashlar Stone in Cyprus: Issues of Provenance and Use. *Mediterranean Archaeology and Archaeometry* 2011(2):37–53.

Pred, Allan 1984 Place as Historically Contingent Process: Structuration and the Time-Geography of Becoming Places. *Annals of the Association of American Geographers* 74(2): 279–297.

Pred, Allan 1990 *Making Histories and Constructing Human Geographies: the Local Transformation of Practice, Power Relations, and Consciousness.* Westview Press, Boulder.

Preucel, Robert W., and Lynn Meskell 2004 Places. In *A Companion to Social Archaeology,* edited by Lynn Meskell and Robert W. Preucel, pp. 215–229. Blackwell, Malden. Massachusetts.

Proshansky, Harold M. 1978 The City and Self-Identity. *Environment and Behavior* 10(2):147–169.

Rapoport, Amos 1988 Levels of Meaning in the Built Environment. In *Cross-Cultural Perspectives in Nonverbal Communication*, edited by F. Poyatos, pp. 317–336. C. J. Hogrefe, Toronto.

Rapoport, Amos 1990 *The Meaning of the Built Environment: A Nonverbal Communication Approach*. 2nd Edition. University of Arizona Press, Tucson.

Richards, Colin 2010 Building the Great Stone Circles of Northern Britain: Questions of Materiality, Identity, and Social Practices. In *Materialitas: Working Stone, Carving Identity*, edited by Blaze O'Connor, Gabriel Cooney, and J. Chapman, pp. 54–63. Prehistoric Society Research Papers, Oxbow Books, Oxford.

Rodman, Margaret C. 1992 Empowering Place: Multilocality and Multivocality. *American Anthropologist* 94(3):640–656.

Russell, James A., and J. Snodgrass 1987 Emotion and the Environment. In *Handbook of Environmental Psychology*, edited by D. Stokols and I. Altman, pp. 245–280. Wiley, New York.

Scarre, Chris. 2010 Stones with Character: Animism, Agency, and Megalithic Monuments. In *Materialitas: Working Stone, Carving Identity*, edited by Blaze O'Connor, Gabriel Cooney and J. Chapman, pp. 9–18. Prehistoric Society Research Papers, Oxbow Books, Oxford.

Schaeffer, C. F. A. 1952 *Enkomi-Alasia: Nouvelles Missions en Chypre, 1946–1950*. Klincksieck, Paris.

Smith, Michael E. 2007 Form and Meaning in the Earliest Cities: A New Approach to Ancient Urban Planning. *Journal of Planning History* 6(3):3–47.

South, Alison K. 1980 Kalavasos-Ayios Dhimitrios 1979: A Summary Report. *Report of the Department of Antiquities, Cyprus*:60–68.

South, Alison K. 1984 Kalavasos-Ayios Dhimitrios 1984. *Report of the Department of Antiquities, Cyprus*:14–41.

South, Alison K. 1988 Kalavasos-Ayios Dhimitrios 1987: An Important Ceramic Group from Building X. *Report of the Department of Antiquities, Cyprus* (pt. 1):223–228.

South, Alison K. 1989 From Copper to Kingship: Aspects of Bronze Age Society Viewed from the Vasilikos Valley. In *Early Society in Cyprus*, edited by E. Peltenburg, pp. 315–324. University of Edinburgh Press, Edinburgh.

South, Alison K. 1991 Kalavasos-Ayios Dhimitrios 1990. *Report of the Department of Antiquities, Cyprus*:131–139.

South, Alison K. 1995 Urbanism and Trade in the Vasilikos Valley in the Late Bronze Age. In *Trade, Contact, and the Movement of Peoples in the Eastern Mediterranean. Studies in Honour of J. Basil Hennessy*, edited by S. Bourke and J. Descoeudres, pp. 187–197. Mediterranean Archaeology Supplement 3, Sydney.

South, Alison K. 1997 Kalavasos-Ayios Dhimitrios 1992–1996. *Report of the Department of Antiquities, Cyprus*:151–175.

South, Alison K. 2008 Feasting in Cyprus: A View from Kalavasos. In *Dais: the Aegean Feast. Proceedings of the 12th International Aegean Conference, University of Melbourne, Centre for Classics and Archaeology, March 2008*, edited by Louise Hitchcock, Robert Laffineur and Janice L. Crowley, pp. 25–29. Université de Liège, Liège.

South, Alison K., and Pamela Russell 1993 Mycenaean Pottery and Social Hierarchy at Kalavasos-Ayios Dhimitrios. In *Wace and Blegen: Pottery as Evidence for Trade in the Aegean Bronze Age, 1939–1989: Proceedings of the International Conference Held at the American School of Classical Studies at Athens, December 2–3, 1989*, edited by C. Zerner, pp. 303–310. Amsterdam.

Swiny, Stuart, G. R. Rapp, and Ellen Herscher, eds. 2003 *Sotira Kaminoudhia: an Early Bronze Age Site in Cyprus*. American Schools of Oriental Research, Boston.

Taçon, Paul S. C. 1991 The Power of Stone: Symbolic Aspects of Stone Use and Tool Development in Western Arnhem Land, Australia. *Antiquity* 65:192–207.

Thompson, Victor D., and C. Fred T. Andrus 2011 Evaluating Mobility, Monumentality, and Feasting at the Sapelo Island Shell Ring Complex. *American Antiquity* 76(2):315–344.

Tilley, Christopher 2004 *The Materiality of Stone: Explorations in Landscape Phenomenology.* Berg, Oxford.

Trigger, Bruce G. 1990 Monumental Architecture: A Thermodynamic Explanation of Symbolic Behaviour. *World Archaeology* 22(2):119–132.

Trigger, Bruce G. 2003 *Understanding Early Civilizations.* Cambridge University Press, Cambridge.

Tringham, Ruth 1995 Archaeological Houses, Households, Housework, and the Home. In *The Home: Words, Interpretations, Meanings, and Environments,* edited by D. N. Benjamin, pp. 79–107. Avebury, Brookfield, Vermont.

Tuan, Yi-Fu 1977 *Space and Place: the Perspective of Experience.* University of Minnesota Press, Minneapolis.

van Dyke, R. M., and S. E. Alcock 2003 Archaeologies of Memory: An Introduction. In *Archaeologies of Memory,* edited by R.M. Van Dyke and S.E. Alcock, pp. 1–13. Blackwell, Oxford.

Webmoor, Timothy, and Christopher L. Witmore 2008 Things Are Us! A Commentary on Human/Things Relations under the Banner of a "Social" Archaeology. *Norwegian Archaeological Review* 41(1):53–70.

Wilson, Peter J. 1988 *The Domestication of the Human Species.* Yale University Press, New Haven.

Wright, James C., ed. 2004 *The Mycenaean Feast.* American School of Classical Studies at Athens, Princeton, New Jersey.

Wright, G. R. H. 1992 *Ancient Building in Cyprus.* E. J. Brill, Leiden.

Xenophontos, C. 1985 Appendix VIII: Kition Building Stone and its Resources. In *Excavations at Kition V, The Pre-Phoenician Levels,* edited by V. Karageorghis and M. Demas, pp. 431–437. Department of Antiquities, Nicosia, Cyprus, Nicosia.

Zerubavel, E. 2003 *Time Maps: Collective Memory and the Social Shape of the Past.* University of Chicago Press, Chicago.

CHAPTER EIGHTEEN

Performance and Monumentality in the "Altar of Tukulti-Ninurta"

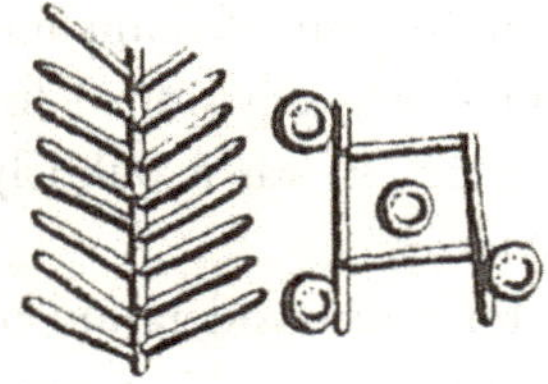

Stephanie M. Langin-Hooper

Abstract *The Ancient Near Eastern monument known as the "Altar of Tukulti-Ninurta" is traditionally analyzed as a divine symbol-socle used in the cult cella of the Ištar Temple at Aššur. This chapter—which refers to the "Altar" by its ancient term* nemedu—*presents a reevaluation of the monument's archaeological context, as well as a consideration of comparative art historical evidence. Both datasets suggest that the* nemedu *in question was actually intended for use outside the temple doorway. Based on this understanding of the* nemedu's *functional context, a more public viewership must be reconstructed for the monument, necessitating, in turn, new approaches to the supposedly self-referential relief on the monument's face, as well as new interpretations of the viewer-object relationship(s) in which the monument participated. The chapter proposes that the combination of the monument's public viewership, its intimate relief depiction of the king's body, and the performances generated by the monument's material properties, created a community of shared ritual action that bridged the usual social and physical divisions between the king and his nonroyal subjects. This unprecedented effect made the* nemedu *a powerful monument, but also a problematic one, perhaps necessitating the* nemedu's *eventual decommissioning and storage.*

The "Altar of Tukulti-Ninurta" is an Ancient Near Eastern monument from the Temple of Ištar at Aššur, dating to the Middle Assyrian period (thirteenth century B.C.) in the northern region of modern-day Iraq. The monument was found in a secondary context within a temple storage room, along with two similar objects. Walter Andrae, the excavator of the Ištar Temple, proposed that the monument's original location was the temple cella, where it would have functioned as a symbol socle or cult pedestal for a deity. The hypothesized cella location and cultic purpose for the monument have not been significantly reevaluated since Andrae's results were published in 1935—and, indeed, continue to be implied by scholarship's use of the name, "Altar of Tukulti-Ninurta." In order to avoid the cultic implications of the terms *altar* or *symbol-socle,* the monument is discussed hereafter using the Akkadian term *nemedu* (which roughly translates as "seat," and which is referenced in an inscription on the monument itself), and is specifically referred to as "Nemedu A."

In this chapter, I reevaluate Andrae's data and propose that Nemedu A was not intended for use inside the cult cella of the Ištar Temple. This reconstruction is based on a reevaluation of the archaeological record, as well as an examination of comparative visual evidence. Based on this analysis, I argue that Nemedu A was envisioned for use outside the temple, next to the temple doorway. In this location, it was a publicly accessible monument intended (at least in part) for a nonroyal viewer.

Such a spatial and social context for the monument allows for a reconsideration of the human-object interactions that it conditioned. A new reconstruction of this monument's performative aspects is offered, which explores how the monument's small size, spatial positioning, and figural relief enticed viewers into assuming particular poses and kneeling postures before the *nemedu.* In its agentive power, Nemedu A should perhaps be considered a "monument" in the secondary, transitive sense, which Osborne, in his introduction to this volume, has proposed reviving. A relational approach to monumentality, which emphasizes the specific human interactions and Middle Assyrian social environment in which Nemedu A was involved, is utilized throughout this chapter. The conclusions reached have a significant impact on how this ancient monument should be understood: not as a private altar for communication between king and god, but rather as a representational monument, which commemorated royal-divine interaction and made it more accessible to the public.

THE SEVEN NEMEDU MONUMENTS OF TUKULTI-NINURTA I

Tukulti-Ninurta I (r. 1243–1207 B.C.) is among the best-known kings of the Middle Assyrian period. Tukulti-Ninurta I's reign was a time of expansion for the Assyrian state, as this king conquered Babylonia to the south, northern Syria to the west, and made forays into the mountainous regions to the north and east of Assyria (Kuhrt 1995:355–358; Van De Mieroop 2007:181–182). It was also an era of large-scale building projects: Tukulti-Ninurta I founded the new settlement of Kar-Tukulti-Ninurta, and also substantially rebuilt many structures within the ancient capital city of Aššur (Andrae 1935; see also discussion in Moortgat 1969:116–120). Among these was the Temple of Ištar (Figure 18.1), which had been in existence since at least the third millennium B.C. (Andrae 1922). When Tukulti-Ninurta I rebuilt this particular temple, he changed the ground plan substantially: he added an antechamber between the temple doorway and the main cella, and also elevated the cult niche up a set of stairs.[1] The use of this dra-

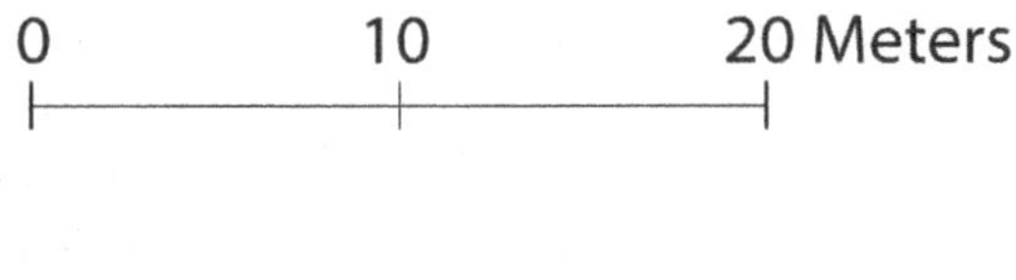

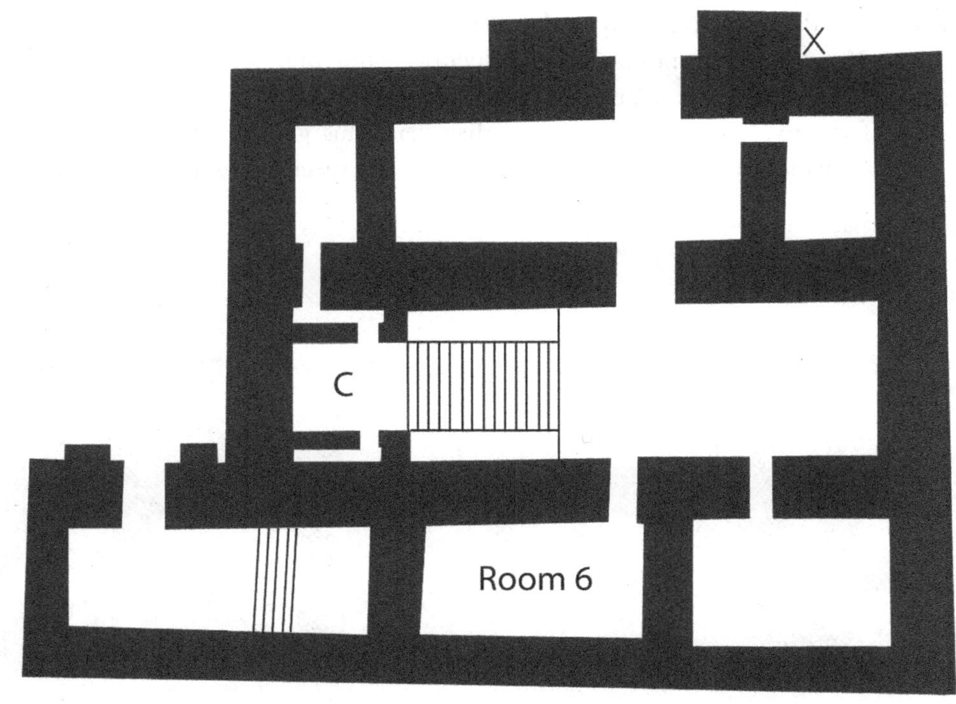

X marks the location of Nemedu B
C marks the location of the cult niche

FIGURE 18.1 Floor plan of the Ištar Temple, Aššur, during the Middle Assyrian period. Room 6 is the excavated location of Nemedus A, C, and D. Adapted from plan in Andrae 1935:Plate 1 (artist credit for adapted version: Jennifer Fechik).

matically new architectural plan suggests that Tukulti-Ninurta I was actively rethinking the use of space in the Ištar Temple to create something different from what was offered by previous structures. One of the major features of the new plan was the placement of the cult niche and statue, which were now up a set of stairs and significantly removed from the temple entrance. The interior space of the temple, and the locations of objects within that space—even crucial things, such as the cult statue—were not designed to be traditional repetitions of earlier Assyrian temple plans (for discussion of these changes, as well as earlier temple plans, see Andrae 1935:15–108). Rather, something new was created, which held contemporary relevance for Middle Assyrians.

It was in this newly renovated temple that Tukulti-Ninurta I placed several monuments, including the *nemedu* that is often referred to—and misleadingly singled out—by the formal name "Altar of Tukulti-Ninurta" (Figure 18.2). This *nemedu* was one of four similarly shaped, carved stone blocks found at the Ištar Temple at Aššur, all of which have been dated to the reign of Tukulti-Ninurta I (Figure 18.3, Nemedus A-D; Table 18.1). None of these monuments are identical, but they all share a similar silhouette: a roughly square block with a heavy plinth-like base and a semicircular projection at each of the two top corners. Objects that share this general silhouette will be termed "*nemedu*-shaped" throughout this chapter, and the specific *nemedu*s excavated at sites in

FIGURE 18.2 Nemedu A (the "Altar of Tukulti-Ninurta," Ass.19869), from Room 6, Ištar Temple, Aššur; Middle Assyrian period, thirteenth century B.C.; alabaster. Height: 57.5 cm, width: 57 cm, depth: 22.5 cm. (photo: bpk, Berlin/Vorderasiatisches Museum, Staatliche Museen, Berlin, Germany/Art Resource, NY).

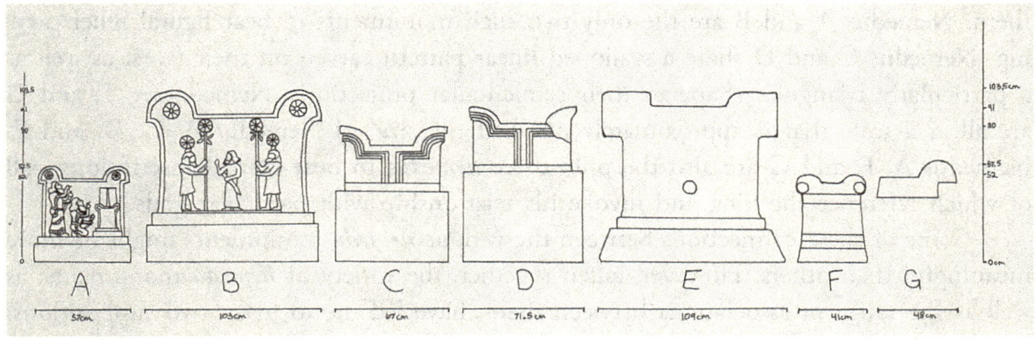

FIGURE 18.3 Scale diagram of the Seven *Nemedu*s of Tukulti-Ninurta I. Middle Assyrian period, thirteenth century B.C. Nemedu A = Ass.19869; Nemedu B = Ass.20069; Nemedu C = Ass.19835; Nemedu D = Ass.19868; Nemedu F = Ass.17178+Ass.17883; Nemedu G = Ass.17177 (artist credit: Jennifer Fechik; editing by Jerry Langin-Hooper).

Assyria will be termed by letter designations, originally assigned by Andrae, to prevent confusion (making the "Altar of Tukulti-Ninurta" into "Nemedu A").[2]

Three additional *nemedu* monuments dating to the reign of Tukulti-Ninurta I are also known from other locations. Nemedu E (see Figure 18.3) was discovered at Kar-Tukulti-Ninurta (Andrae 1935:72–73). Nemedu F and Nemedu G (see Figure 18.3) were found near the gate of the Temple of Aššur at Aššur, and are dated to the period of Tukulti-Ninurta I on the basis of their inscriptions, which name the king (Haller and Andrae 1955:72). These three examples bring the total number of known *nemedu* monuments of Tukulti-Ninurta I to seven.

Although all seven of these monuments share the *nemedu*-shape and are dated to the Tukulti-Ninurta I period,[3] there are also significant formal differences between

TABLE 18.1
MIDDLE ASSYRIAN *NEMEDU* MONUMENTS AND THEIR FINDSPOTS

Letter designation of Nemedu	Aššur Excavation Number	Excavated location
Nemedu A	Ass.19869	Room 6, Ištar Temple, Aššur
Nemedu B	Ass.20069	outside temple doorway, Ištar Temple, Aššur
Nemedu C	Ass.19835	Room 6, Ištar Temple, Aššur
Nemedu D	Ass.19868	Room 6, Ištar Temple, Aššur
Nemedu E	[none; from Kar Tukulti-Ninurta]	Kar Tukulti-Ninurta
Nemedu F	Ass.17178+Ass.17883	gateway area, Aššur Temple, Aššur
Nemedu G	Ass.17177	gateway area, Aššur Temple, Aššur

them. Nemedus A and B are the only two such monuments to bear figural relief carving. Nemedus C and D share a scalloped linear pattern carved on their faces, as well as a particularly triangular shape to their semicircular projections. Nemedus A, F, and G are all at a scale that is approximately one-half the size[4] of Nemedus B, C, D, and E. Nemedus A, F, and G are also the only three *nemedu* to bear textual inscriptions—all of which reference the king and invoke his relationship with particular gods.[5]

Some of these connections between the various *nemedu* monuments might be more meaningful than others. However, taken together, the variety of *nemedu* monuments, as well as the range of associations between them, have led me to make two suppositions: (1) that Tukulti-Ninurta I may have been experimenting with new forms of monumentality (particularly with reference to his relationship with the gods), similar to the architectural renovations seen in the new layout of the Ištar Temple at Aššur; and (2) as part of this process, multiple classes or varieties of *nemedu* were developed. In particular, I see Nemedus A, F, and G as distinct from the others, because of both their diminutive size and their carved inscriptions. However, I additionally see strong connections between Nemedus A and B because of their shared representational imagery. These connections between *nemedus*—and, indeed, the acknowledgment that seven *nemedus* of Tukulti-Ninurta I existed, rather than the one "Altar" which is usually discussed in scholarship—has a significant impact on how the monumental affect of Nemedu A (the "Altar of Tukulti-Ninurta") can be understood.

ARCHAEOLOGICAL CONTEXT OF NEMEDU A

Contrary to what might be expected, Nemedu A was not found in either of the Ištar Temple's most sacred spaces, the cella or the cult niche. Rather, this *nemedu*—along with Nemedus C and D—was discovered in Room 6, a storeroom in the temple that had been sealed (Figure 18.4).

The excavator of Aššur, Walter Andrae, suggested that these monuments were placed in Room 6 only after their cultic use life had ended (1935:67). In his catalogue entry, Oscar Muscarella also emphasized the secondary nature of the archaeological context of Nemedu A (1995:112). While Nemedus C and D were set into the brick pavement of Room 6, Nemedu A was found resting in debris, tipped to the right and angled backward, with its decorative side facing the wall—not a positioning that would be expected for a monument on display or in use.[6]

The original use location of Nemedu A is thus not archaeologically indicated. Walter Andrae suggested that it, along with the other two monuments in Room 6, originally stood in the cult cella (as repeated, and accepted, by, among others, Bahrani 2003:187; Muscarella 1995:112). The reconstruction of a cella context seems to have been based not so much on archaeological evidence as an art historical interpretation of the scene represented on the front of Nemedu A. In this image, the king, shown in duplicate, is both standing and kneeling before a *nemedu*-shaped monument bearing an unidentified object on its top. Scholars have generally assumed that the most appropriate location for such a worship interaction would have been inside the cult cella. This interpretation

FIGURE 18.4 Excavation photo of Room 6 of the Ištar Temple, Aššur; Middle Assyrian period, thirteenth century B.C. Reprinted from Andrae 1935:Plate 12, Image d.

has been supported with evidence from several cylinder seal impressions that might show similar types of monuments bearing divine symbols being used inside the temple (see below). In this cultic interpretation, the *nemedu* is thought to be a largely private object—viewed only by an elite group of priests and the king himself, in addition to the gods—which mediated a personal interaction between a king and a deity (for elaboration on this view, see Bahrani 2003:188–201). Such interpretations are predicated on the hypothesis of a cella context for Nemedu A, which has not been challenged since Andrae's initial determination.

However, no *nemedu*-shaped objects were found in the cult cella of the Ištar Temple, nor of any other temple. As already stated, Nemedus A, C, and D were discovered in Room 6 of the Ištar Temple. Nemedus F and G were found at the nearby Aššur Temple, but in the area of the gate, not near the cella. Nemedu E was found similarly distant from any cella context, although Andrae postulates (without offering any evidence) that "[w]ahrscheinlich gehörte dieser Sockel zum Bestände des Aššur-Tempels in Kar-Tukulti-Ninurta" (1935:72–73). With so little evidence for the use of *nemedu*-shaped objects in Middle Assyrian temple cellas, other contextual possibilities can and should be considered.

A more likely possibility for the use context of Nemedu A is suggested by the *in situ* location of Nemedu B. This monument—which, like Nemedu A, features representational carving—was also discovered at the Ištar Temple. However, Nemedu B was found just outside the doorway to the temple (see Figure 18.1). This monument appears to have been in a primary context. Andrae disregarded the possibility that Nemedu B was intended to be situated by the temple doorway through his assertion that the ground beneath Nemedu B was somewhat rough and uneven (1922:108). However, the excavation photograph (Figure 18.5) seems to contradict Andrae, as Nemedu B appears to be stable and lined up with a statue in a display context.

Nevertheless, based on his evaluation of the ground stability, Andrae claimed that Nemedu B was (like Nemedus A, C, and D) intended to be used inside the temple cella, and had been temporarily removed and placed beside the temple door during temple ren-

FIGURE 18.5 Excavation photo of the main doorway area of the Ištar Temple, Aššur; Middle Assyrian period, thirteenth century B.C.; with view of Nemedu B and a Neo-Sumerian style statue (reprinted from Andrae 1922:108).

ovations (1922:108). While such a scenario is theoretically possible, it requires a curious contortion of the archaeological evidence and leaves several questions unanswered: for instance, why would the temple renovators never have moved Nemedu B back inside, if it was sacred and important enough to belong in the temple cella? And why would Nemedu B have been placed outside in the first place, if there was ample space available in Room 6 to accommodate the other *nemedus*? The existence of such logical conundrums indicates that Andrae himself may have been predisposed to think of *nemedus* as a kind of altar, and so he might have been searching for any explanation for why none of the *nemedus* were found in a cult cella. If that assumption is removed, the simplest explanation—that Nemedu B was placed outside, next to the temple doorway, because that was its appropriate location—seems more likely.

The archaeological context of Nemedus F and G also supports this interpretation. As mentioned previously, these two *nemedus* were excavated at the Aššur Temple in Aššur, but not in the temple cella. Like Nemedu B, these two monuments were discovered near the entrance to a temple; in this case, the gate area of the Aššur Temple (Haller and Andrae 1955:72). While both Nemedu F and Nemedu G were found in disturbed stratigraphy, and so their precise orientation cannot be determined, it seems significant that they share a temple entrance context with Nemedu B.

All of this contextual evidence has a particular relevance for the interpretation of Nemedu A (the "Altar of Tukulti-Ninurta"). Of the seven *nemedus* of Tukulti-Ninurta I, Nemedu A has strongest formal ties with Nemedu B (through shared use of representational imagery) and Nemedus F and G (through shared size, and shared royal inscriptions). All three of these *nemedus* were found in temple entrance contexts, thus it seems logical to conjecture that Nemedu A was likewise intended for use near a temple entrance, prior to its secondary deposition in a debris-ridden corner of Room 6 in the Ištar Temple.

ART HISTORICAL EVIDENCE FOR
TEMPLE ENTRANCE PLACEMENT OF NEMEDUS

Comparison with other Ancient Near Eastern art objects offers further evidence for the placement of *nemedu* monuments outside temple doorways. Such a positioning appears in the temple plan on the lap of Gudea's Statue B (Figure 18.6), from the site of Tello (ancient Girsu), southern Mesopotamia, dating to the Neo-Sumerian period (c. 2100 B.C.). This schematic drawing represents the plan of a temple, which Gudea claimed had been sent to him from a god by means of a dream. While the plan is not particularly detailed, and contains no information about the interior structure of the temple, it does take care to show a small symbol just outside one of the doorways into the temple. The shape of this symbol is visually very similar to the silhouette of Nemedu A. This position of a *nemedu*-shaped symbol outside the door on Gudea's temple plan provides further support for reconstructing such a placement for some of the Middle Assyrian *nemedus*.

The presence of this detail on Gudea's temple plan additionally indicates that the placement of such a monument outside the temple door was a crucial feature of *external*

FIGURE 18.6 Gudea Statue B, Tello (ancient Girsu), southern Mesopotamia; Neo-Sumerian period (c. 2100 B.C.). *Nemedu*-shaped symbol in bottom left corner of temple plan is boxed in photograph. Musée du Louvre (photo: Erich Lessing/Art Resource, NY).

temple architecture, and worthy of inclusion on the schematic plan even while many other details were omitted. The depiction of this detail also reinforces that the *neme-du*-shaped monument was not a part of the temple's interior, nor was its presence or appearance a secret. The interior of the temple—which would presumably have contained even more important architectural features and objects, including the cult cella and its cult statue—is left completely blank on Gudea's plan. That the interior of the temple is not depicted may be a testament to its private or sacred nature. Thus, the *nemedu,* as an object outside the temple walls, seems to have been important, but also accessible to the sight and knowledge of the public.

Although almost one thousand years separate the reign of Gudea from the Middle Assyrian period of Tukulti-Ninurta I, as well as the differing geographical location of northern versus southern Mesopotamia, the Middle Assyrians seem to have emphasized a connection between Gudea's culture and their own. Positioned outside the doorway to the Ištar Temple at Aššur—and immediately next to Nemedu B—stood an uninscribed statue (mentioned previously, and seen in Figure 18.5), carved in a Neo-Sumerian style and possibly dating to the Neo-Sumerian period (Andrae 1922:108). It thus appears that Neo-Sumerian period statuary of Gudea and his contemporaries was available to the Middle Assyrians, and that this visual repertoire held significance for them.[7] As such, it seems entirely plausible that the Middle Assyrians would have known about, and followed, Gudea's positioning of *nemedu*-shaped monuments outside the main temple doors.

Additional evidence for the Middle Assyrian use of *nemedu* monuments outside temple doors can be gleaned from representations on several Middle Assyrian cylinder seals. These seals depict small pedestals with the characteristic shape of the *nemedu,* and show them in the center of temple doorways (Andrae 1935:16; Moortgat 1944:43–44; Muscarella 1995:113). As mentioned above, scholars have typically understood these seals as showing a compressed perspective view of cultic practice inside the temple cella (Frankfort 1996:132). Such interpretations, while possible, are nevertheless tied to the conjecture that *nemedu*-shaped monuments were intended for altar-like use inside the temple's most sacred space. When not regarded through the prism of such assumptions, the imagery on these Middle Assyrian seals provides strong evidence that a physical proximity and visual connection existed between *nemedu*-shaped monuments and temple doorways.

From the archaeological and visual evidence discussed above, it is plausible that at least some of the Middle Assyrian *nemedu*s, including Nemedu A (the "Altar of Tukulti-Ninurta"), were originally intended to be displayed at the entrances to temples. In this location, far from the inner sanctum of the cella—indeed, outside in broad daylight—there would have presumably been a certain amount of public viewing, reception, and interaction with these monuments.

The Representational Imagery of Nemedu A

Before continuing on to the implications of such a public context for the interpretation of Nemedu A, it is first necessary to discuss the issue of the representational imagery shown on the face of this monument (see Figure 18.2). As mentioned previously, this carving is often taken by scholars as a self-referential image, wherein Tukulti-Ninurta I is shown interacting with Nemedu A itself (Bahrani 2003:185–201). The purported self-referentiality of this image is one of the major reasons why scholars have proposed that Nemedu A belonged in the cult cella, where it was part of the deity's cultic equipment and used in private interactions between king, priests, and gods. However, with my new reconstruction of Nemedu A's location (outside the temple, in a public space), this self-referentiality needs to be questioned.

The *nemedu* (hereafter called the "depicted *nemedu*") shown in the representational imagery of Nemedu A is undoubtedly similar to the object on which it was carved. Such similarities would have drawn the viewer's attention to duplications between the depicted scene and the real-life scene of Nemedu A in context with the objects and people who surrounded it (more on this below; also see Bahrani 2003:185–201). It is crucial to recognize, however, that the depicted *nemedu* and Nemedu A are only similar—they are not identical. Several differences between the depicted *nemedu* and Nemedu A are evident.

First, the depicted image shows a blank monument, with no representational imagery carved on it. This difference may or may not have been significant—Zainab Bahrani has convincingly pointed out, with reference to this monument, that Assyrian expectations for mimesis in imagery differed from modern ones (2003:189–190, 201). I would suggest, however, that the difference between the figural imagery on Nemedu A and the uncarved face of the depicted *nemedu* can best be viewed in light of the fact that two carved *nemedu*s (Nemedu A and B) and two uncarved *nemedu*s (Nemedu C and D) were found at the Ištar Temple. It would be more compelling to argue that the lack of representational imagery on the depicted *nemedu* was not meaningful if similarly uncarved *nemedu*s did not exist in full-sized versions.

Additionally problematic for identifying the depicted *nemedu* as self-referential is that it is shown being used as a pedestal for a divine symbol, often thought to represent the god Nusku, who is named in the monument's text (see, for example, Bahrani 2003). However, the evidence does not suggest that the monument itself was used in this way. Nemedu A does not contain a hole, clamp, or other fitting for the insertion of such a symbol, thus seeming to refute the traditional interpretation of this monument as a "symbol socle."[8] Even if such a symbol did not require a firm fitting—in other words, if it could simply sit on top of the *nemedu*—the physical properties of this particular monument do not make it a likely candidate. The top surface of Nemedu A is quite narrow, measuring only 22.5 cm deep. The other three *nemedu*s found at the Ištar Temple (Nemedus B, C, and D) are more than twice as deep, and thus present a much greater surface area on which to place a divine symbol. Again, we cannot assume that modern expectations of mimesis apply to Assyrian *nemedu* imagery. However, if any of the *nemedu*s at the Ištar Temple were meant to function in a manner similar to that shown in the depicted image, Nemedu A was physically the least qualified to do so.

A third factor complicating the equation of the depicted *nemedu* with Nemedu A is the issue of height. The height of Nemedu A is just 57.7 cm at its highest point. The two other monuments (Nemedus C and D) with which it was found in Room 6 of the Ištar Temple, both of which lacked figural imagery, were almost twice this height (see comparison in Figure 18.3). Similarly, Nemedu B, which was found *in situ* outside the temple door, was 103 cm high. The small stature of Nemedu A not only sets this monument apart from its companions at the Ištar Temple as a relatively unimposing object, but also further calls into question the self-referentiality of its carved image. In the image, the depicted *nemedu* is shown in proportion to the standing and kneeling figure of Tukulti-Ninurta I. As can be seen in Figure 18.2, the height of the depicted *nemedu* reaches to the waist of the standing king, and just below the ear of the kneeling king. Thus, the depicted *nemedu* should be considerably larger than Nemedu A. Again, while the rules of proportion were not always followed in Ancient Near Eastern art, this obvious size differential should be viewed in light of the fact that the three other *nemedu*s found in the Ištar Temple (Nemedus B, C, and D) were of sufficient height to match the proportions observed in the representation. The image of Tukulti-Ninurta I standing and kneeling before a monument was carved onto the only one of the four Ištar Temple *nemedu*s that was actually too small to have functioned as the depicted *nemedu* does.

The possibility still exists, of course, that the depicted image was intended to be fully self-referential, and that any disparities that modern viewers might see between the depicted *nemedu* and Nemedu A would have been unnoticed or unimportant to an Assyrian viewer. However, as with Andrae's interpretation of the archaeological evidence and reconstruction of a cella context for the *nemedu*s, such analyses seem to have overlooked the simplest explanation of the available evidence. The depicted *nemedu* is tall, presumably deep enough to support a standing object, and uncarved. Two of the four *nemedu*s found at the Ištar Temple fit this description, while Nemedu A does not. An even more compelling size and visual match is offered by Nemedu E, which—although found at Kar-Tukulti-Ninurta, not Aššur—indicates that near-exact replicas of the depicted *nemedu* existed in full-sized versions. The reference point for the depicted *nemedu* might conceivably have been one of these other objects (Nemedu C, D, E, or an unrecovered parallel), rather than Nemedu A itself.

Thus, I propose that the depicted *nemedu* on Nemedu A was not intended to be a strictly self-referential representation. Once we move away from self-referentiality as the primary lens through which to analyze Nemedu A, new interpretive possibilities are accessible—possibilities in which it is not necessary to limit the range of potential actors capable of performing a duplication of the depicted actions (kneeling and standing before a *nemedu*) to the king alone. When combined with the new reconstruction of a temple doorway location, it becomes conceivable to reconstruct a nonroyal audience viewing and interacting with this monument.

"Performing" Nemedu A

Based on the evidence presented above, I have suggested that Nemedu A was originally intended for placement at the doorway to the Ištar Temple. A temple doorway location would have been a fairly public area, potentially accessible to nonroyal viewers. Once accepted, this spatial setting can explain a great deal about the visual program of this monument and provide a justification for features that make less sense in a cella context.

As described above, Nemedu A is unique among the seven *nemedu*s of Tukulti-Ninurta I in combining the features of representational imagery, diminutive stature, and textual inscription. From a perspective of monumentality, this combination seems somewhat incongruous. Text and image are often used to transform a "stone" into a "monument" (see Thomas this volume), and so Nemedu A does seem to qualify for the label; but, in terms of its dimensions alone, Nemedu A seems oddly "nonmonumental." Several of the other contributions in this volume emphasize the role of scale in making a monument; in the Ancient Near East, in particular, bigger is almost always better when it comes to monumental construction (see discussion in Osborne's introduction to this volume). However, Nemedu A is one of the smallest of Tukulti-Ninurta's *nemedu*s and gives the overall impression of being rather short and squat. Assuming that the *nemedu* was not resting on another platform—and there is no evidence that it was (indeed, the lower section of Nemedu A is already carved into the shape of a graduated plinth, rendering an additional base superfluous)—this means that the image represented on its surface was placed low to the ground, making it difficult to see, especially when the viewer was standing. Indeed, in order to see the image well, the viewer is physically required to bend over, stoop, or kneel. Thus, this short, squat monument with its low-placed image does more than just visually depict an action or event. It also activates and conditions specific actions from its audience.

Stooping or kneeling is not the action that one most often associates with the viewing of monuments. In the case of Nemedu A, however, such movements seem particularly fitting. The specific actions of bending and kneeling were encouraged not only by the positioning of the image on the monument, but also by the represented imagery itself. The carved relief shows a similar interaction between human body and stone monument, in which the person (usually understood as Tukulti-Ninurta I) approaches and then kneels before a *nemedu*. While there are many ways in which a viewer could lower his or her head in order to see the image clearly, one posture in particular— kneeling on both knees, with the toes flexed forward to brace the foot—is specifically suggested to the viewer. Therefore, the image represented on the *nemedu* does not just require a bodily movement; it directly elicits through the power of suggestion a precise performance and pose. By molding the body of its human viewer, the *nemedu* shapes the circumstances of its own viewing. The imagery on the monument entices and pulls the viewer into performing an action that clearly echoes that of the royal figure before the divine symbol (see Figure 18.7).

FIGURE 18.7 Author (Stephanie Langin-Hooper) kneeling before Nemedu A ("Altar of Tukulti-Ninurta") in the Vorderasiatisches Museum, Berlin. The museum displays Nemedu A on a pedestal (for which there is no archaeological evidence) and back-to-back with Nemedu C (note the significantly larger dimensions of Nemedu C) (photo: David Stanton).

The elicitation of a specific human performance is unique to this one *nemedu*. The other six *nemedu*s of Tukulti-Ninurta I are either much larger or lacking in figural imagery, and none of them so explicitly necessitate, as well as condition, a kneeling pose from their human viewer. The only other *nemedu*s that might have created similar human-object interactions are Nemedus F and G. These two *nemedu*s share with Nemedu A a similar size (which would suggest kneeling for close inspection) and a similar use of text carving. The carved text may be especially significant, as it gives the *nemedu* a communicative aspect, which could be recognized even if the viewer could not read the inscription. Thus, Nemedu F and Nemedu G might also have inspired viewers to bend and kneel for a closer look. However, Nemedu A takes this object-human interaction to a more complicated level, through the use of eye-catching representational imagery which, of all possible subjects, showed a human performance similar to that elicited through its own physical properties.

For those of us from the Western (and, particularly, the Christian) tradition, kneeling before an image, especially one connected with deity worship, seems to be a relatively obvious response. However, the carved image on Nemedu A represents the first time in any known Assyrian artwork that the king was shown kneeling before a presumably divine entity (Muscarella 1995:113). In earlier artworks, the pious king was always shown walking or standing, not kneeling.[9] It would therefore seem that the portrayal of the kneeling king—as well as the recruitment of viewers into performing similar kneeling actions—was not an unintentional perpetuation of earlier tradition, but rather a carefully cultivated artistic innovation.

One effect of this innovation was to connect the monument's viewer with the Assyrian king on a physical and personal level, to a degree that is fairly rare in Ancient Near Eastern art. By showing a scene of the king interacting with the gods on a quasi-public monument outside the temple, Nemedu A became a window into the king's private sphere. Members of the outside world could imagine themselves directly observing the king's pious actions. This insight into a sacred and privileged world, where only a very few could physically enter, would have been a rare spectacle. The physical features of the monument—the short, squat stature, and the position of the image—enhanced this effect and even suggested to the viewer that he or she could do more than observe: he or she could actually participate. Through mimicking the king's actions as portrayed on the surface of the monument—kneeling like he kneels, before a similarly shaped object—the body of a public viewer became parallel to, and almost synonymous with, the body of the king. As such, the viewer became a collaborator in the king's piety, reinforcing his actions through repetition of them.

This repetition might, of course, be an illusion. There is no way of knowing if Tukulti-Ninurta I knelt before a *nemedu*-shaped monument in the course of his worship practices. As has been emphasized throughout this chapter, no such monuments were found in temple cellas, where the majority of the king's worship activities presumably took place. As an alternative, I might propose that Room 6 of the Ištar Temple was not actually a storeroom, but rather a kind of cultic room (although undoubtedly not the main cultic room), which was only later used for storage. If Room 6 was used in this way, perhaps Tukulti-Ninurta I did kneel before a *nemedu*. If so, the *nemedu* in question would most likely have been Nemedu C and/or Nemedu D, which might explain the slightly different shape that these *nemedus* took, and why they were set into the brick pavement of the floor as seemingly permanent fixtures (a situation that seems odd in a storeroom context). Such a possibility is conjectural, but is worth mentioning here in order to illustrate that the traditional scholarly view that royal prayer practices took place before a *nemedu*-shaped object placed in the temple cella is a similar conjecture, and one that is based on less archaeological evidence.

From the perspective of the ancient nonroyal viewer, whether or not the king actually engaged in worship practices before any *nemedu* was immaterial to the functionality of Nemedu A's representational imagery and physical properties. Nemedu A provided contact with the king's body and his interaction with the gods on an unprecedented level. The members of the public who knelt before the monument were allowed access to the ritual actions of the king in a physical, almost visceral, way, if only for the fleeting moments of performative mimicry. Thus, Nemedu A established a community centered on the king's ritual actions (whether real or imagined), which transcended the physical and social divide that would otherwise be present.

DISUSE AND STORAGE OF NEMEDU A

This connection between the king and the nonroyal viewer may have been as problematic as it was powerful. In the art of the Ancient Near East, there is generally an enforced distance between the viewer and the king, which this monument caused to break down in ways that might have been considered troubling. To return to the archaeological evidence discussed previously, Nemedu A was the only one of the three monuments found in the Ištar Temple's Room 6 to be discarded in a debris pile, at the back of the room, set askew and facing the wall, while the other two *nemedus* (Nemedus C and D) were set into the floor pavement. The fact that this *nemedu* faced the wall may be especially significant, as this positioning would have hidden the carved relief.

The *nemedus* that Nemedu A most closely resembles—Nemedus F and G (through the sharing of similar size and textual inscription), and Nemedu B (through the sharing of figural representation)—escaped such an ignoble fate, and were found in external contexts near temple doorways. The reason for this difference in ultimate use and disposal of the monuments may relate to the particular combination of features and unique aspects of Nemedu A. Nemedus F and G, while interactive—calling out to a viewer through their inscriptions, and inviting the viewer to kneel through their diminutive size—did not go so far as to show representational imagery. The references to the king are included in the text of each *nemedu,* connecting them both to his royal presence, but in a less direct and personal way than if his body had been represented.

Similarly, Nemedu B also escaped the fate of being placed in storage, and was found *in situ* outside the Ištar Temple's door. Like Nemedu A, Nemedu B (Figure 18.8) includes representational imagery of the king. However, the physical properties of this monument are very different: it is much larger, and thus does not invite the viewer to

FIGURE 18.8 Nemedu B (Ass.20069), from main doorway area of the Ištar Temple, Aššur; Middle Assyrian period, thirteenth century B.C.; alabaster. Height: 103 cm, width: 103 cm, depth: 40 cm. Archaeological Museum Istanbul (photo: Gianni Dagli Orti/The Art Archive at Art Resource, New York).

kneel. No textual inscription is carved on its surface, so Nemedu B is lacking in that communicative aspect and in the declaration of the royal name. Additionally, and perhaps most crucially, Nemedu B shows Tukulti-Ninurta I in a more formal and distant way, flanked by supernatural beings.[10] The king shown on Nemedu B is not accessible, and the viewer cannot create even the illusion of duplicating his actions.

The seemingly long-term temple doorway display of Nemedus B, F, and G, when contrasted with the rather unsympathetic treatment and storage of Nemedu A, suggests that Nemedu A, for all its popularity with modern scholars, may have been viewed at the time as unsuccessful. Its unique performative qualities created a relationship between the body of the viewer and the body of the king that may ultimately have been viewed as being too close, too personal, thus requiring the retirement and storage of Nemedu A in the sealed-off Room 6 of the Ištar Temple.

CONCLUSION

In this chapter, I have argued that the monument traditionally known as the "Altar of Tukulti-Ninurta" (Nemedu A) should be reevaluated. Through a new consideration of archaeological and visual evidence, I suggest that the original location of this monument was outside the Ištar Temple at Aššur, next to the temple doorway. This external, quasi-public context has significant implications for the way in which the monument should be interpreted. Rather than the private object of royal contemplation and worship, it was a representational monument, which commemorated that royal-divine interaction and made it more accessible to the public. Indeed, in keeping with the themes of this volume, I would suggest that it is, in fact, its representational nature that makes Nemedu A a monument—a site of community formation and shared performance—as opposed to a functional and private part of the deity's cultic equipment.

In this, my theoretical approach to Nemedu A as a monument follows that proposed by Osborne in this volume's introduction, in which a relational approach to monumentality is advocated. If, as Osborne argues, a monument gains its monumentality through specific, culturally conditioned "interaction with people around it" (Osborne this volume: 8), then Nemedu A is a monument (at least in part) *because* of the human performances that its physical features and spatial positioning encouraged. The otherwise troubling (and, thus, often ignored) issue of Nemedu A's diminutive scale is transformed through this relational approach: rather than an incongruous formal property inhibiting this object's classification as a "true" monument, the small size of Nemedu A actually enhanced its monumentality by encouraging people to interact with the object in a public, performative way. Nemedu A's representational imagery, which has been the dominant focus of previous research on this object, is only one aspect of the complex interplay between individuals, object(s), space, and society which this monument shaped, and in which it participated.

Specifically, I have proposed that the unique design of Nemedu A elicited bodily performances in its viewers that closely paralleled those of the king. This performative nature of the monument created a connection between viewer and king that was rooted in a visceral, physical experience, and thus broke down the traditional barriers between royal and nonroyal spheres that existed in the Ancient Near East. While this made the power of the monument especially compelling, it also seems to have been problematic—to the extent that the monument was hidden, facing the wall in a debris-ridden corner of a storage room, while a more rigid and remote portrayal of the king replaced it. Through this new analysis of the archaeological and visual evidence for the "Altar of Tukulti-Ninurta," a very different picture of the monumentality and reception of this monument is achieved.

ACKNOWLEDGMENTS

I would like to thank James Osborne, as well as the faculty and students of the Institute for European and Mediterranean Archaeology at SUNY Buffalo, for inviting me to participate in the Fifth IEMA Visiting Scholar Conference and for being such gracious hosts. Additionally, I would like to thank my fellow participants and audience members at that conference for their enthusiasm for my subject and many helpful remarks on my work.

This chapter owes a significant debt to the unpublished ideas of Marian Feldman, who first suggested to me that the "Altar of Tukulti-Ninurta" was situated outside the doorway of the Ištar Temple, and Brian Brown, who noticed the similarity of the "Altar of Tukulti-Ninurta" to the symbol shown on Gudea's temple plan. I am grateful to them for sharing their insights and beginning my own interest in this under-studied monument. I would like to additionally thank Marian Feldman, Allie Terry-Fritsch, James Osborne, and the three anonymous peer reviewers for reading drafts of this article and offering numerous suggestions for improvement. All errors remain, of course, my own.

Notes

1. These temple renovations are dated to the reign of Tukulti-Ninurta I through the discovery of numerous inscribed objects, such as bricks and tablets, including the dramatic foundation deposit of "a huge stone block, five weighty lead tablets, two silver tablets, and two gold tablets," all inscribed with Tukulti-Ninurta I's dedicatory text (Grayson 1987:253). For a discussion of this evidence, see Andrae (1935:15–108). For translations of the foundation texts documenting Tukulti-Ninurta I's renovations and rebuilding of the Ištar Temple, see Luckenbill (1926:62–66); also Grayson (1987:253–263).

2. The original comparison of these *nemedu*s, discussed using letter designations, can be found in Andrae (1935:57–73). Note that although Andrae (1935:59 Figure 21) utilizes the same letter designations adopted throughout this chapter in his diagram comparing the seven *nemedu*s, he inverts the assignment of letters for Nemedus A and B in his discussion in the text. Thus, the "Altar of Tukulti-Ninurta" is referred to as "A" in Andrae's diagram, but "B" in Andrae's text (1935:59, 67–71). The Aššur excavation numbers for these *nemedu*s are as follows: Nemedu A = Ass.19869; Nemedu B = Ass.20069; Nemedu C = Ass.19835; Nemedu D = Ass.19868; Nemedu F = Ass.17178+Ass.17883; Nemedu G = Ass.17177. Nemedu E was found at Kar-Tukulti-Ninurta, so it does not have an Aššur excavation number.

3. The four uninscribed monuments are dated to the reign of Tukulti-Ninurta I based on their archaeological context, as well as their visual and physical similarities to the three inscribed *nemedu*s (all of which can be securely dated to Tukulti-Ninurta I's reign on paleographic grounds). The seven *nemedu*s discussed in this chapter represent some of the only evidence for the use of such monuments in Assyria, and it is possible that their use *in Assyria* is a unique innovation of Tukulti-Ninurta I's reign. Babylonia provides earlier evidence of *nemedu*-shaped monuments: a *nemedu*-shaped symbol is shown on a seated statue of Gudea (discussed in this chapter), and depictions of *nemedu*s can also be found on *kudurru*s (Andrae 1935:58). Tukulti-Ninurta I's use of *nemedu* monuments may therefore be closely linked to his conquests of (and, thus, contact with) Babylonia. Andrae himself postulated Babylonian influence when he first published the *nemedu*s from the Ištar Temple (1935:58). The Assyrian use of these monuments—as evidenced by the monuments themselves, as well as depictions of them on Assyrian seals (see discussion in this chapter)—does not seem to have continued past the Middle Assyrian period. It is possible that this cessation of *nemedu*

use was due, at least in part, to the unsuccessful career of Nemedu A (as postulated in this chapter), as well as to Babylonia's regained independence. For more on this possibility, see notes 7 and 9.

4. Only part of Nemedu G was recovered from the excavations of Aššur, and therefore its complete dimensions remain unknown. Due to the size and proportions of the fragment, Andrae reconstructed the original height of Nemedu G as approximately equal to that of Nemedu F (1935:59), and I concur with his assessment.

5. All three of the textual inscriptions on Tukulti-Ninurta I's *nemedu*s reference interactions between king and god(s). The translations are as follows:

> Nemedu A: "Nemed(u) of the god Nusku, chief vizier of Ekur, bearer of the just scepter, courtier of the gods Aššur and Enlil, who daily repeats the prayers of Tukulti-Ninurta, the king, his beloved, in the presence of the gods Aššur and Enlil and a destiny of power [for him] within Ekur . . . may he [pronounce . . . the god Ašš]ur, [my] lord . . . forever." (Grayson 1987:279–280)

> Nemedu F: "I built the holy dwelling of the god Aššur, [my lord], and established (it) as the residence of the king [of the gods, the great] mountain. May a [later] prince restore [its] dilapidated (portions and) [return] my inscribed name to [its] place. (Then) the god Aššur [will listen] to his prayers." (Grayson 1987:293–294) [Note that although this text does not specifically name Tukulti-Ninurta I, it can be securely dated to his reign based on epigraphy and word choice (see Grayson 1987:293).]

> Nemedu G: "To Aššur, the great lord, father of the gods, his lord, Tukulti-Ninurta, prefect of Enlil, priest of Aššur, son of Shalmaneser, priest of Aššur, son of Adad-nirâri, priest of Aššur. The peace of Aššur, lord of Mount Abeh, his mountain which he loves, and wherein he has commanded (me) to build a lofty abode, his sure favor I ask." (Luckenbill 1926:66–67; see also Grayson 1987:293; Haller and Andrae 1955:72) [Note that Andrae (1935:73) mistakenly associates this text with Nemedu F, found in two pieces and known by the excavation numbers Ass. 17178 and Ass. 17883. However, in publishing the cuneiform text, Schroeder (1922:26, Number 54) accurately associated this text with Nemedu G (excavation number Ass. 17177). Andrae's 1935 mistake was more explicitly corrected by Haller and Andrae (1955:72), and further discussed by Grayson (1987:293), all of whom associate this text with Nemedu G.]

6. Andrae's suggestion for a cult cella context for all three monuments in Room 6 also obscures the differences between the circumstances of their archaeological deposition. Of the three *nemedu*-shaped monuments found in Room 6 of the Ištar Temple, Nemedu A is the only one that is obviously not in its original context. The other two *nemedu*s in Room 6 (Nemedus C and D) were set into the brick pavement of the floor, potentially at a different floor level than that on which Nemedu A rests. It is thus possible that Room 6 was the original context of Nemedus C and D.

7. It seems likely that renewed Assyrian interest in, and knowledge of, Neo-Sumerian arts was directly due to Tukulti-Ninurta I's conquests of Babylonia. It is possible that the display of a Neo-Sumerian period statue, as well as the sudden flourishing of *nemedu* monuments, was intended (at least in part) as a display of cultural appropriation and control over Babylonia. A similar effect might have been intended by the choice to dedicate one of the shrines in the newly renovated Ištar Temple to the goddess *Bēlit-Akkadî* ("Lady of the Akkadians")

(Grayson 1987:260–261). This dedication invokes the patronage of a deity connected both with southern Mesopotamia and, more specifically, with an earlier era in that region's history, when Babylonia was primarily known as the "Land of Sumer and Akkad." Tukulti-Ninurta I himself also claimed a connection with this ancient Babylonian past when he became the first Assyrian to assert that he was *šar māt Šumeri u Akkadî* ("King of the Land of Sumer and Akkad")—significantly choosing to use this "old traditional name for southern Mesopotamia" more frequently than he used *Karduniaš*, the contemporary name given to Babylonia by the Kassite rulers whom Tukulti-Ninurta I had defeated (Kravitz 2010:125; also Cifola 2004).

In the case of the temple dedication, Tukulti-Ninurta I, or someone functioning in his place, seems to have changed his mind about coopting Babylonian religious heritage in this particular way, as the name *Bēlit-Akkadî* was scratched out of the dedication tablet, and the name of the goddess *Dinitu* was added instead, as the deity to whom the shrine was dedicated. As pointed out by Grayson (1987:261), these changes to the text "suggest major ideological changes were taking place under" Tukulti-Ninurta I—changes that, I would add, seem to have been closely connected with religious and artistic traditions imported from southern Mesopotamia.

8.   The interpretation that the *nemedu*s were intended to be symbol-socles was first put forth by Andrae (1935:57), and has been accepted and repeated by many subsequent scholars (Baffi Guardata and Dolce 1990:201; Bahrani 2003:187; Muscarella 1995:112).

9.   Earlier Babylonian art features kneeling figures similar to the image of Tukulti-Ninurta I depicted on Nemedu A. Several Kassite seals show a kneeling figure, who can in some instances be identified as the king (Matthews 1990:70–71, 84–85; see also discussion in Porada 1948:69), and an Old Babylonian bronze statuette depicts a kneeling figure (although named as a servant of the king, Hammurabi, not the king himself) (André-Salvini 2008:7). However, only in the Middle Assyrian period are *nemedu*-shaped monuments and kneeling Assyrian kings found in Assyrian art (for the kneeling Assyrian king shown on Middle Assyrian seals, see Matthews 1990:Number 536; Moortgat 1941:81–84; Porada 1948:Plate LXXXIII, Number 598E; Wiseman 1958:19–22; for a kneeling royal figure depicted on Middle Assyrian painted pottery, see Andrae 1923:Plate 26, 27c; for *nemedu*-shaped monuments depicted on Middle Assyrian seals, see Moortgat 1944:43–44). Even in the Middle Assyrian glyptic, both are relatively rare motifs. It is interesting to note that the two motifs (the kneeling Assyrian king and the *nemedu*-shaped monument) do not seem to have occurred together, even on Middle Assyrian seals—further indicating the experimental (and perhaps ultimately unsuccessful) nature of Nemedu A.

The lack of popularity for images of the kneeling Assyrian king may be linked, particularly in the Neo-Assyrian period, to the association between kneeling or groveling gestures and the postures used to portray (inferior) foreigners in Neo-Assyrian art (Cifarelli 1998). Loss of control over Babylonia might also have been responsible for the posture's unpopularity with the kings who followed Tukulti-Ninurta I, for whom the use of the kneeling posture might have been a visual appropriation of Babylonian royal imagery.

10.   Ornan (2009:115) discusses the change in imagery from Nemedu A to Nemedu B in terms of a trend in Assyrian arts "to avoid the portrayal of major deities." Although this is a different analytical approach to the relief carvings than the one offered in the present chapter, Ornan's observations similarly highlight the viewer's feeling of enforced distance that is strongest with Nemedu B.

REFERENCES CITED

Andrae, Walter 1922 *Die archaischen Ischtar-Tempel.* Ausgrabungen der Deutschen Orient-Gesellschaft in Assur, A: Baudenkmäler Aus Assyrischer Zeit, Vol. IV. Wissenschaftliche Veröffentlichung der Deutschen Orient-Gesellschaft (WVDOG) 39. J.C. Hinrich'sche Buchhandlung, Leipzig.

Andrae, Walter 1923 *Farbige Keramik aus Assur und Ihre Vorstufen in Altassyrischen Wandmalereien.* Scarabaeus Verlag G.M.B.H., Berlin.

Andrae, Walter 1935 *Die jüngeren Ischtar-Tempel in Assur.* Ausgrabungen der Deutschen Orient-Gesellschaft in Assur, A: Baudenkmäler Aus Assyrischer Zeit, Vol. V. Wissenschaftliche Veröffentlichung der Deutschen Orient-Gesellschaft (WVDOG) 58. J.C. Hinrich'sche Buchhandlung, Leipzig.

André-Salvini, Béatrice 2008 *Babylone: L'album de l'exposition.* Musée du Louvre Éditions, Paris.

Baffi Guardata, Francesca, and Rita Dolce 1990 *Archeologia della Mesopotamia l'età Cassia e Medio-Assira,* Archaeologica 88. Giorgio Bretschneider Editore, Rome.

Bahrani, Zainab 2003 *The Graven Image: Representation in Babylonia and Assyria.* University of Pennsylvania Press, Philadelphia.

Cifarelli, Megan 1998 Gesture and Alterity in the Art of Ashurnasirpal II of Assyria. *The Art Bulletin* 80(2):210–228.

Cifola, B. 2004 The Titles of Tukulti-Ninurta I after the Babylonian Campaign: A Re-evaluation. In *From the Upper Sea to the Lower Sea: Studies on the History of Assyria and Babylonia in Honour of A.K. Grayson,* edited by Grant Frame with the assistance of Linda Wilding, pp. 7–15. Nederlands Instituut voor het Nabije Oosten, Leiden.

Frankfort, Henri 1996 *The Art and Architecture of the Ancient Orient.* Yale University Press, New Haven and London. Originally published 1954.

Grayson, A. Kirk 1987 *Assyrian Rulers of the Third and Second Millennia BC (TO 1115 BC).* University of Toronto Press, Toronto, Buffalo, and London.

Haller, Arndt, and Walter Andrae 1955 *Die Heiligtümer des Gottes Assur und der Sin-Šamaš-Tempel in Assur.* Ausgrabungen der Deutschen Orient-Gesellschaft in Assur, A: Baudenkmäler Aus Assyrischer Zeit, Vol. IX. Wissenschaftliche Veröffentlichung der Deutschen Orient-Gesellschaft (WVDOG) 67. Verlag Gebr. Mann, Berlin.

Kravitz, Kathryn F. 2010 Tukulti-Ninurta I Conquers Babylon: Two Versions. In *Gazing on the Deep: Ancient Near Eastern and Other Studies in Honor of Tzvi Abusch,* edited by Jeffery Stackert, Barbara Nevling Porter, and David P. Wright, pp. 121–129. CDL Press, Bethesda.

Kuhrt, Amélie 1995 *The Ancient Near East c. 3000–330 BC,* vol. I. Routledge, New York and London.

Luckenbill, Daniel D. 1926 *Ancient Records of Assyria and Babylonia, Volume I: Historical Records of Assyria from the Earliest Times to Sargon.* University of Chicago Press, Chicago.

Matthews, Donald M. 1990 *Principles of Composition in Near Eastern Glyptic of the Later Second Millennium B.C.* Orbis Biblicus et Orientalis Series Archaeologica (OBOSA) 8. Universitätsverlag, Fribourg, Switzerland.

Moortgat, Anton 1941 Assyrische Glyptik des 13. Jahrhunderts. *Zeitschrift für Assyriologie und vorderasiatische Archäologie* 47(1–2):50–88.

Moortgat, Anton 1944 Assyrische Glyptik des 12. Jahrhunderts. *Zeitschrift für Assyriologie und vorderasiatische Archäologie* 48(1):23–44.

Moortgat, Anton 1969 *The Art of Ancient Mesopotamia: The Classical Art of the Near East.* Phaidon, London and New York.

Muscarella, O.W. 1995 Royal Monument: Cult pedestal of the god Nusku. In *Assyrian Origins: Discoveries at Ashur on the Tigris: Antiquities in the Vorderasiatisches Museum, Berlin,* edited by Prudence Harper, Evelyn Klengel-Brandt, Joan Aruz, and Kim Benzel, pp. 112–113. The Metropolitan Museum of Art, New York.

Ornan, Tallay 2009 In the Likeness of Man: Reflections on the Anthropocentric Perception of the Divine in Mesopotamian Art. In *What Is a God? Anthropomorphic and Non-Anthropomorphic Aspects of Deity in Ancient Mesopotamia,* edited by Barbara Nevling Porter, pp. 93–151. Eisenbrauns, Winona Lake, Indiana.

Porada, Edith 1948 *Corpus of Ancient Near Eastern Seals in North American Collections: The Collection of the Pierpont Morgan Library,* vol. I. The Bollingen Series XIV. Bollingen Foundation and Pantheon Books, Washington, D.C.

Schroeder, Otto 1922 *Keilschrifttexte aus Assur historischen Inhalts,* vol. II. Ausgrabungen der Deutschen Orient-Gesellschaft in Assur, E: Inschriften. J.C. Hinrich'sche Buchhandlung, Leipzig.

Van De Mieroop, Marc 2007 *A History of the Ancient Near East ca. 3000–323 BC.* 2nd ed. Blackwell, Malden, Massachusetts, and Oxford.

Wiseman, D.J. 1958 The Vassal-Treaties of Esarhaddon. *Iraq* 20(1):i–ii, 1–99.

CHAPTER NINETEEN

Visualizing the Dynamics of Monumentality

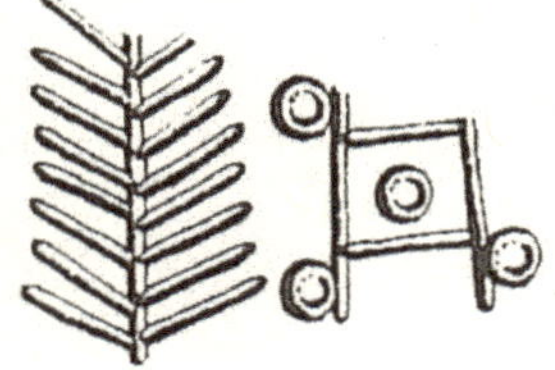

Willeke Wendrich

Abstract *The ancient Egyptian temple complex in Karnak, dedicated to the god Amun-Ra, is the embodiment in stone of struggles for power, establishment of authority, legitimization of rule, religious fervor, inclusion, exclusion, remembering, and forgetting. A three-dimensional virtual reality reconstruction of the Karnak temple complex enables researchers to trace its architectural development over time. The model allows reconstruction of the layout of and routing through the temple in its various phases of development. Speculation regarding which parts were roofed, hidden, and inaccessible to ordinary people can be tested by visualizing the building in its different stages. The emphasis on the development over time allows an approximation of the effects and meaning of the many extensive modifications. Furthermore, the model enables the reconstruction of the original placement of statues, and reliefs, which are found in museum collections worldwide, and allows for a representation of the presence and involvement of human beings in the architecture and the festival routing which was an important part of the yearly ceremonial cycle.*

INTRODUCTION: THE KARNAK TEMPLE COMPLEX

In its present state, the Temple of Amun-Ra in Karnak is a sprawling monumental landscape built over a period of more than 1,500 years (Figure 19.1). Contrary to most archaeological reconstructions, which focus on recreating what once was there, understanding the development of Karnak necessitates removing the overburden of later buildings, to understand what the temple looked like at any particular moment in time.

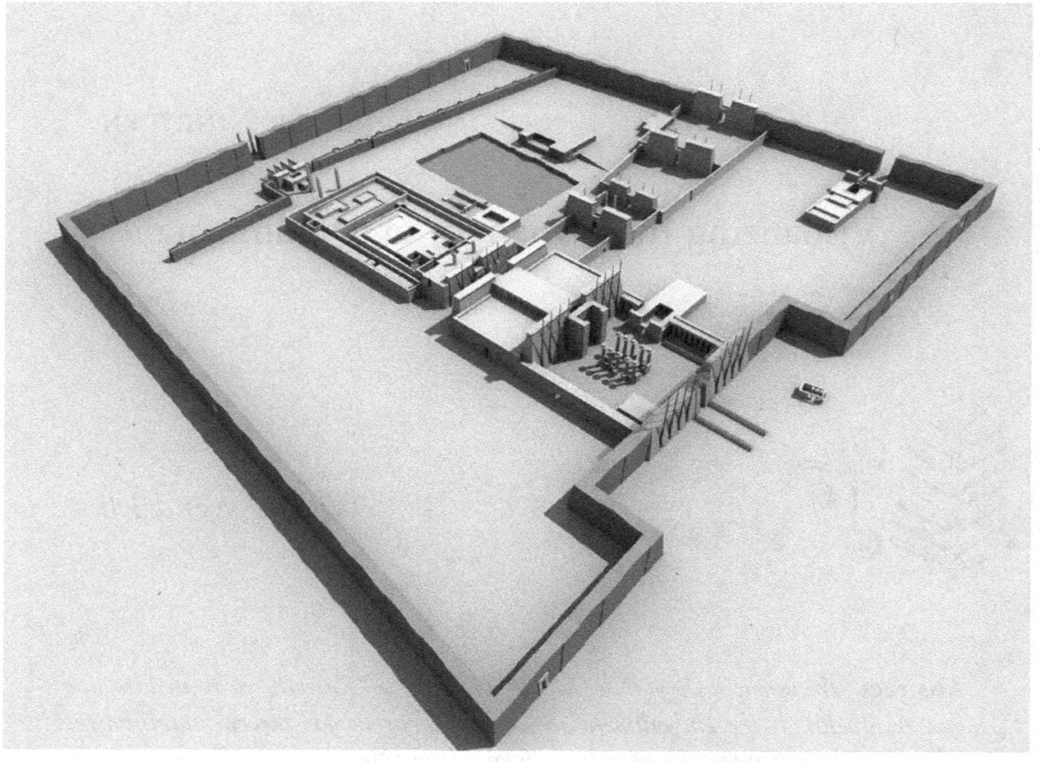

FIGURE 19.1 Reconstructed plan of the Temple of Amun-Ra at Karnak around 360 B.C. (Digital Karnak).

Starting as a small mudbrick temple in the Middle Kingdom (c. 1975–1640 B.C.), and perhaps even earlier, Karnak Temple and its priests were the recipients of royal donations in the form of building projects and agricultural estates which served to maintain the service of its main god Amun-Ra. Throughout history, almost every Egyptian king contributed some architectural elements. Senusret I (c. 1971–1926 B.C.) built a small, highly decorated shrine, which was probably placed in front of the temple to celebrate his jubilee.[1] The New Kingdom Pharaoh Amenhotep I (c. 1523–1502) embellished the temple, by replacing part of the mudbrick walls with stone, adding a calcite shrine to house the sacred barque, the boat-shrine on which the god traveled during processions, in the inner part of the temple. He also built an accompanying limestone chapel, which probably originally stood opposite that of Senusret I in front of the temple (Figure 19.2).[2] By the middle of the New Kingdom during the reign of Amenhotep IV (c. 1349–1332 B.C.) the two shrines had been removed and the stone blocks used in the foundation of later buildings. Even this pharaoh, who abolished the god Amun-Ra and changed his name from *Amen*hotep to Akhen*aten*, built his temple to the god Aten immediately east of the major temple in Karnak (Figure 19.3).[3]

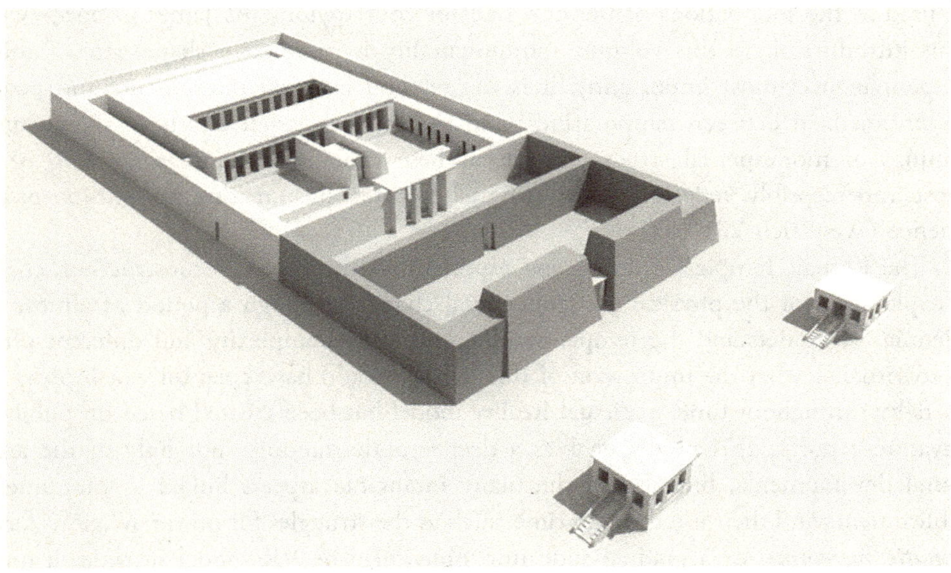

FIGURE 19.2 Karnak Temple in the time of Amenhotep I (c. 1523–1502 B.C.). Note the left limestone chapel, mirroring the much older "white chapel" built out of calcite under Senusret I (c. 1971–1926 B.C.) on the right (Digital Karnak).

During the continuous building and refurbishing process the architectural additions of predecessors often lost their prominent physical (and undoubtedly also conceptual) positions. Sometimes entire buildings were hidden from view, built in or taken apart and reused elsewhere in a less significant place. In some cases they were ruthlessly buried

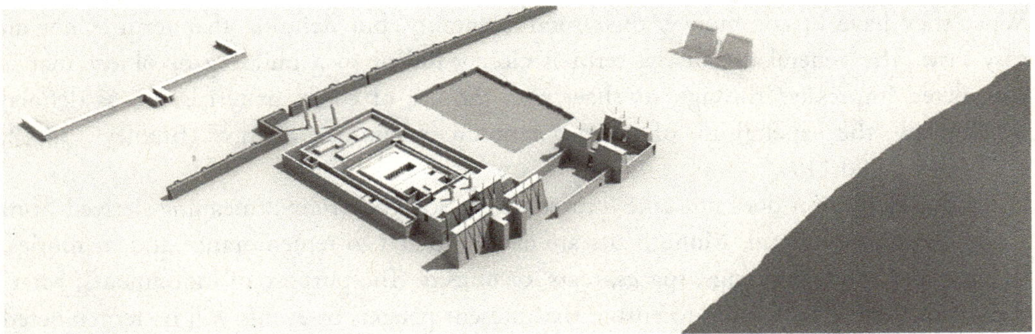

FIGURE 19.3 Karnak Temple in the time of Amenhotep IV (c. 1349–1332 B.C.). The temple at this stage had not only an east-west oriented axis, but was also expanded to the south, alongside the sacred lake and parallel to the Nile. Amenhotep IV's temple, the Gem Pa-Aten is located outside the Eighteenth Dynasty mudbrick enclosure wall, to the east (Digital Karnak).

and used as the foundations of the new halls or court pylons. As James Osborne writes in his introduction to this volume, monumentality is more than shape, size, visibility, and permanence; most importantly, it is the relation between monuments and people. The tension field between temporariness and permanence is felt clearly in the changing meanings of monumental structures. Often these changing meanings are not, or are almost imperceptibly, reflected in the material culture, thus creating the illusion of permanence (Wendrich 2010).

The Karnak Temple Complex, and especially its diachronic reconstruction, enables the exploration of the physical and conceptual changes through a period of almost two millennia. To understand the temple complex in all its complexity and different phases and to visualize what the impression of this temple would have been on worshippers and passers-by throughout time, a Virtual Reality model has been created based on published excavation reports. This model enables a deeper understanding, not only of the architectural developments, but also of the many intangible aspects linked to monumental establishments and their use through time, such as the struggles for power, religious fervor, *damnatio memoriae,* or a gradual slide into oblivion. The VR model provides a means to do a three-dimensional diachronic study of the use of space. It enables an analysis of the strategic decisions taken by priesthood and royalty in relation to the legitimization of power. Furthermore, the monument reflects not only religious and ritual changes, but also shifting attitudes toward history, memory, and the consideration of the contributions of forebears.

WHOSE MONUMENTS?

Monuments are among the most visible archaeological remains, and yet they are decidedly under-studied as a phenomenon in the broader context of surviving ancient remains (Bradley 1985:1). This probably is related to the fact that monuments are classified quite narrowly within distinct functional groups, such as temple, tomb, or landscape feature. What they have in common is their monumentality, but defining that term is not an easy task. The general use of the term is closely linked to a building or object that is considered impressive through its sheer size, the use of costly materials, or, as defined by Bradley, "the expenditure of unusual amounts of human energy" (Bradley 1985:2; cf. Trigger 1990:119).[4]

That definition does not take into consideration the original meaning derived from Latin *monēre,* to remind. Monuments are closely linked to remembrance and memories, be they structures, buildings, spaces, texts, or objects. The purpose of monuments, whatever form they take, is often to ensure that present persons or events will be remembered in the future. In other words, a monument records events, such as the lives and achievements of persons or groups in the present that are to be commemorated as a future past (Assmann 2011:149). It demonstrates that those who establish a monument have a strong perception of the importance of history and their place within it. The type of remembering that is expressed in monuments differs markedly from personal memories, through its communal character and its endorsement by official entities. Monuments are usually erected by organized groups or communities coordinating the efforts to construct a lasting dedication. The communality of the effort results in a depersonalized, often canonized memory, an "official" version of how a particular history is to be remembered. In contrast, I would classify memorials as a broader term, one that includes monuments, but also, at least in the outset, spontaneous, often perishable, grassroots communal initiatives, which at some point may become canonized into a more structured form. The outpouring of sympathy in the form of a carpet of flower bouquets after the death of Princess Diana comes to mind. In the following pages, I will first outline the nature and different aspects of monumentality in the ancient Egyptian context. This is followed by a discussion of how a virtual reality model of the Karnak Temple Complex has been employed to investigate and illustrate these Egyptian principles of monumentality as an expression of cultural memory, as defined by various authors.

WHO REMEMBERS?

Memories of individuals are unique experiences, which sometimes are recorded, for instance in a diary or an autobiography, but are not meant to be shared. When personal memories are made public they become a very different entity. Whether they are written down or expressed in another way, they become shared, and part of the communal memories of a group, period, or particular situation. Collective memory is a social phenomenon, a process of conveying common or shared memories that evoke reactions and emotions. Most often, the collective memory is expressed through verbal communication and spans at most a limited number of generations (Halbwachs 1992). Cultural memory (*kulturelle Gedächtnis*) is a redefinition and more precise rendering by Jan Assmann of the more general term *collective memory* (Assmann 1988, 1992, 2011; Halbwachs 1992). Building on Maurice Halbwachs's introduction of the term *collective memory* in the 1920s to indicate the social construct of remembering, Assmann analyzes the various forms of collective memory and elucidates the many aspects of the term.

There is a difference between remembering and preparing a memory of something or someone. The first can be individual or collective, the latter is by definition meant to be shared and part of the realm of cultural memory. The monument is the quintessence of the prepared memory irrespective of the person(s) or group(s) involved. The sheer size and expenditure of energy and means involved in most, if not all, monumental endeavors brings to the fore another important aspect of cultural memory: the involvement of authorities who condone or initiate the planning and execution of the monument. Without the approval of those who control space, placement, and materials, the erection of monuments cannot be realized. This has immediate implications for the type of remembering that is allowable, as well as the form of remembering. Personal accounts might be part of a monumental display in modern democracies, but not in the theocracy or autocracy that characterized ancient Egyptian society.

In ancient Egypt, monuments were erected by the religious or royal establishment. The Karnak Temple Complex is without doubt the most distinctive and blatant example of the combination of priesthood and royalty engaged in a struggle for power. Renewing, rebuilding, and adding substantial extensions to the temple was a means to pay homage to the gods, and ensure the support of the powerful priesthood of Amun-Ra. The name of the pharaoh who initiated a particular building phase was invariably inscribed in prominent positions on the temple walls or columns. During the time of Ramesses II these inscriptions were gouged deeply into the stone, because usurpation of monuments was a common occurrence and the deep carvings were meant to prevent the next king from claiming credit. In between some of those deeply carved pharaohs' names, traces of earlier kings' names can be found (Brand 2010), so the kings' builders, while usurping monuments of others, tried to avoid the same fate befalling Ramesses' name. If we compare the royal sphere with that of the elite (commoners being virtually invisible) we need to consider examples beyond Karnak. Individuals were allowed to erect their own monuments, but explicitly with the blessing of, and perhaps sometimes even paid for by Pharaoh. The Middle Kingdom Story of Sinuhe, for example, ended with the protagonist, who fled Egypt after hearing rumors of a conspiracy against the king, returning to Egypt at the end of his lifetime. Contrary to his trepidations and fears of receiving punishment for his perceived part in the conspiracy, the king's son welcomes him with open arms and builds a house and a tomb for him (Lichtheim 1973:233), although perhaps the monumental inscription at the entrance of the tomb of Hetep-her-Akhet reflected more realistic royal contributions: "I made this tomb because I was honored by the king, who brought me a sarcophagus" (Lichtheim 1973:16).

Interesting cases are the examples of two high officials in the time of Ramesses II who included so-called kings lists in their tombs. The overseer of works Tenroy, who was buried in Sakkara, the necropolis of the capital Memphis, listed cartouches with the names of 58 kings on a tablet in his tomb (of which at present 47 survive). The list started with king Anedjib of Dynasty 1, ends with Ramesses II, and excluded the kings of the First Intermediate Period, the Second Intermediate Period, the Amarna Period, and Queen Hatshepsut. In other words, the monument included a highly redacted listing of "approved" rulers. Likewise, Amenmes, who was a priest of the cult of the deified first king of the Middle Kingdom "Amenhotep of the forecourt," had himself depicted in his tomb in Thebes giving offerings to Amenhotep I, the founder of the Twelfth Dynasty, and twelve other kings. Each king was facing Tenroy and had his name inscribed in a cartouche. Monuments were, therefore, a royal prerogative, shared, but not controlled by the elite. Only during the so-called Intermediate Periods when the central power broke down did local elites have the possibility to exercise agency in the erection of monumental tombs.

WHAT IS REMEMBERED?

Monuments have been erected to commemorate a person, a group, or an event. The reason why a person is remembered is most often related to either social position or lifetime achievements. In present-day monuments clear shifts in trends have been noted. An increasing number of monuments commemorate victims of wars, accidents, or terrorist attacks (Savage 1997, 2009). Such disastrous periods and events and their aftermath have left a scarring imprint on the collective memory of a society. In addition to honoring an individual for his (rarely her) accomplishments, individuals may represent an entire group. The remembrance of death, most often of deaths that are emotionally perceived as unexplained, untimely, or unfair, warrants memorials, while death in large numbers is often commemorated with a more formal monument. However, cultural memory is not static or unchangeable. An interesting recent example is a monument erected in the city of Amsterdam, dedicated to General Van Heutsz. He was honored because as military governor of Aceh, he ended a 25-year-long war in Indonesia. This military success of 1913 was celebrated with the erection of a monument in 1935. From the very start the Van Heutsz Monument also became the focus of protests against colonial rule, suppression, and even alleged war crimes by the Dutch army. At least four attempts have been made to blow up the monument with dynamite, the last in 1984. In 2001, the Amsterdam city council decided to redesign, rename, and rededicate the monument and in 2007 the "Memorial for the Relation between Indonesia and the Netherlands" was inaugurated. It includes important moments in the history of the relationship, such as first contact in 1596 and the recognition of Indonesia's independence in 1949. Still, the cultural memory of the "old" monument lingers, and in 2011 the monument was once more severely damaged.[5]

Cultural memory is, as Assmann highlights, strongly related to power and can be either retrospective or prospective (Assmann 2011:54). In ancient Egypt, retrospective memory was very common and often linked to legitimization of power through illustrious ancestors (real or imagined). The prime example of this were the king lists, mentioned above. These were documents or inscriptions, composed as early as the Old Kingdom period, which list the names of previous kings, including information such as the capital at that time, and important events such as festivals or ceremonies (Kemp 2006:61–65; Uphill 2003). The purpose of these lists was not to write history, nor to commemorate the great deeds of past kings, but to put the present ruler firmly in the line of succession. Even though the "ancestors" were not directly related, the fact that the current king appeared on the same monument as the rulers from the past was itself a powerful endorsement, a statement of fact.

For this reason alone, one would perhaps expect a kings list to be a royal prerogative, and for most of Egyptian history this seems indeed to have been the case. But the two examples of Tenroy and Amenmes cited above did not fit that mold. What purpose would it have served them to remember the ancestors of their king? The text inscribed on the tablet in Tenroy's tomb was actually quite explicit: Tenroy asked the kings in a prayer to grant him a share of the daily offerings that were made to them in the temple of Ptah at Memphis (Kemp 2006:62). Tenroy and Amenmes were ensuring, therefore, not so much the retrospective memory of the line of kingship as the prospective memory of having their own names remembered and their postmortem persons fed and taken care of in the afterlife. The daily offerings from temples all throughout Egypt were redistributed to the living, as is apparent from the explicit outline of the offering ritual, such as depicted on the east interior wall of the Hypostyle Hall of Karnak Temple. In seven scenes the "reversion of offerings" was depicted, accompanied by seven spells to be recited during the ritual (Figure 19.4) (Sullivan 2008). The notion that nonroyal (albeit high-ranking) individuals such as Tenroy and Amenmes expected to share in the daily offerings made on behalf of the king found a parallel in the phenomenon of the placement of statues in the forecourt of Karnak Temple. By the late Ptolemaic or early Roman period the courts of the temple were cluttered to the extent that the priesthood decided to bury the statues in the forecourt of the seventh pylon. It was a good solution in the Egyptian mindset. The cache, which was rediscovered in 1905, ensured that the statues of the forebears, many of whom were high priests of Amun-Ra at Karnak, were still included in the sacred precinct, without hampering the daily tasks and future statue

FIGURE 19.4 Reversion of offerings: daily ritual. Karnak, west face of the southeast wall of the Hypostyle Hall (photo: Carrie Zarnoch/Digital Karnak).

placements of the living (Legrain 1905). With its emphasis on the afterlife, Egyptian efforts to remember and be remembered were always related to a concern that at some point in time family or paid priesthood would stop remembering and stop caring for the deceased. This was not just an emotional danger, but a severe physical one, because if the dead were devoid of offerings, they were believed to fall on hard times in the afterlife, which implied very real suffering into eternity.

One of the most impressive types of monuments within the Karnak complex are the obelisks erected by several rulers. To carve out a monolithic needle of 20 to 30 m long without steel tools, by pounding the hard granite bedrock with slightly harder diorite, then transport the stone weighing more than 100 tons on special ships down the Nile, 300 km to Karnak or 900 km to Heliopolis, was an enormous feat of ancient engineering and logistics. The first pair of obelisks was erected by king Thutmose I (c. 1504–1492 B.C.) in the Festival Hall in Karnak, just west of the fourth pylon. It was dedicated by Thutmose I to "his father Amun-Ra."[6] A second pair, at 28 m high was commissioned by his son Thutmose II, to be placed next to his father's 20 m high pair, and dedicated to Thutmose I. Thutmose II died before these obelisks were finalized and the task to erect them fell to his sister and wife Hatshepsut.[7] During her rule, Hatshepsut erected six obelisks: two dedicated to Thutmose I, two at the eastern side of the temple complex,[8] lining what probably was an eastern entrance, and two in commemoration of her sixteenth regal year.[9] These latter were placed in the Wadjet Hall, an area of the temple which Hatshepsut completely refurbished. Reliefs on the four sides of the obelisk depicted Hatshepsut as pharaoh, giving offerings to the god Amun-Ra.[10] She commemorated the enormous technological feat of erecting these two 30 m high obelisks in a relief on the wall of a red quartzite barque chapel she also had built (Figure 19.5).

FIGURE 19.5 Block from Hatshepsut's Red Chapel showing the queen dedicating her two obelisks to the god Amun-Ra (photo: Carrie Zarnoch/Digital Karnak).

Apart from her many additions to the Karnak Temple Complex Hatshepsut also built a rock cut tomb in the Valley of the Kings and a magnificent "mansion of millions of years," a temple dedicated to an eternity of ongoing priestly services to the deceased female king. Every king of the New Kingdom followed the same pattern of a decorated tomb hidden in the desert of the west bank of the Nile and a very prominent temple on the edge of the cultivation. These temples are often called "memorial temples," and this suggests they were a form of prospective cultural memory. They were not established, however, to ensure that future generations remembered, but to safeguard the ongoing provisions for the deceased. These temples were all endowed with their own agricultural fields, the yield of which supported the priesthood and the continuation of the cult that benefited the king in the afterlife.

It was probably also Hatshepsut who started building the north-south axis of the temple, which over the centuries would expand to the most important ceremonial route in ancient Thebes. Under her rule two festivals were either initiated, or, more likely, emphasized. These were the Opet Festival and the "Beautiful feast of the Wadi." Both involved yearly processions of the god Amun (hidden in a shrine, carried on the sacred barque), the first from Karnak to the temple in Luxor, the second to visit the dead on the west bank.

Hatshepsut was probably seven years regent, and ruled for 22 years as king. Thutmose III (c. 1479–1425 B.C.) became sole king after her death, for approximately 34 years. During this time he expanded the Karnak Temple Complex even more than Hatshepsut had done by erecting two more obelisks, (re-)constructing the sacred lake, redesigning Hatshepsut's Wadjet Hall, and creating an enormous festival hall at the east side of the Karnak temple.[11] In that area he established a "hall of the ancestors," another one of those king lists, and the traditional legitimization of rule, rather than a narrowly defined retrospective memorization of previous rulers.

Access to Remembering

Many of the Egyptian monuments with the most direct objective of eliciting remembering (either retrospective or prospective) were located in tombs or parts of temples with limited public access. This raises the question of who had access to the monument, and whether access was actually necessary in order for the monument to effectively fulfill its function. It is not clear whether tombs prepared for high officials were open and accessible before the owners' deaths, but after the burial only the forecourt of most tombs could still be visited. In the Old Kingdom period, this was the place where the biography of the tomb owner was inscribed, and is thus a clear form of prospective memory where the tomb owner prepared the monument for himself. These biographies were very explicit (to the point that we would consider shameless bragging) about the tomb owner's accomplishments. Similarly, statues placed in the temple forecourt facilitated that high officials would be remembered. The prominence in the landscape of the New Kingdom royal memorial temples, or "mansions of millions of years," ensured an ongoing reference to the power of a particular king. Although the purpose of these establishments was to ensure ongoing priestly service, the many temples abandoned in antiquity tell us that collective memory lasted only a few generations.

The Karnak Temple Complex provides ample evidence of building programs undertaken by pharaohs to ensure that they would be remembered by the gods and priesthood. To what extent was the king's memory a concern among the population? Most of the building activity in the early New Kingdom concentrated on the construction of the most sacred part of the temple, an area that was off-limits to anyone but the high priest. The Hall of Ancestors, built by Thutmose III, was at the very back of the temple in his festival hall and access would have been severely restricted. Access by the population to the gods venerated in the grand Egyptian temples was limited to the festivals, when the gods would leave the temple. An exception is perhaps the so-called Contra Temple, built at the back of the Temple of Amun-Ra by Thutmose III, between the two obelisks that Hatshepsut erected there, and closing off the putative eastern entrance (Figure 19.6).[12] The small chapel gave access to persons who were not allowed to enter the temple proper. A similar function seems to have been given to the temple of "Amun-Ra-who-hears-prayers," which was built in the east gate of the New Kingdom temenos wall, around the "unique

FIGURE 19.6 The contra temple (the small building between the two obelisks at the right) and the temple of the hearing ear, or "Amun-Ra-who-hears-prayers" near the single "Unique Obelisk," closing off the eastern entrance through the Eighteenth Dynasty enclosure wall (Digital Karnak).

obelisk" erected by Thutmose IV. Most of the construction was done under Ramesses II, but probably refurbishing an earlier temple (Gallet 2013).[13]

Remembering implies forgetting, and this is well illustrated by the building sequences at Karnak: what was to be remembered was foregrounded or newly built; what should no longer be remembered, or what was no longer relevant was literally taken down. Sometimes the buildings that were demolished had simply lost their meaning, but the destruction could also be part of a purposeful program of erasing the memory (*damnatio memoriae*). The ironic result at Karnak is that what was forgotten or supposed to be forgotten has been best preserved. Entire shrines were taken down and used in the foundations of later buildings, or as fill for the enormous pylons. A small open-air museum at Karnak houses several of these buildings, which could be completely reconstructed, after the blocks were discovered and excavated. Examples are the calcite chapel (known as "the White Chapel") of Senusret I,[14] the first pharaoh whose name has been attested at Karnak; the limestone chapel of Amenhotep I, a replica of Senusret's chapel and originally probably installed opposite the latter outside the temple wall (Figure 19.1)[15]; the "Red Chapel" of Hatshepsut[16]; and the peristyle hall built by Thutmose IV.[17] The two white chapels on the west side of the temple entrance provide an interesting sequence of remembering. The fact that Amenhotep I built a replica of Senusret's chapel is testimony not only to remembrance, but respect for his ancestor and quite possibly an eagerness to emulate his illustrious predecessor. Both chapels were probably incorporated in the Festival Hall of Thutmose II. In some cases, demolition was almost as immense a task as building. Amenhotep III tore down the entire pylon and festival hall built by Thutmose II, including the White Chapel and the Limestone Chapel. This large-scale demolition was needed to create space for the third pylon,[18] but it was also indicative of Amenhotep's attitude toward these previous kings.

The demolition of buildings reflects which pharaohs were forgotten, or forgettable, but also which pharaohs were meant to be erased from memory. It was mentioned above that Thutmose III made changes to Hatshepsut's Wadjet Hall. These changes were considerable to the point that most of Hatshepsut's building program became invisible. The wooden columns and partial roof that she had built (Figure 19.7) were replaced by enormous stone columns and the entire hall was re-roofed with stone slabs. Hatshepsut's obelisks were completely hidden because they were encapsulated in the walls of a stone gateway. Only the tops of the obelisks were visible above the roof, but at ground level they were completely obscured (Figure 19.8). The names of Hatshepsut on the obelisks were left intact. Her barque shrine, known as the "Red Chapel," was dismantled and only the door jambs and lintels were reused. The rest of the beautifully decorated shrine was taken apart. Late in his rule, Thutmose III embarked on what has been characterized as a *damnatio memoriae,* removing Hatshepsut's name and destroying much of her statuary. The reason for this has been interpreted as an act of revenge of Thutmose III against a shrewd stepmother (Hayes 1973:317),[19] but recent reconstructions of the timing of these acts of destruction lead to another interpretation. It was not an impulsive decision shortly after her death, but a deliberate program executed when Thutmose III had been sole ruler for at least 20 years. Hatshepsut was the last in the direct female line of the

Thutmoseids, and although Thutmose III's son, the later Pharaoh Amenhotep II, was directly related in the male line, there may have been concerns about the succession (Roth 2005). On some of the blocks of the Red Chapel Hatshepsut's name and figure were hacked out, but on others they were left intact, which probably indicates that after the replacement of the chapel by Thutmose III's granite chapel, the blocks were left somewhere on the temple grounds and only the ones that were accessible were damaged. Approximately 40 years later the blocks were used as fill in the foundation of the third pylon, built under Amenhotep III.

A clear-cut case of *damnatio memoriae* was the destruction of the four Aten temples that were built in the Theban region. Starting under Amenhotep III and his son Amen-hotep IV/Akhenaten, a clear attempt was made by the court to diminish the enormous power of the priesthood of Amun-Ra (Kemp 2012; Kozloff 2011; Kozloff et al. 1992). The expansions to the Karnak temple were accompanied by donations of land to ensure the continued ritual and political support of the Amun priesthood, severely hollowing out the material and political power of the throne. Amenhotep IV closed the temples to Amun and in the first three years of his reign built a temple to the sun-god Aten. Textual references to the existence of at least four structures have been found, but the location of only one of these, the Gem Pa-Aten has been identified. It was built immediately east of the temenos wall of the Amun precinct (Figures 19.3, 19.9)[20] out of small sandstone blocks, a breach with architectural tradition, as were the layout and design of the temple. In the sixth year of his reign Akhenaten moved his political capital from Memphis and

FIGURE 19.7 Hatshepsut's Wadjet Hall, 3D visualization (Digital Karnak).

FIGURE 19.8 Enclosed obelisks of Hatshepsut and reconfiguration of the Wadjet Hall by Thutmose III (Digital Karnak).

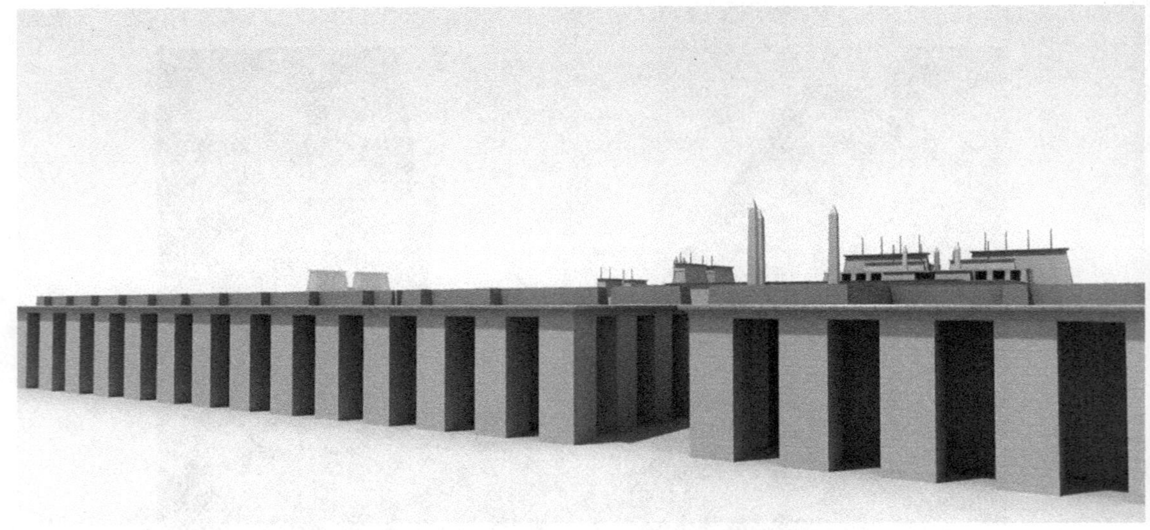

FIGURE 19.9 Gem Pa-Aten, looking toward southwest. Reconstruction of the colonnade built outside the enclosure wall of the precinct of Amun-Ra. The colonnade originally had colossal statues in front of each square pillar depicting Amenhotep IV wearing different crowns (not reproduced in the VR model) (Digital Karnak).

religious capital from Thebes to a new city in Middle Egypt, Akhetaten, "the Horizon of the Aten." This revolution in religion, politics, social relations, and art only lasted the lifetime of the king. After his demise the country went back to the old ways, and one of Akhenaten's successors, Horemheb, dismantled the Aten temples in Thebes and used the talatat blocks as fill in the second, ninth, and tenth pylons (Figure 19.10).

Equally important as access to remembering is access to being remembered. Part of cultural memory in ancient Egypt was the conviction that the afterlife is eternal, real, and dependent on the actions of the living. While royalty and high officials can afford to build monuments, ordinary farmers cannot and their hope for the afterlife is dependent on how long their family remembers and can afford to bring regular offerings.

MATERIALITY OF REMEMBERING

Memories are fleeting and personal. Cultural memory is meant to be shared and therefore requires a "storage system" in which what is memorable is encoded, stored, saved, and retrieved through a shared understanding (Assmann 2011:9). The forms in which memories can be coded differ widely. A particularly poignant feature in the landscape might be understood as representing an event or a social group. Landscape modification or transformation, in the form of moving earth, or transporting and raising stones, is

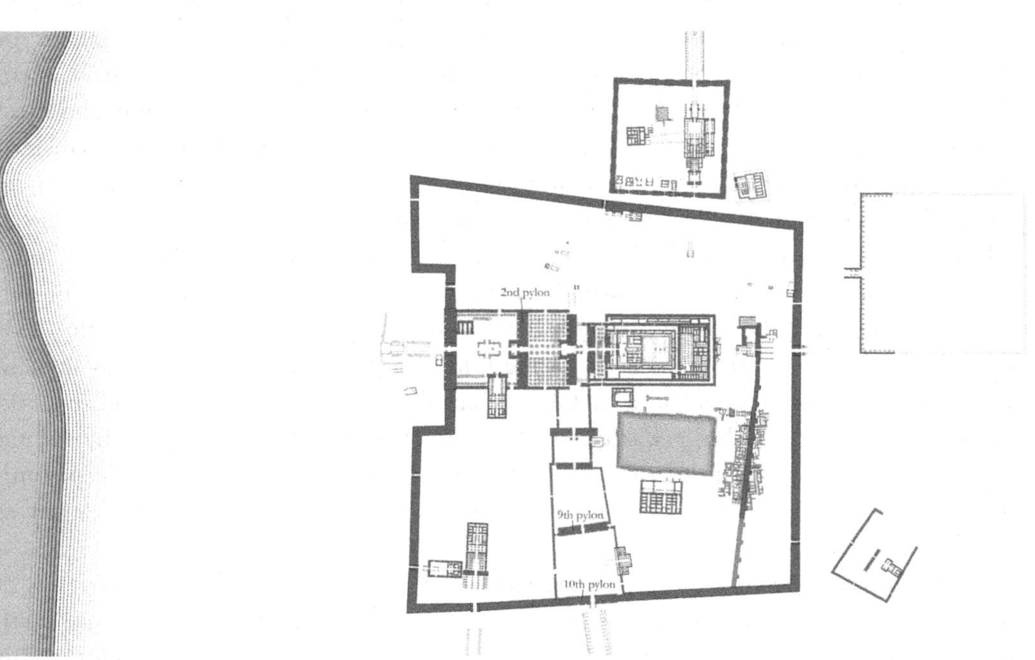

FIGURE 19.10 Location of the 2nd, 9th, and 10th pylons, the core of which were built with blocks from the dismantled Gem Pa-Aten (Digital Karnak).

another form of inscribing cultural memory on a place (Bradley 1998). Art and writing are two incredibly powerful technologies to encode, save, transfer, and decode memory. The combination of art, writing, and building, as the ultimate landscape modification, is what we encounter in ancient Egypt. The size, shape, and character of Egyptian monuments varies widely, but as the word *monumental* in daily use reflects, monuments are unforgettable because of their impressive size, shape, cost, effort, position, or location.

Cultural memory in ancient Egypt was invariably linked to existence in the afterlife and this was reflected in the selection of materials used. Tombs were made for eternity, and already in the royal tombs of the Early Dynastic Period the pottery was therefore replaced with hard stone vases, while the textile cover was represented by a thin gold square tied around the neck of the vessel with a golden fillet. The use of stone in temples and tombs expanded from vessels to architecture. The Djoser Complex in Sakkara is a prime example of the representation in stone of natural materials, such as reed or wooden pillars and grass matting (Kemp 2006:146).

The earliest phases of the Karnak Temple Complex were built of mudbrick, and the first architectural augmentations probably consisted of a replacement of the mudbrick shrine with one of local sandstone. The first real evidence for embellishment of the temple dates to the Middle Kingdom. King Senusret I replaced the sandstone shrine with one of limestone and installed a calcite altar.[21] He also built a small shrine of calcite, which was probably installed outside the temple walls, the so-called White Chapel mentioned above. Replacing local sandstone with nonlocal limestone signified an investment in transportation, which was even more true of the calcite chapel and altar. Calcite, or "Egyptian alabaster," was quarried 450 km north at Hatnub, deep inside the Eastern Desert (Harrell 2012, 2013). The effort and investment needed to carve out and erect obelisks was even more impressive and shows that not only the selection of materials, but also the sheer effort of transportation, a technological feat that would only be matched with difficulty today, demonstrated the importance of the monument. Aswan red granite, the material of which these obelisks were made, was an aesthetically attractive stone, but the major appeal would have been to show control over resources and power to command the carving, transportation, and handling of giant monoliths. This was a true royal prerogative. As early as the Old Kingdom, Aswan granite was used in the pyramid temple of Menkaura in Giza, while the black basalt floor of the pyramid temple of Neussere in Abusir was quarried in the Western Desert north of the Fayum Depression, and the diorite of the statue of King Khephren came from the deep south of the Western Desert, west of present day Abu Simbel in an area simply known as "Khephren's Quarry" (Harrell 2013).

The use of rare or expensive materials was just one aspect of the materiality of remembering. The walls and pillars of Senusret's White Chapel were inscribed with hieroglyphic texts and images recalling the king's *heb-sed,* the festival in honor of his jubilee. The technique used for the inscriptions was raised relief, in which the entire stone surface was carved away, leaving the signs and scenes that adorn the monument. This was the most exquisite and laborious type of creating a relief and together with the high quality fine-grained almost translucent material it gives a breathtaking effect even today. Color traces show that the hieroglyphs and scenes were originally painted using yellow, white, blue, and red. Expenditure of effort thus went hand in hand with a carefully composed textual and pictorial program. The White Chapel was probably originally used in the *heb-sed* as a pavilion in which the double throne of Upper and Lower Egypt would have been located. In the early New Kingdom it was refurbished and used as a barque shrine. At that time the memory of Senusret I and his jubilee were apparently still present. Amenhotep I even copied the White Chapel (see above), using white limestone, rather than calcite.

FUNCTION OF MONUMENTS IN REMEMBERING

Monuments are the lasting embodiment of shared beliefs (Bradley 1985:7) and thus have an important social function in the creation and maintenance of group identity at several moments in their existence. At the time of construction the creation of a monument is a powerful unifying factor, or can prove to be a divisive issue, as illustrated with the example of the Van Heutsz monument in Amsterdam. During its existence a monument's meaning commonly shifts, because circumstances, group dynamics, interests, and focus change, resulting ultimately in "forgotten monuments." At the time of their demolition, by natural disaster, decay, or demolition, some of the original emotions may be remembered and reawakened. The time span that a monument lasts varies greatly and is partly dependent on how much it allows reinterpretation, giving it new meaning in different times, evoking different associations.

Cultural memory is a very specific form of shared belief, whose purpose is to strengthen the group by rendering history into myth. Guided by a specialized tradition bearer (such as a priest, shaman, or king), cultural memory usually poses a mythic origin of the group, and stages formalized festivals (Assmann 2011:41). The function of monuments in ancient Egypt is to bear witness to an age-old unchanging unification of Egypt under the wise leadership of the king, whose main task is to maintain cosmic order. In the iconography, architecture, and texts continuity is stressed, resulting in a seemingly stable, unchanging, monolithic society. This is a very misleading impression, because changing attitudes and interpretations are presented in traditional forms, while the underlying meaning has changed over time (Kemp 2006:61; Wendrich 2010).

EXPERIENCING ANCIENT MONUMENTS

In Egyptian Arabic the term that is often translated as "monument" is "*Athaar*," literally "remnants," a term that reflects the presence of impressive ruins in the landscape from a culture that preceded, but is in many aspects not closely linked to the present. Egyptian schoolchildren are given a very rudimentary overview of Egyptian history, but they do visit the monuments. Pharaonic history is a cause for pride, and the monuments now represent inherent "Egyptianness." Being Egyptian and Islamic is contrasted by many Egyptians with being Arab. The Copts have staked out an even stronger claim of being the true heirs of ancient Egypt, as expressed, for instance, in ancient Egyptian names given to their children. Thus, in the Egyptian mind the monuments are not forgotten relics, but very much part of the living culture.

Although the standing ruins of the great temples are impressive, for Egyptian schoolchildren and foreign tourists alike, it is difficult to understand their development, meaning, and function. Visiting the Karnak temple is a bewildering experience: the great hypostyle hall is immensely impressive, and there is a fascinating statue of a giant dung beetle right next to the sacred lake, but in spite of extensive reconstructions it is very difficult to understand the layout and development of the enormous complex.

Even for an Egyptologist who is well versed in the architectural history of the temple, recognizing the various sections of the sprawling complex is difficult. Much of the Karnak temple has been taken away. Many of the limestone walls have ended up in medieval and postmedieval lime kilns. Two of the most impressive obelisks were transported to Istanbul and Rome, and the statues that were placed in the open courts are now in museums all over the world. The sacred areas of the temple that originally were kept in darkness are roofless and blasted by sunlight.

THE USE OF VIRTUAL REALITY IN UNDERSTANDING MONUMENTALITY

In 2008 UCLA developed a three-dimensional Virtual Reality model of the Karnak Temple Complex, based on published excavation reports. The model has several purposes. In the first place, it is meant to reflect the current state of knowledge and although some speculation (e.g., about the original height of some of the walls) is unavoidable, the model stays as close as possible to a reconstruction based on firm archaeological evidence. The model is, therefore, not designed specifically to provide an immersive experience. For instance, although we know that many of the reliefs, pillars, and pylon faces were brightly colored, color has only been indicated in places where there are actual paint traces visible (e.g., in the Akhmenu).[22] The second purpose is to provide a chronological overview of the development of the complex. A time slider allows the user to explore the modifications made to the temple, and experience the gradual changes from a birds' eye view, as well as from any place inside the temple. For decennia color-coded plans of the complex have tried to accomplish the same, but although such plans can show the expansion of the temple complex, it is incapable of indicating which parts of the temple were moved or dismantled. In the third place, a virtual reconstruction, in contrast with a physical one, enables testing of alternative theories, expression of the level of (un)certainty, and incorporation of ambiguity (Bodenhamer 2010). Only a few parts of the temple have been preserved to roof height, while evidence for the dismantled parts of the temple mostly enables a reconstruction of shape and size, but not of original location. The model includes several uncertain reconstructions of, for instance, many of the wall heights, which parts were roofed, routing, entrances, and original placement of several smaller chapels. Users of the realtime VR model can embark on a three-dimensional diachronic study of the development and consider the purpose of the many modifications the temple has undergone (Sullivan 2008; Sullivan and Wendrich 2009).

At this moment the online version of Digital Karnak contains screen shots and videos generated from the full realtime VR model. The model cannot be run from an online source, because it requires considerable computing power to do so and requires the use of software developed at UCLA (VRnav), or a gaming engine such as Maya.

The placement of reliefs, such as the Daily Ritual, in the model in their original position enables researchers to study the texts and visual sequences in context. The lighting can be adapted to what it would have been at certain times of the day, or the year. Seen at their original height, sometimes obscured by pillars, built in by architectural modifications, it is likely that many of these texts were not legible for the priests doing service in the temple. Their inscription had, therefore, a more fundamental ritual function, related to the establishment of the monument as an eternal presence and a repetition of ritual by the mere presence of the relevant scenes and texts. Similarly, statues can be virtually placed back in their original position, allowing a reconstruction of the temple furnishings and use of space, as well as the meaning of a particular statue in a specific place (Favro 2011).

The VR model helps to explore the dynamics of memory and monumentality. Even though cultural memory establishes a mythical situation in which the monument is static and eternal, in reality Karnak was in constant flux. Not only was the temple complex a dynamic entity due to the continuous changes made to the architecture and layout, but it was the stage setting for a large number of rituals. The movement through the temple, on a daily basis and during the many festivals, is another aspect that is aided by using a three-dimensional reconstruction based on exact measurements. Comparing the length and width of the sacred barque with the dimensions of the temple access gates and corridors allows a reconstruction of the possible routes the procession took.

Less tangible is the impression of walking through the high-ceilinged halls of this enormous complex, the experience of being left standing outside the gates, or joining the crowds at the contra temple. As said above, the purpose of the 3D-VR model is not to create a "near real" ancient environment. Nevertheless, interaction of a user with the model does allow a certain degree of embodiment within space and place (Lock 2010:97–100). Virtual Reality allows us to reinsert the human dimension, not only in comparison to the monumental scale, but also as an agent in experiencing space (Favro 2006).

Conclusion

Using a virtual reality model of the enormous monumental structure that is the Karnak Temple Complex allows us to better understand three important aspects, which would be difficult to tease out by using archaeological publications alone. The first is the incorporation of a time slider, which permits a more ready understanding of changes made to the complex over time. This does not only involve the additions, new pylons, courts, and temple elements, but most importantly the erasures. Akhenaten's Gem Pa-Aten temple was torn down, which in itself was an effort on monumental scale, for the unequivocal purpose of *damnatio memoriae*. The demolition by Amenhotep III of the Festival Hall of Thutmose II, including the White Chapel of Senusret I and the Limestone Chapel of

Amenhotep I probably had a very different meaning: not a purposeful erasure of memory, but a removal of what had become obsolete through forgetting. Even though Amenhotep I and III had the same throne name, they were six generations apart. The situation with all the changes made by Hatshepsut and Thutmose III is extremely interesting and illustrates yet another element of cultural memory through monumentality. Hatshepsut's emphatic presence in Karnak may be explained by a need to legitimize her rule. It is a matter of debate whether Thutmose III's equally extensive building program should be attributed to the same necessity, because his rule was well established. It may, however, have been directed against political factions who might have been stressing the female line of succession, and thus threaten the throne of Thutmose III's son.

The second important aspect of the VR model is that the construction is three-dimensional, forcing decisions and discussions on the original height of walls, roofed versus open areas, presence of doors, windows, roof constructions, pillar shapes, and a host of other elements. These reconstructions are based on measurements of existing architectural features and a number of criteria that are listed in a log that accompanies the model and specifies what the decisions are based on and what is conjecture or speculation.

Third, the model is clad in photographs of the present state of the temple, but could be used to place old photographs or drawings, made when the wall reliefs were more intact, back in their architectural context. Also, the placement of statuary, obelisks that have been removed, and the reconstruction of color patterns based on paint traces enhances the usefulness of the model as a research tool for contextual or experiential studies.

Studying Karnak in detail using the VR model does not diminish the awe one cannot help to feel for this monumental temple complex. The model and the accompanying Web site provide yet another important enhancement: by repeating the names of the pharaohs who built at Karnak, the forgotten ones, and even the ones that were erased from history, are all remembered, reestablished, and according to Egyptian belief, rejuvenated.

NOTES

1. http://dlib.etc.ucla.edu/projects/Karnak/archive/query?period_id=20.
2. http://dlib.etc.ucla.edu/projects/Karnak/archive/query?period_id=11.
3. http://dlib.etc.ucla.edu/projects/Karnak/archive/query?period_id=38.
4. see also the *Oxford English Dictionary*: "The quality of being monumental, or grandly imposing; an instance of this." http://www.oed.com/view/Entry/238260.
5. http://www.buitenbeeldinbeeld.nl/Amsterdam_Z/Van_Heutsz.htm; http://www.historischnieuwsblad.nl/nl/nieuws/2845/van-heutsz-monument-moet-blijven-confronteren.html.
6. http://dlib.etc.ucla.edu/projects/Karnak/feature/ObelisksOfFestivalHallEastPair.
7. http://dlib.etc.ucla.edu/projects/Karnak/feature/ObelisksOfFestivalHallWestPair.
8. http://dlib.etc.ucla.edu/projects/Karnak/feature/ObelisksAtContraTemple.
9. http://dlib.etc.ucla.edu/projects/Karnak/feature/ObelisksOfWadjetHall.
10. Ibid.
11. http://dlib.etc.ucla.edu/projects/Karnak/feature/Akhmenu.

12. http://dlib.etc.ucla.edu/projects/Karnak/feature/ContraTemple.
13. http://dlib.etc.ucla.edu/projects/Karnak/feature/RamessesIIEasternTemple.
14. http://dlib.etc.ucla.edu/projects/Karnak/feature/WhiteChapel.
15. http://dlib.etc.ucla.edu/projects/Karnak/feature/AmenhotepILimestoneChapel.
16. http://dlib.etc.ucla.edu/projects/Karnak/feature/RedChapel.
17. http://dlib.etc.ucla.edu/projects/Karnak/feature/ThutmoseIVPeristyleHall.
18. http://dlib.etc.ucla.edu/projects/Karnak/feature/PylonIII.
19. Hatshepsut was the daughter of Thutmose I and married to her brother Thutmose II. When her spouse died she became regent for Thutmose III, the young son of Thutmose II, and a minor wife. After nine years as regent she proclaimed herself king and co-ruler with Thutmose III.
20. http://dlib.etc.ucla.edu/projects/Karnak/feature/AtenTemples.
21. http://dlib.etc.ucla.edu/projects/Karnak/feature/MiddleKingdomCourt.
22. http://dlib.etc.ucla.edu/projects/Karnak/feature/Akhmenu.

REFERENCES CITED

Assmann, J. 1988 Kollektives Gedächtnis und kulturelle Identität. In *Kultur und Gedächtnis,* edited by J. Assmann and T. Hölscher, pp. 9–19. Suhrkamp, Frankfurt am Main.

Assmann, J. 1992 *Das kulturelle Gedächtnis: Schrift, Erinnerung und politische Identität in frühen Hochkulturen.* Beck, Munich.

Assmann, J. 2011 *Cultural Memory and Early Civilization: Writing, Remembrance, and Political Imagination.* 1st English ed. Cambridge University Press, New York.

Bodenhamer, D. J. 2010 The Potential of Spatial Humanities. In *The Spatial Humanities. GIS and the Future of Humanities Scholarship,* edited by D. J. Bodenhamer, J. Corrigan, and T. M. Harris, pp. 14–30. Indiana University Press, Bloomington and Indianopolis.

Bradley, R. 1985 Consumption, Change and the Archaeological Record: The Archaeology of Monuments and the Archaeology of Deliberate Deposits. Occasional paper, University of Edinburgh. Department of Archaeology, Edinburgh.

Bradley, R. 1998 *The Significance of Monuments: On the Shaping of Human Experience in Neolithic and Bronze Age Europe.* Routledge, London, New York.

Brand, P. 2010 Usurpation of Monuments. In *UCLA Encyclopedia of Egyptology,* edited by W. Wendrich, Los Angeles http://digital2.library.ucla.edu/viewItem.do?ark=21198/zz0025h6fh.

Favro, D. 2006 In the Eyes of the Beholder: Virtual Reality Re-Creations and Academia. *Journal of Roman Archaeology Supplementary Series* Number 61:321–334.

Favro, D. 2011 Meaning in Motion, A Personal Walk Through Historical Simulation Modeling at UCLA. In *Visualizing Statues in the Late Antique Roman Forum, Methodological Essays.* http://inscriptions.etc.ucla.edu/index.php/statues-and-memory/methodological-essays/.

Gallet, L. 2013 The Temple of Amun-Ra-Who-Hears-Prayers. In *UCLA Encyclopedia of Egyptology,* edited by W. Wendrich. Los Angeles.

Halbwachs, M. 1992 *On Collective Memory.* Translated by L. A. Coser. The Heritage of Sociology. University of Chicago Press, Chicago.

Harrell, J. 2012 Building Stones. In *UCLA Encyclopedia of Egyptology,* edited by W. Wendrich. Los Angeles. http://digital2.library.ucla.edu/viewItem.do?ark=21198/zz002c10gb.

Harrell, J. 2013 Ornamental Stones. In *UCLA Encyclopedia of Egyptology,* edited by W. Wendrich. Los Angeles.

Hayes, W. C. 1973 Internal Affairs from Tuthmosis I to the Death of Amenophis III. In *The Cambridge Ancient History vol. 2, part 1, The Middle East and Aegean Region, c. 1800–1380 BC*, edited by I. E. S. Edwards, C. Gadd, N. G. L. Hammond, and E. Sollberger. Cambridge University Press, Cambridge.

Kemp, B. J. 2006 *Ancient Egypt: Anatomy of a Civilization*. 2nd ed. Routledge, London, New York.

Kemp, B. J. 2012 *The City of Akhenaten and Nefertiti: Amarna and Its People. New Aspects of Antiquity*. Thames and Hudson, London.

Kozloff, A. P. 2011 *Amenhotep III: Egypt's Radiant Pharaoh*. Cambridge University Press, Cambridge, New York.

Kozloff, A. P., B. M. Bryan, L. M. Berman, E. Delange 1992 *Egypt's Dazzling Sun: Amenhotep III and His World*. Cleveland Museum of Art in cooperation with Indiana University Press; Distributed by Indiana University Press, Cleveland, Bloomington.

Legrain, G. 1905 *Les récentes découvertes de Karnak*. Imprimerie Nationale, Cairo.

Lichtheim, M. 1973 *Ancient Egyptian Literature; A Book of Readings. Volume I: The Old and Middle Kingdoms*. University of California Press, Berkeley.

Lock, G. 2010 Representations of Space and Place in the Humanities. In *The Spatial Humanities. GIS and the Future of Humanities Scholarship*, edited by D. J. Bodenhamer, J. Corrigan, and T. M. Harris, pp. 89–108. Indiana University Press, Bloomington, Indianopolis.

Roth, A. M. 2005 Erasing a Reign. In *Hatshepsut: From Queen to Pharaoh*, edited by C. H. Roehrig, R. Dreyfus and K. A. Keller, pp. 277–281. Metropolitan Museum of Art, New York.

Savage, K. 1997 *Standing Soldiers, Kneeling Slaves: Race, War, and Monument in Nineteenth-Century America*. Princeton University Press, Princeton.

Savage, K. 2009 *Monument Wars: Washington, D.C., the National Mall, and the Transformation of the Memorial Landscape*. University of California Press, Berkeley, Los Angeles.

Sullivan, E. 2008 The Daily Ritual. In *Digital Karnak* http://dlib.etc.ucla.edu/projects/Karnak/assets/media/resources/DailyRitual/guide.pdf.

Sullivan, E., and W. Wendrich 2009 An Offering to Amun-Ra: Building a Virtual Reality Model of Karnak. In *Information Technology and Egyptology in 2008*, edited by N. Strudwick. Gorgias Press, Piscataway.

Uphill, E. P. 2003 The Ancient Egyptian View of History. In *"Never Had the Like Occurred": Egypt's View of Its Past*, edited by J. Tait, pp. 15–29. Encounters with Ancient Egypt. University College London Press, London.

Wendrich, W. 2010 Epilogue: Eternal Egypt Deconstructed. In *Egyptian Archaeology*, edited by W. Wendrich, pp. 274–278. Wiley-Blackwell, Oxford.

CHAPTER TWENTY

From Memorials to Imaginaries in the Monumentality of Ancient North America

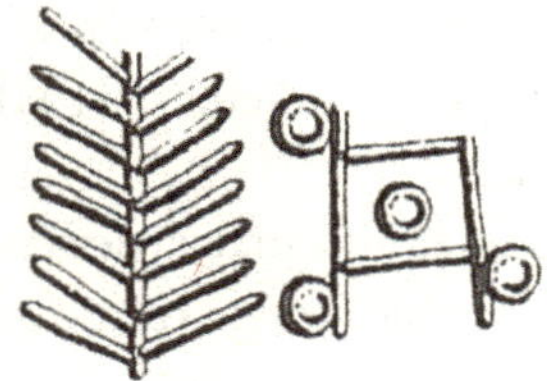

Timothy R. Pauketat

Abstract *Recent animist and relational theories encourage us to analyze the forward-looking, experiential, and sensory aspects of monumentality. A salient characteristic of monumentality in the ancient Americas is the emphasis on refurbishment or renewal. From great pyramids and structured subterranean deposits in Mesoamerica to Great Houses in the Southwest and mounds in the Eastern Woodlands, monuments were frequently if not regularly cleaned, enlarged, and rededicated. In addition, great roads, earthen enclosures, platforms, and sepulchral tumuli were built and rebuilt to channel the movements of living people with respect to the dead and to other moving forces of the cosmos. The sensory effects of such movements, in combination with the qualities of objects and practices caught up in the same, emphasize experience-in-the-now—or the past-in-the-present— rather than recollection of some past. That monuments were portals between pasts, presents, and futures was probably afforded by specific physical or experiential qualities which enabled cosmic connections and transdimensional experiences that did much more than commemorate pasts (Sassaman 2012). Monuments, to be monuments, constitute imagined social futures.*

Theories of memory and materiality in archaeology have encouraged researchers to analyze monuments as sites of intentional or unintentional memory work, sometimes with profound historical implications (Jones 2007; Joyce 2004, 2008; Pauketat 2000; Pauketat and Alt 2003). Contingent on their durability, most if not all monuments would seem to possess commemorative qualities, either via official or unofficial inscriptions and incorporated practices (Connerton 1989). Hence, some monuments might also be considered public memorials, those official or communal constructions designed to embody social memories. Monuments, in short, commemorate (see Osborne, chapter 1). But they also do more than this.

Recent sensuous and relational theories in archaeology focus on engagements of people with each other and with other animate and inanimate things, powers, substances, and spaces (Alberti and Bray 2009; Alberti et al. 2011; Knappett and Malafouris 2008). Human social relationships are always components of more extensive and extended social fields where the causal powers that induce people to do what they do are variously distributed among those animate and inanimate entities. In short, that which motivates people to act in some way is contingent on the relational webs within which people are entangled (see Hodder 2011). The actions of people are contingent on the biographies of things, the genealogies of practices, the histories of places and, significantly, the phenomenal or experiential properties of people, places, and things (Pauketat 2013a). Monuments are among the places and things with such properties.

Monuments, I maintain, are dynamic interlocutors of human affairs that articulate numerous relationships. For such reasons, Osborne (this volume) calls for a relational approach to monumentality. Monuments inspire, motivate, and actively engage people, places, and things, if not also the moving cosmos. In a myriad of ways, monuments shape futures for people (Sassaman 2012). In this chapter, I highlight evidence for this statement in the form of the refurbishment or renewal of earthen, masonry, and wooden monuments and monument-like cultural features—specifically roads—in Mesoamerica and the American Southwest and Midwest. This evidence suggests that monuments have imaginary qualities. In other words, monuments enable people to look beyond this world, and sometimes possess transdimensional properties (see also Baires et al. 2013). Monuments are seldom just commemorations of the past. Rather, like formal roads that connect people, places, and things, monuments are portals to other futures and other worlds.

FROM MEMORIES TO PROPHECIES

Much Western scholarship has focused on the commemorative qualities of special sorts of places or constructed features, including monuments, that revivify events, social movements, or peoples. These "places of memory" (*lieux de mémoire*) form the terrain of social life (Nora 1989). They embody values and emotions and constitute an ongoing negotiation of meanings and memories (Basso 1996; Rodaway 1994). This is the case owing to their materiality, which is to say the material dimension of practices and experiences. Some monuments, for instance, will certainly call forth memories and, being interconnected to a web of social relationships, have their own biographies (Jones 2007).

However, monuments and other places, objects, and bodies might also provoke reactions and emotions independent of their biographies, much like impressionist paintings or optical art (following Gell 1998). This is a second characteristic of materiality that involves the sensuality and perceptual affordances of the material itself (Ingold 2000; Jones and Boivin 2010; Jones and MacGregor 2002; MacGregor 2008; Richards 1996). Depending on the physical properties of some thing—its visibility, reflectivity, angularity, tactility, resonance, durability, etc.—people's encounter with it will be constrained or enabled in distinctive and definite ways. A sparkling obelisk attracts the eye and stimulates optic nerves. A cavernous room or dark passageway alters the temporality of experience. A great red-plastered enclosure colors in some ways the emotional state of those inside. A pyramid blocks some views yet allows others, perhaps directing the eye to distant or heavenly alignments (Pauketat 2013a).

All such things may also be commemorative, at least to the extent to which they are enmeshed in the remembered associations of people. But the sensuous qualities of things and places, including monuments, are more than simply mnemonic. They are the material dimension of human imagination. They are imaginaries.

Psychoanalyst Jacques Lacan (1977) identified imaginaries as belonging to one of three intersecting orders of cultural experience, the other two being the symbolic (or representational) and the real. Today, few researchers would strictly adhere to this triadic model, instead recognizing, perhaps counterintuitively, that imaginaries are real. Just this sense is my intent, which is consistent with contemporary relational and phenomenological theories that do not separate mind and matter, subject and object, or thought and action (Alberti and Bray 2009; Knappett and Malafouris 2008; Meskell 2004). To them, an imaginary is a nexus, site, or object in which a multiplicity of experiences, practices, and relationships are mediated (Shepherd 2007). Imaginaries might be as small as a portable object or a rock-art glyph and as large as a landscape (Whitridge 2004).

An array of material and architectural examples from Mesoamerica, the American Southwest, and the Eastern Woodlands will help us understand the nature of imaginaries (Figure 20.1). In the indigenous American past, many found objects, crafted articles, substances, places, and monuments might have possessed power or the ability to articulate human experience with the greater forces of the cosmos. A colorful stone, unusual fossil, or ancient artifact might have served a talisman (Boivin 2008). Some chipped-stone item, say an eccentric obsidian blade from the Hopewell culture in Ohio, might have afforded transdimensional relations with other worlds of the living or dead (Hall 1997; Seeman 2004). Ingested substances, such as tobacco smoke, cacao, peyote, or the black drink enabled a heightened state of awareness critical to communicating with spirits, ancestors, or the gods.

Especially in North America, such objects and substances were often kept in "medicine bundles," wrapped packages that were carefully curated in special buildings and opened only on special occasions (Pauketat 2013a, b; Zedeño 2008). Knowledge of the powers of these bundles was passed from spirit guides, ancestors, or deities to the bundle holder through dreams and visions (Irwin 1994). Well-known Plains-Prairie and southeastern Indian ceremonials, such as the Sun Dance, the Okipa, and the Green Corn Ceremony were all tethered to bundles and were performed in and around associated monumental spaces and shrines (Archambault 2001; Voget 1984; Witthoft 1949). These ceremonials had spread from one group to another over the centuries in much the same way as more recent religious movements, via the distribution and reanimation of sacred articles in mass performances (Mooney 1973).

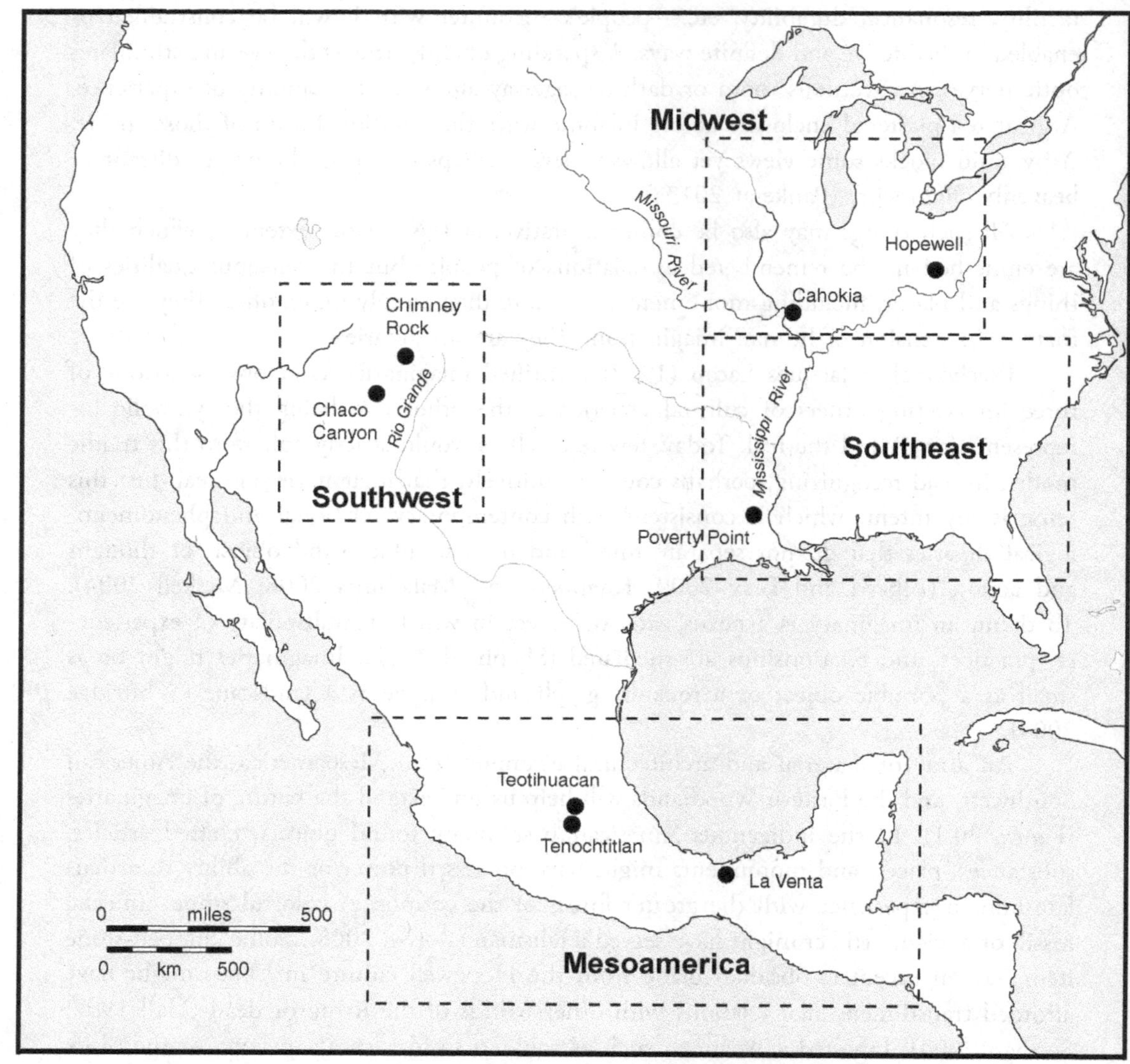

FIGURE 20.1 Map of North American cultural regions and key sites mentioned in the text.

The leaders of such religious movements were not scribes or genealogists but visionaries and prophets. Their monuments—sacred posts, post circles, shrines, temples, and earthen pyramids—were *not* primarily built to commemorate. Rather, they were built to enable people to engage the cosmic and the numinous. We might call such monuments portals, since they enabled movements between worlds or dimensions. As such they are imaginaries that afforded forward-looking relationships with other people, powers, and beings.

Pyramids and Portals

Doubtless, experiencing the powers of the cosmos was a powerful if not dangerous business that would have seldom been done carelessly. Not only might certain spaces, objects, substances, and people have been more or less able or qualified to channel such forces, but special preparations might have been required in order for the convergence to occur properly. For instance, locations might need to be cleaned, purified, and rebalanced to rid them of the chaos and pollutants that accumulate in the mundane world.

In pre-Columbian America, such sacred activities included the refurbishment and reconstruction of great politico-religious architecture. Certainly, the monumental cores of Mesoamerican ceremonial centers and cities, beginning with the Olmec, were periodically renewed, reconditioned, or rebuilt (Clark and Colman 2008; Coe and Diehl 1980; Gillespie 2008). The associated monuments included both visible and buried creations, as in pavements of stones that were laid down, covered over, reopened, repaved, and reburied. People from outside the centers often traveled to such ceremonial places along roads and avenues, some of which were highly formalized, for the special events (Snead et al. 2009). Once there, work commenced on the pyramids and pavements, among other things, few of which were single-event constructions.

Rather, even the largest pyramids were routinely and periodically enlarged. Later stages were built directly atop the earlier ones. The result was a series of nested stages that many have suggested were tied to political interregna and cycles of time (Anderson 1996; Gillespie 2008; Hally 1996). At the Aztec imperial city of Tenochtitlan, for instance, stone pyramids and pavements were built over earlier stages during a two hundred year time span (Figure 20.2). There are few compelling functional explanations for such refurbishments

FIGURE 20.2 Series of superimposed stone courtyard pavements (each marked with an arrow) at the foot of the Templo Mayor, Mexico City.

and enlargements. The periodicity of construction has been linked to great political inaugurations, military victories, and calendrically based religious ceremonies (Hassig 2001).

The same has been said of the earthen pyramids of the Mississippian peoples of eastern North America (A.D. 1050–1600) and, to lesser extent, the Great Houses of the early Puebloan Southwest (A.D. 860–1150). In the Mississippian case, major earthen-pyramid stage enlargements have been characterized as memorials to political leaders (Anderson 1994; Hally 1996). In the Southwest, documented pulses of masonry construction have been considered as indicators of Chacoan political development, with the construction of roadways in and out of Chaco Canyon possibly related to these pulses (Lekson 2006).

Similar roadways and formal processional avenues are known from the great Hopewellian centers of the Ohio and Mississippi valleys, where earthen constructions sometimes bear a striking resemblance to later Mississippian monuments, prompting some to consider them representations of timeless, pan-Eastern cultural narratives (but see Pauketat and Alt 2003). But great Hopewell ceremonial complexes, especially in Ohio, include great community-scale enclosures built of earth with some evidence for later resurfacing and enlargement (Greber 2009; Greber and Shane 2009). Moreover, Hopewellian earthwork constructions in the Midwest (150 B.C.–A.D. 400) are seldom identified as having a political basis, presumably owing to the perceived lack of institutionalized hierarchy at that time in the midcontinent (see Anderson and Mainfort 2002; Carr and Case 2005; Charles and Buikstra 2006).

The Hopewell case allows us to question commonplace assumptions that monuments, especially those in eastern North America, had primarily political and commemorative functions. Were these constructions and their associated practices, or those of the later Puebloan and Mississippian worlds, simply *representations* of things, stories, people, or places remembered, renewed, or rededicated? Certainly such views do not square with explanations offered by many indigenous builders of public and ceremonial architecture in the historic-era Plains and Eastern Woodlands. Plains Indian medicine lodges, medicine wheels, and world-center shrines, they say, actively gather or focus community and cosmic relationships; they do not simply memorialize them (see Eddy 1974; Hall 1985; Knight 1989). The embankments of the Hopewell centers of Ohio and later Southeastern flat-topped, four-sided mounds were "navels" or portals between the sky and earth and the living and dead (Knight 1989). A feature that linked the order of heaven and earth was, in essence, an *axis mundi* (Eliade 1987).

Building, Plastering, and Passage in the Southwest

Many ancient and extant pueblos in the American Southwest physically reference prominent physical features in their positioning or alignment (Ashmore 2007). At Chaco, in northwestern New Mexico, Great Houses were sometimes positioned adjacent to precariously balanced rock columns or standing vertical cliffs (Figure 20.3). At Wupatki, in northeastern Arizona, a Great House was built in the shadow of an active volcano (Lekson 2009). Elsewhere, pueblos were located to face mountains wherein resided ancestors and gods who might periodically visit the pueblo as rain clouds (Schaafsma 1999). Hence,

FIGURE 20.3 A vertical rock slab in Chaco Canyon.

one might reasonably conclude that the masonry complexes commemorated these natural landscape features and their resident supernatural powers. The formal roads of the Southwest might have done likewise. Some led to and from Great Houses. Others seem intended to pass by, but not go directly to, long-abandoned Great Houses. Still others simply marked directions and some have monumental staircases. Whatever their specific attributes, various researchers suspect that these avenues were intended for more than living travelers. They might have connected the places and spirits of the past with living people and pueblos of the present (Mills 2002; Van Dyke 2007). These roads, that is, were routes between worlds.

So too might have been masonry constructions themselves. The distinctive masonry styles used in the walls of the Great Houses of the Chacoan region, for instance, were mimetic of the natural sandstone cliffs of Chaco Canyon itself (Van Dyke 2004). Yet their distinctive masonry was not intended to be seen by later visitors. Instead, the builders plastered it over, possibly giving the constructions an inherent invisible power. Into the historic era, plaster itself assumed the status as an interlocutor between the living and dead, with murals of the Katsina gods being painted on fresh plaster with each significant ritual renewal of the sacred space (Adams 1991; Schaafsma 1994). Such acts of plastering possibly opened a portal between people and the ancestors or dieties, much like wearing of Katsina costumes (which virtually presenced the spirits and gods through the movements of the living).

As is obvious in the case of plastered walls, commemoration was probably not the principal intention of southwestern masons, road builders, plasterers, or painters. Indeed, like the roads, Chacoan Great Houses and later pueblos were aligned to natural features, to each other, to the unseen, and at a larger scale to various rising and setting positions of the sun and moon (Sofaer 2008). Standing in various positions in and around these masonry monuments thus situated oneself at the interstices of an orderly, aligned universe, constituting a "hierophantic" experience that physically and emotionally linked human beings with the supreme powers of the cosmos (Eliade 1987, 1991). The point was not merely to inscribe some location with knowledge of the past, but to emplace and embody the cosmos in the present.

Certainly, such hierophantic experience would have been memorable, but these masonry constructions, roads, and pavements—owing to their performative aspects—were imaginaries first and foremost. They inspired, connected, and animated relationships between people and the cosmos.

MOUND-CONSTRUCTION PERIODICITY IN THE EAST

The empirical evidence of mound stratigraphy is one of the various reasons to conclude that a similar imaginary quality was present in indigenous public constructions in eastern North America. While there are clear cases of great mounds having been thrown up in short order (Kidder 2010; Pauketat et al. 2010; Sherwood and Kidder 2011), recent excavations of even the largest of these mounds (at the Archaic-period site of Poverty Point and the early Mississippian city of Cahokia) indicate an astonishing degree of ritualized construction complexity. In one well-known mound excavation at the Mississippian-era city of Cahokia, the excavator remarked that the pyramid appeared to have been under constant renovation (Pauketat 1993). Later excavators have recognized in Cahokian earthen construction an obsession with alternating layers of light and dark fills that seem to intentionally ignore long-term engineering problems, especially the instability of alternating sand and clay mantles (Figure 20.4).

Indeed, the early Mississippian pyramids were routinely comprised of several stage enlargements capped with alternating "blanket mantles" of light and dark or friable and dense clays, silts, and sands (Knight 1989). In a half-dozen well-documented cases, the light-and-dark fills were laid down in rapid succession during single construction events (Pauketat 2013a; Pauketat et al. 2010; Sherwood and Kidder 2011; Sullivan and Pauketat

FIGURE 20.4 A section through a Cahokian mound at Horseshoe Lake, St. Clair County, Illinois.

2008). That is, a layer of light-colored sediment was packed onto a mound followed immediately by a layer of dark-colored sediment. In at least four of these cases, additional light and dark mantles were added immediately following the first pair.

While it is yet possible to label such construction practices as acts of purification, they were never merely commemorative acts. This is because, historically, earth in the

Great Plains and Eastern Woodlands was uniformly understood to be one of the fundamental life forces or animate powers of the cosmos (Dorsey 1894; Howard 1981; Murie 1981). As such, earth was considered to be a "Witness," which is to say a transcendental substance that enabled spirits and deities to see what people were doing on earth. Thus, adding light and dark colored earth was more than a passive act of purification. It was an opening of a conduit, if only for a moment, to the most holy powers of the cosmos. As noted earlier, earthen pyramids, or most any earthen architecture in eastern North America, were said to be navels or portals by later Mississippians (Knight 1989).

Pulses of construction may well have corresponded with a ritualized life-cycle event of an important person, but the practice of earthen construction was a hierophantic window to the great beyond and the powers that dwelt there. The act of building itself, not the final mound, was the most important component of the pyramid (Pauketat 1993). The engagement of earth and sky or humanity and cosmos in the moment, not the remembrance of some mythical or genealogical past, was the most important quality of mounds.

This is best exemplified in a series of likely pilgrimage shrine complexes located in the treeless hills east of the city of Cahokia (Figure 20.5). There, 15 to 20 miles from the main complex near a processional avenue that exits the region to the southeast, sit three major and an uncounted number of minor shrine complexes, their mounds, marker posts, and buildings aligned to a series of moonrises and moonsets associated with that celestial body's long 18.6-year cycle (Pauketat 2013a). In excavations at one of the large complexes, known as the Pfeffer site, the opening and closing of semi-subterranean pole-and-thatch temples and subterranean pits was preceded by the deposition of yellow

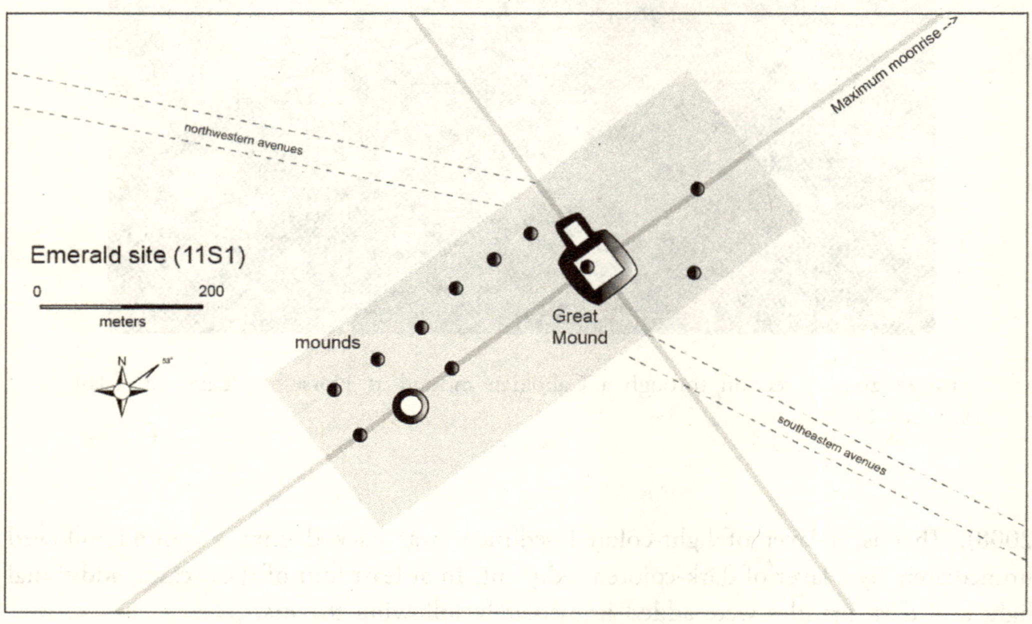

FIGURE 20.5 Schematic plan of the Emerald site, Cahokia region, ca. A.D. 1100, showing mounds, avenues, and organizational axes.

and black mantles. In the case of the lined pits, special ashy fills and burned objects from rituals elsewhere on site were then buried there. The idea appears to have been to animate the locations, affording Witnessing events, which involved the careful disposal of ritual substances (Pauketat 2008). Excavations into the pyramid of a second large site revealed similar structured earthen deposits atop each stage of the main platform mound. Elsewhere I have suggested that the periodicity of monumental construction at this the Emerald site was tied not primarily to human political events, but to a sequence of moonrises that occur once every generation (Pauketat 2013a).

Imagining the Imaginary in Monumentality

Like so many Native American sacred places, monumental pyramids, temples, Great Houses, and possibly roads were never merely dedicated places of memory that then inscribed a landscape with meaning and clothed it with narratives. Rather, indigenous American monuments were alive, so to speak. They were proactive. They were sites of cosmic engagement that articulated a multiplicity of relationships, human and otherwise. People came to them along roads and processional avenues to move through them into their collective futures in the presence of the past, but seldom, if ever, simply to memorialize that past. They still come to them for the same reasons today, as when pilgrims visit buildings such as the Kukulcán pyramid at Chichen Itza or Teotihuacan's Pyramid of the Sun on the day of the vernal equinox (Figure 20.6).

FIGURE 20.6 Pilgrims climbing the staircase of the Pyramid of the Sun, Teotihuacan, Mexico, on the vernal equinox, 1995.

The movements through such sacred spaces and their larger landscapes were sometimes highly formalized. Roadways themselves were more than transportation corridors. They were an integral part of what we might think of as a process of Witnessing (Pauketat 2013a). Even the Aztec king Moteuczomah made regular (monthly) processions north to the ancient city of Teotihuacan, probably less to remember what had transpired there and more to connect with the mystical powers that yet resided among its ruins (Hassig 1985).

But if the histories of places and the inscriptive powers of monuments matter less in the Americas than some might suspect, what then makes a monument monumental? Why did Moteuczomah make routine visits to Teotihuacan? Why did pilgrims travel to the great imaginaries of the Southwest, Midwest, and Southeast? Why the obsessive layerings of masonry, plaster, and earth?

These places, it seems, possessed the power to attract and articulate a multiplicity of social and cosmic relationships. Whether roads, Great Houses, or pyramids, the principal power of things monumental was realized via alignment and positioning. Monuments are those features or fixtures that, owing to their shape, directionality, or materiality, anchor or impel the diverse movements and relational convergences of the human and nonhuman world. Size matters here, but so does color, texture, and a host of other sensory properties (e.g., Hurcombe 2008; Jones and Boivin 2010; Knappett and Malafouris 2008). Object biographies, practical genealogies, and cultural histories matter as well, but so does the pure physicality of the construction or the site.

Such an experiential definition of monuments, one that emphasizes the imaginary rather than the commemorative (or affordance rather than meaning) is not restricted to human constructions. There are, of course, natural monuments (following Bradley 2000). Monument Valley in Utah, Chimney Rock in Colorado, the Grand Canyon in Arizona, or the mighty Mississippi in the American heartland are all monuments in a sense—in some cases officially designated by governments as National Monuments—because they are dynamic interlocutors of human affairs. They inspire, motivate, and actively engage people by disproportionately articulating social relationships to other places, substances, moving celestial objects, and the great beyond. I would suggest that the most monumental of all, those with the greatest historical impact, are precisely the ones that articulate our visions of a future world with the fundamental powers of the cosmos and social order.

Indeed, I also suggest that such qualities are the defining elements of monuments worldwide to varying degrees. Monuments, to be monuments, must be more than big memorials. They must possess the qualities of monumentality, the foremost of which is the imaginary. We do not merely see them and remember. We feel them and imagine.

ACKNOWLEDGMENTS

I am most grateful to James Osborne for organizing the monumentality conference and including a New World perspective, and to Peter Biehl, director of IEMA at the University of Buffalo, for his future-oriented oversight of the IEMA conference series. Reinhard Bernbeck provided a venue for an earlier presentation that morphed into this chapter, and Ross Hassig suggested some pertinent points regarding the Aztec. All shortcomings are mine alone.

References Cited

Adams, E. C. 1991 *The Origins and Development of the Pueblo Katsina Cult.* University of Arizona Press, Tucson.

Alberti, B., and T. L. Bray 2009 Animating Archaeology: Of Subjects, Objects, and Alternative Ontologies. *Cambridge Archaeological Journal* 19(3):337–343.

Alberti, B., S. Fowles, M. Holbraad, Y. Marshall, and C. Witmore 2011 "Worlds Otherwise": Archaeology, Anthropology, and Ontological Difference. *Current Anthropology* 52(6):896–912.

Anderson, D. G. 1994 *The Savannah River Chiefdoms: Political Change in the Late Prehistoric Southeast.* University of Alabama Press, Tuscaloosa.

Anderson, D. G. 1996 Fluctuations Between Simple and Complex Chiefdoms: Cycling in the Late Prehistoric Southeast. In *Political Structure and Change in the Prehistoric Southeastern United States,* edited by J. F. Scarry, pp. 231–252. University Press of Florida, Gainesville.

Anderson, D. G., and R. C. Mainfort, eds. 2002 *The Woodland Southeast.* University of Alabama Press, Tuscaloosa.

Archambault, J. 2001 Sun Dance. In *Handbook of North American Indians, Plains, Part 2 of 2,* edited by R. J. DeMallie, pp. 983–995. Smithsonian Institution, Washington, D.C.

Ashmore, W. 2007 Building Social History at Pueblo Bonito: Footnotes to a Biography of Place. In *The Architecture of Chaco Canyon, New Mexico,* edited by S. H. Lekson, pp. 179–198. University of Utah Press, Salt Lake City.

Baires, S. E., A. J. Butler, B. J. Skousen, and T. Pauketat 2013 Fields of Movement in the Ancient Eastern Woodlands. In *Archaeology After Interpretation,* edited by B. Alberti, A. Jones, and J. Pollard. Left Coast Press, Walnut Creek, California.

Basso, K. H. 1996 *Wisdom Sits in Places: Landscape and Language Among the Western Apache.* University of New Mexico Press, Albuquerque.

Boivin, N. 2008 *Material Cultures, Material Minds: The Impact of Things on Human Thought, Society and Evolution.* Cambridge University Press, Cambridge.

Bradley, R. 2000 *An Archaeology of Natural Places.* Routledge, London.

Carr, C., and D. T. Case, eds. 2005 *Gathering Hopewell: Society, Ritual, and Ritual Interaction.* Kluwer Academic/Plenum, New York.

Charles, D., and J. Buikstra, eds. 2006 *Recreating Hopewell.* University Press of Florida, Gainesville.

Clark, J. E., and A. Colman 2008 Time Reckoning and Memorials in Mesoamerica. *Cambridge Archaeological Journal* 18(1):93–99.

Coe, M. D., and R. A. Diehl 1980 *In the Land of the Olmec: The Archaeology of San Lorenzo Tenochtitlan.* University of Texas Press, Austin.

Connerton, P. 1989 *How Societies Remember.* Cambridge University Press, Cambridge.

Dorsey, J. O. 1894 A Study of Siouan Cults. In *Eleventh Annual Report of the Bureau of Ethnology,* pp. 351–554. Government Printing Office, Washington, D.C.

Eddy, J. A. 1974 Astronomical Alignment of the Big Horn Medicine Wheel. *Science* 184:1035–1043.

Eliade, M. 1987 *The Sacred and the Profane: The Nature of Religion* (originally published 1959). Harcourt Brace, San Diego.

Eliade, M. 1991 *The Myth of the Eternal Return or, Cosmos and History* (originally published 1954). Princeton University Press, Princeton.

Gell, A. 1998 *Art and Agency: An Anthropological Theory.* Oxford University Press, Oxford.

Gillespie, S. D. 2008 History in Practice: Ritual Deposition at La Venta Complex A. In *Memory Work: Archaeologies of Material Practices,* edited by B. J. Mills and W. H. Walker, pp. 109–136. School for Advanced Research Press, Santa Fe.

Greber, N. O. B. 2009 Field Data and Summary Comments. *Midcontinental Journal of Archaeology* 34(1):171–186.

Greber, N. O. B., and O. C. Shane III 2009 Field Studies of the Octagon and Great Circle, High Bank Earthworks, Ross County, Ohio. In *Footprints: In the Footprints of Squier and Davis: Archeological Fieldwork in Ross County, Ohio,* edited by M. J. Lynott, pp. 23–48. Midwest Archeological Center, National Park Service, Lincoln, Nebraska.

Hall, R. L. 1985 Medicine Wheels, Sun Circles, and the Magic of World Center Shrines. *Plains Anthropologist* 30:181–193.

Hall, R. L. 1997 *An Archaeology of the Soul: Native American Indian Belief and Ritual.* University of Illinois Press, Urbana.

Hally, D. J. 1996 Platform-Mound Construction and the Instability of Mississippian Chiefdoms. In *Political Structure and Change in the Prehistoric Southeastern United States,* edited by J. F. Scarry, pp. 92–127. University Press of Florida, Gainesville.

Hassig, R. 1985 *Trade, Tribute, and Transportation: The Sixteenth-Century Political Economy of the Valley of Mexico.* University of Oklahoma Press, Norman.

Hassig, R. 2001 *Time, History, and Belief in Aztec and Colonial Mexico.* University of Texas Press, Austin.

Hodder, I. 2011 *Entangled: An Archaeology of the Relationships between Humans and Things.* Wiley-Blackwell, West Sussex, UK.

Howard, J. H. 1981 *Shawnee! The Ceremonialism of a Native Indian Tribe and Its Cultural Background.* Ohio University Press, Athens.

Hurcombe, L. 2008 A Sense of Materials and Sensory Perception in Concepts of Materiality. *World Archaeology* 39(4):532–545.

Ingold, T. 2000 *The Perception of the Environment: Essays in Livelihood, Dwelling and Skill.* Routledge, London.

Irwin, L. 1994 *The Dream Seekers: Native American Visionary Traditions of the Great Plains.* University of Oklahoma, Norman.

Jones, A. 2007 *Memory and Material Culture.* Cambridge University Press, Cambridge.

Jones, A., and S. MacGregor, eds. 2002 *Colouring the Past: The Significance of Colour in Archaeological Research.* Berg, Oxford.

Jones, A. M., and N. Boivin 2010 The Malice of Inanimate Objects: Material Agency. In *The Oxford Handbook of Material Culture Studies,* edited by D. Hicks and M. C. Beaudry, pp. 333–351. Oxford University Press, Oxford.

Joyce, R. A. 2004 Unintended Consequences? Monumentality as a Novel Experience in Formative Mesoamerica. *Journal of Archaeological Method and Theory* (11):5–29.

Joyce, R. A. 2008 Practice in and as Deposition. In *Memory Work: Archaeologies of Material Practices,* edited by B. J. Mills and W. H. Walker, pp. 25–39. School for Advanced Research Press, Santa Fe.

Kidder, T. R. 2010 Hunter-Gatherer Ritual and Complexity: New Evidence from Poverty Point, Louisiana. In *Ancient Complexities: New Perspectives in Precolumbian North America,* edited by S. M. Alt, pp. 32–51. University of Utah Press, Salt Lake City.

Knappett, C. and L. Malafouris, eds. 2008 *Material Agency: Towards a Non-Anthropocentric Approach.* Springer, New York.

Knight, V. J. Jr. 1989 Symbolism of Mississippian Mounds. In *Powhatan's Mantle: Indians in the Colonial Southeast,* edited by P. H. Wood, G. A. Waselkov and M. T. Hatley, pp. 279–291. University of Nebraska Press, Lincoln.

Lacan, J. 1977 *Écrits: A Selection*. Norton, New York.

Lekson, S. H., ed. 2006 *The Archaeology of Chaco Canyon: An Eleventh-Century Pueblo Regional Center*. School for Advanced Research Press, Santa Fe.

Lekson, S. H., ed. 2009 *A History of the Ancient Southwest*. School for Advanced Research Press, Santa Fe.

MacGregor, G. 2008 Elemental Bodies: The Nature of Transformative Practices During the Late Third and Second Millennium BC in Scotland. *World Archaeology* 40(2):268–280.

Meskell, L. M. 2004 Object Worlds in Ancient Egypt: Material Biographies Past and Present. Berg, London.

Mills, B. J. 2002 Recent Research on Chaco: Changing Views on Economy, Ritual, and Society. *Journal of Archaeological Research* 10:65–117.

Mooney, J. 1973 *The Ghost-Dance Religion and Wounded Knee*. Dover, New York.

Murie, J. R. 1981 *Ceremonies of the Pawnee, Part I: The Skiri*. Smithsonian Contributions to Anthropology, Number 27. Smithsonian Institution Press, Washington, D.C.

Nora, P. 1989 Between Memory and History: *Les Lieux de Mémoire. Representations* 26:7–24.

Pauketat, T. R. 1993 *Temples for Cahokia Lords: Preston Holder's 1955–1956 Excavations of Kunnemann Mound*. Memoirs of the University of Michigan Museum of Anthropology, Number 26. University of Michigan, Ann Arbor.

Pauketat, T. R. 2000 The tragedy of the commoners. In *Agency in Archaeology*, edited by M.-A. Dobres and J. Robb, pp. 113–129. Routledge, London.

Pauketat, T. R. 2008 Founders' Cults and the Archaeology of *Wa-kan-da*. In *Memory Work: Archaeologies of Material Practices*, edited by B. Mills and W. H. Walker, pp. 61–79. School for Advanced Research Press, Santa Fe.

Pauketat, T. R. 2013a *An Archaeology of the Cosmos: Rethinking Agency and Religion in Ancient America*. Routledge, London.

Pauketat, T. R. 2013b Bundles in/of/as Time. In *Big Histories, Human Lives: Tackling Problems of Scale in Archaeology*, edited by J. Robb and T. R. Pauketat. School for Advanced Research Press, Santa Fe.

Pauketat, T. R., and S. M. Alt 2003 Mounds, Memory, and Contested Mississippian History. In *Archaeologies of Memory*, edited by R. M. Van Dyke and S. E. Alcock, pp. 151–179. Blackwell, Oxford.

Pauketat, T. R., M. A. Rees, A. M. VanDerwarker, and K. E. Parker 2010 Excavations into Cahokia's Mound 49. *Illinois Archaeology* 22:397–436.

Richards, C. 1996 Henges and Water: Towards an Elemental Understanding of Monumentality and Landscape in Late Neolithic Britain. *Journal of Material Culture* 1(3):313–336.

Rodaway, P. 1994 *Sensuous Geographies: Body, Sense, and Place*. Routledge, London.

Sassaman, Kenneth E. 2012 Futurologists Look Back. *Archaeologies: Journal of the World Archaeological Congress* 8(3):250–268.

Schaafsma, P. 1994 *Kachinas in the Pueblo World*. University of New Mexico Press, Albuquerque.

Schaafsma, P. 1999 Tlalocs, Kachinas, Sacred Bundles, and Related Symbolism in the Southwest and Mesoamerica. In *The Casas Grandes World*, edited by C. F. Schaafsma and C. L. Riley, pp. 164–193. The University of Utah Press, Salt Lake City.

Seeman, M. F. 2004 Hopewell Art in Hopewell Places. In *Hero, Hawk, and Open Hand: American Indian Art of the Ancient Midwest and South*, edited by R. V. Sharp and R. F. Townsend, pp. 57–71. Chicago Art Institute and Yale University Press, Chicago and New Haven.

Shepherd, N. 2007 Archaeology Dreaming: Post-Apartheid Urban Imaginaries and the Bones of the Prestwich Street Dead. *Journal of Social Archaeology* 7(1):3–28.

Sherwood, S. C. and T. R. Kidder. 2011 The DaVincis of Dirt: Geoarchaeological Perspectives on Native American Mound Building in the Mississippi River Basin. *Journal of Anthropological Archaeology* 30:69–87.

Snead, J. E., C. L. Erickson, and J. A. Darling, eds. 2009 *Landscapes of Movement: Trails, Paths, and Roads in Anthropological Perspective*. University of Pennsylvania Museum of Archaeology and Anthropology, Philadelphia.

Sofaer, A. 2008 *Chaco Astronomy: An Ancient American Cosmology*. Ocean Tree Books, Santa Fe.

Sullivan, L. P. and T. R. Pauketat 2008 Cahokia's Mound 31: A Short-Term Construction at a Long-Term Site. *Southeastern Archaeology* 26:12–31.

Van Dyke, R. M. 2004 Memory, Meaning, and Masonry: The Late Bonito Chacoan Landscape. *American Antiquity* 69:413–431.

Van Dyke, R. M. 2007 *The Chaco Experience: Landscape and Ideology at the Center Place*. School for Advanced Research Press, Santa Fe.

Voget, F. W. 1984 *The Shoshoni-Crow Sun Dance*. University of Oklahoma Press, Norman.

Whitridge, P. 2004 Landscapes, Houses, Bodies, Things: "Place" and the Archaeology of Inuit Imaginaries. *Journal of Archaeological Method and Theory* 11(2):213–250.

Witthoft, J. 1949 *Green Corn Ceremonialism in the Eastern Woodlands*. University of Michigan, Museum of Anthropology, Occasional Contributions 13, Ann Arbor.

Zedeño, M. N. 2008 Bundled Worlds: The Roles and Interactions of Complex Objects from the North American Plains. *Journal of Archaeological Method and Theory* 15:362–378.

Contributors

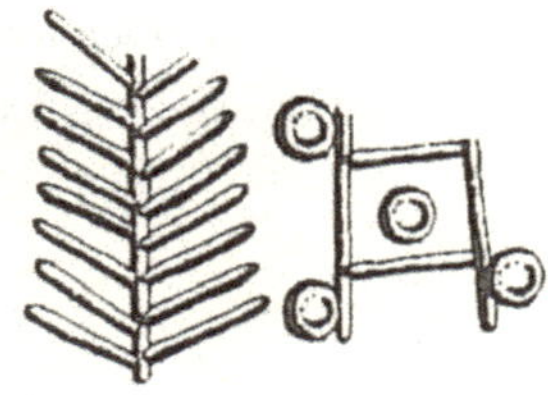

Annetta Alexandridis, Associate Professor, Department of History of Art and Visual Studies, Cornell University

Christoph Bachhuber, Postdoctoral Fellow, Center for Area Studies, Lecturer, Institute of Ancient Near Eastern Archaeology, Freie Universität Berlin

Peter Bogucki, Associate Dean for Undergraduate Affairs, School of Engineering and Applied Science, Princeton University

Dietrich Boschung, Professor of Classical Archaeology, Institute of Archaeology, University of Cologne

William Caraher, Associate Professor, Department of History, University of North Dakota

Oliver Dietrich, Research Assistant, Orient Department, German Archaeological Institute

Kevin D. Fisher, Assistant Professor, Department of Classical, Near Eastern, & Religious Studies, University of British Columbia

Claudia Glatz, Lecturer in Archaeology, School of Humanities, University of Glasgow

Álvaro Ibarra, Assistant Professor, Department of Art History, College of Charleston

Michael J. Kolb, Professor, Department of Anthropology, Northern Illinois University

Stephanie M. Langin-Hooper, Assistant Professor and Karl Kilinski II Endowed Chair of Hellenic Visual Culture, Art History Department, Southern Methodist University

Johannes Müller, Professor and Chair of Prehistoric Archaeology, Institute of Pre- and Protohistoric Archaeology, University of Kiel

Jens Notroff, Research Assistant, Orient Department, German Archaeological Institute

Mirko Novák, Professor for Near Eastern Archaeology, University of Bern, Institute of Archaeological Sciences

James F. Osborne, Postdoctoral Fellow in Archaeology, Joukowsky Institute for Archaeology and the Ancient World, Brown University

Grant Parker, Associate Professor of Classics, Stanford University, Extraordinary Professor of Ancient Studies, Stellenbosch University Associate Professor

Timothy Pauketat, Professor, Departments of Anthropology and Medieval Studies, University of Illinois at Urbana-Champaign

Daniel T. Potts, Professor of Ancient Near Eastern Archaeology and History, Institute for the Study of the Ancient World, New York University

Klaus Schmidt†, Senior Researcher, Orient Department, German Archaeological Institute

Göran Therborn, Professor Emeritus of Sociology, University of Cambridge, Affiliated Professor of Sociology, Linnaeus University

Edmund Thomas, Lecturer, Department of Classics and Ancient History, Durham University

Willeke Wendrich, Professor of Egyptian Archaeology and Digital Humanities, Department of Near Eastern Languages and Culture, University of California, Los Angeles

Index

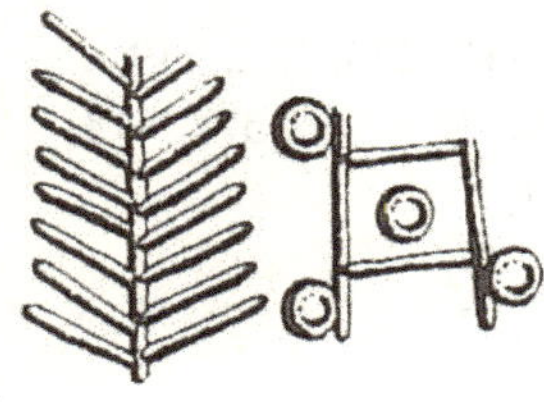